Community Psychology

Linking Individuals and Communities

Community Psychology

Linking Individuals and Communities

SECOND EDITION

JAMES H. DALTON
Bloomsburg University

MAURICE J. ELIAS
Rutgers University

ABRAHAM WANDERSMAN
University of South Carolina

Australia • Brazil • Canada • Mexico • Singapore
Spain • United Kingdom • United States

Community Psychology:
***Linking Individuals and Communities*, Second Edition**
James H. Dalton, Maurice J. Elias and Abraham Wandersman

Publisher: Vicki Knight
Acquisitions Editor: Marianne Taflinger
Assistant Editor: Jennifer Keever
Editorial Assistant: Lucy Faridany
Marketing Assistant: Natasha Coats
Marketing Communications Manager: Kelley McAllister
Project Manager, Editorial Production: Megan E. Hansen
Creative Director: Rob Hugel
Art Director: Maria Epes
Print Buyer: Rebecca Cross
Permissions Editor: Bob Kauser
Production Service: Merrill Peterson, Matrix Productions
Copy Editor: Vicki Nelson
Cover Designer: Paula Goldstein
Cover Image: Tony Anderson/Getty
Compositor: International Typesetting and Composition
Printer: RR Donnelley/Crawfordsville
Cover Printer: Phoenix Color Corp

Printed in the United States of America

1 2 3 4 5 6 7 10 09 08 07 06

Library of Congress Control Number: 2006923040

Student Edition: ISBN 0-534-63454-0

Thomson Higher Education
10, Davis Drive
Belmont CA 94002–3098 USA

For more information about our products, contact us at:
Thomson Learning Academic Resource Center
1-800-423-0563

For permission to use material from this text or product, submit a request online at
http://www.thomsonrights.com.
Any additional questions about permissions can be submitted by e-mail to
thomsonrights@thomson.com.

To my wife Carolyn, whose companionship, love, and wisdom sustain me daily; to my sister Mary Hannah, who exemplifies courage; and to the memory of Heath and Sally Dalton, who taught by example the integration of faith and action.—J.H.D.

To my wife Ellen, with gratitude for her love and cherished support always; and to Agnes and Sol Elias, whose unwavering support has served as the springboard for my accomplishments.—M.J.E.

To my wife Lois, whose love and wisdom make me happy and wiser; and to my father Irving Wandersman and in memory of my mother Hadassah Wandersman, who saw great things in me and nurtured me.—A.W.

Brief Contents

PART IV Preventing Problem Behavior and Promoting Social Competence

PART V Promoting Community and Social Change

Contents

Forewords

I have always been somewhat in awe of textbook writers. How do they muster the temerity, the chutzpah, to define a field? How do they find the time to gain a detailed understanding of research that is reasonably distant from their own and to lay it out clearly for others? Writing a text is a prodigious amount of work. The best texts convey the excitement of a field to students who are just beginning to explore it, but also offer new insights and make new connections for old-timers. This text succeeds along these dimensions. It is lucid and inviting, scholarly and comprehensive.

There are two other ways this book excels, one conceptual and one pedagogical. Conceptually, we humans think of ourselves as the center of the universe. We tend to make attributions of causal responsibility for events to people's characteristics, intentions, and actions rather than to the situations in which people find themselves. The tendency is so pervasive that social psychologists dub it the "fundamental attribution error." Psychologists who study personality or psychopathology may be particularly disposed to focus on personal characteristics as explanations for behavior and for successes and failures. Clinical psychologists may be particularly prone to attempt to change outcomes by changing individuals or the ways that they think about their world. Community psychologists, on the other hand, focus on the contexts of human behavior. They try to understand how our behavior and outcomes are influenced by our culture, the physical and social environments in which we live, and the resources at our disposal. The authors of this book succeed in helping students to switch figure and ground, to focus on contexts as influences on behavior and as targets for change. Of course, ignoring individual differences, like ignoring context, would lead to an overly simplistic view of the world, and Dalton, Elias, and Wandersman do not fall into that trap. But they make a contextual perspective compelling.

Pedagogically, the authors take their own advice, derived from research on successful educational and preventive programs: "Learning is promoted by actively working with materials and situations and with creating our own meanings" (p. 289).

The book is full of exercises inviting students to try out the concepts in its pages, and to apply the ideas to themselves and their own communities. The authors are clearly master teachers who have thought not just about how to present material clearly to passive readers, but how to orchestrate students' engagement as active participants in learning. This may be unusual in a text, but is not a surprise to anyone who knows the authors. For more than a decade Jim Dalton and Mo Elias have run the "Education Connection," a clearinghouse of resources, syllabi, and exercises used by faculty teaching community psychology courses around the country. Mo Elias won the ethnic-minority mentoring prize from the Society for Community Research and Action (the professional society of community psychologists). Abe Wandersman, winner of the award for Distinguished Contributions to Theory and Research from the same organization, has also mentored a number of dissertations that have won its annual dissertation prize. Dalton, Elias, and Wandersman care about scholarship and care about teaching. It shows.

Marybeth Shinn
Professor of Psychology, New York University

This book is more than a traditional college textbook written to introduce an undergraduate student to a field of study. This book is different. It does orient the reader to the key topics of the field of community psychology, like designing, evaluating and implementing prevention and community development programs. More important, this book is a resource for those students and citizens who wish to carry out community-based programs where they live and work.

The three authors are informed and discriminating guides to escort the reader on a tour through the multiple facets of community psychology. They have constructed a comprehensive examination of the field. More important, they have expanded the view of the field from being perceived as a restricted and enclosed academic discipline. They have opened up the field's contributions for appraisal and public use. The success of the book is that readers become aware that knowledge of community psychology does not exist only in the pages of this book. Though there *are* plentiful ideas, findings, precepts and practical help in its pages, the impact of the book is that *readers can take these ideas and use them for their personal contributions to their own communities*. After reading this book, readers can feel confident to carry out their own adaptations of community psychology.

Readers' efforts to do their own community psychology is buttressed by a trust that the material in the book has benefited from give and take and feedback with the very persons who were the intended beneficiaries of this book. In this sense, the ideas presented here have been pretested: trying them out in authentic places where people live their lives. The knowledge presented here is creditable because the findings and concepts have resulted from very active immersion in a variety of community settings. There has been accountability in the research process so that consumers, clients, and citizens have had a voice in the creation of the work. The reader can safely take these ideas as plausible beginnings for their own community work.

This book was not written just to impress an audience with the vitality or quality of community psychology. A nice side effect of the authors' point of view is that community psychology is presented as an accessible field. I was personally delighted to discover these qualities.

This book is a testimony to those community psychologists who have been developing the field over its first 40 years. There is a substantial set of workable and tested ideas now available. The persons referenced in this book have been breaking new ground by developing research or demonstration projects and prevention programs with the active participation of residents of the communities in which the work was done. The insights and knowledge presented here are the work of university faculty and students and community psychologists outside the university. Their combined efforts have produced clarity about the concrete steps and actions needed to anchor and sustain community psychology efforts.

This book is also a testimony to how unique and vigorous community psychology is. Although community psychologists make up a very small portion of the total number of psychologists, the work illustrated here has contributed to a major redefinition of what topics are included within the larger province of psychology. As a result, psychologists have shifted away, for example, from a primary focus on illness, disease, and dysfunction. Increasingly, the ways and means of developing social competencies and sources of personal strength are at the top of agendas for more inquiry and understanding.

The promotion of mental health, an aspiration of many professionals and citizens after World War II, is now being realized. Community psychologists, as illustrated in this book, are understanding how the skills and know-how that enhance an individual's mental health are learned and nurtured. In addition, more and more community psychologists are attempting to understand a community's capacity to generate support systems for these newly acquired competencies.

The book expresses an exciting quality of the field. It presents the various methods being used by community psychologists in designing and evaluating community programs. This is refreshing in that there is not just one short list of preferred ways to understand the topics of community psychology; the reader is encouraged to select the method that fits the circumstances of the program and community. A diversity of methods within the repertoire of the community psychologist also means the field can respond much better to the cultural needs of people who live in diverse communities. The science of community psychology is a science of adaptation to the unique cultural conditions of people. This well-documented concept is central to the field and is clearly apparent throughout the entire book.

The topics of social competencies and mental health are topics about the linkages between the attributes of social environments and the qualities of persons who live in them. This is a testimony to community psychology's successful efforts to bring about a shift in how psychologists in general think about prevention; prevention is increasingly understood to be the development of positive qualities of persons and the development of social settings. Each of the 15 chapters point out how these foci on health and context have been liberating adventures. The authors create enticing opportunities for the reader to learn more about and participate in these adventures.

James G. Kelly
Davis, California
Emeritus Professor of Psychology, University of Illinois at Chicago

Preface

We invite you to join us for this book's journey through the exciting field of community psychology! We came to community psychology because it engaged our minds, our values, and our lives. We hope this book does that for you.

To enliven the journey and to engage you actively in learning, we have included a number of exercises, questions, and examples, including extended examples and stories, to stimulate your thinking about persons in communities. We build on the strengths of our first edition, which was praised by teachers and students for its exercises and applications. Community psychology is a way of thinking that can be applied to many life situations and communities. This textbook reflects that perspective.

We intend this book to be useful for upper-level undergraduate students and graduate students in psychology and related fields. We also seek to provide an overview of community psychology for community psychologists, citizens, and professionals in other fields. Finally, we seek to make conceptual contributions to community psychology, posing issues for scholars and activists in our field to consider, and adding to the ongoing conversation that allows our field to evolve.

We wrote all of our chapters with extensive mutual feedback and revision. Nonetheless, in the interest of full disclosure, each chapter had a primary author whose perspective shaped it the most. James Dalton is primary author for Chapters 1–8, 12, 13, and 15; Maurice Elias for Chapters 9–11; Abraham Wandersman for Chapter 14. Elise Herndon co-authored Chapter 8 and provided material for Chapter 1.

We also want you to know that we donate one-tenth of our royalties to the Society for Community Research and Action (SCRA), an international body of community psychologists and scholars in related fields. To learn more about SCRA, or to become a member, see its website at http://www.scra27.org/

ACKNOWLEDGMENTS

This book would not have been conceived or written without the support of many individuals and of the multiple communities in which we live. Jean Ann Linney first conceived of this book and continued to encourage us after other commitments precluded her continuing with it. Elise Herndon wrote the first draft of Chapter 8, assisted with later drafts, wrote the sections on "Elaine" in Chapter 1 and 8, and provided a personal account for a box in Chapter 8. Marianne Taflinger, our editor at Wadsworth, skillfully mixed persistence and forbearance in helping us to finish this edition and do it well. Jim Kelly and Beth Shinn wrote forewords and encouraged us in many ways. We thank each of these colleagues for their support.

In our first edition, we acknowledged many individuals who had influenced our perspectives on community psychology and community life. For this edition, we also thank many colleagues and students who have given us comments and suggestions in class, at conferences, on surveys, and by e-mail. Our students especially have been patient in reading drafts, writing responses, testing exercises, and enduring our mistakes. Tracy Fox, a Bloomsburg University student, provided excellent proofreading. We also acknowledge the value of reading recent community psychology textbooks by other authors, especially those by Murray Levine, Douglas Perkins, and David Perkins; Jennifer Kofkin Rudkin; Geoff Nelson and Isaac Prilleltensky; Karen Duffy and Frank Wong; and John Scileppi, Elizabeth Teed, and Robin Torres. All of these make valuable contributions to the ongoing conversation of our field.

Our reviewers' support and critiques were genuinely thoughtful and valuable. We especially thank Jean Hill, New Mexico Highlands University, for an extended, insightful, influential review. We also thank our other reviewers, whose work we much appreciate: Bill Berkowitz, University of Massachusetts, Lowell; Craig Brookins, North Carolina State University-Raleigh; Rik D'Amato, University of Northern Colorado; Eros DeSouza, Illinois State University; Joseph Durlak, Loyola University, Chicago; James Emshoff, Georgia State University; Kelly Hazel, Metropolitan State University; Marc Levy, Southern Oregon University; Mercedes McCormick, Pace University; Clifford O'Donnell, University of Hawai'i; Loretta Simons, Widener University; Jennifer Woolard, Georgetown University.

Jim Dalton also thanks especially the members of Millville (Pennsylvania) Meeting of the Religious Society of Friends (Quakers), who have sustained him spiritually and cheerfully throughout the writing of both editions of this book. Maurice Elias thanks his colleagues at the Collaborative for Academic, Social, and Emotional Learning (www.CASEL.org) and all of our partners, whose sustained dedication to children, and to the families, schools, and communities who nurture them, inspires him to be a better community psychologist and teach others to do the same. Abe Wandersman thanks his students and former students for their valuable contributions to theory, research, and action that make community psychology valuable to our communities. He also thanks Kevin Everhart and David DuBois for their contributions on mentoring in chapter 14.

Finally, we deeply thank our families, whose love, patience, and support always nurture and enrich our lives.

April 2006
James H. Dalton
Maurice J. Elias
Abraham Wandersman

To Instructors

CHANGES IN THE SECOND EDITION: OVERVIEW

We have been gratified that teachers and students have told us that our first edition excited them, deepening and broadening their visions of their own lives, of the promise of community life, and of the field of community psychology. Kenneth Maton's (2003) review in *Contemporary Psychology* also praised our first edition as "well-written, innovative and informative" (p. 186) and cited its attention to ecological context and to community psychology values as particular strengths. In this second edition, we have built on those themes of personal involvement, attention to values, and broadened, multilevel perspectives.

We have made extensive changes to many chapters while retaining their strengths. These revisions are based on the many suggestions for improvement that we have received from colleagues, students, and reviewers (we are thankful for all of these). We also have field-tested our chapters with students in our classes, both undergraduates and graduate students, and have carefully considered their suggestions.

As instructors and students requested, in this edition we present additional personal and community narratives and extended examples to enliven our writing. We also expand our coverage of social policy research and advocacy, interdisciplinary perspectives on communities (e.g., the concept of social capital), and interventions to enhance neighborhood and community life. We portray community psychology as now more international, more attentive to human diversity, and more attuned to the nuances of social and cultural contexts than ever before. Perhaps most important, we convey the distinctive perspective of community psychology in ways that speak to the realities of students' lives and concerns. For instance, we provide narratives illustrating how ordinary citizens working together have transformed their communities and engaged in social change. In some chapters, we also illustrate in livelier detail how community concepts can usefully broaden the perspective of clinically minded students.

We retain many distinctive features of our first edition, which are seldom available in other community psychology texts. These include whole chapters on the development of the field, research contexts and methods, concepts of community (including sense of community), concepts of human diversity, exemplary prevention programs, implementation of prevention programs, citizen participation, and program evaluation. We also retain our pedagogical focus and features, especially exercises to begin chapters and at the end of chapters.

CHANGES IN THE SECOND EDITION: SPECIFIC CHAPTERS

Reviewers, especially students, told us that more stories would enliven our introductory chapters. Chapter 1 now highlights two extended, vivid examples. One concerns "Elaine," whose story illustrates how individual life is intertwined with community and macrosystem processes and how clinical treatment can be strengthened by understanding ecological levels of analysis and identifying community resources. The second example describes how Debi Starnes (2004), a community psychologist, implemented community psychology values in her work on the Atlanta, Georgia, City Council. In addition, we highlight specific personal examples from Rhona Weinstein's (2002a) *Reaching Higher,* an important critique of teaching and learning in schools. We retain two sections that provided memorable examples for students: the nine-dot problem as the opening exercise and the metaphor of musical chairs for understanding homelessness.

Chapter 2, on the history of community psychology, now focuses on the emergence and development of the field over the last 60 years. At reviewers' request, we have strengthened coverage of the international growth and global context of the field, Barbara Dohrenwend's and Marie Jahoda's conceptual contributions, influential early settings in the field, and the articulation of empowerment, feminist, critical, and liberatory perspectives. We continue to use Levine and Levine's (1992) concepts of historical forces, Ryan's (1971; 1994) concepts of victim blaming and Fair Shares/Fair Play, and Rappaport's (1981) concept of divergent reasoning needed to appreciate multiple truths in multisided debates. Although our political perspective is progressive, we also focus on common ground between conservative positions and community psychology, at least in a U.S. context. Our text is one of only two current texts in the field to devote a full chapter to the importance of these historical trends for the field today.

Chapters 3 and 4, the research methods chapters, include new coverage of feminist community psychology research, constructivist and critical approaches, and detailed coverage of methods and examples from the 2002 Chicago conference on participatory community research (Jason et al.,2004). Reviewers suggested these changes. Chapter 4 contains added coverage of community case studies, experimental social innovation and dissemination, and integrating quantitative and qualitative methods, as well as updated examples of community psychology studies. Ours is one of only two current community psychology textbooks to cover community research methods in this depth.

Chapter 5 presents fundamental ecological concepts of the field and was praised by our users. In this edition, we now discuss Moos's (2002, 2003) recent integrative papers on contexts, and activity setting concepts (O'Donnell, Tharp, & Wilson, 1993). This chapter also contains enhanced, updated coverage on neighborhoods and personal life (Shinn & Toohey, 2003) and neighborhood-level change initiatives.

We have changed the order of our chapters on community concepts and human diversity. Chapter 6 now covers concepts of community, including recent work on sense of community (e.g., Fisher, Sonn, & Bishop, 2002), and on Putnam's (2000) *Bowling Alone*, a widely recognized work on social capital. We also cover community psychologists' applications and critiques of both concepts. We describe how community concepts can be applied to spiritual communities, community service learning, and online communities. Ours is the only textbook in the field to devote an entire chapter to these important issues.

Chapter 7 now covers concepts of human diversity. Our first edition was the first community psychology textbook to devote a chapter to these topics, and this edition builds on its strengths. As users suggested, we link dynamics of oppression more clearly with liberation and social transformation. We analyze issues of conflict between culture and liberation through the work of Ortiz-Torres, Serrano-Garcia, and Torres-Burgos (2000). We include more coverage of identity development and update our coverage of individualism-collectivism, including critiques of the concept. Throughout, we continue to emphasize that there are many dimensions of human diversity and that every individual has a place on each dimension.

As users asked, we (with Elise Herndon) revised Chapter 8 to emphasize more vividly how a community-ecological perspective can inform individual/family coping and mental health services. We present a comprehensive, multilevel conceptual framework that emphasizes contextual processes and resources, positive outcomes, and points for interventions ranging from social advocacy to clinical treatment, all illustrated with additional details from the example of "Elaine" first presented in Chapter 1. Elise Herndon also provides a personal account of her personal recovery from a severe accident. and provides perspective on the recent upheavals caused by Hurricanes Katrina and Rita along the U.S. Gulf Coast, based on her prior work experiences in disaster mental health services. Our updated coverage of mutual help groups (including online mutual help) now appears in this chapter.

Chapters 9, 10, and 11 present key concepts, exemplars, and issues of prevention and promotion, a distinctive strength of our first edition (Maton, 2003). Chapter 10 includes more recent programs while retaining classic exemplars of prevention approaches and an extended example of how multiple programs could promote the coping of a specific family. Our updated Chapter 11 remains a ground-breaking analysis of the importance of implementation and context in preventive efforts. It is the only chapter of its kind in a community psychology textbook, praised by many users and in a published review (Maton, 2003).

Chapters 12 and 13 form a unit in their focus on how community and social change intertwine with individual lives. Users asked that we include more actual stories from the rich literature on these topics, and we have done so. Chapter 12 begins with three personal stories of citizen engagement in community decisions and social policy, later profiles a fourth community activist, and examines two qualitative studies of personal sociopolitical development. These narratives vividly illustrate how community and social change intertwines with individual lives as well as how seemingly ordinary persons become leaders in advocacy that transforms localities and society. We integrate these stories with later conceptual discussions. As users also requested, Chapter 12 also now contains a distinctive, interdisciplinary analysis of multiple concepts of power and empowerment. We also update coverage of empowering community settings and dilemmas of empowerment, which were strengths of our first edition (Maton, 2003).

Chapter 13 begins with six engaging stories of community and social change, then uses them to illustrate our analysis of seven approaches to such change. As users requested, we expand our coverage of policy research and advocacy, with examples drawn from community psychology advocacy on homelessness (Shinn, Baumohl, & Hopper, 2001). Chapter 13 reflects a multilevel, ecological perspective on empowerment and change in communities and societies, a perspective that emphasizes community psychology values as well as concepts and methods. Our goals are to help students to understand how community and social change are linked to their lives and to inspire them to personal involvement in efforts for community and social transformation that express their values.

Chapter 14 opens with examples of how evaluation and program improvement are pervasive in everyday life, then expands and updates its coverage of how citizens can use evaluation methods to monitor and strengthen community programs, including an emphasis on empowerment evaluation. Only one other community psychology text contains a chapter on program evaluation, and no other text presents the distinctive perspective of our chapter, which integrates community program development with program evaluation and evaluation concepts with practical methods.

Chapter 15 gives a concluding overview. We add coverage of Kelly's (1971) qualities for the community psychologist, for its intrinsic value in crystallizing the spirit of community psychology and to unite the history and future of the field. We also seek to promote students' optimism for their own engagement in community and social change, and we add additional real-life, hopeful stories of such change. We conclude with an exercise, asking students to envision their own ideal future community and society.

ALTERNATIVE ORDERINGS OF CHAPTERS

Community psychology course instructors have their own favorite ways to organize the concepts and themes of the field. In revising our second edition, we make it more convenient to arrange your own ordering of its chapters while still building on the core concepts of the field and fostering student recognition of interrelated strands among community psychology concepts. Some possible chapter orderings follow. All of our suggestions use Chapters 1–2 to introduce the field, although some instructors may choose to rely on Chapter 1 alone.

After the introductory chapters, you may proceed directly to Chapters 5–7 (ecology, community, diversity). To highlight an empowerment perspective early, you also may use Chapters 12 (empowerment and citizen participation) and 13 (empowerment and community and social change) much sooner than they appear in the book.

If your course has many clinically minded students (this includes graduate students in clinical or counseling psychology, but it is also the implicit focus of many undergraduates), enlarging their perspective to think ecologically and preventively may be an important goal. To engage their interest, you might assign Chapter 8 (coping) early, to highlight the integration of clinical and community concepts. Alternatively, Chapters 8–11 (coping and prevention/promotion) can form an integrated unit on coping and prevention at some point in the course. Chapter 14 could be added to illustrate how local program evaluation can improve program implementation and quality. However, full coverage of community psychology requires covering Chapters 5–7 and 12–13 at some point.

You may wish to assign Chapter 14 (program evaluation) following the research focus of Chapters 3–4, to illustrate how the logic of scientific thinking can be adapted to practical community program monitoring and improvement. Some instructors assign Chapters 3, 4, and 14 near the end of the course. After chapters on ecology, community, diversity, and empowerment, the emphasis in Chapters 3, 4, and 14 on participatory research and cultural anchoring may have deeper meaning. Our students also have found Chapter 14 useful for an evaluation component in papers proposing a community intervention.

These are only some of the possible orderings of chapters in this text. We encourage you to develop your own approach.

PEDAGOGY

Many instructors and students consider our engaging pedagogy to be a distinctive strength of our textbook. We remain committed to integrating pedagogy into the text to promote student reflection, insight, application, and action. This includes an emphasis on the outline for each chapter as an "advance organizer," opening exercises to promote student interest and application of concepts, use of headings, tables and boldface to highlight key terms, chapter summaries that point students to the principal themes and concepts in the chapter, and suggested readings and websites for further exploration. At the beginning of Chapter 1, we orient students to pedagogical features that they should use in the section *Suggestions to Students: How to Use This Textbook.*

We call your attention to the Brief Exercises at the end of each chapter and to the Interchapter Exercises that follow some chapters. These are resources for you to use in class to foster student application of concepts individually, in small groups, or in whole-class discussion. Some involve out-of-class projects.

The first Brief Exercise in Chapter 1 describes a format, developed by Maurice Elias, for students to write reflective reactions to each chapter. We use this format in our classes for at least some chapters and encourage you to adapt the format to the needs of your own course. We have found it highly valuable in understanding both what students think and feel and what they do and do not understand in the text.

Interchapter Exercises (following Chapters 4, 5, 8, and 9) are either longer exercises or tools for analyzing readings in the community psychology literature. Our Instructor Manual gives additional longer exercises and projects. Many of these have been featured in the Community Psychology Education Connection, which Maurice Elias and Jim Dalton founded in 1982 and which appears in *The Community Psychologist* newsletter for members of the Society for Community Research and Action. To learn more about SCRA or to become a member, see its website at http://www.scra27.org/

This textbook can be packaged with the InfoTrac® College Edition online search service, which enables you to read articles in selected recent periodicals. Those include some journals that community psychologists read, such as the *American Journal of Community Psychology.* InfoTrac® College Edition also includes popular periodicals where students can read about current social and community issues.

About the Authors

Eric Foster/Bloomsburg University

I am Professor of Psychology at Bloomsburg University in Pennsylvania. I grew up in Floyd, Virginia, and received a bachelor's degree from King College, in Tennessee, and a doctorate from the University of Connecticut. With Maurice Elias, I developed the Community Psychology Education Connection, a resource for teachers of community psychology courses that now appears in *The Community Psychologist*. In Bloomsburg, I have played leadership roles in the Task Force on Racial Equity, which works for social change on issues of human diversity and social justice. I also work with the Frederick Douglass Learning Community, which brings together first-year Bloomsburg University students of varied racial and ethnic backgrounds to live together in a residence hall, take courses together, and build a shared community. Students in this learning community appear in the photo for Chapter 15.

I originally became interested in community psychology because it seemed related to the strengths and limitations of community that I experienced while growing up in a small rural town as well as to concerns of social justice that I developed while growing up in the South during the years of the civil rights movement and Great Society anti-poverty programs. During college, my involvement in a faith-based community service learning experience in inner-city Newark, New Jersey, deepened these interests. I met Maurice Elias on my first day of graduate school at UConn. Although we came from very different backgrounds, we became lasting friends and colleagues. Abe Wandersman and I later met and became friends at a biennial conference of the Society for Community Research and Action (SCRA).

The happiest outcome of graduate school for me was meeting my wife Carolyn, whose mix of genuine love, companionship, and Connecticut Yankee practicality made this book possible. Carolyn and I have two children, Craig and Julia, and are active in the Friends (Quaker) Meeting in Millville, Pennsylvania. By the time you read this, we hope to have returned to one of our favorite hobbies: hiking in the Appalachian Mountains.

James H. Dalton, Ph.D.

Maurice Elias

I am Professor of Psychology at Rutgers University. I received my doctorate from the University of Connecticut and my B.A. from Queens College, City University of New York. Starting in 1979, I co-developed the Social Decision Making–Social Problem Solving Project, which received the 1988 Lela Rowland Prevention Award from the National Mental Health Association and has been recognized as a model program by the U.S. Department of Education's Expert Panel on Safe, Drug Free Schools, the National Association of School Psychologists, the Character Education Partnership, and other national groups.

Currently, I am a member of the Leadership Team of the Collaborative for Academic, Social, and Emotional Learning (CASEL) and a Trustee of the Association for Children of New Jersey and the H.O.P.E Foundation. With colleagues at CASEL, I was senior author of *Promoting Social and Emotional Learning: Guidelines for Educators,* published by the Association for Supervision and Curriculum Development and circulated to over 100,000 educational leaders in the United States and internationally, wrote a document commissioned by the International Bureau of Education and UNESCO, and collaborated on related works that can be found at www.CASEL.org. I have written numerous books and articles on prevention and have served in various capacities for SCRA, most recently working as part of a team establishing a practice journal for the field.

Born in the Bronx, New York, I was taken to Yankee Stadium many times at an early age and imprinted as a lifelong fan. This has generalized to other sports, particularly college basketball. Another impassioned pursuit is Jewish Education and its attendant commitment to making the world a better, more socially just place for all, something shared deeply with my wife Ellen and children Sara and Samara. As a family, we feel a deep sense of mission about closing the gaps that seem to be growing in our society and worldwide. For these and related reasons, the field of community psychology has been deeply fulfilling for me, personally and professionally.

Maurice J. Elias, Ph.D.

University of South Carolina

I am Professor of Psychology at the University of South Carolina–Columbia. I received my Ph.D. from Cornell University and my bachelor's degree from the State University of New York at Stony Brook. I perform research and program evaluation on citizen participation in community organizations and coalitions and on interagency collaboration. I am co-author of *Prevention Plus III* and co-editor of *Empowerment Evaluation: Knowledge and Tools for Self Assessment and Accountability.* I have published many other books and articles and have served on a number of national advisory committees for prevention. I received the 1998 Myrdal Award for Evaluation Practice from the American Evaluation Association. In 2000 I was elected SCRA president and in 2005 received the SCRA Award for Distinguished Contributions to Theory and Research. In a project with the Centers for Disease Control and Prevention, I am working on the development of empowerment evaluation systems in the areas of intimate partner violence prevention and sexual violence prevention.

I was born in a displaced persons camp in Germany, the son of two Holocaust survivors. I came to the United States at 9 months of age and grew up in Brooklyn, New York. I date my quest to improve the quality of people's lives to age 6, when my sister died from what I later understood was medical malpractice. Though the death of any child is a family tragedy, her death was all the more tragic because each child born to a Holocaust survivor is viewed not only as a precious treasure, but as a living repudiation of Hitler and his racist beliefs.

Entering Stony Brook in 1967 was a transforming experience in my life. Stony Brook was a hotbed of the social change being played out in the larger society. I changed my major from pre-med to psychology and looked to the social sciences for a career. I also met Lois Pall at Stony Brook, and we married shortly before we began graduate study in psychology at Cornell. Lois was a source of personal support and intellectual growth at a time when I was struggling "to learn how to think." At Cornell, I majored in social/personality psychology but cobbled together a broad curriculum, also studying child and family psychopathology, social organization and change, and environmental psychology. When I took my first teaching job at George Peabody College, Bob Newbrough introduced me to the new field of community psychology.

I am very grateful to my wife Lois and sons Seth and Jeff for attempting to keep me real and grounded, and for loving me. My linkages with family, extended family, community, and society are what life is about.

Abraham Wandersman, Ph.D.

Community Psychology

Linking Individuals and Communities

1

What Is Community Psychology?

HIRB/Index Stock

A MESSAGE TO READERS

Welcome to community psychology, and to our textbook!

Humans seek communities. Relationships with others are at the center of our lives. Individual lives and community life are intertwined. This book is about the many ways in which that intertwining occurs.

Our writing is influenced by our points of view (on some issues, we hold more than one per author). Throughout the book, we strive to be comprehensive and to discuss alternative views fairly. Yet our writing is inevitably the result of our experiences and perspectives. Those with different experiences and perspectives may view things differently. We respect that. This book is designed to lead to discussions, enabling you to develop and express your own views, and to understand those of others.

We hope that you finish this book with several accomplishments: a better understanding of community psychology, a greater appreciation of the intertwining of individual, community and society; a greater awareness of your own values; a willingness to consider with respect the many sides of community and social issues; and a passionate engagement in changing your communities and society for the better. We came to community psychology because it engaged our minds, our values, and our lives. We hope this book does that for you.

SUGGESTIONS TO STUDENTS: HOW TO USE THIS TEXTBOOK

Before we begin, please consider these suggestions on how to use this textbook. They will help you learn and retain more by organizing your learning and promoting personal involvement in what you read.

- We begin each chapter with a chapter outline. It is an advance organizer to structure your learning. Before reading the chapter, scan the outline for the major topics of the chapter. Review it again after reading the chapter.
- As you read, pay attention to headings in the chapter, which often contain key terms. Other key terms are boldfaced in the chapter text and listed in italics in the chapter summary. Lists of key concepts also may be listed in tables that appear in the text. For class or quizzes, be able to define and give examples of these key terms.
- The text of most chapters begins with an exercise that asks you to think and often to write about something. Take time to do this: it helps make the later reading more interesting. In some chapters, we also insert thought exercises or questions elsewhere in the chapter.
- We suggest recording (or at least thinking about) your reactions to each chapter after you read it. We give a format for doing this in the first Brief Exercise for Chapter 1. This format involves Revelations, Emotions, Questions, and Disagreements. Doing this helps you learn more from the reading, and participate more in class discussions.
- After each chapter we give a few Brief Exercises to apply your learning. Do these if possible. Your instructor may assign some of them or use them in class.
- We also give a few Recommended Readings and Recommended Websites after each chapter. These can extend your learning about what you read.
- Some chapters are followed by Interchapter Exercises that apply concepts from the prior chapter in more depth than the Brief Exercises. Some Interchapter Exercises are activities for you to do. Others are formats for critical reading of further sources beyond the text.
- Your textbook comes with the InfoTrac online search service that enables you to read articles in selected recent periodicals. Those include some

journals that community psychologists read, such as the *American Journal of Community Psychology.* InfoTrac also includes popular periodicals where you can read about current social and community issues.

OPENING EXERCISE

Before you begin reading this chapter, study Figure 1.1, often known as the nine-dot problem, and try to solve it. Keep at it for at least several minutes before consulting Figure 1.2 on a following page for the answer.

Were you surprised by the answer in Figure 1.2? Here's an account by one author of this book (Jim Dalton).

> The first time I encountered this problem (in Watzlawick, Weakland, & Fisch, 1974), I diagrammed alternative solutions for a number of minutes, then gave up. I was surprised how simple the answer was! I had committed the error that most people commit when they encounter this problem: I made an assumption that was not given in the instructions or the diagram. The 3 × 3 array of nine dots seemed to me to create a square box, and I tried to draw all four straight lines within that box. Not only was that assumption unnecessary, it actually made the problem impossible to solve.
>
> The real problem was my mistaken assumption (and my increasing frustration as attempted solutions failed). The box was a frame through which I viewed the nine-dot array, a frame that highlighted and limited what I saw there. Of course, that frame was more powerful because I did not recognize or question it. That is why it is so important to be able to think "out of the box" and question assumptions.

Community psychology concerns relationships among societies, communities, and individuals. These are considerably more complex than the nine-dot problem in Figure 1.1. Yet this simple puzzle contains a key message of this textbook. The assumptions that we make about a problem, especially when we are unaware that we are making them, determine the ways that we

FIGURE 1.1 Instructions: Devise a way to draw four straight lines that pass through all nine dots, without lifting your pencil from the paper and without retracing a line

SOURCE: From Watzlawick, Weakland, & Fisch (1974, p. 25).

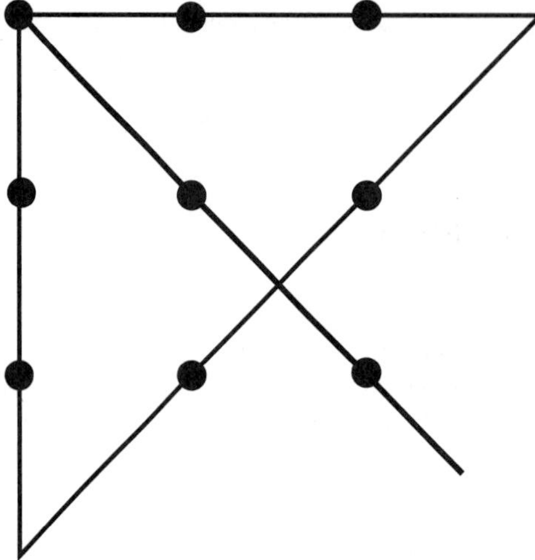

FIGURE 1.2 Answer to the nine-dot problem in Figure 1.1
SOURCE: From Watzlawick, Weakland, & Fisch (1974, p. 27).

approach and try to solve it. Our cultural background, personal experiences, education, and biases (and sometimes the biases that came with our education) help shape those assumptions, which may actually prevent effective responses to the problem. Our assumptions thus can become the real problem. If we ignore how problems are framed, we will be imprisoned by those frames (Seidman & Rappaport, 1986). In this book, we hope to broaden your thinking about framing problems. Community psychologists think outside the traditional boxes of psychology to define problems and generate interventions at many levels, not just with individuals.

Actually, there are no truly individual problems or interventions. Everything that humans do takes place in social contexts: in a culture, a locality, a setting (such as a workplace, school, playground, or home), and a set of personal relationships. A child matures, for instance, within many social contexts. When a client arrives for a psychotherapy session, he or she brings a personal set of life experiences (in social contexts), as does the therapist. They form a relationship that is rooted not only in who they are as persons, but in cultural, gender, social, economic (e.g., who pays for treatment, and how does that affect it?), and other contexts. Even the atmosphere of the waiting room, interpreted in cultural terms, makes a difference.

In this chapter we will first discuss how community psychology involves a shift of perspective from the viewpoint of most of psychology. We then elaborate the community psychology perspective by describing some of its basic assumptions about persons, contexts, and two types of change. We offer a definition of community psychology, then discuss two conceptual frameworks central to the field: ecological levels of analysis (multiple layers of social contexts), and seven core values of the field. This chapter is the first of two that introduce and define community psychology in Part 1 of this book. In Chapter 2 we trace the historical development and current contexts of community psychology.

COMMUNITY PSYCHOLOGY: A SHIFT IN PERSPECTIVE

To further explore the community psychology perspective, let's consider two real-life problems. Each involves a shift in perspective: from focusing only on individuals to considering how individuals, communities and societies are intertwined. The first is a simple but memorable analogy; the second a more detailed analysis of how individual and social problems are intertwined.

Homelessness as Musical Chairs

Many citizens assume that people become homeless because they have mental disorders or other personal problems. This represents an individualistic view, focused on how homeless persons and families are different from those with housing. However, even though research has identified a number of individual and situational risk factors for homelessness, all of them are more common among persons who do *not* become homeless (Shinn, Baumohl, & Hopper, 2001). A different view is that homelessness can be described as a game of musical chairs (McChesney, cited in Shinn, 1990). In fact, the best predictor of the extent of homelessness in a community is the ratio of available, affordable housing units to the number of persons and families seeking them (Shinn, Baumohl, & Hopper, 2001). In a game of musical chairs, this is the ratio of available chairs to the number of players.

Of course, individual variables do influence who becomes homeless. These may include income, coping skills, severity of personal problems, or having family or friends who provide temporary shelter. To continue the musical chairs analogy, these factors determine who gets available seats and who is left standing, *but not how many chairs are available.*

A study of solely individual-level variables in homelessness misses this larger reality. A social program for homelessness that focuses only on factors such as treating individual mental disorders or promoting job-interviewing skills may reshuffle which persons become homeless and which do not, yet do nothing about availability of housing. Addressing community or societal problems such as homelessness requires a shift in perspective. Within this broader perspective, community psychologists have much to contribute (e.g., Shinn, 1992; Toro, 1999).

Elaine: Multiple Contexts of Clinical Depression

"Elaine" (a pseudonym) telephoned a counseling center asking if they had anyone on staff like Dr. Kevorkian, the physician known for assisting suicide. Her husband was terminally ill, and Elaine wanted to end his life and then hers. Under the circumstances, she reasoned, everyone would be better off. Elaine felt no pleasure in life, couldn't eat or sleep, and lacked energy to do even simple tasks. She met the diagnostic criteria for Major Depressive Disorder in the DSM-IV (American Psychiatric Association, 1994). Although Elaine's problems seem like a simple case of depression, examining the contexts of her problems reveals important stressors, resources, and avenues for interventions (Wandersman, Coyne, Herndon, McKnight, & Morsbach, 2002; personal communication, Elise Herndon, September 5, 2003).

Elaine's family context seemed bleak. Her husband had responded to his illness by extensive alcohol abuse and impulsive spending. With credit cards offered in unsolicited mail, he ran up debts far beyond the family's income. When a major flood damaged their home, he spent the government disaster grant instead of making repairs. The only family income was his disability payments, which were too little to pay the debts and would end with his death. The family was in danger of losing their home. Her husband did not want Elaine to work, drive, or become involved in financial affairs. Their son also abused substances, exhibited anxiety and depressive symptoms, and was violent, at times threatening Elaine. Elaine's mother, her only neighbor within walking distance, was also ill and relied on Elaine to care for her.

Elaine had no friends or support outside the family. She lived in a rural area with no neighbors within walking distance, and she could not drive. She had no history of employment, had left school at age 15, and had few marketable skills. Her rural Southern U.S. community was geographically dispersed and offered few community services.

Treatment: An Ecological Approach Staff at the counseling center took an ecological approach to treatment, implementing a plan with multiple elements: antidepressant medication for Elaine, individual and family home visits with counseling and case management, help with obtaining government disaster assistance and debt counseling, promoting better communication between Elaine's husband and his physician, encouraging Elaine to seek wider sources of support. These approaches involve one shift of perspective, from focusing only on Elaine's personal and family situation to promoting involvement with community resources.

Elaine benefited from this approach. She stopped enabling family members, her husband stopped his alcohol abuse and spending, and her son entered treatment for substance abuse. Elaine and her husband began attending a nearby church and made new, supportive friends. With her son's help, Elaine learned to drive, broadening her sources of support. The family's money problems did not disappear, but together they were managing them better. With family life improved, Elaine's "sunny disposition" and coping skills returned, and medication was discontinued (Wandersman et al., 2002, p. 22).

Potential Community and Macrosystem Approaches Another shift of perspective flows from asking these questions: How many cases like Elaine's go unnoticed? What can communities do to prevent or lessen the suffering of people like Elaine? More accessible mental health and other services are an important partial answer, but providing trained professionals to treat everyone with psychological problems would be impossibly expensive. Citizens, psychologists, and decision makers also must address needs and resources at community and societal levels, not just focus on individuals.

Wider social forces cannot be ignored in cases like Elaine's. Economic decisions by powerful others have hit U.S. communities hard, as jobs have disappeared while executives and investors benefit. Global and local economic forces help create many personal and family difficulties, and limit public and private funding for community services. Also, even though Elaine's family members contributed to their personal and financial problems, wealthier people with similar failings have far more resources for dealing with such problems. Inequalities of wealth and opportunity are growing in many societies, including the United States. This inequality is associated with poorer health and other negative outcomes for everyone, not just those with low incomes (American Psychological Association, 2000; Lott & Bullock, 2001).

Gender beliefs and practices, from family to society, created a context in which Elaine became the overburdened caretaker in her family. She had no sources of outside support and little voice in family decisions; the men did little work but exercised control. Like many in her circumstances, Elaine had not been encouraged to think of pursuing education, making connections outside the family, making financial decisions, or even driving, as things women do.

How can psychologists address issues such as these? In this book, we will discuss a number of responses to this question. Here's an overview:

Prevention/promotion programs reduce the future likelihood of problems, for instance, by strengthening personal skills for social-emotional coping, school achievement, or other goals; by promoting parenting or family resilience; or by acting to reduce future community levels of drug abuse.

Consultation with organizations, such as workplaces, focuses on roles, decision making, communication, and conflict in the organization to promote employee job satisfaction or effectiveness of human services or schools.

Alternative settings arise when traditional services are not helpful for some populations: for example, women's centers, rape crisis centers, and self-help organizations for persons with specific problems. In Elaine's situation, a women's center, as well as self-help groups for persons in recovery from addictions or coping with disabilities, would have been helpful. For instance, Liang, Glenn, and Goodman (2005) discussed Reaching Out About Depression, a community program for women based on a feminist model. It pairs women advocates with low-income women coping with depression, providing personal support and advocacy based on feminist concepts and sharing of power in relationships.

Community development at grassroots levels helps citizens organize to identify local issues and decide how to address them. *Community coalitions* bring together citizens and community institutions (e.g., religious congregations, schools, police, business, human services, government) to address a community problem together instead of with separate, uncoordinated efforts.

Participatory research, in which community researchers and citizens collaborate, provides useful information for action on community issues. *Program evaluation* helps to determine whether community programs effectively attain their goals and how they can be improved.

Policy research and advocacy includes research on community and social issues, efforts to inform decision makers (government officials, private sector leaders, mass media, the public) about courses for action, and evaluation of the effects of social policies. Community psychologists are engaged in advocacy regarding homelessness, peace, drug abuse, positive child and family development, and other issues. One goal of this book is to introduce you to tools for advocacy, as a citizen or professional, at levels from local to international.

Any reader of this book is quite likely to participate in community initiatives such as these in the future, whether as community psychologist, clinical-counseling psychologist. or other health professional, educator, researcher, parent, or citizen. One goal of this book is to give you tools for doing so.

Understanding diverse cultures, including your own, requires another shift of perspective. Cultural traditions of individuals, families, and communities provide personal strengths and resources for effective action. Community psychology emphasizes understanding each culture's distinctiveness while not losing sight of its core values and of shared human experiences. A further goal of this book is to provide you with some tools for learning about and working in diverse cultures.

PERSONS, CONTEXTS, AND CHANGE

The shifts of perspectives that we have described involve underlying assumptions about two questions. How do problems arise? How can change occur? Next, we describe some assumptions among community psychologists about these questions.

Persons *and* Contexts

Some of our most important assumptions about problems concern the importance of persons and contexts. Shinn and Toohey (2003) coined the term **context minimization error** to denote ignoring or discounting the importance of contexts in an individual's life. **Context** (a term we will use throughout this book) refers to the encapsulating environments within which an individual lives: family, friendship network, peer group, neighborhood, workplace, school, religious or community organization, locality, cultural heritage and norms, gender roles, social and economic forces. Context minimization errors lead to psychological theories and research findings that are flawed or that hold true only in limited circumstances. These errors can also lead to therapy interventions or social programs that fail because they attempt to reform individuals without understanding or altering the contexts within which those individuals live.

A key concept of social psychology is the *fundamental attribution error* (Ross, 1977), the tendency of observers watching an actor to overestimate the importance of the actor's individual characteristics, and underestimate the importance of situational factors. When we see someone trip on a sidewalk, we often think, "How awkward," or wonder if the person has been drinking. We seldom look to see if the sidewalk is flawed. Context minimization is similar, but this term refers to contexts and forces that include those beyond the immediate situation. Cultural norms, economic necessities, neighborhood characteristics, and the psychological climate of a workplace are examples. Contexts influence our lives at least as much as individual characteristics do. This is not to say that personal characteristics do not matter, or that individuals are not responsible for their actions, but to recognize the impacts of contexts. Community psychologists seek to understand people within the social contexts of their lives and to change contexts in order to promote quality of life for persons.

Consider the multiple contexts that influence a child in a first-grade public school classroom. The personalities of teacher and students certainly influence the classroom context, but so do the relationships of the teacher with each child and each child's parents. Teachers and students also relate to others in the school. The class occurs in a physical room and school located in a wider neighborhood and community, which can support or interfere with learning. Relationships among administrators, school board, and citizens (and taxpayers) certainly influence the classroom environment, as do community, state, and national attitudes and policies about education. Actions to improve learning for students in that first-grade classroom will need to change multiple contexts (see especially Weinstein, 2002a).

Persons and Contexts Influence Each Other Community psychology is about the *relationships* of persons and contexts. These are not one-way streets. Contexts affect personal life, whereas persons, especially when acting together with others, influence and change contexts. Riger (2001) called for community psychology to appreciate how persons respond to contexts and how they can exercise power to change those contexts.

Persons influence context when citizen efforts in a neighborhood lead to improved police coverage, neighboring connections among residents, assistance for battered women, affordable housing, or action to reduce pollution by a neighboring factory. Persons who share a problem or illness influence context when they form a mutual help group to support each other. Community psychology seeks to understand *and* to improve individual, community, and societal quality of life. One of our goals for this book is to whet your appetite for involvement in community and social action in ways that draw on your personal strengths and community resources.

Reading This Book "in Context" As you read this book, we expect that at times you will disagree with or recognize limitations to what we write. Respectful disagreement is important in community psychology. Community psychologist Julian Rappaport playfully yet seriously proposed Rappaport's Rule: "When everyone agrees with you, worry" (Rappaport, 1981, p. 3). Diversity of views is a valuable resource for understanding multiple sides of community and social questions.

As you read this book, identify your specific life experiences that lead you to agree or disagree, and identify the social contexts of those experiences. If possible, discuss these with your instructor, a classmate, or your class. It is our observation that many disagreements in communities and societies are based on differing life experiences in different contexts. It is important to discuss those experiences with respect and to understand them. That discussion can deepen your own and others' learning.

First-Order and Second-Order Change

In community psychology, shifts of perspective and recognition of persons and contexts involve acting to change contexts in order to improve individual and community life. To do that, a further shift in perspective is needed.

Writing of the family as a social system, Watzlawick et al. (1974) distinguished between two kinds of change. **First-order change** alters, rearranges, or replaces the individual members of a group. This may resolve some aspects of the problem. However, in the long run the same problems often recur with the new cast of characters, leading to the conclusion that the more things change, the more they remain the same. Attempting to resolve homelessness by counseling homeless individuals without addressing the supply of affordable housing represents first-order change.

Try a thought experiment suggested by community psychologist Seymour Sarason (1972) to analyze the educational system. Criticisms of schools, at least in the United States, often focus blame on individuals or collections of individuals: incompetent teachers, unmotivated or unprepared students, or uncaring parents or administrators. Imagine changing every individual person in the school: firing all teachers and staff and hiring replacements, obtaining a new student population, and changing every individual from the school board to the classroom, yet leaving intact the structure of roles, expectations, and policies about how the school is to be run. How long do you think it will be before the same issues and criticisms return? If you answer, "Not long," you are seeing the limits of first-order change. Sometimes it is enough, but often it is not.

A group is not just a collection of individuals; it is also a set of relationships among them. Changing those relationships, especially changing shared goals, roles, rules and power relationships, is **second-order change** (Linney, 1990; Seidman, 1988). For instance, instead of preserving rigid lines between bosses who make decisions and workers who carry them out, second-order change involves collaborative decision making. Instead of rigid lines of expertise between mental health professionals and "patients," it involves finding ways that persons with disorders may help each other in self-help groups. Here are some more detailed examples.

Reaching Higher: Second-Order Change in Schools How can schools create "contexts of productive learning" for all students (Sarason, 1972)? Currently in the United States, the No Child Left Behind law seeks to reform schools by relying on standardized testing and drastic penalties for students and schools that fail. This represents first-order change within the assumptions and roles of the existing system.

Articulating a different approach to improving student learning, Rhona Weinstein began her 2002 book *Reaching Higher* with the story of "Eric" (pseudonym), a 10-year-old who had never learned to read. Tests showed no learning disability, but years of tutoring had been no help.

> A visit to his classroom, however, provided more of the story. Eric was a member of the lowest reading group, which was called the "clowns." Among its members were the sole ethnic minority child, a nonreader, an overweight

> child, and so on. Comparing the climate of the highest and lowest ability reading groups was exceedingly painful. In the highest group, the pace was lively, the material interesting, and the children active. In the lowest group, the work was repetitive, remedial, and dull. Upon following the children out to recess, I found that the friendship patterns matched the reading group assignments, but that the members of the lowest reading group stood alone and isolated, even from each other.
>
> So I suggested changing the context for learning instead of trying to change the child—that is, that Eric be moved up to the middle reading group. I also insisted on a contract specifying that he remain there for a three-month trial and that I would provide extra tutoring and psychological help to support his learning. A lengthy battle ensued. In a classic catch-22, both Eric's teacher and the principal asked for proof that Eric was capable of handling the material in the middle reading group. I argued that we would not have proof until the educational context was changed and Eric's anxiety about learning was relieved. I finally won approval. Eric was promoted to the middle reading group and slowly but surely began to read and participate in classroom life. By the end of the school year, he had reached grade level in his reading skills and he had friends. He proudly showed them off to me, his arms linked with theirs, as I walked the school halls.
>
> . . . But I kept thinking about the other Erics left behind in the lowest reading groups. . . . (2002a, pp. 2–3)

Weinstein's experience with Eric inspired her to study and create better contexts for learning in schools. She learned that students from many backgrounds experience poor contexts for learning. For instance, her twin sons, one with a visual problem from birth complications, were treated very differently in their public schooling. After only two months of first grade, the principal told Weinstein and her husband that their son with the visual problem would never be "college material like his brother" (Weinstein, 2002a, p. 19). School professionals began offering exciting classes and learning opportunities for the "talented" son, but not for the "learning-disabled" son. Parents and son had to fight this disparity throughout his schooling. With determined parental support for each son to learn in his own way, both eventually excelled in school and college.

Weinstein and her associates (Weinstein, 2002a,b; Weinstein, Gregory, & Strambler, 2004) have shown how teachers can use a wider range of techniques to teach and motivate all students, enabling them to become active learners. This leads to gains in their educational achievement. To broaden their skills, teachers need their own contexts of productive learning: administrative and peer support, and opportunities to experiment and learn. That will require changes in school systems' routines, and in public beliefs, to support the view that every child can learn if taught appropriately. All of these steps change role relationships, representing second-order change.

Oxford House: Second-Order Change in Recovery from Substance Abuse
Traditional professional treatments for substance abuse have high recidivism rates. Methods that rely more on persons in recovery helping each other offer

promising alternatives. One example is twelve-step groups such as Alcoholics Anonymous. Another is Oxford House, a network of residential settings (Ferrari, Jason, Olson, Davis, & Alvarez, 2002; Jason, Ferrari, Davis, & Olson, 2006; Suarez-Balcazar et al., 2004).

Many recovery homes (halfway houses) are located in areas of higher crime and drug use, have crowded and time-limited accommodations, and impose rules that limit resident initiative and responsibility. Some of these limitations reflect the reluctance of the larger society to support or have day-to-day contact with persons in recovery. In contrast, Oxford Houses offer more spacious dwellings in lower-crime residential neighborhoods. Residents are required to be employed, pay rent, perform chores, and remain drug-free. The resident may chose whether to be involved in professional treatment, mutual help (e.g., twelve-step) groups, or both. Separate Oxford Houses exist for women and men. Each house is governed democratically, with officers chosen by residents but without professional staff. Current residents vote on applications to join the house; a resident who returns to drug use or who is disruptive can be dismissed by a similar vote. The new resident joins a community in which there is support, shared responsibility, and shared decision making.

Oxford Houses represent second-order change because they alter the usual roles of patient and staff, making persons in recovery more accountable for their own behavior *and* for each other, in a context of equality and shared community. Evaluations indicate positive outcomes and reduced recidivism.

Listening Partners: Second-Order Change among Women The Listening Partners Program blended feminist and community psychology principles to provide peer groups for young mothers in Vermont (Bond, Belenky, & Weinstock, 2000). Its participants were low-income European-American women living in isolated rural circumstances, although many of its principles could be extended to other groups.

In Listening Partners, groups of young mothers meet weekly with local women leaders. Groups empower women to construct personal stories of their lives and strengths, learn from and support each other, and develop skills in addressing problems. Leaders minimize status distinctions between leader and participant (altering role relationships). Evaluations showed that women in Listening Partners groups (compared to a control group) strengthened qualities of "developmental leadership" in their lives, families, and communities. As one participant described her progress:

> I think a lot more about things and whether or not they can be changed. If they can, then I try to think of [things] I can do to change them. If they can't be changed, then I try to think of ways of dealing with them. . . . Now I care about other people and myself. I have a new self-assuredness—that I can do it right *and* that I have rights. (Bond, Belenky, & Weinstock, 2000, p. 720)

Listening Partners involves second-order change because it addresses societal injustice and enables changes in role relationships in women's lives, promoting individual growth within the bonds of community.

Limits of Change in Social Contexts Even second-order change does not "solve" community and social problems. Attempts to resolve community and social issues represent a problem resolution *process* rather than problem *solving*. Every resolution creates new problems or challenges: unintended consequences, altered alignments of human or material resources, new conflicts involving human needs and values. This is not a reason to give up. The process leads to real improvements *if* communities and societies carefully study both history and likely future consequences (Sarason, 1978).

For example, the school reforms discussed earlier will create challenges (Elias, 2002; Sarason, 2002; 2003a; Weinstein, 2002a,b). Creating contexts of productive learning for all will surely meet resistance, some of it legitimate. Resources are limited in schools and communities. Questions will include: Who benefits from the inequities and shortcomings of the educational system as it exists now? Who will benefit from proposed changes? Is there any common ground for compromise? Where will the necessary money, skills, and leadership come from? What will happen over time? These and other questions are critical aspects of community change.

WHAT IS COMMUNITY PSYCHOLOGY? A DEFINITION

Based on these shifts in perspective, we can now define community psychology more completely. At first, the ideas of community and psychology can seem contradictory. Community suggests the idea of persons coming together in some shared endeavor or at least geographic proximity: e.g., groups, neighborhoods, and larger structures. Psychology has traditionally concerned individual cognition, emotion, motivation, behavior, development, and related processes. In Western cultures, individual and community often have been considered opposing interests. Is community psychology an oxymoron, a contradiction in terms?

A paradox exists when two seemingly contradictory ideas turn out, upon further analysis, to be interrelated, not contradictory (Rappaport, 1981). That is true of individual and community, which are intertwined in a number of ways (Shinn, 1990). Community psychologists see quality of life for individuals, for communities and for societies as inextricable.

Keeping in mind the diversity of community psychologists' interests and personal views, we offer this definition of the field:

> Community psychology concerns the relationships of individuals with communities and societies. By integrating research with action, it seeks to understand and enhance quality of life for individuals, communities, and societies. Community psychology is guided by its core values of individual and family wellness, sense of community, respect for human diversity, social justice, citizen participation, collaboration and community strengths, and empirical grounding.

Let's unpack this definition. Community psychology concerns the multiple relationships among individuals, communities, and societies. We define community broadly. An individual lives within many communities, at multiple levels: family, networks of friends, workplace, school, voluntary association, neighborhood and wider locality, even cultures. All of these exist within larger societies and ultimately within global context. The individual must be understood in terms of these relationships, not in isolation. This means that community psychology is actually interdisciplinary, drawing on the concepts and methods of many other disciplines, including public health, community development, human development, anthropology, sociology, social work, geography, and other fields. The principal professional society for the field is named the Society for Community Research and Action, in recognition of this interdisciplinary focus.

Community psychology's focus is not on the individual or on the community alone, but on their linkages (as in the title of this book). The field also studies the influences of social structures on each other: how citizen organizations influence the wider community. Yet that understanding is always tied in some way to how these structures affect or involve individuals.

Community psychology also is committed to developing valid psychological knowledge that is useful in community life. In the community psychology perspective, knowledge is constructed through action. The community psychologist's role has often been described as that of a **participant conceptualizer** (Bennett et al., 1966, pp. 7–8), actively involved in community processes while also attempting to understand and explain them, as aptly summarized in these statements:

> If you want to understand something, try to change it. (Dearborn, cited in Bronfenbrenner, 1979, p. 37)
>
> There is nothing so useful as a good theory. (Lewin, cited in Marrow, 1969)
>
> If we are afraid of testing our ideas about society by intervening in it, and if we are always detached observers of society and rarely if ever participants in it, we can only give our students ideas about society, not our experiences in it. We can tell our students about how society ought to be, but not what it is like to try to change the way things are. (Sarason, 1974, p. 266)

Community psychology research is intertwined with community and social action. Findings from research are used to build theory *and* to guide action. For example, a program developed in a high school setting to prevent violence can generate greater knowledge of the problem, of adolescent development, of the local school and community, and of how to design future prevention programs. Moreover, community psychology research and action are collaborative, based on partnerships with the persons or communities involved.

Community psychology research and action are rooted in the seven core values listed in our definition. To elaborate on our definition, we next turn to surveying the levels of relationships and social contexts within which we live, then to detailing those seven core values.

ECOLOGICAL LEVELS OF ANALYSIS IN COMMUNITY PSYCHOLOGY

As individuals, we live within webs of social relationships. Urie Bronfenbrenner (1979) originated a concept of levels of analysis (describing levels of social contexts) that is influential in developmental psychology and community psychology. Our discussion of ecological levels is partly based on Bronfenbrenner's approach, but our frame of reference is the community, not just the developing individual. Thus our approach differs in some details from his (see also different concepts of ecological levels in Maton, 2000; Moane, 2003; Nelson & Prilleltensky, 2005).

Thinking in terms of ecological levels of analysis helps to clarify how a single event or problem has multiple causes. For instance, factors that contribute to a child's problems in school may include forces at multiple levels. Powerful adults at school, locality, national, and global levels make policy decisions that affect the quality of education the child receives. Family members, friends, and teachers have a great impact, but even their thinking and values are influenced by the school system, locality, cultural, societal, and even global levels. Have people ever urged you to become educated for competing in a global economy?

Thinking in terms of ecological levels of analysis also helps to illustrate multiple answers to an important question for community psychology: What is a community? Although originally tied to place or a locality, the term *community* has come to refer to sets of relationships among persons, at many levels, whether tied to place or not. Thus, a classroom, sorority, religious congregation, online virtual community, or cultural group (e.g., the Mexican American community) may be considered a community.

Figure 1.3 illustrates our typology of ecological levels of analysis for community psychology. The most **proximal** systems, closest to the individual and involving the most face-to-face contact, are closer to the center of the diagram. The more **distal** systems, less immediate to the person yet having broad effects, are toward the outside of the diagram. The boundaries between each level are more gradual than the diagram suggests; for instance, some organizations such as small businesses or community groups are so small that they have many of the psychosocial qualities of microsystems. The examples in italics in Figure 1.3 are illustrative and do not represent all groups at each level.

Bronfenbrenner (1979) described the webs of relationships surrounding the individual using the metaphor of the Russian nesting doll. A nesting doll is egg shaped and contains a succession of smaller dolls. Each doll, when opened, reveals a smaller doll inside. The nesting doll metaphor calls attention to how the smallest doll exists within layers of larger dolls, just as each individual exists within layers of contexts. Figure 1.3 is based on this metaphor: proximal systems are nested within broader, more distal systems. However, the nesting doll metaphor is incomplete, omitting the relationships among levels. Individuals, societies, and the levels between them are interdependent. Indeed, community psychology is based on that interdependence.

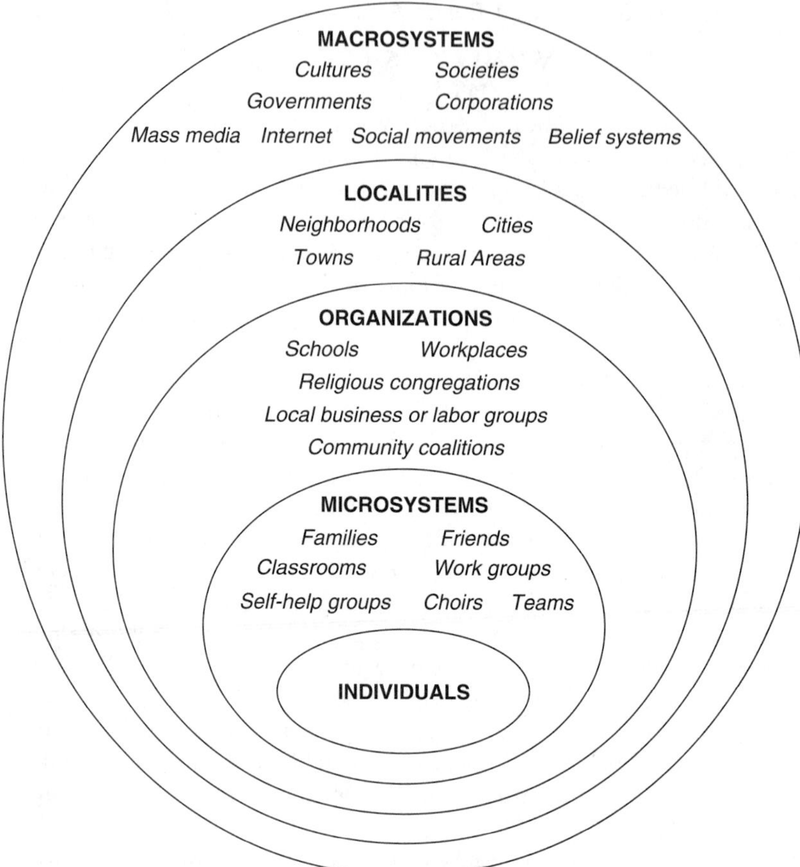

FIGURE 1.3 Ecological Levels of Analysis for Community Psychology

Individuals

Consider the smallest doll to be the individual person, nested within the other levels. The person chooses his or her relationships or environments to some extent, and influences them in many ways; likewise, they influence the person. Each person is involved in systems at multiple ecological levels, such as family and friends, workplace, and neighborhood. Much research in community psychology concerns how individuals are interrelated with social contexts in their lives. For example, a recent special journal issue examined the human costs of underemployment (Dooley & Catalano, 2003).

Community psychologists and others in related fields have developed individually oriented preventive interventions in communities, effective in reducing problems such as difficulties in the social and academic development of children, adolescent behavior problems and juvenile delinquency, adult physical health and depression, HIV/AIDS, difficulties during family transitions such as parenting and divorce, and family violence (we will discuss these in detail in Chapters 9–11). Many preventive approaches promote social-emotional competence, skills for adapting to challenging contexts and to ecological transitions from one context to another, such as entering school or becoming a parent (Weissberg & Kumpfer, 2003).

Microsystems

In the nesting doll metaphor, the first encapsulating doll represents the level of analysis just beyond the individual: microsystems. Microsystems are environments in which the person repeatedly engages in direct, personal interaction with others (Bronfenbrenner, 1979, p. 22). They include families, classrooms, friendship networks, scout troops, athletic teams, musical groups, residence hall wings, and self-help groups. In microsystems, individuals form interpersonal relationships, assume social roles, and share activities (Maton & Salem, 1995).

Microsystems are more than simply the sum of their individual members; they are social units with their own dynamics. For instance, family therapists have long focused on how families function as systems beyond their individual members (Watzlawick et al., 1974). Microsystems can be important sources of support for their members and also sources of conflict and burdens.

The concept of a **setting** is important in community psychology. In this psychological usage of the term, setting is not simply a physical place, but an enduring set of relationships among individuals that may be associated with one or several places. A chapter of a self-help group is a setting, even if its meeting place changes. Physical settings such as playgrounds, local parks, bars, or coffee shops may provide meeting places for microsystems. The term *setting* is applied to microsystems and to larger organizations.

Individuals in different contexts use microsystems in different ways. For instance, one study in a predominantly European-American university found that family support was more important during the first year of college for African-American students, who had fewer peers on campus, whereas peer support was more important for European Americans, who had more peers available (Maton et al., 1996).

What are the most important microsystems in your life? Are these microsystems part of wider settings such as a neighborhood, university, or business?

Choose one microsystem. What resources does it provide for you? What challenges or obligations does it present?

Name something that you would like to change about one of the microsystems in your life. Why?

Organizations

The next larger encapsulating doll represents the organizational level. Organizations are larger than microsystems and have a formal structure: a title, mission, bylaws or policies, meeting or work times, supervisory relationships, and so on. Organizations studied by community psychologists include human service and health care settings, treatment programs, schools, workplaces, neighborhood associations, cooperative housing units, religious congregations, and community coalitions. These are important forms of community. Employed persons often introduce themselves by where they work, for instance.

Organizations often consist of sets of smaller microsystems. Classes, activities, departments, staff, administrators, and boards make up a school or college. Departments, shifts, or work teams make up a factory or restaurant. Religious congregations have choirs, religious classes, and prayer groups. Large community organizations usually work through committees. However, organizations are not simply the sum of their parts; the dynamics of the whole organization, such as its organizational hierarchy and its informal culture, are important.

In turn, organizations can be parts of larger social units. A local congregation may be part of a wider religious body, or a retail store part of a chain. A neighborhood association offers a way for citizens to influence city government. The largest organizations, such as international corporations, political parties, or religious denominations, are macrosystems (to be defined later).

What are the most important organizations in your life?

Do you participate in these organizations through smaller microsystems? Are these organizations part of larger localities or systems?

Choose one organization. What resources does it provide for you? What challenges does it present?

Name something that you would like change about an organization in your life. Why?

Localities

The next encapsulating doll represents the locality level. Although the term *community* has meanings at many levels of analysis, one prominent meaning refers to geographic localities, including rural counties, small towns, urban neighborhoods, or entire cities. Localities usually have governments, local economies, media, systems of social, educational and health services, and other institutions that influence individual quality of life.

Localities may be understood as sets of organizations or microsystems. Individuals participate in the life of their shared locality mainly through smaller groups. Even in small towns, individuals seldom influence the wider community unless they work alongside other citizens in an organization or microsystem. An association of neighborhood residents is an organization, but the entire neighborhood is a locality. That neighborhood may also host microsystems of teen friends, adults who meet for coffee, and parents and children who gather at a playground. However, a locality is not simply the sum of its citizens, microsystems, or community organizations. Its history, cultural traditions, and qualities as a whole community surround each of those levels.

Neighborhoods are important in individual lives, and community and developmental psychologists have begun to study them. A recent research review (Shinn & Toohey, 2003) concluded that neighborhood conditions (in both urban and rural areas) are linked to children's health, personal distress, academic achievement, employment opportunities, behavior problems, delinquency, teenage childbearing, and being a victim of violence. Parenting strategies that are adaptive in safer neighborhoods differ from strategies adaptive in riskier neighborhoods (Gonzales, Cauce, Friedman, & Mason, 1996). Among adults, neighborhoods affect fear of crime, anxiety, depression, and sense of community (Shinn & Toohey, 2003).

An example of the linkage between organizations and localities is the recent emergence of community coalitions, comprised of representatives of various community groups and organizations, formed to address wider community issues such as drug abuse or health concerns.

What localities are important in your life?

Describe a locality that you live in or have lived in. What are its strengths? Limitations? What would you change about it if you could? What organizations are important in this locality? How is it affected by larger social forces?

Macrosystems

Macrosystems, represented by the largest nesting doll, include societies, cultures, political parties, social movements, corporations, international labor unions, multiple levels of government, international institutions, broad economic and social forces, and belief systems. Community psychology's perspective ultimately needs to be global.

Macrosystems exercise influence through policies and specific decisions, such as legislation and court decisions, and through promoting ideologies and social norms. Ideals of individual autonomy greatly influence U.S. culture and the discipline of psychology. Mass media communicate subtle forms of racial stereotyping, and cultural expectations for thinness, especially for women. Macrosystems also form contexts within which the other levels function, such as the economic climate affecting businesses. Yet systems at other levels can influence macrosystems through social advocacy, or through actions such as buying locally grown foods.

An important level of analysis that we include under macrosystems is the population. A population is defined by a broadly shared characteristic, such as gender, race, ethnicity, nationality, income, religion, sexual orientation, or having a physical or mental disability. Populations can be a basis of a broad form of community, such as the Jewish community or the gay community. However, not all individuals within a population will identify with it as a community.

Many studies in community psychology concern more than one level of analysis. For instance, a study of rural Midwestern U.S. families revealed that economic stress (macrosystem) on families (microsystem) lowered adolescents' (individual) sense of control in their lives and increased symptoms of anxiety and depression (Conger, Conger, Matthews, & Elder, 1999).

What does your nationality and/or ethnicity mean to you? What are its strengths?

How do the job market and other economic forces affect your daily life? Your future plans?

Do you have personal experiences with immigration or living in another culture? What did you learn from these?

SEVEN CORE VALUES IN COMMUNITY PSYCHOLOGY

> Our personal values about relationships, accountability, social change priorities, and our personal political world view all shape our priorities and agenda for community work. (Bond, 1989, p. 356)
>
> Our work always promotes the ends of some interest group, even if we do not recognize that explicitly. (Riger, 1989, p. 382)

Awareness of values is crucial for community psychology. But what exactly do we mean by values? Values are deeply held ideals about what is moral or good. They have emotional intensity; they are honored, not lightly held. Values may concern ends (goals), or means (how to attain goals), or both. They are social; we develop values through experiences with others. Individuals hold values, but so do families, communities, and cultures. Values may be rooted in spiritual beliefs or practices, but can also be secular. Many values conflicts involve choices about which of two worthy values is more important in a given situation (Nelson & Prilleltensky, 2005; O'Neill, 1989; Rudkin, 2003; Schwartz, 1994; Snow, Grady, and Goyette-Ewing, 2000).

In community psychology, discussions of values are useful for several purposes. First, values help clarify choices for research and action. Even defining a problem is a value-laden choice, strongly influencing subsequent action (Seidman & Rappaport, 1986). Public definitions of community and social problems reflect the worldviews of the powerful and help to maintain the status quo. Attending to values can lead to questioning those dominant views. For community psychologists, deciding whether to work with a particular organization or community requires attention to values. Sometimes the community psychologist may conclude that his or her values do not match those of a setting, and choose not to work together (Isenberg, Loomis, Humphreys, & Maton, 2004).

Second, discussion of values helps to identify when actions and espoused values do not match. Consider a community leader who helps to found a neighborhood social center to empower teens who are gay, lesbian, bisexual, or questioning their sexuality. The leader decides how to renovate the space and plans programs, allowing the youth themselves little say. Despite the leader's intent, this actually disempowers the youth (Stanley, 2003). The leader "talks the talk" but doesn't "walk the walk."

Or consider an alternative high school that seeks to empower students, their families, and teachers (Gruber & Trickett, 1987). Yet when decisions are to be made, the teachers have sources of day-to-day information and influence that students and parents lack; teachers thus dominate the discussion. Despite the espoused values of all involved, the organizational practices do not empower students and families. The problem is not individual hypocrisy, but an organizational discrepancy between ideals and actual outcomes.

TABLE 1.1 Seven Core Values in Community Psychology

Individual and family wellness	Citizen participation
Sense of community	Collaboration and community strengths
Respect for human diversity	Empirical grounding
Social justice	

Third, understanding a culture or community involves understanding its distinctive values. For instance, Potts (2003) discussed the importance of Africanist values in a program for middle-school African-American youth. Native Hawai'ian cultural conceptions of health are closely tied to values of *'ohana* and *lokahi*, family and community unity, and of interdependence of the land, water, and human communities. A health promotion program in Native Hawai'ian communities needs to be interwoven with these values (Helm, 2003).

Fourth, community psychology has a distinctive spirit (Kelly, 2002a), a shared sense of purpose and meaning. That spirit is the basis of our commitment, and what keeps us going when obstacles arise. It is thoughtful, but also passionate and embodied in action.

In our experience, the spirit of community psychology is based on seven core values, listed in Table 1.1. We begin with the value most closely linked to the individual level of analysis, proceeding to those more closely linked to community and macrosystem levels. This order is *not* a ranking of these values' importance. Our discussion of these seven values is influenced by, yet different from, the discussions of values by Isaac Prilleltensky and Geoffrey Nelson (2002; Nelson & Prilleltensky, 2005; Prilleltensky, 1997, 2001). These seven values, based on our experiences, are just one way of summarizing the field's values. Each individual and working group within the field must decide on what values will be central to their work. Our discussion here is intended to promote discussion of these values and the issues they raise for community life. As Bond (1989) and Riger (1989) asserted in quotations at the beginning of this section, community psychology will be guided by some set of values, and serve someone's interests, whether we realize it or not. Better to discuss and choose our values and how to put them into action.

Debi Starnes, a community psychologist, provided examples of how she applied each value in her leadership on the Atlanta, Georgia, City Council (Starnes, 2004). These examples illustrate how one committed person can make a difference, by speaking out and working cooperatively with others.

Individual and Family Wellness

Wellness refers to physical and psychological health, including personal well-being and attainment of personal goals (Cowen, 1994, 2000a,b,c). Indicators of wellness include symptoms of psychological distress, and measures of positive qualities such as resilience, social-emotional skills, personal well-being, and life satisfaction. These and similar indicators are often outcome criteria for community psychology interventions.

Strengthening families can promote individual wellness. Community prevention programs that focus on child development often address parent and family functioning. However, individual and family wellness are not synonymous. For instance, when violence or other exploitation of family members is ongoing, preserving the family conflicts with the individual wellness of those victims.

Individual/family wellness is also the focus of clinical psychology and related fields. Community psychology goes beyond, yet complements, clinical methods by placing individual wellness in the context of ecological levels of analysis. One of the events leading to the founding of community psychology in the United States was a study showing that professional clinical treatment for all who need it would be prohibitively expensive and impossible in practice (Albee, 1959). (Albee's analysis is even more believable now in the era of managed health care.) Clinical care is valuable, but not available to all, and often not to those who need it most (Felner, Felner, & Silverman, 2000).

To promote individual/family wellness, community psychologists have studied and developed community interventions focused on: prevention of maladaptive behavior, personal and family problems, and illness; promotion of social-emotional competence, and of health; social support networks and mutual help groups; intervention programs in nonclinical settings such as schools and workplaces; and advocacy for changes in social services, laws, policies, and programs to promote health and mental health.

> In her work on the Atlanta City Council, Starnes promoted the value of individual and family wellness by heading an action group that produced policies and programs for homeless persons and families. This led to developing services along a continuum of care: emergency shelter care, transitional housing, self-sufficient housing for living independently, job training, supportive housing for homeless persons with serious mental illness, and a resource opportunity center and management information system that coordinated services among 70 agencies serving the homeless. These services also helped cut costs since they diverted homeless persons from emergency rooms and jails. (Starnes, 2004, p. 3)

Starnes' efforts benefit both homeless persons and families, and the community at large. Prilleltensky (2001) proposed the concept of **collective wellness** to refer to the health of communities and societies. Cowen's (1994, 2000c) descriptions of wellness include concepts of empowerment and social justice. Certainly individual and community well-being are interwoven, and collective wellness is an attractive general principle. It is involved with the next five values that we discuss.

Sense of Community

Sense of community is the center of some definitions of community psychology (Sarason, 1974). It refers to a perception of belongingness, interdependence, and mutual commitment that links individuals in a collective unity (McMillan & Chavis, 1986; Sarason, 1974). Community psychologists have studied sense of community, for instance, in neighborhoods, schools, and classrooms, mutual help groups, faith communities, workplaces, and Internet virtual environments, (e.g., Fisher, Sonn, & Bishop, 2002; Newbrough, 1996). Sense of community is a basis for community and social action as well as a resource for social support and clinical work.

The value of sense of community balances the value of individual/family wellness. The emphasis in Western cultures and in their fields of psychology is on the individual, which in its worst forms can foster selfishness or indifference to others (Bellah, Madsen, Sullivan, Swidler, & Tipton, 1985; Sarason, 1974). Building sense of community goes beyond individualism to a focus on interdependence and relationships. From a community psychology perspective, quality of life for individual and community ultimately depend on each other.

Yet sense of community is not always positive. It can involve distancing "insiders" from "outsiders." It can be bolstered by ignoring or attacking diversity within a community, creating injustice or a deadening conformity. It is not a cure-all. In especially risky neighborhoods, withdrawal from the community may be adaptive for adults or children (Brodsky, 1996). Thus, this value must be balanced with other values, especially social justice and respect for diversity.

> In her work in Atlanta, Starnes (2004, p. 4) promoted this value through several initiatives. Atlanta has become a leader in replacing large, concentrated public housing units with attractive, well-built, mixed-income communities. Starnes was considered naïve for championing the mixing of middle-income and lower-income residents, but the first project in her district was such a success that six more similar public housing communities have been re-built. These have increased feelings of community across social class lines. In addition, Starnes helped initiate Community Redevelopment Plans for seven Atlanta neighborhoods affected by the 1996 Olympics development. Finally, she helped initiate new Quality of Life zoning and building ordinances requiring street planning and housing features that encourage neighboring. For instance, those ordinances promote having services within walking distance and having front porches and sidewalks so that people can see each other and chat more.

Respect for Human Diversity

This value recognizes and honors the variety of communities and social identities, based on gender, ethnic or racial identity, nationality, sexual orientation, ability or disability, socioeconomic status and income, age, or other characteristics. Understanding individuals-in-communities requires understanding human diversity (Trickett, 1996). Persons and communities are diverse, defying easy generalizations and demanding that they be understood in their own terms.

This is not a vague respect for diversity as a politically correct attitude. To be effective in community work, community psychologists must understand the traditions and folkways of any culture or distinctive community with whom they work (O'Donnell, 2005a). That includes appreciating how the culture provides distinctive strengths and resources for living. Researchers also need to adapt research methods and questions to be appropriate to a culture. This is more than simply translating questionnaires; it involves a thorough reexamination of the aims, methods, and expected products of research, in terms of the culture to be studied (Hughes & Seidman, 2002).

Respect for diversity does not mean moral relativism; one can hold strong values while also seeking to understand different values. For instance, cultural traditions differ in the power they grant to women; religious traditions vary in their teachings about sexuality. Respect for diversity also must be balanced with the values of social justice and sense of community: understanding diverse groups and persons while promoting fairness, seeking common ground, and avoiding social fragmentation (Prilleltensky, 2001). To do that, the first step is usually to study diversities in order to understand them. A related step is to respect others as fellow persons, even when you disagree.

> Starnes (2004, p. 5) described how she promoted respect for diversity in Atlanta by strengthening affirmative action policies, insurance coverage for domestic partners in gay and lesbian couples, and related ways of addressing past and present discrimination (matters of both social justice and respect for diversity). The housing initiatives just discussed involved promoting neighboring and community ties among diverse groups. Starnes represented a district with plenty of socioeconomic, racial, and other forms of diversity, and her job required considerable cultural competence to represent her constituents. Starnes also pointed out that Atlanta now has women in a majority on City Council, and as mayor, city attorney and chief operating officer (playfully known as "chicks in charge"). A familiar experience in community organizations is that most of the volunteers and local leaders are women, and women are now assuming leadership roles in a variety of larger contexts.

Social Justice

Social justice can be defined as fair, equitable allocation of resources, opportunities, obligations, and power in society as a whole (Prilleltensky, 2001, p. 754). It is central to some definitions of community psychology (Nelson & Prilleltensky, 2005; Rappaport, 1981).

Social justice has two meanings especially important here. **Distributive justice** concerns the allocation of resources (e.g., money, access to good-quality health services or education) among members of a population. The community mental health movement that arose in the United States in the 1960s was a distributive effort to provide mental health services to more citizens. Who determines how such resources are distributed? That is the question of **procedural justice,** which concerns whether processes of collective decision making include a fair representation of citizens. Thus distributive justice concerns the outcomes of a program or social policy; procedural justice concerns how it is planned and implemented (Drew, Bishop, & Syme, 2002; Fondacaro & Weinberg, 2002).

Psychology's record of support for social justice in the U.S. has been mixed. It has sometimes been at the forefront of social justice struggles, as in the involvement of psychologists Mamie and Kenneth Clark and others in research cited in the 1954 school desegregation case, *Brown v. Board of Education.* However, psychological research and practice has also had the effect of supporting sexism, racism, and other injustices, as in the area of intelligence testing (Gould, 1981; Prilleltensky & Nelson, 2002). The tradition of liberation psychology, rooted in Latin America, and the related fields of critical psychology and feminist psychology, exemplify psychological pursuit of social justice (Bond, Hill, Mulvey, & Terenzio, 2000a,b; Martin-Baro, 1994; Montero, 1996; Prilleltensky & Nelson, 2002; Watts & Serrano-Garcia, 2003).

A social justice perspective is often most concerned with advocacy: for social policies (laws, court decisions, government practices, regulations), and for changes in public attitudes, especially through mass media. Yet it can also guide clinical work with members of oppressed populations, and research on psychological effects of social injustice or changes in social policy.

Social justice involves concern for wellness of all persons and an inclusive vision of community and recognition of human diversity. Procedural justice is especially related to values we present next: citizen participation in making decisions and genuine collaboration between psychologists and community members.

In practice, pursuit of social justice must be balanced with other values and with inequalities in power that are difficult to change (Prilleltensky, 2001). For instance, psychologists who have worked with survivors of state-sponsored violence in Guatemala and South Africa have found that pursuing full accountability of perpetrators of past violence and greater power for survivors (social justice) must be balanced with other aims: individual healing (wellness), community and national reconciliation (sense of community), and the realities of who continues to hold power in communities and society (Lykes, Blanche, & Hamber, 2003).

> In Atlanta, Starnes (2004, p. 4–5) and other Council members addressed their concern with social justice through sponsoring a city living wage policy, which would raise the minimum wage for employees of city services and of contractors serving the city. When business representatives told her that she did not understand the "ripple effects" of that policy, she replied that she did indeed understand ripple effects, and that was why she proposed the raise! Starnes also helped pioneer a system of community courts using principles of restorative justice for nonviolent crimes, such as cleaning up graffiti and performing community service. In a related initiative, arrested prostitutes are now offered help through treatment and services for the homeless. Recidivism and costs have decreased. The housing reforms, affirmative action policies, and services for the homeless discussed earlier also promoted social justice.

Citizen Participation

This value refers to democratic processes of making decisions that allow all members of a community to have meaningful involvement in the decision, especially those who are directly affected (Prilleltensky, 2001; Wandersman & Florin, 1990).

Grassroots citizen groups, neighborhood organizations, and community-wide prevention coalitions promote citizen participation. It also refers to the ability of a community to participate in decisions by larger bodies (e.g., macrosystems) that affect its future. Citizen participation is related to the concepts of empowerment and procedural justice (Fondacaro & Weinberg, 2002; Rappaport, 1981; Zimmerman, 2000). It is fundamental to the community psychology perspective.

Citizen participation does not automatically lead to better decisions. Sometimes citizens do not consider the rights and needs of all individuals or groups. Thus this value must be balanced with values of sense of community, social justice, and respect for diversity. This can lead to conflict among competing views and interests. However, simply avoiding conflict by limiting citizen participation is often worse for those values than promoting free debate.

> Atlanta is divided into 24 neighborhood planning units. Proposed city policies (e.g., zoning) are sent to these groups for discussion and input. Starnes (2004, p. 4) referred to these sessions as "raucous democracy," but that passionate involvement of citizens means that their voices are heard, that elites find it difficult to make decisions in private, and that citizens and neighborhoods have a say in decisions that affect them. Starnes herself is a former chair of one of these groups. The community development plans growing out of the Olympics (mentioned earlier) also brought citizens and professional planners together as partners in making decisions.

Collaboration and Community Strengths

Perhaps the most distinctive value of community psychology, long emphasized in the field, involves *relationships* between community psychologists and citizens, and the *process* of their work.

Psychologists usually relate to community members as experts: researchers, clinical or educational professionals, organizational consultants. That creates a hierarchical, unequal relationship of expert and client, useful in some contexts but often inappropriate for community work. Psychologists also traditionally address deficits in individuals (e.g., diagnosing mental disorder), whereas community psychologists search for personal and community strengths that promote change. Community psychologists do have expertise to share with communities. However, they also need to honor the life experiences, wisdom, passionate zeal, social networks, organizations, cultural traditions, and other resources (in short, the community strengths) that already exist in a community. Building on these strengths is often the best pathway to overcoming problems (Maton, Schellenbach, Leadbeater, & Solarz, 2004).

Further, community psychologists seek to create a collaborative relationship with citizens, so that community strengths are available for use. In that relationship, both psychologist and citizens contribute knowledge and resources, and both participate in making decisions (Kelly, 1986; Prilleltensky, 2001; Tyler, Pargament, & Gatz, 1983). For instance, community researchers may design a study to meet the needs of citizens, share research findings with citizens in a form that they can use, and help use the findings to advocate for changes by decision makers. Developers of a community program would involve citizens fully in planning and implementing it.

Collaboration is best pursued where psychologist and community share common values. Thus it is crucial for community psychologists to know their own values priorities, and to make careful choices about whom to ally with in the community. It also means that the differences in views that emerge must be discussed and resolved fairly.

> Community psychologist Tom Wolff was engaged by a community health coalition to work with local citizens to plan health initiatives. He held an evening meeting open to all citizens. At such a meeting, one might expect to discuss community health education campaigns, the need for a community clinic, early screening programs, or mutual help groups. Instead, the most important need identified by many citizens was for street signs! Wolff barely contained his amazement. Yet recently in this community, emergency medical care had been delayed several times, with serious consequences, because ambulances could not locate residences.
>
> Wolff duly noted this concern, then sought to turn the conversation to matters fitting his preconceptions. However, the local citizens would not have it; they wanted a plan for action on street signs. When that need had been met, they reasoned, they could trust the health coalition to work with them on other issues. Wolff then shifted to working with the citizens to get the municipality to erect street signs. Instead of pursuing his own agenda, he worked with citizens to accomplish their goals. His actions illustrate the values of citizen participation and collaboration (Wolff & Lee, 1997).
>
> In Atlanta, Starnes (2004, p.4–6) noted how her work as an elected official often involves listening to and mediating between competing interests whose advocates hold strong, emotional views. She cited a pressing need in government for community psychologists with mediation skills. Starnes uses her community psychology process and collaborative skills every day, and has a lively appreciation of the strengths of her constituents and of the city at large.

Empirical Grounding

This value refers to integrating research with community action, basing (grounding) action in empirical research findings whenever possible. This uses research to make community action more effective, *and* makes research more valid for understanding communities. Community psychologists are impatient with theory or action that lacks empirical evidence, and with research that ignores the context and interests of the community in which it occurred.

Community psychologists use both quantitative and qualitative research methods (we discuss both in Chapter 4). Community psychologists prize generating knowledge from a diversity of sources, with innovative methods (Jason, Keys, Suarez-Balcazar, Taylor, & Davis, 2004; Martin, Lounsbury, & Davidson, 2004).

BOX 1.1 Education and Careers in Community Psychology

Community psychologists hold master's or doctoral degrees. Doctoral and master's programs fall loosely into three types.

- Free-standing community psychology programs focus on community psychology.
- Programs in community-clinical psychology, or with a specialty track in counseling, allow students to pursue training in both community and clinical-counseling areas.
- Interdisciplinary community programs integrate community psychology with related psychological fields such as applied developmental or applied social psychology, or with disciplines outside psychology such as human development and community development.

Some programs also offer coordinated studies for degrees in fields such as law, planning, social work, or public health. A master's degree typically takes two years of full-time study after the bachelor's degree; a doctorate (usually Ph.D.) four to six years full time, after the bachelor's degree. Some master's-level programs also admit part-time students. Some programs encourage students to have work experience before beginning graduate study. See your instructor or another member of the psychology faculty for advice about graduate school.

Graduate programs in community psychology are profiled at the Society for Community Research and Action website:
http://www.scra27.org/scraprograms.html

Community psychologists perform a variety of duties, typically specializing in one or more of these areas:

- research on community issues, program evaluation, or social policy
- advocating for changes in social policies
- work as or with elected officials on social policies
- developing and coordinating prevention/promotion programs
- working with alternative settings
- administering community services and programs
- consulting with community agencies, schools, or workplaces
- coordinating community coalitions
- academic teaching, research, and administration
- with clinical-counseling training, psychological treatment

As you can see from this list, community psychologists work at many ecological levels, from individuals to macrosystems. Their work expresses the seven core values described in this chapter.

Community psychologists work in many settings, including youth and family services; health promotion programs; substance abuse prevention settings; community prevention/promotion programs; domestic violence and rape crisis centers; criminal justice settings; mental health services; national, state, and local advocacy organizations; community development organizations; community coalitions; private foundations and funding organizations; executive and legislative branches of government; and academia. This is only a suggestive list. One beauty of community psychology is that its perspective can be useful in many settings. If you have a particular interest that you do not see here but are intrigued by community psychology, there is probably a pathway for you in the field.

Community psychologists tend to be both idealistic and practical in their work. Their work often is a *vocation* in its original sense: a calling or leading that one follows, in which actions express deeply held values. We don't know any wealthy community psychologists, but the ones we know love their work.

Community psychologists believe no research is value free; it is always influenced by researchers' values and preconceptions, and by the context in which the research is conducted. Drawing conclusions from research thus requires attention to values and context, not simply to the data. This does not mean that researchers abandon rigorous research, but that values and community issues that affect the research are discussed openly, to promote better understanding of findings.

Starnes (2004, p. 5–6) has advocated basing decisions of Atlanta government on empirical evidence whenever possible. She admitted that she had only mixed success. Yet methods abound for using research evidence to inform government decisions, evaluate community programs, and assist neighborhood associations. Moreover, Starnes noted that community problems and decisions are growing more complex, requiring more knowledge and analytical ability and providing a challenge for community psychologists.

Conclusion: Values in Context

No discipline commands unanimity among its members, and community psychologists in particular can be a skeptical, questioning lot (recall Rappaport's Rule). These core values therefore must be understood in terms of how they complement, balance and limit each other in practice (Prilleltensky, 2001). For instance, individual wellness must be balanced with concern for the wider community. Collaborating with local community members is a time-consuming approach that can slow the completion of research. Promoting a local sense of community or cultural identity does not necessarily promote a wider concern for social justice. Community life and a wise community psychology require accommodations among these values, rather than single-minded pursuit of one or two.

Moreover, abstract ideas such as individual/family wellness, social justice, respect for diversity, and sense of community can mean very different things to different persons or in different contexts (Riger, 1999). These seven core values must be elaborated and applied through example and discussion. As you read this book, seek a way to discuss values questions respectfully with others. Part of the appeal of community psychology is that values issues are on the table to be discussed.

Box 1.1 describes the education, work settings, and professional activities of community psychologists. These are tangible ways that community psychologists express their values, in work involving multiple ecological levels of analysis.

CHAPTER SUMMARY

1. Community psychology concerns the relationships of individuals with communities and societies. By integrating research with action, it seeks to understand and enhance quality of life for individuals, communities, and societies. Community psychology emphasizes collaboration with community members as partners in research or action. Community psychologists are *participant conceptualizers* in communities, engaged in community action and in research to understand that action.
2. Compared to other psychological fields, community psychology involves a shift in perspective. The focus of community psychology is not on the individual alone, but on how the individual exists within a web of *contexts:* encapsulating environments and social connections. Persons and social contexts influence each other. Discounting the influence of social contexts is the *context minimization error.*

3. *First-order change* alters or replaces individual members of a group or community; *second-order change* alters the role relationships among those members. Examples of second-order change include changing schools to provide contexts of productive learning for all students, changing systems for recovery from substance abuse, and empowering young mothers. Every action creates new challenges, yet these can be an improvement over time.
4. Community psychologists study *ecological levels of analysis. Individuals* are nested within *microsystems* such as families, friendship networks, classrooms, and small groups. Microsystems often are nested within *organizations* such as schools and workplaces. Organizations are nested within wider *localities*, such as neighborhoods. Localities are nested within *macrosystems* such as societies and cultures. Microsystems are the most *proximal* (closest) level to individuals, whereas macrosystems are the most *distal* (farthest away), yet all influence individual lives. A *setting* is an enduring set of relationships among individuals that may be associated with one or several physical places. It may apply to microsystems or to organizations.
5. Values are important in community psychology. They help clarify issues and choices in research and action, facilitate questioning of dominant views of social issues, and promote understanding how cultures and communities are distinctive.
6. Community psychology is based on seven core values: *Individual and family wellness, Sense of community, Respect for human diversity, Social justice, Citizen participation, Collaboration and Community strengths, and Empirical grounding. Distributive justice* concerns whether resources in society are allocated fairly; *procedural justice* concerns whether decision-making processes are inclusive. These seven core values are interrelated. Pursuit of one value, without consideration of the others, leads to one-sided research and action.

BRIEF EXERCISES

1. Consider each of these questions about the chapter:
   What were the most important revelations or insights for me?
   What emotional reactions did I have, at what points in the chapter, and why?
   What questions do I have now about the topics of this chapter?
   With what might I disagree? How is that related to my own life experiences?
   (We recommend using this format for all chapters in this book. Discuss your answers with a friend, classmate, your instructor, or in class.)
2. What are your answers to these questions of vision and values? Discuss them with others.
   How would you define an ideal personal life?
   How would it be related to community and society?
   What core values would guide this life?
   How would you define an ideal community?
   How would it enable a good life for individuals? Families?
   What organizations would exist in this community? Why?

What would be the core values of this community? Why?
How would you define an ideal society?
How would it enable a good life for individuals, families, and communities?
What would be core values of this society? Why?

3. Review the seven core values of community psychology. Discuss your answers with others.
   Which of these resonate most with your own values? Where might you disagree?
   Thinking about communities in your own life, what other values are important to you?
   What examples of conflicts among these values can you think of?
4. Read a recent article in a community psychology journal that is interesting to you. Describe which of the seven core values it addresses. You can access the *American Journal of Community Psychology* through the InfoTrac search service that comes with this textbook.
5. List at least five important social problems or issues facing your community or society. Choose one of these and answer these questions:
   Which community psychology values are relevant to this issue, and why?
   How does this issue involve factors at individual, microsystem, organizational, locality, or macrosystem levels?

RECOMMENDED READINGS

Rappaport, J., & Seidman, E. (Eds.). (2000). *Handbook of community psychology.* New York: Kluwer/Plenum.

Shinn, M., & Toohey, S. M. (2003). Community contexts of human welfare. *Annual Review of Psychology, 54,* 427–460.

 RECOMMENDED WEBSITES

The Community Psychology Net
http://www.communitypsychology.net

Information about community psychology and links to other community psychology sites. Useful for students, citizens and community psychologists.

Society for Community Research and Action
http://www.scra27.org/

Website of the international professional body of community psychology. Information on SCRA mission and goals, membership benefits, interest groups, listservs, graduate schools, and job opportunities in community psychology, conferences and activities (including those for students).

 INFOTRAC® COLLEGE EDITION KEYWORDS

community(ies), community psychology

2

How Has Community Psychology Developed?

HIRB/Index Stock

OPENING EXERCISE

> History is the parent—at present, a largely unrecognized parent—of psychology's concerns. (Rogler, 2002, pp. 1020)

Consider for a few moments the impact on your life of the terrorist attacks of September 11, 2001, and their many consequences across the world. Are there ways in which your personal life is different since then? How? Are the communities in your life different? How? Is your society different? How? If you live outside the United States, was September 11 as important in your society as it has been in the U.S.? Why or why not? Have other recent historical events been more important in your nation or in your own life? How?

Now consider your education in the field of psychology or related fields. Does that education help you understand the personal impact of historical, cultural, social, political, and economic forces in our lives? (The forces that led up to September 11, and that flowed from it, are examples.) What other sources of knowledge are needed?

Like persons and communities, academic fields are influenced by their historical contexts. In this chapter we consider how community psychology is developing as a distinctive field. Community psychology today flows from its history, which has contexts, settings, characters, and turns of plot. At many points there are multiple stories. That history becomes the present and future, and it includes you as a student, a citizen, perhaps a future psychologist.

Our perspective is not the only way to view the history of community psychology. Indeed, our goal is to stimulate you to think critically, for yourself and in dialogue with others, about the field. We focus on community psychology in the United States but also recognize its international roots and that it is now a global field.

Community psychology in the U.S. is usually considered to have originated at a conference of psychologists in Swampscott, Massachusetts, in 1965. Yet the story does not start there. The Swampscott conference did not occur in a vacuum—it was nested in the historical and cultural context of mid-twentieth-century U.S. society and psychology. In fact, community psychology was evolving before Swampscott, and it has continued to grow. We must go back "before the beginning" (Sarason, 1974) to set the stage. First, we consider some characteristics of psychology, the parent field of community psychology.

INDIVIDUALISTIC SCIENCE AND PRACTICE IN PSYCHOLOGY

> If [early psychologists] had put not one but two or three animals in a maze, we would have had a more productive conception of human behavior and learning. (Sarason, 2003b, p. 101)

Psychology, especially in the United States, has traditionally defined itself as the study of the individual organism. Even social psychologists have studied primarily the cognitions and attitudes of individuals. The tradition of behaviorism, which does emphasize the importance of environment, has seldom studied cultural-social variables. Psychodynamic, humanistic, and cognitive perspectives have focused on individuals rather than on their environments. This stance has had considerable benefits, but also some limitations that led to the emergence of alternative viewpoints, including those of community psychology.

Psychology did not have to develop with so much focus on the individual. Defining psychology as the study of how individuals are related to their sociocultural environment is implicit in the early works of John Dewey and Kurt Lewin (Sarason, 1974, 2003b). In 1896, Lightner Witmer's Psycho-Educational Clinic opened in Philadelphia, the first psychological clinic in the United States. Concerned with educational problems of children, Witmer asserted that every child can learn, altered teaching methods to fit the needs of each child, and worked collaboratively with public schools, anticipating later themes of community psychology (Levine & Levine, 1992). Despite this example, later psychological practice focused on individual disorders and on professional assessment and treatment, primarily with adults.

Psychology in Cultural Perspective

For most of its history, psychology has been primarily conceptualized, researched, and practiced by European-American men, often with research participants from the same background. When women were studied directly, it was often within a male-centered theoretical framework. The experiences of persons of differing racial and ethnic backgrounds were seldom studied until recently, and often within an ethnocentric Western cultural framework. This legacy assumed that individuals are largely independent of each other. Interdependence in relationships, and the relationships of individuals to communities, was considered secondary or ignored (e.g., Miller, 1976; Riger, 1993; Sarason, 1974, 1994; 2003b; van Uchelen, 2000).

In a classic challenge to this thinking, Kenneth Gergen (1973, p. 312) argued that in cross-cultural perspective, many psychological concepts would seem much different. High self-esteem, prized in Western, individualistic cultures, could be considered an excessive focus on oneself in cultural contexts that emphasize interdependence among group members. Similarly, in many world contexts, seeking to control events and outcomes in one's life might communicate a lack of respect for others. Social conformity, something to be resisted in the worldview of Western individualism, could be interpreted in a different cultural context as behavior cementing the solidarity of an important group. This is not to say that individualistic concepts are mistaken, simply that they are not universal.

Power and control are psychological concepts especially influenced by individualistic thinking (Riger, 1993; van Uchelen, 2000). Psychologists often have focused on whether an autonomous individual can exercise control over his/her circumstances. Believing that you hold such internal control, in general, is often associated with measures of psychological adjustment in individualistic contexts (Rotter, 1966, 1990). This approach assumes an independent self with a clear boundary between self and others. While applicable in individualistic contexts, such a view does not hold in contexts where interdependence is prized: in non-Western cultures, or in close-knit communities in Western cultures (van Uchelen, 2000). Individuals in those contexts assume that to exert control, they must cooperate with others. This weakens the psychological distinction between "internal" and "external" control. Moreover, feminist thinkers (e.g., Miller, 1976; Riger, 1993) have noted that psychological conceptions of control often equate pursuit of one's goals or interests with dominating others. Yet greater control of one's circumstances often can be pursued through cooperation (Shapiro, Schwartz, & Astin, 1996; van Uchelen, 2000).

These examples are only a few of the issues for which cultural awareness is needed in psychology. Many areas of the discipline, including community psychology, are now beginning to study individuals within cultural and social contexts. Yet as we shall see in this and later chapters, this is not always easily put into practice.

Individualistic Practice

Professional psychological practice also focuses primarily on individuals. The psychometric study of individual differences has long been linked to testing in schools and industry. Individuals are measured, sorted, and perhaps changed, but the environments of school and work seldom receive such scrutiny. In addition, much psychotherapy is based on assumptions of individual primacy. The client focuses inward to find new ways of living that yield greater personal happiness. Concern for others is assumed to automatically follow from this concern for self (Bellah, Madsen, Sullivan, Swidler, & Tipton, 1985; Wallach & Wallach, 1983). This approach is often helpful for those whose lives are in disarray. However, it may overlook interpersonal, community and social resources for recovery. As a general philosophy of living, it emphasizes self-fulfillment and says little about commitment to others. An individualistic perspective frames the ways we picture ourselves, the discipline of psychology, and our communities and society. As with the nine-dot problem in Chapter 1, unless we are aware of those frames, they can imprison our thinking.

Changing settings, communities, or society is often necessary to improve quality of life for individuals. Our point is not that individually based research, testing, and psychotherapy are useless, but that psychology relies heavily on individualistic tools when others are also needed. Community psychology seeks to identify and work with those other tools.

Community psychology represents both a reaction to the limitations of mainstream psychology and an extension of it. The field developed through this tension and continues to experience it today. To understand how the field has developed, we begin by considering U.S. society in the mid-twentieth century.

COMMUNITY PSYCHOLOGY EMERGES IN THE UNITED STATES

During the 1930s and 1940s, the United States and its allies overcame a disastrous economic depression and won the Second World War. The war effort reached into every home, challenging and strengthening national solidarity. Women entered the paid workforce in unprecedented numbers. Many of them were laid off at war's end, yet their competence had been established and helped fuel later feminist efforts. African Americans and other persons of color served their country and returned home less willing to tolerate racial discrimination. American troops of Japanese ancestry earned recognition for bravery, while at home

Japanese Americans were incarcerated in detention camps. Anti-Semitism, openly practiced in academia and elsewhere, lost influence in the wake of the Holocaust. The postwar G.I. Bill sent many veterans to college and broadened the focus of universities. Widespread psychological problems among combat veterans led to the rise of clinical psychology.

These events set in motion important changes in U.S. society during the 1950s and 1960s that led to the emergence of community psychology (Wilson, Hayes, Greene, Kelly, & Iscoe, 2003). We will describe five forces that influenced this emergence (admittedly, this framework oversimplifies the many factors involved). All five forces reflect increasingly community-oriented thinking about personal, community, and social problems. (See Levine, Perkins, & Perkins [2005] for a detailed alternative account of these origins.)

A Preventive Perspective on Problems in Living

> No mass disorder afflicting humankind has ever been eliminated or brought under control by attempts at treating the affected individual. (Gordon, quoted by Albee in Kelly, 2003)

The first of these forces involved the development of a preventive perspective on mental health services, influenced by the concepts of the discipline of public health. Public health is concerned with preventing illness more than with treating it. Prevention may take a variety of forms: sanitation, vaccination, education, early detection, and treatment. Moreover, public health takes a population perspective, focusing on control or prevention of disease within a community or society, not merely for an individual. As implied in the quotation, long-term successes in controlling diseases such as smallpox and polio have come from preventive public health programs, not from treating persons already suffering from the disease (treatment is humane but does not lead to wider control of disease). Applied to the area of mental health services by psychiatrists Erich Lindemann, Gerald Caplan, and their colleagues, a public health perspective emphasized environmental factors in mental disorder, early intervention in psychological problems, community-based services rather than isolation in hospital settings, and using community strengths to prevent problems in living (Caplan, 1961, Klein & Lindemann, 1961; Lindemann, 1957).

Lindemann emphasized the importance of life crises and transitions as the points of preventive intervention for mental health services. His best-known study concerned families coping with bereavement (Lindemann, 1944). A tragic fire at the Coconut Grove nightclub, in Boston, was near a clinic where Lindemann worked. Many survivors needed help, far more than clinic staff could serve with the usual psychodynamic treatment approaches. Lindemann was certain that the trauma experienced by many people would lead to even more psychological and family problems in the future. Rather than waiting for full-blown disorders to develop, Lindemann developed education about coping and support for the bereaved to have a preventive effect.

In 1948, Lindemann built on this approach in helping to found the Human Relations Service in Wellesley, Massachusetts, which provided consultation with parents and teachers, educational workshops, support groups, crisis intervention, and short-term therapy. Service staff collaborated with citizens and community leaders such as clergy and school officials. This foreshadowed the community psychology value of community collaboration and strengths and embodied altering of role relationships and second-order change. An early director of the Human Relations Service, Donald Klein, became a founder of community psychology. The HRS provided a setting for research by psychologists, sociologists, and anthropologists interested in mental health and public health (Felsinger &Klein, 1957; Kelly, 1984; Klein, 1984, 1995; Klein & Lindemann, 1961; Lindemann, 1957; Spaulding & Balch, 1983). Interest in community services and prevention resulted in a 1955 conference where Lindemann, Klein, and others described their work and suggested future possibilities for a field to be called "community mental health" (Felsinger & Klein, 1957; Strother, 1957; Wilson et al., 2003).

In 1953, psychologist John Glidewell joined Margaret Gildea and associates with a public health department in St. Louis County, Missouri, to establish programs in schools and with parents to prevent behavior disorders in children (Glidewell, 1994; Glidewell, Gildea, & Kaufman, 1973; Kelly, 2003). In 1958, Emory Cowen and colleagues began the Primary Mental Health Project in the elementary schools of Rochester, New York, seeking to detect early indicators of school maladjustment in students and intervene before full-blown problems appeared (Cowen, in Kelly, 2003; Cowen, Pedersen, Babigian, Izzo, & Trost, 1973; Cowen et al., 1996). Like the Human Relations Service, these innovative programs involved collaboration with community members that helped to initiate second-order change. They also evaluated their efforts with empirical research. Thus they helped to forge the community psychology values of wellness, community collaboration, and empirical grounding.

Although it was not within a public health framework, another early program in schools was noteworthy. Seymour Sarason and colleagues at the Yale Psycho-Educational Clinic began collaborating with schools and other institutions for youth in 1962. (Sarason took the Clinic's name from Lightner Witmer's early clinic.) Through working alongside school staff, Clinic staff sought to understand "the culture of the school" and to identify and foster "contexts of productive learning" to promote youth development. The Clinic focused on understanding and changing settings, not just individuals, taking an ecological approach that foreshadowed important community psychology themes (Sarason, 1972, 1982, 1988; 1995; Sarason, in Kelly, 2003).

Although prevention initiatives represented important innovations, they encountered sharp resistance by advocates of traditional clinical care and did not yet enter the mainstream of either psychiatry or clinical psychology (Strother, 1987).

Reforms in the Mental Health System

[As a Quaker conscientious objector to war, Wilbert Edgerton was assigned in 1942 to alternative service in a state mental hospital. Here he describes his experiences.] They had more patients than beds, more patients than blankets.

> It was run like a feudal estate that turned money back to the state every year. . . . One of our group documented all these things and brought it to the state legislature, which had a special session and appropriated more money for all the state hospitals. . . . This is an example of how, if you take action, good things can happen. (Edgerton, 2000)

A second force leading to the emergence of community psychology involved sweeping changes in the U.S. system of mental health care. These began with World War II and continued into the 1960s (Humphreys, 1996; Levine, 1981; Sarason, 1988). After the war, a flood of veterans returned to civilian life traumatized by war. The Veterans Administration (VA) was created to care for the unprecedented numbers of veterans with medical (including mental) disorders. In addition, the National Institute of Mental Health (NIMH) was established to coordinate funding for mental health research and training. Both of these federal administrations decided to rely heavily on psychology (Kelly, 2003).

These events led to a rapid expansion of the field of clinical psychology and continue to influence it today. Clinical training became a specialized program within university psychology departments. Clinical skills were primarily learned in medical settings (often VA hospitals, working with adult male veterans). This approach was codified at the Boulder Conference in 1948. Its emphasis on individual psychotherapy with adults was a product of the needs of the VA and the treatment orientation of a medical model. The child-family focus and environmental perspective of Witmer's and other early psychological clinics, another possible pathway for the new field, was largely overlooked. This was an important missed opportunity (Humphreys, 1996; Sarason, 2003b).

Also emerging in the postwar society was a movement for reform in the quality of mental health care (Levine, 1981; Sarason, 1974; Spaulding & Balch, 1983). Journalistic accounts and films documented inhumane conditions in psychiatric hospitals, and citizen groups such as the National Association for Mental Health advocated reform. Advances in psychotropic medication made prolonged hospitalization less necessary, strengthening reform efforts. After his formative experience in a mental hospital quoted earlier, Wil Edgerton helped pioneer efforts to improve community mental health services through advocacy and collaboration with community groups (Edgerton, 2000, 2001). Under Robert Felix, the NIMH became a key setting for psychologists interested in preventive and community innovations (Goldston, 1994; Kelly, 2002b, 2003).

A further problem with mental hospitalization at the time was that hospital care did not prepare patients for living in the community upon release. In 1960, George Fairweather and colleagues at a Palo Alto, California, VA hospital began developing and evaluating an innovative program, the Community Lodge, to address this problem (Fairweather, 1979, 1994; Fairweather, Sanders, Cressler, & Maynard, 1969; Kelly, 2003). (Their sample of male veterans illustrated the narrowing of focus associated with the VA.) The Community Lodge research documented that men with severe mental disorders, whom professionals considered unfit to live in the community, could in fact live very well in a supportive community, monitoring each others' functioning and even running a small business

BOX 2.1 Marie Jahoda: A Foremother of Community Psychology

The work of Marie Jahoda, a social psychologist, foreshadowed and influenced today's field of community psychology. In 1930, Jahoda and her associates formed an interdisciplinary team to research the psychological effects of unemployment (Jahoda, Lazarsfeld, & Zeisel, 1933/1971). They studied Marienthal, an Austrian village where the principal workplaces closed as worldwide economic depression deepened. Their study was the first to connect unemployment with psychological experiences, which ranged from resignation and despair to practical coping and hardy resilience. The research team focused on studying the community as well as individuals using documents, questionnaires, interviews, individual and family histories, and participant and nonparticipant observation. They collaborated as partners with community members and found practical ways to serve the community. They sought to understand Marienthal in its own terms, not to test hypotheses for generalization to other locales. Their research has influenced much later work, including community psychology research today (Fryer & Fagan, 2003; Kelly, 2003). When fascists took power in Austria, Jahoda was jailed, then allowed to emigrate to Britain; she later lived in the United States (Unger, 2001).

Partly because of her research on resilience and strengths among Marienthal families, in the 1950s the U.S. Joint Commission on Mental Health asked Jahoda to lead an interdisciplinary committee to define positive mental health, not simply as absence of mental disorder but as the presence of positive qualities. The group's report identified criteria of positive mental health, including a strong personal identity, motivation for psychological growth, pursuit of values, resilience under stress, independent choices and actions, empathy, and adequacy in love, work, play, and interpersonal relations. Jahoda and associates concluded that positive mental health is a value-laden concept influenced by social context. For instance, they argued that for Western cultures, autonomy is a key component of positive mental health, but that it may be less important elsewhere (Jahoda, 1958; Jahoda, in Kelly, 2003). The report defined qualities of persons, but not of conditions that might foster mental health. Yet it was an important advance, foreshadowing current concepts of community psychology and positive psychology.

with minimal professional supervision. The Community Lodge emphasized mutual help, relatedness, and accountability to the community, rather than individual treatment. When Fairweather approached mental health administrators about widespread adoption of the Lodge model, however, few were interested in an approach that so boldly empowered persons with mental disorders. Fairweather's core emphases are still influential in community psychology today: humanitarian values in mental health care, developing innovative programs, evaluating their effectiveness in rigorous field experiments, and disseminating the results widely (Hazel & Onanga, 2003; Seidman, 2003).

In 1961, the federally sponsored Joint Commission on Mental Illness and Mental Health recommended sweeping changes in mental health care (Joint Commission, 1961). In one of the commission's studies, psychologist George Albee (1959) reviewed recent research that documented surprisingly high rates of mental disorders, compared this with the costs of training clinical professionals, and concluded that the nation could never afford to train enough professionals to provide clinical care for all who needed it. Albee and others called for an emphasis on prevention. Psychologist Marie Jahoda headed efforts to broaden thinking about mental illness by defining qualities of positive mental health, a forerunner of current concepts of wellness, resilience, and strengths (see Box 2.1). Jahoda also advocated identifying conditions that inhibited personal mental health and altering those conditions through prevention and social change (Albee, 1995;

Kelly, 2003). However, in their final report most Joint Commission members remained committed to individualized professional treatment (Levine, 1981).

As a response to the Joint Commission report, the NIMH proposed a national system of community mental health centers (CMHCs; Goldston, 1994; Levine, 1981). With the support of President Kennedy, whose sister suffered from a mental disorder, and through timely advocacy by members of Congress, NIMH, and the National Mental Health Association, Congress passed the Community Mental Health Centers Act in 1963. CMHCs were given a different mandate than traditional psychiatric hospitals, including care for persons with mental disorders in the community, crisis intervention and emergency services, consultation with community agencies (e.g., schools, human services, police), and prevention programs (Goldston, 1994; Kelly 2003; Levine, 1981). The Wellesley Human Relations Service was to be a model for these services. The CMHC approach, with federal funding, strongly influenced the emergence of community psychology.

Group Dynamics and Action Research

> Kurt Lewin was not concerned with research topics considered "proper" within psychology, but with understanding interesting situations. . . . Lewin was a creative person who liked to have other people create with him. (Zander, in Kelly, 2003; Zander, 1995)

A third force influencing the development of community psychology originated in social psychology: the group dynamics and action research traditions that began with Kurt Lewin (Kelly, 2003; Marrow, 1969; Zander, 1995).

Lewin spent much of his career demonstrating to laboratory-based psychologists and to citizens that social action and research could be integrated in ways that strengthen both. He is known for asserting that "there is nothing so practical as a good theory" (Marrow, 1969). Lewin was a founder of the Society for the Psychological Study of Social Issues (SPSSI), long an important voice in U.S. psychology. During the 1940s, as a Jewish refugee from Nazi Germany, he became interested in how the study of group dynamics could be used to address social and community problems.

The first community problem with which the Lewin action research team became involved was not primarily a mental health issue. The team was asked to help develop methods to reduce anti-Semitism in Connecticut communities and began conducting citizen group discussions (Cherry & Borshuk, 1998; Marrow, 1969, pp. 210–211). The insistence of citizens that they be included when psychologists analyzed these discussions, and their disagreement with those psychologists' views, led Lewin's team to focus on group dynamics and to the creation of training group methods (T-groups; Bradford,Gibb, & Benne, 1964). After Lewin's death, his students and others founded the National Training Laboratories (NTL) in Bethel, Maine, a center for professionals and citizens to learn about the dynamics within and between groups in everyday life (Kelly, 2003; Marrow, 1969; Zander, 1995). The NTL workshops (still offered today) focus on the development of skills for working in groups and communities. They are not therapy or support groups and are not clinical in orientation. Instead, they embody social-psychological

BOX 2.2 Exemplary Early Settings in Community Psychology

Community psychology emerged not simply from the work of individuals but from trailblazing *settings,* many of them situations in which psychologists and citizens worked together. We chose four early settings for a closer look: Wellesley Human Relations Service, Community Lodge, Yale Psycho-Educational Clinic, and Primary Mental Health Project. We have described their work elsewhere in this chapter. Here we focus on the personal-emotional meaning of these settings and how they involved collaboration with citizens, appreciation of community strengths, and second-order change in role relationships. Those themes appear especially clearly in interviews with early community psychologists conducted by James Kelly and students (excerpted in Kelly, 2003).

The Wellesley Human Relations Service was founded at the request of community leaders. Though other mental health professionals asserted their special knowledge of mental disorders and treatment, Erich Lindemann, the HRS's first leader, stressed the importance of learning from citizens and enabling them to take responsibility for the mental health of their community. Donald Klein (1995) described preparing for a meeting with community leaders in which he planned primarily to inform them of what the Service could do for their community. "No, no," Lindemann told him, "it's what we can learn *from them* that's important."

Even in interviews conducted decades later, key interpersonal qualities come through when Don Klein and Jim Kelly discuss their years with the Human Relations Service: a certain gentleness, an appreciation of community strengths and of listening carefully, an attention to personal relationships. These are rooted in part in Lindemann's leadership style, Klein's experiences with the National Training Laboratories (based on Lewin's group dynamics work), and the experience of working alongside citizens as partners in Wellesley (Klein, 1995; Kelly, 1997, 2003).

The Community Lodge went further, creating a setting that empowered men with psychological disorders. George Fairweather and colleagues at a VA hospital began by seeking to improve group therapy with their patients. Their experiences and research eventually led them to finding that a group of men with serious psychological disorders, working together and helping each other in their own daily lives, could live together successfully outside the hospital. The success of the Community Lodge contradicted many professionals' assumptions about the capabilities of persons with mental disorders. Its success principally resulted from the emergence of unrecognized strengths and mutual support among its participants. Fairweather's folksy, common-sense style and facilitative-consultative role supported that emergence.

An important point in any community partnership comes when citizens assert control. Fairweather later described the poignant moment when the first Lodge members thanked him for his efforts but also stated, "It's time for you to go." Fairweather termed this a "horrible moment for a professional," yet he understood and accepted their decision. The Lodge had become its own community, and the presence of a professional, however well-intentioned and supportive, would hinder its future development. The original Lodge and others have enjoyed sustained success (Fairweather, 1994; Kelly, 2003).

Seymour Sarason described the Yale Psycho-Educational Clinic as having three aims: to understand the "culture of the school" and how that often inhibits productive learning, to gain that understanding

concern with group dynamics. This approach, which ran counter to the prevailing individualism and laboratory focus of psychology, involved a collaborative partnership of professionals and citizens.

Several early community psychologists (Don Klein, Jack Glidewell, Wil Edgerton) worked with NTL, thus linking the group dynamics and action research tradition with innovations in prevention and community mental health (Edgerton, 2000; Glidewell, 1994; Kelly, 2003; Klein, 1987, 1995). The Lewinian focus on action research, in collaboration with citizens, was a forerunner of community psychology research today. The importance of personal relationships and group process can be seen in four exemplary early settings in community psychology, profiled in Box 2.2.

experientially through performing services in schools, and to model for university students the everyday practical involvement of their faculty in schools (Sarason, in Kelly, 2003). These goals indicate a willingness to step outside the usual research methods, to ask open-ended questions and learn from rigorous analysis of personal experience, and to take risks to promote learning.

At the outset, Sarason and his colleagues were not entirely sure what they were looking for, or what roles and findings might evolve in their work. Murray Levine described his first job at the Clinic as being to "go out to the schools and find a way to be useful". A smiling Sarason later told students how he applied for grants to support the Clinic, yet was unable to specify exactly what he meant by "culture of the school" or what research methods he would use to study it. His proposals were rejected twice. Yet the Clinic's approach eventually led to influential books, papers, and concepts that permeate community psychology today. Clinic staff analyzed their experiences intensively in Friday staff meetings. These involved deep, wide-ranging scrutiny of personal experiences and events at the school, asking tough questions about their meaning (Levine, in Kelly, 2003; Sarason, 1995; Sarason, in Kelly, 2003).

The Psycho-Educational Clinic experience was deeply personal for its staff and students. Many influential community psychologists testify to the Clinic's importance in their lives. Rhona Weinstein's innovative work in schools began there (we described her work with "Eric" in Chapter 1). Sarason intervened on her behalf when her application was rejected by those at Yale who did not desire to admit women (Weinstein, 2005). Murray Levine still carries his key to the old Clinic building, a token of his personal attachment to the people there (Levine, in Kelly, 2003).

Emory Cowen has been described by George Albee as "the tallest oak in the forest of prevention" (Albee, 2000, pp. xiii). Much of his stature came from the Primary Mental Health Project (PMHP) and Center for Community Study (now Children's Institute) that Cowen founded and headed at the University of Rochester.

Cowen and colleagues (Cowen, Hightower, Pedro-Carroll, Work, Wyman, & Haffey, 1996; Cowen in Kelly, 2003) have described how PMHP grew from several mental health revelations of the 1950s: that we lack enough personnel to help all children in need; that early identification of young children with academic, behavioral or emotional problems, and prompt intervention, would forestall later, more intractable problems; and that paraprofessionals building positive relationships with at-risk children and helping them learn key coping skills could accomplish at least as much as professional services. In 1963, Cowen and his team developed the role of Child Associates, paraprofessionals working under professional supervision in schools, providing support and tangible assistance to children. Cowen and his teams of colleagues and students built PMHP from a pilot project in a single school to over 2000 schools worldwide. The Center for Community Study broadened its focus over the years to include action research on topics such as social problem-solving skills training in schools, preventive services for children of divorce, and child resilience. Its work in prevention and Cowen's (1994, 2000a) concept of wellness helped shape community, developmental, clinical and school psychology. Many influential community psychologists worked with Cowen on PMHP or other projects; a recent volume honored his conceptual contributions and innovative community work (Cicchetti, Rappaport, Sandler, & Weissberg, 2000).

Movements for Social Change and Liberation

> . . . psychology is worse than worthless in contributing to a vision which could truly liberate—men as well as women. . . . In brief, the uselessness of present psychology (and biology) with regard to women is simply a special case of the general conclusion; one must understand the social conditions under which women live if one is going to attempt to explain the behavior of women. . . . But it is clear that until social expectations for men and women are equal, until we provide equal respect for both men and women, our answers to these questions will simply reflect our prejudices. (Weisstein, 1971/1993, pp. 197, 207, 208)

> I am sure that we all recognize that there are some things in our society, some things in our world, to which we should never be adjusted.... We must never adjust ourselves to racial discrimination and racial segregation. We must never adjust ourselves to religious bigotry. We must never adjust ourselves to economic conditions that take necessities from the many to give luxuries to the few. We must never adjust ourselves to the madness of militarism, and the self-defeating effects of physical violence. (King, 1968, p. 185)

A fourth force influencing the development of community psychology in the U.S. involves movements for social change and liberation. The civil rights and feminist movements most directly influenced psychology, but the peace, environmental, antipoverty, and gay rights movements also were important. These movements are associated in the popular mindset with the 1960s, although all had much longer historical roots. They reached a crescendo during the 1960s and early 1970s, bringing their grievances and ideals to national attention.

The ideals of these social movements had several commonalities (Kelly, 1990; Wilson et al., 2003). One was the challenging of hierarchical, unequal role relationships: between European Americans and people of color; men and women; experts and citizens, persons of heterosexual and homosexual orientations; and the powerful and the oppressed. Youth often assumed leadership: college students sat in at segregated lunch counters, participated in Freedom Rides through the segregated South, led antiwar protests, and organized the first Earth Day. Values common to these movements match well with some core values of community psychology: social justice, citizen participation, and respect for diversity (Wilson et al., 2003).

Another commonality of these social movements was that they sought to link social action at the local and national levels. Advocates in each movement pursued change in local communities and nationally. "Think globally, act locally" became a familiar motto. The movements advocated changes at each of the ecological levels that we delineated in Chapter 1. For instance, the various groups in the civil rights movement used different approaches. For decades, the NAACP employed policy research and legal advocacy in the courts. Other organizations used community mobilizing approaches: time-limited mass demonstrations that attracted media attention (Freedom Rides, Birmingham and Selma campaigns, the March on Washington). Less recognized local people pursued long-term community organizing for voter registration and other aims, an approach that generated fewer famous names but many enduring community changes (Lewis, 1998; Payne, 1995). Women, including Ella Baker, Fannie Lou Hamer, and Septima Clark, often were local leaders (Collier-Thomas & Franklin, 2001). All of these changes coincided with the emerging power of national television to portray social conflicts to national audiences. It became more difficult to deny the existence of racism (Wilson et al., 2003).

A few psychologists played a policy advocacy role in the civil rights movement. The research of Kenneth and Mamie Clark, African-American psychologists, was cited in the 1954 Supreme Court desegregation decision in the case of *Brown v. Board of Education*. The Clarks' research, which originated in Mamie Clark's master's thesis, compared children's reactions to dolls of differing skin colors to measure the self-esteem of African-American and European-American children. Advocacy and research, including court testimony, by Kenneth Clark and members of SPSSI was important in the NAACP lawsuits against segregated schools (e.g., Clark, 1953; Clark, Chein, & Cook, 1952/2004). However, the reaction of the professional psychological establishment was mixed. Other psychologists testified to defend segregation. Clark later came to believe that the social science advocacy that led to the 1954 Court decision had underestimated the depth of racism in the United States (Benjamin & Crouse, 2002; Keppel, 2002; Lal, 2002).

Feminism also shares many aims with community psychology (Mulvey, 1988). One of the key insights of feminism is that "the personal is political": even personal relationships are influenced by power dynamics and societal beliefs that oppress women. This is consistent with an ecological levels perspective. Both feminism and community psychology call attention to inequalities in role relationships, such as professional-client or male-female. Both perspectives emphasize peer support and organizing members of a community as methods of change; women's consciousness-raising groups were a key institution in the advance of feminist views. Both also promote advocacy at macrosystem levels. Of course, there are differences, principally that feminism arose as a social movement willing to take risks (Mulvey, 1988), whereas community psychology originated as an academic discipline.

In 1968, psychologist Naomi Weisstein gave an address with the spirited title "Psychology Constructs the Female: Or the Fantasy Life of the Male Psychologist" (quoted earlier; Weisstein, 1971/1993). Weisstein's paper has been described as an "earthquake . . . shaking the foundations of psychology" (Riger, in Kelly, 2003), a formative event for many women in community psychology and women's studies. Weisstein questioned whether psychology at the time knew anything about women at all, after years of research that systematically excluded women or interpreted their responses from men's perspectives. Moreover, she emphasized the importance of social context in shaping choices and acts as well as the ways in which contexts constrained women's choices. Her critique was one of many founding statements of feminist scholarship that has transformed concepts and methods of inquiry in many disciplines, including community psychology. Moreover, Weisstein and others in the women's movement were activists in their communities, founding settings to support women's development and advocating for social change (Dan, Campbell, Riger, & Strobel, in Kelly, 2003).

As the social change movements of the 1960s progressed, many psychologists became convinced that citizen and community action was necessary to bring about social change on multiple fronts and that psychology had a role to play (Bennett et al., 1966; Kelly, 1990; Sarason, 1974; Walsh, 1987). In 1967, Martin Luther King, Jr., addressed the APA, calling for psychologists to study and promote youth development, citizen leadership, and social action, especially among African Americans (King, 1968). Yet the vision of a socially involved psychology was not widely supported in the field. King's speech was arranged by activist psychologists, including Kenneth Clark, over the objections of APA leaders (Pickren & Tomes, 2002).

The Undercurrent of Optimism

> We had just won a huge war, the biggest ever. And we had started from way back—we had been about to get whipped. If we could do this, we could do anything, including solving all the social problems of the U.S.: race relations, poverty.... There was a sense of optimism... a messianic zeal.... We believed that we could change the world, and we felt that we had just done it.
>
> Solving social problems is sobering.... To win wars, you kill people and destroy things. To solve social problems, you must build things, create things. (Glidewell, 1994)

Glidewell's remark illustrates an underlying support for all four forces we have described: optimism about the solution of social problems. That optimism is very American in nature (Kelly, 1990; Levine & Levine, 1992; Sarason, 1994), and it supported the emergence of community psychology.

In 1965, the Johnson Administration initiated a collection of federally funded Great Society programs, popularly known as the War on Poverty. These included educational initiatives such as Head Start, job training and employment programs, and local community action organizations. Federal funders of community mental health and of the War on Poverty looked to the social sciences, including psychology, as a source of scientific solutions to social problems. This attitude grew out of a very American faith in science and technology, based on experiences in World War II and the Cold War, and gaining clearest expression in the space program. That faith has since been replaced by a more sober sense of the real but limited utility of social science for social change, reflected in Glidewell's remarks.

The Swampscott Conference

In May 1965, 39 psychologists gathered at the seaside resort of Swampscott, Massachusetts, to discuss training psychologists for new roles in the CMHC system (Bennett et al., 1966; Kelly, 2003; Klein, 1987). As was typical of psychology and most sciences and professions at the time, the conferees were almost all European-American men (Rosenblum, in Kelly, 2003; Walsh, 1987). (One woman, Luleen Anderson, attended and helped author the conference report.) Yet most of the group described themselves as atypical psychologists because their involvement in community work had transformed their interests and skills (Bennett et al., 1966). Many were forging new connections among academic researchers, mental health professionals, and citizens. At Swampscott, they took over a conference called to design a training model for community mental health and made it a founding event for the new, broader field of community psychology.

The new field would concern "psychological processes that link social systems with individual behavior in complex interaction" (Bennett et al., 1966, p. 7). It would not be limited to mental health issues or settings and would be distinct from community mental health, although the two would overlap.

Conferees agreed on the concept of *participant conceptualizer* (recall this from Chapter 1) to describe the community psychologist, who would act as a community change agent as well as conduct research on the effectiveness of those efforts. They discussed roles for community psychologists: consulting with schools and community agencies, developing prevention programs, advocating for community and social change, and collaborating with citizens. They also called for interdisciplinary collaboration and humility in the face of complex community dynamics (Bennett et al., 1966).

There also was disagreement at Swampscott. Some conferees endorsed a public health prevention model for community psychology. In contrast, Robert Reiff spoke passionately about the limitations of community mental health approaches, the advantages of a community action approach, and his work with indigenous nonprofessionals recruited for their practical knowledge of their communities (Reiff, 1966). These perspectives foreshadowed tensions in community psychology today. Wisely, the Swampscott conferees opted to present multiple views, not to seek premature consensus (Bennett et al., 1966; Rosenblum, in Kelly, 2003).

Swampscott was an energizing turning point for its participants and for those who soon flocked to the emerging field. Many had felt isolated in traditional academic and clinical settings and rejoiced to find colleagues with similar visions and values. "We found each other!" is a common memory among Swampscott participants. Thirty years later, describing the impact of Swampscott to a student audience, Donald Klein spontaneously smiled, drew himself up, and with enthusiasm in his eyes and voice asserted "the excitement of the conference is still as if it happened yesterday" (Klein, in Kelly, 2003).

COMMUNITY PSYCHOLOGY: DEVELOPING AN IDENTITY

After Swampscott, U.S. community psychology gradually developed its own distinctive identity and diverged from community mental health. In 1973, two journals devoted to the field were established in the United States: the *American Journal of Community Psychology* and the *Journal of Community Psychology.* Graduate training programs were developed. Influential textbooks appeared (by dates of first editions: Murrell, 1973; Heller & Monahan, 1977; Rappaport, 1977; Levine & Perkins, 1987), and helped shape the field's developing identity (Revenson & Seidman, 2002).

Changes in Community Mental Health

The community mental health movement burgeoned in the 1960s. A number of community-oriented psychologists began working in CMHCs. They consulted with human services, police, and schools; performed evaluation research; directed prevention programs; and often also provided clinical services. Community mental health and community psychology remained closely intertwined for a decade after Swampscott (Goodstein & Sandler, 1978). However, community-oriented consultation and prevention proved difficult to fund, especially as federal funding shrank in the 1970s and 1980s. Sources that describe the community mental health movement in detail include Bloom (1977), Golann and Eisdorfer (1972), Levine (1981), and Heller, Jenkins, Steffen, and Swindle (2000).

Deinstitutionalization accelerated as persons with mental disorders were discharged from psychiatric institutions into communities. Continuing advances in medications for mental disorders supported this trend, but less humane reasons were also involved. Deinstitutionalization enabled governments to cut costs but led to dumping of persons with severe mental disorders into communities without adequate care (Levine, 1981; Linney, 1990). In essence, U.S. society has taken money out of mental hospitals but has seldom shifted that money to community mental health services. Moreover, the public was not adequately prepared for living alongside persons with serious mental disorders, leading to community resistance to CMHC programs (Heller et al., 2000). Many persons with mental disorders have ended up in the criminal justice system. A few exemplary community mental health programs have survived, such as Assertive Community Treatment (Bond et al., 1990). But the funding climate in the United States has not been friendly since 1980.

Lack of community involvement in the CMHC system contributed to its demise. Its top-down approach offered a single, uniform concept, the professionally operated CMHC, to meet the mental health needs of diverse communities with differing conceptions of mental disorder and health. Unlike the Wellesley model, efforts to involve indigenous helpers, community leaders, and spiritual or work settings were often minimal. The "community" to be served by each center was defined by a "catchment area" defined by professional planners, not natural community boundaries (Hunter & Riger, 1986). This made it difficult to match CMHC programs with cultural values. CMHC advocates also underestimated resistance by mental health professionals and the public to the CMHC reforms (Heller et al., 2000). A final factor was change in federal government funding, from community mental health to the War on Drugs, which we will discuss later in this chapter.

The Limitations of Government-Mandated Social Change

After 1968, U.S. political leaders and citizens began to question War on Poverty programs (Wandersman, 1984; Moynihan, 1969). Some programs lacked clear objectives and pursued well-intentioned yet contradictory or unrealistic aims. In addition, the federal government could not fund both the Vietnam War and the War on Poverty. Political rhetoric about erasing poverty raised public expectations unrealistically high; when quick "victories" in the "war" on poverty did not appear, public support diminished. Despite public perceptions, U.S. poverty rates (especially for children) did fall from 1965 to 1970, the period of the War on Poverty (U.S. Census Bureau, 2005).

Some Great Society initiatives had lasting positive effects. Two examples are Head Start for young children and their families, and Upward Bound for adolescents. One reason for their staying power is that many U.S. voters are willing to support some extra education for disadvantaged children, but not social change to address the roots of those disadvantages. Head Start could also point to research findings documenting the long-term gains for program participants, when it is implemented with high quality and with follow-up during the school years (Schweinhart & Weikert, 1988; Zigler, 1994). However, Head Start is also an example of a War on Poverty program established with the optimistic expectation that an intervention with 4-year-olds could prevent poverty (Zigler, 1994). In practice, Head Start has been limited to largely educational and family outcomes, worthy in themselves, and helpful in helping participants lift themselves out of poverty, but not likely to eradicate poverty on a wide scale (Rudkin, 2003). (Our point is not a criticism of Head Start staff, who in our experience are highly competent, or of Head Start participants, who often make major changes in their lives. Moreover, Head Start is not funded well enough to serve all families who are eligible.) The same logic often applies to poverty that we noted for homelessness in Chapter 1: individual and family-focused programs are humane and often helpful to their participants but do not address wider economic and social causes.

The central dilemma of War on Poverty programs was this: effectively addressing social problems means creating some form of social change. Yet it is difficult, perhaps impossible, for government/taxpayer-funded programs to challenge government and society to change. For instance, Great Society funding often mandated participation by citizens in community program planning. When these groups challenged political elites, those elites found ways to weaken or eliminate the programs (Wandersman, 1984).

Blaming the Victim: Thinking about Social Issues

Understanding the rise and fall of community mental health centers and War on Poverty programs demands that we next consider two ways of thinking about social issues. One concerns how we think about problems, the other, how we think about interventions. Both will be important throughout this book.

Psychologist William Ryan's 1971 book, *Blaming the Victim,* provided a classic critique of individualistic thinking about social problems. It had widespread impact and was important in the development of community psychology. When we assume that problems such as poverty, drug abuse, personal/family distress, educational failure, crime, or unemployment are caused by deficits within individuals, we ignore larger factors such as economic factors, discrimination, or lack of access to good-quality health care. (These larger factors are usually rooted in macrosystems.) Even if we assume that personal deficits are caused by one's family, or by "cultural deprivation," we still locate the deficit within the person, and still ignore larger factors. Ryan (1971), coining a now-popular term, called this thinking **blaming the victim.**

For instance, in a community with underfunded schools, in neighborhoods where violence is common, and where many students do poorly on standardized tests, are we to blame the individual students? Their parents? Something about their community's culture? (All of these can be ways of blaming victims.) Or might we ask: Why are schools in some communities underfunded? How can the larger society help fund better education for all? What can be done to make all children safe? What community resources could be involved? Are the tests really valid measures of learning, and who decided to use them? These questions address social conditions at multiple ecological levels (see Weinstein, 2002a).

Ryan also questioned whether researchers, policy makers, or others who have never directly experienced a social problem (e.g., poverty) have the best viewpoint for analyzing it. They (often, *we*) tend to have a middle-class perspective that is not an accurate understanding of poverty's everyday realities. For someone who grew up with the blessings of family and community advantages, success in school and life may seem largely to the result of personal characteristics or effort (especially if he or she does not recognize how important those blessings are). For persons in poverty and other oppressive conditions, however, success is heavily influenced by social and economic factors; sadly, the effects of their personal efforts are limited by those factors. In addition, researchers and policy makers often overestimate the accuracy of the statistics on which they depend (Ryan, 1971, provided many examples). Many programs that Ryan criticized were "liberal" social and educational programs of the War on Poverty. These can blame victims especially if they focus on individual, family, or "cultural" deficits of program participants, fail to address economic and sociopolitical roots of social problems, and overlook individual and community strengths.

Certainly it is also true that personal effort and responsibility do count in life. Nor is every person with a problem necessarily a victim; the term *victim* has been trivialized and stretched far beyond Ryan's original usage (see Sykes, 1992, for a critique). Yet Ryan drew attention to how social conditions can create or worsen seemingly personal problems and to how we often are trained to ignore those conditions. For Ryan, improving the quality of community life means addressing social and economic root causes.

Bottom-Up and Top-Down: Contrasting Approaches to Social Change

Whatever our theories about causes of a community or social problem, we can address that problem in either of two ways. Both are important for citizens and community psychologists to understand; both were involved in the social initiatives of the 1960s.

Bottom-up approaches originate at the grassroots level, among citizens rather than among professionals or the powerful. They reflect attempts by ordinary people to assert control over their everyday lives. They reflect the experiences and ideas of people most affected by a community or social problem (Fawcett et al., 1995). **Top-down** approaches are designed by professionals, community leaders, or similar elites. These may be well intentioned and grounded in research findings yet also inevitably reflect the life experiences, worldviews, and interests of the powerful, and usually preserve the existing power structure (perhaps with some reform). They also often overlook the strengths of a community (Kretzmann & McKnight, 1993).

Professional mental health care represents a top-down approach, self-help groups a bottom-up approach. Centralizing decisions in city hall offices is a top-down approach; enabling neighborhood associations to make local decisions is a bottom-up approach. Relying only on psychologists or other professionals to design a program to prevent drug abuse is a top-down approach; involving citizens in making decisions about that program is a bottom-up approach.

Neither approach is always best. Values of social justice, citizen participation, and collaboration and community strengths are linked to bottom-up approaches. Yet outside resources (funding, expertise) are often easier to acquire with a top-down approach, which also may better apply research findings on effective programs elsewhere. The two approaches can complement each other, as when mental health professionals and mutual help groups collaborate or when psychologists and citizens collaborate on research that assists the community.

Community mental health was mainly a top-down approach, although with more accountability to citizens than mental hospitals. Some War on Poverty programs were bottom-up approaches, but it was these that often clashed with powerful elites as we described. Other War on Poverty programs had more top-down qualities, and as Ryan pointed out, also had the limitations of perspective that accompany a top-down approach. Yet as we will describe throughout this book, in other contexts both top-down and bottom-up approaches have achieved notable successes in addressing community and social problems.

Conceptual Frameworks for Community Psychology

During the 1970s, several community psychologists proposed conceptual frameworks that helped define the field and distinguish it from community mental health. These have continued to be influential.

Emory Cowen's (1973) *Annual Review of Psychology* chapter, "Social and Community Interventions" (the first devoted to this topic), was both an indication of the importance of community psychology and of the difficulty in defining it. Reviewing scholarly articles concerned with community mental health, he found less than 3 percent with a prevention focus and noted little in common among many community interventions. Nonetheless, he identified a number of interventions, principally dealing with child or youth development, and often focused on disadvantaged populations and collaboration with local citizens. Cowen called for more emphasis on prevention.

James Kelly, Edison Trickett, and associates proposed concepts from biological ecology, such as interdependence and cycling of resources, as useful analogies in community psychology (Trickett, Kelly, & Todd, 1972; Kelly, 1979a). In their view, ecological concepts would enhance understanding of how individual coping or adaptation varied in social environments (e.g., schools) with differing psychosocial qualities. This approach suggests understanding how environments and individuals are interrelated.

In 1974, Seymour Sarason published *The Psychological Sense of Community,* a critique of the field. He proposed that community psychology abandon its individualistic focus on mental health services and embrace a broader concern with the "psychological sense of community." Community psychologists could conceptualize and intervene in what Sarason saw as the defining problem of U.S.

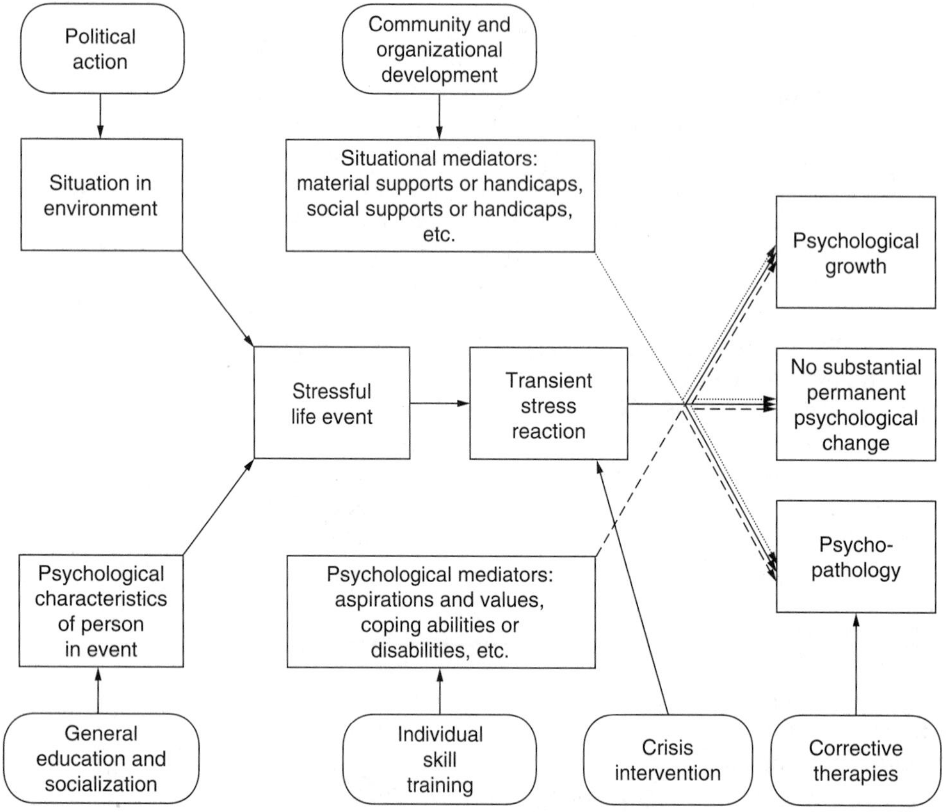

FIGURE 2.1 Dohrenwend's Ecological model
SOURCE: From Dohrenwend (1978).

society, the individual's disconnection from others. Sarason argued that community psychology should focus broadly on the relationships between individuals and their communities rather than just on the psychological adjustment of individuals.

Barbara Dohrenwend's (1978) ecological model of problems in living offered a comprehensive overview of many emerging community psychology themes (see Figure 2.1). She recognized both situational and individual causes of stressful life events, and both situational and individual mediating factors that could offset those stressors. Dohrenwend also emphasized strengths in the person as well as resources in the environment and recognized that the outcome of coping with stress could be positive psychological growth, not just relief of symptoms. These are now familiar notions, but they were innovations at the time. She also identified a number of interventions that community psychology could pursue to support persons coping with stress, ranging from individual skills training to public education, community development, and political action. She noted how these differed from clinical treatment and crisis intervention while placing both community and clinical approaches in an overarching model of coping.

The Austin Conference

In April 1975, over 100 community psychologists and students from the United States and Puerto Rico gathered at the University of Texas in Austin for a second conference on training. This time, the focus clearly concerned community psychology (Iscoe, Bloom, & Spielberger, 1977; Iscoe, in Kelly, 2003).

Prevention of psychological problems and promotion of social competence, especially in schools, represented one important theme at Austin. A second theme concerned social advocacy to address issues such as poverty, racism, and sexism. Austin's conference participants were more diverse than Swampscott's, reflecting a third theme of emerging diversity. The perspectives of women and persons of color began to be heard, although these groups were concentrated among students and junior professionals, not among senior professionals. Reports from working groups of African Americans, Hispanics, and women called for translating espoused values of the field into tangible changes in training, research, and action (Iscoe et al., 1977).

The trends we have discussed in this section led to a divergence of community mental health and community psychology, which had begun at Swampscott and accelerated after Austin. Although community mental health remained focused on mental health services, community psychology expanded its focus to schools, workplaces, neighborhoods, community development, and advocacy for social change. Individual/family wellness remained an important concern of community psychology, but the field gradually began to focus on other values as well, such as sense of community, social justice, respect for diversity, and citizen participation.

BROADENING THE FOCUS OF THE FIELD

Since the Austin conference, community psychology has continued to develop a distinctive identity, broadened its focus and methods, and sought ways to put its core values into action.

An International Community Psychology

During the 1970s, community psychology developed among psychologists throughout Latin America, largely independent of North American trends (Comas-Diaz, Lykes, & Alarcon, 1998; Montero, 1996). The Latin American movements for community psychology and liberation psychology grew out of social psychology and social change movements rather than from clinical psychology. In some countries (e.g., Chile, Guatemala), these trends were a response to repressive government regimes and overt conflict. These developments were influenced by liberation theology, which blended many values of Christianity and Latin American liberation struggles. At the community level, liberation theology and psychology emphasized empowerment of citizens and struggle against injustice (Martin-Baro, 1994). Another influence was the approach of Brazilian educator and activist Paulo Freire (1970/1993), who focused on new methods of education as means of raising consciousness of the impact of social conditions on personal lives, and as a beginning point for social transformation. Freire focused on practical, local initiatives for social change.

A distinctive Latin American community social psychology emerged, more concerned with social critique and with liberation than North American community psychology at the time. Emphasizing democratic participation, social justice, concepts of power and ideology, and social change, it established a presence in Puerto Rico, Venezuela, Brazil, Mexico, Cuba, and other countries (Montero, 1996, 2002).

The 1970s and early 1980s saw the emergence of community psychology on other continents. The origins differed somewhat: in South Africa, opposition to apartheid was a unifying force; in Germany, social movements for women and the environment played a role; in Australia, New Zealand, and Canada, disenchantment with purely clinical concepts was important. Today, community psychology is a burgeoning international field. Learning from and working with indigenous peoples is a theme in several countries—for instance, the Maori in New Zealand, Aboriginal peoples in Australia, and Mayan peoples in Guatemala (Glover, Dudgeon, & Huygens, 2005; Lykes, Blanche, & Hamber, 2003; Wingenfeld & Newbrough, 2000). The *Journal of Community and Applied Social Psychology* carries articles from an international array of community psychologists. Training programs and practitioners now exist across Latin America, Europe, Japan, New Zealand, Australia, Israel, South Africa, Canada, and elsewhere.

Empowerment and Related Perspectives

In the late 1970s and 1980s, Julian Rappaport's (1977, 1981, 1987) focus on empowerment and cultural diversity emerged as a central part of community psychology's identity. In his 1977 textbook, Rappaport argued that a pernicious effect of traditional psychological science and practice has been to perpetuate the notion that one standard of psychological adjustment fits all and to develop helping services that hold a diversity of peoples to that standard. Despite the good intentions of its providers, this functions as a system of social control. Moreover, traditional psychological services perpetuate inequalities of power, placing persons with problems in living in a dependent position that helps maintain their problems.

Rappaport's 1981 paper was a turning point for the field. He critiqued prevention as a one-sided approach. Like clinical treatment, prevention was being provided largely by a professional class of helpers and educators within social systems (e.g., mental health care) that offered clients few opportunities for self-determination. A wiser approach, Rappaport asserted, would focus on the rights of citizens, provide choices among types of helping, and promote the positive psychological effects of exercising choice and power. He argued that community psychologists must seek truly collaborative relationships with citizens, especially those with less access to resources of social power and funding. As an example of this approach in action, Rappaport and colleagues soon embarked on a program of research with mutual help organizations and other forms of informal, nonprofessional helping (e.g., Luke, Rappaport, & Seidman, 1991).

Rappaport's later papers (e.g., 1987, Wiley & Rappaport, 2000) have identified how prevention, wellness, and empowerment can be complementary notions, all needed for community psychology.

Feminism and community psychology coexisted for decades with less integration than one might expect, but a distinctively feminist perspective has become influential in the field. Liberation concepts and critical community psychology also are gaining ground. Each of these perspectives has distinctive concepts and aims, yet all emphasize core values of social justice, respect for human diversity, collaborating with oppressed groups, and an activist approach to research and social change. All also emphasize power dynamics at multiple ecological levels and involve tensions with the worldviews and policies of the powerful. Because we as community psychologists have the privileges of a professional class, these perspectives also help us understand our own limitations and biases (Angelique & Culley, 2000, 2003; Bond, Hill, Mulvey, & Terenzio, 2000a,b; Bond & Mulvey, 2000; Mulvey, 1988; Nelson & Prilleltensky, 2005; Swift, Bond, & Serrano-Garcia, 2000; Watts & Serrano-Garcia, 2003).

Collaborative, Participatory Research

Empirical grounding is a distinctive core value of community psychology. The field has always sought to integrate research with action in communities. Yet rigorous, systematic inquiry and genuine collaboration with citizens in research can be opposing goals, difficult to combine in practice. Describing the early years of the two major U.S. community psychology journals, two early editors mentioned the importance of establishing the emerging field's legitimacy by publishing research that would be methodologically respectable in mainstream psychology (Glidewell, 1994; Newbrough, 1997). The field attained that goal, but at a price: the quantitative, experimental, individualistic psychology of the time limited the creativity of early community psychology research. Reviews of articles in community psychology journals found that research focused on individual-level phenomena, seldom studied higher ecological levels, and seldom attended to human diversity (Bernal & Enchautegui-de-Jesus, 1994; Loo, Fong, & Iwamasa, 1988; Lounsbury, Leader, Meares, & Cook, 1980; McClure et al., 1980; Novaco & Monahan, 1980; Speer et al., 1992).

Two major conferences in community psychology, held in Chicago in 1988 and 2002, broadened the methodological imagination of the field. The 1988 conference explored "adventuresome" research methods and was a gateway to expanded use of qualitative and innovative quantitative research methods (Tolan, Keys, Chertok, & Jason, 1990). The 2002 gathering highlighted participatory research with communities (Jason, Keys, Suarez-Balcazar, Taylor, & Davis, 2004).

Reviews of community psychology journal articles in the 1990s found a broadening of focus, moving from primarily mental health concerns to multiple community issues. There also was increased concern with social action, a greater proportion of studies of community samples, and a growing feminist community psychology (Angelique & Culley, 2000, 2003; Martin et al., 2004). Recent years have seen more published works on diversity topics (e.g., Schneider & Harper, 2003; Watts & Serrano-Garcia, 2003), but many more are needed. A recent special journal issue concerned innovative approaches to making community research more useful for communities (Wandersman, Kloos, Linney, & Shinn, 2005). A recent book, by community and developmental psychologists and other scholars, applied research findings to social policy for children, families, and communities (Maton, Schellenbach, Leadbeater, & Solarz, 2004).

In 1987, the Division of Community Psychology of the American Psychological Association, the principal U.S. body of community psychologists, began holding biennial conferences devoted solely to presenting and discussing recent research and action in community psychology. In 1990, this group changed its name to the Society for Community Research and Action (SCRA). This change recognized several trends in the field that continue today. First, the field has a growing international membership. Over half of the members of community psychology professional organizations now live outside the United States (Toro, 2005). It also has developed an interdisciplinary focus beyond the boundaries of psychology, linking with fields such as public health, applied anthropology, community development, and women's studies. Third, the integration of research and action has become a distinct hallmark of the field, deserving explicit mention in its name. These themes are reflected in the topics discussed at recent biennial conferences.

CONSERVATIVE SHIFTS IN SOCIAL CONTEXTS

As it has developed a distinctive identity, community psychology also has coped with changing social and political contexts. Beginning in the 1970s, but especially after 1980, U.S. society became more politically conservative, as did some other countries with active fields of community psychology, including Britain, Canada, Australia, and New Zealand.

In the 1980s, the community-social perspective on social issues that had led to community psychology in the United States was supplanted by strongly biomedical views. This change was propelled in part by genuine advances in biomedical research and treatment. However, the pendulum swing also was the result of social forces. As society and government became more conservative, funding agencies called for psychological research on biomedical causes of mental disorders, and researchers' interests followed suit (Humphreys & Rappaport, 1993).

Federal attention also shifted from mental health to substance abuse. Mental health had been an emphasis of progressive presidents (Kennedy, Carter), and conservatives sought their own issues for activism. In the 1980s, President Ronald Reagan declared a War on Drugs. It focused on causal factors for drug abuse within the individual, such as genes, illness, and willpower. It also greatly expanded the use of police and prisons. The federal prison population doubled during the Reagan administration; most of the increase was in drug offenders (Humphreys & Rappaport, 1993).

Research followed this trend. Psychological journals for the years 1981–1992 contained 170 articles for drug addiction and personality and only three references for drug addiction and poverty; similar findings appear if similar index terms are searched. Similarly, primary federal funding for research on homelessness was provided by the Alcohol, Drug Abuse and Mental Health Administration, not the Department of Housing and Urban Development. Research thus focused on the subgroup of homeless persons with substance abuse and mental disorders rather than on affordable housing and employment, issues that affected all homeless persons (Humphreys & Rappaport, 1993; Shinn, 1992).

After declining during the 1960s and remaining largely steady during the 1970s, the proportion of children living in poverty rose after 1980. In the early 1980s and early 1990s, it returned to mid-1960s levels (U.S. Census Bureau, 2005). Homelessness became a visible problem in many U.S. cities.

In the United States at least, this generally conservative period has persisted into the twenty-first century, with some ups and downs in intensity, and with either political party in power. This prevailing perspective poses challenges and opportunities for community psychology. Many citizens and opinion leaders fail to recognize the impact of complex social and economic forces on personal life. Faced with many voters suspicious of government, elected officials continue to cut taxes and slash funding for many community and social programs. Community programs that are growing tend to focus on helping individuals and families change, especially if they fit with conservative worldviews, such as some faith-based initiatives. For instance, involvement in self-help groups and spiritual small groups (not dependent on government funding) has burgeoned (Kessler, Mickelson, & Zhao, 1997; Wuthnow, 1994). Community programs involving sexuality (e.g., teen pregnancy, HIV prevention, sexual orientation) are especially controversial. Before we discuss how community psychologists respond to these shifts in public perspective, we must consider some lessons to be drawn from the history we have already described about the relationships of community psychology and its social contexts.

Defining Social Issues in Progressive and Conservative Eras

Murray Levine and Adeline Levine (1970, 1992), a community psychologist and a sociologist, wrote a classic historical analysis of how social and political forces in the United States have shaped public beliefs about social problems and helping services. Their historical work concerned services to children and families in the early twentieth century, but their analysis also fits several trends in the history of community psychology.

Levine and Levine proposed a simple hypothesis. In times that are socially and politically more progressive, human problems will be conceptualized in environmental (e.g., community, societal) terms. Progressive times are not necessarily associated with one political party but are marked by optimism about the possibility of lessening social problems as varied as poverty, drug abuse, crime, psychological disorders, and the educational and behavioral problems of children. In the common sense of a progressive period, social causes of such problems will be emphasized, and community or social interventions will be developed to address these causes. Persons are to be helped by improving their circumstances or resources, giving them greater freedom and choice in their lives. Not all political progressives will endorse an environmental view, but a progressive trend in society overall tends to strengthen it.

During more politically conservative times, the same problems will be conceptualized in individualistic terms, emphasizing individual causes. The common sense of the era will locate problems within the biological, psychological, or moral makeup of the individual. These individual deficits must be remedied by changes in the individuals themselves, and programs to help them will seek to change the individuals (and perhaps families). This will enhance their ability to cope with environmental circumstances. Conservative times are not necessarily tied to one political party, but to pessimism about whether social problems can be lessened, or to the belief that individual changes are more important than wider social change. Not all political conservatives will endorse an individualistic view, but a conservative trend in society overall tends to strengthen it.

Social forces influence how a problem is defined and what is done to address it. They also define what research is considered worth doing (and funding), and how that research is applied in practice. As we have noted, community psychology in the U.S. arose in the 1960s, a progressive time that emphasized social and economic root causes of social problems. As we described, since the 1980s individualistic thinking has dominated research and funding on topics such as mental health, drug abuse and homelessness. Psychological research and practice cannot be insulated from such swings in social-political-public thinking.

The differences between more progressive and more conservative periods, and between individualistic and environmental perspectives, are not absolute (Levine & Levine, 1992). In any historical period, both perspectives are voiced, and some historical periods are difficult to categorize as one or the other. Moreover, the worldview of individualism, focused on individual happiness and autonomy, often outweighs other American ideals (Bellah et al., 1985; Lipset, 1996). A focus on individuals becomes most dominant in more conservative times yet is powerful even in progressive times. Recall that Ryan's *Blaming the Victim* criticized the individualistic focus of some War on Poverty programs despite their funding by a liberal Democratic administration. The vision of family values and of religion held by some conservatives opposes what they believe is excessive individualism in the wider culture. At a personal level, the authors of this book know some political conservatives who are deeply embedded and active in communities, and some political progressives who are not.

Both individualistic and environmental perspectives hold truth; neither completely accounts for personal and social difficulties. Environments (including macrosystems) *and* personal factors and choices shape our lives. Yet progressive and conservative advocates articulate very different goals for social policy and community life, and these often reflect differences along the lines we are discussing. As Levine and Levine showed, the political contexts of the time influence which of those ideas are more widely accepted.

Fair Play and Fair Shares: Contrasting Definitions of Equality

The individualistic and environmental perspectives that we have described correspond to Ryan's (1981, 1994) discussion of two differing definitions of the cherished American value of equality. The **Fair Play** definition of equality seeks to assure rules of fairness in competition for economic, educational or social advancement. The central metaphor is that of a race, with everyone starting at the same place, and rules of competition that treat all individuals similarly. If the rules of the race are fair, Fair Players accept great inequalities of outcome in the competition, assuming that those inequalities are caused by differences in individual merit, talent or effort. "The Fair Player wants an equal opportunity and assurance that the best get the most" (Ryan, 1994, p. 28).

A Fair Play orientation often leads to agreement with statements such as "The most important American idea is that each individual would have the opportunity to rise as high as his talents and hard work will take him" (Ryan, 1994, p. 29). Examples of Fair Play social policies include basing educational and employment decisions on test scores and flat rates of taxation (all income groups are taxed the same percentage).

Ryan (1981, 1994) described an alternative perspective of **Fair Shares,** which means concern not only with fairness of procedure but also with minimizing extreme inequalities of outcome. Adopting a Fair Shares perspective does not preclude Fair Play rules, but it goes beyond them to consider other factors. The central metaphor of the Fair Shares perspective is a family or community taking care of all of its members. For instance, Fair Shares involves limiting accumulation of wealth so that everyone has some minimum level of economic security. Although achieving absolute equality is impractical, a Fair Shares approach seeks to avoid extreme inequalities (Ryan, 1994).

Fair Sharers tend to agree with statements such as "For any decent society, the first job is to make sure everyone has enough food, shelter, and health care," and "It simply isn't fair that a small number of people have enormous wealth while millions are so poor they can barely survive" (Ryan, 1994, p. 29). Examples of Fair Shares social policies include universal health care, enriching educational opportunities for all students (not just the gifted), affirmative action in college admissions and employment, and progressive taxation (in which persons with higher incomes pay a higher percentage).

Ryan (1981, 1994) emphasized that although both perspectives have value, Fair Play thinking dominates American discussions of equality and opportunity. Yet Fair Play presumes that all participants in the race for economic and social advancement begin at the same starting line, and that we only need to make sure the race is conducted fairly. In fact, few citizens really believe that all persons share the same economic or educational resources, the same chances of employment in well-paying jobs, or the same starting line for advancement. In the United States, as in many countries, a very small proportion of the population controls a very large proportion of the wealth. In our view, and in the view of many community psychologists, some methods of strengthening Fair Shares seem necessary to set up truly Fair Play.

Opposing Viewpoints and Divergent Reasoning

Social issues involve opposing viewpoints. In many cases, opposing views can both be true (at least, hold some important truth). Already in this book we have discussed several such oppositions: persons and contexts; first-order and second-order change; potential conflicts among community psychology core values; individualistic and environmental perspectives on social issues; progressive and conservative viewpoints; Fair Play and Fair Shares.

Recognizing important truths in opposing perspectives forces us to hold both in mind, thinking in terms of "both/and" rather than "either/or" (Rappaport, 1981). (This thinking has roots in the dialectical philosophies of Hegel and Marx, but it is different from either system.) Rappaport (1981) advocated **divergent reasoning:** identifying multiple truths in the opposing perspectives; recognizing that conflicting viewpoints may usefully coexist; resisting easy answers. This is *not* to say that attempts to address social problems are useless. But the best thinking about social issues takes into account multiple perspectives and avoids one-sided answers.

Dialogue that respects both positions, rather than debate that creates winners and losers, can promote divergent reasoning. A good metaphor for this process, often suggested in feminist theory (Bond, Belenky, & Weinstock, 2000; Reinharz, 1994) is a frank yet respectful conversation among multiple persons. It involves boldly setting out one's views in one's own voice, but also careful listening to others and recognizing that many positions hold some truth. Divergent reasoning recognizes conflict between differing perspectives as a path to knowledge. It is not a search for complete objectivity, but a process of learning through dialogue. In community psychology, that conversation is often multisided, not simply two opposing poles.

Divergent reasoning also involves questioning the status quo or commonly accepted view of an issue (Rappaport, 1981). In discussion of a social issue such as poverty, there is often a dominant, widely accepted view, and an opposing pole that is largely ignored. The dominant view serves the interests of the powerful by defining the issue and terms of debate. Psychology has often adopted or been co-opted by dominant views rather than questioning them (Gergen, 2001; Humphreys & Rappaport, 1993; Riger, 1993; Ryan, 1971, 1994; Sarason, 1974, 2003b). Often this happens as psychologists and citizens think solely in individual terms, ignoring the importance of contexts (Shinn & Toohey, 2003). Questioning the status quo often involves listening carefully to the voices of persons who have direct experience with an issue, especially those whose views have been ignored. For instance, research that investigates the experiences and perspectives of persons with mental disorders can illuminate their strengths and focus on their rights to make decisions in their own lives as well as their needs for treatment and support (Rappaport, 1981).

Finally, divergent reasoning requires humility. No matter how strong your commitment to your own point of view, it is likely to be one sided in some way, and there is likely to be some truth in an opposing view. Remember Rappaport's Rule: "When everyone agrees with you, worry."

Community Psychology Responses to Conservative Contexts

Opportunities for community psychology research and action do exist in conservative times. Sarason (1976) articulated the "anarchist insight" (with which many conservatives agree) that government interventions for social problems may undermine the sense of community and mutual aid among citizens. Lappe and DuBois (1994) and Wolff (1994) noted that many conservatives and progressives agree that social problems must be addressed at the community level, where many community psychologists are engaged.

Some very influential perspectives in community psychology are related to conservative as well as to progressive thinking. For instance, Sarason's (1974) concept of sense of community and Rappaport's (1981) concept of empowerment are both locally focused and reflect a skeptical view of top-down government interventions. Both also differ from most conservative views in important ways, especially in their focus on challenging the status quo. Yet there is some potential common ground.

Jean Ann Linney (1990) delineated three trends that offer windows of opportunity for community psychology in the United States during conservative times. Her advice is still timely. First, as power shifts from federal to state and local governments, community psychologists can more easily collaborate with legislators, executive agencies, and other policy makers. Second, a lack of trust in government, characteristic of a conservative period, has fostered a number of grassroots movements at the community level. That bottom-up approach is consistent with both conservative ideals of local self-reliance and community psychology core values of citizen participation and sense of community.

Third, the budget-cutting cost consciousness of conservative governments may paradoxically open opportunities for community innovations, if those programs can show that their costs are lower than traditional approaches. This is especially true in the areas of health and mental health, where professional treatments have been very expensive. Pressures for cost containment in mental health care may force clinical psychology to reconsider its emphasis on psychotherapy and focus more on prevention, mutual help, and other less expensive alternatives (Humphreys, 1996).

An example of the fiscal benefits of a preventive program is provided by longitudinal follow-up evaluations of the High/Scope Perry Preschool program, one of the models for Head Start (Schweinhart & Weikert, 1988). These studies included cost-benefit analyses that demonstrated long-term benefits to taxpayers of $23,000 for every year that a child was enrolled in this high-quality preschool for economically disadvantaged children. Compared with controls, graduates of the program were less likely to use special education services in their school years, less likely to need welfare assistance as adults, less likely to be imprisoned, and paid more taxes as adults. Thus, a program that may appear at first to be a costly program actually saved money in the long run.

In addition, there is considerable diversity among conservative views. In the United States, economic conservatives often emphasize personal liberty in ways that sometimes converge with community psychology's emphasis on respecting human diversity. Social conservatives, especially those whose views have a genuinely religious basis, often are concerned with addressing poverty and some forms of injustice. Faith-based settings can be resources for community action.

It would be heedless of history to forget that some conservative views are narrowly individualistic, victim-blaming perspectives (Levine & Levine, 1992; Rappaport, 1981; Ryan, 1971, 1994). Such views often fail to understand or appreciate human diversity, and often keep money and resources in affluent communities rather than using them where they are needed most. Many politically conservative ideas of strengthening community and of empowerment differ greatly from what most community psychologists mean by those terms. Yet psychology in general, and community psychology in particular, have been criticized for a lack of politically conservative members and viewpoints (Redding, 2001). This can lead to one-sided thinking and action. Useful dialogues can occur between conservatives and progressives in community psychology classrooms and in community settings.

In conservative times, indeed at all times, community psychologists of any political persuasion need to be explicit about their values, understand differing values, support their claims with research findings, search for common ground with those who differ, and engage in divergent reasoning about community life.

THE GLOBAL CONTEXT OF COMMUNITY PSYCHOLOGY

The future of community psychology is global. Distances among diverse cultures, communities, and persons are shrinking. Communication media, travel, trade, cultural exchange, and, sadly, exploitation and violence are becoming global in scope. In the United States, we often hear that the September 11, 2001, terrorist attacks altered our world. Yet globalization and its effects developed well before that day, shaped its events, and continue to accelerate.

Globalization actually forms one pole of another pair of opposing viewpoints: "globalization from above and indigenization from below" (Tehranian & Reed, quoted in Marsella, 1998). **Globalization** refers to the centralizing effects of market capitalism, advertising, mass media, and values of individualism and economic output. **Indigenization** refers to consciousness of traditional collective values and community bonds of indigenous ethnic cultures and local communities (see also Friedman, 2000; Stiglitz, 2003). Of course, there exist a diversity of local peoples, with a diversity of responses to the different aspects of globalization. Yet the interface of globalizing markets and traditional cultures does influence individual and community life across the world. Indigenous resistance to globalization is increasing as local communities seek to conserve their identities and values.

Both indigenization and globalization reflect important human aspirations. The forces of global capitalism create many challenges to community psychology values of social justice, appreciating community strengths, and citizen participation. Yet indigenous cultures also have their injustices and limitations. The freedoms of Western democracies also are powerful and appealing to many. Community psychologist Anne Brodsky's (2003) *With All Our Strength* illustrates an interweaving of these themes: she studied the Revolutionary Association of the Women of Afghanistan, an indigenous network of Afghan women who seek women's empowerment and democratic freedoms yet are committed to living in Afghan society.

Marsella (1998) proposed a "global-community psychology" to study the global community: links between economic and political forces of globalization, the development and destruction of diverse cultures and local communities, and how these are related to the psychological functioning of families and individuals.

It would recognize and promote the diversity of world cultures, seek to understand them on their own terms, and accept that Western psychological principles are only one form of psychology among many. A community psychology that is truly contextual is positioned to expand its understanding to take a global perspective. However, adopting that stance poses several challenges for the field: increased understanding of the experiences of diverse peoples, even more participatory approaches to research, learning from community psychologists outside the United States, and careful consideration of how to apply core community psychology values in action. We will consider these issues in more detail in Chapters 3 and 7, and we will include examples throughout this book.

CONCLUSION

> When those of us working in this field in the early 1960s began, we were innocent of the questions as well as of the answers. Now at least we are developing an intellectual framework within which diverse experiences make some sense. We can at least ask questions that are more meaningful than ones we were able to ask 40 years ago. (Levine, Perkins & Perkins, 2005, p. 9)

Community psychology is still maturing as a field. Even the most experienced community psychologist is still a student of relationships between individual and community life, at many ecological levels. Every generation of students builds on the experiences of prior generations yet reinvents community psychology in new contexts.

CHAPTER SUMMARY

1. Psychology in the United States has been influenced strongly by *individualism* and has defined itself as the study of the individual with little attention to social context. Psychological practice is also individualistic, which is useful in many ways but also one sided and limited.
2. Community psychology emerged in the United States during the mid-twentieth century. Among the many forces that led to this development, we identified five important ones: (a) a preventive perspective; (b) reforms in mental health care; (c) action research and group dynamics; (d) social change movements such as civil rights and feminism; and (e) optimism about solving social problems. The Swampscott conference in 1965 identified community psychology as a new field.
3. During the 1960s and 1970s, the field of community psychology in the United States diverged from that of community mental health. Changes in the mental health system and limitations of government social programs influenced this split. *Blaming the victim* occurs when social problems or programs are defined by focusing only on individual causes, not social factors. *Top-down* approaches to change are designed by the powerful, whereas *bottom-up* approaches reflect the ideas of ordinary citizens. Both have advantages and limitations.

4. During the 1970s, conceptual frameworks appeared for community psychology: prevention, an ecological perspective, sense of community, and multiple interventions to promote coping. The field developed a distinctive identity after the 1975 Austin conference.
5. Community psychology is now an international field. Community social psychology emerged in Latin America with a distinctive social change focus. Empowerment, feminist, liberation, and critical perspectives have become important, and collaborative, participatory research methods have emerged.
6. During the 1980s, in the United States and elsewhere, the sociopolitical context grew more conservative. The Levine and Levine hypothesis predicts that in politically progressive times environmental explanations of social problems will be favored, leading to programs to change community environments. In conservative times, individualistic explanations of social problems will be favored, leading to programs to change individuals. These two perspectives are also related to two definitions of equality. *Fair Play,* a more conservative view, defines fairness in terms of rules for fair competition for economic success. *Fair Shares,* a more progressive view, defines fairness in terms of providing basic necessities for all.
7. For community psychology, thinking about social issues requires *divergent reasoning:* understanding how opposing viewpoints may both hold truth, responding to such conflicts with "both/and" rather than "either/or" thinking and being open to dialogue with those who hold different views, and questioning the status quo while searching for viewpoints that are not being voiced or recognized.
8. Conservative times provide challenges and opportunities for community psychology. Areas of common ground between the field and conservative views include skepticism about top-down programs, a focus on local decision making, the recognition that some community programs have long-term impacts that offset their costs, and the fact that some community psychology core values may appeal to economic conservatives while others appeal to social conservatives.
9. The global context is important for the future of the field. This involves understanding the conflicts of global capitalism and indigenous cultures and requires more broadening of focus for the field.

BRIEF EXERCISES

1. Interview your instructor or another person in community psychology about his or her personal history of involvement in the field. Ask about influential teachers, readings, and experiences. Ask what communities or settings were influential in his or her professional development. Ask what energized your instructor to enter the field and also about his or her related interests outside the field.

2. Interview one or more older adults about social contexts and their lives. Focus on links between broad social conditions and their personal experiences. Depending on the person, you might ask about the Great Depression, World War II, the upheavals of the Sixties, or immigration, unemployment, changes in women's roles, or other experiences in their lives. Ask what communities, settings, or groups were influential in their lives.
3. Discuss these questions with a classmate: How has your education in psychology been individualistic? Has it helped you understand the personal impacts of environments/contexts (beyond the immediate family)? How or how not? What psychology areas or courses do you think about as you consider these questions?
4. Discuss with a friend or classmate: Choose a social problem and discuss how it affects you personally, even if indirectly. Similarly, how does globalization affect you personally?

RECOMMENDED READINGS

Revenson, T., D'Augelli, A., French, S., Hughes, D., Livert, S., Seidman, E., Shinn, M., Yoshikawa, H. (Eds.) (2002). *A quarter century of community psychology: Readings from the American Journal of Community Psychology.* New York: Kluwer/Plenum. [Classic articles from community psychology's history, with four essays on the development of the field.]

Ryan, W. (1971). *Blaming the victim*. New York: Random House [especially first chapter]. Or: Ryan, W. (1994). Many cooks, brave men, apples, and oranges: How people think about equality. *American Journal of Community Psychology, 22*, 25–36.

RECOMMENDED VIDEODISC

Kelly, J. G. (Director/Producer) (2003). *Exemplars of community psychology* [DVD]. Society for Community Research and Action. Available through: SCRA Membership Office, 1800 Canyon Park Circle, Building 4, Suite 403, Edmond, OK 73103 USA. Email: scra@telepath.com

Excerpts from interviews of pioneering community psychologists and others on the early development of the field in the U.S. Their personal stories often reveal sources of ideas, support, emotion, and conflict not addressed in print. Many quotations in this chapter are from these interviews.

INFOTRAC COLLEGE EDITION KEYWORDS

blaming the victim (or victim blaming), history and *community psychology, history* and *community mental health, Swampscott*

3

The Aims of Community Research

HIRB/Index Stock

INTRODUCTION

> Isn't it a pleasure when you can make practical use of what you have learned? (*Analects of Confucius*, cited in Reid, 1999, p. 90)

> My department colleagues asked me, "Where have you been? We haven't seen you in three days!" I told them I had been out collecting data. "Oh? In whose laboratory?" [they asked]. "In St. Louis County," I said. "It's a great laboratory." (Glidewell, 1994)

Jack Glidewell evaluated one of the first preventive mental health interventions in schools during the 1950s. As he asserted, communities offer rich opportunities for research. This is an ancient concern: the Chinese sage Kung Fu Tzu (known in the West as Confucius) spent his life seeking to integrate knowledge with action and community governance (Reid, 1999).

Community research does involve giving up at least a portion of what makes the laboratory a useful setting: control. The laboratory psychologist largely controls the choice of phenomena to study, the perspective from which to study them, methodology, treatment of participants during the procedure, format in which those participants provide data, analysis of data, interpretation of findings, and reporting of results. That control promotes clarity of conclusions and the production of some forms of knowledge. Of course, the researcher must make all these choices within accepted ethical limits. Yet the degree of control granted the psychological researcher in the laboratory is great.

However, although many individuals (e.g., students in introductory psychology courses) are willing to briefly participate in a laboratory experiment, few citizens are willing to cede control in the settings where they and their families live every day: school, work, family, neighborhood, or mutual help group. The settings that are most significant for community psychology research are also the most important to their inhabitants.

In this chapter we present a different view of control: *sharing* control with community members can *enhance* the knowledge gained from community research. Well-designed community research, conducted within a collaborative relationship with a community, can yield insights not available in the laboratory. Sharing control does not mean giving it up. In a collaborative relationship, both community members and researchers plan and implement research. In this chapter, our goal is for you to better understand and respect the interests of communities as well as the methods of community psychology research.

This chapter is the first of two on community research. In Chapter 4, we describe specific methods of community psychology research. By reading both chapters, we hope that you learn how community research becomes richer by embracing and seeking to understand the complexities of community life.

Questions for Conducting Community Research

Community research can support or harm communities, so values are involved in every step of that research. Community psychology is committed to the value of empirical grounding; research is central to our identity. Yet each community research project must resolve questions about the relative priority of several other values: citizen participation and collaboration, social justice, respect for human diversity, and searching for community strengths. These issues can be summarized in this general question: *Who will generate what knowledge, for whom, and for what purposes?*

Seymour Sarason (1972) spoke of the important time *before the beginning* of a community initiative. In that period, the persons involved become aware of a problem or challenge to be addressed, trying to make sense of the problem and what to do about it. This concept also fits well with the early stages of a research project, well before a design is chosen and data collected. Important, overarching issues for community psychology research can be summarized in terms of the following four questions. After summarizing these questions, we will take up each in detail in the rest of the chapter.

1. What Values Stances Shall We Take? Community psychology researchers need to be clear on their fundamental values and their assumptions about research and its relation to community and social action. Researchers need this clarity before approaching a community to conduct research, although their ideas about these issues will also be influenced by their experiences with community members.

2. How Shall We Promote Community Participation and Collaboration in Research Decisions? The most distinctive quality of community psychology research is its process of conducting research within a participatory, collaborative relationship with citizens and communities. That distinctive approach developed from the practical experiences and careful reflection of community psychologists and researchers in related fields. They grapple with questions such as these: How, specifically, can researchers and citizens collaborate in planning and conducting research? How can that collaboration be empowering and productive for both? How can respectful relationships among researchers, community members, and research participants best be created and maintained?

3. How Shall We Understand the Cultural and Social Contexts of This Research? Community research always occurs within a culture, perhaps more than one. Often the cultural assumptions and experiences of researchers differ from those of community members, so an early task is for researchers to deepen their knowledge of the community with whom they seek to work. Community researchers also may seek or need to address questions of human diversity beyond culture, such as gender, sexual orientation, ability-disability, social class. A related concern is whether the research will take account of strengths of the individuals, communities and cultures studied.

4. At What Ecological Levels of Analysis Shall We Conduct This Research? Community researchers make decisions, explicitly or implicitly, about the level(s) of analysis they will focus on. The history and practices of psychology draw attention to individual processes, but community psychology seeks to attend to social systems at higher levels. Such choices of focus are better made explicitly.

WHAT VALUES STANCES SHALL WE TAKE?

Recall the nine-dot problem in Chapter 1: unrecognized assumptions often prevent resolution of problems. Similarly, unrecognized assumptions influence researchers' choices of which phenomena to study, from which perspective, within which framework of methods and values. Those assumptions concern one's most basic ideas of what constitutes social-scientific knowledge and how it can best be used. We begin by contrasting three different views of what constitutes knowledge and how to obtain it.

Three Philosophies of Science for Community Psychology Research

A philosophy of science refers to one's beliefs about what scientific knowledge is, through what methods it is obtained, and how it is related to action. You may never have thought of yourself as having a personal philosophy of science, but your ideas about research and how to do it (perhaps as you learned it in prior psychology courses) reflect a philosophy of science. We will discuss three general philosophies of science for community psychology research. Each is actually a family of related approaches, not a single school of thought. Riger (1990, 1992), Campbell & Wasco (2000, pp. 779–783), and Nelson and Prilleltensky (2005, pp. 239–248) provide succinct overviews, and our summary here especially relies on these sources.

In psychology, **positivism** has been the dominant philosophy of science. Positivism has assumed many forms, but a few common elements important in psychology are these: pursuit of objectivity and value-free neutrality in research, an ultimate goal of understanding cause-effect relationships, hypothesis testing with control of extraneous factors to clarify cause and effect, and measurement as the source of data. Positivist science seeks to construct generalized laws based on research findings that are applicable to many circumstances. If you have taken prior courses in psychological research methods, what you learned there was influenced by the perspective of positivism.

This vision of research (admittedly oversimplified here, as an introduction) has come under increasing criticism. No observer is value free; for instance, one is always a member of a culture and influenced by it. Moreover, the particular qualities of cultures, historical circumstances, and settings limit the "generalizability" of research findings from one context to another (Gergen, 1973, 2001). These and other critiques have led to **postpositivist** approaches that recognize that no researcher is truly objective, yet seek to reduce biases as much as possible. Postpositivist approaches in community psychology adapt experimental methods and psychological measurement to community settings.

Constructivist (sometimes termed *contextualist* or *postmodernist*) philosophies of science take a different approach (Campbell & Wasco, 2000; Gergen, 2001; Kingry-Westergaard & Kelly, 1990; Montero, 2002; Nelson & Prilleltensky, 2005). Instead of pursuing the ideal of value-free objectivity, constructivists assume that knowing occurs in a relationship and is a product of a social connection between researcher and research participant. This emphasis on knowing through connection, collaboration, and mutual understanding is a particular emphasis of qualitative research and of some feminist researchers (see Campbell & Wasco, 2000; Riger, 1992; Stein & Mankowski, 2004). Constructivist approaches seek to understand a particular social context and what it means to the people who experience it (e.g., what having schizophrenia means for the person and his or her family; Stein & Wemmerus, 2001). Testing hypotheses about causes and effects becomes less important. For these purposes, qualitative research methods, such as interviewing, often provide the best techniques. Of course, the viewpoint of the researcher can still influence findings. The idea is not to eliminate researcher bias, which constructivists consider impossible, but to put the assumptions of the researcher on the table to be discussed and evaluated. This puts responsibility on researchers to make their assumptions explicit and to describe carefully the relationships in which research was conducted, reporting faithfully the words and ideas of research participants.

Critical philosophies of science take a third position, related to contructivism yet distinct from it (Campbell & Wasco, 2000; Nelson & Prilleltensky, 2005). They assume that knowledge is shaped by power relationships created and maintained by social institutions and belief systems. The gender, race, ethnicity, social class, and other social positions of the researcher and research participant strongly influence what they experience in everyday life because these positions reflect greater or lesser degrees of social power. Critical approaches put responsibility on researchers to recognize and question their own position in social systems and how this affects research. Critical researchers also take an activist stance, conducting research that can lead to challenging injustice. Critical community research may use specific research methods drawn from either postpositivist or constructivist approaches. Some feminist and liberation approaches to community psychology reflect a critical philosophy of science. Of course, an activist stance influences research choices and findings, so (as with constructivist approaches) this puts responsibility on the researchers to make their assumptions and viewpoints explicit.

Thus, "before the beginning" of research, positivist, constructivist and critical philosophies of science have different aims. They are based in different ideas of the roles of researcher and research participant, different conceptions of how to use research, different ideas about how to deal with researchers' values and assumptions, even different conceptions of what is "knowledge." Much useful community research has postpositivistic features, especially use of measurement and experimentation modified to fit community settings. Constructivist approaches have become influential in community psychology in the last two decades, especially fitting the field's emphasis on a collaborative researcher-community relationship. Critical approaches also have become influential, in part because they call attention to integrating research and action and to the importance of social systems. All three philosophies of science are useful in community psychology research, and a study may incorporate elements of more than one of these three philosophies. Our main point here is to advocate that community researchers make explicit choices about these issues in planning their research.

Taking Sides: Research on Controversial Social Issues

Community researchers must decide how their research will relate to action. A postpositivist approach to social problems seeks concrete, pragmatic answers supported by research findings. It applies (with modifications) the scientific methods and findings of psychology to society. Much social science research assumes this stance, which dominated the early development of community psychology.

Some aspects of this approach are useful. For instance, how does a nation or a community prevent the spread of AIDS, or improve child health, or reduce violence in schools? Community research can identify causes of these problems, develop programs or social policies to address those factors, and evaluate their effectiveness. The U.S. Institute of Medicine approach to prevention science involves such a process: research on factors that lead to health or behavior problems, using that knowledge to develop prevention programs, testing their effectiveness in controlled studies, then disseminating the most effective programs for replication in other settings (Mrazek & Haggerty, 1994).

However, the usefulness of such research depends on social consensus in definition of problems, causes, and appropriate responses (Price, 1989). That consensus often does not exist. Even with public health problems that are clearly defined and for which causal factors are understood (e.g., the diagnosis and transmission of HIV infection), there is often great controversy about prevention methods (e.g., needle exchange, education about condoms). Conflicts mushroom when citizens cannot even agree on the definition of the problem and its causes, as with many issues of sexuality, child and family problems, and drug use, for instance. A research team may use what they believe are common-sense definitions of problems and solutions, only to have their findings rejected by those who disagree with their premises. Price (1989) described his own experience in testifying before Congress about community programs for reducing teen pregnancy, preventing child abuse, and coping with marital separation, only to receive the response that such programs undermined the institution of marriage and family values. Thus, Price (1989, p. 157) argued that many social dilemmas are better understood as social conflicts than as social "problems" to be "solved" (see also Sarason, 1978). Those conflicts involve competing values.

Does such conflict mean empirical research on social and community issues is useless? Price argued not. Instead of seeking to be value neutral, researchers can acknowledge that social issues involve multiple positions, each with different value assumptions, different definitions of the problem, different theories about its causes and effects, different interventions to prevent or treat it. Even when rigorous scientific methods are used, each side will tend to generate empirical findings that reflect its assumptions. Thus, researchers with strongly held values can take sides consistent with their values and bear witness when their findings are relevant to those debates (Price, 1989). Such research will provide one of several perspectives on the issue at hand. This view fits with constructivist and critical philosophies of science.

Researchers must still be intellectually honest, recognize the value of opposing views, use defensible methods, and be willing to present findings that turned out contrary to their assumptions (Nelson, Prilleltensky, & MacGillivary, 2001, p. 671). Yet boldly and explicitly stating one's premises and values actually can improve research by clarifying the assumptions on which it is based.

With whom does a community researcher take sides? One's personal values are the most important guide. Another guideline is to look for whose viewpoints are missing in the debate over a social issue (Friere, 1970/1993; Price, 1989; Rappaport, 1981; Riger, 1990). Discussion of social issues is often dominated by the powerful, who define the problem and set the terms of debate. Their ideas become the conventional wisdom about the problem. Thus an important role of community researchers is to identify a community whose views are being overlooked and to conduct research that helps bring attention to the experiences and views of that community. This provides broader knowledge of the issue and also may identify community strengths and resources. This approach can be termed **attending to unheard voices**.

The metaphor of **voice** comes from feminist thinkers (Belenky, Clinchy, Goldberger, & Tarule, 1986; Reinharz, 1994; Riger, 1990). In their view, positivist methods and theories in psychology obscured and distorted women's experiences and knowledge. Women's voices—their words, intuitions, and insights—have not been clearly heard or understood. This obscuring of voices has also happened to other groups not well represented among researchers: for example, persons of color, low-income persons, and those with physical or mental disabilities. Students in schools are seldom asked for their experiences and views in research on teaching and learning (Weinstein, 2002a). Reinharz (1994) noted that researchers cannot give voice to excluded groups or individuals; voice is something one develops oneself. Yet researchers can create ways to listen to and learn from voices of diverse persons and can help bring their voices into psychology's knowledge base.

Attending to unheard voices involves beginning research from the standpoint of the less powerful individuals within social systems—the people who are most affected by the practices of social system(s) (e.g., global economy, workplace, mental health services, school system, or university) but who have the least control over those practices. Study the issue through their experiences, from their point of view, to understand the multiple social systems that affect them. That knowledge can then be used to advocate for social change to improve their lives and perhaps quality of life for the whole community or society as well. Rappaport (1981) advocated this approach in his early discussions of empowerment. It is especially consistent with critical philosophies of science (Nelson and Prilleltensky, 2005).

Many forms of feminist community psychology (e.g., Bond, Hill, Mulvey & Terenzio, 2000a,b; Salina et al., 2004) illustrate research that takes sides. Feminist researchers are often explicit about values and premises, attend to unheard voices, and conduct valid scholarly research that supports an activist approach to social change. They also call attention to how multiple ecological levels are intertwined, examining how macrosystems, organizations, and interpersonal forces are connected to oppression and liberation of women (recall the feminist slogan: "The personal is political"). Feminist community researchers often admit that their own life experiences influence their perspectives, seek to be explicit about their assumptions, and seek to learn from others' perspectives. Research becomes a process of personal development and interpersonal bonding, not simply an intellectual undertaking—a distinctively feminist theme.

Cris Sullivan and associates worked with community women's advocates and survivors of domestic violence to develop a program in which paraprofessional advocates worked with women with abusive partners. The researchers took sides, based on feminist values and analysis, but also used randomized experimental designs with representative samples. Their studies demonstrated that battered women involved in the advocacy relationship reported less violence, more social support, and better perceived quality of life than those in a control group (Bybee & Sullivan, 2002; Sullivan, 2003).

Community researchers can take sides in many community contexts. Participatory community research (Jason, Keys, Suarez-Balcazar, & Davis, 2004) also takes sides to work collaboratively with citizens in communities and attend to unheard voices. For instance, consider a middle-class community that develops a program to prevent drug abuse among its youth. The program funders require evaluation of the program's effectiveness. In a positivist approach, the evaluation researchers would maintain a neutral stance, distant from the program, making most or all of the choices about the evaluation research. In contrast, empowerment evaluation methods (see Chapter 14) focus on working with the program, helping to clarify its goals and initial planning, providing feedback on how it is actually implemented, and evaluating its outcomes. Important voices to consider would include the community's youth. This approach creates a partnership that continually improves program quality over time, instead of issuing a one-time verdict on program effectiveness from an outsider's perspective (Fetterman, 2002). Both approaches have value; our point here is that taking sides (in this case, empowerment evaluation) is a legitimate approach, generating knowledge not provided by an outside evaluation.

HOW SHALL WE PROMOTE COMMUNITY PARTICIPATION AND COLLABORATION IN RESEARCH DECISIONS?

> The first time I ever did research, I'll never forget it.... I went through eleven organizations; they all turned me down. So Baake called some guy... and said will you be kind to Chris Argyris and let him come into your bank and interview some people.... So I went in and interviewed fifty people, did my study.... And I went and gave the people some feedback, and they said "We like this. Would you come in now and do a total bank study?" Which I did.... I got almost diametrically opposed data. And I had interviewed twenty-five of the same people that I interviewed before.... I had nineteen of them come into a room, and I said "You can tell me what's going on." They said "Professor, it ain't so difficult. Four weeks ago, it was be-kind-to-Chris week. So some of us answered the questions in a way, who cares, and some said what the hell, it's not threatening, tell the truth. Now you come back as a consultant/researcher. Those of us who are now frightened distort the data, and those who think they might get some help give you the truth." (Argyris, in Lawler et al., 1985, quoted in Kelly, 1986, p. 583)

It is clear from this anecdote that the quality and usefulness of research data depends on the context in which it is collected, and especially on the relationship between researcher and research participants. When the researcher's position, power, and purposes changed, so did the nature of what employees told him. Argyris was performing organizational research, but similar issues pervade community psychology research.

One metaphor for the researcher-community relationship is that of guest and host (Robinson, 1990). Research is conducted by guests in a host community; among the good manners that might be expected of such guests are full disclosure of their intent and methods, seeking permission for their activities, respect for host wishes and views, and meaningful thanks for hospitality. Researchers receive the gift of cooperation by the community in providing data; reciprocating that gift involves providing products of that research in a form useful to the community. Another metaphor for this relationship is a collaborative partnership, with both parties having some degree of choice and control, and with open communication, compromise, and respect regarding those choices. Each partner brings unique resources to the shared work. Participatory community research is not a "noble sacrifice" by researchers; it involves rewards and costs for both researchers and community members (Isenberg, Loomis, Humphreys, & Maton, 2004).

These metaphors imply a concern for the long-term interests of the community. The partnership metaphor especially involves participation by community members in planning and conducting research. The approaches we will discuss have been termed **participatory community research, participatory action research, action research, collaborative research** and **community science** (Jason et al., 2004; Kelly, Ryan, Altman, & Stelzner, 2000; Reason & Bradbury, 2001; Tolman & Brydon-Miller, 2001; Trickett & Espino, 2004; Wandersman, Kloos, Linney, & Shinn, 2005). Many of these are intellectual descendants of Lewin's action research efforts in the 1940s.

Many researchers have exploited communities as "pockets of needs, laboratories for experimentation, or passive recipients of expertise" (Bringle & Hatcher, 2002, pp. 503–504). The metaphor of "data mining" fits the approach of researchers who conduct community research that benefits the researchers but not the community studied. Those communities understandably are reluctant to cooperate with future researchers. Though collaborative methods are not a panacea for such difficulties, they do address issues of control and avoiding exploitation.

These issues become even more important if the research involves an intervention or action program. The problem to be addressed, the specific objectives of the intervention, how it is implemented and evaluated, are all issues to be decided. Long-term commitment by researchers is needed if the intervention is to be incorporated into the everyday life of the setting (Primavera, 2004).

Issues of research process involve values, emotions, personal relationships, and resolving conflicts. Researchers need not only an intellectual understanding of the issues involved, but also social-emotional insight and skills. Genuinely collaborative research often leads to personal change for both citizens and researchers. Cultural misunderstandings, power differentials, divergent values, and other factors create challenges yet also can lead to richer personal understanding and better research (Jason et al., 2004; Primavera & Brodsky, 2004; Sarason, 2003a).

In this section, we review specific approaches to facilitating researcher-community partnership, and citizen participation in research decision making, at each stage of community research: before the beginning, defining the topic, collecting data, interpreting and reporting findings, and actions based on findings. At each step, we present approaches that maximize participation by community members. We do not advocate that these methods are useful or appropriate in every context. Community research varies along a spectrum from minimum to maximum community participation. Each community and research project requires a different matching of researcher and citizen roles (Pokorny et al., 2004). For further reading, we especially recommend several resources (Bond, Hill, Mulvey, & Terenzio, 2000b; Bringle & Hatcher, 2002; Brodsky, 2001; Fisher & Ball, 2003; Hazel & Onanga, 2003; Hughes & Seidman, 2002; Jason et al., 2004; Kelly, Ryan, Altman, & Stelzner, 2000; Nelson et al., 2001; Primavera & Brodsky, 2004; Tolan et al., 1990; Wandersman et al., 2005).

Partnership "Before the Beginning"

The research partnership begins with entry of researchers into the community. Entry issues include the following.

Who are the researchers, what institutions support or fund them, and what are their purposes? Are researchers invited into the community? By whom, and under what terms? Who are the community representatives, and are they representative of the community? Who will benefit from research in this community?

The resources of researchers and the host community must be assessed. From researchers, these may include funding for programs or staff positions for community members. To build true collaboration, both sides will need to devote time and effort and to decide how to share control. Not every community needs or wants the same resources from researchers: an economically oppressed community may look for economic resources; a more affluent community may need emotional support for persons with chronic illness (Nelson et al., 2001). Community members also offer resources, such as practical knowledge of the community and culture, social networks, and access to community settings.

Interdependence of researchers and citizens must be built through interpersonal relationships. That involves plenty of informal face-to-face contact, getting to know each other without the barriers of expertise and titles. For community researchers, important interpersonal skills include accurate self-awareness of one's emotions and of how one appears to others, self-disclosure in the process of building trust, and clear communication of aims, viewpoints, and values. Having community members explain their community and culture to researchers, in an atmosphere of learning and respect, is valuable. Humility and willingness to learn are essential. Volunteer community service, and informal socializing with community members, can be helpful. It is important for researchers to recognize differences in social status, power, culture, and life opportunities between researchers and community members, and to acknowledge how those can limit the perspectives of researchers (we will discuss this more in the section on culturally anchored research).

Researchers may need to demystify the images many citizens hold about research. To promote effective communication within the team, researchers must be willing to find a vocabulary that is commonsensical yet not condescending. Language communicates power, and the use of words such as "empirical" can alienate citizens. Researchers also need to learn from community members' experiential, cultural, "insider" knowledge.

Research Decisions

Creating a **community research panel**, comprised of representatives of community organizations and other citizens, allows researchers to communicate and negotiate with community members. It also improves the ability of researchers to understand the cultural characteristics of the community, and provides a way for the community to hold researchers accountable. Instead of a panel, researchers can establish a formal relationship with an existing body in the community, such as a tribal council or neighborhood association.

The community research panel and research team plan the research. Some examples of issues for the research team to negotiate include whether to use a control group (which does not receive a promising program), whether observers of mutual help group meetings are acceptable, the format and questions for questionnaires, and even where original data will be kept and how its confidentiality can be assured.

These and similar decisions have tradeoffs. For instance, lack of a control group may limit the evaluation of a program's effectiveness. Open-ended interviews fit the folkways of many communities better than standardized questionnaires but make it more difficult to develop reliable, valid measurements and use a large sample. Negotiating methodological or practical decisions with the community takes time and involves compromise. Yet genuine collaboration with community members can increase the validity of measurement, as researchers craft more appropriate methods, and research participants take the research more seriously. (Have you ever completed a survey hurriedly because you had no investment in the results?) Studies with mutual help groups that involved the group as a genuinely collaborative partner have had very high response rates (Isenberg et al., 2004). Creating a positive relationship with a community affords returning there for future studies. The tradeoffs must be considered in each study and community.

A participatory approach can involve experimental methods. The research on advocacy with battered women conducted by Sullivan (2003) and associates (described earlier in this chapter) involved women's shelters, community advocates, and survivors of abuse in decisions about all aspects of the research, including development of assessment questions and measures. The most difficult decision involved whether to use an experimental design, randomly assigning women to the advocacy program or to a control group that received the usual shelter services. The community members resisted the randomization at first but eventually were convinced of its fairness and of the value of carefully evaluating the actual effects of the program.

Another step in the community-researcher partnership is interpretation of results. One useful step is to present results to the community research panel, or other community members, asking for their interpretations. Researchers and citizens can consider questions such as: Are these results surprising? Is further refinement of methods needed? How can these results be useful to the community? How might they harm the community?

Interdependent relationships grow from tit-for-tat reciprocity, in which each partner focuses on satisfaction of his or her own interests, to focusing on outcomes that benefit both partners over the long term in an atmosphere of trust (Bringle & Hatcher, 2002). Affirming shared values and long-term aims fosters this development, especially when conflicts arise. That does not mean an end to conflicts but builds a climate in which to resolve them. It also is important to share credit for successes and work together to address challenges and conflicts. Important interpersonal skills for making collaborative research decisions include providing interpersonal support, asserting and accepting disagreement, avoiding defensiveness, sharing power, and recognizing and managing conflicts. Close monitoring and discussion of these issues fosters relationship development. Primavera (2004) described the ebb and flow of relationships in a university-community partnership for a family literacy program.

In Chapter 1, we discussed the Oxford House movement, in which persons in recovery from substance abuse live together and promote each other's recovery without professional supervision. This nationwide movement began in a Chicago recovery home without any researcher or professional involvement. Over 12 years, Oxford House and a research team from DePaul University have developed a collaborative partnership that has benefited both. The DePaul team entered the relationship with an interest in innovative models of recovery and believed that involving Oxford House members in all phases of the research would enhance its validity and practical value. Oxford House members and researchers meet weekly for an open exchange of ideas and monitoring of ongoing research; these meetings are open to any Oxford House member. Likewise, Oxford House meetings, even when sensitive topics are discussed, are open to researchers. Both partners worked to promote trust in the relationship. The research began with student researchers attending Oxford House activities and conducting interviews with residents to learn about the process of recovery at Oxford House from the residents' perspective. This qualitative research became the basis for later quantitative studies. Research design and assessment instruments were discussed thoroughly and approved by Oxford House representatives. In grant-supported studies, the staff who recruited participants and collected data were current or former Oxford House residents, approved by Oxford House representatives and the research team. The partnership has built the capacity of the research team to understand and measure the utility of the Oxford House approach, while also building the capacity of Oxford House staff to perform their own ongoing evaluation and program development. Researchers have become advocates for Oxford House, and worked with the movement in establishing new houses for women with children (Suarez-Balcazar et al., 2004).

Research Products and Impact

Research typically generates scholarly reports such as journal articles, books, and conference presentations. These publications further the researchers' careers but usually do little for the community.

Important questions concern products of research: Who is actually benefiting from this research? Will researchers share their findings with community members, in a form useful to them? Did citizens gain knowledge, skills, funding, or other resources to pursue their own goals? Have the researchers and the community members built an ongoing alliance for future collaborations? Even broader issues arise when macrosystems are also considered: Will the research methods or findings promote social justice? Will research products accurately portray the strengths of the individuals, communities, or cultures studied? How can the research inform future decisions by citizens, communities, organizations, governmental bodies, or other groups?

To report results of studies on citizen participation in block associations in Nashville neighborhoods, Chavis, Stucky, and Wandersman (1983) and a citizens' panel developed workshops for block association leaders. Community members and researchers led these workshops. Researchers discussed their research in common-sense terms, presented their results, and asked for feedback and interpretations by the citizens. Participants broke into small groups, listed priority problems for their neighborhood, and devised action plans. The workshops enriched the researchers' understanding of their results and facilitated action by the community. Adaptations of this approach have been adopted widely in community research (Jason et al., 2004).

Examples of additional research products might include reader-friendly newsletters for citizens, opinion essays or letters to the editor in newspapers, articles in popular magazines, interviews on broadcast media, expert testimony in legislative hearings or in court, advocacy reports or visits to policy makers, teaching formal or informal courses, contributing to community art projects, and developing educational role-plays, skits or other performances (Stein & Mankowski, 2004). While conducting interviews on the psychological effects of unemployment, Fryer and Fagan (2003) used a hand-held computer to calculate eligibility for government entitlements and programs (for those who were willing to share the financial information needed). This was the first time those benefits had been helpfully explained to many participants.

Psychopolitical Validity Prilleltensky (2003) proposed that community psychology research be evaluated not only in terms of methodological (often positivist) forms of validity, but also in terms of two other criteria, which are part of his concept of psychopolitical validity.

First, does the research account for the influence of macrosystem and other social forces, especially social injustice, on the lives of individuals and communities? Were these forces measured or studied in the research, and discussed with community members? Second, does the research promote the capacity of research participants and community members to understand macrosystem forces and to become involved in liberating social change? For instance, did citizens gain skills in understanding injustice, articulating their views, forming alliances, resolving conflicts, gaining power, making decisions, and similar capacities for advocating their community's interests?

Pursuing these goals involves careful thinking not only "before the beginning" but also about what happens "after the ending."

Limitations of Participatory Approaches

Participatory, collaborative community research methods have limitations. Not all community psychology research needs to be participatory. For instance, naturalistic assessment of community physical environments or analyses of archival data do not require participatory methods (although a collaborative approach can enhance the research) (e.g., Kuo, Sullivan, Coley, & Brunson, 1998; Perkins & Taylor, 1996).

Participatory methods are time consuming and risky for citizens, who often must master new roles that can be empowering but also take time, effort, and skill development. The extent of that commitment should be chosen by the citizens and respected by the researchers. Moreover, participation by some citizens in research decisions opens them to criticism by other community members displeased by the methods or findings. Researchers must respect the wishes of community panel members for private rather than public involvement (Chataway, 1997).

The university environment presents obstacles to participatory research by faculty and students. Many graduate programs need more training for the sensitivity, communication, and negotiation that conducting research with full citizen participation involves, especially across cultural boundaries (Nelson et al., 2001). Moreover, universities often demand publications more quickly than participatory community research allows, in forms not useful to communities.

Although participatory methods level to some extent the hierarchical, unequal relationship between researchers and community members, some power differentials seem inherent in conducting research. Using participatory methods does not magically erase these differentials, which must be acknowledged and dealt with. Even participatory research may have unintended negative consequences for the community. Researchers must be vigilant regarding the process and actual outcomes of their work (Bond, 1990; Burman, 1997; Isenberg et al., 2004).

Terms such as *participatory* and *collaborative* have multiple meanings, which can be divergent or even contradictory (Trickett & Espino, 2004). We have emphasized the commonalities of a number of participatory-collaborative approaches, but further reading is best focused on the diversity of different approaches (see resources that we have cited).

Participatory approaches provide specific ways to enact core community psychology values, and embody the Swampscott ideal of the *participant conceptualizer.* They represent a distinctive contribution of community psychology to academic research and to communities.

HOW SHALL WE UNDERSTAND THE CULTURAL AND SOCIAL CONTEXTS OF THIS RESEARCH?

All research, even a laboratory study, occurs within a culture, perhaps more than one. However, understanding diverse cultures, populations, and settings is essential for community psychology. It is especially important that community researchers study a variety of cultures and communities, especially those that have been ignored by mainstream psychology. Researchers also need to understand how they themselves are affected by culture. In this section, we will focus on a few specific cultural issues in conducting research. We leave for Chapter 7 a larger analysis of cultural and related concepts for understanding human diversity.

Four Methodological Issues Involving Culture

Cultural assumptions influence every research decision. Yet psychologists have only recently considered how these assumptions limit the meaning and interpretation of our research findings (Sue, 1999; Tebes, 2000). Recently, cultural variables have been included in many studies without adequate reflection about what is meant by these constructs, why they may be important for a given study, and how they are to be measured or assessed.

For instance, suppose a study finds that Hispanic adolescents dropped out of school more often than European American teens, a seemingly simple empirical effect. Yet such a finding is useless, even harmful, as a basis for designing social policy or prevention programs, unless important conceptual questions are answered. Were confounds such as socioeconomic status, effects of stereotyping and discrimination, access to educational opportunities, and first language (English or Spanish) controlled in this study? Is this difference due to the result of factors within Hispanic cultures or to external economic forces or discrimination? Which Hispanic ethnicities (e.g., Mexican American, Puerto Rican, Cuban, Dominican) were represented in the sample? How might these specific ethnic groups differ from each other? How many Hispanic adolescents were recent immigrants or longer-term U.S. residents? Are cultural factors best understood in a "between-group" study that compares two ethnic or cultural groups, or by "within-group" studies that focus on one culture? These questions illustrate the methodological issues we describe next (see Bernal, Trimble, Burlew, & Leong, 2003; Hughes & Seidman, 2002).

How Is Cultural or Ethnic Identity Assessed? These and similar concepts are often assessed with simple box checking based on the participant's self-reported choice among a limited set of categories. For instance, on a questionnaire, "Asian American" may be the only available category for Americans of Japanese, Vietnamese, Indian, and other ancestries (the category is even wider if Pacific Islanders are included). Related issues include: Is there a coding scheme for multiethnic or biracial responses? Are one's first language, birthplace and parents' birthplaces, and length of residence in the country assessed? What is the extent of one's personal identification with an ethnic or cultural tradition? If researchers rely on simple box checking, even with more specific boxes to check, they assess only the surface of ethnocultural identification, not its deeper reality (Frable, 1997; Trimble, Helms, & Root, 2003). Deeper identification rather than simple categorization also may be an issue for concepts such as sexual orientation, ability-disability, and religion or spirituality.

Assumptions of Population Homogeneity A related issue concerns accurately understanding the diversity within every culture. An assumption of population homogeneity (Sasao & Sue, 1993) categorizes all members of a cultural group as alike and overlooks differences among them. Research in social categorization suggested that this results from the cognitive tendency to think about members of one's cultural in-group in more detail than persons outside it (Kelly, Azelton, Burzette, & Mock, 1994). Thus, people understand members of their own culture in complex ways, as individuals and as members of various groups or categories. Yet people think more simplistically about members of other cultures or communities and tend to categorize them in more general terms. This is ethnocentrism, although often inadvertent. It also reflects lack of detailed knowledge and experience with phenomena we wish to understand in the communities where they occur. Forming a collaborative relationship with community members helps to counteract assumptions of population homogeneity.

For instance, Hamby (2000) found considerable differences in cultural gender norms among the 512 recognized American Indian cultural communities in the United States (e.g., Seneca, Zuni, Apache). Also important are differences between generations of immigrant groups (e.g., first-generation immigrants from Mexico, second- and third-generation Mexican Americans) as well as gender, socioeconomic, or other differences within ethnic or racial categories (Goodkind & Deacon, 2004; Hughes & Seidman, 2002). In studies of alcohol use among Americans of Japanese ancestry, findings from samples in Hawai'i differed from those on the mainland (Sasao & Sue, 1993). At the individual level, some members of an ethnic population may consider their ethnicity a very important aspect of their personal identity and others do not. Characteristics such as gender make a great deal of difference in worldview and life experiences in any culture.

Assumptions of Methodological Equivalence A third issue concerns equivalence of research methods across cultures (Burlew, 2003; Hughes & Seidman,

2002). Such assumptions can occur even when cultural differences are not the topic of research or recognized by researchers. Linguistic equivalence of questionnaires or other measurement instruments is the simplest example. Tanaka-Matsumi and Marsella (cited in Hughes et al., 1993) found that the English clinical term *depression* and the closest Japanese translation *yuutsu* were not equivalent. When asked to define them, U.S. citizens described internal states such as "sad" and "lonely," whereas Japanese described external states such as "dark" and "rain." Careful checks on translation can reduce but not eliminate such problems.

Issues of scale equivalence refer to whether choices on questionnaires or other measures mean the same thing across cultures. Hughes and Seidman (2002) cited evidence that African-American and Hispanic participants were more likely to use the extremes of Likert scales, whereas European-American respondents were more likely to use the intermediate areas of such scales. More generally, the quantitative approach of Western psychology is unfamiliar in many cultures. Goodkind and Deacon (2004) discussed how they developed qualitative and quantitative methods for research with two groups of refugee women: Hmong women from Laos and Muslim women from the Middle East, Afghanistan, and Africa.

Between-Group and Within-Group Designs A between-group design compares two or more cultural groups, for instance African Americans and European Americans, on variables specified by the researchers. Its strength is that such comparison can yield knowledge of differences between cultures. One major drawback is that the researchers' own cultures will affect their design, assessment, and interpretation of differences. Also, the equivalence of procedures, setting, and measurements in both cultures is difficult to assure. Finally, without a deep understanding of both cultures, it is difficult to avoid interpreting differences as a deficit or weakness in one of the cultural groups. Thus, between-group studies are vulnerable to producing results that "blame cultures" for problems, rather than considering cultural strengths and effects of external factors such as economic and political forces.

Researchers using a within-group design study a cultural group in more depth, on its own terms. Comparisons and differences between cultures are not the focus. This approach fosters understanding of why distinctive cultural practices exist. In addition, subgroups within the culture (e.g., based on socioeconomic status or length of U.S. residence) can be understood more clearly. Population-specific psychologies study psychological aspects of specific cultures or cultural groups, such as African, Mexican, Polish, or Japanese (Kim & Berry, 1993; Potts, 2003). For psychological understanding of most cultures, a deeper understanding is needed first, in the near future (Hughes & Seidman, 2002). Moreover, a recent review of studies in a major community psychology journal found that between-group studies were more likely to emphasize deficits of a culture or population, whereas within-group studies more often emphasized strengths (Martin, Lounsbury, & Davidson, 2004).

Conducting Culturally Anchored Research

What can researchers do to recognize issues of culture and respond to them? The first steps begin with yourself. Cultivate an understanding of how your own culture and experiences have shaped your worldview. In addition, adopt a "stance of informed naivete, curiosity, and humility" in learning about another culture: an awareness of your own limited knowledge and a genuine willingness to learn (Mock, 1999). Recognize that this learning will be an ongoing process.

This learning cannot be cultivated in isolation. Seek experiences and personal relationships that promote learning about your own culture and the culture in which you seek to do research. Those experiences may be informal socializing, attending community celebrations and events, or more structured interviews with interested community members. What you do may be less important than how you do it, with respect and willingness to listen. Examples include the following.

Create safe settings for discussion where researchers and citizens can personally explore difficult issues of culture and power: how each person's own culture influences and limits his or her worldview; strengths of different cultural worldviews and values; personal effects of social injustice and oppression; how to plan research to promote empowerment of community members; and access to resources that are wanted by the host community.

Bernadette Sanchez studied mentorship among Mexican-American adolescents (Keys, McMahon, Sanchez, London, & Absul-Adil, 2004, pp. 185–186). She read ethnographies about Mexican-American communities, attended meetings of a Mexican student organization, and participated in social activities. These steps deepened her own cultural understanding of the Mexican-American community and adolescents there. Before interviewing research participants, she shared information about herself: why she was pursuing a doctoral degree and her interest in the education of Latino/as. During the interview, she also shared her own experiences with family and mentoring relationships when appropriate. This mutuality encouraged participants to respond more fully to her questions. After she analyzed the interviews, she met with nine participants to discuss her findings, check her interpretations, and hear their views.

Susan McMahon and Roderick Watts (2002) studied ethnic identity among urban African-American youth. For this study, McMahon, a European-American woman, worked with Watts, an African-American man. McMahon examined her own cultural background and how it shaped her own identity, spent much time talking about her interests with African Americans in the school and community, conducted observations and focus group interviews to test measures for validity and cultural equivalence, and sought to understand how economic and sociopolitical barriers affect the lives of African-American youth (Keys et al., 2004, p. 189).

James Kelly and his associates (Kelly et al., 1994; Kelly et al., 2004; Tandon et al., 1998) pursued a long-term research project on the nature of leadership in an African-American community in Chicago, collaborating with a panel of community leaders there. Those local leaders, with the support of the researchers, actually designed the interview used in the research. The researchers' original conceptions of leadership focused on personal qualities of individual leaders. However, the leaders on the panel articulated a collective definition of leadership, based on their experiences in working together, and consistent with their African heritage. They used the metaphor of making soup to describe the importance of both individual contributions and group experiences. The research team's perspective, rooted in the individualism of psychology, was expanded by this encounter with different cultural assumptions.

One valuable way to learn about cultures is to study its narratives: the shared stories that express important values, historical events, folkways, and emotions. Gary Harper and associates collaborated with Project VIDA, a community-based organization in Little Village, a Mexican-American neighborhood in Chicago (Harper, Bangi, et al. 2004; Harper, Lardon, et al. 2004). Project VIDA conducts HIV prevention programs for adolescent Latinas and for Latino gay, bisexual, and questioning youth. Harper and associates read Latino/a magazines and newspapers, especially those for Latina adolescents. They visited Little Village repeatedly, learning about cultural murals and the neighborhood's decorative gateway, shopping and eating locally, attending (and dancing at) cultural events, and meeting Project VIDA staff and Little Village residents. They sought to learn stories associated with Mexican culture, Little Village, and individuals involved with La Vida. Meetings with project staff began with sharing of food and personal stories, a reflection of Mexican culture. The study itself used individual and group interviews to elicit stories from adolescent participants and program staff about culturally based expectations that can promote or hinder HIV prevention among Latino/a adolescents.

Gerald Mohatt, Kelly Hazel, and associates (2004) also drew on narratives in research on sobriety in Alaska Native communities. They took a strengths perspective by studying personal stories of pathways to sobriety. They developed a collaborative research relationship with a coordinating council composed mostly of Native Alaskans while negotiating steps of the research with a number of Native Alaskan tribal boards and village councils. Tribal elders rejected the idea of monetary payment for participation, saying that their participation was not for sale and that many persons would participate to contribute to the community. Institutional review boards required that tapes of interviews be destroyed after the research, but the elders also rejected this notion, pointing out the usefulness of tapes for future prevention activities. The researchers developed procedures for each participant to choose whether to receive payment or donate it to charity, and to choose whether to allow retention of tapes with confidentiality assured. When recruitment of participants greatly outpaced all expectations (152 persons volunteered for an initial study requiring only 36 participants), the elders insisted that each volunteer be interviewed to respect their willingness to help. Researchers developed a briefer interview process for this purpose. Researchers also had to forge compromises between federal funders who desired quantitative methods and Native preference for qualitative interviews that allowed them to tell their own stories. The patience of Native representatives and the research team was rewarded with a rich archive of interviews that expressed cultural strengths and provided a basis for sobriety promotion in Native communities.

An Example: The Akwesasne Study

Santiago-Rivera, Morse, Hunt, and Lickers (1998) reported on the process of building a collaborative partnership between university-based researchers and the Mohawk Nation of Akwesasne, a community located along the St. Lawrence River between the United States and Canada. Their work illustrates many aspects of the participatory approach and of culturally anchored research.

The Mohawk Nation of Akwesasne faces serious environmental contamination from outside corporations' dumping of pollutants (e.g., fluorides, cyanide, PCBs) into the land, water, and air. Ms. Katsi Cook, a Mohawk midwife and community leader, headed efforts to obtain support for a study, funded by an external grant, of the effects of PCB exposure on the health of Akwesasne citizens. Santiago-Rivera and colleagues became involved as part of that study.

The researchers and their Mohawk hosts worked through a process developed by the Akwesasne Task Force on the Environment, a Mohawk group. The researchers found that they had to adapt their communication style to facilitate dialogue with community members. They limited use of scientific vocabulary. They spent much time listening to the experiences and views of many community members and sought education in Mohawk beliefs, customs, language, and the history of the community. Mohawk beliefs about their spiritual relationship with the land made environmental contamination a deeply emotional and spiritual matter. Customs regarding interpersonal relationships affected every aspect of data collection and research planning. The researchers had to learn Mohawk culture sufficiently to gain the trust of their community partners.

Akwesasne Task Force members had many questions for the Santiago-Rivera research team: How will this benefit us? How will you assure confidentiality of data? Will you follow a research protocol and methods that we approve? Who will own and keep the data? Who will be employed with the research grant money?

Researchers and the Akwesasne Task Force worked together to assess the cultural appropriateness of all measurements and materials and to field-test all methods and materials in a small pilot study with Akwesasne citizens. Those participants also discussed their concerns about measurements with the research team and suggested changes. The researchers and task force negotiated roles for carrying out research, including hiring and training Mohawk staff for data collection and supervisory responsibilities. All original data would remain in the Akwesasne community, an Akwesasne committee would review all research to assure that it had followed agreed-on procedures, and an Akwesasne Task Force member would be coauthor of any published reports.

The researchers and community also devised workable means of resolving disagreements. The Mohawk method is to do this by discussion and consensus. The researchers had to adjust their schedules and styles to participate in this approach; balancing the time needed for consensus and the reporting deadlines of the granting agency was a problem. However, the commitment of both the

Akwesasne and the researchers led to successful resolutions of these issues and completion of research that benefited both parties.

AT WHAT ECOLOGICAL LEVELS OF ANALYSIS SHALL WE CONDUCT THIS RESEARCH?

For any study, the researchers choose the ecological level(s) of analysis. Questions about ecological levels are actively debated in community psychology. The challenge is addressing the interrelationships among these differing levels of analysis, not just studying one level in isolation.

For example, in a study of protective factors for adolescent resistance to drug use, what variables should be included? Individual strengths? Microsystem factors, such as family and peer influences? Neighborhood characteristics? Cultural values and resources? Economic factors? Political influences on drug laws and enforcement?

Shall a study of neighborhood empowerment focus on the effects of a block association on its individual members, or on the functioning of the block association as an organization or on its effectiveness in improving the quality of life in the neighborhood as a whole? Will the research take into account the effects on neighborhoods of macrosystems, such as economic forces and decisions by governments and corporations?

Examples of the Importance of Considering Levels of Analysis

Phenomena such as social support or citizen participation can be viewed through different lenses at different ecological levels. Let's consider two examples.

Social Support Networks Do senior citizens receive support from individuals only, or do microsystems and organizations also provide support, beyond that from individuals? Felton and Berry (1992) conducted a study of social support networks among senior citizens at a hospital geriatric clinic. Their interview questions, following standardized, often-used procedures, asked respondents to name individuals who provided important support to them. Yet Felton and Berry's respondents provided some initially puzzling answers. Although asked for individuals, many gave answers like "all my nieces and nephews," "my grandchildren," and "the people at my senior center." Almost one-third of the respondents named such groups, not an individual, at least once. In total, about 10 percent of the support sources listed were groups. When interviewers asked for clarification, most respondents insisted that they meant a group, and that it was the group as a whole, not particular individuals, who provided support. (Notice that Felton and Berry then listened to and reported the words of these respondents, whose ideas did not fit the original measurement procedure.)

What do we make of this finding? Social support has usually been understood and measured as a process occurring between two individuals. This has kept much of the research on social support at the individual level (Felton & Shinn, 1992). Yet clearly social support also occurs in groups (Maton, 1989), especially in microsystems. Those groups provide support and a sense of community even when the individual members change. Maton (1989) found that highly supportive religious congregations, mutual help groups, and senior centers provided significant aid to members facing a variety of stressors. In fact, the sense of belonging within such an organization or microsystem (social integration) may be as important as social support from individuals (Felton & Shinn, 1992).

Neighborhood Citizen Participation What predicts citizen participation in neighborhood associations? Perkins, Florin, Rich, Wandersman, and Chavis (1990) analyzed predictors of citizen participation as part of the Block Booster Project, an action research project conducted in urban neighborhoods. They focused on city blocks and block associations formed by residents. When Perkins and colleagues compared individuals' extent of participation in block associations, the citizens who participated more included those who owned their homes (vs. renting), who had lived longer on the block, and who had higher incomes (this is consistent with prior research). Then Perkins et al. computed means for these three residential and income variables for each block and compared blocks, not individuals, on the extent of their residents' participation. In that block-level analysis, none of the three income/residence factors were associated with participation.

What does this mean? Perkins et al. (1990, p. 106) interpreted it this way. Within a block, the individuals most likely to participate were long-time residents, homeowners, and those with higher incomes. Yet blocks with few long-term, homeowning, or higher-income residents still mustered as much citizen participation overall as blocks with many of these residents. In their study, this appeared to be because the sense of community among residents of the block as a whole was more important for participation than the individual characteristics of its residents.

If Perkins et al. had not compared blocks as well as individuals, they would have concluded that owning a home, having a higher income, and being a long-term resident are the most important factors in citizen participation. These variables are difficult to change and would give dispiriting news to residents of lower-income neighborhoods attempting to improve the quality of neighborhood life. Instead, the more accurate picture emerges that these demographic factors make a difference within a block, but blocks without these resources can mobilize other resources (e.g., sense of community) to increase participation. Their analysis revealed not only differences by level of analysis, but also suggested community strengths for lower-income neighborhoods.

How Can Ecological Levels Be Studied?

How can researchers study the characteristics of levels beyond the individual, such as microsystems, organizations, and communities? These cannot solely be studied by administering individual measures familiar to psychologists. Individuals within a classroom, organization, or even locality may be interdependent members of a community, which complicates statistical analysis and interpretation (Shinn & Rapkin, 2000). Community psychology seeks to answer questions about the effects of larger ecological units on individual lives. Following are a few ideas, a suggestive but not exhaustive list.

In Chapter 5 we describe the idea of measuring the social climate of a setting (Moos, 1984, 1994, 2003). In a number of studies, Moos and associates measured the psychological characteristics of environments such as classrooms and mental health treatment settings. They did this by using questionnaires to ask individuals about their perceptions of qualities of the environment, which are summed to measure constructs such as supportiveness of relationships among setting members, how task-oriented the setting is, and how clear the goals and rules of the organization are. These are subjective ratings, based on individual judgments. When scores are combined for everyone in the setting, the mean level of perceived supportiveness for a classroom, for instance, can be used to compare it to other classrooms. However, this approach has limitations. For instance, an overall mean level of perceived supportiveness among employees in a workplace does not reveal if there are systematic differences in perceptions between female and male employees (Shinn, 1990; Shinn & Rapkin, 2000).

More objective measures of a small group or organization can be provided by independent outside observers (Shinn, 1990). Roberts and colleagues (1991, 1999) used trained, independent observers to conduct behavioral observations of a self-help group. Their studies yielded important findings about social support exchanged in such groups.

An intermediate approach uses key informants to provide information on an organization or community. Allen (2005) studied the effectiveness of community coordinating councils by interviewing and surveying members and leaders. Chesir-Teran (2003) suggested methods for measuring heterosexism in high schools through surveys, interviews, physical observation, and archival records.

Another approach is to identify and count changes in a community as a whole. Fawcett and associates have developed a variety of such measures (Fawcett et al., 1995). Examples include a new high school peer-helping program to reduce drug abuse, a new radio station policy prohibiting glamorization of drug use, and creation of training courses for clergy in drug abuse prevention efforts for their congregations. Speer, Hughey, Gensheimer, and Adams-Leavitt (1995) used archival data to measure the impact of community advocacy organizations. Over a three-year period, they counted the number of stories in major metropolitan newspapers on two such organizations and the number of ideas emphasized by each group that appeared in these stories. Such measures are especially useful in longitudinal studies of community change.

In Chapter 5 we describe ecological concepts that community psychologists use to think about these issues. Two chapters in the *Handbook of Community Psychology* (Rappaport & Seidman, 2000) provide useful reviews of these issues. Linney (2000) described ecological concepts and assessment methods. Shinn and Rapkin (2000) provided detailed discussions of conceptual and methodological issues for community research involving multiple ecological levels.

Multiple ecological levels are embedded in the term *community psychology.* Researchers in the field choose ecological level(s) of analysis for every study, even if only by default. Research is improved by making those choices explicit and by addressing factors at multiple ecological levels.

CONCLUSION

Our format of four questions for community research may seem to imply that a research team answers these four questions in a sequence. Actually, these choices are interdependent and not necessarily sequential. It is not unusual for an existing partnership with a community organization to influence the researcher's choice of phenomenon, perspective, and level of analysis for a study. Or a researcher may study her own culture or population, often within an existing relationship with a specific community. What is certain is that all four questions are involved in community research, whether explicitly chosen by the researcher or implicitly assumed without reflection. Community research always occurs within a culture and a community, always concerns levels of analysis, and always studies a phenomenon from a particular framework of values. Our purpose in this chapter has been to help you become more aware of these questions, and thus more capable of making explicit, reasoned choices in performing community research. In the next chapter, we turn to specific research methods.

CHAPTER SUMMARY

1. Communities provide useful settings for research. Conducting community research involves explicitly answering four questions: What values stances shall we take? How shall we promote community participation and collaboration in research decisions? How shall we understand the cultural and social contexts of this research? At what ecological levels of analysis shall we conduct this research? These four questions involve aspects of a larger question: *Who will generate what knowledge, for whom, and for what purposes?*
2. Three philosophies of science underlie much community psychology research. These concern definitions of science, scientific knowledge, proper research methods, and proper uses of research findings. *Positivist* views emphasize objectivity, measurement, experimentation, hypothesis testing to discover cause and effect, and generalizing findings to other settings. *Post-positivist* views, a later development of positivism, assume that no researcher is truly neutral but seek to minimize bias with measurement and experimentation. *Constructivist* views emphasize a connection between researcher and participant, the particular setting where research occurs, and understanding

participants' experiences and their meaning to participants, not just causes and effects. *Critical* views emphasize how social forces and belief systems influence both researchers and participants as well as researchers' responsibility for integrating research with social action. Each philosophy of science has advantages and limitations. Our main point is to encourage explicit decisions by researchers about values and philosophy of science.

3. Social issues also affect community research. A positivist approach defines social problems and seeks to test solutions with scientific research. A problem with this is that social issues are often conflicts between competing perspectives offering different definitions of the issue. Community researchers can address controversial issues by explicitly *taking sides*, conducting research that provides information from one perspective on the issue. *Attending to unheard voices*, the views and strengths of persons who are affected by social issues and policies but who hold little power, is one such approach.
4. We described *participatory, collaborative community research* processes: "before the beginning" of research, making research decisions, and products of research. Developing a *community research panel* is one way to involve citizens in these decisions. *Psychopolitical validity* concerns whether the research process empowered citizens to become involved in liberating social change to benefit their communities. Participatory research involves tradeoffs. Each researcher-community partnership will have its own level of optimal involvement.
5. Understanding the cultural and social contexts of a community is important. Four research issues involve culture: (a) how cultural and ethnic identity are assessed; (b) challenging assumptions of *population homogeneity*, that everyone is similar within a cultural group; (c) *methodological equivalence* of research methods and measures across cultures; and (d) whether it is more valuable to study differences between cultural groups or study one cultural group in detail (*between-group* or *within-group* studies).
6. Much community research concerns multiple ecological levels of analysis. We illustrated how thinking in levels-of-analysis terms helps to clarify confusing findings on social support networks and neighborhood citizen participation. We gave suggestive examples of how ecological levels above the individual may be studied.
7. The four questions for community research are not a sequence, but they are interrelated. We advocate making explicit choices about each question.

BRIEF EXERCISES

1. Identify a controversial issue in your community or society with which you have personal experience in some way.
   What are the opposing sides on this issue?
   What persons, communities, or voices are unheard or discounted?

How might community psychology research help in understanding those voices?
What groups or organizations should be involved in a community research panel for this research? Why?

2. Read a recent article in a community psychology journal that is interesting to you. (You can access the *American Journal of Community Psychology* through the InfoTrac search service that comes with this textbook. Articles that we have cited in this chapter make good examples.) Does this article:

   Take more of a positivist, constructivist, or critical approach? How?
   Take sides in a debate on a social or community issue? Attend to unheard voices? How?
   Use a participatory or collaborative approach to working with citizens or communities? How?
   Describe explicitly how collaborative community relationships were developed? Describe these.
   (This seldom appears in journal articles in detail, but some articles we cited do so.)
   Illustrate methods of culturally anchored research that we discussed? How?
   Make explicit what ecological levels of analysis were involved in the study? Which levels?

3. If you intrigued by the idea of participatory community research, consider the skills that we mentioned in the chapter as important for this work (interpersonal and methodological). Which of these are strengths that you have now? Where, and with whom, could you learn more of these skills? With what communities and cultures are you interested in doing research?

RECOMMENDED READINGS

Bond, M., Hill, J., Mulvey, A., & Terenzio, M. (Eds.) (2000a, b). Special Issues: Feminism and community psychology [Parts I and II]. *American Journal of Community Psychology, 28(5,6).*

Hughes, D., & Seidman, E. (2002). In pursuit of a culturally anchored methodology. In T. Revenson, A. D'Augelli, S. French, D. Hughes, D. Livert, E. Seidman, M. Shinn & H. Yoshikawa, (Eds.), *Ecological research to promote social change: Methodological advances from community psychology* (pp. 243–255). New York: Kluwer/Plenum.

Jason, L., Keys, C., Suarez-Balcazar, Y., Taylor, R., & Davis, M. (Eds.) (2004). *Participatory community research: Theories and methods in action.* Washington, DC: American Psychological Association.

Primavera, J. & Brodsky, A. (Eds.). (2004). Special issue: Process of community research and action. *American Journal of Community Psychology, 33(3/4).*

INFOTRAC COLLEGE EDITION KEYWORDS

positivism(t), constructivism(t), postmodern(ist), feminism(t) and *research, community research, participatory community research, participatory action research, collaborative research, culturally anchored research, psychopolitical validity, ecological level(s), levels of analysis, multi-level*

4

Methods of Community Psychology Research

Stan Mason

INTRODUCTION

What specific research methods do community psychologists use?

In this chapter we discuss qualitative and quantitative community research methods, introducing each approach in its own terms. We highlight specific methods, with summaries of their strengths and limitations, and examples of actual studies. We also examine how qualitative and quantitative methods can be integrated in a single study. Our overall themes are these.

- Qualitative and quantitative methods yield complementary forms of useful knowledge.
- Choice of methods must depend on the questions to be answered in the research.
- Both qualitative and quantitative methods can be used in participatory-collaborative community research of the type we discussed in Chapter 3.
- Multiple methods often strengthen a specific study.
- Contextual and longitudinal perspectives often strengthen community research.

- Community psychology is best served by a diversity of forms of knowledge and methods of research.

QUALITATIVE METHODS

Let's begin with a study that illustrates the power of qualitative methods. Catherine Stein and Virginia Wemmerus (2001) studied how a sample of families of adults with schizophrenia responded to their family members' illness. They interviewed 22 individuals from six families, including the ill family member (person with schizophrenia). (Studies of families with members with schizophrenia seldom include the ill member. One goal of this study was to attend to their unheard voices.) This sample is small and limited in diversity; more studies are needed. Yet the authors' use of qualitative methods yielded a rich, compelling account of family life not provided by other studies and led to actions beyond a research report (Stein & Mankowski, 2004).

Stein and Wemmerus interviewed all participants, asking open-ended questions about their perceptions of the onset and course of the schizophrenia, the impact of that illness on the family, family caregiving efforts, and expectations for the future. The researchers' "passionate listening" allowed participants to "think out loud" about the meaning of their experiences, and to share hurt, vulnerabilities, and strengths. The experience led the researchers to consider how society (including themselves) contributes to the pain of coping with schizophrenia and to consider the hopes, strengths, and active coping of families and persons with schizophrenia (Stein & Mankowski, 2004, p. 28).

Stein and Wemmerus reported their findings in terms of a life course perspective: the ways in which schizophrenia had interrupted what families considered "a normal life" for their family member in early or middle adulthood; the losses and grief that ensued; the efforts of the ill member and the family to recover or achieve the social roles of "a normal life" (e.g., daily activities, work, social life, intimate relationships); and their expectations for the future. These excerpts convey participants' efforts to live socially valued roles and suggest the immediacy and emotional impact of attending to unheard voices:

> From Martin's mother, describing the onset of his illness: "Well, mothers are supposed to fix things. And all I could do was, you know, try to get help . . . . It's devastating to understand that [your child has] a lifelong illness and it's going to be hard for him, a lot harder for him than it is for me, and it's devastating for me."
>
> From Martin's sister: "Martin's not fine in any sense of the term, but he's doing fine. He's living independently, he can go do his own shopping, he can go to the doctor's, and he can drive a car."
>
> From Donna, who was a wife, mother of two, and a teacher when her schizophrenia began: "I never dreamed when [my children] were born that I'd get that sick, and have [my children] move away and live with my brother. That was hard. Very hard."

> From Mary, who has coped with schizophrenia for 11 years: "This Thanksgiving was different. I had my own Thanksgiving here with my husband. And it turned out to be a success. We had a couple and a single person. We had our own turkey, sweet potatoes, lima beans, gelatin salad and the couple brought a pumpkin pie. My first Thanksgiving since I've been married." (Stein & Wemmerus, 2001, pp. 734, 735, 738, 739; names are pseudonyms)

In reading these remarks, if you experience some of their anguish, longing, courage, pride, and other feelings, that illustrates the emotional power of qualitative methods.

The researchers' commitment to understanding the role of the ill member in family life led to uncovering of a striking finding: when family members were asked about their preparations for future caregiving with their ill family member, none of the six families had discussed those issues with that ill member, despite abundant evidence of the families' caring involvement (Stein & Wemmerus, 2001, p. 740). That omission did not result simply from family dynamics, but from societal attitudes about persons with schizophrenia, and suggests more active efforts by both families and the mental health system to include persons with mental illness in decisions about their lives and care.

This research led to a publication and to Stein's developing of a course in which clinical psychology graduate students learn about schizophrenia through being paired with persons coping with the illness. Through shared learning activities, these persons teach the future clinicians about daily coping with the illness (Stein & Mankowski, 2004).

Common Features of Qualitative Methods

Qualitative methods have a long history in psychology (Maracek, Fine, & Kidder, 1997; Stewart, 2000). The clinical case history is a qualitative method. Other examples include Dollard's (1937) study, *Caste and Class in a Southern Town* and Rosenhan's (1973) infiltration of psychiatric units by pseudopatients, "On Being Sane in Insane Places," *Women's Ways of Knowing* (Belenky, Clinchy, Goldberger, & Tarule, 1986) advocated the importance of qualitative approaches for understanding women's experiences. Qualitative research includes a diversity of methods, yet most of them share the following common features.

1. **Contextual meaning.** The principal aim of qualitative research is to understand the meaning of a phenomenon for persons who experience it, in the contexts of their lives. This involves allowing persons to "speak in their own voices" as much as possible, although interpretation by the researcher is also involved. Contextual understanding represents a form of insider knowledge, although it is generated in part by discussions with an outsider (the researcher).
2. **Participant-researcher relationship.** Contextual meaning is created within a personal, mutual relationship between research participant and researcher that may be emotional as well as intellectual. These methods thus

are especially apt for collaborative research with community members and for understanding cultural contexts.

3. **Sampling.** The researcher develops a close relationship with a sample of persons, often through one or more particular community settings. The sample of persons is usually small to facilitate the level of detail needed. Researchers may also rely on their own experiences as sources of information.
4. **Generalization.** Generalization of findings is less important than understanding meaning among the persons sampled. Researchers may generalize findings by identifying converging themes from multiple studies or cases.
5. **Listening.** As much as possible, the researcher sets aside preconceptions and attempts to understand the persons or setting on their terms, in their language and context. Attentiveness, asking open-ended questions, and providing freedom for interviewees to structure their own responses are preferred over standardized questionnaires (which often reflect researchers' preconceptions or theories).
6. **Reflexivity.** Researchers also seek to be reflexive: stating their interests, values, preconceptions, and personal statuses or roles as explicitly as possible, both to the persons studied and in the research report. They also re-examine those assumptions in light of what they learn from the research participants. This makes potential biases and assumptions as transparent as possible.
7. **Thick description.** Qualitative data in psychology usually are words. The researcher seeks specific "thick" description of personal experiences, detailed enough to provide convincing evidence of realism. This also affords later checking for significant details and patterns. Other researchers can also use these detailed notes or transcripts to check the validity of analysis and interpretation.
8. **Data analysis, interpretation.** The processes of data collection, data analysis, and interpretation overlap, and the researcher moves back and forth among them. Analysis often consists of identifying (coding) repeating themes or separating and comparing distinct categories or stages. For instance, a researcher may use a question-ordered matrix (Sonn & Fisher, 1996, p. 421), in which questions form the columns, individual interviewees the rows, and answers by each participant the entries in each cell. This framework promotes comparison of responses. Researchers can test the validity of themes or categories by collecting and analyzing more data. Multiple coders and checks on intercoder agreement are used to strengthen reliability.
9. **Checking.** Usually after several rounds of refinement through data collection and analysis, the researcher may check themes and interpretations by presenting them to informants or other community members for correction, clarification, and interpretation.
10. **Multiple interpretations.** It is possible to have multiple interpretations or accounts of a topic. However, an account should be internally consistent and compelling in terms of its realism and thick description.

(Useful resources include Brodsky, 2001; Brydon-Miller & Tolman, 1997; Cosgrove & McHugh, 2000; Denzin & Lincoln, 1994; Langhout, 2003; Miles & Huberman, 1994; Miller, 2004; Miller & Banyard, 1998; Rapley & Pretty, 1999; Rappaport, 1990, 1993, 1995, 2000; Reinharz, 1994; Riger, 1990; Stein & Mankowski, 2004; Stewart, 2000; Tolman & Brydon-Miller, 2001.)

Acts of Qualitative Research How do qualitative researchers conduct a study? Catherine Stein and Eric Mankowski (2004) identified four essential steps in qualitative study (they focus on qualitative interviewing). They termed these steps *acts* because they progress like acts in a play. The four acts put the ten qualities we just covered into a narrative sequence, with human characters, and also integrate them with participatory approaches that we described in Chapter 3.

Act One, **Asking,** involves identifying the persons to be studied and making explicit the researchers' assumptions and values. This involves our first two questions for community research in Chapter 3 (concerning values and community participation), and common features 1–4 in our earlier list. (Note that Asking here does not involve interviewing, which comes in the next step.)

For Stein and Mankowski, qualitative research is directly connected to social justice and social change, and it explicitly takes sides. They noted that qualitative methods can be used not only to attend to unheard voices of marginalized groups, but also to understand and critique the conceptions of privileged groups. Either approach can promote social change. For instance, Stein and Wemmerus (described earlier) studied families of persons with schizophrenia, including the often-ignored views of ill family members. Mankowski, on the other hand, studied men's support groups and intervention groups for men who battered women. Many, but not all, of their experiences reflected the power of their gender roles.

Rebecca Campbell and associates described how they designed recruitment flyers to offer an emotionally safe, respectful setting for interviewing women who were survivors of rape and how they circulated these in community locales frequented by women (Campbell, Sefl, Wasco, & Ahrens, 2004). Participants attested to the emotional power of the flyers in their decision to participate in the study, feeling safe, respected, and able to share personal experiences in ways that would help other women.

Act Two, **Witnessing,** concerns how researcher and participant create knowledge through developing a relationship. The researcher poses open-ended questions, the participant describes experiences and ideas, and the researcher provides an attentive, empathic, affirming audience. Participants' words are recorded in some way. In the Campbell et al. (2004) study of rape survivors, interviewers formed an emotional bond with participants that facilitated participants' ability to tell their stories and (for many) the experience of some healing of their trauma by participating in the interview.

Witnessing requires that the researchers put aside their own preconceptions as much as possible and be open to the words and experiences of the participants. Moreover, their relationship may lead to transformation for both researcher and participant. Both may get more than they expected in terms of intense emotions, personal revelations, and motivation or accountability for engaging in personal, community, or social change (see also Campbell, 2002; Stewart, 2000). This involves common features 5–7.

Act Three, **Interpreting,** is analysis of the information gathered in asking and witnessing, making wider sense of patterns in the experiences of participants. This act raises the question: Whose story is this? Is the primary purpose to communicate the experiences and voices of participants (their stories), or to classify, analyze, or critique those experiences (the researcher's story)? Also, is there one underlying story, or many stories, among participants? The researcher creates meaning by "transforming 'participant stories' into 'research stories'" (Stein & Mankowski, 2004, p. 22). This involves common feature 8. That meaning must explain the participant stories, so reflexivity, checks on interpretation, and acknowledgment of multiple possible interpretations (features 6, 9, and 10) are needed.

For instance, in the Stein and Wemmerus (2001) study of families with a member with schizophrenia, the researchers recorded and transcribed all interviews with participants, and independently read each repeatedly to identify themes in the participant comments. They then discussed and agreed on themes, and excerpted quotations that reflected each. Themes concerned similarities and differences among families and among individuals within families. To test the reliability and coherence of their findings, the researchers then had two assistants match the excerpted quotations with the themes. Further discussion among researchers and assistants led to refinement of theme categories, and eventually to agreement on several key themes (Stein & Wemmerus, 2001, p. 732). The participants' words and experiences did not always fit the researchers' preconceptions, which required refinement of themes (Stein & Mankowski, 2004).

Stein and Mankowski argued that researchers have legitimate authority to make interpretations that challenge participants' views, but that such interpretations are best made explicit so that others can evaluate them. Brodsky et al. (2004) described negotiating agreement on interpretations among members of a research team.

Act Four, **Knowing,** involves the products of qualitative research and whether these are used to further the interests or capacities of research participants. This includes not only academic research reports, but also other arenas. Stein developed an innovative course pairing graduate students in clinical psychology with persons with schizophrenia, who taught the future clinicians about everyday life with schizophrenia. Mankowski developed a YMCA class, regional conferences, and radio appearances to promote men's discussion of sexism and dismantling sexist roles.

Even though these four acts form a sequence, some moving back and forth among them is characteristic of qualitative research. Each specific qualitative research method conducts each act in somewhat different ways, and researchers can shape each act to the circumstances in their study.

Qualitative methods are very useful for attending to unheard voices of marginalized groups, and reducing (but not eliminating) power differentials between researcher and participant. They also afford a deeper, contextual understanding of a culture, community, or population. They can highlight emotions and generate insight and passion. However, they do not simply express the views and voices of participants. The researcher's assumptions and interpretations are always involved, even with open-ended questioning and discussion (Miller, 2004; Rapley, & Pretty, 1999). These methods create knowledge within a relationship between researcher and participant.

The grounding of qualitative research in the researcher-participant relationship is both a strength and source of potential limitations. This relationship not only generates knowledge, but may also lead to friendship or to meaningful personal change and social action. However, dilemmas may arise as the researcher moves from witnessing to interpreting. Participants may find their views described or critiqued in ways they do not like and feel betrayed in proportion to the degree of trust that they had established. Researchers may be reluctant to analyze or critique the views of persons with whom they are personally connected. Even with informed consent at the outset and participant checking of interpretations later, problems may arise. A participatory approach to research decisions facilitates discussion of such dilemmas (Paradis, 2000; Stein & Mankowski, 2004; Stewart, 2000).

We next discuss four types of qualitative methods: participant observation, qualitative interviews, focus groups, and case studies. These are only some of the available qualitative methods. (The following sources present other qualitative methods, including discourse analysis, conversation analysis, and concept mapping: Campbell & Salem, 1999; Cosgrove & McHugh, 2000; Denzin & Lincoln, 1994; Miller & Banyard, 1998; Rapley & Pretty, 1999; Stewart, 2000; Tandon, Azelton, Kelly, & Strickland, 1998.)

Participant Observation

Many community researchers, especially if they conduct participatory research, perform at least some participant observation. It is a key component of ethnographic research in anthropology and other social sciences. For some studies, participant observation is the primary method. Both words in its title are important. Participant observation involves careful, detailed observation, with written notes, interviews or conversations with citizens, and conceptual interpretation. It is not just a description or a memoir. Yet it is also participation, as the researcher becomes a member of a community or a collaborator in its efforts, an actor in community life. This provides at least some of the experiential insider knowledge of community members, whereas the researcher also strives to maintain something of the outsider perspective.

Strengths and Limitations Participant observation is the method of choice for a researcher seeking maximum insider knowledge and depth of experience in a community. The participant observer knows the setting thoroughly and can communicate its essence vividly. This method also maximizes the researcher-community relationship and allows thick description of many aspects of community life.

However, that depth of knowledge comes at a price. First, the focus on one setting necessarily means that generalizability to other settings is a problem.

This limitation can be reduced by visiting other settings, usually in less depth but long enough to discern the applicability of one's findings.

A second issue concerns whether the researcher's experiences and records are representative of the setting and its dynamics. The participant observer relies at least in part on field notes as data, often supplemented by other methods such as interviews. The researcher's notes, analysis, and interpretation can be affected by selective observation, selective memory, and selective interpretations. Findings can also be affected by an unrepresentative sample of informants or of situations studied (e.g., observations of formal meetings but not informal caucuses or personal contacts). Researchers need to report explicitly their value commitments relevant to the study, and whether they took sides in a controversy, so that readers can judge the effects of these choices on data collection and interpretation.

Another problem is that the researcher is influencing (at least weakly, but perhaps strongly) the phenomena or community under study. Field notes and interpretations should explicitly indicate the extent of the researcher's influence on the actions of others so that the impact of the researcher's participation can be assessed.

A final limitation is the role conflict created by playing both participant and observer roles (Wicker & Sommer, 1993). An ethical and personal problem concerns what the researcher tells the members of the community about the research. For instance, the more forthrightly the researcher speaks of taking field notes, the more suspicious or less revealing the community members may be. On the other hand, research ethics, truthfulness, and norms of neighborliness require that some explanation of one's research intent and methods be made. Playing the role of both insider and researcher can be stressful. Striking a balance between these is an important part of gaining entry, forming a relationship, and seeking to benefit the community.

A Participation Observation Study Caroline Kroeker (1995, 1996) used this method to study the community functioning of peasant agricultural cooperatives in Nicaragua.

> The main portion of the research was done through 7 months of participant observation in one agricultural cooperative in Nicaragua and four follow-up visits. I lived in the cooperative, observing formal and informal meetings. I shared their living conditions and food, in exchange for assisting in the education of the children and in a peer adult education program. By living among them, I was able to integrate, listen, engage in many conversations, ask questions, and determine subtle feelings and meanings. The notes of the cooperative's meetings, conversations and observations were supplemented by documents and observations of processes and interactions in the village and in the town close to the cooperative. The research also included a general study of other cooperatives in Nicaragua through a literature review, interviews of key informants, and visits to 15 cooperatives around the country. (Kroeker, 1995, p. 754)

These sources of data provided thick description of the cooperative as a community. To analyze her data, Kroeker (p. 754) categorized the information she had collected, identified patterns and causal links, and developed interpretations of their meaning. This was a reiterative process involving several repetitions of data collection and analysis. She identified alternative interpretations of her findings and weighed the evidence for each interpretation.

Kroeker's (1995, 1996) reports presented themes including the importance of consciousness raising and development of skills in citizen participation along with the difficulties of strengthening these skills in a context where such citizen leadership had not been possible (and where many outsiders still did not believe it workable). One of her principal findings was the importance of *accompaniment,* a process of mentoring and support for emerging leadership skills that Kroeker herself was able to provide to the cooperative members. This role encouraged local leaders. Kroeker's willingness to work in collaborative, empowering ways with cooperative members benefited the cooperative and enriched her findings.

Qualitative Interviewing

Interviewing a sample of individuals has become a popular qualitative research format in community psychology. The interview is often open ended or minimally structured to promote participants' describing their experiences in their words. Samples are usually small to facilitate interviewing and analysis in depth. The researcher is not necessarily a participant in the community under study but usually does assume a role of collaboration or extended contact with interviewees.

Strengths and Limitations Qualitative interviewing allows flexible exploration of the phenomenon of interest and discovery of aspects not anticipated by the researcher. It is based in a strong relationship between researcher and participant. It involves attending to the voices of participants and thick description of their experiences. It can challenge the researcher's preconceptions and affords contextual understanding of a community, culture, or population.

Interviewing has several advantages over participant observation. Data collection can be more standardized, limiting biases of selective perception, memory, and interpretation. Interviews can be recorded and transcripts prepared so that analysis can be based on participants' actual words. Analysis can also be standardized and performed by multiple, independent raters, not just the interviewer, which increases reliability and validity. The interviewer can develop a relationship with the setting and participants that is mutual and trusting yet with less role conflict than participant observation. Of course, all these also mean that the insights developed from interviews are less direct than those from participant observation.

These advantages require intensive study of a small sample, which means that generalizability of findings is often limited. Also, the time required for research interviews may subtly exclude participants in marginalized groups or demanding circumstances (Cannon et al., cited in Campbell & Wasco, 2000). Differences of interpretation between participants and researchers do create challenges (Stein & Mankowski, 2004).

The Stein and Wemmerus (2001) study of families with a member with schizophrenia, described earlier, provides an example of a qualitative interviewing study.

Focus Groups

A focus group discussion is an interview with a group. It generates thick description and qualitative information in response to questions or discussion topics posed by a moderator. Using focus groups, researchers can assess similarities and differences among individuals and allow participants to elaborate on ideas and themes by reacting to each other, not just to an interviewer. Hughes and DuMont (1993) offered an introduction to the use of focus group research methods in community psychology.

In focus group research, the group, not the individual, is the unit of analysis: The sample size is one for each group. Individual comments are not independent of other group members; indeed, one of the purposes of the focus group is to elicit discussion. Each group is usually composed of 6–12 participants who share some characteristic of concern to the researchers: for example, the same race, gender, culture, or age; similar occupations; or the same health problem. This homogeneity helps to promote free discussion and ability of participants to be able to identify with each other's experiences. A group of strangers is preferred to minimize the effects of prior personal contacts. Multiple focus groups are needed to provide broader information and to compare populations (husbands vs. wives, for example). However, as with qualitative interviewing, samples are seldom representative of a large population. The goal is to generate contextual understanding.

The moderator's responsibilities include creating an environment conducive to free discussion, speaking in language comfortable to all participants, ensuring that all members participate, eliciting both agreement and disagreement, and balancing between being nondirective and covering all topics of interest to the researchers. The moderator uses a discussion guide that includes topics to be discussed and that moves from general topics to specific phenomena relevant to the research. Analysis of focus group data is similar to the process of analyzing individual qualitative interviews.

Strengths and Limitations These are similar to those of qualitative interviewing. However, focus groups have several advantages over other qualitative methods. Researchers can structure discussion and learn about topics of interest and personal experiences of others more easily than with participant observation. Compared to individual interviews, focus groups allow greater access to shared knowledge and mutual discussion. They also allow researchers to observe social interaction among group participants, perhaps revealing behavioral patterns unavailable in individual interviews. However, a focus group moderator has less flexibility to ask for elaboration, control changes of topic, or learn about individuals in depth than an interviewer of individuals. Focus groups are especially useful for gaining cultural understanding. They also can help explore a topic, or test questionnaires, prior to quantitative studies.

Studies Using Focus Groups Hirokazu Yoshikawa and associates (2003) used focus groups to understand the experiences and lessons learned by front-line peer educators in a community agency conducting HIV prevention programs in communities of Asian/Pacific Islanders in New York City. These workers knew their communities and cultures well and were rich resources for understanding effective, culturally anchored techniques for disseminating information and influencing behaviors that often transmit HIV. The researchers convened focus groups for workers with different populations (youth, gay/bisexual/transgender persons, women, heterosexually identified men). Their protocol questions concerned "success stories" of effective outreach and behavior change as well as how the peer educators adapted their techniques to different ethnic groups, populations of different immigration and socioeconomic statuses, and ethnic, mainstream U.S. and gay communities. Yoshikawa et al. developed categories of responses, refining these through reviews of interview transcripts until they had interjudge agreement on matching respondent comments to categories. For instance, categories concerned cultural norms about sexuality, strategies used for peer educator outreach, and specific risk and protective behaviors. The results showed the influence of culture, social oppression, and immigration status on HIV-related behaviors, and effective, culturally appropriate methods of addressing these.

As other examples, Hughes and DuMont (1993) convened focus groups to learn how African-American parents socialize their children to deal with racism. Dumka, Gonzales, Wood, and Formoso (1998) used focus groups with families in four cultures in their locality (African Americans, European Americans, Mexican Americans, and Mexican immigrants) to learn about parenting adolescents in these cultures. In both studies, focus groups helped develop and refine measures for later quantitative studies.

Case Studies

The case study method, usually conducted on individuals in clinical psychology, can be applied to an organization or a locality (Bond & Keys, 1993; Mulvey, 2002). Community psychologists also can study an individual in relation to the settings in that person's life (Langhout, 2003). They may conduct multiple case studies so that comparisons can be made. For instance, Wasco, Campbell, and Clark (2002) interviewed eight advocates who worked with rape victims about how the advocates coped with the emotional trauma encountered in their work and about personal and organizational resources that promoted coping. Neigher and Fishman (2004) used multiple case studies to describe planned change and evaluation in five community organizations.

Case studies provide a bridge connecting qualitative and quantitative approaches. A case study may rely on any or all of the qualitative methods we have described. It may also use qualitative **archival data** (i.e., from archives or records) such as minutes of group meetings, organizational policy manuals, or newspaper stories. Archival data can also be quantitative records such as police statistics, records of attendance at programs, or quantitative evaluations of whether a program attained its goals. Case studies also can use other quantitative measures such as questionnaires. Later in this chapter we will describe case studies using both qualitative and quantitative methods.

Strengths and Limitations Like participant observation, a case study can examine in depth a single person, setting, or locality. Case studies are excellent for understanding the nuances of cultural, social, or community contexts. They can afford thick description and contextual understanding. By using multiple data sources, subjective biases can be checked. The longitudinal focus of most case studies is also useful. Although case-study researchers cannot study causes and effects with experimental control, they can identify complex patterns of causation in natural settings.

Their focus on a single case is also the principal limitation for case study methods. Generalizability of findings to other settings is uncertain. Researchers can include multiple case studies in one analysis, but that may weaken some of the strengths just described. Involvement in the setting or locality studied may create insider-outsider role conflicts, as discussed earlier.

The use of archival records presents both advantages and problems. Written records can provide information on meetings or other events not attended by the researcher and remembered imperfectly by interview informants. Archival records also can document events in the history of an organization or community. However, researchers who review archival data may not discover the processes that they are most interested in. For instance, conflict and compromise preceding a group decision are usually omitted or sparingly recorded in meeting minutes.

A Case Study Using Qualitative Methods Anne Brodsky (2003) used a variety of qualitative methods to study the Revolutionary Association of the Women of Afghanistan (RAWA). Her book, *With All Our Strength,* describes the history, philosophy, actions, resilience, and sense of community shared by the members of this remarkable Afghan women's movement. Since 1977, RAWA has advocated forcefully yet nonviolently for women's and human rights and for a democratic, secular government in Afghanistan. It is outspoken and independent of the various invading armies, Afghan warlords, and governments during this period. Founded in 1977 by a 20-year-old college student, RAWA promotes feminist values that defy both traditional Afghan patriarchal values and the stereotypes of Afghan women widely held in the outside world. RAWA members (all volunteers, all women) publish advocacy materials and maintain a website, document and publicize abuse and atrocities, aid women suffering from many forms of trauma, distribute humanitarian assistance, conduct literacy and educational classes for women and girls, work with men who share their goals, hold protest rallies in Pakistan, and conduct international outreach (Brodsky, 2003, pp. 2–3). These activities have generated such fierce opposition that RAWA is a clandestine, underground organization that nonetheless engages in public actions. Though RAWA's struggle is ongoing, it has made a difference in Afghan life, and offers a vision for the future that continues to inspire Afghan women and men.

Brodsky was especially interested in how RAWA acted and sustained itself as a community. She was also interested in their shared resilience in the face of vigorous and violent opposition and of many setbacks and losses, including the assassination of Meena, RAWA's founder (Brodsky, 2003). Her use of a research framework and methods based in feminist qualitative research fits well with the feminist philosophy of RAWA, with the need to take Afghan culture and context into account, with the need to attend to emotions in RAWA members and in the researcher, with the fact that RAWA is a clandestine organization and that a participatory-collaborative research relationship was necessary, and with the goal of empowering RAWA and other feminist organizations through the research (pp.7–9).

Brodsky used multiple qualitative methods (pp. 9–12). She has been very involved with RAWA's outreach in the United States for several years. For this research, Brodsky visited Pakistan and Afghanistan in 2001 and 2002, beginning prior to September 11, 2001 and the U.S.-led war in Afghanistan. She individually interviewed over 100 members and supporters of RAWA, women and men, in Afghanistan and Pakistan. Interviews often lasted 2–3 hours, and many persons were interviewed more than once. Brodsky also conducted group interviews and spent many hours in participant observation and informal conversations with RAWA members, visited 35 RAWA projects in ten localities in Pakistan and Afghanistan, and reviewed archival records and sources. Most of her interviews were conducted in Dari, an Afghan language, with a translator who was a RAWA member. (Brodsky knew the language well enough to serve as a check on accuracy of translation.) Certainly the research is affected by the use of a RAWA translator and by Brodsky's ongoing commitment to RAWA, but these factors built the trust necessary for this research in this context.

Brodsky's findings are rich and contextual. She describes the strong sense of community within RAWA, consistent with its feminist ideals and practices and with the collective orientation of Afghan culture. Resilience in the face of trauma and violent opposition is another theme. Both community and resilience are expressed in the commitment of RAWA members to their ideals, and the emotional caring and practical support offered among RAWA members. Two interview excerpts express these themes, and illustrate the emotional power of qualitative methods.

> From a member who joined RAWA in a refugee camp: "I found everything; I escaped out of my grief and sadness. There were classes, the handicraft center, and I found these people serving the rest of the people of Afghanistan and going toward the lightness . . . . [B]y lightness I mean education . . . . RAWA giving education, hope and enables us to serve our people."
>
> From Mariam (pseudonym): "When I first attended a RAWA function I found that they chanted the slogans that were stuck in my throat; they spoke the words that I didn't dare speak." (Brodsky, 2003, pp. 245, 248)

Two Concluding Issues

We conclude this section by discussing two overarching issues for qualitative methods: how they elicit narratives and meaning and how they address the criteria of reliability, validity, and generalizability.

Narratives in Qualitative Research Qualitative methods often tap narratives. Narratives have a plot, or sequence of events, and meaningful characters and settings. They may be individual stories or cultural myths. They provide insights into psychological themes and convey emotions and prized values in memorable ways (Rappaport, 1993, 1995, 2000). For instance, the Stein and Wemmerus (2001) study elicited narratives from the lives of families of persons with schizophrenia. Mulvey's (2002) case study of Lowell, Massachusetts, was organized as a narrative. Harper, Lardon et al. (2004) illustrated the power of narratives to convey Mexican American cultural meanings.

Rappaport (2000) defines **narratives** as being shared by members of a group. A community or setting narrative communicates events, values, and other themes important to the identity and sustainability of that group. Cultural myths and traditions also are narratives. **Personal stories** are individuals' unique accounts, created to make sense of their own lives. Personal identity is embedded in a life story. Qualitative research methods can be designed to elicit shared narratives or personal stories or both. Both are studied in anthropology, sociology, and cognitive, personality, and developmental psychology (Rappaport, 1993, 1995, 2000). They can be analyzed for descriptive details and abstract themes. They are one of the best ways to attend to unheard voices and to understand a culture or community.

Reliability, Validity, Generalizability Students educated in the thinking of positivistic, quantitative methods may question the reliability, validity, and generalizability of qualitative methods. It is important to remember that the aims of qualitative methods are different than those of much quantitative research. In a qualitative study, sensitivity to participants' interpretations is more important than standardization. Yet many qualitative methods use scientific criteria analogous to the reliability and validity criteria of a more positivist approach.

For qualitative methods, reliability is usually a matter of interrater reliability among multiple readers who are coding or categorizing verbal data. Generalizability of findings to other persons or populations is more limited than with larger studies but is usually not the aim of the qualitative study. However, the thick description generated by qualitative research allows readers to understand more deeply the persons and contexts being studied, and to compare them with other samples. Moreover, the connection of researcher and participant in qualitative studies allows clarifying and elaborating of what those participants mean by their responses to questions, an issue of validity overlooked in standardized questionnaires.

Qualitative research addresses validity in part by **triangulation,** the use of different methods to understand the same phenomenon. These can be interviews and personal observation, use of several informants who can be expected to have different viewpoints, use of multiple interviewers, or use of quantitative measures along with qualitative information. Triangulation in qualitative studies is analogous to use of multiple measures of a variable in quantitative research. In addition, the thick, detailed description of experiences in qualitative research provides convincing realism and details that allow judgment of validity. A common goal of qualitative research is not only to provide intellectual evidence of validity, but also **verisimilitude,** eliciting a personal experience in a reader similar to the original experiences of the research participant. For example, recall the quotations earlier in this chapter from families of persons with schizophrenia or the Afghan women of RAWA (Stein & Wemmerus, 2001; Brodsky, 2003). If you experienced the emotional power of their words, that's verisimilitude.

> "Whether numbers or words, data do not speak for themselves." (Marecek et al., 1998, p. 632)

Bias affects both qualitative and quantitative methods. Choices of what to study and of how to interpret findings are matters of theory and values, whatever the method. **Reflexivity** (discussed earlier in this chapter and in Chapter 3), including explicit statements of the researcher's perspective are useful in any study. Regardless of method, multiple interpretations of complex phenomena will arise because diverse persons and groups have different perspectives. Both qualitative and quantitative methods can illuminate those perspectives.

QUANTITATIVE METHODS

We now turn to methods that emphasize measurement, statistical analysis, and experimental or statistical control. They address different purposes and questions than qualitative methods. Quantitative methods are historically based in a positivist philosophy of science, but they can be used with other approaches to research. Although general differences certainly exist between qualitative and quantitative approaches, they are not a simple dichotomy.

Common Features of Quantitative Methods

A great diversity of quantitative methods exists. However, most quantitative methods in community research share some common features. We don't wish to repeat all of what you may have learned in previous methodology courses, so the following list focuses on features that offer clear contrasts with qualitative methods and highlights how quantitative methods can be adapted to community research.

1. **Measurement, comparisons.** The principal aim of quantitative methods is to analyze measurable differences along variables and the strength of relationships among those variables. They facilitate understanding variables, predicting outcomes, and understanding causes and effects. Quantitative research can generate "outsider knowledge" that affords comparisons across contexts.
2. **Numbers are data.** Although some variables are categorical (e.g., an experimental program compared to a control group), the purpose is almost always to study their relationship to measured variables.
3. **Cause and effect.** One important objective is to understand cause-effect relationships. This can lead to prediction of consequences and inform social

action to promote desirable changes. Experiments and similar methods are often used to evaluate the effects of social innovations, programs, or policies. Nonexperimental quantitative studies identify empirical relationships that can eventually lead to knowledge of causes and effects and to social innovation.

4. **Generalization.** Another important objective is to derive conclusions that can be generalized at least to some extent across contexts, settings, and communities (e.g., empirical findings showing that a prevention program or social policy is effective is many communities).
5. **Standardized measures.** Standardized measurement instruments are preferred to ensure reliable, valid measurement. The flexibility and contextual sensitivity of qualitative methods are lost, but comparability of findings across studies and control of extraneous variables are increased.

Next, we discuss four specific types of quantitative methods in community psychology research: quantitative description, randomized field experiments, nonequivalent comparison group designs, and interrupted time-series designs. These are only some of the available quantitative methods for community research. (These sources present others: Langhout, 2003; Luke, 2005; Revenson et al., 2002; Shadish, Cook, & Campbell, 2002.)

Quantitative Description

Quantitative description methods include a variety of procedures, including surveys, structured interviews, behavioral observations of community settings, epidemiological studies, and use of social indicators (i.e., census data, crime and health statistics). They are quantitative but not experimental: they do not involve manipulation of an independent variable. They can be used for purposes such as the following.

- to compare existing groups (e.g. women's and men's perceptions of crime)
- to study associations between survey variables (e.g., correlation of family income with health or changes over time in adolescent sexual attitudes)
- to measure characteristics of community settings (e.g., measure the frequency of emotional support and advice-giving in mutual help groups)
- to conduct epidemiological studies to identify factors predicting the presence or absence of an illness (e.g., behaviors that increase or decrease risk of HIV infection)
- to study relationships between geographic-spatial and social environments (e.g., correlation between density of liquor stores and crime rates in neighborhoods)

Statistical analyses may include correlation, multiple regression, path analysis and structural modeling, and even *t* tests and analyses of variance to compare naturally occurring groups. These studies may be *cross-sectional,* sampling only one point in time, or *longitudinal,* sampling repeatedly over time.

Quantitative description usually samples more individuals than either qualitative studies or experiments. This facilitates statistical analysis and generalizability. To enable a study of this breadth, these methods rely on previous knowledge and/or exploratory research to determine which variables to study, how to measure them, and whom to sample. Qualitative research is very useful for this exploration.

Correlation and Causation Early undergraduate education in psychology typically contrasts correlation and causation. Just because two factors are associated statistically, you learned, does not mean that one causes another. The causation could just as easily run in the opposite direction than you think (B causes A rather than A causing B). Or the causal factor may be a third variable that determines both correlated variables (C causes both A and B).

Under some conditions, however, nonexperimental designs can be used to identify causal patterns and test causal hypotheses. The simplest case involves precedence in time: If change in A is correlated with change in B, yet A consistently precedes B, a causal interpretation (A causes B) is more warranted (although a third variable still may be involved). A theoretical model, based on prior knowledge of relationships among A, B, C, and other related variables, strengthens causal inference from nonexperimental data. Such causal inference relies on statistical control of extraneous variables, not experimental control.

Community Surveys Surveys of community samples, using standardized questionnaires or other measurements, are quantitative description methods. For instance, Fleishman et al. (2003) conducted longitudinal surveys of well-being in a large, multiethnic, nationally representative U.S. sample of HIV-infected persons. Using the statistical method of cluster analysis, they identified four coping styles among the respondents: active-approach, distancing, blame-withdrawal, and passive. Also, a disturbing finding of this survey was that members of several more socially marginalized groups (women, racial/ethnic minorities, and injection drug users) had less social support than men, whites, and those who had not used injection drugs. This suggests a need for more understanding and support for HIV-infected persons in these groups among health professionals and society (Fleishman et al., 2003, p. 201).

Community surveys can focus on organizations as the unit of analysis. Community coalitions bring together representatives of various segments of a locality to address an issue such as domestic violence (Allen, 2005) or promoting positive youth development (Feinberg, Greenberg, & Osgood, 2004). Feinberg et al. conducted structured interviews with representatives of 21 local Communities That Care coalitions and derived quantitative measurements from them. Results indicated that community readiness and internal functioning of the coalition as a group were the factors related to for perceived coalition effectiveness. Allen (2005) surveyed and interviewed representatives of 43 local domestic violence coalitions, finding that perceived effectiveness was most related to having an inclusive climate of shared decision making and active membership participation.

Epidemiology These methods are useful for community research concerned with health and mental health. Epidemiology is the study of the frequency and distribution of disorders and of risk and protective factors for them. It is usually a precursor to more experimental studies of causal factors of these disorders and is essential to practical planning of prevention and treatment. Epidemiology is most often used in the discipline of public health, but it is also used in the social sciences (e.g., Mason, Chapman, & Scott, 1999).

Two basic epidemiological concepts are incidence and prevalence. **Incidence** is the rate of *new* occurrences of a disorder in a population within a specific time period (usually a year). It is thus a measure of the frequency of the onset of a disorder. **Prevalence** is the rate of *existing* occurrences of a disorder in a population within a time period. It includes both new cases and continuing cases of the disorder that began before the time period studied. Both concepts are usually expressed as rates (e.g., the number of cases per thousand persons in the population). The incidence-prevalence distinction is important for community psychology. Prevention is more concerned with incidence, the frequency of new cases. Prevalence, the rate of existing cases, is relevant to mutual help or mental health services policy.

When incidence and prevalence rates have been determined for a population, epidemiological research is focused on identifying risk and protective factors. **Risk factors** are associated with increased likelihood of a disorder. These may be causes of the disorder or simply correlated with it. Exposure to stressors or lack of coping resources are examples of risk factors. **Protective factors** are associated with lesser likelihood of a disorder; they may counteract or buffer the effects of the disorder's causes or simply be correlated with other factors that do so. Personal or cultural strengths and support systems are protective factors.

Mapping Physical and Social Environments The increasing availability of Geographical Information Systems (GIS) methods offer a rich new resource for studying relationships between physical-spatial aspects of communities and their psychosocial qualities (Luke, 2005). GIS methods can be used to plot onto a map any data available for spatial locations. Archival data sources can include census information on population density or average household income, or social indicators such as neighborhood crime rates or density of liquor stores. Community survey data can also be entered in GIS databases if associated with respondents' residences (Van Egeren, Huber, & Cantillon, 2003). GIS data and resulting maps can be used for quantitative statistical analysis or for visual searching for spatial patterns (a more qualitative approach). For instance, in a study of Kansas City neighborhoods, Hughey and Whitehead (2003) found lack of access to high-quality food statistically related to rates of obesity and density of liquor outlets related to rates of violent crime. GIS also can be used to track changes in localities over time.

Strengths and Limitations Quantitative description methods have a number of strengths. Standardized measurement affords statistical analysis, and large samples that provide greater generalizability. These methods can be used to study variables that cannot be manipulated in an experiment. Epidemiological research can be used to identify risk and protective factors and evaluate the outcome of preventive efforts.

Finally, these studies often identify factors that can be targeted for social or community change, even without experimental knowledge of specific causes and effects. One need not know all the cause-effect relationships for youth violence, for instance, in order to identify risk and protective factors and to initiate change efforts.

These methods have several limitations, however. They rely on prior knowledge to select and measure variables and populations. Study of causes and effects is limited, as we have discussed.

Also, except for GIS approaches, the knowledge provided by these studies is usually *decontextualized,* gathered from individuals but not associated with existing settings, communities, or cultures. This approach can increase breadth of sampling, but it limits knowledge of contextual factors. The focus of epidemiological research on disorders also limits its utility for community psychology (Linney & Reppucci, 1982). Community psychology is concerned with overall psychological well-being, including but not limited to disorders. When mental disorders are studied, difficulties of accurate diagnosis and measurement make epidemiology more difficult than with physical disease. Also, community psychology's focus on promotion of strengths includes identifying protective factors for disorders but goes beyond that to concern development of positive qualities.

Experimental Social Innovation and Dissemination

Fairweather's (1967) concept of experimental social innovation (later amended to include dissemination of findings, thus ESID) is the community research approach closest to the classic laboratory experiment. Yet it also involves explicit awareness of social values and the gritty world of community action. ESID is an enduring contribution to community psychology (Hazel & Onanga, 2003; Seidman, 2003). Fairweather's Community Lodge program (described in Chapter 2) was the prototype of this approach (Fairweather, Sanders, Cressler, & Maynard, 1969).

Experimental social innovation is based on careful groundwork "before the beginning." The social or community problem is carefully defined, an experimental innovation (e.g., community program or social policy) to address that problem is specified, and the innovation itself is planned.

A hallmark of Fairweather's experimental social innovation is evaluating the effects of the innovation in an experimental design. Researchers conduct a longitudinal study in which the innovation is implemented and compared with a control or comparison condition. In experimental terminology, the independent variable is the comparison of the social innovation to a control condition. Dependent variables are measurements of the outcomes of the program. If effective, the findings and knowledge of how to implement the innovation are then disseminated to other communities and decision makers (Hazel & Onanga, 2003; we discuss dissemination more fully in Chapter 11). The ESID method addresses the ethical imperative that the effects of social actions be evaluated.

We will discuss three research methods as forms of experimental social innovation: randomized field experiments, nonequivalent comparison group designs, and interrupted time series designs.

Randomized Field Experiments

This is the most rigorous form of experimental social innovation. Participants (individuals or settings) are randomly assigned to experimental or control groups. These are compared at a pretest before the implementation of the experimental social innovation, at which they are expected to be equal on measures of dependent variables. They are compared again at posttest(s), when they are expected to differ because of the effects of the innovation. Follow-up posttests can continue over several years.

The experimental social innovation represents the experimental condition. The control condition can often be "treatment as usual" under existing policy or practices. For example, in Fairweather's Community Lodge study (Fairweather et al., 1969), men in a psychiatric hospital were assigned to either the Community Lodge program or to the usual treatment and aftercare procedures for the hospital. Another experimental approach is to compare two different innovations with each other, such as two contrasting prevention programs in a school (Linney, 1989). A third approach is to provide the experimental innovation to members of the control group after the posttest. They serve first as a control group, then receive the innovation, minimizing ethical problems with their not receiving it originally.

A key issue is the method of assignment to experimental and control conditions. If this is random, many confounding variables are controlled. These include individual differences in personality, coping skills, social support networks, and life experiences that may affect their responses to the innovation. Confounds also include differences between groups in demographics such as gender, age, race, culture, and family income. In the laboratory, random assignment is taken for granted, but in the community it must be achieved by collaboration and negotiation with community members (Sullivan, 2003).

Strengths and Limitations Randomized field experiments are unsurpassed for clarity of cause-effect interpretation—for example, in testing effects of a social innovation. With greater control over confounding factors, researchers can make more confident interpretations of its effects. Moreover, if experimental studies demonstrate the effectiveness of a social innovation, advocacy for it can be more effective. For instance, randomized field experiments have helped to document the effects of many preventive interventions and increase the credibility of prevention efforts generally (Weissberg, Kumpfer, & Seligman, 2003).

However, experiments require substantial prior knowledge of the context to propose social innovations worth testing and to choose measurements. A useful sequence might be to conduct qualitative studies to understand the context and key variables, then quantitative descriptions to specify risk and protective factors and refine measurements, then developing an experimental social innovation and conducting an experiment to evaluate its effectiveness. Even during the experiment, qualitative or individualized quantitative methods are helpful to understand differences in outcomes and whether these resulted from the intervention (Lipsey & Cordray, 2002).

The intrusiveness of experiments also raises issues of control in community settings. Permission is needed to collect quantitative data (often in multiple waves) and to randomly assign participants to experimental conditions. Those decisions must be explained and negotiated with community members.

Evaluating Advocacy for Women with a Randomized Field Experiment Cris Sullivan (2003) described how she worked with community survivors of domestic violence and staff in women's advocacy centers in order to consider questions such as: What community resources do battered women need to prevent further abuse? How can understaffed women's advocacy settings address these issues and empower battered women (Sullivan, 2003, pp. 296–297)?

Sullivan and her community collaborators then worked together to design the Community Advocacy Project, an innovation in which university students were trained as advocates for battered women (beyond the usual training for volunteers in women's shelters). These advocates were trained for one semester in a practicum course, then worked during a second semester with community women to devise individualized safety plans for each woman and to help carry out those plans. The latter involved advocating directly with community agencies and resources needed to carry out those plans, and working with the women to empower them to devise and implement their own future plans (pp. 298–299).

The researchers and community collaborators decided to evaluate the project with a randomized field experiment. This was not an easy decision. The needs of battered women were so immediate, and the prospect of project effectiveness so intuitively obvious, that they were reluctant to assign some women to a control group. Eventually, the community members were convinced by these arguments: at the time of the research there were not enough resources to offer the advocacy program to all women; the program sounded promising but was unproven and could even be counterproductive (as a woman established her own life, the batterer might become more violent to reassert control); an experiment was the best way of determining its effectiveness; the fairest method of assigning women to the advocacy or control conditions was randomization. The project became the experimental condition, and the usual shelter services comprised the control condition. Community members also participated fully in creating and choosing measures of program effectiveness (p. 297).

At the conclusion of the intervention, and in follow-up assessments over two years, battered women who worked with student advocates in the Community Advocacy Project were less likely than women in the control group to experience further violence, were less depressed, had more social support and better perceived quality of life, and reported greater success in obtaining needed resources. Sullivan is conducting studies with an expanded form of the project and helped obtain funding for expanded shelter staffing to provide expanded advocacy and to train volunteers for expanded advocacy (pp. 300–301).

Evaluating a Community Development Initiative with a Randomized Experiment Paul Florin, David Chavis, Abraham Wandersman, and Richard Rich (1992) used a randomized experimental design to evaluate the effects of the Block Booster Project, a training program for leaders in neighborhood block associations in New York City.

The Block Booster Project worked with local block associations in working-class and middle-class neighborhoods in Brooklyn and Queens. The sample included predominantly European-American, predominantly African-American, and racially diverse neighborhoods. Each association is formed for a city block, encompassing the area of both sides of one street, one block long. Enhancing the functioning of those citizen participation associations is critical to their viability; many such associations start up, then become inactive within a year or two. The Block Booster staff worked with 27 block associations. For all of these, staff conducted a survey of block residents.

Block Booster staff then randomly assigned 18 block associations to an experimental condition. Two leaders from each association participated in a workshop on strengthening block associations and participated in ongoing meetings and consultations with Block Booster staff. Nine other associations were assigned to a control condition, which had only a written report on the survey and some telephone technical assistance. (Note that this study uses associations, not individuals, as the unit of analysis.)

When they were contacted 10 months after the workshops, 44 percent of control associations had already become inactive, whereas only 22 percent of associations in the experimental condition had become inactive. The Block Booster Project thus cut the attrition rate in half. In a context where many associations become inactive quickly, this example provides sound evidence of effectiveness (Florin et al., 1992).

This finding leaves open the question of what exactly caused the better performance of the experimental group. However, in follow-up interviews, leaders in the experimental group remembered specific survey findings about their associations and reported using their workshop learning and materials, indicating the effectiveness of the workshops (Florin et al., 1992).

Nonequivalent Comparison Group Designs

For a variety of reasons, many settings simply cannot support random assignment to experimental and control conditions. For instance, seldom can a school randomly assign some children to an innovative classroom and others to a control classroom. Even if they did, the students may mix at lunch or recess so much that the independence of experimental and control conditions is greatly reduced. Providing the innovation to all students in a grade and comparing their outcomes to another school or to students in a previous year means, of course, that assurance of equivalence between groups is lost. Comparing a sample of schools rather than a sample of individuals (making the unit of analysis the school, not the individual) may be prohibitively expensive.

Yet many of the strengths of the experiment can be retained if researchers are creative about working around such obstacles. Using a nonequivalent comparison group is a common approach.

Nonequivalent comparison group designs are used whenever assignment to experimental or comparison condition is something other than random. For instance, different classrooms within a school or different schools within a region may serve as experimental and comparison conditions. Assignment to classroom or choice of school is not random, but the classes or schools may be similar. The choice of comparison group is critical to generating interpretable results. In schools, student socioeconomic status, race, gender, and age are examples of variables to equate as much as possible in the two groups. Teacher demographics, school size, and curriculum also need to be similar (Linney & Repucci, 1982).

Strengths and Limitations Using an existing group as a comparison condition is practical and less intrusive than randomized experiments. However, the control of confounding factors is much weaker, and clarity of interpretation and confidence in conclusions is decreased. Researchers in this situation must collect as much data as possible on factors that may confound the comparison. This allows them to document the similarity of the two conditions or to use those variables as statistical controls. For instance, researchers may be able to show that the average family income of the experimental and control conditions was similar, or to control effects of family income statistically. The ultimate goal is to weaken or eliminate plausible competing explanations for findings.

Evaluating School Reforms with a Nonequivalent Comparison Group Rhona Weinstein and associates used qualitative and quantitative methods to study how teacher expectations and school curriculum policies affect student performance. Weinstein described this multiyear program of research in *Reaching Higher* (Weinstein, 2002a; Weinstein et al., 1991). They implemented practical reforms to enhance learning for students not considered capable of college preparatory courses in an urban California high school. Our concern here is with the empirical evaluation of that intervention, conducted with a nonequivalent comparison group design. It used both quantitative and qualitative methods.

"Los Robles High School" (a pseudonym), a mid-sized urban school in an aging, run-down building, drew students from both wealthier and lower-income areas. Over two-thirds of the students, but only one-fifth of the teachers, were members of ethnic minority groups. School student achievement scores were below the state median, yet the school also ranked high in the number of graduates admitted to the selective University of California system. The school staff culture held a bimodal view of the students: some were very talented and hard working, others were not, and little could be done to change this. Weinstein and her team discovered that students assigned to lower-track curriculum in ninth grade, based on tests that often underestimated their strengths, were assigned to classes that did not prepare them for college. These classes often were taught with uninteresting materials and teacher-centered methods that did not generate discussion. Students in this track were disproportionately African American (68%). Classes for honors students, in contrast, were often discussion oriented and used challenging yet interesting materials. Similar situations are all too common in U.S. schools (Weinstein, 2002a, pp. 209–211).

Weinstein and her team implemented an ongoing series of workshops with some teachers (volunteers) of reputedly lower-ability ninth-grade classes. Workshops focused on the importance of challenging and motivating students to higher performance, involving all students more actively in classroom learning, involving parents, and using more challenging yet interesting materials (often from the honors curriculum). Teachers met and discussed their efforts to alter teaching strategies and classroom climate. Weinstein's team worked with them to devise responses to obstacles. A year of these workshops showed positive results, but also the need for training more teachers and for curriculum reform and administrative changes. These became the next goals of the project (pp. 211–227).

A team of school staff and university researchers worked collaboratively to plan the research evaluating project effectiveness. Qualitative analysis of meeting records indicated positive shifts in teacher expectations, teaching strategies, and curriculum policy. The research also used a quantitative comparison of grades and other records for 158 students involved in classes in the project (the experimental group) and grades and records for a demographically similar group of 154 students from the previous two years' classes (the nonequivalent comparison group). Analyses statistically controlled prior differences between students in achievement. Project students attained higher overall grades and had fewer disciplinary referrals than comparison students in the first year of the project. They also were less likely to leave the school in subsequent years. The project's effects on grades ebbed after one year. This also suggests the need for curriculum reform and wider teacher training to spread the positive changes throughout the school.

These outcomes cannot be as confidently attributed to the project as in a randomized design. Possible confounding differences between the experimental group and comparison group could have included subtle changes in the student body between comparison and experimental years, events during the experimental year that altered student performance, or changes in teacher grading practices (Weinstein et al., 1991). Yet there were many qualitative signs of project effectiveness. For the first time, lower-track students were excited about school, despite challenging readings and writing assignments (Weinstein 2002a, p. 228). These are promising findings that suggest directions for genuine school reform.

Interrupted Time-Series Designs

Another approach is the use of interrupted time-series designs. In the simplest case, this involves repeated measurement over time (a time series) of a single case (an individual, organization, locality, or other social unit). In an initial baseline period, the participant or setting is monitored as measurements of dependent variables are collected. This provides the equivalent of a control condition. Then the social innovation (e.g., program, policy) is introduced while measurement continues. Data collected in the baseline period are compared to data collected during or after the innovation was implemented. This is termed an *interrupted* time-series design because the innovation interrupts the series of measurements. This approach combines time-series measurement with an experimental manipulation, providing a useful design for small-scale experimental social innovation when a control group is not available.

Strengths and Limitations Time-series designs are practical. They also afford understanding of change over time in a specific context, such as one community, while standardizing measurement and minimizing extraneous confounds.

However, a time-series design with one group still is open to a number of external confounds (Linney & Reppucci, 1982). These include seasonal or cyclical fluctuations in the variables measured. An example is that the number of college students who seek counseling rises as final exams approach. If seeking counseling is used as a dependent variable in a time-series study, researchers must take this seasonal rise into account. A further confound concerns historical events that affect the variables measured. An example is negative national publicity about tobacco use at the same time as implementation of a local anti-tobacco prevention program for youth. If youth tobacco use drops, the publicity may have been the real cause, not the local prevention program. Finally, findings from a single case or community, even over a long time period, may not generalize to other communities.

A key issue for time-series designs is the number of measurements in the baseline and experimental periods (Linney & Reppucci, 1982). Social innovations may have gradual or delayed effects difficult to detect in a short time-series design. Seasonal or cyclical fluctuations (confounds) in the dependent variable may be detected if the time series is long enough.

Multiple-Baseline Designs This is a form of interrupted times-series design that reduces the problems of external confounds and generalizability. Think of this design as a set of time-series studies, each conducted in a different community and compared to each other. The experimental social innovation is implemented at a different time in each community so that effects of an external historical factor (happening at the same time for all communities, such as national publicity about tobacco use) will not be confounded with the innovation. If measures of the dependent variable show a change soon after the implementation of the innovation, at a different date in each community, confidence can be stronger that the innovation caused this effect. This also provides some evidence of generalizability. In effect, the design tests whether findings from one community can be replicated in other communities, within a single study (Biglan, Ary, Koehn, et al., 1996).

The multiple-baseline design combines the strengths of the interrupted time-series and nonequivalent comparison group designs. However, the multiple communities studied are still nonequivalent (assignment of individuals to them is not random), and differences among them still exist that complicate interpretation. However, it is a useful way to combine repeated measurement, contextual study of a single community and replication across communities.

A Community-Level Multiple-Baseline Study Can a community intervention emphasizing positive reinforcement reduce tobacco sales to youth, in multiple communities? Anthony Biglan and colleagues addressed this question. They studied whole localities, using multiple-baseline, time-series methods (Biglan et al., 1996). They analyzed the antecedents and consequences of illegal sales of tobacco products to youth by retail merchants, devised an intervention, and evaluated its effectiveness in a multiple-baseline design in localities in rural Oregon.

In each town, the research team and local community members organized a proclamation by community leaders opposing tobacco sales to minors. Community members then visited each merchant to remind them of the proclamation and to give the merchant a description of the law and signs about it for posting. A key element was intervention visits to merchants by teen volunteers seeking to purchase tobacco products. If the clerk asked for identification or refused to sell, the volunteer handed the clerk a thank you letter and a gift certificate donated by a local business (positive reinforcement). If the clerk was willing to sell, the volunteer declined to buy and gave the clerk a reminder statement about the law and proclamation. The researchers periodically provided feedback to merchants about their clerks' behavior in general (but not about individual clerks). In addition, community members publicly praised clerks and stores who had refused to sell, in newspaper articles, ads, and circulars (again providing reinforcement).

Measurement of intervention effectiveness was conducted with assessment visits to stores by teens seeking to purchase tobacco. These measurement visits were separate from the intervention visits and did not provide reinforcement of refusals to sell or reminders of the law. Teens simply asked to buy tobacco, then declined to buy if a clerk was willing to sell. Over 200 volunteer youth, males and females age 14 to 17, participated as testers. Attempts to buy were balanced by gender.

Researchers measured effectiveness of the intervention by locality, not by individual store, because they had implemented a community intervention. The dependent variable was the proportion of stores in a community willing to sell tobacco to youth in assessment visits by youth. The researchers studied four small towns; all had fewer than 6,000 residents, mostly European American.

Biglan et al. collected baseline assessments in each community before implementing the intervention, then comparing those data to similar assessments during and after the intervention. They conducted up to 16 assessment periods in each town. They used multiple-baseline techniques by conducting the intervention at one time in two communities, and later in the other two.

In two communities, Willamina and Prineville, clerks' willingness to sell during assessment visits clearly decreased following the intervention. These differences were statistically significant. The intervention occurred at different times in these two communities, indicating that the intervention, not an extraneous factor, caused the reduction. In Sutherlin, a third town, willingness to sell decreased, but not immediately after the intervention began. In Creswell, the fourth town, baseline willingness to sell was somewhat lower than elsewhere, and the intervention did not make a significant difference. Unknown local community factors influenced the intervention's effectiveness.

The generalizability of these findings may be limited, because the sample was only a small number of relatively similar localities. In addition, it is not clear which element of the intervention accounted for its success (e.g., community proclamation, reinforcement of clerk refusals to sell, feedback to merchants, or the combination of these). Yet the intervention package, in most communities, was effective in reducing retail clerks' willingness to sell tobacco to youth. Biglan et al. noted that preventing sales in one community does not necessarily mean youth will not use tobacco, because they may obtain it from adults or in other communities. However, both behavioral analysis and common sense suggest that the more difficult it is to obtain tobacco, the less likely that youth will begin to use it.

INTEGRATING QUALITATIVE AND QUANTITATIVE METHODS

Qualitative and quantitative methods can be used in a single study to offer the advantages of both perspectives (Lipsey & Cordray, 2000; Maton, 1993). We next discuss three examples of case studies that used both types of methods to study a locality, a student in relation to a school setting, and planned change in five organizations.

A Case Study of a Locality Anne Mulvey (2002) conducted a case study of the city of Lowell, Massachusetts. She examined changes over 15 years in perceptions of Lowell residents about safety and quality of life. During this time, Lowell experienced ups and downs in the local economy and an increase in immigrants, especially from Southeast Asia (the most recent of many immigration waves in Lowell, going back over 150 years). Describing Lowell in a contextualized way was the principal purpose of the study, not generalization to other cities.

Mulvey's database was a series of structured interview surveys of Lowell residents conducted by graduate students in a research methods class. The surveys included quantitative items and brief open-ended questions. Most interviews took 30–45 minutes. A total of 840 residents were sampled over 15 years in nine neighborhoods. The neighborhoods varied in average household income as recorded in census data. (Note that this average measures a characteristic of the neighborhood, not the household income of an individual respondent.) Mulvey also collected crime statistics during the period from police reports. She and two assistants read open-ended comments and developed reliable categories to code these. Qualitative findings helped her elaborate and interpret trends found in the quantitative analyses.

The surveys asked about perceptions of safety and quality of life for the respondent's neighborhood, about quality of life for Lowell as a whole, and about perceived safety in downtown Lowell. Gender was the most important predictor of perceived safety: women felt less safe than men. Residents of lower-income neighborhoods felt less safe and perceived a lower quality of life than residents of higher-income neighborhoods. Perceptions of safety and quality of life varied somewhat over time, consistent with economic trends, although residents rated their neighborhoods positively in all periods. Open-ended comments chiefly concerned safety and immigrant groups. Some of the latter were positive, but many about youth were negative. This hostility seemed greater in the 1990s than in the 1980s, although actual crime rates (other than domestic violence) dropped during the 1990s.

A Contextual Case Study of an Individual Regina Langhout (2003) used a case study of "Daniel" (pseudonym), a third-grade African-American student, to illustrate how qualitative and quantitative methods can both be used to understand relationships between persons and settings. Langhout used qualitative interviewing to elicit Daniel's descriptions of classroom, playground, and other settings in his school. These helped to understand his emotions, actions, strengths, and relationships with peers and adults, including the racial context of his school. His words revealed his understanding of teacher attitudes and behavioral expectations that emphasized discipline more than learning and that unfairly targeted African-American boys. (Daniel's perceptions were consistent with an audit of the school by the U.S. Office of Civil Rights.)

Langhout also employed multidimensional scaling and social network analysis to quantify Daniel's perceptions of these settings. These techniques employ numerical methods and statistical analysis but are scaled by each child's own answers to open-ended questions. The multidimensional scaling revealed that Daniel's positive feelings were strongest in places where he had more freedom (library, lunchroom, gymnasium, one part of the playground) and privacy. Daniel also liked settings where he had more of a leadership role (he was a bathroom and lunchroom monitor for younger students). In the social network analysis, Daniel reported positive social ties in the gym, but only a few such ties in the classroom, a disliked place. Both qualitative and quantitative methods documented positive experiences and even leadership in some settings, but also a sense of being marginalized in the classroom (note the similarity with Weinstein's studies discussed earlier).

Multiple Case Studies of Organizational Change William Neigher and Daniel Fishman (2004) reported multiple case studies of planned change in five organizations: a New Jersey religious philanthropy, a foundation that supports citizenship development for immigrants in California, a Kentucky network of family resources centers, a national organization promoting innovative programs in schools for social and citizenship development, and a New Jersey school district that implemented innovative teaching of social-emotional literacy skills. These organizations differ in mission and level of complexity, yet all were using a planned change process of goal setting and planning, designing new policies and programs, implementing and carefully monitoring these, evaluating their overall effectiveness, and reflecting on lessons learned for the future. The evaluations collected both qualitative and quantitative data, including archival sources.

Neigher and Fishman's analysis focused on similarities and practical steps in the planned change process across the different settings.

CONCLUSION

On the next page, Table 4.1 summarizes the distinctive features, strengths, and limitations of the qualitative and quantitative methods described in this chapter. That summary is simplified to save space, so remember that each set of methods has nuances and can be applied in many ways. There is plenty of room for creative imagination in designing community research.

Six themes run through this chapter. First, qualitative and quantitative methods tap different sources of knowledge and complement each other. As you probably noticed, the limitations of one are often the strengths of the other. No single approach provides a royal road to knowledge. For instance, the studies by Stein and Wemmerus and by Brodsky especially illustrated the power of research participants' voices, tapped by qualitative methods. The studies by Sullivan, Florin et al., and Biglan et al. showed how experiments can address significant community and social issues. A second theme is that much can be gained by integrating qualitative and quantitative approaches in one study to provide differing perspectives. The studies by Weinstein, Mulvey, and Langhout exemplified this theme.

Third, a longitudinal perspective often enhances community research. Studying changes over time reveals the workings of communities in ways not available in cross-sectional analysis. Studies by Sullivan, Florin et al., Weinstein, Biglan et al., and Mulvey illustrated this theme. Qualitative studies by Kroeker and Brodsky also addressed the history of the settings they studied.

Fourth, both qualitative and quantitative approaches can be used within a participatory-collaborative partnership with community members. Many studies we have described embody this theme.

Fifth, no one method is best for every research question. Community researchers would be wise to respect and know how to use both qualitative and quantitative methods. Ideally, the nature of the research question to be studied would play an important role in choosing methods. Realistically, every community researcher cannot be equally competent with qualitative and quantitative methods; some specialization is to be expected. Yet the student of community psychology needs to be familiar with both approaches. Community psychology as a field is best served by a diversity of forms of knowledge and methods of research.

It is important to think of our two research chapters as a unit. Chapter 3 concerned the importance of social values in community research; of participatory, collaborative research in partnership with community members; and of sensitivity to cultural and social contexts and multiple ecological levels. Chapter 4 illustrates specific methods for conducting community research along those lines to provide knowledge useful to a community and to the world beyond it.

TABLE 4.1 Comparison of Community Research Methods

Method	Distinctive Features	Strengths	Limitations
Qualitative Methods			
Participant observation	Researcher "joins" community or setting as a member, records personal experiences and observations	Maximum relationship with community, thick description, contextual understanding	Generalizability limited, sampling and data collection are not standardized, researcher influences setting studied, insider-outsider role conflict
Qualitative interviewing of individuals	Collaborative approach, open-ended questioning to elicit participant words and experiences, intensive study of small sample	Strong relationship with participants, thick description, contextual understanding, flexible exploration of topics, more standardized than participant observation	Generalizability limited, less standardized than quantitative methods, interpretation may create insider-outsider role conflict
Focus group interviewing	Similar to qualitative interviews but conducted with a group to elicit shared views	Similar to qualitative interviews but allows group discussion, especially useful for cultural understanding	Similar to qualitative interviews except less depth of understanding of individual
Case studies	Study of single individual, organization, or community over time (can use qualitative and quantitative methods)	Understanding setting in depth, understanding changes over time, thick description, contextual understanding	Generalizability limited, less standardized than quantitative methods, limitations of archival data, interpretation may create insider-outsider role conflict
Quantitative Methods			
Quantitative description	Measurement and statistical analysis of standardized data from large samples without experimental intervention	Standardized methods, generalizability, study of variables that cannot be experimentally manipulated	Reliance on prior knowledge, often decontextualized, limited understanding of cause and effect, epidemiology focuses on disorder
Randomized field experiments	Evaluation of social innovation, random assignment to experimental and control conditions	Standardized methods, control of confounding factors, understanding of cause and effect	Reliance on prior knowledge, difficulty in obtaining control groups in community settings, generalizability limited
Nonequivalent comparison group designs	Similar to field experiments without random assignment to conditions	Standardized methods, some control of confounds, practicality	Reliance on prior knowledge, less control of confounds than randomized experiments, generalizability limited
Interrupted time series designs	Longitudinal measurement of one or more settings before and after intervention; may use multiple-baseline design	Measurement in context, practicality, longitudinal perspective	Reliance on prior knowledge, less control of confounds than randomized experiments, generalizability limited (multiple-baseline design better)

CHAPTER SUMMARY

1. Community research methods can be divided into *qualitative* and *quantitative* methods, largely on the basis of whether the data studied are in verbal or numerical form. Each method has characteristic strengths and limitations. Qualitative methods often provide knowledge of what a psychological or community phenomenon means to those who experience it. Quantitative methods often provide knowledge useful in making statistical comparisons and testing the effectiveness of social innovations or programs.
2. Qualitative methods have a long history in psychology. In the chapter we described ten common features of these methods. They usually involve intensive study of a small sample. The goal is to understand *contextual meaning* for the research participants, in their own terms, through a personal *participant-researcher relationship.* The researcher uses open-ended questions and listens carefully to participants' language in order to generate *thick description* of participants' experiences. Data are usually words. Data analysis often involves interpretation of themes or categories in participant responses, often refined through checking of interpretations with participants. Multiple interpretations are acceptable. Stein and Mankowski described four acts of qualitative research: *asking, witnessing, interpreting,* and *knowing.*
3. We discussed four qualitative methods: *participant observation, qualitative interviewing* (of individuals), *focus group interviewing,* and *case studies.* Qualitative methods often tap shared *narratives* and *personal stories* of individuals. Qualitative methods address reliability, validity, and generalizability differently than quantitative methods. Validity for qualitative methods often concerns *triangulation, verisimilitude,* and *reflexivity.*
4. Quantitative research emphasizes *measurement, comparisons, cause-effect* relationships, *generalization* across multiple contexts, and often experimentation. Data are numbers. *Standardized measurements* with established reliability and validity are preferred. Statistical analysis is the dominant method of analysis.
5. Quantitative description includes a variety of methods involving measurement but not experimental manipulation of variables: for example, community surveys, epidemiology, and use of geographical information systems. Although correlation is not causation, description can sometimes be used for conclusions about causes. In epidemiology, important concepts include *incidence, prevalence, risk factor,* and *protective factor.*
6. In community research, an important use of experimental methods is *experimental social innovation,* in which social innovations are tested for effectiveness. Methods include *randomized field experiments, nonequivalent comparison group designs,* and *interrupted time-series designs,* the latter sometimes in a *multiple-baseline* format.
7. Qualitative and quantitative methods can be integrated in a single study or in multiple related studies, to offer the advantages of both approaches.

8. Table 4.1 summarizes the distinctive features, strengths, and limitations of eight specific qualitative and quantitative methods often used in community research. Six themes of this chapter are summarized in the Conclusions.

BRIEF EXERCISES

1. Consider these questions, and discuss them with a classmate.
   Which methods in this chapter would I like to use in research of my own? Why?
   Where and from whom could I learn the skills to conduct this research?
2. Choose a controversial social or community issue that you care about. Propose a community research study using at least one of the specific research methods or designs described in this chapter. Discuss the strengths and limitations of your choice.
3. Read an empirical research article in a journal of community psychology or a related field. (You can access the *American Journal of Community Psychology* through the InfoTrac College Edition search service that comes with this textbook.) What specific research methods does it use? What are their strengths and limitations for the topic of this research? What was the most interesting thing you learned from the article? What might you disagree with about this research?

RECOMMENDED READINGS

Hazel, K., & Onanga, E. (Eds.). (2003). Experimental social innovation and dissemination [Special issue]. *American Journal of Community Psychology, 32* (4).

Revenson, T., D'Augelli, A., French, S., Hughes, D., Livert, D., Seidman, E., Shinn, M., & Yoshikawa, H. (Eds.). (2002). *Ecological research to promote social change: Methodological advances from community psychology.* New York: Kluwer Academic/Plenum.

Stein, C., & Mankowski, E. (2004). Asking, witnessing, interpreting, knowing: Conducting qualitative research in community psychology. *American Journal of Community Psychology, 33,* 21–36.

INFOTRAC COLLEGE EDITION KEYWORDS

qualitative, quantitative, qualitative and *methods* or *research, quantitative* and *methods or research, community research, participant observation, focus group(s), case study(ies), narrative(s), epidemiology(ical), experimental social innovation, experiment(al), time series, multiple baseline*

INTERCHAPTER EXERCISE

Analyzing a Community Research Report

The purpose of this exercise is to use the concepts from Chapters 3 and 4 to analyze a study in community psychology or a related field. Choose a journal article or other research report that presents an empirical research study. If you can, choose an article on an issue or topic about which you care deeply. Record the full reference so you can identify and cite it later.

Analyze the study using the following questions. (Not all questions will apply to all studies.) Add your own questions if needed. Identify both the strengths and limitations of the research.

Purposes

1. What were the purposes of this study?
2. Was this study descriptive, studying an existing issue? Or did it evaluate the effects of a social program, policy, or other change?
3. Did the researchers take sides on a controversial social issue? Did the study sample marginalized populations or unheard voices? Did it address an issue of social justice?
4. What ecological levels of analysis did this study concern?

Relationships with Community

(These issues may be difficult to discern in published works.)

5. Did the researchers work with community members in a participatory-collaborative relationship? How? What decisions about conducting the research were shared, in what ways?
6. Did the study make a positive difference in the community in which it was conducted? Did the researchers provide products of the research to that

community, in a form that could be used by citizens? Did the study strengthen or empower the community to pursue its own goals after the study was completed?

Sampling

7. What culture(s) was studied in this research? Was this a within-cultural-group or between-cultural-groups study? Did the researchers report steps to assure that their concepts and methods were applicable in the culture(s) they studied?
8. How were the specific participants in this study chosen? Were they studied in a specific context: e.g., a community setting, organization, locality, or culture?
9. How diverse was the sample studied? Consider the multiple dimensions of human diversity (see Chapter 7 for a list of these). Did the study sample populations often underrepresented in psychological research?

Methods and Analysis

10. What research methods did this study use? Were these among the research methods described in Chapter 4?
11. Did this study use multiple methods, measures, data sources, or other means of triangulation?
12. How were the data analyzed? If qualitative analyses were used, what procedures were used for coding themes or categories, and for assuring agreement on these among multiple judges? If quantitative analyses were used, are they appropriate for these data? Was the sample size sufficient for the statistics used?

Findings and Validity

13. What were the most important findings? (Choose about three or fewer.)
14. Did the study identify strengths of a population, community, or culture? What strengths?
15. If the study reported on whether a social innovation, intervention, program, or policy attained its goals: What goals were attained? How were they measured or assessed? Can you think of any other factors (i.e., confounds) that might also account for the findings? Can you identify possible unintended negative consequences that might have occurred?
16. Are you convinced of the truth of the researchers' conclusions or claims? Why?

Personal Reactions

17. What emotions did you experience while reading or thinking about this study? Why? Is that evidence of verisimilitude?

18. How could you apply the findings of this study in communities in your own life?
19. What do you think were the principal limitations of this study? How might your views be based in your own experiences?
20. If the study is a recent one, consider writing an e-mail to its principal author. What questions do you have that you would like the author to answer? What would you suggest for a further study on this issue, and why?

5

Understanding Individuals within Environments

HIRB/Index Stock

OPENING EXERCISE AND INTRODUCTION

Take a moment to remember, as fully as you can, your first visit to the college or university you now attend (or one you attended earlier). What do you recall about the college as a setting—about its atmosphere, its "feel" for you as an individual? Was it a quiet, tree-lined campus, or did it have the excitement of an urban university? Did you feel welcomed? Did you sense that people like you live, study, or work here, or did you feel different in some important way? Write a few notes on these memories.

Now take a longer view. How has this college environment affected you as an individual? How have your experiences in this environment shaped your learning, personal development, friendships, vocational plans, and personal well-being?

What have you learned here? What values have you developed or strengthened? Briefly list a few of these changes.

How well do you know your classmates other than your immediate friends? How well do you know the faculty and staff? What help do you provide to or receive from each of these groups? Write briefly about whether you are satisfied with these aspects of your college experience.

Can you identify the following resources on your campus: A place where you like to socialize? A quiet place to study? A place and person you would seek for help with a personal-emotional problem? A place where scholarly discussion happens outside class? A place for group study? A place to exercise? A place for commuter students to meet? Access to parking or to public transportation? Other resources? List these briefly.

Finally, assume a critical stance. What changes would you suggest to improve your college or university environment? That includes changes in the physical campus, services, policies, staff or student makeup, or anything else. List your suggestions.

These questions reflect the concepts community psychologists and others have developed to understand the interaction of environments (e.g., a college) and persons in everyday life. This study of persons in ecological context has been a central theme for community psychology. The 1965 Swampscott conference report identified "the reciprocal relationships between individuals and social systems" (Bennett et al., 1966, p. 7) as an essential focus of community psychology.

For a century, ecological context has been implicitly recognized as important for understanding human behavior. At the turn of the twentieth century, Lightner Witmer and the staff of the early child development clinics did their work in the settings where children lived and went to school, making changes in those settings to help children learn. The Chicago School of sociology (e.g., Park, 1952) documented the importance of neighborhood and city environments for personal life. Kurt Lewin (1935; Marrow, 1969) argued that behavior is a function of person *and* environment. Theories of personality proposed by Murray (1938), Rotter (1954), and Bandura (1986) emphasized the interaction of person and situation, although applications of their concepts focused on individuals. Environmental psychology arose at about the same time as community psychology, investigating how physical (usually built) environments influence behavior. Even advocates of genetic perspectives argue that environments interact with individual factors (Buss, 1995). However, the specific ways that contexts and individuals interact are not well understood. Psychology has focused on individual variables, devoting much less attention to environmental processes.

Examples of the interplay of individual and environment are all around us. How did you select a university to attend? Financial considerations? Academic offerings or reputation? Social atmosphere? Distance from home? All of these are contextual factors interacting with your needs or preferences. Or think about how decor, music, and seating contribute to the ambiance of a restaurant. In a band, a workplace, or a family, an individual may stand out at a given moment, but to understand that individual's actions one must understand his or her relationship to the environment.

In this chapter we examine concepts and community research regarding ecological context. First, we describe six ecological perspectives for community psychology. Second, we review research and action regarding the interplay of neighborhood, family, and personal life. Finally, we highlight two exemplary community programs that created or altered ecological contexts to improve quality of life for individuals.

This chapter is the first of four chapters to focus on key concepts in community psychology. All concern contexts. Chapter 6 will cover concepts of community, Chapter 7 concepts and issues of human diversity, and Chapter 8 a contextual perspective on coping.

CONCEPTUAL MODELS OF ECOLOGICAL CONTEXT

In this section we describe six ecological models used in community psychology to describe environments and their impact on individuals. As you read about each one, keep in mind the levels of analysis that we introduced in Chapter 1. Some of the models can be used at multiple levels; others fit one or two levels best.

Ecological Psychology and Behavior Settings

In 1947, Roger and Louise Barker, Herbert Wright, and colleagues began studying the lives of children in a town they referred to as "Midwest" (actually Oskaloosa, Kansas). In this small town, they aimed to understand children's lives in context (Barker, 1968; Barker & Wright, 1955; Barker & Associates, 1978). The Barker family moved to Midwest to live and with their colleagues opened the Midwest Field Station. After gaining the trust and cooperation of Midwest residents, they and their associates began careful, systematic, naturalistic observations of all aspects of children's everyday lives. Barker (1978, p. 3) termed this approach studying the "stream of behavior," rather than breaking that stream into bits and choosing only some bits to understand apart from the whole. They soon discovered that they could not study children's lives in context without including the whole town.

> The truth is that we soon became overwhelmed with individual behavior. We estimated that the 119 children of Midwest engaged in about one hundred thousand behavior episodes daily.... We sampled behavior in such divergent places as the drugstore, the Sunday School classes, the 4-H Club meeting, and the football games.... At this point, we stopped focusing exclusively on the behavior of individuals and saw for the first time a thing that is obvious to the inhabitants of Midwest, namely, that behavior comes in extraindividual wave patterns that are as visible and invariant as the pools and rapids of Slough Creek, west of town. The Presbyterian worship services, the high school basketball games, and the post office, for example, persist year after year with their unique configurations of behavior, despite constant changes in the persons involved. These persisting, extraindividual behavior phenomena we have called the standing behavior patterns of Midwest. (Barker & Wright, 1978, pp. 24–25)

Ecological psychology, the theory and methodology developed in Midwest, is an important basis of both environmental and community psychology. Barker and colleagues studied Midwest, and eventually a similar English town ("Yoredale") and other settings, by observing physical and social environments where community life was created and sustained. They were interested not in individual personalities, but in patterns of behavior characteristic of a behavior setting regardless of which individuals were there (Barker, 1965, 1968; Barker & Associates, 1978; Barker & Schoggen, 1973; Barker & Wright, 1955). Their work has been extended by others (e.g., Schoggen, 1989; Wicker, 1979).

Behavior Settings Barker (1968) developed this concept as the primary unit of analysis for ecological psychology. A behavior setting is defined by having a place, time, and a standing pattern of behavior. Thus, the behavior setting of a third-grade class in Midwest met weekdays in one classroom at the school, proceeding through a program involving predictable teacher and student behavior, largely regardless of which individuals were present. The drugstore behavior setting had wider time boundaries and more turnover of "inhabitants" (customers and staff), but it occurred in a single place and involved standing behavior patterns, again regardless of the individuals present. Some behavior settings were embedded within larger behavior settings, such as classes within a school. Others stood alone, such as a service station. Some occurred only occasionally, such as a wedding or talent show, whereas others were daily events. Barker (1968, p. 106) and colleagues identified 884 behavior settings in Midwest in 1963–1964; almost all could be grouped into five categories: government, business, educational, religious, and voluntary associations.

A behavior setting is not simply a physical place. The sanctuary of the Methodist church in Midwest was a physical setting but not a behavior setting. Instead, several behavior settings occurred within it, each with a time and standing behavior pattern, such as worship services, choir practices, and weddings. In contrast, a small retail shop comprised a single behavior setting. The physical setting and the behavior setting are *synomorphic,* or matched in their structure. The seats in a lecture hall face the speaker, for example, whereas seats in a committee meeting room face each other. Each makes possible the standing behavior pattern of the setting.

In Barker's perspective, persons in a behavior setting are largely interchangeable; the same patterns of behavior occur irrespective of the specific individuals. Barker further hypothesized that behavior settings have rules, implicit or explicit, that maintain the standing behavior pattern (Barker, 1968, pp. 167–171). These rules can be seen in specific behavior patterns.

- **Program circuits,** such as an agenda for a meeting, guide the standing behavior pattern.
- **Goal circuits** satisfy goals of individuals, such as a customer purchasing an item or a member participating in a worship service.

The rules also incorporate control mechanisms to channel or limit individual involvement.

- **Deviation-countering circuits** involve training individuals for roles in the behavior setting and correcting their behavior to improve role performance.

- **Vetoing circuits** occur when individuals are excluded from the behavior setting.

The purpose of ecological psychology is to identify behavior settings and to understand the physical features and social circuits that maintain them.

A baseball game provides an illustration (Barker, 1968). The game is a behavior setting, a standing pattern of behavior, occurring within a given time and place. The field defines the physical environment alone but reveals little about the game. Similarly, we would not be able to understand the game or individual players' acts by focusing on each player in isolation (the common individual-level focus of psychological research). Imagine, for example, a film showing the first baseman alone, without the context of the field or of plays not involving the first baseman. Very little could be learned about what this player is doing and why, and it would be quite difficult to predict this player's behavior. By observing the context of the entire behavior setting, the program circuits or rules become clearer. So do the relationships among players during the game. Barker (1968) suggested that it is the combination of the physical field, game time, and the standing patterns of behavior among players (and fans) that constitute the behavior setting of a baseball game.

Identifying behavior settings, as initially performed in Midwest, was an exceedingly lengthy process. Barker and colleagues spent over a year in an exhaustive description of the behavior settings in Midwest (Barker & Wright, 1955). Behavior setting methodology has been applied in schools (Barker & Gump, 1964; Schoggen & Schoggen, 1988), churches (Wicker, 1969), mutual help groups (Luke, Rappaport, & Seidman, 1991), and work settings (Oxley & Barrera, 1984). Wicker (1979) suggested methods of sampling to streamline the procedure.

Underpopulated Settings A second contribution of Barker's ecological approach has been the study of "manning" theory (Barker, 1968). Schoggen (1989) adopted the terms *underpopulated* and *optimally populated* settings.

In a classic study, *Big School, Small School,* Barker and Gump (1964) compared involvement of students in extracurricular activities (one form of behavior settings) in large and small high schools in Kansas (enrollments ranged from 35 to over 2,000). In the smaller schools, they found greater levels of student involvement in performances and in leadership roles as well as higher levels of student satisfaction and attachment to school. Larger schools showed a slightly greater number of opportunities for involvement. Yet students in smaller schools were twice as likely to participate in active ways, and on average they participated in a wider variety of activities. Barker and Gump also found that students in smaller schools perceived more responsibility to volunteer for activities. They often reported a sense that even if they weren't talented in a particular activity, their help was needed. The larger schools had higher rates of uninvolved, marginal students with little sense of commitment to the school or social connection with school peers or staff.

Studies in a variety of settings have established that the critical factor is the ratio of the number of roles available in a behavior setting compared to the number of individuals available to play those roles (Wicker, 1979, 1987). An optimally populated setting has as many or more players than roles. Settings easily recruit enough members to fill their roles; other students are marginalized or left out. Barker (1968, p. 181) theorized that vetoing circuits (behaviors that screen out potential members) would be especially common in these settings because there are plenty of replacements available. A large school will probably have tryouts for athletic teams, musical groups, dramatic productions, and so on; only the most talented will be able to participate. Barker and Gump (1964) found that larger schools contained more optimally populated settings.

An underpopulated setting has more roles than members. That increases members' sense of responsibility for maintaining the setting and offers them the chance to develop skills they otherwise might not have learned. It may also increase the diversity of persons participating in the setting, attracting unused resources. For example, a shy person who otherwise would not try out for a school play is pressed into service, developing social skills or perhaps revealing hidden talents. In addition, members of an underpopulated behavior setting would engage in deviation-countering circuits rather than vetoing circuits. They would invest time and effort in teaching the skills needed for a role in the setting rather than excluding the person. This strategy makes sense if members are needed to play roles necessary for maintaining the setting. Barker and Gump (1964) found that smaller schools contained more underpopulated settings. Of course, members in an extremely underpopulated setting will "burn out"; the setting may even be disbanded. Yet moderate understaffing may lead to positive outcomes for individuals (greater skill or personal development) and setting (greater commitment among members).

These concepts fit the organizational strategies of GROW, a mutual help organization for persons with serious mental illness. GROW deliberately limits the size of local chapters, creates leadership roles for all members, and maximizes members' sense of responsibility for group functioning. These methods promote the personal development and mutual commitment of members and illustrate practical benefits of an underpopulated behavior setting (Luke et al., 1991; Zimmerman et al., 1991).

Contributions and Limitations Ecological psychology has generated an enduring body of concepts and research and has influenced the development of other ecological perspectives in community psychology. The concepts of behavior setting and underpopulated settings represent two especially important contributions.

One limitation is that Barker and associates focused on behavior, largely discounting cultural meanings and other subjective processes. A second limitation is that behavior setting theory focuses on how behavior settings perpetuate themselves and mold the behavior of individuals. This is one side of the picture, but it underplays how settings are created and changed and how individuals influence settings (Perkins, Burns, Perry, & Nielsen, 1988). Having originally been developed in a small-town setting, this emphasis on stability rather than change is understandable yet limited in scope. Third, the effects of underpopulated and optimally populated settings have not always been replicated in later studies, and their relationship to individual adjustment and behavior appear more complicated than behavior setting theory suggests (Perkins et al., 1988). (See Schoggen, 1988, for a defense of behavior setting concepts on these points.)

Activity Settings

Clifford O'Donnell, Roland Tharp, and Kathleen Wilson (1993) developed the concept of activity settings. Although similar to ecological psychology in focusing on settings, activity setting theory takes subjective experiences and cultural-social meanings into account. O'Donnell et al. were influenced by the Russian developmental theorist Vygotsky, by the constructivist approaches that we described in Chapter 3, and by working in Hawai'i and Pacific cultural contexts.

An activity setting is not simply a physical setting, and not just the behavior of persons who meet there, but also the subjective meanings that develop there among setting participants, especially **intersubjectivities:** beliefs, assumptions, values, and emotional experiences that are shared by setting participants. Key elements of an activity setting include the physical setting, positions (roles), people and the interpersonal relationships they form, time, and symbols that setting members create and use. Intersubjectivity develops over time as persons in the setting communicate, work together, and form relationships. They develop symbols, chiefly language but also visual or other images, to express what they have in common. This perspective calls attention to cultural practices and meanings.

In many spiritual settings, for instance, sacred written works and vocabulary, visual art, and music are important symbols whose meaning is both intensely personal and widely shared. Much of what is important about any culture is intersubjective, widely understood within the culture yet difficult to communicate to outsiders. Even within one culture, families and organizations develop intersubjective uses of language and gesture that outsiders cannot understand and that reflect important insider attitudes.

Activity setting theory offers a broader conception of social settings than ecological psychology. It has been used to study child development, juvenile delinquency, education, and community interventions. It is especially useful in working across cultural boundaries, as O'Donnell and associates have shown in their work in Hawai'i, Micronesia, and elsewhere (O'Donnell, Tharp, & Wilson, 1993; O'Donnell & Yamauchi, 2005; Gallimore, Goldenberg, & Weisner, 1993).

Four Ecological Principles

Adapting concepts from the biological field of ecology, James Kelly, Edison Trickett, and colleagues postulated four ecological principles as a framework for community psychology: interdependence, cycling of resources, adaptation, and succession (Kelly, 1966, 1970a, 1979a, 2006; Kelly, Ryan, Altman, & Stelzner, 2000; Trickett, Barone, & Watts, 2000; Trickett, Kelly, & Todd, 1972). These concepts have been very influential in understanding ecological context. You should understand them as characteristics of settings, not of individuals. Workplaces, for instance, differ in the extent of interdependence among workers, in what resources are cycled, and in what individual skills are needed to adapt to the setting. Of course, these setting factors influence individual life greatly in schools, families, workplaces, and other settings.

Interdependence As with biological ecosystems, any social system has multiple related parts and multiple relationships with other systems. Changes in one of these affects the others: they are interdependent (Trickett, Kelly, & Todd, 1972). For a public school, interdependent components include students, teachers, administrators, secretaries, janitors and other staff, parents, board members, and district taxpayers. Actions of any of these groups can affect everyone else. State and national governments, and local and international economies, also affect even local schooling. For a business firm, interdependent components include stockholders, board members, executives, employees, their families, suppliers, and customers.

Consider the ecology of a family, for example. If one family member gets the flu, everyone else is affected in one way or another. If a young child is sick, an older member of the family will likely miss work or school to stay at home with the sick child. Others in the family may also become ill in turn. If the primary caregiver gets the flu, meal preparation, washing, transportation, and a host of other daily operations for every other member of the family are affected. The change may be temporary, with the system returning to its previous state after a few days. Other changes in one member are longer lasting, such as having an ailing grandparent join the household.

A corollary of the principle of interdependence is that any change in a system will have multiple consequences, some of them unanticipated and perhaps unwanted. Similarly, change efforts within a system may be thwarted because interdependent components of the system are not addressed. For instance, a teacher may introduce cooperative learning techniques in a classroom, only to face resistance from students, if the wider culture or many parents strongly endorse individual competition in education.

Cycling of Resources Kelly's second principle is closely related to interdependence. It specifies that any system can be understood by examining how resources are defined, used, created, conserved, and transformed (Trickett, Kelly, & Todd, 1972). In social settings, resources are exchanged among members of the setting.

> An ecological perspective assumes that there are many more resources within a social setting than are perceived to be available. (Kelly, Ryan, Altman, & Stelzner, 2000, p. 137)

Personal resources include individual talents, knowledge, experiences, strengths, or other qualities that can contribute to other persons or to the setting. Social resources occur in relationships among members of the setting, including shared beliefs, values, formal rules, informal norms, group events, and shared sense of community. Even physical aspects of a setting are resources: a library with both rooms for group study and quiet nooks for individual study, for instance.

What resources are important for a family? Time, nurturance, attention, emotional support, and money are some examples. By examining the cycling of resources, one can begin to characterize family priorities and connections. Similarly, what resources (especially intangible ones) are cycled among students at your university? Information is exchanged in many forms, such as advice on courses, professors, social life, job possibilities. Emotional support, practical assistance, and tutoring also are resources often exchanged.

You may not recognize how family members are resources useful to you until you encounter a stressful life event they have lived through and can advise you about. An acquaintance who is a physics major may mean little to you until you take a physics course. A quiet person who understands others well is a valuable resource for a group but may be overlooked among more outspoken members. An implication of Kelly's approach is to search any environment (family, organization, neighborhood) for resources (tangible or intangible) that may contribute to individual or system well-being.

Stack's (1974) classic study of a low-income African-American community highlighted patterns of resource sharing. In The Flats (a public housing community with limited financial resources), residents shared furniture, child care, food stamps, and money beyond their own families. For example, a member of the community loaned furniture to a neighbor for an extended period of time, and that neighbor had previously cared for her child while she was looking for work out of town. To an outsider, this exchange of resources may seem risky for families with little money, but it made sense to those within the system. Resources were allocated to those who needed them, and today's provider may be tomorrow's recipient. Stack's detailed study of this system documented the interdependence of the members and their cycling of resources.

Adaptation The third ecological principle concerns the transactions between person and environment. This is a two-way process: individuals cope with the constraints or demands of an environment, and environments adapt to their members (Trickett, Kelly, & Todd, 1972). Recall how you adapted to the demands of your first job, for instance. To adapt, you probably learned new skills without losing your unique identity. Environments also adapt to their members. Think about the changes in a family precipitated by events such as the birth of a child, a teen getting a driver's license, or a mother entering college. A community organization that does not respond to its members will find it difficult to retain member involvement or attract new members. Individuals and social systems adapt to each other (Kelly et al., 2000).

Social settings also adapt to the larger environments of which they are an interdependent part (Kelly et al., 2000). A local school system, for instance, adapts yearly to changes in the requirements and funding of local, state and national government, as well as to changes in the student makeup of the schools. Changes in technology, the economy, and cultural ideas about education also affect local schools.

For an illustration of the adaptation principle, list the skills you have needed for effective learning and coping in the college environment. Examples may include good note taking, knowing how to study for an essay versus for a multiple-choice test, making conversation and new friends, resolving roommate conflicts, time management, money budgeting, resilience after setbacks, and asking for help. Whether you learned them before entering college, or have learned them here, these skills indicate the adaptive demands made by the college environment. Moreover, a college that does not offer multiple ways to learn these skills is likely to experience difficulty in retaining students. Adaptation involves values as well as skills. A class that values individual competition, for instance, will reward different behavior from its students than one that prizes cooperation.

A further implication of the adaptation principle is that every environment demands different skills. Skills students need are somewhat different from those for factory workers or homemakers or police officers. Effective parenting in dangerous neighborhoods is more directive, setting more rules and firmer limits, than effective parenting in safer neighborhoods (Gonzales, Cauce, Friedman, & Mason, 1996).

Succession Ecologies and social systems change over time. Interdependence, resource cycling, and adaptation must be understood in that perspective (Trickett, Kelly, & Todd, 1972). This principle applies to families, settings and communities. How many times have you heard that "you have to work at keeping a marriage healthy"? Over time, patterns of partner interdependence, the cycling of resources such as emotional support, and adaptation of each partner to the other can change without their noticing. The nature of the relationship changes, perhaps with the partners drifting apart. At the cultural level, the forms of marriage have been changing in Western societies over the last century, another process of succession that affects individual life. Divorce and living together while unmarried are more frequent. Single parenting and same-gender partnering also are more common. These changes in forms of marriage are influenced by larger social and cultural forces and in turn influence individual choices about marriage.

An implication of succession is that before psychologists plan an intervention in a system, they need to understand that system's history. They also should consider carefully the likely consequences of the intervention, including possible unintended consequences.

The rise of mutual help (self-help) groups, largely without professional planning or intervention, provides an example of large-scale succession. Mutual help has become an important element in mental health care, especially regarding addictions, violence against women and coping with chronic illnesses. In addition, local mutual help groups involve all four ecological principles. Their primary purpose is to strengthen individual adaptation of its members. Interdependence is encouraged, often including individual contacts outside the group meetings. Social support, information, and other resources are exchanged. Persons who often think of themselves as needing resources have the uplifting experience of providing resources to others. How a local self-help group maintains itself, especially after its pioneers move on, is a matter of succession.

Contributions Kelly's four principles provide distinctive, useful concepts for describing the dynamics of social environments. They address aspects not emphasized in other approaches, such as resources and succession. Kelly et al. (2000)

specified how ecological concepts can guide the development of preventive interventions in community settings. Speer and Hughey (1995) applied these ecological concepts to describe how a community organizing approach mobilized citizens for effective social action.

In addition, Kelly, Trickett, and associates (e.g., Kelly, 1979b, 1986; Kingry-Westergaard & Kelly, 1990; Tandon et al., 1998; Vincent & Trickett, 1983) have applied the ecological principles to research and intervention in the community. This includes establishing an interdependent relationship between researchers and host community, identifying and cultivating community members who can be resources for the research, and anticipating unintended effects of research or intervention. The writings of Kelly and associates eloquently express values of genuine interdependence with community members and appreciation of community resources. This perspective underlies many of the aims of community research we discussed in Chapter 3.

Social Climate Dimensions

Many psychological effects of environments are best assessed in terms of persons' perceptions of the environment and its meaning. Rudolf Moos and colleagues developed the Social Climate Scales to assess the shared perceptions of a setting among its members (e.g., Moos, 1973, 1994, 2002, 2003). They have also applied social climate concepts within models of individual coping (Holahan & Moos, 1994; Holahan, Moos & Bonin, 1997; Moos, 1984, 1996, 2002; Moos & Holahan, 2003).

Social climate scales exist for microsystem and organizations including workplaces, families, university residence halls, psychiatric inpatient settings, correctional settings, community treatment settings, supported community living facilities, military units, and classrooms (Moos, 1994). They have been used in a number of countries and languages (e.g., Moos & Trickett, 1987). Social climate scales are based on three primary dimensions used to characterize any setting; each has subscales depending on the type of setting measured (Moos, 1994).

Relationships This dimension concerns mutual supportiveness, involvement and cohesion of members (Moos, 2002). The Classroom Environment Scale, which measures high school classroom environments, contains subscales on the extent to which students are involved in and participate in class, the extent of affiliation or friendship they report among classmates, and the amount of support they perceive from the teacher (Moos & Trickett, 1987). The Family Environment Scale (Moos & Moos, 1986) includes subscales on how cohesive and how expressive the members perceive their family to be, and the extent of conflict they perceive. Coworker cohesion and supervisor support are measured in work settings (Moos, 2002). These constructs are conceptually related to Kelly's principles of interdependence and cycling of resources just discussed.

Personal Development This concerns whether individual autonomy, growth, and skill development are fostered in the setting (Moos, 2002). The Classroom

Environment Scale contains a subscale on competition among students (Moos & Trickett, 1987). The Family Environment Scale (Moos & Moos, 1986) includes subscales concerning the independence accorded individual family members and the family's emphasis on achievement, intellectual-cultural pursuits, recreation, and moral-religious concerns. In work settings, worker autonomy and pressure on workers are measured (Moos, 2002). These environmental demands are related to Kelly's principle of adaptation.

System Maintenance and Change This dimension concerns the emphasis in the setting on order, clarity of rules and expectations, and control of behavior (Moos, 2002). The Classroom Environment Scale contains subscales concerning the extent to which class activities are organized and orderly, the clarity of rules, the strictness of the teacher, and the extent to which innovative activities and thinking are welcomed (Moos & Trickett, 1987). The Family Environment Scale (Moos & Moos, 1986) includes scales on the extent of control exerted by parents. In work settings, variables such as managerial control and encouragement of innovation are measured (Moos, 2002). These are conceptually related to Barker's behavior setting programs and deviation-countering circuits, and to adaptation in Kelly's framework.

Research on Social Climates Moos' social climate scales include items that reflect each of these dimensions. Persons in the setting complete these items to report their perception of that setting. These responses are aggregated to form a profile of the shared perceptions of the environment (Moos, 1994, 2002).

Social climate scales are useful in consultation and program development (Moos, 1984). A consultant may have setting members complete two forms of a social climate scale: the Real Form to report current setting functioning, and the Ideal Form to report how they desire the setting to be. The consultant then presents the aggregated group scores on both forms, and the group discusses how to change the environment to become more like the shared ideal profile.

Social climate scores have been statistically related to measures of individual well-being such as job satisfaction and psychological adjustment (Repetti & Cosmas, 1991). For instance, high school classrooms that emphasize competition and teacher control, but not teacher support and student involvement, have greater absenteeism (Moos, 1984). Juvenile delinquency treatment programs that score higher on support, autonomy, and clarity of expectations have lower rates of recidivism (Moos, 1975). Treatment settings perceived as less supportive by clients and/or staff, and that lack clear rules and procedures, have higher dropout rates (Moos, 1984). Of course, these are generalizations across many settings; social climate scales also can be used to study a particular juvenile treatment program, for instance.

Generalizing across many studies and settings, Moos (2003) identified three general themes. A balance of emphasis in a setting on personal relationships, personal development, and setting organization often promotes setting performance, individual performance, and individual well-being. Highly structured families, work settings, and communities often promote cohesion, but they can also foster conformity and inhibit minority views and personal growth. The quality of personal relationships often affects how much long-term influence a setting has on individuals.

Beyond Social Climate: Additional Setting Qualities Moos and associates also have identified three other important aspects of setting social environments, all of which can affect social climates (Moos, 2003; Timko, 1996). These are *physical features* of the setting, *organizational policies and norms,* and *suprapersonal factors,* or the aggregate individual characteristics of setting members. An example of suprapersonal factors is that being in a residence hall where many students engage in binge drinking is different from a hall where few students do, or that being in a college where most students are business majors is different from one where most students are art majors (Moos, 2003).

Contributions and a Limitation Social climate scales measure important but intangible aspects of settings, such as supportiveness, clarity of expectations, and individual growth. They connect subjective perceptions with setting characteristics in a way that behavior-setting theory does not. The conceptual value and ease of use of social climate scales has fostered research and practical applications in a variety of settings, generating a rich literature of empirical findings. Social climates influence important individual outcomes.

The chief limitation of social climate scales is that individuals or subgroups within the setting may see its social climate differently. For instance, Raviv, Raviv, and Reisel (1990) reported differences between teachers and students in the same classroom, and Trickett, Trickett, Castro, and Schaffner (1982) found differences between students and independent observers. These discrepancies suggest social climate measures are influenced by one's personality or social role in the setting, not just by the setting's overall characteristics. For instance, if the mean score (for a sample of setting members) is midway on a social climate scale (e.g., supportiveness), it could mean at least two things. It may indicate unanimous perceptions of medium supportiveness, or it may reflect two polarized camps of setting members, one group perceiving a very supportive setting but the other a very unsupportive setting. The same environment may generate quite different perceptions among women and men, for example. Thus, social climate scores should be examined carefully for variation among individuals or subgroups in the setting (Moos, 2003; Shinn, 1990).

Social Regularities

Settings often create predictable relationships among their members, and those qualities persist over time regardless of the individuals involved. Edward Seidman (1988, 1990) proposed that settings be understood in terms of these social regularities, defined as the routine patterns of social relations among the elements (e.g., persons) within a setting (Seidman, 1988, pp. 9–10; 1990, pp. 92–93). Seidman's focus is not on individual personalities, but on relationships between individuals.

Think back over your schooling for a moment. Who asks most of the questions in the school or college classroom? If your answer is the teacher, you've noticed a social regularity (Sarason, 1982; Seidman, 1988). Why is this so predictable, despite the diversity of teachers and students and levels of education? Both teachers and students often focus on attributes of persons (e.g., boring teachers, lazy students). Instead, might this regularity have to do with assumptions (of both teachers and students) about the roles and relationship of teacher and students and about how learning takes place? Perhaps even about power in the classroom?

To discover social regularities, search for patterns of behavior that reveal roles and power in relationships among setting members, such as teacher-student, therapist-client, employer-employee, parent-child. Roles are enacted in a specific setting (similar to Barker's behavior setting and standing pattern of behavior). However, the social regularity perspective goes beyond behavior-setting theory in attending to what role relationships reveal about power, resources, and inequalities in a setting (Seidman, 1988).

Another social regularity in schools concerns racial desegregation. A historical social regularity is that U.S. schools have been a sorting mechanism for separating students by achievement or test scores, then preparing them for different roles in society. Segregated schools once also sorted students by race. When the courts mandated an end to segregation, communities brought African-American and European-American students into the same schools. Yet both research and common sense observation reveal that in many schools a new form of sorting takes place. On the basis of (mainly White) staff perceptions of their abilities, and on test scores that may not fairly measure those abilities, Black (and often Latino/Latina and Native American) students are assigned disproportionately to classes and curricula that limit their ability to apply for college and their future attainments (Linney, 1986; Seidman, 1988; Weinstein, 2002a,b). By sorting on this basis, school systems continued (in modified form) the social regularity of racial separation. The new form of sorting is often unintentional rather than segregation by law. Nonetheless, it affects students' lives.

A final example of a social regularity concerns professional psychotherapy and mutual help for persons with mental disorders (Seidman, 1988). In a professionally conducted group, members may fall into more passive "patient behavior" even when the professional seeks to promote mutual help. By contrast, in a mutual help group conducted by members, all of whom who have experienced the same problem, members exchange helping. In studies comparing the social climates of professionally conducted groups with peer-led groups, members of peer-led groups rated their groups as more cohesive and as fostering more independence (Toro, Rappaport, & Seidman, 1987; Toro et al., 1988). These differences are rooted in the social regularities of the different groups.

Contributions The concept of social regularities calls attention to role relationships and power. It also offers a way of understanding why it often seems that the more things change in a setting, the more they remain the same. Often, attempts to change a setting, such as a school, are undermined by social regularities, power, and role relationships that were not changed. Only if those social regularities are altered is the system itself changed (Linney, 1986; Seidman, 1988). Identifying social regularities requires rich understanding of a setting. Methods for doing this include naturalistic observation, case study, and ethnographic approaches. Once regularities are identified, quantitative methods may also be used.

Environmental Psychology

Environmental psychology examines the influence of physical characteristics of a setting (especially built environments) on behavior (Saegert & Winkel, 1990; Timko, 1996). Environmental psychology in the United States arose at about the same time as community psychology. Its founders were primarily social psychologists interested in the physical environment and behavior. Both fields emphasize a shift of perspective from individual to individual-in-environment, research conducted in field settings, and applications to social action (Shinn, 1996b).

Environmental Stressors A major focus of environmental psychology is the study of the psychological effects of environmental stressors, such as noise, air pollution, hazardous waste, and crowded housing (Rich, Edelstein, Hallman, & Wandersman, 1995; Saegert & Winkel, 1990). For instance, the psychological effects of two notable incidents from the late 1970s have been researched intensively and longitudinally. At Love Canal, near Niagara Falls, New York, residents discovered in 1977 that they were living above a chemical waste dump when birth defects began appearing. The effects of that disaster, and of citizen activism in response, were studied by Adeline Levine and associates (Levine, 1982; Stone & Levine, 1985). The Three Mile Island nuclear plant near Harrisburg, Pennsylvania, had a serious accident in which radiation was released in 1979; the stressful effects of this accident on nearby residents have been studied over time (Baum & Fleming, 1993). In both cases, uncertainty about the levels of actual exposure to radiation or toxic substances and inconsistencies in public statements by industry and government officials exacerbated the stressful effects of the event (see also Wandersman & Hallman, 1993). After the Three Mile Island incident, blood pressure remained elevated, immune-system functioning depressed, and symptoms of posttraumatic stress more common among nearby residents than in comparison samples. These effects did not dissipate for nearly 10 years (Baum & Fleming, 1993).

Environmental Design Environmental psychologists also study the psychological effects of architectural and neighborhood design features. Examples include studies of enclosed work spaces, windows, and other aspects of housing design (Sundstrom, Bell, Busby, & Asmus, 1996). For a personal example, consider arrangement of furniture in indoor spaces on your campus or in your workplace. The psychology department of one of the authors recently remodeled common space in the department offices to redirect traffic flow and conversation areas away from working staff. Students and faculty responded by regularly moving chairs to resemble the old arrangement, presumably to recreate the social spaces. In the department of another author, a common area for students has some seats in a circle, a few student carrels, snack machines, and faculty mailboxes nearby and is located between the hallway and psychology department offices. This creates a social space in which faculty and students can encounter each other outside class as well as a corner for study when the space is quiet. Yet the competition for space on campus is keen, and periodically this social space must be vigorously defended against administrative attempts to use it for offices.

Environmental design also concerns neighborhood-level processes. A study of a large public housing project in Chicago found that greenness, the presence of trees and other vegetation, in public spaces was associated with stronger social ties, sense of safety, and adjustment to the neighborhood (Kuo, Sullivan, Coley, & Brunson, 1998). However, as Jane Jacobs noted in her classic 1961 book, *The Death and Life of Great American Cities,* in order to promote safety, greenery must not interfere with openness to public view and safety.

The New Urbanism movement in residential architecture and neighborhood design encourages community. Plas and Lewis (1996) studied Seaside, Florida, a community designed along New Urbanist lines, with building codes that require front porches and low picket fences for each house and town design with walkways to the town center and beach and limited automobile access. Businesses are accessible on foot from anywhere in the community. These features encourage neighboring and are based on study of older, established towns and neighborhoods with a strong sense of community (e.g., Jacobs, 1961). Surveys, interviews, and naturalistic observation in Seaside indicated that these features did encourage neighboring contacts and sense of community (Plas & Lewis, 1996). In Atlanta, city council member Debi Starnes (2004) helped create similar planning guidelines.

However, studies in other locales show that physical design does not always promote sense of community as intended (Hillier, 2002). For instance, in the 1960s, planners of the new town of Columbia, Maryland, put all mailboxes for a block together to encourage neighboring, yet the new residents demanded mailboxes at their houses. In addition, a convenience store was planned within a short walk of every house, yet residents preferred to drive a few minutes to larger stores in the town center and the convenience stores failed (Wandersman, 1984, p. 341). Part of the problem may have been contextual: the principles used by the Columbia planners are useful in urban neighborhoods and small towns, where walking to corner stores is familiar, but Columbia is a suburb, where residents expect to drive to supermarkets. Citizen participation in planning also is important (Jacobs, 1961). In Atlanta, citizen input occurs in neighborhood planning meetings, where controversy is common but where plans can be discussed and improved (Starnes, 2004).

Contributions By emphasizing the importance of the physical environment, environmental psychology complements the more social perspective of the other approaches. Although its focus is different from that of community psychology, there are significant areas of overlap.

TABLE 5.1 Key Ecological Concepts for Community Psychology

Ecological Psychology
behavior setting; optimally populated, underpopulated settings
Activity Settings
intersubjectivity
Ecological Principles
interdependence; cycling of resources; adaptation; succession
Social Climate Dimensions
relationship; personal development; system maintenance and change
Social Regularities
Environmental Psychology
environmental stressors; environmental design

Comparing the Perspectives: An Example

Key concepts from the six ecological frameworks are listed in Table 5.1. To compare these six perspectives, consider a play to be performed by students in a high school setting.

A high school play is a behavior setting. It has boundaries of time (for practices and performances) and space (an auditorium or theater). It has a standing pattern of behavior: during the performances, actors, audience, and others behave in predictable ways and locate themselves in predictable places. These behavior patterns indicate the program circuit or agenda: to perform a play to entertain an audience.

If the setting is underpopulated, having fewer participants than roles or functions to be filled, the principles of ecological psychology would predict that setting members (director, cast, and crew) would seek to recruit additional help and be likely to take on extra roles or tasks. They would engage in more deviation-countering circuits, teaching needed skills and keeping members involved. A person with no drama experience may be pressed to join the cast or crew, developing new skills or revealing hidden talents. If, in contrast, the setting is optimally populated, vetoing circuits are likely; a member who cannot learn a role or task can be replaced easily. There will be auditions for parts, and only the best actors will be accepted. Other students will become marginalized. If many students seek to be involved in the play, the staff could create the benefits of underpopulated settings by having two casts of different actors perform the play on alternate nights or stage a second production with different actors (Wicker, 1973).

Performing a play is not just following a literal script; it involves recreating a world on stage that involves the relationships among actors and seeks to engage the audience. Actors seek an intangible chemistry between themselves and with the audience. That intersubjectivity is the focus of activity-setting theory (O'Donnell,

Tharp, & Wilson, 1993). Engaging theater communicates intersubjective meanings through words, gestures, set, costumes, lighting, and perhaps music. The bonding that occurs among actors and crew during the long hours and shared work of a production also creates intersubjectivities.

How could the high school play be described in terms of Kelly's ecological principles? By working together, students and faculty build interdependent ties. This provides a basis for exchange of resources such as encouragement, instruction (especially from the director), and socializing. In addition, the play has interdependent relationships with other settings within the school. Its existence allows students who are not outstanding in other areas (e.g., academics, athletics) to feel connected with others, contribute to school life, and perhaps to shine, becoming recognized for their work (Elias, 1987). The play is also a way for the school to connect with and be recognized in the community.

Resources may be cycled between the play and the school as a whole. In a school in which drama is prized, money, facilities, student interest, and overall support will be plentiful; in one that does not prize drama, the play will receive little of these. Availability of resources also depends on the strength of interdependent relationships built between the drama faculty and administration, parents, school board members, and others. In turn, the play may generate a flow of resources from the community to the school. For instance, families, friends, and businesses may contribute resources such as props, costumes, food for intermission, and encouragement.

Adaptation for students involved in the play will involve learning skills in performance, set design, lighting, and so on. All members may have to help in publicizing and managing the production. These skills may also have adaptive value in the larger environments of school or community, such as future employment. In addition, the play will occur within a pattern of succession. It may be the first such production or the latest in a line of successful, well-attended productions; the latter may have more resources available but also place higher expectations on the cast and crew.

To apply Moos's social climate dimensions, members of the production (including director, actors, and crew) could complete questionnaires about their perceptions of the production environment. If they generally agree that play members were actively involved and supported each other well, and if they believe the director was supportive, scores will be high on Relationship dimension scales. Questions on that dimension might also assess conflict among members. The Personal Development dimension would concern whether participating in the play provided them opportunities to develop skills or experience personal growth. System Maintenance and Change items would measure their perceptions about how organized the production was, how much control the director exerted, the clarity of expectations for members' performance, and how much creativity was valued.

If different perceptions of the group social climate occur among subgroups (e.g., director, actors, stage crew; men and women), discussion could focus on what events and processes led to those differences. Using both the Real and Ideal forms of a social climate scale would afford comparisons between the current group functioning and the visions of an ideal group held by all or by subgroups. Conclusions about social climate could be used in planning the next production.

What social regularities (Seidman, 1988) and role relationships are involved here? One concerns the roles of director and actors. The director, usually a faculty member, will assume a powerful role. Choosing the play, making casting decisions, coaching actors, and assuming responsibility for the quality of performance are all functions that the director may perform. With inexperienced actors, that assumption of power may make sense. However, each of these functions could be shared with experienced actors to promote their skill development and personal growth. Such altering of social regularities could also mobilize resources such as hidden leadership talents among the students. It changes the usual role relationship in schools but promotes the educational and perhaps artistic value of the production. (Indeed, using students as directors and in other authority roles seems more common in drama than in other areas of many schools.) The concept of social regularities calls attention to power and resources predictably invested in social roles in the setting and how these may be changed to promote the development of individuals or settings.

Finally, an environmental psychologist would examine how the physical environment can be manipulated to promote the artistic themes of the play. The stage set, lighting, sound, and costumes are not merely backdrops, but artistic elements that help create mood and reflect the progress of the plot. Audience participation could be promoted by altering the room or seating. Actors in character could meet patrons at the door and create an atmosphere of immersion in the play. A play involves the creation of a believable world on stage that engages the audience, using artistic elements that parallel the concerns of environmental psychology.

RESEARCH AND ACTION IN NEIGHBORHOODS

In the remainder of this chapter we illustrate how ecological thinking influences community research and action. Next, we discuss research on how neighborhood contexts intertwine with individual and family lives and interventions to improve neighborhood quality of life.

Research: Neighborhoods, Families, and Individuals

A story by Reid (1999, p. 21) illustrates the impact of neighborhood and societal context on individual and family life. Reid's family, including a ten-year-old daughter, moved from the U.S. to Tokyo. The daughter was soon invited by a new Japanese friend to go on a day trip to a theme park. The trip involved taking multiple trains across Tokyo, waiting in stations between trains, and returning after dark, without any adult to accompany them. Reid objected, thinking of safety in U.S. cities, and was astounded when he called the Japanese mother of the friend and found that she saw no problem with this plan. Reid relented; the girls made their trip in safety and had a great time together.

A different story was told to researchers studying resilient mothers and daughters in a risky urban U.S. neighborhood (Brodsky, 1996; Caughey, O'Campo & Brodsky, 1999, p. 624). A school-age daughter wanted to continue in an after-school program near her home, but that involved coming home after dark when the mother could not accompany her. Even if the mother arranged for other adults to pick her up, they would not be safe after dark. In contexts such as this, parents and others face daunting neighborhood obstacles.

Neighborhoods provide one example of relationships between ecological contexts and the lives of individuals and families. Our contrast of two urban contexts above is somewhat simplistic: both environments have their strengths and local resources, and both have limitations. Studies by community psychologists and others have yielded findings that illustrate the complexity of neighborhoods and of how they are related to family and personal life. Some of that research also demonstrates that much of what we assume about such relationships may be wrong, or at least oversimplified.

For instance, Gonzales, Cauce, Friedman, and Mason (1996) studied predictors of grades in school for a sample of urban African-American adolescents. Their neighborhoods varied in degree of risk (occurrence of crime, gang activity, and violence). Neighborhood risk was a *stronger predictor of grades than family characteristics* such as parent education, family income, and number of parents living in the home. Moreover, neighborhood risk made a difference in what kind of parenting style was associated with higher grades. In lower-risk neighborhoods, teens whose parents were *less* restrictive had higher grades. But in higher-risk neighborhoods, teens whose parents were *more* restrictive had higher grades.

Studies of pregnant mothers provide another example. Women in higher-crime Baltimore neighborhoods had a risk of poor pregnancy outcomes (e.g., premature birth, low birth weight) that was 2.5 times higher than those in lower-crime areas. Moreover, while providing prenatal care and education about pregnancy reduces the risk of poor pregnancy outcomes, this reduction in risk was much less for women living in neighborhoods with high poverty rates and high unemployment than for women in other neighborhoods (Caughey, O'Campo, & Brodsky, 1999). This finding indicates that for women in high-poverty neighborhoods, providing access to prenatal care may not be enough. In Baltimore, the Healthy Start program develops jobs in the community and works to improve housing quality as well as providing prenatal care (Caughey et al., 1999). These problems are also rooted in macrosystem forces, requiring policy changes by governments and corporations.

Understanding Neighborhood Research Before describing other research on neighborhood contexts, we must make a few introductory points.

An exact definition of a neighborhood is somewhat difficult; it is larger than an urban block and smaller than a city. Neighborhoods have somewhat fluid boundaries (Coulton, Korbin, Chan, & Su, 2001; Shinn & Toohey, 2003). A small town may have the qualities of a single neighborhood. Nevertheless, most of us have a rough, intuitive idea of neighborhood.

However, neighborhoods are very diverse, and generalizations have many exceptions. Research on links between neighborhood qualities and individual functioning is in its early stages, with many complexities not understood (Shinn & Toohey, 2003). In addition, even within a neighborhood there may be different areas. Within one Baltimore neighborhood, areas varied greatly in income, rates of home ownership, and unemployment. "Blocks of vacant, boarded-up public housing projects are only a few blocks from streets of well-maintained homes with well-manicured lawns and gardens" (Caughey, O'Campo, & Brodsky, 1999, p. 629).

In addition, neighborhoods, families, and individuals are always changing. Although a neighborhood may appear stable, in fact it may be in the process of gaining or losing population, jobs, or quality and affordability of housing stock. Its ethnic mix or average income level may be changing. It may be in transition from a neighborhood whose residents have lived there for decades to a neighborhood with higher resident turnover, or vice versa. Of course, individuals and families also are continually changing as members mature and their actions and attitudes change over time. Thus, even though many of the characteristics that we will describe may seem to be stable, they are actually snapshots that capture one point in ongoing change.

We will distinguish between **neighborhood risk processes,** which are statistically correlated with problematic individual outcomes such as personal distress, mental disorders, or behavior problems, and **neighborhood protective processes,** which are strengths or resources associated with positive individual outcomes. Protective processes may offset or buffer the impact of risk processes. Risk and protective processes may be different in different neighborhoods.

We also distinguish between **distal processes,** which are broader in scope and indirectly affect individuals, and **proximal processes,** which affect individuals more directly and immediately. Proximal and distal are not absolute categories; they differ along a continuum. We will consider structural neighborhood processes (more distal), neighborhood disorder and physical-environmental stressors (both more proximal), and protective processes, proximal and distal. Our coverage is based on two recent reviews by community psychologists (Shinn & Toohey, 2003; Wandersman & Nation, 1998).

Distal Socioeconomic Risk Processes These involve social and economic or physical characteristics of a neighborhood as a whole that are correlated with individual problems. For example, mental health and behavioral problems, delinquency, cardiovascular disease, and pregnancy problems are, on average, more common in neighborhoods where many residents have low incomes (Shinn &

Toohey, 2003; Wandersman, & Nation, 1998). Another distal social process is residential turnover: in neighborhoods with higher turnover, juvenile delinquency is more common (Wandersman & Nation, 1998).

Distal socioeconomic processes are not limited to cities. In a study in rural Iowa, community disadvantage (computed from community rates of unemployment, receiving of government assistance, and proportion of population with less than high school education) predicted rates of conduct problems among adolescent boys, whereas the proportion of single-parent households in the community predicted conduct problems among adolescent girls (Simons, Johnson, Beaman, Conger, & Whitbeck, 1996).

These neighborhood-level statistics do not mean that low-income or single-parent families themselves are to be blamed for such problems. Economic macrosystem forces (e.g., unemployment) are often the root causes. In any community there will be many exceptions to statistical generalities. Moreover, low-income neighborhoods and families also may have protective processes at work.

Risky Physical Environments Socioeconomic root processes also create hazardous physical environments, which have more direct (proximal) effects on individuals and families. Residents of low-income neighborhoods are more likely to breathe polluted air and drink polluted water. They endure higher levels of traffic noise, which has been shown to limit academic learning in children, and higher exposure to lead, which limits cognitive development. Their neighborhoods have more hazardous traffic crossings and higher child pedestrian injury rates. Low-income neighborhoods often lack sources of healthy food: supermarkets are often hard to find, yet convenience and liquor stores are abundant. Housing is often of lower quality, presenting many health hazards. Overcrowded housing also is associated with psychological distress in children (Evans, 2004; Wandersman & Nation, 1998). As noted earlier, health interventions in low-income neighborhoods are less effective if such environmental problems are not addressed (Caughey et al., 1999).

Neighborhood Disorder Another more proximal approach focuses on processes of neighborhood violence and incivilities (Shinn & Toohey, 2003; Wandersman & Nation, 1998). For instance, about one-quarter of U.S. urban youth witness a murder in their lifetime. Exposure to violence is associated with posttraumatic stress disorder, depression and other distress, aggression, and behavior problems (Shinn & Toohey, 2003).

Incivilities are noticeable signs of neighborhood disruption that raise fears of crime. Physical incivilities include abandoned or dilapidated buildings, litter, vandalism, and graffiti. Social incivilities include public drunkenness, gang activities, and drug trade. Perkins and Taylor (1996) reported that residents of U.S. city blocks with more incivilities (especially physical ones) tended to have greater fears of crime, more depression, and more anxiety than those on neighborhoods with fewer incivilities. Neighborhood disorder also leads to restrictive parenting and even withdrawal from the community by parents concerned for their own and their children's safety (Gonzales et al., 1996; Brodsky, 1996).

Protective Processes Not every neighborhood with statistical risk factors has higher levels of individual problems or distress (Shinn & Toohey, 2003). This leads to inquiring what protective processes may be occurring there. Distal processes that are often protective for individual well-being include having a larger proportion of long-term residents and owner-occupied housing (Shinn & Toohey, 2003). In addition, more proximal processes are protective, such as relationships and sense of community among residents. For instance, in Baltimore neighborhoods that had higher levels of community organization (more voters registered, greater participation in community organizations), women had much lower risk of problems with pregnancy than women in neighborhoods with low levels of such organization. Risks were also lower in neighborhoods with more community services, businesses, and health care (Caughey et al., 1999). In another study of low-income urban U.S. neighborhoods, those where social ties and support among residents were stronger had lower levels of child maltreatment than neighborhoods where these supports were weaker (Garbarino & Kostelny, 1992).

The interactions among macrosystem, neighborhood, family, peer group, and individual factors are considerably more complicated than we have presented here. For instance, Roosa, Jones, Tein, and Cree (2003) presented a model of neighborhood influences on children and families, designed to guide prevention programs. Additional factors in their model include the importance of children's and parents' perceptions of the neighborhood, the importance of peer groups for adolescents and how these interact with neighborhood forces, and ways that prevention programs can enhance families' coping with the impact of neighborhood problems.

Promoting Neighborhood Quality of Life

These protective processes suggest avenues for community interventions. Community health and prevention programs and clinical interventions can link families with community resources such as jobs and child care. Community-level interventions include working with neighborhood associations, efforts to create jobs and improve housing quality and affordability, and policy advocacy to address wider social issues (Caughey et al., 1999; Maton, Schellenbach, Leadbeater, & Solarz, 2004; Wandersman & Nation, 1998).

Cooperative housing initiatives for low-income residents in New York City illustrate the impact of citizen participation in housing decisions (Saegert & Winkel, 1990, 1996). When city government seized buildings from absentee landlords who had not paid taxes, it helped finance sale of the buildings to cooperatives of low-income tenants, who then managed the buildings. Cooperative housing was higher in management quality, safety, freedom from drug activity, and resident satisfaction than city-owned housing or buildings owned by private landlords (Saegert & Winkel, 1996, p. 520). Effective citizen leaders emerged, particularly among women and elderly residents (Saegert, 1989).

The Dudley Street Neighborhood Initiative (DSNI) is an example of neighborhood-based community development. DSNI has transformed an inner-city area of Boston into a thriving neighborhood. In 1984 the area was one-third vacant lots, with unauthorized dumping by trash haulers and frequent arson, while city government looked the other way. The Dudley Street neighborhood now boasts new parks, businesses, community agricultural gardens, playgrounds, and community centers. Vacant lots have been rehabilitated for homes and community uses, over 400 new homes built, and over 500 housing units rehabbed. Street life is vibrant and safe. All this has been planned and implemented by local residents working through DSNI, which has more than 3,760 members. Outside grants and city collaboration have helped, but DSNI citizens insisted on and won local control. They use local resources and make decisions for the local community, transforming their community from the inside out. Although there is a healthy diversity of opinion on each DSNI project, there also is a real community spirit and tangible evidence of a transformed community (Dudley Street Neighborhood Initiative, n.d.; Kretzmann & McKnight, 1993; Medoff & Sklar, 1994; Putnam & Feldstein, 2003).

In urban neighborhoods in Nashville and in New York City, citizen block associations have had significantly positive impacts on the block physical environment. In longitudinal studies, improvements (on private as well as public properties) were more common on blocks with block associations (Wandersman & Florin, 2000). Also recall that pregnancy problems are less likely in neighborhoods with more participation in community organizations and more community services (Caughey et al., 1999). These findings from quantitative research and case studies indicate that community development interventions can be effective. (We discuss these in more detail in Chapter 13.) Yet for neighborhoods to thrive, wider social issues also need to be addressed (Caughey et al., 1999; Maton, Schellenbach, Leadbeater, & Solarz, 2004).

CREATING AND ALTERING SETTINGS

Neighborhoods are not the only focus of community interventions. Next we describe two exemplary community psychology interventions that created or changed community settings to promote quality of life for their inhabitants.

The Community Lodge: Creating an Alternative Setting

How can environments be created or altered to enhance their members' quality of life? Changing existing settings is usually not easy, even when one can identify the contextual variables that need to be addressed. Settings, social systems, and individuals within them generally resist change and try to preserve the status quo. The concepts of interdependence, adaptation, and social regularities suggest some ways in which this happens. Another approach to improving individual quality of life is to create a new and different setting, which community psychologists term an **alternative setting.**

The Community Lodge (Fairweather, 1979, 1994; Fairweather et al., 1969) was an early influence on community psychology and community mental health (we described it briefly in Chapter 2). Yet some of its principal elements have never been widely adopted in mental health systems. Those elements happen to be the aspects that pose the most interesting challenges to social regularities of mental health care. The Community Lodge movement exemplifies an alternative setting.

The Community Lodge idea began in a Veterans' Administration psychiatric hospital in the 1950s. After working in psychiatric hospital care for some time, Fairweather and others recognized that the context of the hospital did not promote the aim of independent community living for persons with serious mental illness. In hospital settings, the patient has few opportunities for decision making and autonomy. "Good behavior" usually means following orders. In contrast, once discharged, the individual needs to take initiative, make independent decisions, and form supportive relationships with others.

Fairweather's group developed in-patient group treatments that promoted the ability of men (veterans) with even the most serious mental disorders to participate in group decisions, and to prepare for living outside the hospital. However, even those treatments were not enough; those men, once released, still returned to the hospital at too high a rate after too short a period in the community. The problem, Fairweather and associates realized, was that there was no community setting, set of roles, or adequate support following release from the hospital. Altering regularities within the hospital was not enough.

Fairweather and associates then created an alternative setting, in which patients released from the hospital moved together to a residence in the community (Fairweather, 1979, pp. 316–322, 327–333). An old motel was leased and refurbished for their Lodge. After visiting the new Lodge several times, the members were discharged from the hospital and moved in. After several trial and error experiences, Lodge members became self-governing. They developed Lodge rules that, for instance, made it acceptable to discuss symptoms of mental illness with other Lodge members but not with neighbors. The researchers were surprised that some of the previously most seriously ill persons became active members of the community. With consultation, Lodge members established a janitorial and gardening business and eventually became economically self-supporting. Finally, they felt confident enough that they ended their professional relationship with Fairweather, although infrequent social contacts continued (Fairweather, 1994). A number of Community Lodges now exist in the United States.

Community Lodges have several distinctive features, all involving changed role relationships. The most important and surprising one is that Lodge residents govern themselves. Professionals serve only as consultants and eventually phase out of professional contact. Lodge members assume responsibility for monitoring each other for taking medication, behaving responsibly within and outside the Lodge, and related issues. Lodges decide for themselves, as a group, whether to admit new members or to dismiss members (Fairweather, 1979, 1994).

In controlled studies using volunteers randomly assigned to a Lodge or to ordinary psychiatric aftercare, Fairweather (1979) and Fairweather et al. (1969)

demonstrated that Lodge members, although similar to the control group on background variables, relapsed less often, spent fewer days in the hospital when they did, and spent more days employed than the controls. These differences persisted for five years of follow-up studies. Moreover, the Community Lodge method was less expensive than traditional community aftercare.

By demonstrating the effectiveness of community-based housing and economic ventures, the Community Lodge studies have contributed to the expansion of mental health care in communities since the 1960s. Yet their key element, self-government by members, has seldom been adopted (Fairweather, 1979). Perhaps that is because it undermines a social regularity many professionals believe is essential for helping persons with mental illness: professional supervision and control. As Fairweather often has pointed out, the Community Lodge findings indicate otherwise.

STEP: Altering Social Regularities in School

Think back to your first day of high school. Did you have these concerns: finding classes and your locker, getting lost, worrying about academic requirements and demanding teachers, staying in contact with your old friends in a bigger and more complicated setting, making new friends, avoid hazing or harassment from older students, and finding a way to fit into this new environment?

The School Transitional Environment Program (STEP; Felner & Adan, 1988) was designed to address issues such as these. STEP specifically alters key social regularities characteristic of American public junior and senior high schools. These school transitions are clearly difficult. For most students, academic performance, involvement in school activities, social support from school staff, and self-esteem drop during these transitions (Reyes, Gillock, & Kobus, 1994; Seidman, Allen, Aber, Mitchell, & Feinman, 1994). The long-term effects are particularly serious for the most vulnerable students.

The STEP program has two essential components: "(a) reorganizing the regularities of the school environment to reduce the degree of flux and complexity of the social and physical setting that the student confronts; and (b) restructuring the roles of homeroom teachers and guidance personnel" (Felner & Adan, 1988, p. 114). To address the first component, the STEP program clusters students in groups that are assigned to take many of their primary academic subjects and homeroom together. These academic subjects are offered in locations in close proximity to the homerooms and by a core group of teachers who work together as a team. These simple modifications facilitate forming multiple new peer relationships. They also facilitate students' sense of comfort with the school environment. These effects are especially salient in large urban schools with multiple feeder schools.

The second component of the STEP program involves redefinition of roles for the homeroom teacher. STEP homeroom teachers serve as the primary link between the school and the student's family. The STEP homeroom teacher knows each individual student well, meets with parents, contacts the family if the student is absent, meets with parents, and advises the student on a range of issues. This assures every student a mentoring relationship with an involved adult.

In the initial experimental trial of the STEP program, a randomly selected group of ninth graders participating in the STEP program were compared with a matched comparison sample of students in the same school. Felner and Adan (1988) reported significantly lower school absentee rates and higher grades for STEP program students at the end of the ninth grade. STEP students felt more positively about the school environment, considering it to be more stable, supportive, organized, and understandable. STEP students' self-concept scores remained stable over the year, while those of students not in STEP declined. STEP teachers also reported higher levels of satisfaction with teaching. By the end of tenth grade, fewer STEP students had dropped out of school. Replications of the STEP program in junior high and middle schools, with suburban and rural samples, showed similar results (Felner & Adan, 1988). Thus STEP seems to reduce the stressful effects of school transition, at several different grade levels and in varying locales.

CONCLUSION: ENDURING QUESTIONS

Environments are psychologically important, especially the resources that they offer for individual and community life. However, Moos (2002, 2003) identified four enduring questions about the relationships of individuals and ecological contexts.

1. *How are contexts both powerful and fragile in their influences on individuals? What risks and rewards do these qualities involve?* Neighborhoods, community settings, treatment settings, families, and other contexts can be powerful. Cohesive settings especially exert influence on members' attitudes and actions. Yet that power is also risky: for instance, cohesion and loyalty can become paramount, and differences can be labeled as deficits. "Any setting that is powerful enough to produce constructive personal change is also powerful enough to elicit self-doubt, distress, even suicidal behavior" (Moos, 2003, p. 8). The risks of promoting cohesion and the power of settings must be understood and considered. Building settings that truly respect diverse members and views is challenging.

   Yet the impacts of settings on individual lives also can be fragile, in the sense that when persons are no longer in the setting, its influence often wanes. Research amply demonstrates that although treatment settings, prevention programs, and other community changes may have short-term effects on individuals and communities, these changes are difficult to sustain over the long term. It is critical to find ways to create environments that sustain positive changes.

   Many persons also endure traumatic effects of powerful environments yet find ways to overcome that trauma, and in fact to grow and to develop new strengths. What qualities of both persons and environments support this growth? Moos (2003) notes that case studies can identify personal and environmental processes in such transformations.

2. *How can we understand ecological contexts as dynamic systems that change over time?* Communities, settings, and other contexts have their own histories, which must be understood as an ongoing story of changes. Although the concepts we have presented in this chapter may give the illusion of stability in environments, in fact they are works in progress, changing over time. Families change as their members mature. Neighborhoods change as their social and cultural makeup, economic resources, and institutions evolve. Community organizations often begin in a period of energetic efforts and optimism yet often evolve into predictable forms or disband. We still only partially understand how these changes over time are related to internal forces within the environment and to external influences, such as relations with other settings and macrosystem forces.
3. *How can we clarify the mutual relationships between individuals and contexts?* Studying the characteristics of environments is challenging, given that many of their most psychologically important qualities are subjective (as with the Moos social climate scales). Methods exist for aggregating these into variables describing environments, yet there is still much to be worked out (Moos, 2003; Shinn & Rapkin, 2000). Moreover, the relationships between environments and individuals are reciprocal. Persons certainly select and influence contexts as well as being influenced by them. Teasing out causal patterns is difficult.
4. *How are ecological contexts influenced by culture, ethnicity, gender, and other social processes?* Communities, neighborhoods, settings, and other contexts differ in their cultural, historical, and social characteristics. This is important not only for explaining ecological contexts but also for developing them. For example, to create effective community settings for helping individuals overcome alcohol abuse, cultural and spiritual resources, ways of involving individuals, and shared ritual practices would be different among European Americans in an East Coast suburb and among Native Alaskans in rural villages (Hazel & Mohatt, 2001; Mohatt et al., 2004). A cultural perspective will be needed (O'Donnell, 2005a).

    Concepts of ecological context are central to community psychology. In many ways, the entire field is about understanding how contexts and individuals influence each other. In that sense, the remaining chapters of this text elaborate and extend this chapter.

CHAPTER SUMMARY

1. Ecological context consists of the physical and social aspects of environments that influence individuals. Persons and contexts influence each other. Community psychologists seek to understand the interplay of ecological

context and individual life and to find ways to create or alter contexts to enhance individuals' quality of life.

2. Barker's ecological psychology was developed to study social behavior in everyday context. Barker and associates proposed the concept of *behavior setting*, comprised of a physical place, time, and program or standing pattern of behavior. Behavior settings have *program circuits,* agendas for the setting, and *goal circuits* to satisfy individual needs. They employ *vetoing circuits* to exclude some persons, and *deviation-countering circuits* to teach individuals the skills needed to participate in the setting.
3. Barker and associates also proposed the concepts of *underpopulated and optimally populated settings*. Optimally populated settings engage only some persons, using *vetoing circuits* to exclude others. Somewhat underpopulated settings require participation from many inhabitants to fill needed roles, and thus contribute to greater skill development and mutual commitment. They develop skills and involvement through *deviation-countering circuits* rather than vetoing.
4. O'Donnell and associates proposed the concept of *activity setting* that takes subjective experience of setting participants into account more than behavior setting concepts. Activity settings are based on *intersubjectivities,* or shared assumptions and meanings among participants in a setting.
5. Kelly and associates proposed four ecological principles for describing contexts in community psychology. *Interdependence* refers to the extent of interconnections among persons and among settings. *Cycling of resources* calls attention to how tangible and intangible resources are defined, created, exchanged, and conserved. *Adaptation* refers to the demands made on individuals by the setting, and how individuals cope with those demands. Settings also adapt to the individuals within them, and in relationships with other settings. *Succession* refers to how settings are created, maintained, and changed over time.
6. Moos developed the idea of measuring the *social climate* of environments through the perceptions of their members. In Moos's approach, social climates have three basic dimensions: *Relationship, Personal Development, and System Maintenance and Change.* Social climate scales have been related in research to many measures of setting qualities and individual functioning.
7. Seidman developed the concept of a *social regularity,* a predictable pattern of social behavior in a setting, often a role relationship such as teacher-student. Social regularities involve differences in power between the roles.
8. Environmental psychology concerns the relationships between the physical environment and individual or social behavior. Topics related to community psychology include environmental stress and environmental design of workspaces and neighborhoods.
9. We described an example of how a high school play could be analyzed from each of the six ecological perspectives in this chapter.

10. Neighborhood factors influence family and individual quality of life. In fact, neighborhood stressors may outweigh family and individual factors in importance. We defined neighborhood *risk and protective processes,* including *proximal* forces directly affecting individuals and families, and *distal,* larger forces whose effects may be indirect. These factors included distal socioeconomic factors, risky physical environments, neighborhood disorder, and protective processes such as neighborhood strengths and resources. We also discussed community-level interventions to promote neighborhood quality of life, including the Dudley Street Neighborhood Initiative.
11. Community psychologists are especially concerned with how smaller settings can be altered to improve individuals' quality of life. We described two examples: the Community Lodge, an *alternative setting* for persons with serious mental illness, and the STEP program, which altered social regularities of schools.
12. Moos identified four enduring questions about ecological contexts, about the power and fragility of settings, how settings are dynamic and ever changing, how individuals and environments are related, and how these relationships are affected by cultural and other social processes.

BRIEF EXERCISES

1. Choose two classes you have taken (at any level of education), one that you enjoyed and one you did not. Try to choose classes that are at similar levels of difficulty.

   Describe how these two classes differed as settings. List as many differences as you can (e.g., reliance on lecture vs. group activities, competition vs. cooperation among students, differences in physical classroom or size of class, skills needed for effective adaptation, vetoing vs. deviation-countering circuits, social regularities).

   Explain your variables to a classmate to check the clarity of your reasoning. Find the Classroom Environment Scale (CES; Moos & Trickett, 1987), or use the description of those scales in the chapter, and compare your two classes on your perceptions of relationships, personal development, and system maintenance and change.

   Finally, consider that different students learn best in different types of class environments. For the two classes you described, suggest the types of students who might learn well in each class (related to Kelly's principle of adaptation).
2. Think back over your life experiences and choose an optimally populated behavior setting, in which members equaled or outnumbered available roles, and an underpopulated setting, in which roles outnumbered members. (If you have no immediate ideas, start by analyzing your high school's extracurricular activities.) Describe the two settings, especially their differences. Then answer the following questions.

Did the optimally populated setting generate more marginal members who were not involved or committed to the setting (as Barker and Gump would predict)? Were vetoing circuits common there?

Did the underpopulated setting pull its members into roles through which they developed new skills or greater self-esteem? Did it generate a greater sense of involvement or commitment among members? Were deviation-countering circuits common there?

Which setting was more enjoyable for you as a member? Why?

3. Walk through a residential neighborhood (at home or elsewhere). The best time to do this is early evenings in warm weather. Look for the features that might promote community contacts: front porches where people sit, pedestrian walkways and sidewalks, streets with less automobile traffic and more pedestrian traffic, and public areas where children can safely play while adults can both supervise them and talk to each other. Do these features encourage saying hello, conversation, or other neighborly contacts, even with people you don't know? Does the lack of them discourage such contact? Are there other features that encourage contact?

   Visit common spaces such as parks or playgrounds, no matter how small. Is there pedestrian traffic and neighborly contact? Are spaces open to public view in ways that help keep them safe? Do greenery, benches, or other features promote neighborly contacts (Kuo et al., 1998)?

RECOMMENDED READINGS

Kelly, J., Ryan, A. M., Altman, B. E., & Stelzner, S. (2000). Understanding and changing social systems: An ecological view. In J. Rappaport & E. Seidman (Eds.), *Handbook of community psychology* (pp. 133–159). New York: Kluwer Academic/Plenum.

Moos, R. (2003). Social contexts: Transcending their power and their fragility. *American Journal of Community Psychology, 31,* 1–14.

Shinn, M. & Toohey, S. M. (2003). Community contexts of human welfare. *Annual Review of Psychology, 54,* 427–460.

Wandersman, A., & Nation, M. (1998). Urban neighborhoods and mental health: Psychological contributions to understanding toxicity, resilience and interventions. *American Psychologist, 53,* 647–656.

RECOMMENDED WEBSITES

Dudley Street Neighborhood Initiative (DSNI)
http://www.dsni.org

Describes the history and work of DSNI, an exemplary neighborhood change initiative described in this chapter.

INFOTRAC COLLEGE EDITION KEYWORDS

behavior setting, ecological psychology, environmental design, environmental psychology, microsystem, mesosystem, exosystem, macrosystem, neighborhood, setting, social climate, social regularity(ies)

INTERCHAPTER EXERCISE

Ecological Assessment of a Setting

Chapter 5 presents ecological concepts and research at a number of levels of analysis. In this exercise you will analyze a setting at the microsystem or organization level.

To begin, choose a behavior setting. As defined by Barker and associates, a behavior setting must have:

- a physical time and place
- clear boundaries of space or time to separate it from other settings
- a standing pattern of behavior

This may involve a microsystem or organization; choose a behavior setting other than your immediate family. Choose a setting carefully: one that you know well from personal experience, preferably one that you can observe now. You may choose a setting from your past experience if you remember it very well. Choose one that involves at least 10 people (an arbitrary rule of thumb to ensure enough roles and members to analyze). Some examples include a class, student organization, playground, residence hall wing or unit, small workplace, social club, or religious congregation (or group within it such as a choir or class).

Analyze the setting in terms of each of the following sections. Observing the setting again is a good idea. Doing this with a friend is often more fun.

Physical Setting

Describe the setting's natural, architectural, and furnishing features: its location, size, boundaries, arrangement of space, furniture (and whether it is movable), pathways of travel, greenery (if outdoors). At what times is it used? Is it ever crowded or empty? Can you describe its atmosphere as a physical setting?

Can you suggest useful changes in the physical features of the setting?

Behavior Setting

This part uses concepts drawn from Barker's theory of behavior settings.

Describe the setting's program or standing pattern(s) of behavior. Be as detailed as you can. How many persons are involved? Is there high turnover of persons (e.g., a retail store, playground) or low turnover (e.g., first-grade class)?

Define the goal circuits of the setting. That is, describe the most common goals that a person might pursue in this setting. What reinforcements do persons seek in this setting?

Finally, consider how this setting is related to other behavior settings. Is it part of a larger organization? Does it relate directly to other behavior settings?

Underpopulated and Optimally Populated Settings

Does the setting seem optimally populated or underpopulated? Slightly or very much so?

If the setting seems optimally populated, does it exclude a number of persons who would otherwise be likely to participate (vetoing circuits)? Does it tend to involve individuals only in specialized roles?

If the setting seems underpopulated, does it involve persons in a variety of roles? Does anyone play two or more roles? Are roles left unfilled? How actively does it recruit participants? Do persons in the setting take time to teach members how to play their roles (deviation-countering circuits)? How strong is the commitment of setting participants to this setting?

Can you suggest useful changes in these practices to create more of the benefits of underpopulated settings?

Population/Structural Characteristics

Describe setting participants in demographic terms by gender, race, age, or other categories. How do these demographic characteristics influence how the setting works? For instance, if members of the setting are mainly persons of a certain age or of one gender, how does that affect the atmosphere of the setting?

Social Regularities

Identify one social regularity or predictable pattern of behavior to analyze (recall the example of teachers asking questions more than students). What role relationships does the regularity involve? (For instance, consider the interlocking roles of teacher–student, boss–employee, organization officer–member, staff member–patient.) Are there differences in power based on this regularity?

Can you suggest changes in social regularities to pursue the setting's mission or purpose better?

Social Climate

If your setting is one for which Moos (1994) and associates have developed a social climate scale (see your instructor about this), complete the scale. If you can, find other setting members to complete it as well, and compute the mean and range of scores for each of the subscales. If a scale is not available, review the discussion in the chapter and decide on social climate concepts that can be used to describe the setting.

What changes would you suggest to improve the setting's social climate?

Ecological Principles

This section concerns Kelly's ecological principles. You may be able to use information from other sections here.

How are setting participants interdependent? How frequently do they interact? (See your earlier answers on social climate relationship dimensions.) How could interdependence be enhanced in this setting? Would that be desirable?

What resources, tangible or intangible, exist in the setting? Intangible resources might include knowledge, skills, emotional support, time, energy, commitment, vision for the future, and rituals or traditions of the setting. How are these resources cycled or exchanged in the setting? How could resources be better cultivated or used in the setting?

What demands does this setting place on participants (adaptation)? What skills are needed for participants to adapt to this setting? How can these skills be learned? How could the setting promote learning of these skills?

How has this setting changed over time (succession)? What characteristics of this setting have remained stable over time? What do you foresee for the future of this setting?

Summary

Which of the preceding sections generates the most interesting information about the setting? Are there important things about the setting that are not covered in these questions and concepts? What are the most important things you have learned through this exercise?

6

Understanding Community

Stan Mason

OPENING EXERCISE: COMMUNITIES IN YOUR LIFE

> I have never met anyone—young or old, rich or poor, black or white, male or female, educated or not—to whom I have had any great difficulty explaining what I meant by the psychological sense of community. (Sarason, 1974, p. 1)

What are the important communities in your life? After some reflection, write a list of these. (For simplicity, don't list your immediate family and your network of friends.) Here are some examples, but list any community that is important in your life.

- your extended family, beyond your immediate nuclear family
- a campus organization, club, or team; a recreational club or league
- a workplace
- a group of students taking the same class(es) or in the same program
- a block, neighborhood, or town where you live or once lived
- a religious congregation or group

- a mutual help (self-help) or other support group
- a civic club or group working for change in your society or community
- the college or university you are attending
- an Internet chat room or other online group

Consider why you listed each community. What emotions do you experience in this community?

Finally, identify one time in your life when you felt you were excluded, or treated unjustly, by a community. How did that happen, and how did affect you? (If this arouses strong feelings, find someone trustworthy with whom to talk about them.)

In our experience, the lists that people make in this exercise vary but still have common psychological themes. In some of their communities, people experience a shared emotional bond, a shared identity, and mutual trust, caring, and commitment. Community psychologists call this the psychological sense of community.

However, although each of us can identify important communities in our life, scholars and citizens express concern that communities and sense of community may be declining. Robert Putnam's (2000) *Bowling Alone* documented important shifts in many forms of community involvement in the United States. Public opinion polls have found that individuals' sense of alienation from their communities is at the highest levels ever measured, whereas reported trust in others is at the lowest levels ever measured. Charitable contributions (as proportion of income) declined steadily from 1965 to 1995, leveling off recently. Active involvement in local community organizations also has declined steadily over the last 30 years. These declines are especially serious for organizations that provide volunteer services for youth development and persons in need, since government services for these populations also are being slashed. Informal neighboring and social visiting also are declining, although not as sharply as other indicators. Many forms of citizen participation in government have weakened over 30 years: voting, signing petitions, writing letters to the editor, and volunteering for a political party or campaign (Berkowitz, 1996; Putnam, 2000). Concern about the nature and sustainability of community ties is not solely a U.S. issue. For instance, voting and other forms of political involvement have decreased in many European countries, Japan, Australia, and New Zealand (although often remaining higher than in the U.S.) (Putnam, 2002).

However, the news is not all bad. In the U.S., participation in mutual help groups has increased strongly (Kessler, Mickelson, & Zhao, 1997). Two of every five U.S. adults are involved in a small group that provides caring for its members, a category that includes not only mutual help but also religious study and prayer groups (Wuthnow, 1994). Community service is growing among youth and retirees. Online communication offers new forms of community (Putnam, 2000).

Youth are involved in citizen advocacy. Protesters at the 2004 Republican convention, for instance, greatly outnumbered the famous 1968 demonstrations at the Chicago Democratic convention. "E-activism", using online resources to engage citizens for action, is growing rapidly, often with youthful leadership.

In the 2004 U.S. presidential election, turnout of voters under age 30 increased more than any other age group (Kamenetz, 2005).

What do these trends mean? Is there a decline in community ties or simply a redirection of the forms of community in which citizens participate? Putnam used *Bowling Alone* as his central metaphor and title but admitted that what the data show is decreased participation in organized bowling leagues; people are bowling more often in informal groups (Putnam, 2000, p. 113). Perhaps the most serious concern may be the erosion of connections and mutual understanding across boundaries of social class, income, and race (Wuthnow, 2002).

Discussion of these issues is complicated by the variety of meanings of the term *community.* Its emotional connotations grant it power as a metaphor yet make it difficult to define for research. Community refers to varying ecological levels, from microsystems to macrosystems. Yet that diversity of meaning is not necessarily bad. It allows for creative exploration of conceptions of community at multiple levels, valuable as long as the explorers consider multiple perspectives and their underlying values and avoid one-sided thinking (Rudkin, 2003). Remember Rappaport's Rule: "When everyone agrees with you, worry" (Rappaport, 1981, p. 3). Keep his rule in mind as we turn to defining concepts of community.

WHAT IS A COMMUNITY?

Community has long been a concern in the social sciences. Tonnies (1887/1988) proposed a famous distinction between *Gemeinschaft,* the communal solidarity of preindustrial village life, and *Gesellschaft,* instrumental relationships formed to pursue individual goals. Life involves both types of relationships. Buying groceries does not require a *Gemeinschaft* relationship. However, Tonnies believed that modern Western society undermined *Gemeinschaft* relations. His view was an early statement of the theme of loss of community. Kropotkin (1914/1955) took a different angle. To oppose the Social Darwinist view that evolutionary success inevitably goes to strong, aggressive individuals, Kropotkin amassed evidence from natural and social history that mutual aid in fact promotes survival of individuals and communities. His work provides a reminder of how communities and interdependence are everywhere. Among psychological theorists, Adler (1933/1979) also emphasized the importance of community involvement for both individual well-being and social cohesion.

Seymour Sarason's (1974) book, *The Psychological Sense of Community,* set the tone for how community psychologists think about the relationships between individuals and communities. Sarason defined community as "a readily available, mutually supportive network of relationships on which one could depend" (p. 1). Sarason argued that the "absence or dilution of the psychological sense of community is the most destructive dynamic in the lives of people in our society." Its development and maintenance is "the keystone value" for a community psychology (p. x). He applied the term *community* to localities, community institutions, families, street gangs, friends, neighbors, religious and fraternal bodies, and even national professional organizations (pp. 131, 153). Sarason's emphasis on the yearning for community by lonely individuals reflected only one perspective from which social scientists have studied community (Bernard, 1973; Hunter & Riger, 1986).

Types of Communities

Definitions of community in sociology and in community psychology distinguish between two meanings of the term: community as locality and community as a relational group (e.g., Bernard, 1973; Bess, Fisher, Sonn, & Bishop, 2002).

Locality-based Community This is the traditional conception of community. It includes city blocks, neighborhoods, small towns, cities, and rural regions. Interpersonal ties exist among community members (residents); they are based on geographic proximity, not necessarily choice. When residents of a locality share a strong sense of community, individuals often identify themselves by their locality and friends are often neighbors. In many nations, political representation, public school districts, and other forms of social organization often are delineated by locality.

Relational Community These communities are defined by interpersonal relationships and a sense of community but are not limited by geography. Internet discussion groups are communities completely without geographic limits. Mutual help groups, student clubs, and religious congregations are defined by relational bonds. Although sense of community in localities may have waned in Western societies, individuals seem increasingly involved in relational communities (Hunter & Riger, 1986).

Although relational communities may be based only on friendships or recreation (e.g., bowling league, sorority), many are organizations bound by a common task or mission. Workplaces, athletic teams, religious congregations, women's advocacy organizations, chambers of commerce, labor unions, and political parties are examples.

Locality-based and relational communities form a spectrum rather than a dichotomy. Many primarily relational communities, such as universities and religious congregations, are seated in a locality. An Internet discussion group anchors the purely relational pole of the continuum; a town or neighborhood represents the opposite locality-based pole. The communities you listed in the opening exercise may vary along this spectrum.

Levels of Communities

Communities exist at different ecological levels. These include:

- microsystems, e.g., classrooms, mutual help groups
- organizations, e.g., workplaces, religious congregations, civic groups

- localities, e.g., city blocks, neighborhoods, cities, towns, rural areas
- macrosystems, e.g., the business community, the Filipino community

Moreover, communities are related across levels. Classrooms exist within a school. Localities, in the form of city government, local economy, street layout, school location, and other factors, certainly affect neighborhoods, organizations, and even microsystems (e.g., which children become schoolmates and friends). Macrosystem economic and political forces influence workplaces, schools, community programs, and families. Improving community and individual life often involves change at multiple levels, even macrosystems.

If communities exist at different levels, what is the smallest group that can be usefully called a community? Could your immediate family or your network of friends be considered a community? Certainly these have some of the psychological qualities of communities. However, Hill (1996, p. 434) argued that for conceptual clarity, connections with families and friends should be considered social networks, not communities. She defined community as a larger grouping of individuals who may not know all of the other members yet who share a sense of mutual commitment. In this chapter we exclude immediate families and immediate friendship networks from our discussion of communities as a way to focus our discussion.

Mediating Structures Some groups and organizations connect individuals or smaller groups with a larger organization, locality, or society. Joining them provides a sense of community for the individual and a practical way to participate in the larger community or society. These intermediate communities link differing ecological levels and are called *mediating structures* (Berger & Neuhaus, 1977). For instance, parent-teacher associations, civic clubs, political advocacy groups, and neighborhood associations all offer ways to become involved in wider communities and can give collective voice to their members' views about community issues. They mediate between individuals and the wider community. In a university, student clubs, residence hall organizations, and student government are mediating structures.

Who Defines Communities?

Certainly, communities define themselves, but it is important to recognize that this may require a struggle and that external systems (e.g., government planners, political forces) may be involved. For instance, Sonn and Fisher (1996) studied the sense of community among "Coloured" South Africans, a racist category created by apartheid laws. Despite this artificial, externally imposed categorization, "Coloured" South Africans managed to build shared ideas and commitments that helped them resist racist oppression and that persisted even among those who emigrated to Australia. In Australia itself, discussion of the Aboriginal "community" has often been in terms defined by European Australians in government and academia. Thus it is phrased in Western concepts and often fails to recognize diversity among indigenous Australian peoples (Dudgeon, Mallard,

Oxenham, & Fielder, 2002; Lee, 2000). This also occurs in dominant views of Native Americans and other dispossessed groups. Finally, concepts of what it means to be Australian (or any other national identity) are socially constructed and challenged over time (Fisher & Sonn, 2002).

Hunter and Riger (1986) identified how the definition of communities for U.S. community mental health centers (discussed in Chapter 2) was a top-down, imposed concept of "catchment areas" defined by planners and based on census tracts. Catchment areas did not reflect existing social and cultural boundaries and failed to recognize relational communities, such as mutual help groups, that reached across catchment area boundaries. In a 2001 study of neighborhood boundaries for families and children, census tract definitions of neighborhoods in Cleveland, Ohio, often did not match residents' own drawings of neighborhood maps. Measures of social indicators such as rates of crime and teen childbearing differed depending on whether census or resident maps were used. This would greatly affect both community research and community programs that use census data (Coulton, Korbin, Chan, & Su, 2001).

SENSE OF COMMUNITY

Very important to community psychologists is the strength of bonding among community members, which Sarason (1974) termed the psychological sense of community. He defined it as

> the perception of similarity to others, an acknowledged interdependence with others, a willingness to maintain this interdependence by giving to or doing for others what one expects from them, the feeling that one is part of a larger dependable and stable structure. (p. 157)

David McMillan and David Chavis (1986) reviewed research in sociology and social psychology on the sense of community and group cohesion. Their definition of sense of community resembled Sarason's:

> a feeling that members have of belonging, a feeling that members matter to one another and to the group, and a shared faith that members' needs will be met through their commitment to be together. (McMillan & Chavis, 1986, p. 9)

Four Elements of Sense of Community

What are the specific qualities of sense of community? McMillan and Chavis identified four elements: membership, influence, integration and fulfillment of needs, and shared emotional connection. These elements help translate the overarching theme of a sense of community, which characterizes Sarason's thinking, into measurable constructs for research and specific objectives for action. In their

TABLE 6.1 Elements of the Psychological Sense of Community

Membership
Boundaries
Common symbols
Emotional safety
Personal investment
Sense of belonging, identification with community
Influence
Mutual influence of community on individuals, individuals on community
Integration and Fulfillment of Needs
Shared values
Satisfying needs, exchanging resources
Shared Emotional Connection
Shared dramatic moments, celebrations, rituals

SOURCE: Based on McMillan and Chavis (1986), McMillan (1996).

formulation, all four elements must be present to define a sense of community. No one element is the root cause; all strengthen each other. Our description of these elements is based primarily on McMillan and Chavis (1986) and McMillan (1996). The elements are summarized in Table 6.1.

Choose one community from the list you wrote for the exercise at the beginning of this chapter. Think about it as you read about these four elements.

Membership This is the sense among community members of personal investment in the community and of belonging to it (McMillan & Chavis, 1986, p. 9). It has five attributes. The first attribute, **boundaries,** refers to the necessity of defining what includes members and excludes nonmembers. For a locality, this involves geographic boundaries; for a relational community, it may involve personal similarities or shared goals. Boundaries may be clearly or obscurely marked, and they may be rigid or permeable. They are necessary for the community to define itself. Ingroup-outgroup distinctions are pervasive across cultures (Brewer, 1997). Other qualities of sense of community depend on having boundaries.

Common symbols help define boundaries, identifying members, or territory. Examples include the use of Greek letters among campus sororities, colors and symbols among youth gangs and sports teams, religious imagery, university decals on automobiles, characteristic slang expressions and jargon, and national flags and anthems (Fisher & Sonn, 2002).

In a community with clear boundaries, members experience **emotional safety.** This can mean a sense of safety from crime in a neighborhood. More deeply, it can mean secure relationships for sharing feelings and concerns. Emotional safety in that sense requires mutual processes of self-disclosure and group acceptance (McMillan, 1996).

A member who feels safe is likely to make **personal investment** in the community. McMillan (1996) refers to the latter as "paying dues," although it is often not monetary. Investment indicates long-term commitment to a community, such as home ownership in a neighborhood, membership in a religious congregation, or devotion of time to a charity organization. It can also involve taking emotional risks for the group.

These acts deepen a member's **sense of belonging and identification** with the community. The individual is accepted by other community members, and defines personal identity partly in terms of membership in the community. Individuals may identify with being a resident of a neighborhood, adherent of a religion, member of a profession or trade, student in a university, or member of an ethnic group.

Influence The second element refers both to the power that members exercise over the group and to the reciprocal power that group dynamics exert on members. McMillan and Chavis (1986, pp. 11—12) based their discussion of influence in part on the group cohesiveness literature in social psychology. Members are more attracted to a group in which they feel influential. The most influential members in the group are often those to whom the needs and values of others matter most. Those who seek to dominate or exercise power too strongly often are isolated. The more cohesive the group, the greater is its pressure for conformity. However, this is rooted in the shared commitments of each individual to the group, not simply imposed on the individual. (It does, however, indicate a disadvantage of a strong positive sense of community that we will discuss later.) Thus, the individual influences the wider group or community, and that community influences the views and actions of the person.

Integration and Fulfillment of Needs Influence concerns vertical relations between individuals and the overall community; integration concerns horizontal relations among members. Integration has two aspects: shared values and exchange of resources. Shared values are ideals that can be pursued through community involvement, such as worship in a religious community or improving educational quality.

The second concept refers to satisfying needs and exchanging resources among community members. McMillan (1996) referred to this as a "community economy." Individuals participate in communities in part because their individual needs are met there. Needs may be physical (e.g., for safety) or psychosocial (e.g., for emotional support, socializing, or exercising leadership). Integration is similar to interdependence and cycling of resources in Kelly's ecological perspective (see Chapter 5).

Shared Emotional Connection McMillan and Chavis considered this the "definitive element for true community" (1986, p. 14). It involves a "spiritual bond": not necessarily religious-transcendent, and not easily defined, yet recognizable to those who share it. "Soul" among African-Americans is an example. Members of a community may recognize a shared bond through behavior, speech, or other cues. The bond itself is deeper, however, not merely a matter of behavior. Shared emotional connection is strengthened through important community experiences, such as celebrations, shared rituals, honoring members, and shared stories (Berkowitz, 1996; McMillan, 1996; Rappaport, 2000).

An Overview of Research on Sense of Community

Research on sense of community has concerned both locality and relational communities at multiple levels. Many studies used measurement instruments based on the McMillan-Chavis model; some defined and assessed sense of community in other ways (Buckner, 1988; Glynn, 1986; Puddifoot, 2003). Studies in community psychology have been conducted in the Americas, Asia, Australia, New Zealand, and Europe. Five sources contain a broad sample of this research (Chavis & Pretty, 1999; Fisher, Sonn, & Bishop, 2002; Newbrough, 1996; Newbrough & Chavis, 1986a,b). The following examples give the flavor of sense of community research, but remember that they are only illustrative.

Sense of community has been studied in:

- localities (e.g., Bishop et al., 2002; Brodsky et al., 1999; Farrell et al., 2004)
- workplaces (e.g., Lambert & Hopkins, 1995; Mahan et al., 2002; Royal & Rossi, 1996)
- schools (e.g., Bateman, 2002; Solomon et al., 1996)
- college students (e.g., Loomis et al., 2004; Lounsbury et al., 2003)
- spiritual communities (e.g., Mankowski & Rappaport, 2000a; Trout et al., 2003)
- community organizations (e.g., Brodsky & Marx, 2001; Ferrari et al., 2002; Hughey et al., 1999)
- online virtual environments (Roberts et al., 2002)
- immigrant groups (e.g., Sonn, 2002; Sonn & Fisher, 1996, 1998)
- Afghan women working for women's and human rights (Brodsky, 2003)

Positive sense of community was associated with:

- neighboring and working together on neighborhood projects (e.g., Farrell et al., 2004; Garcia et al., 1999; Perkins & Long, 2002; Prezza et al., 2001)
- participation in neighborhood groups and religious institutions (e.g., Brodsky et al., 1999; Hughey et al., 1999; Kingston et al., 1999; Perkins & Long, 2002)
- believing that working with others to take community action can be effective (e.g., Perkins & Long, 2002; Peterson & Reid, 2003; Speer, 2000)
- voting in city elections (Davidson & Cotter, 1989, 1993), and neighborhoods with higher levels of voter registration (Brodsky et al., 1999)
- resistance to oppression (e.g., Brodsky, 2003; Sonn & Fisher, 1996, 1998; 2003)
- cooperative teaching and learning in schools (Bateman, 2002; Royal & Rossi, 1996; Solomon et al., 1996)

- adolescent identity formation (Pretty, 2002; Pretty et al., 1994, 1996)
- individual well-being, mental health, and recovery from substance abuse (e.g., Farrell et al., 2004; Ferrari et al., 2002; Pretty et al., 1994, 1996; Prezza et al., 2001)

QUESTIONS AND ISSUES FOR DEFINING SENSE OF COMMUNITY

In community psychology, sense of community has been defined and used in a diversity of ways, raising a number of questions and issues. These illustrate the strengths and limitations of the concept.

Elements of Sense of Community

Are the four McMillan-Chavis elements the best way of describing the basic elements of sense of community? Empirical research has established the validity and importance of the overall sense of community construct, but findings have been inconsistent concerning the independence and validity of the four McMillan-Chavis elements. Some studies have generally confirmed them (Bateman, 2002; Obst & White, 2004) or validated them but have also found additional dimensions (Obst, Zinekiewicz, & Smith, 2002). Some researchers found the four elements so highly intercorrelated that they focused only on the overall construct of sense of community (Mahan, Garrard, Lewis, & Newbrough, 2002). Other studies found different dimensions of sense of community (Chipuer & Pretty, 1999; Hughey, Speer, & Peterson, 1999; Long & Perkins, 2003).

These inconsistencies may result in part from problems in the existing measures of sense of community. Existing quantitative scales often lack the richness of examples found in the original Sarason and McMillan-Chavis descriptions (Bess et al., 2002; Chipuer & Pretty, 1999; McMillan, personal communication, August 25, 2003). Qualitative research methods can be useful, but also have limitations (Brodsky, Loomis, & Marx, 2002; Rapley & Pretty, 1999).

Perhaps sense of community is contextual, varying in different cultures and communities. If that is true, the McMillan-Chavis model (or any other single framework) might describe the basic elements in some communities, but other communities would require different conceptualizations. Indeed, that is one way to interpret some of the findings just discussed. Sense of community seems contextual to many community psychologists (Hill, 1996; Bess et al., 2002). For instance, Hughey, Speer, and Peterson (1999) found new dimensions of sense of community among members of locality-based organizations in a U.S. city. New conceptual frameworks may be especially needed in cultures markedly different from the Western ones, for instance among Australian Aboriginal groups (Dudgeon et al., 2002).

A related question: Is sense of community primarily a cognitive-emotional construct, or does it include related behaviors such as acts of neighboring and citizen participation in decision making? The idea of "sense" of community refers to thinking and emotions, such as a feeling of belongingness, of emotional safety, a shared emotional connection. Should measures of sense of community also include actions such as helping neighbors or participating in community organizations (as in Chavis, Hogge, McMillan, & Wandersman, 1986)? Or should such actions be measured separately (Perkins & Long, 2002)? For our introductory purposes, we will discuss the behaviors of neighboring and citizen participation as separate concepts. However, note that David McMillan argues that the cognitions, emotions, and actions of sense of community cannot be separated (personal communication, August 25, 2003).

Levels of Sense of Community

Is sense of community simply in the eye of the beholder, the individual perception of the wider community? Or is it a characteristic of a community as a whole? Most studies have measured sense of community with questionnaires for individuals, analyzed at the individual level. However, in samples of high school and university students, Lounsbury, Loveland, and Gibson (2003) found that personality variables (e.g., extraversion, agreeableness) accounted for up to 25 percent of the variance in how much sense of community students perceived in their school or college. In contrast, a study of residential blocks in urban neighborhoods found substantial agreement among residents of each block in their reports of sense of community there, as well as significant differences in sense of community between blocks (Perkins & Long, 2002). These shared perceptions of block-level community seem to go beyond individual personality differences.

Both personal and neighborhood factors contribute to perceptions of sense of community (Long & Perkins, 2003). It also seems likely that their relative importance would vary in different contexts. For instance, shared sense of community may develop more strongly in residential neighborhoods where individuals may remain for a longer time than in high school or college. The residential street blocks studied by Perkins and Long, although urban, also are smaller communities than a university.

Bess et al. (2002, pp. 8—9) proposed that existing terminology be refined. *Psychological sense of community* would refer to an individual experience of community ties. This is what most psychological researchers have been studying, often omitting the "psychological" modifier. This individual-level variable might vary even among members of the same community and be influenced by both personal characteristics and community experiences. *Sense of community* then would refer to a quality of a community as a whole. It would be based on substantial agreement among members of a community or on some measure of the community at large. This delineation would help lessen confusion, but it does not allow for a term to refer to both levels, as we are doing here, and it is too soon to tell if most researchers will adopt it.

Sense of community is a rich concept. At this point in its development, it is probably better to study it in a variety of ways: with the McMillan-Chavis model and other frameworks, at individual and community levels, with qualitative and quantitative methods, while remaining sensitive to contextual differences.

Narratives and Sense of Community

Narratives are a powerful force for building sense of community, and offer an alternative way to study it. Rappaport (2000) defines narratives as stories shared by members of a group. **Dominant cultural narratives** are familiar to most people in a culture and are communicated through media, books, and shared rituals. They convey values prized by the culture or at least by its most powerful members. For instance, the individual hero is central to many dominant cultural narratives in the United States. The hero's independence is celebrated; how a hero is often interdependent with others is downplayed. Dominant cultural narratives also can exclude those not in the narrative's mainstream, or convey stereotypes about them. **Community narratives** are told within smaller communities and may follow or resist dominant cultural narratives. For instance, in GROW, a mutual help group for persons with serious mental illnesses, community narratives focused on members' personal strengths can help offset a dominant cultural narrative focused on their deficits. Community narratives may emphasize interdependence rather than individualistic heroes. Community narratives offer shared emotional connection, meaning for understanding life, assurance of mutual commitment, and a sense of belonging: all elements of sense of community. In addition, if community narratives are stories of personal and social transformation, they offer resources for change.

Personal stories are individuals' unique accounts, created to make sense of their own lives. One's personal identity is embedded in a life story. Personal stories often draw on shared cultural or community narratives to find meaning. As individuals hear more of the community narratives in a setting of mutual acceptance and belonging, they often weave elements of the community narrative into their own personal stories. They blend the shared social identity with their personal identities. For instance, a person with an illness may adopt the shared narrative of a mutual help group to create a vision for recovery. This convergence of community narrative and individual life stories may be one qualitative indicator of psychological sense of community. It seems likely that the community narratives will also change over time to fit changes in the personal experiences of members. In addition, community research on personal stories and community narratives of marginalized groups can help challenge inaccurate, unjust dominant cultural narratives (Mankowski & Rappaport, 2000b).

Negative Psychological Sense of Community

Does individual perception of psychological sense of community vary only from neutral to highly positive, or can it be negative? Psychological sense of community is negative when a person feels strongly negatively about the wider community

(Brodsky, Loomis, & Marx, 2002). Thus the person may resist community involvement, concluding it will be harmful.

That negative psychological sense of community is what Anne Brodsky (1996) found in a qualitative study of ten resilient single mothers who were living and raising daughters in an urban U.S. neighborhood with high rates of crime and violence. These women were nominated as especially resilient, effective mothers by two sources in their daughters' elementary schools. All were parenting at least one child and working full time or part time. Some were also pursuing education or taking care of other family members. Their views of their neighborhood in general were decidedly negative. They drew a strong boundary between family and neighborhood:

> And when you come into my house it's totally different.... It's my world... when you close that door, leave that world out there. (Brodsky, 1996, p. 351)

Physical and emotional safety, a key characteristic of sense of community in the McMillan-Chavis model, seldom existed in their neighborhood. These mothers also shared few values with many others in the neighborhood. The neighborhood did have some positive resources for parents, and these women were involved in some of them (e.g., resident council, school), especially where involvement directly benefited their children. Yet this involvement did not alter their views of the neighborhood at large. Their strength as persons and mothers involved resistance to neighborhood forces, not sense of community (Brodsky, 1996).

The adaptive value of a negative psychological sense of community is not limited to this sample (Brodsky, Loomis, & Marx, 2002). Consider, for example, a community with limited acceptance of diversity, where conformity pressures are strong. Persons who are not accepted there may strengthen their well-being by distancing themselves from the community and seeking settings where they are accepted.

Brodsky's findings thus raise the question: Is a strongly positive sense of community always "good for you"? Does it always promote individual well-being or resilience under stress? Community psychologists and others may romanticize the idea of sense of community. In many circumstances, it is true that a strongly positive sense of community benefits the individual. Yet it is also clear from Brodsky's findings that sometimes a negative psychological sense of community better promotes well-being.

Multiple Communities in a Person's Life

Individuals belong to many communities (Hunter & Riger, 1986). We form multiple identities as members of multiple communities, such as student, employee, family member, and neighbor. Multiple commitments compete for our time and energy or conflict in important ways. A student may experience a sense of belonging both to the college in which she is enrolled and to her hometown or neighborhood, with friends in both, yet neither of these communities may appreciate her loyalty to the other. Individual adult life is often filled with multiple identities in multiple communities, and balancing of commitments among them. On the other hand, some communities in our lives revitalize us, providing resources and energy for involvement in other communities. Spiritual and mutual help communities can have this effect, but so can an exercise class or musical group. The key to understanding multiple community membership is the role of each community in a person's life. Individuals choose how committed they are to the various communities in their lives (Hunter & Riger, 1986). Community psychology is only beginning to study how these multiple communities interact (Brodsky et al., 2002).

Conflict and Change within a Community

> The psychological sense of community has a virtuous sound, stimulating as it does visions of togetherness and cooperation uncluttered by conflict, controversy and divisiveness. Such visions are hard to resist, but they must be resisted because they are illusory. (Sarason, 1974, p. 11)

Because members of a community also participate in other communities and have multiple identities, diverse **subcommunities** (smaller groups) emerge within a community. Examples include the various communities and identities of students in a college, or residents of various ethnicities or religions in a neighborhood. This diversity can be a strength for a community, but only if it is recognized and valued (Trickett, 1996).

An emphasis on the similarities without attending to the differences in a community is what Wiesenfeld (1996) termed the **myth of "we"** in a community. Romanticizing the psychological sense of community, without recognizing diversity within a community, supports the myth of "we." Wiesenfeld also termed the community's overall shared sense of community as **macrobelonging,** while the diverse other identities or connections that its members have are **microbelongings.** Research on sense of community has focused on macrobelonging, and is only beginning to study diversity of microbelongings.

An example of the myth of "we" occurred among residents of four southeastern U.S. cities in response to Hurricane Hugo (Kaniasty & Norris, 1995). After the hurricane, these communities seemed to unite to help each other. Overall, citizens who suffered greater loss and personal harm received greater amounts of social support from others. A sense of "we" did exist within these communities. However, some groups received less support, especially if they suffered greater harm: African Americans, persons with less education, and unmarried persons. In action, the sense of "we" did not include the entire community. Similar patterns have occurred following other disasters in the U.S. (Kaniasty & Norris, 1995).

Subcommunities based on microbelongings can create conflict. Yet that is where constructive community change often begins (Wiesenfeld, 1996). For instance, the societal transformations of the civil rights movement and the women's movement in the United States began with subcommunities, especially African Americans and women, within the nation and within local communities.

Without attention to microbelongings, conflict, and change, sense of community can become a static concept, supporting an unjust status quo instead of showing the way to constructive social change (see Fisher & Sonn, 2002; Rudkin, 2003). Ignoring conflict, stifling dissent, or excluding subcommunities eventually undermines a community, but constructive resolution of conflict (with attention to microbelongings *and* macrobelonging) can strengthen it.

> A community has changed, is changing, and will change again. (Sarason, 1974, p. 131)

Change is inevitable for communities. Sense of community ultimately is a process. For instance, Loomis, Dockett, and Brodsky (2004) found that it rose among students at one university in response to an external threat, then subsided later. Fisher and Sonn (2002) thoughtfully discuss conflict and change regarding what it means to be an Australian. Similar issues arise in communities at many levels: What does it mean to be a member of this community? How does that reflect the diversity within this community? How do we respond to the challenges of ongoing change?

External Relationships

A danger of strengthening sense of community is the potential that it may increase conflict *between* communities, especially by encouraging prejudice or hostility toward others. Sense of community may be strong in communities that scapegoat outsiders, or in privileged communities that deny problems of poverty and injustice, or in groups whose values are repugnant to many others, such as neo-Nazi or vigilante groups or youth gangs (McMillan & Chavis, 1986, p. 20; Sarason, 1974). This issue is one reason why we asked you to consider an instance of being excluded or treated unjustly by a community in the opening exercise.

These issues concern external relationships between communities. Communities influence other communities, are influenced by them, and are influenced by macrosystems (Hughey & Speer, 2002; Hunter & Riger, 1986). However, those external relationships are not explicitly addressed in the four McMillan-Chavis elements of sense of community, which focus on the internal dynamics of a community. McMillan and Chavis (1986) concluded with a call for building "free, open, accepting" communities, "based on faith, hope, and tolerance" and using sense of community "as a tool for fostering understanding and cooperation" (p. 20). Their model has been used to pursue those important values. However, because it focuses on the internal dynamics of communities, the model does not provide explicit conceptual guidance for that pursuit.

For a practical example of these issues, imagine that you are approached for help with community development by a neighborhood organization whose members are all European Americans. You soon learn that their underlying aim is to exclude persons of color (especially African Americans and Latinos/as) from moving into their neighborhood. Unless those exclusionary aims are changed, strengthening sense of community within the neighborhood would have racist effects (Chavis, personal communication, October, 1987). This dilemma reflects a potential conflict between core values of community psychology: sense of community in one neighborhood versus social justice and respect for human diversity (and, ultimately, individual wellness of all). An ethical response would be to decline to work with the organization unless it genuinely renounced its exclusionary aims.

Constructive change within a community often comes through connections with other communities, through the perspectives of citizens with microbelongings. For instance, the primary author of this chapter (Jim Dalton) grew up in a rural Appalachian community with a strong sense of macrobelonging. Its citizens also had identities based on microbelongings. A historically important transformation there was school desegregation, initiated through a lawsuit by local African-American NAACP members supported by their national organization. Ultimately a federal court imposed desegregation. Community transformation was linked to microbelongings, other communities, and macrosystems.

The issues that we have just discussed involve balancing sense of community, as a value, with other values. Newbrough (1995) argued that traditional concepts of community do not address issues of justice and equality. He proposed a concept of the **just community,** whose members would seek to balance values of community, individual liberty, and equality (social justice), both within the community and in relations with the wider world. His view raises questions such as: How much concern does a community have for other communities? For its own diverse subcommunities and individual members? How is that concern expressed in action?

CONCEPTS RELATED TO SENSE OF COMMUNITY

Sense of community, at individual and community levels, is related to a number of other concepts. We next discuss several of these.

Competent Communities

The concept of a competent community (Cottrell, 1976; Iscoe, 1974) refers to a set of ideal community characteristics for addressing community issues and making decisions. It addresses several issues just discussed.

From his experience in community development, Cottrell (1976) proposed a list of characteristics of a competent community (see Table 6.2). He emphasized the ability of community members to articulate their views and those of their subcommunity, understand the views of other subcommunities, recognize

TABLE 6.2 Qualities of the Competent Community

1. Commitment

Individuals are motivated to engage in shared community work. Community and individuals influence each other.

2. Self-other awareness

Members clearly understand their own and their subgroup's interests and views along with those of other members and subgroups.

3. Articulateness

Members have the ability to state clearly their or their subgroup's views and interests.

4. Communication

Ideas and terms with a shared meaning are used to communicate within the community. These are based on understanding multiple perspectives within the group and lead to genuine collaboration among members and subgroups.

5. Conflict containment and accommodation

A set of agreed-upon procedures exists to recognize and manage conflicts within the community.

6. Participation in decision making

A set of agreed-upon procedures enables members to participate actively in community goal setting, decision making, and implementing of plans.

7. Management of relations with larger society

The community identifies and uses external resources and responds to external demands or threats.

8. Utilization of resources

The community makes the best use of resources and skills among community members and those acquired externally.

9. Socialization for leadership

Work is conducted so that citizens learn skills for participation, leadership, and exercising power and responsibility. This includes transferring power while managing conflict.

10. Evaluation

Action research is conducted on community issues, and effectiveness of programs and policies is evaluated, with use of feedback for improvement.

SOURCE: Items 1–7 are based on Cottrell (1976); items 8–10 are based on Iscoe (1974).

and actively manage conflicts, build mechanisms for true citizen participation in community decisions, and manage relations with other communities and society. These qualities go beyond the McMillan-Chavis model, recognizing the importance of subcommunities (microbelongings), conflict, communication, and external relations. Cottrell also recognized the need for developing citizen leadership skills (e.g., communication, representing a subcommunity). Goeppinger and Baglioni (1985) published a scale to measure Cottrell's concepts.

Citing Cottrell's earlier work, Iscoe (1974) offered three additional concepts. He emphasized identifying and using all the resources available to a community. Iscoe also was concerned with developing citizen leadership, especially the transition of power as community members assume more control over their communities. He also emphasized the importance of action and evaluation research useful for community decisions.

Other Related Concepts

Neighboring Perkins and Long (2002, p. 295) define this as informal contacts and assistance among neighbors. In their view, it involves specific behaviors, while sense of community is strongly emotional and cognitive. It also refers to personal interaction among neighbors, not to participation in neighborhood associations. For instance, in a study of neighboring, Unger and Wandersman (1983, p. 295) asked residents of city blocks: How many of the people on this block would you:

- know by name?
- feel comfortable asking to borrow some food or a tool?
- feel comfortable asking to watch your house while you're away?
- feel comfortable asking for a ride when your car is not working?

Neighboring often occurs between persons who are not close friends but acquainted sufficiently to pass on information and news, recognize mutual interests as neighbors, and provide limited assistance. These contribute to integration and fulfillment of needs. Yet they can occur to some extent even in neighborhoods with little sense of community, and between neighbors who feel little connection to the wider community. Neighboring thus overlaps with sense of community, but can be understood as distinct from it. One study found that Italian localities differed in how closely these two concepts were related (Prezza, Amici, Roberti, & Tedeschi, 2001).

Place Attachment Seldom studied by community psychologists yet important for locality-based communities, this refers to emotional bonding to a particular physical environment and usually to the social ties one has there (Perkins & Long, 2002, pp. 296–297). Environments may vary in scale: a room, a building, a street corner's public space, a neighborhood or college campus, or a hometown or region. In a religious congregation, for instance, the physical space of worship with a cherished community, involving shared rituals and spiritual meaning, evokes both place attachment and sense of community. A research team's meeting room described by Brodsky et al. (2004) is also an example of the importance of place. Neighborhood sense of community is anchored in places there. Even sense of community for an ethnic or national group is often related to a geographic place as well as a society or culture (e.g., Sonn, 2002). These remarks by a geographer express the emotional and social power of places:

> Our lives are full of events that take place, in place.... Places are socially constructed; at the same time they have a physicality and an ecological

> history. . . . Places are charged with energy; they are full of stories that anchor the memories that shape our individual and collective identities. (Flad, 2003)

Citizen Participation As we discussed in Chapter 1, this means having a voice and influence in community decision making. It involves community decisions, not simply community service. Sense of community is a strong predictor of citizen participation in neighborhood associations (Perkins & Long, 2002; Saegert & Winkel, 2004; Wandersman & Florin, 2000). However, citizens may participate in community decisions even if they do not share a strong positive sense of community, so citizen participation can be considered distinct from sense of community. We will discuss citizen participation in detail in Chapter 12.

Social Support This is help provided by others to promote coping with stress. Social support and sense of community overlap but also differ. Certainly a group with a strong sense of community will provide social support; this is one aspect of integration and fulfillment of needs. However, the community in which one feels a sense of belongingness may be much larger, less intimate, than the immediate network of persons who provide support for coping with a specific stressor. Also, sense of community is not solely a resource for coping, but is also related to other important processes, including citizen participation. In Chapter 8, we will discuss social support in detail.

SOCIAL CAPITAL

> If the crime rate in my neighborhood is lowered by neighbors keeping an eye on one another's homes, I benefit even if I personally spend most of my time on the road and never even nod to another resident on the street. (Putnam, 2000, p. 20)

Social capital is probably the best-known concept closely related to sense of community. As we noted early in this chapter, in *Bowling Alone* (2000), Robert Putnam marshaled broad evidence to argue that community ties and civic engagement in the United States have been steadily declining for 30–40 years. His research found declines in involvement in civic associations, political participation, religious congregations, charitable giving, and even trust in fellow citizens. Putnam documented what many had suspected and renewed debates on quality of community life.

Putnam also attempted to explain the causes of this decline. He documented the community involvement of what he termed the "long civic generation" who came of age during the Great Depression and World War II and the failure of succeeding generations to match that commitment. He also identified the rise of television, suburban sprawl and commuting, and increased work time and strain as important contributing factors. These findings, although only suggestive, struck important nerves in the U.S. public. Even if they blamed different causes, diverse social and political observers agreed that Putnam's findings were important.

The evidence that Putnam cited is not the whole picture. Local communities are building social capital, sense of community, and other community strengths (e.g., Perkins, Crim, Silberman, & Brown, 2004; Putnam & Feldstein, 2003; Saegert, Thompson, & Warren, 2001; Wolff, 2001a). We will describe these in Chapters 12 and 13. In this section we will focus on what social capital means and how it is related to sense of community.

Putnam's Social Capital Concepts

The term **social capital** has been used in education, economics, sociology, and political science (Putnam's discipline), but not until *Bowling Alone* did the idea gain wide public interest or much notice in psychology. Putnam defined it thus:

> Social capital refers to connections among individuals—social networks and the norms of reciprocity and trustworthiness that arise from them. . . . civic virtue is most powerful when embedded in a dense network of reciprocal social relations. (Putnam, 2000, p. 19)

This definition makes an analogy to financial capital while highlighting resources that are social, neither material assets nor individual skills or qualities. (Note that this economic analogy risks overlooking the human essence of communities.) Those resources are based in interpersonal relationships, both personal ties and involvement in the wider community. Putnam's definition refers primarily to more objective social connections and secondarily to a more subjective sense of trust (similar to sense of community). His work primarily has concerned localities.

Putnam did not measure social networks directly, instead focusing on behavioral indicators of community involvement measured through surveys, time diaries, and organizational and community records. His analyses of social capital focused mainly on five behavioral forms of community participation: political, local-civic, religious, socializing and neighboring, and community service. (These can overlap, of course.)

Putnam is especially concerned with face-to-face involvement that strengthens relationships and communication about community life. Involvement may be **formal,** through community organizations, or **informal,** through friendships, neighboring, and other social contacts. He relishes the Yiddish distinction between *machers,* persons who make things happen through formal community organizations, and *schmoozers,* who involve themselves in networks of informal contacts. Both create important forms of social capital (Putnam, 2000).

Bonding and Bridging This is a key distinction (Putnam, 2000, pp. 22–23). **Bonding** refers to creating and maintaining strong social-emotional ties, usually in groups of similar persons that provide belongingness, emotional support, and mutual commitment. These internal ties underlie a sense of community and shared identity. Their limitations often are a lack of diversity of members or views and exclusion of outsiders.

Bridging, by contrast, refers to creating and maintaining links between groups or communities. Bridging ties reach out to a broader set of persons than bonding and involve links among people whose life experiences may be very different. Bridging ties are useful especially when diverse groups face a common challenge and need to work together.

Bridging relationships often have what Granovetter (1973) termed the **strength of weak ties.** These are relationships between persons who are not close friends but acquainted sufficiently to recognize mutual interests, pass on information about the community, and act together when needed. A person may bridge by cultivating relationships with people in two different factions, groups, or communities. A community coalition to promote positive youth development may bridge by bringing together persons from diverse parts of the locality, such as schools, religious congregations, police, recreation groups, diverse racial or ethnic communities, and youth themselves. Bridging links also can help a group obtain access to key decision makers in a locality in order to make their concerns heard (Bond & Keys, 1993; Hughey & Speer, 2002). Bonding ties alone seldom accomplish these objectives.

The strengths of bridging links are their reach or breadth of contacts, access to a diversity of views and resources, and ability to support wider community collaboration. However, they seldom offer the sense of community that occurs in bonding groups. Both types of social capital are important. Some relationships or groups can have elements of both. For example, a religious congregation or a community coalition that brings together persons across lines of social class and race, yet builds a sense of shared community, is both bridging and bonding.

Putnam's findings suggest that bridging social capital is weakening in the United States. For instance, involvement is declining in local civic groups and community organizations, where persons are likely to encounter and have to work with others who hold different views. The growing forms of community that Putnam identified often emphasize bonding rather than bridging: small mutual help and religious groups, online communities, and political and religious advocacy groups that rally the like minded (Putnam, 2000, chap. 9). In his findings, only a trend of increasing community service by youth and retirees involves bridging.

Research on Social Capital

Is social capital empirically related to quality of individual and community life? Putnam (2000) presents analyses that go beyond what psychologists often study.

For instance, Putnam's research team compared 48 U.S. states, using a state-level index of social capital compiled from two sources: representative surveys of citizens about formal and informal community involvement and general trust in others, and state-level indicators of citizen participation and community organizations (Putnam, 2000, p. 291). (Alaska, Hawai'i, and the District of Columbia were omitted (p. 487); all are culturally diverse and would have added valuable perspective.) The researchers compared this index to several state-level indexes of social well-being.

Social capital was strongly positively related to differences among states in the widely used Kids Count Index of child health and well-being as well as in educational achievement on standardized tests (Putnam, 2000, pp. 297–300). Among a large set of social variables, social capital was second only to statewide poverty level in predicting these and other outcomes. It also was associated with lower state murder rates. Studies comparing neighborhoods showed that social capital (especially enforcement of informal social norms against violence) is stronger in less violent neighborhoods (pp. 308, 313–314).

State-level social capital was strongly related to an index of overall public health (p. 328). Putnam also reviewed research in psychology, public health, and other fields on social integration and social support, concluding that these are forms of social capital. These protective factors reduce the risk of illness as much as that risk is increased by smoking, obesity, high blood pressure, and lack of exercise (pp. 326–327).

> The more integrated we are with our community, the less likely we are to experience colds, heart attacks, strokes, cancer, depression, and premature death of all sorts. Such protective effects have been confirmed for close family ties, for friendship networks, for participation in social events, and even for simple affiliation with religious and other civic associations. (Putnam, 2000, p. 326)

Incorporating the social support literature illustrates the creative breadth of the social capital concept. Yet differences between social support and wider social capital and sense of community must be kept in mind, as we discussed earlier. The Saguaro Seminar website (listed at the end of the chapter) describes recent findings on social capital.

An Example of Community Psychology Research on Social Capital Community psychologists have begun to adopt the concept of social capital. For instance, Perkins and Long (2002) propose a psychological definition of neighborhood social capital composed of four elements: sense of community, neighboring, and citizen participation (covered earlier in this chapter), and sense of collective efficacy (the belief that neighbors acting together can improve community life). They analyzed data from a study of New York City neighborhoods, finding these four elements to be generally interrelated. Sense of community was significantly related to all three other factors.

Strengths and Limitations of Putnam's Perspective

Putnam (2000) identifies broad trends and calls attention to important forces in communities and societies. His work is important because of its scope, interdisciplinary perspective, and public impact. It complements and extends the thinking of community psychology.

However, Putnam's "high-altitude" breadth of perspective limits sensitivity to context. Much of his team's research compares levels of social capital, aggregated across many types of community involvement, comparing U.S. states. Gender, social class and income, race and ethnicity, culture, urban-suburban-rural contexts, and other dimensions of human diversity certainly influence social capital, but these are seldom in focus in Putnam's analyses. Often they are considered competing explanations to be statistically controlled, not studied in their own right or for how they interact with social capital in specific communities. This focus also does not consider how forms of social capital differ for issues as different as child health and political participation. A later collection of case studies in specific communities addressed some of these limitations (Putnam & Feldstein, 2003).

A second issue is that Putnam's (2000) analyses include data from a number of sources collected in different contexts and not originally designed to measure the concept of social capital. One example, already noted, is incorporating findings on social support and health. As we have discussed, this breadth of usage can be creative, but also can gloss over important differences in meaning.

Finally, an emphasis on local social capital (or local sense of community) can lead to underestimating the importance of macrosystem factors. Corporate decisions, losses of federal funding for effective programs such as Head Start, and other macrosystem forces do affect community life. Strengthening local social capital is certainly important for addressing community problems. Yet in many communities, local resources cannot do it all. Broader social change is also important to address social problems and injustices.

BUILDING COMMUNITIES: THREE EXAMPLES

To illustrate the concepts in this chapter, we now turn to three extended examples of communities and community building: spiritual communities, community service learning, and online communities. Keep in mind, however, that these are only some examples of the diversity of human communities.

Spirituality, Religion, and Communities

> The beauty of the religious and spiritual impulse, at its best, is the humility, person-affirmation, service-orientation, and mainstream culture-challenge which it can engender, along with a glimpse of the reality that we all are part of a larger whole, each of us (and each subgroup) valuable, necessary, and interdependent. (Maton, 2001, p. 611)

Spiritual communities play important roles in community life. They provide sense of community at microsystem, organizational, locality, and macrosystem levels. Their holistic perspectives integrate spiritual, emotional, cognitive, and social aspects of personal life (Mattis & Jagers, 2001). Sarason (1993) noted that sense of community throughout history has usually been inextricably tied to a sense of the transcendent, of spiritual experience beyond oneself and one's immediate world. He asked whether modern forms of community could be sustained without that sense of transcendence. Because of its holistic significance for human and community development, some assert that "spirituality is integral to community psychology as a human science" (Dokecki, Newbrough, & O'Gorman, 2001, p. 499).

U.S. poll respondents have more confidence in religious institutions than any other social institution. Over one-third of volunteer activity is based in religious congregations, and congregations contribute more money to community causes than corporations do (Pargament & Maton, 2000). Spirituality and religion have played important roles in survival of oppressed groups. Spiritual beliefs, practices and communities provide important resources for finding meaning in living and coping with stressors. They comprise important forms of community, contribute important resources to society, and advocate for social justice. Their importance is increasingly recognized in community psychology (e.g., Hill, 1996, 2000; Kloos & Moore, 2000a,b, 2001; Mankowski & Rappaport, 2000a; Maton & Wells, 1995; Pargament, 1997; Pargament & Maton, 2000).

However, the impact of religious and spiritual traditions is not always positive. History reveals many examples of religious exclusion and oppression. Research has indicated that some especially religious U.S. college students are more prejudiced than other students against African Americans, women, gay men, lesbians, and others (Hunsberger, 1995; Pargament, 1997, p. 352; Waldo et al., 1998). As in other communities, religious and spiritual traditions as well as local congregations can have positive and negative effects on persons, communities, and societies (Brodsky, 2000, 2003; Martin-Baro, 1990; Pargament, 1997; Ventis, 1995).

In this section and throughout this book, we define **spirituality** inclusively as beliefs, practices, and communities associated with a personally meaningful sense of transcendence beyond oneself and one's immediate world. This includes but is not limited to religious traditions worshiping a supernatural deity (Hill, 2000; Kloos & Moore, 2000b). Although over 90 percent of U.S. poll respondents believe in God or a higher power, many of them do not associate themselves with religious institutions, and a sizable minority consider themselves spiritual but not religious (Hill, 2000; Pargament & Maton, 2000). Hill (2000, pp. 145—146) defined spirituality as a sense of connection to the human and natural worlds, and awe at mysteries beyond our comprehension. Additional definitions of spirituality include "exploring what it means to be fully human" (McFague, cited in Dokecki et al., 2001, p. 498), and the "search for the sacred" (Hill & Pargament, 2003, p. 65). Rasmussen, following theologian Paul Tillich, defined religion as concerning "ultimate meaning in universal life experiences" (Moore, Kloos, & Rasmussen, 2001, p. 490). As with concepts of community, definitions differ, yet this can be a strength if carefully understood. Community psychologists are concerned with spirituality as expressed in communion with others, not simply individual belief or practice. We use the inclusive term

spiritual communities to refer to religious or spiritual or faith-based institutions, organizations, or settings.

Spiritual communities differ in whether they focus on matters of belief, spiritual experience, or action. Some are primarily concerned with personal salvation, others with broader spiritual growth, community bonding, social service ministries, or prophetic calls for social justice. Many differences are subtle (Kress & Elias, 2000). Examples of spiritual communities studied by community psychologists have included:

- Afrocentric spiritual perspectives (Myers & Speight, 1994)
- spirituality in Native American cultures (Hazel & Mohatt, 2001; Walsh-Bowers, 2000)
- women's spirituality (Molock & Douglas, 1999; Mulvey, Gridley, & Gawith, 2001)
- twelve-step mutual help groups (Humphreys, 2000)
- communities within Judaism, Christianity, Islam, and Buddhism (Abdul-Adil & Jason, 1991; Dockett, 1999; Dokecki et al., 2001; Kress & Elias, 2000; Mattis & Jagers, 2001; Stuber, 2000).

How Are Spiritual Communities Involved in Community Life? Spirituality serves five important community functions (Kloos & Moore, 2000b; Pargament & Maton, 2000). First, it helps meet primary human needs for finding meaning in everyday life (Frankl, 1959/1984; Pargament, 1997). Spirituality provides solace in the face of uncontrollable circumstances and guides active coping with controllable ones. A sense of transcendence provides a way to understand one's life, while spiritual values provide guides for living.

Second, spiritual communities provide sense of community and meet primary human needs for belonging. Many can be described in terms of the four McMillan-Chavis elements. They provide a sense of membership through common rituals and symbols, including rites of passage for membership. These rituals also foster identification with the community. Emotional safety is provided through small-group and one-to-one sharing. The formation of a religious identity can be an important social identity, fostered by multiple religious contexts (Kress & Elias, 2000).

Spiritual communities also foster mutual influence as well as integration and fulfillment of needs. Shared spiritual practices influence individual decisions. In turn, many spiritual settings provide opportunities for members' participation in leadership and decision making (Maton & Salem, 1995). Members of a spiritual community help meet each other's interpersonal, economic, psychological, and spiritual needs. Finally, spiritual communities foster emotional and spiritual bonds based on a deeply shared sense of spiritual transcendence. Small groups, religious education classes, and shared worship foster community (Wuthnow, 1994). Saddleback Church in California, for instance, a congregation of thousands, has many small groups that involve members in face-to-face communities (Putnam & Feldstein, 2003).

Third, spiritual communities provide important community services. Religious involvement among teens and adults has been shown in research to protect against risky behavior and promote well-being (Kloos & Moore, 2000a; Kress & Elias, 2000; Steinman & Zimmerman, 2004). Spiritual communities offer supports for families, parents, and marital partners, including workshops, small-group meetings, and counseling. Many other community services have religious-spiritual bases, from soup kitchens to Habitat for Humanity. The Caroline Center, operated by sisters of a Roman Catholic order, provides job training and an important community for low-income Baltimore women (Brodsky & Marx, 2001). Twelve-step mutual help groups are common and effective forms of healing (Humphreys, 2000). Programs to promote sobriety in Alaska Native communities involve indigenous Native spiritual concepts (Hazel & Mohatt, 2001).

Fourth, spiritual communities are especially valuable for members of oppressed, disenfranchised populations, who lack resources and power in society. These have included, for instance, Native Americans, African Americans and other peoples of color, gay and lesbian individuals, the economically oppressed, and women (Hazel & Mohatt, 2001; Mattis & Jagers, 2001; Potts, 1999; Rappaport, 2000).

Fifth, spiritual communities challenge forces in mainstream culture. In Western cultures, they help to counterbalance mainstream values of individualism and materialism through concern for the public good, for the disenfranchised and for social justice, and for values of compassion and service. Social advocacy, one way that spiritual perspectives challenge mainstream culture, includes public positions taken by nationwide religious institutions and community-level efforts by local faith-based groups (Maton, 2000; 2001). For example, the U.S. civil rights movement involved many faith-based social change initiatives. Community organizing for social justice, based in faith communities, has achieved substantive community changes (Putnam & Feldstein, 2003; Speer, Hughey, Gensheimer, & Adams-Leavitt, 1995). "Basic ecclesial communities" are small spiritual groups that meet for worship, interpersonal support, reflection on spiritual ideals, and taking collective action for social justice and community development (Dokecki et al., 2001; Trout, Dokecki, Newbrough, & O'Gorman, 2003). Not surprisingly, many examples of faith-based advocacy arise among members of oppressed populations.

Of course, some spiritual communities focus on individual salvation or spiritual development, or on community building within the congregation, having little impact on wider community life. Yet when one considers all spiritual communities, these five functions are important contributions to communities and societies.

Narratives, Identity, and Meaning-Making in Spiritual Communities Spiritual and religious narratives express important ideals and build spiritual bonds (Mankowski & Rappaport, 2000a; Rappaport, 2000). The narrative of Passover and the Exodus in Jewish tradition; the ministry, death, and resurrection of Jesus in Christian tradition; and Muhammad's encounters with the angel, call to prophecy, and ascension into heaven in Islamic tradition are examples. Numerous parables in these and other faiths are ways of teaching through narratives.

Spiritual narratives provide resources for individuals seeking to understand their own life experiences (stories). This is especially important at life transitions or when a person or group is demeaned in dominant cultural narratives. For college students questioning their beliefs or struggling with choices, a campus ministry that interprets such questioning as a basis for growth thus provides a positive way of understanding one's own experiences (Mankowski & Thomas, 2000). To an alcoholic who has hit bottom, twelve-step principles offer a community narrative that explains his or her descent into alcoholism and offers a path to recovery validated by other group members' experiences (Humphreys, 2000). To persons wounded by past trauma, many spiritual settings provide narratives of healing and redemption. To spiritual gay men and lesbians, a congregation that offers a positive, strengths-based perspective on their sexuality and spirituality provides a safe haven and a place for spiritual growth. To persons experiencing serious mental illness, a mutual help group offers a focus on strengths and practical coping (Rappaport, 2000).

Spiritual narratives are vessels that carry meaning and values, communicating them to individuals and supporting their personal growth (Stuber, 2000). Meaning-making in spiritual communities can lead to personal and to social transformation. Kenneth Maton, a community psychologist long involved in research with spiritual communities, argued for their importance:

> . . . without incorporating the religious and spiritual domains of the larger community, prevention, empowerment-oriented, and other social action efforts stand little hope of mobilizing the resources, building the scale, and challenging mainstream culture in the ways necessary to make any truly substantive difference in our social problems. (Maton, 2001, p. 610)

Community Service Learning

Community service, unpaid work for community betterment, is increasing in the United States among youth and retirees (Putnam, 2000; Stukas & Dunlap, 2002). Community service learning occurs when educational requirements for community service include a reflective component in which the student writes about or discusses what he or she learned (Eyler, 2002).

The most engaged form of community service learning builds and sustains personal relationships among persons with different life experiences across lines of social class, race, age, culture, or other boundaries. This can strengthen mutual understanding and broaden community ties—bridging social capital that can connect the privileged and the marginalized (Putnam, 2000; Wuthnow, 2002). Settings where this can occur include, for instance, youth development and mentoring programs, tutoring in schools, adult literacy programs, companionship pairings with persons with mental illnesses, and community organizing work. This approach to community service learning builds sense of community:

enlarging boundaries of whom one perceives as a member of one's community; fulfilling mutual needs as service is provided and learning occurs; and often building a shared emotional connection.

Community service, especially service learning linked to an academic course, leads to a number of positive outcomes for students (Astin, Vogelsang, Ikeda, & Yee, 2000; Eyler, 2002; Stukas & Dunlap, 2002):

- learning about another culture, community, or group
- personal-emotional rewards of helping and/or friendship
- increased awareness of personal values, especially sense of social responsibility
- increased skills in analyzing and addressing complex social issues
- increased skills and confidence for community involvement and leadership;
- awareness of privileges and resources that one may have taken for granted
- broader sense of community and interdependence with others
- greater awareness of social issues and willingness to act for social change

Students in the authors' classes frequently report on the value and emotional meaning of community service, involving contacts with persons they otherwise would never have met. College students who volunteered in the community are more likely to become involved in their communities after graduation (Eyler, 2002). Students who engaged in extensive service learning perceived an intertwining of personal growth and service in their own lives (Singer, King, Green, & Barr, 2002).

Few studies have assessed how the relationship affects recipients of community service (Stukas & Dunlap, 2002). Effective community service learning, as with any community-building action, requires attention to relationships between providers and recipients of service (Bringle & Hatcher, 2002; Nadler, 2002). Several approaches can help make the relationship more mutual, a two-way street. Allowing choices to be made by recipients is one step. Creating opportunities for recipients to teach providers in some way is another (interviewing recipients as resources for class papers can be a method for this). Involving recipients of service in planning and evaluating of service (e.g., helping to plan a project; contributing to a discussion of lessons learned) is a further step. Creating enduring relationships, between an individual student and recipient or through continuing involvement of students in a service setting, also builds mutuality. These steps can also deepen the learning component for students by expanding their opportunities for learning from recipients (Eyler, 2002; Werner, Voce, Openshaw, & Simons, 2002).

Online Communities

New forms of community are emerging online: chat rooms, discussion forums, electronic bulletin boards, listservs, and multiuser object oriented (MOO) environments, in which members create characters and interact with each other

(Roberts, Smith, & Pollock, 2002). An online community may be said to exist when "people carry on public discussions long enough, with sufficient human feeling, to form webs of personal relationships in cyberspace" (Rheingold, 1994, cited in Roberts et al., 2002, p. 225). Of course, many people communicate online with others they already know (e.g., instant messaging, e-mail), an important link in busy lives that maintains existing communities. What is new occurs when strangers meet and build community online.

Some online communities are tied to an existing locality and build community ties among citizens there: e.g., Craigslist.org. A mainly relational online community can arrange local events where members meet personally, such as the meetups hosted by the political organization MoveOn.org. Other online communities are purely relational, with membership that can be worldwide.

Roberts et al. (2002) interviewed, online, a sample of individuals in MOO environments. Most believed that their MOO had a positive sense of community. Respondents' comments fit each of the four McMillan-Chavis elements of sense of community. Boundaries are enforced by membership requirements for MOO members and for the fictional characters they create. MOO communities have mechanisms for excluding members whose online behavior does not match community norms. The MOO programming language, and the jargon that develops in conversation, are common symbol systems. In the MOOs studied, there are offices and decision-making procedures allowing mutual influence, and mutual helping occurs (online and in person) that represents integration. MOO users reported strong shared emotional connection. Roberts et al. concluded that MOO environments were a relational community with a shared sense of community.

In online mutual help groups, individuals with a shared problem or concern (e.g., breast cancer, problem drinking) help each other online. This facilitates support among persons unable to attend face-to-face mutual help groups and those who feel especially stigmatized, out of place, or reluctant to attend in person. Research indicates that helping in online mutual help settings resembles helping in face-to-face groups. We will discuss this form of support in more detail in Chapter 8.

Craigslist.org started in San Francisco as e-mail messages from Craig Newmark to his friends about events that he thought they would be interested in. It has evolved to online settings in 175 localities in 34 countries (as of May 2005), with listings for jobs, housing, roommates, community events and information, personal ads, and other categories (Craigslist Online Community, May 2005). It is avowedly noncommercial, providing information for free (job listings do cost advertisers, but not readers), and emphasizing an atmosphere of person-to-person contact. Many Craigslist users become loyal members of what they consider a community with a shared emotional connection, user jargon, and mutual helping. Behavioral norms are enforced; a posting that receives a set number of "flags" (objections) from site visitors is automatically removed. Although individuals visit, not join, local Craiglists, they appear to have many elements of a relational community and locality-based qualities as well (Putnam & Feldstein, 2003, ch. 11).

Online communities can be used for community development and change:

> After taking a cold outdoor shower at the beach one morning . . . a homeless resident of Santa Monica, California discovered that his sweater had been stolen from its overnight hiding place. Using a computer terminal in the public library to access the city's Public Electronic Network (PEN), he asked if anyone could give him another. An affluent PEN user living nearby read his request and met him at the public library with a sweater, soap and razor.
>
> Though they had never met, these two Santa Monica residents were not strangers. They and scores of other had corresponded electronically for several months in a PEN conference item on homelessness. Soon thereafter, this unlikely pair used PEN to convene a face-to-face meeting of those who would develop an action strategy for grassroots change in Santa Monica. (Wittig & Schmitz, 1996, pp. 53–54)

PEN was the first local, public (government-funded; free to users) interactive electronic communication system in the U.S. The PEN Action Group spanned boundaries of social class, education, race and neighborhood. Its diverse members worked together to influence city government decisions, succeeding in establishing a homeless center and a job placement service for homeless persons. For some Action Group members, this was their first experience in citizen activism. Santa Monica's PEN illustrates the democratic, equalizing potential of online communication for citizen participation in collective decision making. Homeless and homed persons were able to hold dialogues, agree on shared goals, and pursue them with collective actions (Wittig & Schmitz, 1996). PEN also illustrates how sense of community, first formed online, can catalyze locality-level change.

Online communities have several advantages for community building. They can transcend geographic distance and social status boundaries. They offer choice for individuals in finding a community and sense of belongingness. The lack of nonverbal communication can be an advantage: stereotypes related to appearance are lessened when race, social class, attractiveness, age, and even gender are unclear. This can facilitate more democratic relationships and power sharing. Lack of nonverbal cues can also be a disadvantage: communication of emotion is more difficult and easily misunderstood. The anonymity of much online communication is a strength and a drawback: it can allow heavily stigmatized individuals to self-disclose and form supportive relationships, but it also can lead to exploitation, mistrust and rudeness ("flaming") (See Center for Safe and Responsible Internet Use, http://csriu.org). Boundaries for membership and behavioral rules must be established somehow for online communities as they are for face-to-face groups and localities. Online communities represent an important new form of community, which can be linked with existing communities or create new ones (Putnam & Feldstein, 2003; Rudkin, 2003).

CONCLUSION

Concepts of community lie at the heart of community psychology yet also involve the questions, issues, and values we have discussed. This chapter is only an introduction to use of these concepts. In later chapters we will discuss in detail other forms of community, such as mutual help groups (Chapter 8) and related topics such as human diversity (next chapter), citizen participation in communities (Chapter 12), and community and social change (Chapter 13).

CHAPTER SUMMARY

1. Involvement in many forms of community is declining in the United States, but other forms are strengthening. We defined *locality-based* and *relational communities.* Communities exist at different ecological levels: microsystems, organizations, localities, macrosystems. *Mediating structures* provide links between individuals and larger communities or society. We discussed issues in who defines communities and their boundaries.
2. *Sense of community* was first proposed as a key concept for the field by Sarason (1974) and defined in more specific terms by McMillan and Chavis (1986). They identified four elements of sense of community: *Membership, Mutual influence* between individual and community, *Integration and fulfillment of needs* among members, and *Shared emotional connection.* The elements and their attributes are listed in Table 6.1. Research on sense of community demonstrates its importance.
3. Questions remain about the sense of community concept. Does it have the four McMillan-Chavis elements, or others, or does it vary in each community? Does it exist as both an individual cognition and a characteristic of a community? How might narratives reveal sense of community? Rappaport defined *dominant cultural narratives, community narratives,* and *personal stories.* These narratives influence each other.
4. A person can have a *negative psychological sense of community,* and have *multiple psychological senses of community* for the multiple communities in his or her life. Multiple subcommunities often exist within a community. The *myth of "we"* overlooks diversity in a community. The shared sense of community is a *macrobelonging*, the smaller subcommunity memberships are *microbelongings*. A community's *external relationships* with outsiders and other communities are important. Sense of community changes over time. Newbrough's concept of the *just community* balances community, freedom, and equality (social justice).
5. Concepts related to sense of community include *competent communities, neighboring, place attachment, citizen participation,* and *social support.* The characteristics of a competent community are defined in Table 6.2.

6. Putnam's (2000) concept of *social capital* refers to connections among citizens, and reciprocity and trust based on them. It may be *formal* or *informal* and may involve *bonding* or *bridging*. Research on social capital demonstrates its importance for community life and society and reveals that many of its forms are declining in the U.S. and elsewhere. Putnam's perspective has strengths and limitations.
7. Religious and spiritual communities represent an important form of community. We defined *spirituality* more broadly than religion. *Spiritual communities* fulfill five functions in communities: providing meaning, sense of community, community services, resources for the oppressed, and challenges to mainstream culture. Shared narratives in spiritual communities promote these functions.
8. Community service learning often involves bridging social capital and has many benefits for students and communities. On-line communities are a growing form of community.

BRIEF EXERCISES

1. Choose a community in your life that has a strong, positive, shared sense of community. Consider these questions about that community, based on the four McMillan-Chavis elements of sense of community:

   Membership:

   How is membership defined? What else do members have in common?
   Are there common symbols shared by members?
   What investment (material, emotional, other) have you made in this community?
   How deep is your sense of emotional safety in this community?
   Is being a member of this group an important identity for you? How?

   Influence:

   How does being in this community influence you as an individual?
   How much influence do you as an individual have on this community?
   If you wanted to influence a decision in this community, how would you do that?

   Integration:

   How are your individual needs fulfilled in this community?
   How do you help fulfill other members' needs?
   What values are shared in this group?

   Shared Emotional Connection:

   Do you feel an emotional bond with other members of the community? How?
   What rituals, celebrations, or other occasions strengthen community bonds?
   What community narratives are shared in this community?

2. Consider how to apply these social capital concepts to your life:
   Are you personally involved in student or community organizations?
   Are you more of a *macher* or a *schmoozer*? How?
   What weak-tie relationships are important in your life? How?
   What communities or networks in your life are settings where bonding is strong?
   What communities in your life provide bridging among different groups?
   Do you know people who provide important bridging between different communities or networks?
   Have you ever been a member of two groups in conflict and helped them understand each other better?
3. Are you involved in community service of any kind? What have you learned from your community service? What emotions have you experienced about it? Has it broadened your sense of community or your sense of social responsibility? Does it involve bridging relationships?

RECOMMENDED READINGS

Fisher, A., Sonn, C., & Bishop, B. (Eds.) (2002). *Psychological sense of community: Research, applications and implications.* New York: Kluwer Academic/Plenum.

McMillan, D. W., & Chavis, D. M. (1986). Sense of community: A definition and theory. *Journal of Community Psychology, 14,* 6–23.

Putnam, R. (2000). *Bowling alone: The collapse and revival of American community.* New York: Simon & Schuster.

Sarason, S. B. (1974). *The psychological sense of community: Prospects for a community psychology.* San Francisco: Jossey-Bass.

Sarason, S. B. (1993). American psychology, and the needs for transcendence and community. *American Journal of Community Psychology, 21,* 185–202.

RECOMMENDED WEBSITES

Saguaro Seminar www.ksg.harvard.edu/saguaro

Website for research and action initiated by Putnam's (2000) *Bowling Alone.*

INFOTRAC COLLEGE EDITION KEYWORDS

community(ies), (psychological) sense of community, social capital, neighboring, (community) service learning, religious or *spiritual* or *faith(-based)* or *spiritually based settings* or *community(ies)*

7

Understanding Human Diversity

HIRB/Index Stock

OPENING EXERCISE

What is human diversity? Let's begin by performing a simple exercise to place yourself in the "diversity of contexts" (Trickett, 1996) in your life. Describing these will not reflect all of what makes you a unique individual, but it will help you to understand some of the cultural and social forces that influence you every day. We encourage you to discuss your thoughts about these questions with a classmate or friend.

What is your gender? How does this influence, for instance, your everyday behavior, your life (including career) planning, or your approach to emotions, friendships, or intimate relationships?

What is your culture or nationality? What is your first language? How do these factors affect your values, life planning, family relationships, friendships? How much experience have you had with other cultures?

How would you describe your race and ethnicity? How does it influence your life, interactions with strangers or friends, language and speech, life planning, choice of college, friendships? How many meaningful relationships do you have with others of a different race or ethnicity? What are the most important contributions that your racial or ethnic group has made to your society?

How do socioeconomic factors affect your life? How did they affect the nature and quality of education in your home community? Your choice of college, or experiences in college? Has a need to hold a time-consuming job, or another economic stressor, interfered with your schooling? How many of your friends come from socioeconomic circumstances different from yours?

What is your age? How does it affect your everyday life, friendships, life planning, and other choices?

What is your sexual orientation? Has understanding your orientation ever been difficult for you? How does your orientation affect your everyday life, friendships, life planning, and other choices?

Do you have a spiritual belief, practice, or background? If you practice it today, how does your personal spirituality influence your values, daily life, and relationships with others? If you are a member of a faith community, what role does it play in your life? Have your life plans been influenced by your spirituality?

We could write similar questions about physical or mental ability/disability, rural/suburban/urban background, or other forms of diversity. Consider those if they are important in your life.

Every person is involved when we discuss human diversity. We sometimes encounter among students and others the assumption that *diversity* refers only to people not included in a European-American, middle-class, heterosexual norm. Yet everyone has a culture, a race, a gender, a sexual orientation, and a place somewhere on each dimension of human diversity. One goal of this chapter is for you to understand your place, and others' places, on each dimension of human diversity.

Fruitful discussion of diversity takes the perspective of *pluralism,* the idea that no culture or group represents the norm. In a pluralistic perspective, every person, culture, or group has a place on each dimension, but none is superior. Each must be understood on its own terms. This perspective does not define differences as deficits, but searches instead for cultural, community and human strengths revealed in human diversity (Trickett, Watts, & Birman, 1994). That is part of what the value of respect for human diversity means in community psychology.

In this chapter we introduce community psychology conceptions of human diversity. First, we briefly describe some of the dimensions of that diversity. Second, we discuss how cultures can be described along a spectrum of individualism-collectivism and the limitations of that portrayal. Third, human diversity is not only cultural, but also involves issues of social power. We describe concepts of oppression and liberation that involve power. Fourth, we examine acculturation and social identities. Finally, we consider what cultural competence means for community psychologists.

BOX 7.1 The Perspective of This Chapter's Primary Author

To the reader it may seem ironic at best to learn that the primary author of this chapter on human diversity is a European-American man, a university professor who has enjoyed a privileged life in many ways, a native of the Southern Appalachians who has lived almost all his life in rural U.S. (mostly Appalachian) towns. Having come to write this chapter by a mixture of circumstance and choice, that irony is not lost on me. I have had good teachers on issues of diversity, many of them not in academia. I have lived for short periods in multiethnic cities, including an inner-city neighborhood in Newark, New Jersey (a community service learning experience during college), and in Honolulu, Hawai'i. I have a viewpoint on issues of human diversity, particularly oppression, which is based in my experiences and in participation in efforts to dismantle forms of oppression.

A limitation of my perspective is that most of my experience with racism, for instance, has concerned two groups: European Americans and African Americans. My life experience is centered in the United States, a further limitation in understanding world cultures. My perspective on human diversity is still developing and has strengths, drawbacks, and omissions. However, that perspective is supplemented by those of my co-authors and of the reviewers of this textbook. All of these sources have broadened and deepened this chapter. (Jim Dalton)

Throughout this chapter we emphasize the theme that understanding human diversity means studying the lives of others and ourselves from a pluralistic perspective while recognizing how our own values affect our perspective. The meaning of this chapter is dependent on each reader's context and experiences (see Box 7.1). As a team of authors, we invite you to sample the ideas here, measure their meaning against your own experiences, and seek broader experiences that educate you further in issues of human diversity.

KEY DIMENSIONS OF HUMAN DIVERSITY FOR COMMUNITY PSYCHOLOGY

The dimensions we emphasize here certainly do not exhaust all the forms of human diversity, but they do represent concepts frequently addressed in community psychology research and action. Our definitions are brief, designed only to provide an orienting overview. Our major point is that human diversity has multiple dimensions, including ones not listed here.

Culture

"Cultural diversity" has become a buzzword as the world's societies have become more interdependent. The term *culture* has been stretched to refer not only to ethnic and cultural groups but also to nation-states, religious groups, racial groupings, and corporations (Betancourt & Lopez, 1993).

What is culture, and how are cultures diverse? After decades of debate, anthropologists and other social scientists have not settled on a single definition of culture, but certain key elements are identifiable (Lonner, 1994). It does not explain anything to say, "Astrid behaves in a certain way because she is Swedish"

(Lonner, 1994, p. 234). To understand cultural influences on Astrid's actions in a certain situation, we need to specify a Swedish cultural element that shapes her actions in that situation. That element must be reflected in other aspects of Swedish culture. These might include a behavioral norm taught to children, a tradition reflected in literature or in religious or political documents, a concept for which the Swedish language has a word, or a folk saying. Shared language, social roles, and norms for behavior are cultural expressions important to psychologists (Triandis, 1994). Culture is often expressed in what the group seeks to transmit (e.g., by education) to younger generations. In multicultural societies with heterogeneous populations, boundaries between cultural groupings are often somewhat fluid. Culture is an essential dimension for community psychologists to study (O'Donnell, 2005a).

Race

Race has long occupied a *quasi-biological* status in Western psychological thought (Zuckerman, 1990). That quasi-biological definition of race has often provided an intellectual basis for assumptions of racial superiority. Biological and psychological racist assumptions supported, for instance, Nazi theories of Aryan superiority, colonialist theories of European superiority, restrictive U.S. immigration laws, and histories of slavery and segregation in the United States and apartheid in South Africa. The damage done to human lives by thinking of race in biological terms makes it doubly important to define race carefully.

Psychologists, anthropologists, and biologists have concluded that biological race differences are not meaningful (American Anthropological Association, 1998; Betancourt & Lopez, 1993; Helms, 1994; Jones, 2003; Smedley & Smedley, 2005; Zuckerman, 1990). Human racial groups are biologically much more alike than different. When racial differences appear, as in IQ scores, differences are attributable to social and economic variables, not race per se.

Yet race does have psychological and social meaning in many societies: as a socially constructed set of categories related to inequalities of status and power (Jones, 2003; Smedley & Smedley, 2005). Race is important because racism makes it so. In the United States, European Americans often need pay little attention to race because most seldom encounter racial prejudice. However, persons of color are often made acutely aware of their race. That difference in life experiences and perspective reflects a powerful set of social dynamics. Racial distinctions in U.S. life are based on a history of slavery and segregation and the assumptions of White supremacy that were used to justify them. Today's differences in sociopolitical and economic power are maintained by persistent (often unrecognized) versions of those assumptions of superiority (Jones, 2003; Smedley & Smedley, 2005; Sue, 2004).

Race is not simply ethnicity. Race is "socially defined on the basis of physical criteria" (Van den Berghe, cited in Jones, 1997, p. 347), That is, people make racial distinctions based on assumptions about observable physical qualities such as skin color. Ethnicity is "socially defined on the basis of cultural criteria" (Van den Berghe, cited in Jones, 1997, p. 358), such as language, national origin, customs, and values, having little to do with physical appearance (see Birman, 1994, Helms, 1994, and Jones, 1997, on concepts of race, ethnicity, and similar terms).

An example of the significance of race for those of different ethnic or national backgrounds is that in the United States, persons of largely African ancestry include at least three groups: those with long ancestries in the U.S., those of Afro-Caribbean background, and recent immigrants from various parts of Africa. Yet all share experiences associated with racism in the United States.

No terminology is entirely satisfactory to describe the racial diversity of U.S. and many other societies. When discussing race in this chapter in the U.S. context, we use general racial category terms (e.g., European American) when necessary to refer to broad groupings defined by racial criteria rather than by specific ethnicity. Where relevant, we discuss specific ethnic groups (e.g., Puerto Ricans, Japanese Americans). We use other racial terms if used by authors whose works we are describing. When we use the terms *Black* and *White,* primarily for brevity, we capitalize them to remind you to think of these categories as socially constructed categories rather than biological races. Finally, when needed, we use the term *persons of color* to refer to all persons of ancestry other than European. This term sometimes is necessary to discuss the effects of racism that targets multiple groups. In other nations, different categories and terms will be necessary.

Use of almost any terminology and definition of race perpetuates racial oppression in some way. Yet community psychology, at least in the United States, cannot ignore race, despite the drawbacks of our vocabulary for discussing it (Helms, 1994; Suarez-Balcazar, 1998; Trickett et al., 1994).

Ethnicity

Ethnicity can be defined as a social identity, based on one's ancestry or culture of origin and modified by the culture in which one currently resides (Helms, 1994, p. 293; Jones, 1997, p. 358). The term is related to the Greek *ethnos,* referring to tribe or nationality. Ethnicity is defined by language, customs, values, social ties, and other aspects of subjective culture (Birman, 1994; Jones, 1997). In psychological research, it may refer to a simply demographic category, cultural qualities shared by a group or population, or ethnic identity, the extent to which an individual incorporates ethnicity into one's sense of self (Birman, 1994, pp. 262–263). It is important to know which is meant in a given study.

Some broad categories often used in U.S. research combine multiple ethnicities. Hispanic or Latino/Latina (Latino denotes men, Latina, women) may refer to persons of Puerto Rican, Cuban, Dominican, Mexican, or many other ancestries. Many ethnicities and nationalities exist among Asian Americans. Native Americans represent a diversity of tribal and cultural traditions.

Physical appearance can vary greatly within an ethnic group. Ethnicity is also not simply nationality: India, for instance, is a very multiethnic nation, and even Japan has multiple ethnic groups.

Ethnicity often involves an interaction of at least two cultures. Being Chinese American is not simply being Chinese but is defined by the interaction (including conflict) of Chinese and U.S. cultural contexts (Sasao & Sue, 1993).

Gender

Differences between females and males provide a distinction that has been the basis of socially constructed concepts and definitions of "sexual" differences. Gender refers to how those differences are interpreted and reflected in attitudes, social roles, and social institutions, including distribution of resources and power. Gender is not simply a demographic category, but represents important psychological and social processes (Gridley & Turner, 2005; Mulvey, Bond, Hill, & Terenzio, 2000). Gender is also an important aspect of one's identity or sense of self (Frable, 1997).

Sexual Orientation

This is best understood as a spectrum from exclusively heterosexual to exclusively homosexual, with intermediate points. It refers to an underlying orientation involving sexual attraction, romantic affection, and related emotions. Because of widespread social pressure to be heterosexual, sometimes enforced with violence, outward social behavior does not necessarily correspond to an underlying orientation elsewhere along the spectrum (Gonsiorek & Weinrich, 1991). Sexual orientation is distinct from gender identity, one's sense of being psychologically male or female, and from gender role, one's adherence to social norms for masculinity and femininity (e.g., dress, appearance). Being gay, lesbian, or bisexual is a social identity important for many persons (Frable, 1997). The importance of this dimension is increasingly recognized in community psychology (D'Augelli, 2003; Harper, 2005; Schneider & Harper, 2003).

Social Class, Socioeconomic Status

This dimension may be defined primarily in terms of income or material assets, or as a composite concept that also includes occupational and educational status. Income or educational level also may be studied alone.

Social class comprises a key dimension for community psychology. Although often studied only as a demographic descriptor, social class actually marks differences in power, especially economic resources and opportunities (Ostrove & Cole, 2003). It influences identity and self-image, interpersonal relationships, socialization, well-being, living environment, educational opportunities, and many other psychological issues (American Psychological Association, 2000; Bradley & Corwyn, 2002; McLoyd, 1998). (See Ehrenreich, 2001 for a personal account of the psychological and economic aspects of living on low wages.) Psychologists have only belatedly attended to psychological issues related to social class (Lott & Bullock, 2001; Ostrove & Cole, 2003).

Ability/Disability

Most persons will experience a physical or mental disability at some time in their lives. A disability creates life experiences different from those of fully "able" persons. Challenges of stigma, exclusion, and justice arise for persons with disabilities.

Community psychology has focused research and action on issues concerning mental and physical disabilities (e.g., Fawcett et al., 1994; Kloos, 2005; White, 2005).

Age

Children, adolescents, and younger and older adults differ in psychological concerns, developmental transitions, and community involvement. Aging also brings changes in relationships and power for families, communities, workplaces, and society (Gatz & Cotton, 1994).

Localities

Differences among localities affect individual lives in many ways, creating differences in life experiences that comprise a form of human diversity. Localities are often said to differ along a dimension of rural/suburban/urban communities, but other examples of localities include resort communities or urbanized areas within an otherwise suburban locality. An example of how locality affects personal life or community action is that rural areas are often marked by geographic dispersion, limited human services, and stable, insular social networks that can make it difficult for newcomers or outsiders to establish trust (Bierman et al., 1997, Muehrer, 1997). Transportation is a challenge for almost any community innovation. Community conflict must be approached more carefully when you are likely to encounter last night's opponent at work or in town today. Distinctive land-use conflicts can arise between agriculture and housing when population density rises, as in the conflicts between local planners and Amish farming families described by Bennett (2003).

In contrast, diversity and change are hallmarks of urban life. Skills in understanding multiple forms of human diversity, in establishing new interpersonal relationships, and in adapting to changing circumstances are important in urban life. Relationships between the physical environment and personal life are also different. Jacobs (1961) provided a classic analysis of how land use planning in a city must differ from a suburb or small town. Suburban and rural residents often value privacy, and feel safe when they know people personally. City residents cannot expect to know everyone, so safety in public is found in numbers, even with strangers. Safety is enhanced by public spaces that are open to public view and frequently visited, and limited in spaces that lack these qualities (e.g., seldom-used subway stops or streets, shrubbery that obscures views in public parks).

Finally, disadvantaged urban and rural areas have far fewer economic resources than many suburban and affluent urban ones. This shapes the resources available for schools, human and health services, and key community institutions and organizations.

This is not to say that all urban, rural or other communities, or their individual members, are alike. Each locality is distinctive. The categories that we have discussed are only general guides to a richness of local and particular communities. However conceptualized, life experiences in differing localities comprise one form of human diversity.

Spirituality and Religion

Spirituality and religion concern community psychology because of their importance for personal well-being and the importance of spiritual institutions and communities. As we noted in Chapter 6, we use the inclusive terms *spirituality* and *spiritual* to refer to religious traditions and to other perspectives concerned with transcendence.

Spirituality and religion interrelate with culture and ethnicity. It is impossible to understand many cultures without understanding their religious institutions and spiritual practices. Yet religion and spirituality are not simply cultural. Moreover, many religions and spiritual traditions are multicultural, and many cultures contain multiple religious and spiritual communities. These interrelationships can be complicated. Birman (1994) discusses the dilemmas faced in the U.S. by Jewish refugees from Russia to the United States. In Russia they were considered a nationality (connoting ethnicity) and sometimes even a physically distinctive race; Judaism as a religion was not important to many. In the U.S., their Jewishness was often perceived in religious terms and their nationality considered to be Russian, which astounded many of these immigrants.

Other Dimensions, Intersectionality

These ten dimensions, though important for community psychology, reflect only some forms of human diversity. Other important dimensions include nationality and generational differences in immigrant families. These dimensions provide a "high-altitude" overview; none describes a specific population or community. In addition, these dimensions are not independent of each other. The meanings of culture, race, and ethnicity especially converge. Human diversities are complex; languages often fail to reflect that complexity.

In any given situation, many forms of diversity may be psychologically important. Often most important is **intersectionality** (Ostrove & Cole, 2003), when several dimensions overlap. Multiple injustices of racism, sexism, and classism burden low-income women of color, for instance. Social myths often confuse issues and perpetuate stereotypes, especially of race and social class. For instance, when we say "welfare recipient," we seldom think of low-income European Americans (Ostrove & Cole, 2003). Yet thinking in multiple dimensions helps identify strengths, such as spirituality, cultural resources, and peer support networks. Moreover, a person may form multiple identities based on race, sexual orientation, and spirituality, among other factors.

INDIVIDUALISM-COLLECTIVISM: A SPECTRUM OF CULTURES

To increase employee productivity, a Texas corporation told its employees to look in the mirror and say "I'm beautiful" 100 times before coming to work. For much the same purpose, a Japanese supermarket in New Jersey

> told its employees to begin each workday by telling another employee that he or she is beautiful. (Markus & Kitayama, 1991, p. 224)

> All cultures, in one way or another, negotiate some mixture of individual identity and collective identity. (Dudgeon, Mallard, Oxenham, & Fielder, 2002, p. 255)

Imagine a spectrum of human cultures as varied as the visible light spectrum from infrared to ultraviolet. As an introduction, we will contrast briefly two general pathways of living, most clearly represented in the areas near the poles of this spectrum (Greenfield, Keller, Fuligni, & Maynard, 2003; Kagitçibasi, 1997; Kim, Triandis, Kagitçibasi, Choi, & Yoo, 1994; Markus & Kitayama, 1991; Triandis, 1994; van Uchelen, 2000). The first quotation illustrates such contrasts, which are useful for introducing some of the diversity along the spectrum. Yet remember that this comparison of extremes can be overly simplistic, as highlighted in the second quotation.

Consider one way of living in which parents wish to impart these lessons to their children: high self-esteem, taking initiative to succeed as individuals, and resisting peer pressure. In a different way of living, however, the same characteristics might be considered an excessive focus on self and lack of respect for others. That second way emphasizes cooperation and supportive relationships. What the first way considers conformity, the second way views as teamwork (Gergen, 1973; Greenfield et al., 2003).

The first way of living emphasizes individual self-reliance, assertion, competition, and achievement. Important tasks of growing up include developing an **independent self,** with a sense of one's unique identity, and a strong, clear boundary between oneself and others. Dependence on others is to be avoided.

The second way of living emphasizes security and harmony within groups. Individual achievement is to be attained through group success. Growing up includes cultivating an **interdependent self,** with a more open boundary between self and others. Identity is defined in terms of relationships with others and membership in communities. Being ostracized by others is to be avoided.

Cultural psychologists describe cultures embodying the first way of living as **individualistic** and cultures embodying the second way as **collectivistic.** Of course, no culture or community can be entirely one or the other. As the second quotation that opened this section indicates, all cultures and persons balance individual independence and collective interdependence (Dudgeon et al., 2002). Also, although collectivistic practices clearly go back much further in human history than individualistic ones, collectivistic cultures are not just traditional, "primitive," or less economically developed. Japan, for instance, is an economically developed society with many collectivistic norms, interwoven with growing individualistic practices (Markus & Kitayama, 1991; Reid, 1999). **Individualism-collectivism** is better understood as a spectrum along which cultures and communities vary. It is useful for understanding cultures as long as you remember that it is a broad theme with many exceptions.

Examples of Individualism-Collectivism Contrasts

Differences along the individualism-collectivism spectrum can color conceptions of self and emotion. For instance, Markus and Kitayama (1991) listed eleven emotional states recognized in the Japanese language but not in English; many of these concern other-focused feelings of communion and respect. This emphasis on interdependence is similar to African ideas of the extended self (Nobles, 1991), Mayan concepts of knowing (Greenfield et al., 2003), and feminist concepts of relatedness (van Uchelen, 2000).

Among the !Kung people of southern Africa, Fiji Islanders, and indigenous First Nations peoples in western Canada, wellness is viewed as a collective quality, not as an individual characteristic. Psychological, social, and spiritual resources for healing are *synergistic:* available to everyone and expanded through collective singing, dancing, and other activities. When asked about strengths that promote wellness, members of First Nations in Canada (similar to Native Americans in the U.S.) mentioned cultural traditions and family and community ties, not individual qualities. Mutual help groups also offer a form of collective healing (Katz, 1984; van Uchelen, 2000).

Differences in family life also may reflect these patterns of an individualism-collectivism spectrum. Parents in Puerto Rico, Mexico, Nigeria, Cameroon, Japan, and China emphasized responsibility to others, especially family and elders, more than independence, assertion and self-esteem. German, Dutch, and European-American parents did the opposite (Greenfield et al., 2003). Certainly there was diversity among parents within and among these societies, and parents in all societies valued both independence and interdependence in their children to some extent. Yet a broad group difference emerged in what parents fostered more strongly in their children.

A similar pattern emerged in studies of adult children's involvement with their aging parents. Greater interdependence with aging parents was endorsed in Indonesia, the Philippines, Thailand, and Turkey, whereas greater independence of parents and children was emphasized among European Americans. This does not mean that European Americans were unwilling to care for their parents, but a broad group difference in priorities was significant (Kagitçibasi, 1996, cited in Greenfield et al., 2003, p. 471). Similar differences can appear within a society. Family loyalty is an important and often-researched cultural value and behavioral norm among Latino/as, Asian Americans, Native Americans, and African Americans (Marin & Gamba, 2003).

Such differences in worldviews can become practical conflicts. For instance, parents from a culture that primarily values education in terms of children's social skills and demeanor and school teachers emphasizing Western concepts of learning and independence may not understand each other or collaborate well, especially if language differences obscure nuances of meaning (Greenfield et al., 2003).

The pattern also is reflected in attitudes about equality. When individualistic views dominate, inequality of resources is more accepted as an outcome of competition among independent selves. Helping another is considered desirable but voluntary. When interdependence is emphasized, equality among group members is prized and rewards are more likely to be shared (Kagitçibasi, 1997). For instance, the difference between the salary of the lowest-paid and highest-paid employees in a Japanese corporation is usually far less than in U.S. corporations (Reid, 1999). (Recall concepts of Fair Play and Fair Shares values in Chapter 2.)

However, even in strongly collectivistic cultures, help is not extended to all. Many collectivistic cultures grant authority to men, elders, chiefs, religious leaders, or members of higher castes, not to every person equally (Triandis, 1994). Also, in a collectivistic culture, one is obligated to other members of one's group (e.g., extended family, ethnic group, nationality), but not to persons outside that group (Hofstede, 1994). Ingroup-outgroup distinctions also occur in more individualistic societies (Brewer, 1997).

Sense of community overlaps with collectivism but also is distinct from it. Collectivism is a way of describing pervasive cultural forces reflected in many aspects of a person's life. Sense of community describes connection within one community or setting. Even in strongly individualistic cultures some groups have a strong, positive sense of community. Also, in more individualistic cultures one has greater choice of which communities to join. In many collectivistic cultures community membership is often ascribed (e.g., one is born into them) rather than chosen.

Limitations of Individualism-Collectivism Concepts

Individualism-collectivism helps to understand some aspects of diverse cultures, but it has limitations. First, there is variation along the individualism-collectivism spectrum even within a culture. For example, dominant U.S. cultural and political institutions are individualistic. Yet some U.S. communities have established more collectivistic ways of living, such as spiritual communities, ethnic cultures, and women's collectives. The student culture of many U.S. high schools, where acceptance by a group is paramount, has collectivistic aspects. Some athletic teams emphasize teamwork over individual recognition.

Second, all cultures change over time, and world cultures are becoming more interdependent, their differences less clear cut. Many more collectivistic cultures are incorporating individualistic practices, particularly in work settings as global capitalism expands. The worldwide reach of Western media and cross-cultural personal contacts also increase the interweaving of differing cultures, complicating easy generalizations (Fowers & Richardson, 1996; Hermans & Kempen, 1998; Tyler, 2001, pp. 185–187).

Third, individualism-collectivism is only one spectrum along which cultures differ. Cultures differ in their orientation to time, including whether time is understood as linear or nonlinear; an emphasis on short-term or long-term perspectives, and the extent to which efficiency and promptness are valued. They also differ greatly, for instance, in gender roles and opportunities for women; in attitudes about authority and its proper forms; and in communication styles (Jones, 1997; Triandis, 1994).

Fourth, it is easy to oversimplify another culture by viewing it only in contrast to one's own. For instance, Australians and others of European descent tend to view Aboriginal peoples, who have lived in Australia for at least 40,000 years, as a uniform "community" or culture, despite the diversity of indigenous Australian peoples. (Even the single term *Aboriginal* contributes to this.) This oversimplification easily leads to romanticizing indigenous peoples as unselfish and primitive (i.e., the opposite of Western cultures) (Dudgeon et al., 2002; Lee, 2000). Similar conceptions influence European-American views of Native Americans, who represent a diversity of cultures. Thinking in terms of dichotomies misunderstands another culture as an exotic Other, a simple opposite of the familiar, not as diverse persons and communities to be understood in their own terms (Tyler, 2001).

Fifth, concepts of individualism-collectivism are useful only for describing broad themes across many cultures. They provide a general view and do not illuminate the unique qualities of a specific culture. Indigenous or population-specific psychologies have arisen to study specific cultures (Kim & Berry, 1993; Watts, 1994). Psychological descriptions of African-American culture, for instance, have emphasized the importance of its African roots (e.g., Jones, 1997, pp. 483–493; Potts, 2003). Most community research and action occurs in a specific cultural context, so knowledge of that context is its most important cultural prerequisite.

Finally, it is impossible to understand many communities solely in cultural terms. Our next section explores how issues of social justice, oppression, and liberation are also important in human diversity.

CONCEPTS OF LIBERATION AND OPPRESSION

> Whenever you feel like criticizing anyone, he told me, just remember that all the people in this world haven't had the advantages that you've had. (Fitzgerald, 1925/1995, *The Great Gatsby,* p. 5)

Consider these facts about U.S. society:

- Among full-time, year-round employees, in 2004, the average woman received 77 percent of the income of the average man (U.S. Census Bureau, 2005).
- Median household income in 2004 for Whites was $49,000, for Hispanics was $34,200 (70% of the White median), and for Blacks was $30,100 (61% of the White median) (U.S. Census Bureau, 2005).
- Inequality of household income is increasing steadily. From 1979 to 2001, incomes (adjusted for inflation) rose 81 percent for the highest-earning 5 percent of the population, but gains for the lower four-fifths of the population were much lower. This is a marked change from the post–World War II era (1947–1979), when income gains were similar for all segments of the population. In 1960, the average corporate chief executive's income was 41 times the average worker's income; in 1997, it was 115 times more (Inequality.org, 2004; Lott & Bullock, 2001; U.S. Census Bureau, 2005).

- Upward economic mobility is decreasing; compared to earlier periods, fewer people are now moving from lower-income groups into higher ones (Inequality.org, 2004; Scott & Leonhardt, 2005).
- Wealth (net worth, not yearly income) is highly skewed. The wealthiest 1 percent of the population control 33 percent of the nation's private assets, more than the combined assets of nine-tenths of the population (Inequality.org, 2004).
- Large income gaps between rich and poor are correlated with lower life expectancy for the entire population, not just the poorest (American Psychological Association, 2000).
- In 2004, about one in every six U.S. residents, and about one in every nine children, had no health insurance. Among Blacks and Hispanics, these figures are much higher (U.S. Census Bureau, 2005). Illness is more common among those with the lowest incomes (American Psychological Association, 2000).
- In 2004, about one in every eight residents, and more than one in every six children, lived in poverty as defined by federal standards (which do not consider housing costs). Among Whites, about one in eleven lives in poverty; among Blacks, about one in four; among Hispanics, over one in five (U.S. Census Bureau, 2005). If a definition of poverty that includes housing costs were used, poverty rates would be about twice as high (Lott & Bullock, 2001).
- Income from one minimum-wage job falls far short of what is needed to pull a family with two children out of poverty (Lott & Bullock, 2001).
- The rate of child poverty in the U.S. is higher than in 16 developed countries (Lott & Bullock, 2001).
- Growing up in sustained poverty places children at higher risk of many problems and illnesses (Bradley & Corwyn, 2002; McLoyd, 1998). Many low-income families are resilient, but they face daunting money-related challenges.

These and similar differences among persons and families do not result from cultural factors. They are better understood in terms of power and access to resources. To understand such differences, concepts of liberation and oppression are needed (e.g., Bond, Hill, Mulvey & Terenzio, 2000; Fanon, 1963; Freire, 1970/1993; Martin-Baro, 1994; Miller, 1976; Prilleltensky & Gonick, 1994; Nelson & Prilleltensky, 2005; Tatum, 1997; Watts, 1994; Watts & Serrano-Garcia, 2003; Watts, Williams, & Jagers, 2003).

Oppression: Initial Definitions

Oppression occurs in a hierarchical relationship in which a dominant group unjustly holds power and resources and withholds them from another group (see Nelson & Prilleltensky, 2005, p. 106; Prilleltensky & Gonick, 1994; Tatum, 1997; Watts et al., 2003). The more powerful group is termed the **dominant** or

privileged group; the less powerful is the **oppressed** or **subordinated group.** Oppressive hierarchies are often based on ascribed characteristics fixed at birth or otherwise outside personal control, such as gender or race.

For instance, the oppressive system of racism in the United States creates a privileged group of White persons and subordinate groups of all others: African Americans, Latinos/Latinas, Asian Americans, and Native Americans. Sexism creates privileges for men and subordinates women. "Ableism" creates privileges for persons without physical or mental disabilities and subordinates those with them. Heterosexism privileges heterosexuals and subordinates lesbians, gay men, and bisexuals. Classism privileges those with economic power and resources and subordinates everyone else, especially those of lowest incomes.

Oppressive systems may also create intermediate groups. South African apartheid and British colonialism in India, for instance, created classes such as "coloured" South Africans and "Anglo-Indians," subordinated by the dominant class but more privileged than the lowest classes (Sonn & Fisher, 2003). Classism operates along a continuum in many Western societies; middle classes are more privileged than those with lowest incomes, yet still they are still less powerful and often manipulated by the wealthy. In U.S. history, some immigrant groups were only gradually accepted by dominant Anglo-American groups. Racism in the U.S. today often has different effects among diverse persons of color.

Resources controlled by a dominant or privileged group may include economic resources, status and influence, sociopolitical power, interpersonal connections among elites, the power to frame discussion of conflicts (often exerted through media and educational systems), representation in political and corporate offices, and even inequalities in marriage and personal relationships. Perhaps most insidious are ideologies and myths to convince members of subordinated groups that they actually are inferior. This sense of inferiority is termed **internalized oppression.**

Members of privileged groups are granted resources, opportunities, and power not by their own efforts but by oppressive systems (McIntosh, 1998). Members of a privileged class may not recognize or consent to this state of affairs, yet they are granted the privileges anyway. In the United States, many White persons oppose racism, but they are privileged by systems that operate in racist ways. Similar statements apply to individuals in other privileged groups, such as men, the wealthy, and heterosexuals.

Subordinated groups are denied access to much power and many resources without their consent. However, they are not powerless. They may resist injustice in many ways, direct and indirect. The strengths of their cultural heritage may provide resources for doing this. Subordinated groups may also develop ways of coping with oppression and protecting themselves. For instance, women who are victims of battering often learn to interpret the nuances of their partners' moods (Tatum, 1997). The subordinated group may comply overtly with oppressors yet create personal identities revealed only with other members of their group, as "coloured" South Africans did under apartheid (Sonn & Fisher, 1998, 2003).

Oppressive systems have long historical roots. Those systems, not individuals currently living within them, are the sources of injustice (Prilleltensky & Gonick, 1994; Freire, 1970/1993). For instance, to dismantle sexism, **patriarchy** (the system of unearned male power) is the opponent, not individual men. In fact, patriarchy harms men as well as women: for instance, by the emotional restriction and costly competitiveness of masculine role expectations. The harm is less for a privileged group than for subordinated groups, of course. Yet dismantling oppression liberates privileged and oppressed from a system that dehumanizes both (Freire, 1970/1993). This perspective on oppressive social systems is consistent with a community psychology perspective (Mulvey, 1988).

In complex societies, multiple forms of oppression exist. Steele (1997) summarized evidence that in the United States, even the best African-American students are affected by racist stereotypes, and even the most mathematically talented women are similarly affected by stereotypes about women's mathematical ability. Moreover, the same individual can be privileged by one oppression while being subordinated by another. In the United States, Black men are oppressed by racism and privileged by sexism; White women are oppressed by sexism and privileged by racism; working-class and low-income White men are oppressed by socioeconomic classism and privileged by racism and sexism.

Consider for a moment ways in which you may be a member of privileged groups in some ways and of subordinated groups in other ways. Box 7.2 illustrates some personal aspects of privilege and subordination.

Oppression: Multiple Ecological Levels

The power relationships of the larger society are often mirrored at multiple ecological levels in macrosystems, communities, organizations, microsystems, and individual prejudices (Freire, 1970/1993; James et al., 2003; Watts, 1994).

Breathing "Smog": Social Myths Oppressive hierarchies are sustained in part by widely accepted myths that rationalize them (Freire, 1970/1993; Prilleltensky & Nelson, 2002; Watts, 1994). Blaming the victims of macrosystem economic forces is one example (Ryan, 1971). As a result, members of dominant groups and even subordinated groups often fail to recognize how systems of oppression are creating injustices. Tatum (1997) likened this process to "breathing smog." After a while, one doesn't notice it; the air seems natural.

One example of "smog" can be a false reading of differences in educational attainment or income. Values of individualism channel our thinking to interpret these as the result of individual effort or ability. Although these qualities do count for something, it is also true that oppressive systems reward effort and ability among members of the privileged group while often ignoring the same qualities among members of the subordinated group. Recognizing this injustice, especially for members of the privileged group, would call into question cherished beliefs about individual freedom, something that many persons would rather not think about. So when Whites earn more than other racial groups, or men earn more

BOX 7.2 Unearned Privileges

My wife and I work in the same building at the same university. When I need to work late, I do so without reservations about my personal safety. For men, our campus is safe even late at night. I don't think about whether anyone else is on my floor or who has access to the building. When I walk to my car, I don't need to be alert. However, if she works late, my wife thinks about all of these things. In this society we tolerate a great deal of men's violence toward women, of which sexual assault is but one example. It is clear that I (and other men) have a privilege that my wife (and other women) do not share.

Consider a second form of privilege. When my wife and I wish to hold each other's hand or embrace in public, we do so without concern for our safety. As a teenager and college student, I was free to talk with friends about whom I was dating or wished to date. No one told crude jokes about persons of my sexual orientation. I did not have to agonize about what my sexual orientation was or about whether to tell my parents about it.

This privilege is not available to one of my closest friends, who is a lesbian. She has been harassed. If she is open about her sexuality, she may be excluded from some of the major institutions of society: many religious congregations, marriage, adopting a child, careers involving working with children. If she hides her sexuality, she must deal with the personal cost to her integrity and well-being. Finally, the danger of murderous violence is always there for her, at some level of awareness.

Consider a third form of privilege. Many of my Black friends and colleagues have noted that almost every day, in ways large or small, they are unpleasantly reminded of their race. Though these reminders may be indirect or unintentional, their effects are nonetheless real. Moreover, I have learned that the direct, intimidating incidents of racism are more common than I had realized, even today. In contrast, European Americans may go for years without being confronted with the meaning of our racial status. European Americans are freer (if we wish) to pursue our education, career aspirations, and leisure time almost solely in the company of people of our race. When a conflict occurs and one needs to assert oneself with a superior at work, the manager of a retail business, or the teacher of one's children at school, or when one must call the police, we can be much more confident that we will be dealing with a person of our race. European Americans also can much more easily arrange to protect our children from adults who may harm them on the basis of their race (McIntosh, 1998).

A fourth form of privilege involves the advantages of middle-class life compared to the lives of those with less income and less access to good housing and health care, educational opportunities, and other resources. My childhood and adolescence in rural Appalachia provided me with experiences across social class boundaries, and (thanks largely to my parents) with some awareness of social-economic causes. Later, I spent one college summer working in a faith-based social program in inner-city Newark, New Jersey. That was an education for me about racism, classism, and resistance to oppression. In other college summers, I worked in construction jobs near home, a different experience across class boundaries. These experiences influenced me for life, pushing me to develop a critical awareness of inequality.

Privileges of gender, race, sexual orientation, and class are not earned. Moreover, the privileges that, for instance, accrue to being male are not something I (or many other men) support; I would much rather live in a society in which women are safe and as privileged as men. Life in such a society would be freer for both women and men. The same is true regarding other forms of oppression. It seems to me and to many others that those of us who are members of privileged groups, although we did not create these forms of oppression, have a responsibility to work to dismantle them. (Jim Dalton)

than women, we are predisposed to interpret those differences in individual terms, ignoring broader factors. Rice (2001) reviews studies that indicate such social myths especially harm women in poverty.

In fact, an oppressive system often works best when a few members of an oppressed group break through to enjoy the privileges of the dominant group. They may be tokens accepted only for public relations, or perhaps they are the best at assimilating the values and behaviors of the dominant class. Their success seems to offer a lesson about the importance of individual effort. Yet research shows that these individuals are often held to higher performance standards than members of the privileged group (Ridgeway, 2001).

The Role of Mass Media Print media, television, movies, radio, and the Internet comprise a very influential macrosystem. The presence and status of women, persons of color, and other oppressed groups have increased in U.S. mass media in the last half-century. Yet mass media continue to provide misleading images of oppressed populations.

Often the poor are simply ignored in mainstream news; Wall Street and economic-corporate news are headlined while unemployment is sporadically mentioned and economic inequality seldom covered. When news stories do cover poverty, they frequently ignore macrosystem factors such as low wages and high housing costs. Although U.S. drug users and dealers are most often European-American men, in news and crime shows they most often appear as urban African American and Latino men. Low-income women also are portrayed negatively (Gilliam & Iyengar, 2000; Bullock, Wyche, & Williams, 2003). Gilens (1996) investigated coverage of poverty in major U.S. news magazines, finding that although African Americans comprised less than one-third of persons living in poverty, every person pictured in news magazine stories about the "underclass" was African American. This bias had real effects: public opinion polls cited by Gilens showed that U.S. citizens consistently overestimated the proportion of the poor who are Black.

Neighborhood Racial "Tipping Point" Oppression can also exist at the neighborhood level. Hacker (1992, pp. 35–38) reviewed research on the racial "tipping point" in U.S. residential neighborhoods, especially involving White and Black residents. Most White residents will remain in a racially mixed neighborhood only if the proportion of persons of color remains below about 8 percent. Once that tipping point is passed, a predictable sequence occurs. White residents move out, often quickly, and no Whites move in. Blacks, often seeking an integrated neighborhood, move in only to find the area becoming all-Black or nearly so. What makes this more than simply a matter of individual prejudice is the predictable tipping point of about 8 percent, a surprisingly uniform figure across the nation and well below the proportion of Blacks or other persons of color in the general population.

Institutional Oppression: Workplaces Organizational policies can have discriminatory effects, even when administered by well-meaning individuals. For instance, reliance on standardized test scores in college admissions can exclude otherwise promising students of color and those who are economically disadvantaged.

The "glass ceiling" for women in organizations is another example. Studies of work communication show that in mixed-sex groups men talk more, make more suggestions, use more assertive speech and gestures, and influence group decisions more often. These acts indicate the use of power in a group, and studies indicate that both women and men accept male leaders who use them competently. Yet when women use these actions to lead assertively, the response is often different. Many men and even women feel discomfort, and emotional backlash is more likely to occur, even if not voiced openly. Assertive women managers, for instance, are more likely to be considered hostile than equally assertive men (Heilman, 2001). The source of discomfort is that assertive women contradict subtle, socially constructed (and unjust) expectations about who can legitimately exercise these forms of power (Carli, 1999, 2003; Ridgeway, 2001; Rudman & Glick, 2001). In other words, assertive women are challenging hierarchical systems of oppression. The discomfort and backlash even among other women indicates that an established system of power and roles is involved, not simply men.

Reviews of psychological research also indicate that women's work performance, even when identical to men's, still is often rated less positively (Carli, 1999, 2003; Crosby, Iyer, Clayton, & Downing, 2003; Heilman, 2001). When men and women submit otherwise identical resumes for jobs, men's resumes are often evaluated more positively (Ridgeway, 2001). Even when undergraduate students were asked in several studies to hire a student for a campus job, both men and women raters preferred men over equally qualified women (Carli, 1999).

Pager (2003) conducted a field experiment to test the roles of race and criminal record in hiring. Four male testers answered advertisements for entry-level positions in the Milwaukee area in 2001. Two were White, one presenting credentials with no criminal record, the other presenting otherwise identical credentials but also reporting a (fabricated) felony conviction for selling cocaine and serving 18 months in prison. Two other testers were Black, with the same credentials and manipulation of criminal background. Testers appeared in person to apply for positions (they rotated which individual presented evidence of a criminal record). The pairs applied for a total of 350 jobs. Very few employers actually checked applicants' references; most seemed to accept their self-reports. The dependent variable was the rate of job offers or call-backs for further interviews from employers.

The results showed that Whites received call-backs or offers more than twice as often as Blacks. In fact, Whites reporting a felony drug conviction were more likely to receive call-backs or job offers than Blacks with no criminal record at all. Similar studies in other U.S. localities have found similar racial discrimination (Crosby et al., 2003; Pager, 2003).

Many social-psychological studies show that individuals who believe themselves free of prejudice nonetheless can behave in discriminatory ways (Jones, 1997, 1998). The widespread discrimination documented by Pager (2003) and others is an institutional and societal issue, not simply an individual matter.

Institutional Oppression: Schools In the United States, schools are often believed to be the pathway to racial integration and to upward economic mobility. For some this is true. Yet they often simply perpetuate existing race and class differences (Fine & Burns, 2003; Hochschild, 2003; Lott, 2001). One reason is residential racial segregation (see the tipping point research discussed earlier).

In addition, reliance on local funding of schools, and great disparities of wealth among school districts, creates much richer opportunities for some students than others. Within schools, tracking of students, largely based on test scores, shunts students of color and those from lower-income families disproportionately into lower-quality classes that do not prepare them for college or competitive jobs (Lott, 2001; Weinstein, 2002a).

Intergroup Relations and Individual Prejudices Research on intergroup relations in social psychology demonstrates that as humans we often hold positive attitudes about our in-group (who we see as similar to ourselves), while stereotyping and even holding prejudices about out-group members (those we see as different). Members of both dominant and subordinated groups thus may hold stereotypes and prejudices about the other group.

However, an insight of the liberation perspective is that not everyone's stereotypes and prejudices have the same effects. If a person is in a more powerful role (e.g., employer, teacher, police officer, elected official), his or her biases have greater effects on others. Members of privileged groups have more influence in their organizations, communities, and societies. Members of the subordinated group are not free of prejudices, but theirs are less powerful because their subordinated status limits their influence. For instance, in U.S. society, both Whites and persons of color are likely to hold at least some stereotypes and prejudices toward the other. Yet white persons as a group dominate economic, political, and social institutions (e.g., access to employment, housing, education, mortgages and loans, favorable mass media coverage, political power). The biases of powerful Whites become part of an interlocking set of social arrangements that perpetuate this control of resources; in short, a system of racism (Jones, 1997). All Whites, even those who oppose racism, benefit from this system; inevitably they are privileged by it. Similar dynamics perpetuate other forms of oppression.

Table 7.1 summarizes principles of the liberation perspective.

The Liberation Perspective: A Call to Action

> Liberation in its fullest sense requires the securing of full human rights and the remaking of a society without roles of oppressor and oppressed. (Watts, Williams, & Jagers, 2003, p. 187)

The liberation perspective is not just an intellectual analysis, it is a call to action. It explains injustices and names an opponent: the oppressive system. The aim is to change the system, to emancipate both the privileged and the oppressed (Freire, 1970/1993). First-order change in this context would mean that the currently oppressed group simply replaces the currently privileged group in power, a reshuffling within the oppressive system. Second-order change dismantles the oppressive system and its inequalities. That is the aim of liberation.

Members of the subordinated group usually understand the system of oppression better than those who are privileged by it. Frequent participation in relationships where one is privileged dulls the awareness of the privileged person, making

TABLE 7.1 Assumptions and Concepts of the Liberation Perspective

1. Oppression occurs in a hierarchical relationship in which a dominant group unjustly holds power and resources and withholds them from another group.
2. The more powerful group is the dominant or privileged group; the less powerful is the oppressed or subordinated group. A person's group membership is often determined by birth or other factors beyond one's personal control.
3. Resources controlled by a dominant group may include economic resources, status and influence, sociopolitical power, interpersonal connections, and the power to frame public discussion of issues.
4. The oppressive system grants unearned privileges to members of the dominant group, whether or not they recognize or consent to them.
5. The oppressed group resists oppression, directly or indirectly, with the power they have.
6. Multiple forms of oppression exist. An individual may be privileged by one form of oppression and subordinated by another.
7. Oppression involves multiple ecological levels: macrosystems, localities, organizations, interpersonal relationships, and individual prejudices.
8. Social myths rationalize an oppressive system. Tatum (1997) likened this process to "breathing smog": after a while, the workings of the oppressive system seem natural.
9. Because they experience its consequences directly, members of the oppressed group often understand an oppressive system better than members of the dominant group.
10. Any individual may have prejudices, but those of the dominant group are more damaging because they interlock with the power of oppressive systems.
11. Liberation theory is a call to action, to work collectively to dismantle oppressive systems.
12. Oppression dehumanizes both oppressor and oppressed. To truly dismantle it, those who oppose it must aim to liberate both the oppressed group and the dominant group from the oppressive system.

SOURCE: Freire (1970/1993), Miller (1976), Nelson & Prilleltensky (2005), Olsson, Powell, and Steuhling (1998), Prilleltensky and Gonick (1994), Tatum (1997), Watts (1994), Watts & Serrano-Garcia (2003).

injustices seem natural (breathing smog). Yet the same encounters can lead to insights by the subordinated. For instance, European Americans are seldom forced to confront the existence of racism, but members of other racial groups have perhaps daily experience with it. This means that liberatory efforts need leaders from the subordinated group to sustain awareness of where the real issues lie. Paulo Freire, (1970/1993), an important theorist of liberation, holds that three resources are needed for dismantling of oppression. The first is critical awareness and understanding of the oppressive system. Second is involvement and leadership from members of the subordinated group. Third is collective action; solely individual actions are difficult to sustain against powerful opposition.

When Culture and Liberation Conflict

> Culture, we believe, cannot become a haven for oppression, but must instead be a space where respect for diversity and participation in the development of new values leads all of us closer to health, dignity, and freedom. (Ortiz-Torres, Serrano-Garcia, & Torres-Burgos, 2000, p. 877)

When cultural traditions contribute to oppression, and conflict with liberating aims, how can this conflict be addressed or resolved? The values and practices of some cultures victimize women overtly or prescribe restrictive social roles for them (note that this is often interpreted as honoring or protecting women). Many traditional collectivistic cultures grant greater authority to men, some elders, or members of higher castes. Individualistic cultures offer much individual freedom but can tolerate great inequalities and undermine concern for the dispossessed.

Bianca Ortiz-Torres, Irma Serrano-Garcia, and Nelida Torres-Burgos (2000) addressed these issues in an article titled "Subverting Culture." As part of an HIV prevention initiative, their aim was to promote the capability of Puerto Rican women to negotiate use of safer-sex precautions with male sex partners.

That aim conflicts with two cultural values. *Marianismo* defines the culturally feminine role in many Latino/a cultures: a vision of the ideal woman as chaste and virginal, nurturing with men yet obedient to them, based on the Christian image of the Virgin Mary. It leads to sexuality as a topic for only private conversation and often to young women knowing little about their own sexuality. By extolling virginity, *marianismo* can be protective against risky sexual behavior. However, its role in suppressing discussion and understanding of sexuality, and emphasis on obedience to men, also leaves many women less knowledgeable and powerful in sexual situations. *Machismo* defines the masculine role, emphasizing virility and sexual prowess. In sexual situations, the *marianismo-machismo* combination grants men greater power than women, for whom the contradictory cultural expectations are more difficult (e.g., being chaste vs. pleasing one's partner).

In focus groups and individual interviews, Latina college students (in Puerto Rico and New York City) reported emotional and interpersonal obstacles to discussing safer sex, negotiating with lovers for condom use, nonpenetrative sexuality, and other self-protective actions. Fears of rejection, feelings of hurt and anxiety, men's assertion that these actions demonstrated a lack of trust, and women's own love for their partners were obstacles mentioned by participants. These are universal concerns, but in the context of *marianismo-machismo* values and roles, they are especially powerful.

However, no culture is completely static or unchanging. Women's movements in many cultures have challenged traditions and practices that victimize and disempower women. Moreover, women disadvantaged by cultural values often have cultural resources as well. In the study by Ortiz-Torres and associates, these included social support from other women, the impact of women's movements within the culture, and contact with different gender roles in other cultures. Ortiz-Torres et al. conclude that feminist community psychologists inside Latino/a culture can work to promote sexual education and open discussion of women's sexuality, to challenge values and practices that harm women, and to build women's personal negotiating skills and social support. These efforts can use traditional *marianismo* conceptions of abstinence and of protecting women so that they can build families and serve others. Yet they can also advocate condom use, nonpenetrative sexuality, and women's power to make decisions and to negotiate as equals in sexual situations.

Three key conclusions emerge about conflicts between culture and liberation. The first is that cultural values often contain contradictions. Cultural values such as *marianismo* and *machismo* have long histories, but so do values for protecting Latina women. Similarly, to oppose cultural norms underlying men's violence against women among some Southeast Asian immigrants to the United States, women's activists advocated for traditional Southeast Asian cultural values of protecting women (Silka & Tip, 1994, p. 518).

A second point is that cultures are continually evolving in response to external and internal conditions, including contacts with different cultures and diversity within the culture. Efforts for cultural transformation enter a stream of ongoing changes in a culture.

Finally, to be legitimate, cultural transformation needs to be initiated from inside the culture by its own members. Ortiz-Torres et al. developed their intervention as cultural insiders. Similarly, Afghan women initiated the Revolutionary Association of the Women of Afghanistan to advocate for women's and wider human rights in their own nation (Brodsky, 2003). For outsiders to impose their conceptions on a culture raises many questions of social justice. Within a culture, advocating for cultural change is legitimate.

Contributions and Limitations of the Liberation Perspective

The liberation and cultural perspectives are complementary. Liberation concepts call attention to the workings of power, often obscured in a cultural perspective.

A limitation of the liberation perspective is that by emphasizing the different positions of privileged and subordinated groups, it may underestimate the diversity within each of those groups. Not all women are identical in resources, power, or viewpoint, for instance, nor do all Mexican Americans speak with one voice. A second limitation is that in its emphasis on social systems, liberation theory can portray members of subordinated groups merely as victims, unless their cultural strengths and resistance to oppression are explicitly recognized.

A third limitation can arise when liberation concepts are used in action. Oppression creates conflict between dominant and subordinated groups. That conflict often is based on real, undeniable injustices. Yet the ideal of liberating both the oppressor and the oppressed may be difficult to sustain in the heat of that conflict. Discussion may be dominated by blaming of individuals or groups, rather than blaming social myths and practices. Research on intergroup conflicts shows that avoiding these obstacles requires commitment to shared goals as well as to addressing injustice (Jones, 1997). The long-term value of liberation concepts lies in how well they lead to Freire's (1970/1993) vision of liberating both oppressor and oppressed.

IDENTITIES AND ACCULTURATION

> One ever feels his two-ness,—an American, a Negro; two souls, two thoughts, two unreconciled strivings; two warring ideals in one dark body, whose dogged strength alone keeps it from being torn asunder.

> The history of the American Negro is the history of this strife,—this longing to attain self-conscious manhood, to merge his double self into a better and truer self. In this merging he wishes neither of the older selves to be lost. . . . He simply wishes to make it possible for a man to be both a Negro and an American. (DuBois, 1903/1986, p. 365)

In this famous passage, W. E. B. DuBois addressed a conflict of two identities that cannot be easily merged. His African ancestry and American experience promised mutual enrichment, yet forces of oppression prohibited their merging. DuBois himself eventually left the U.S. because racism prevented an integration of these two identities.

Neither the cultural nor the liberation perspectives fully address how individuals resolve such questions. A third perspective is needed, a focus on social identities. A person has not only unique personal characteristics, but also multiple social identities. These are based on race, ethnicity, gender, sexual orientation, religion and spirituality, or other social or cultural distinctions that influence one's sense of "who I am." Two theories influence how community psychologists think about social identities: identity development and acculturation theories. Community psychologist Dina Birman has written and performed research on these issues (Birman, 1994, 1998; Birman, Trickett, & Buchanan, 2005).

Identity Development Models

Psychologists have proposed models of social identity development for Americans of African, Asian, Latino, and White ancestry and status, U.S. ethnic minorities in general, feminists, and gay men, lesbians and bisexuals (e.g., D'Augelli, 1994; Helms, 1994; Phinney, 1990; Rickard, 1990). These models focus on how social identities develop, usually in late adolescence and early adulthood. They assume a sequence of stages (Frable, 1997; Helms, 1994; Phinney, 2003; Trimble, Helms, & Root, 2003).

Most begin with a stage of unexamined identity in which the person identifies with mainstream cultural ideals, ignoring or denying social group status (e.g., racial, ethnic, gender, or sexual orientation). That is challenged by life experiences that make social group status salient (this may involve experiencing or witnessing discrimination, or feeling in a minority status).

The person begins to explore his or her social or cultural status and heritage, forming a new identity around these themes. This often involves a period of immersion in activities and gatherings of the social group. This stage may begin with anger about discrimination and oppression by dominant groups but leads to a focus on the strengths of the social group or cultural heritage.

The individual internalizes the newly formed social identity, strengthening commitment to the social group, then emerges into transformed relations with mainstream culture. For instance, for gay men and lesbians, the experiences of "coming out" to others are important developmental steps at this stage (Rosario, Hunter, Maguen, Gwadz, & Smith, 2001).

Social identities are especially salient for oppressed groups as they explore the realities of oppression and seek strengths in their own heritages (Birman, 1994; Helms, 1994; Phinney, 2003; Varas-Diaz & Serrano-Garcia, 2003). For instance, in samples of African-American youth, stronger ethnic-racial identity was correlated with more active coping with stressors and fewer aggressive acts (Caldwell, Kohn-Wood, Schmeelk-Cone, Chavous, & Zimmerman, 2004; McMahon & Watts, 2002). Yet members of privileged groups also develop social identities as they become aware of human diversity, social boundaries, and injustices (e.g., White identity development; Helms, 1994).

Identity development models have some limitations (Frable, 1997). A person may not go through all the stages, or may not go through them in order, or may repeat stages. This variation suggests that the stages are better understood as *states,* different ways of viewing the world, but not necessarily in a developmental sequence. These models also may be difficult to apply to multiethnic individuals. It is also important to recognize the intertwining of multiple social identities within a single person (e.g., gender, social class, spirituality) (Frable, 1997; Hurtado, 1997).

Sellers, Smith, Shelton, Rowley, and Chavous (1998) proposed and validated a new model of African-American racial identity that addresses such limitations. Rather than a hierarchy of stages, their model focuses on multiple dimensions of racial identity. It recognizes that the salience of racial identity is influenced by situational and larger contextual factors and that an individual may hold multiple social identities. It focuses on the cultural, historical, and personal experiences of African Americans and on multiple ideologies and worldviews among that population.

Many identity development models explicitly address issues of oppression and liberation (Birman, 1994). They also make sense of many persons' lived experiences and help to explain some dynamics of relations between social groups, especially in high school and college. Tatum (1997; 2004) answered a question often asked by White students, "Why are all the Black kids sitting together in the cafeteria?" She used developmental theories to describe how African-American students (and by extension, other subordinated groups) sitting together are often in a stage of immersion: responding to experiences (often discriminatory) that made their racial status salient and exploring the resources and strengths of their peers and heritage.

Acculturation Models

- A family leaves civil war in their home country and immigrates to Canada.
- A student leaves his native Korea to attend graduate school in the United States.
- A young Navaho must choose between career advancement that would mean leaving his home reservation, weakening ties to his family and culture, or staying home in jobs that will mean less income and prestige.

- An African-American student must choose whether to attend a predominantly African-American college or a predominantly European-American one.
- An Asian American and a Mexican American, college friends, talk a lot about how to balance a future career with loyalty to their families. They realize that they are experiencing differences between mainstream U.S. cultural trends and their own cultural backgrounds.
- A student is the first from her working-class family to attend college. Although she makes friends and succeeds academically, she feels out of place on campus and realizes that she is experiencing subtle pressure to identify with the more affluent world of her classmates. She is ambivalent about this.

These examples pose two questions. To what extent do persons continue to identify or maintain relationships with their culture of origin? To what extent do they identify or maintain relationships with the host or dominant culture?

Psychological acculturation refers to changes in individuals related to the contact between two (or more) cultures that the person experiences (Birman, 1994). Culture here is used in a general sense that may also refer to ethnicity, nationality, race, or other dimensions of diversity. Although psychological acculturation focuses on the individual, it cannot be separated from the contact between larger cultural groups (Birman, 1994). For instance, to understand the individual acculturation of a Japanese-American college student, one must understand not only Japanese cultural heritage, but also the historical discrimination faced by Japanese Americans. Contact of cultural groups usually involves change by each of them to some extent (although one may dominate the others politically or economically). The individual is nested within a two-way process of group contact (Birman, 1994). For some, more than two cultures are involved.

A terminological note: In some writings, *acculturation* has meant identification with the dominant or host culture, and loss of ties to one's culture of origin. Following Berry (1994, 2003) and Birman (1994) we will term that *assimilation*. Also, *enculturation* refers to developing within one's culture of origin, not involving change through relations with another culture (Birman, 1994).

Psychological acculturation may be behaviorally expressed, for instance, in choices of language, clothing, food, gender roles, childrearing strategies, or religious affiliation. It may also be internally expressed: one's personal identity, values, emotions, aspirations, and spirituality are grounded in culture. Berry (1994) proposed a model of psychological acculturation to describe experiences of immigrants adjusting to a new (host) culture; it can be extended to address other subordinated, minority, or indigenous groups. Berry's model assumes that in acculturation the individual identifies with one or the other culture, with both, or with neither. This leads to the four strategies listed in Table 7.2 (Berry, 1994, 2003; Berry & Sam, 1997; Birman, 1994; LaFromboise, Coleman, & Gerton, 1993). You should understand these four strategies as blending into each other, not as simple, sharply demarcated categories.

TABLE 7.2 Four Acculturative Strategies*

	Identification with Dominant Culture	
Identification with Culture of Origin	**Stronger**	**Weaker**
Stronger	Biculturality	Separation
Weaker	Assimilation	Marginality

*Strategies blend into each other. Thus we have labeled identification with each culture in relative terms: *stronger* and *weaker.*

SOURCE: Berry (1994, p. 126).

Separation Individuals pursue this strategy if they identify with their culture of origin, develop language and skills primarily for participating in that culture, live primarily within communities of that culture, and interact with the dominant culture only in limited ways (e.g., work or other economic exchanges). (If members of the dominant culture act in this way, while reserving political, economic, and social power for their group, *segregation* is the appropriate term.) Separation has been a recurrent theme (and one adaptive strategy) in the histories of African Americans, French-speaking Canadians, Native Americans, and immigrants to many countries who live and work in their own ethnic communities.

Assimilation On the other hand, if individuals give up identifying with their culture of origin to pursue identification with the language, values, and communities of the dominant culture, they are assimilating. Assimilation is an acculturation strategy used by some immigrants, refugees, and similar groups in a new host culture. The idea of the "melting pot" for immigrants to the United States has usually meant assimilation to the dominant Anglo-American culture.

Some form of behavioral (but not internal) assimilation may be the only strategy available under powerful systems of oppression. In such circumstances, some members of a subordinated population may be able to pass as a member of the dominant group. *Passing* involves behavioral assimilation in public coupled with a different cultural identification in private. Many lesbians and gay men, especially in adolescence, respond to heterosexist oppression by passing. However, passing exacts a psychic price because it involves keeping secrets and maintaining a divided identity.

Assimilation may be impossible for individuals and groups who differ from the dominant cultural group in obvious ways such as skin color. In a society marked by strong discrimination, even the most sincere and thorough attempts at assimilation by members of such groups may be rebuffed. The first stage of many ethnic and racial identity development models involves attempts to assimilate by persons of color, who abandon it when they are rebuffed by discrimination by European Americans (Phinney, 2003).

Marginality This occurs if individuals do not or cannot identify with either their culture of origin or with the dominant culture. This strategy may not

TABLE 7.3 Characteristics of Bicultural Competence

Identity Factors
Strong individual identity
Strong cultural identity
Cognitive/Emotional Factors
Knowledge of both cultures
Positive attitude toward both cultures
Sense of bicultural efficacy
Social/Behavioral Factors
Communication competence in both cultures
Behavioral skills in both cultures
Social support networks in both cultures

SOURCE: LaFromboise et al. (1993, pp. 402–409).

be chosen, but can result from loss of contact with one's culture of origin combined with exclusion from the dominant culture. It is the strategy usually associated with the greatest psychological distress (Berry & Sam, 1997; LaFromboise et al., 1993, Vivero & Jenkins, 1999). Note that this involves not only being marginalized by a dominant culture (something that may happen with separation as well), but also loss of contact or participation with one's culture of origin.

Integration, Biculturality If individuals identify or participate in meaningful ways with both their culture of origin and the dominant culture, they are using a strategy that Berry (1994) termed *integration,* a strategy others consider *bicultural* (Birman, 1994; LaFromboise et al., 1993). It deserves a longer description.

Bicultural Competence

LaFromboise et al./ (1993) defined eight characteristics of bicultural competence, summarized in Table 7.3.

The first two characteristics concern aspects of one's identity. A **strong individual identity** is crucial. This involves self-awareness and ability to distinguish one's values and choices from others. A **strong cultural identity,** based on integration with one's culture of origin, is also crucial. This identification with one's cultural roots is a resource for development of bicultural competence, providing a secure base from which to explore and learn about the second culture. Identification with one's culture of origin is also an emphasis of identity development models (Birman, 1994). Without identification with at least one culture, a person may possess knowledge and skills of two cultures but may not be deeply identified with either. That state resembles biculturality in behavior but emotionally is more like marginality.

Three further characteristics are cognitive and emotional. The first involves sufficient **knowledge of both cultures:** cultural beliefs, social institutions, and everyday social norms. The individual may find ways to integrate differing values, or need to know how and when to conform one's behavior to one culture or the other. The second characteristic is having **positive attitudes about both cultures,** being able to recognize strengths in each, and holding both in positive regard. The third is a sense of **bicultural efficacy,** the belief or confidence that one can live satisfactorily within both cultures without compromising one's cultural and personal identity. (Note that conditions of oppression can make the latter two aspects difficult.)

LaFromboise et al. cited studies showing that many American Indian children developed greater knowledge of the dominant Anglo-American culture as they moved through school, while also maintaining allegiance to tribal interpersonal norms. In universities in which Anglo-American norms were dominant, bicultural American Indian students knew more about strategies for academic achievement than American Indian peers immersed mainly in their tribal culture. Yet the bicultural students were also more likely to enroll in courses and participate in cultural activities based on American Indian cultures.

Bicultural competence also involves three social/behavioral factors. **Communication competence** in the languages of both cultures and a **repertoire of behavioral skills** in both cultures are necessary. For instance, studies of Latino/Latina and American Indian college students in the United States indicate that possessing academic and social skills for both the dominant culture and the culture of origin promoted personal adjustment to college (LaFromboise et al., 1993).

Finally, bicultural competence involves cultivating **social support networks** within both cultures. (LaFromboise term this *groundedness.*) These networks promote learning bicultural skills and attitudes and provide emotional support for persisting in the face of cultural conflicts and obstacles. Such networks are stronger if they include both bonding ties (e.g, family, friends) and bridging ties for information and contacts.

There are many ways to be bicultural. Some involve strong identification with one's culture of origin and behavioral participation in the dominant culture but not deeper identification with it (Birman, 1994; Ortiz-Torres et al., 2000). This may especially fit the experiences of members of social groups faced with persistent discrimination. For others, particularly immigrant groups, a bicultural strategy may involve identification with both one's culture of origin as well as a deepening identification over time with the dominant culture (Birman, 1994; Phinney, 2003).

The Need for a Contextual Perspective

Two ancient stories from Jewish tradition illustrate the value of acculturation strategies other than biculturality for a small cultural group within a powerful, oppressive society. Joseph, a Jew sold into slavery in Egypt by his brothers, assimilated to Egyptian society, rose to power, and became the

> instrument for preserving Jewish culture in a time of famine. Years later, Moses, a Jew reared by Egyptian royalty with little knowledge of his cultural heritage, learned about that heritage, then led a separatist movement and exodus from Egypt. In different ways, both Joseph and Moses helped preserve their culture. (adapted from Birman, 1994, p. 281)

What is the most adaptive psychological acculturation strategy? As with Joseph and Moses, that depends on the context (Birman, 1994; Trickett, 1996).

Bicultural integration is not necessarily common. For instance, in a study of adolescents whose families had immigrated from Latin America to Washington, D.C., most adolescents were either highly involved in Hispanic culture and social networks (separation) or in wider American culture and networks (assimilation); few were highly involved in both (Birman, 1998). A study of adolescents in Russian Jewish families who had immigrated to the U.S. found similar results (Birman, Trickett, & Vinokurov, 2002). Among a sample of New York City residents of Puerto Rican ancestry, only about one-fourth were bicultural. About one-third were predominantly involved in Puerto Rican culture (separation), one-fourth were involved predominantly in U.S. culture (assimilation), and the remainder uninvolved in either culture (marginality) (Cortes, Rogler, & Malgady, 1994). Many members of immigrant groups pursue bicultural strategies, particularly family members born in the United States, but not all do (Phinney, 2003).

Bicultural integration also is not necessarily adaptive: findings on acculturation and personal adjustment, for adolescents and for adults are mixed (Birman et al., 2002; Shen & Takeuchi, 2001; see also Berry & Sam, 1997; LaFromboise et al., 1993; Phinney, 1990, 2003).

A contextual perspective on acculturation is necessary, asking what cultural qualities (language, social behavior, deeper identity) are important in a given context, and what outcomes (e.g., personal adjustment, academic performance) are most important there. The specific circumstances of the social group and the attitudes of the host society are also influential. Other important factors may include gender, social class, sexual orientation, religiosity, family dynamics, and the qualities of the setting: e.g., school, workplace or neighborhood (Chun & Akutsu, 2003; Santisteban & Mitrani, 2003; Hughes, 2003; Hurtado, 1997; Phinney, Horenczyk, Liebkind, & Vedder, 2001; Sasao, 1999; Shen & Takeuchi, 2001; Ying, 1995). A study of adolescents from the former Soviet Union in two U.S. communities found a number of differences between communities in the dynamics of acculturation and adaptation for these youth (Birman, Trickett, & Buchanan, 2005).

Both social identity development and acculturation are far more complex processes than we have portrayed in our introduction here. Both must be understood as related to multiple ecological levels (see these sources for discussion of complexities: Berry, 1994, 2003, Birman, 1994; Birman, Trickett, & Vinokurov, 2002; Chun, Organista, & Marin, 2003; Helms, 1994; Jones, 2003; Marin & Gamba, 2003; Phinney, 2003; Phinney et al., 2001; Trimble, 2003; Trimble, Helms, & Root, 2003).

A further contextual question is: What specific qualities of communities or community settings promote identification with one's culture of origin yet also strengthen appreciation of other communities and cultures, and a wider sense of unity and "affirmative diversity" (Jones, 1994; Kress & Elias, 2000)?

For example, how can teaching strategies, curricula, learning communities, community service learning, and other aspects of college life promote outcomes such as students' cultural awareness, identity development, adaptation to college, and sense of wider social responsibility? (See, for instance, Maton, 2000, pp. 43–44; Stukas & Dunlap, 2002; Zirkel & Cantor, 2004.) Allport (1954) proposed conditions for effective intergroup education, such as equal status among diverse groups, and personal experience in working together toward shared goals. Are those concepts useful in creating settings in college (e.g., Gurin, Nagda, & Lopez, 2004)? How can colleges recognize and promote the strengths of identification with one's culture of origin (e.g., Tatum, 2004)? Are desirable setting qualities contextual—for example, different for White and Black students in predominantly White or historically Black colleges (Brower & Ketterhagen, 2004)? Similar questions can be asked about schools and other settings for children and youth as well as for adult development; and not only about race or ethnicity but also about other social identities such as gender, sexual orientation, and spirituality.

IMPLICATIONS FOR COMMUNITY PSYCHOLOGISTS

The concepts in this chapter have a number of implications for community psychology. In Chapter 3 we discussed implications for conducting community research. Here we focus on personal cultural competence among community psychologists and on cultural appropriateness of community programs.

Individual Cultural Competence

Community psychologists seek to understand communities by working within them, which often requires competence for working across cultural boundaries. Definitions and descriptions of cultural competence for community researchers and practitioners vary (e.g., Canning, 1999; Harrell, Taylor, & Burke, 1999; Mock, 1999; Resnicow, Braithwaite, Ahluwahlia, & Baranowski, 1999; Sasao, 1999), but often contain the following elements (note that several elements parallel the characteristics of bicultural competence described earlier):

- knowledge of the characteristics, experiences, beliefs, values, and norms of the cultural group with whom one is working
- respect for these cultural elements without assumptions of superiority or inferiority
- interpersonal-behavioral skills for working within the culture

- supportive relationships within the culture with whom one is working, and in one's own culture;
- "a professional stance of informed naiveté, curiosity, and humility" (Mock, 1999, p. 40), involving awareness of one's limited knowledge and a commitment to learn
- awareness of how one's own culture and experiences have shaped one's worldview
- a viewpoint that development of cultural competence is an ongoing process, not a simple achievement

These qualities involve not only cognitive knowledge and behavioral skills, but also attitudes. Those include a curiosity about, and genuine respect for, the strengths of a cultural tradition as well as a willingness to address differences in privilege and personal experiences with power.

Designing Culturally Sensitive Community Programs

Culturally sensitive or appropriate community programs must address many aspects of the culture for which they are designed. These are best developed in genuine collaboration with members of the local culture and community. Writing from a health promotion perspective, Resnicow et al. (1999) proposed a useful distinction for describing cultural issues in designing community programs, borrowed from linguistics: the surface structure and deep structure of a community program.

Surface structure involves observable aspects of a program: race, ethnicity, and gender of its staff; language(s) used; choice of cultural elements such as food or music; and setting. These elements are important, but surface structure alone may not be enough to make a program effective. For instance, Sasao (1999) found that simply having Asian-American staff in a clinical service for Asian Americans did not resolve all cultural differences between therapists and clients. As another example, simply being a Black psychologist is not enough to secure the trust of a Black community; that trust must be built (Jordan, Bogat, & Smith, 2001).

Deep structure involves core cultural beliefs, values, and practices. The deep structure of a culture requires historical, psychological, and social knowledge of the culture. For instance, some Latino/Latina and African cultural beliefs emphasize supernatural causes for illness as well as natural causes (Resnicow et al., 1999). These multiple explanations of illness will affect willingness to report symptoms, choice of indigenous healers or Western health professionals, and many health-related behaviors. A health promotion outreach program for these populations must address those issues. Potts (2003) described a school program that drew on African cultural and spiritual concepts to promote African-American youth development. Helm (2003) described how health promotion in Native Hawai'ian communities must draw on community and cultural beliefs about interconnection of land and water, community and health. Harper et al. (2004) described culturally sensitive sexuality initiatives in a Mexican-American community. The sexuality intervention for young Latinas that we described earlier illustrated deep structural elements, addressing values of *marianismo* and *machismo* (Ortiz-Torres et al., 2000). Jumper-Thurman, Edwards, Plested, and Oetting (2003) assessed community readiness in Native American, Hispanic, and Anglo communities to create culturally valid interventions in each. Deep structural cultural programs may appeal most to persons pursuing separation or bicultural strategies, not those seeking assimilation or who are marginalized. Effectiveness of culturally sensitive programs needs to be evaluated in research (Resnicow et al., 1999).

Alaska Native Spirituality and Sobriety Alaska Native indigenous communities are using their cultural heritages to create community climates of sobriety, helping individuals and communities prevent and promote recovery from substance abuse (Hazel & Mohatt, 2001; Mohatt et al., 2004). These provide an example of culturally anchored community initiatives, developed by community members, which address both surface and deep structure.

Alaska Native peoples are diverse (Yupik, Inupiat, Athapascan, Tlingit, Haida, and others). Yet they share some common cultural elements, especially spiritual perspectives, and these are key aspects of the Native sobriety movement. Common spiritual elements include beliefs in a Creator, the spirituality of all living beings, the intermingling of the spiritual and material worlds, and the importance of personal awareness of spiritual forces. These offer rich resources for community sobriety initiatives.

Native leaders summarized cultural elements related to sobriety in four interrelated realms of living: physical, emotional, cognitive, and spiritual. Persons and communities promote sobriety in the physical realm by using Native healing and traditional foods; by participation in Native cleansing rituals, dancing, singing, and other arts; and by subsistence gathering and hunting. In the emotional realm, individuals foster sobriety by experiencing joyful and painful emotions, connecting with family and community, and practicing forgiveness. In the cognitive realm, they can learn and take pride in cultural legends, history, and practices; by learn the culture's language, and by take responsibility for self, family, and community. Sobriety in the spiritual realm involves opening one's eyes to the spiritual world, connecting with ancestors, meditation, prayer, and using dreams and visions as guides (Hazel & Mohatt, 2001). Promoting sobriety involves all four realms, strengthening individual development and family and community bonds. Mohatt et al. (2004) described how program developers worked with Native leaders to develop culturally appropriate evaluation methods.

CONCLUSION

Two important overall questions remain. First, does this chapter's perspective on human diversity lead to moral relativism, endorsing all value systems (e.g., Nazism, religious intolerance, or oppression of women) as equally morally compelling?

Simply put, no. The perspective of this chapter is concerned with understanding human diversity in context. This involves comprehending other persons and cultures in their own terms, especially their strengths. This often leads to discerning one's own assumptions and values and to deeper awareness of both others and oneself. This process is not easy or simple, but only with such pluralistic, contextual understanding can informed, principled moral stances on human problems be built.

Overarching values, such as the seven values we have proposed for community psychology, help to address such issues. As we discussed in the earlier section When Culture and Liberation Conflict, action based on principled values such as social justice, by *citizens acting collectively within their own culture,* can lead to personal and social transformation. Of course, the ways that community psychologists think about social justice or other values are rooted in their own cultural experiences. Yet community psychologists and others working for change, such as the empowerment of women, can ally themselves with members of other cultures or communities who hold *similar values within their cultural context.*

Second, with all our emphasis on how humans differ across cultural, racial, ethnic, gender, and other boundaries, how can we understand what humans have in common? On what shared basis can multicultural, diverse communities or societies be constructed and sustained?

This question requires some historical perspective. The question may presuppose the desirability of earlier times that seemed harmonious to members of privileged groups because both they and members of subordinated groups "knew their place." It is also important to note that Western social scientists often have assumed that their concepts and perspective were universal and later found those ideas were ethnocentric. Perspectives differ on how best to address this question (e.g., Fowers & Richardson, 1996; Hall, 1997; Sue, 2004). Searching for common ground on overarching values may help as long as we remember that each person's perspective is inevitably limited by their own cultural experiences.

Certainly there is much that is universal in human experience, but we can understand it only if we also understand how others view that experience differently. As one of psychology's founders, William James, asserted: "There is very little difference between one person and another, but what little difference there is, is very important" (cited in Hall, 1997, p. 650).

CHAPTER SUMMARY

1. Important dimensions of human diversity for community psychology include culture, race, ethnicity, gender, sexual orientation, socioeconomic status or social class, ability/disability, age, locality, and spirituality. These dimensions can be separated conceptually, but they may converge in community life. Pluralism involves the assumption that everyone has a position

somewhere on these dimensions and that each position is to be understood in its own terms. *Intersectionality* is when two or more of these dimensions overlap.

2. One important dimension of cultural diversity is *individualism-collectivism*. This is a spectrum along which cultures differ, including conceptions of a more *independent self* or *interdependent self*. Individual and group thinking, emotions and behavior are influenced by whether a culture is more individualistic or collectivistic, although all cultures must deal with tensions between individual and collective identities. However, the individualism-collectivism concept has limitations: (a) individualistic and collectivistic communities exist even within cultures; (b) world cultures are becoming more interdependent; (c) it is only one dimension along which cultures differ; (d) understanding another culture as simply the opposite of one's own is inaccurate; (e) it is useful only for describing broad themes of cultural differences, not for understanding any specific culture well.
3. Not all human diversity is the result of cultural forces. Power and access to resources also create group differences. The *liberation perspective* describes social systems of oppression and aims of liberation. Oppression creates an inequality of power between a *dominant, privileged group* and an *oppressed, subordinated group,* often on grounds of factors such as gender or race that an individual cannot change. Oppression is more than prejudice; it is based in social systems that affect privileged and subordinated groups regardless of whether they like it or not. There are multiple systems of oppression (e.g., racism, sexism) working at multiple ecological levels (e.g., social myths, mass media stereotypes, neighborhood tipping point). Those in subordinated groups often resist oppression, but *internalized oppression* occurs when they believe that they really are inferior. *Patriarchy* is an example of an oppressive system that subordinates women but harms both women and men. Thus dismantling it would have benefits for both. Key elements of liberation theory are summarized in Table 7.1.
4. When culture and liberation conflict, attention to values is needed, and change needs to come from persons and values within the culture. Every culture has some diversity of values and changes over time; these can be bases for cultural challenge and transformation.
5. Limitations of liberation theory include the following: (a) it may underestimate diversity within dominant or subordinated groups; (b) the oppressed group may be portrayed merely as victims; and (c) it may emphasize conflict between groups to the exclusion of shared goals.
6. *Social identity development* models have been proposed for racial, ethnic, sexual orientation, and other groups. Most assume stages of identity that include an opening stage of unexamined identity, followed by stages of exploration, often within one's own group, and higher stages of forming a social (e.g., racial) identity and learning to relate to both one's own group and the wider

world. These models do address issues of oppression and identity. However, many people do not follow the stage sequence, so the "stages" might better be considered "states."

7. The *acculturation* perspective concerns individual adaptation to the interaction of two cultures or groups. Four acculturative strategies can be identified: *separation, assimilation, marginality,* and *biculturality* (or *integration*). (See Table 7.2.)
8. *Bicultural competence* refers to skills and conditions needed for effective adaptation to a second or dominant culture while retaining identification with one's culture of origin. Its eight factors are summarized in Table 7.3. Although evidence supports the value of the bicultural strategy in many circumstances, it is not always the wisest acculturative strategy.
9. *Cultural competence* for community psychologists consists of qualities that promote genuine understanding and collaboration with members of a culture. Culturally sensitive community programs address the *surface structure* and *deep structure* of a culture.
10. Understanding and respecting human diversity does not mean moral relativism: one can hold strong values while seeking to understand other views. Better understanding of multiple forms of human diversity is needed.

BRIEF EXERCISES

1. Experiential learning about human diversity is best done with other people, especially those who are different from you in race, gender, social class, sexual orientation, or other dimension of diversity. In addition, experiences that bridge cultural, racial, or other boundaries often involve emotions that must be understood and preconceptions that can be difficult to recognize at first. For those reasons, we recommend that you seek experiences at your campus multicultural center or other setting (on or off campus) for learning about dimensions of human diversity. Make time for this. It's potentially one of the most meaningful parts of your education. Visit the setting and attend lectures, workshops, or other presentations. Talk with staff or students there and indicate your interest in learning, and listen to learn. Be patient; don't try to become an instant expert. Be persistent; don't be discouraged by an initial experience that doesn't happen as you wanted it. Recognize that students there may be interested in talking with you, but they also have other commitments.

   Of course, the best learning often occurs in personal relationships where trust is built and understanding unfolds over time. Cultivating these across boundaries of diverse groups can be an important part of your education.
2. Discuss your responses to the exercise that begins this chapter with classmates or friends. The more diverse the group for discussion, the better. The

Muilticultural Pavilion and Understanding Prejudice websites in the list of recommended websites have other exercises that may work better for you.

3. Read a community psychology journal article that concerns at least one dimension of human diversity. (You can access the *American Journal of Community Psychology* through the InfoTrac College Edition search service.) Consider these questions: What dimension(s) of human diversity did this article concern? Did the study concern themes of individualism-collectivism, liberation and oppression, or acculturation? If the study concerned an intervention within a culture, did it focus on surface structure or deep structure?

RECOMMENDED READINGS

Bond, M., Hill, J., Mulvey, A., & Terenzio, M. (Eds.) (2000). Special issue part I: Feminism and community psychology. *American Journal of Community Psychology, 28*(5).

Freire, P. (1993). *Pedagogy of the oppressed.* New York: Continuum. (Original work published 1970.)

Jones, J. M. (1997). *Prejudice and racism* (2nd ed.). New York: McGraw-Hill.

Trickett, E. J. (1996). A future for community psychology: The contexts of diversity and the diversity of contexts. *American Journal of Community Psychology, 24,* 209–235.

Trickett, E. J., Watts, R. J., & Birman, D. (Eds.). (1994). *Human diversity: Perspectives on people in context.* San Francisco: Jossey-Bass.

Watts, R., & Serrano-Garcia, I. (Eds.) (2003). Special issue section: The psychology of liberation: Responses to oppression. *American Journal of Community Psychology, 31,* 73–204.

RECOMMENDED WEBSITES

American Psychological Association Public Interest Directorate
http://www.apa.org/pi/programs.html

Information on Public Interest Directorate programs on psychological aspects of diversity topics.

Multicultural Pavilion
http://www.edchange.org/multicultural/

Information, exercises, and links to related sites on many dimensions of human diversity. Primarily education topics.

Understanding Prejudice
http://www.understandingprejudice.org

Exercises, information, and links on a variety of prejudice and social justice issues.

National Index of Violence and Harm
http://www.manchester.edu/links/violenceindex/

Information on this quantitative index of violence and inequality and changes over time.

INFOTRAC COLLEGE EDITION KEYWORDS

acculturation, bicultural(ity), culture(al), diversity, social (racial, ethnic) identity(ies), liberation, oppression; or listing any dimension of diversity from the chapter, e.g., *aging,* or any category term, e.g., *Japanese, Asian American*

8

Understanding Coping in Context

Elise Herndon is co-author of this chapter.

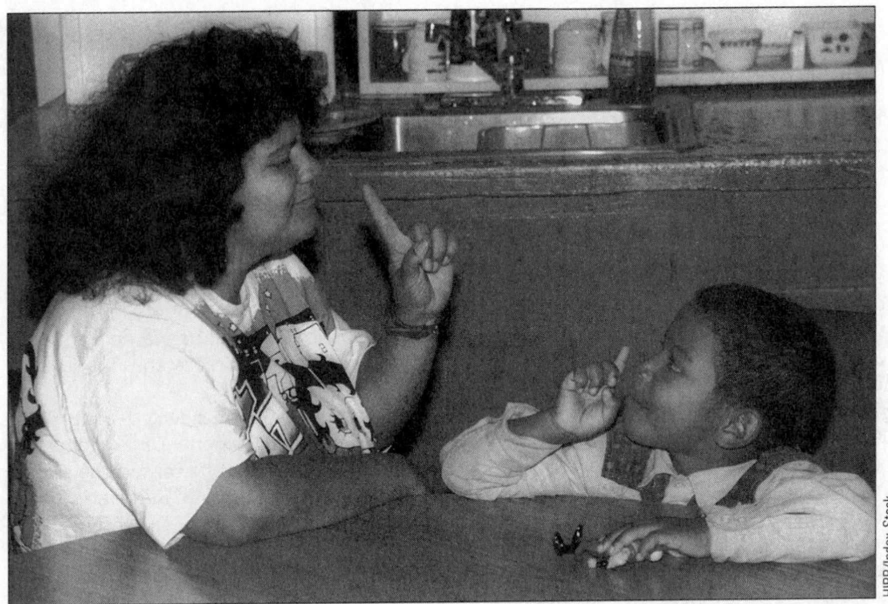
HIRB/Index Stock

OPENING EXERCISE

Think of an important stressful experience in your life. It may have been a single event: serious illness or injury, or flunking an important test. It may have been a life transition: beginning college or graduate school, becoming a parent, divorce, loss of a job, bereavement. It may be a long-term situation: living on a low income, a chronic illness, or having to balance several demanding roles such as mother, wife, student, and worker. It may be an experience that fits none of these categories well.

Consider the following questions about your experience.

- What was stressful about it for you?
- Was it a short-term or single event, or a long-term situation?
- What resources helped you cope with this stressful experience? For instance: support from others, coping or other skills, beliefs or practices that sustained you, money, time.
- What things did you do to cope with this experience?
- Are you a different person now as a result of this experience? What did you learn, or how did you grow, through this experience?

Box 8.1 contains answers to these questions by two authors of this chapter.

BOX 8.1 Personal Experiences with Stress, Coping, Resources, and Thriving

The following accounts by two authors of this chapter illustrate some of the processes in this chapter.

Passage to Adulthood

When I was 21, in the summer between my junior and senior years of college, my mother died after long being ill with cancer. My father, sister, and I knew her death was coming, even welcomed it with relief; her cancer had been very painful. But it still came hard, with an emptiness and sense of great loss. Several things about that experience still stand out for me, decades later.

Within hours, friends from our church and town began what is a bereavement tradition in many communities: delivering home-cooked food for us and the mourners who would join us. This and many other acts of kindness continued for days.

The next few days were a blur as we attended to the duties and rituals of bereavement in our culture. Some of those were not easy, but they were helpful, even inspiring. I felt I belonged in an extended family and community. I cannot count the ways that my family and I received support from others. Cultural and religious traditions and rituals helped make her life and death meaningful to me.

Sometime later that summer, while still recovering emotionally, I realized that I now had to grow up, especially to make decisions for myself. Like most mothers, mine had been a close personal guide even when I disregarded her advice. Her passing was a turning point for me. With the support of my family, friends, and my academic mentor, and with spiritual support, the next year was a time of spiraling growth, a year of making choices, the beginning of adulthood. (Jim Dalton)

The End of the Road

It was dark and drizzling rain on a warm March night as I drove to spend the evening with my fiance. There were few houses or landmarks on the rural county road I was traveling, but I felt reassured that I'd be warned of the approach of the T-shaped intersection by the rumble strips that signaled the stop ahead.

Suddenly I was struck by the unexpected sight of another road crossing my path. I experienced a moment of disorientation, then realized that I'd missed the stop and was flying through the intersection. Resurfacing work had obliterated the rumble strips.

In the next moment, I was airborne as I sailed over the embankment at the end of the road. My thoughts raced as I quickly sized up the situation and my options. I concluded there was nothing that could be done until the car had landed and come to a stop. I marveled at how clear my thoughts were and vaguely wondered why my life wasn't flashing before me.

Finally, the car landed with a dull, bone-crushing thud and continued its forward motion into a grove of pine trees and scrub oaks. I prayed that I would not hit one. I realized that the deeper the car was propelled into the forest, the less likely I would be found, and the farther I'd have to make my way out. If my injuries were extensive, that might not be possible. The car finally

COPING: AN ECOLOGICAL-CONTEXTUAL FRAMEWORK

In this chapter we offer a community psychology view of stress, coping, social support, and their outcomes, emphasizing how persons are embedded in multiple contexts. We also hope to show how community and clinical psychology intersect and complement each other in addressing stress and coping. We highlight contextual and community processes, leaving details of individual coping processes to more individually oriented textbooks and resources. However, we believe that both community-contextual and clinical-individual perspectives are needed for understanding the dynamic experiences and outcomes of stress and coping. In coping, individual and contextual processes are intertwined (Sandler, Gensheimer, & Braver, 2000).

came to a stop, slowed by the low scrubs and brush in the forest. I hadn't hit a tree, but once I had recovered my breath, I could quickly tell that I was too badly injured to move.

I don't know how long I sat there. I struggled to calm myself and deal with the intense feeling of fear that flooded me. Once I was calm, I began to consider what action, if any, I could take at this point. In spite of my circumstances, I was lucid and alert.

In what seems like both an instant and an eternity, I heard a voice say, "Are you okay?" A man and his wife had been passing by when they saw my car cross the intersection. Realizing there was no road on the other side, they turned around to investigate. I quickly said a prayer of thanks before answering his question. I told him that I thought my back was broken and my ankles were fractured. He stayed there beside me while we waited for the ambulance, bolstering my courage with his steady presence and comforting words.

When at last the emergency medical personnel arrived, they spoke to me, did a cursory examination, then lashed me to a back board and loaded me into the ambulance. I think I made a joke of some kind because I remember laughter, but I don't recall what was said. As we drove away, one EMT held my hand, softly speaking words of reassurance.

In the ambulance, I made a resolution that whatever adversity I might face, I would find a way to have a meaningful life. I remembered when I was a child seeing greeting cards created by a woman who was completely paralyzed, painted with a brush clenched in her teeth. I thought, "I'm artistic. I could do that."

During the weeks I lay in the hospital and the months of recovery that followed, I was fortified by an outpouring of support from family and friends. Fresh flowers were forbidden in ICU, but a dear friend sent a small basket of artificial fruit held by a tiny elf. It was a strange little gift, but whenever I looked at it I was reminded of the love of those who were thinking of me. When I was transferred from ICU, the flowers, cards, visits, prayers, and small acts of kindness from family, friends, and even the hospital staff sustained me. My fiance kept fresh roses in my room and stayed with me whenever he could to make sure my needs were met. My doctors, nurses, and physical therapists provided professional care and refused to give up on my recovery.

I did recover, beyond all expectations, and I mark this event as a key turning point in my life. Some of the chronic health repercussions have been challenging, but I've grown as a result of the experience. I have a deeper spiritual faith, a stronger belief in human goodness, and greater confidence in my own resiliency. I'm more determined now, and I'm much clearer about my priorities. Perhaps most important of all, I now believe that even the most difficult circumstances can be gifts in disguise. (Elise Herndon)

Figure 8.1. illustrates the conceptual framework of this chapter. It identifies key processes and outcomes, relationships among them, and points for constructive interventions. It is based on frameworks by Barbara Dohrenwend, Rudolf Moos, and Abraham Wandersman and associates (Dohrenwend, 1978; Moos, 2002; Wandersman, 1990; Wandersman, Morsbach, McKnight, Herndon, & Coyne, 2002). This framework is suggestive; we present it to stimulate your own thinking about the processes involved. Causal pathways among these processes are complex and often involve cycles among multiple processes. There are many useful ways to understand these relationships. Nonetheless, this framework makes a good conceptual scaffold for this chapter.

In this chapter we draw case examples from Elise Herndon's work in a community mental health program for flood and hurricane victims in a rural region of the southeastern United States. Many of these concern "Elaine" (a pseudonym),

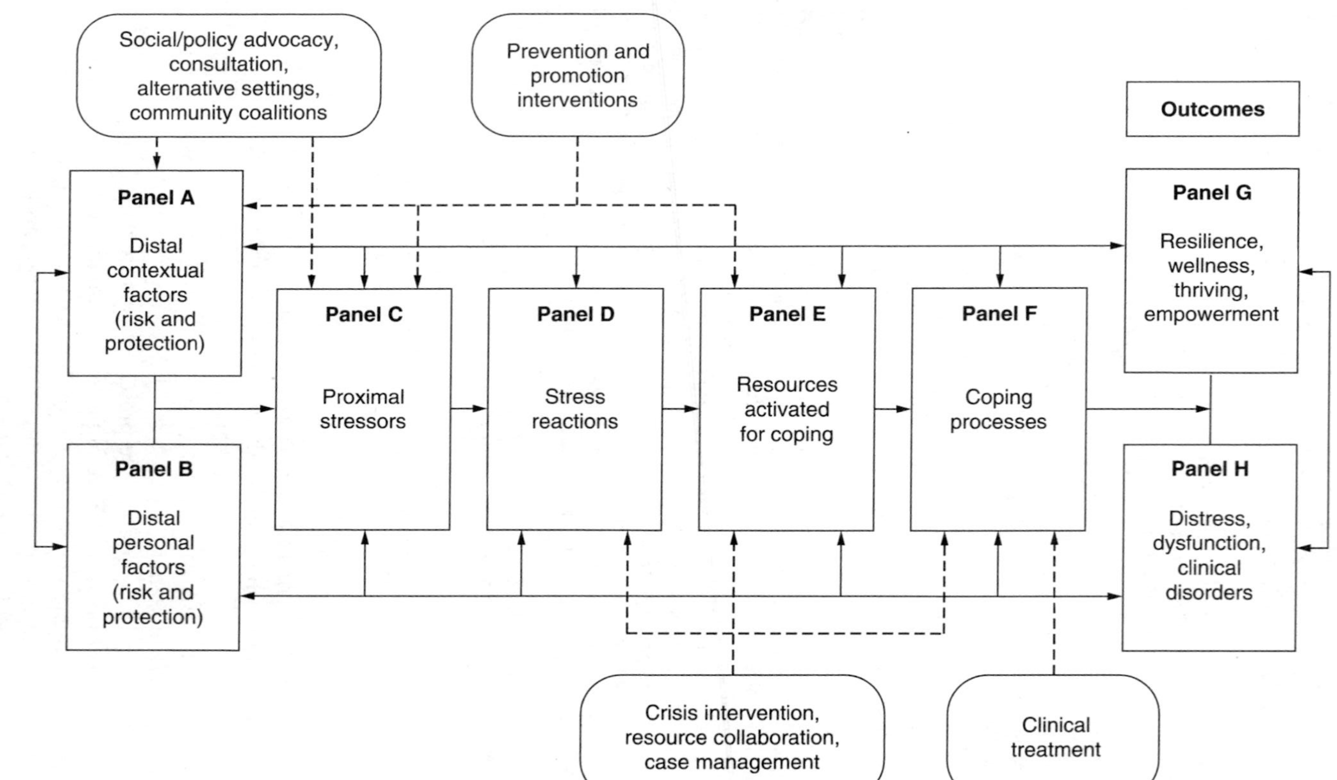

FIGURE 8.1 Potential relationships among ecological levels, coping processes, and interventions

whom we introduced in Chapter 1. Elaine was a flood victim who called a crisis line when she was depressed and suicidal. Her experiences and others we discuss illustrate the value of employing an ecological approach.

Risk and Protective Processes

In our ecological framework, we distinguish between **risk processes** (or risk factors), which are correlated with problematic individual outcomes such as personal distress, mental disorders, or behavior problems, and **protective processes** (or factors), which are strengths or resources associated with positive individual outcomes (we also used this distinction in Chapter 5 in discussing neighborhoods). Risk and protective processes exist at multiple ecological levels, from individual qualities to macrosystem forces.

Risk processes often make it difficult to sustain desired or expected social roles. An example is a family in which the mother has a chronic illness. For children, this could comprise a genetic risk of contracting the same illness. Furthermore, if the mother is chronically ill, she may be unable to drive the children to friends' houses or to school for activities or programs. The father may be burdened with her care and less available to spend time with the children or help them with homework. Neither parent may be able to maintain working contacts with their children's teachers. The mother's illness may affect the family's income and health care expenses. Thus the mother's illness, although only one of many factors in the family's life, may be related to academic or social problems for the children and to the family's economic and social well-being.

Protective processes, in contrast, provide resources for coping and often represent strengths of persons or communities. Bronfenbrenner (1979) asserted that the presence of an "irrationally caring" adult is the most essential protective factor for children. He meant that children benefit when they know someone unconditionally cares about them. Other protective processes may involve personal qualities such as optimism, interpersonal resources such as friends, community resources such as religious congregations or school programs or recreational opportunities, and macrosystem resources such as affordable health care. Sense of community and social capital in neighborhoods and organizations can be protective factors.

In our example of a family whose mother has a chronic illness, suppose this family had several caring relatives who were available to help the family and encourage the children. Add a caring school environment and a teacher who realizes these children need some special help. With these protective influences, the risk of negative outcomes for these children may be significantly reduced.

Protective processes are related to the concept of resilience, an individual's capacity to adapt successfully and function competently despite exposure to stress, adversity, or chronic trauma. Resilience is common, surprisingly so to psychologists who are trained to search for deficits rather than strengths. Although problems remain with how resilience is defined and measured, it is important in understanding coping (Bonanno, 2004; Luthar, Cicchetti, & Becker, 2000; Masten, 2001).

At times, resilience is addressed as though it were a trait. For example, Garmezy's (1971) early work referred to "invulnerable children." However, it often results from a combination of individual and environmental processes (Luthar, Cicchetti, & Becker, 2000). Perhaps there were key people who showed help and caring or tangible resources at key moments. Recognizing environmental influences, consistent with a community psychology perspective, suggests pathways for action involving multiple ecological levels, not just individuals. In the ecological framework in Figure 8.1, we include resilience as an outcome, involving adapting effectively despite adverse circumstances. However, the capacity to achieve that outcome often involves distal contextual and personal processes.

Protective processes are also related to the idea of personal and community strengths. For instance, "at-risk" adolescents often thrive as their personal strengths are identified, enhanced, valued, and linked to areas of difficulty (Brendtro, Brokenleg, & Van Bockern, 1990; Elias & Cohen, 1999). Recent work in the positive psychology movement is legitimizing the study of personal strengths and bringing this concept into the mainstream of psychology (Seligman & Csikszentmihalyi, 2000a). However, positive psychology focuses on individual qualities, often lacks a developmental perspective, and is isolated from innovations in primary prevention and competence promotion intervention research (Cowen & Kilmer, 2002). In community psychology, strengths are defined at multiple ecological levels beyond the individual, including those of cultural traditions, neighborhoods, organizations, and friendship networks (Maton, Schellenbach, Leadbeater, & Solarz, 2004). In addition, community and preventive interventions bolster competence in social and emotional competencies (e.g., Albee & Gullotta, 1997; Cherniss, 2001; Weissberg & Kumpfer, 2003). Thus, to fully understand strengths, a community perspective complements the positive psychology perspective.

Distal Factors

Beginning at the left of Figure 8.1, Panels A and B depict the distinct yet interrelated influences of distal contextual and personal factors. **Distal factors** are predisposing processes, which directly and indirectly shape stressors, resources, coping processes, and outcomes. They are distal in relation to stress reactions and coping (Panels D and F in Figure 8.1). Stress and coping play out differently in different contexts and for different persons. Both influence what stressors occur, how stress is understood and experienced, what resources are available and used, and what coping strategies the person chooses. Distal factors may be relatively stable characteristics such as gender or personal temperament or more dynamic processes such as economic trends, neighborhood crime, and family conflict. (However, all distal factors are dynamic processes in the sense that they change over time.) Both Panel A and Panel B include both risk and protective processes.

In Figure 8.1, distal factors are distinct from **proximal processes,** which are more immediately related to stress and coping. Proximal processes include precipitating stressors such as bereavement or a natural disaster (Panel C) and resources activated for coping (Panel E). A person with many distal risks may nonetheless cope very well if proximal stressors are mild or if proximal resources are available. Conversely, although many persons may endure a proximal stressor such as a hurricane, the most vulnerable are often those with many distal risk factors and few proximal resources.

Distal Contextual Factors These include ongoing environmental conditions in various life domains. Cultural traditions, beliefs, practices or rituals, and institutions can provide meaning and strength in difficult times, as noted in Box 8.1. Yet they also can create stressors, for instance in the ways that many cultures foster unequal workloads and limit opportunities for women. In a multicultural society, cultural influences include those from the dominant culture as well as that of other relevant cultures. Economic conditions at multiple levels, from global to local, also introduce both stressors and opportunities. Social and political forces affect individuals (for instance, in the form of discrimination) or through policies that limit it. An ongoing environmental hazard such as toxic waste near a community poses both biological and psychological risks. As we discussed in Chapters 5 and 6, neighborhood processes such as violence, sense of community, or informal neighboring influence individual well-being. The social climate of a school, classroom, or workplace, and the social regularities defined by social roles and power dynamics, also shape individual lives. Finally, the dynamics of family life and of interpersonal relationships provide both stressors and resources for individuals.

Distal contextual factors may also be chronic stressors that involve long-term resource scarcity (not the more sudden changes that we label proximal stressors) (Wandersman & Nation, 1998). Examples include poverty, environmental pollution, noise, crowding, neighborhood crime, lack of health care, and family role demands such as caregiving for a sick relative or parenting a challenging child. The effects of chronic environmental conditions may be cumulative, such as the combined effects of poverty, crowding, and a chronic illness. Ongoing family conditions, such as parental alcoholism or chronic illness, may be both chronic stressors for the affected family member and contextual factors for the children in such families that increase their risk of dysfunction (Barrera, Li, & Chassin, 1995). As we mentioned in Chapter 5, stressors include long-term exposure to toxic wastes and neighborhood hazards (Evans, 2004; Levine, 1982; Wandersman & Nation, 1998; Wandersman & Hallman, 1993).

Distal Personal Factors These include: genetic and other biological factors; personality traits such as shyness or extraversion; ongoing individual conditions such as chronic illness; and continuing effects of prior life experiences such as child maltreatment. As with contextual factors, distal personal factors may act as stressors or resources and play a risk or protective role. Dispositional optimism, for example, promotes a positive appraisal of stressors and effective coping (Scheier, Carver, & Bridges, 2001). Because these factors are well-covered in other sources and our emphasis is contextual, we do not review them in detail here.

The boundary between contextual and personal factors is permeable and fluid. A chronic illness, for example, is not only a personal issue. The personal

TABLE 8.1 Distal Factors in Coping

Contextual*
Cultural traditions, practices
Economic conditions
Social, political forces
Environmental hazards
Neighborhood processes
Setting social climates
Social regularities
Family dynamics
Personal*
Biological, genetic factors
Personal temperaments, traits
Chronic illness or similar conditions
Ongoing effects of prior life experiences

*These are illustrative categories, not exhaustive lists.

impact of the illness is influenced by sociocultural interpretations of the illness, how disabling it is considered to be, and how individuals with that illness are expected to behave. Although family dynamics are contextual, they interact closely with a wide range of personal factors.

See Table 8.1 for an illustrative summary of distal factors.

Elaine: Distal Factors Elaine had become depressed and suicidal while caring for her husband during his terminal illness, and her situation was complicated by her mother's chronic illness and her husband's and son's behavior problems. Distal contextual factors that shaped Elaine's situation included long-standing poverty and living in a mobile home on a flood plain. Cultural gender expectations placed Elaine in multiple caregiver roles with little assistance from the men in the family. Family dysfunction included substance abuse by Elaine's adult son, who was living at home, and impulsive spending of the very limited family resources by her husband. Elaine and her family were isolated in their rural community: neighbors were distant, and there were few community helping services or other community resources (these were limited due to macrosystem economic and political forces, as we discussed in Chapter 1). This lack of resources was worsened by Elaine's personal limitations: she could not drive, had little formal education and few job skills, and had little experience in family finances (which are also reflections of the impact of macrosystems, including gender roles).

Proximal Stressors

Panel C in Figure 8.1 includes proximal stressors, termed proximal because of their precipitating, relatively direct relationship to stress and coping. Stressors are demands that represent a threatened or actual loss or scarcity of resources (Hobfoll, 1988; 1998; Lazarus & Folkman, 1984). Stressors are risk factors involving both individuals and environments. They vary in duration, severity, quantity, personal meaning, and point of impact. In addition, the boundary between proximal and distal-chronic stressors is not always simple. For instance, traumatic events such as rape or combat may evoke distress for years following the incident. Here we present four types of proximal stressors, but these categories overlap to some extent, and other useful categories exist.

In our framework, stressors are first presented as antecedents, prior to appraisal and coping. However, stressors and coping responses shape each other to some extent (see feedback arrows in our model). Maladaptive coping efforts create additional stressors that may lead to vicious spirals. For instance, avoidant coping such as binge drinking can create stressors at work or school and in personal relationships. Adaptive coping can add to resources and reduce stressors, as indicated in our model by arrows leading from coping responses back to resources.

Major Life Events Holmes and Rahe (1967) pioneered a study of the impact of major life events. Their Social Readjustment Rating Scale is a standardized list of stressful life events such as bereavement, divorce, and job loss. Based on empirical studies, each event is assigned a point value to estimate the amount of change or adjustment it requires of the individual. The sum of these points represents an individual's degree of exposure to stress. Researchers in this arena have found reliable, moderate correlations between life-event scores and the occurrence of illness.

The work of Holmes and Rahe spawned a number of studies with varied populations and stressors. However, this approach has a number of shortcomings (Sandler et al., 2000). Correlations of life-events scores and outcomes have been relatively modest, accounting for only 9–10 percent of the variance in scores (Hobfoll & Vaux, 1993). In addition, because stressors are defined as events requiring adaptive change, the lists include both "entrances," such as marriage or the birth of a child, and "exits," such as widowhood or unemployment. Studies indicate that exits tend to have a stronger association with psychological distress and illness than entrances (Thoits, 1983; Vinokur & Selzer, 1975). Furthermore, such standardized lists of life events are not sensitive to the cultural, economic, and personal meaning of those events to the individual (Mirowsky & Ross, 1989). Divorce, for example, is given a single score regardless of its cultural acceptability or the variability of its impact. Finally, uncontrollable and unpredictable events have been found to be particularly stressful, yet these dimensions are not measured by most life-events scales (Thoits, 1983).

Life Transitions These produce an enduring change in a person's life context, requiring the learning of new skills or assumption of new roles. Examples include the bereavement and the car accident in Box 8.1. Or recall the transition for you when you entered college or graduate school. Making that transition may have required you to expand your academic, interpersonal, time management, or decision-making skills. The impact of a life transition (e.g., impact of divorce on children) is contextual, each transition requires its own coping skills, each has its own cultural-social meaning (e.g., attitudes about divorce), and persons bring different personal and social resources to the transition.

Transitions from elementary to middle and high school can be stressful, especially in large school systems that diminish individual contacts between students and staff. Seidman and associates studied multiracial samples of low-income adolescents in New York City, Baltimore, and Washington, D.C. After the transition to junior high school, grades, preparation for school, involvement in school activities, social support from school staff, and self-esteem all dropped. Engagement with peers increased, but this was not necessarily constructive, because students reported that peers' values were becoming more antisocial (Seidman, Allen, Aber, Mitchell, & Feinman, 1994). At the transition to high school, similar but less negative effects occurred (Seidman, Aber, Allen, & French, 1996). Similar effects occurred among low-income, mainly Hispanic students in Chicago, where students moved directly from elementary school to high school. Decreases occurred in student grades, attendance, and perceptions of support from family, peers, and school staff (Gillock & Reyes, 1996).

These declines in academic engagement are especially serious given the developmental importance of the early adolescent years (Seidman, Aber & French, 2004). These studies document a loss of resources for many youth. Social support from adults, especially at school, decreases. In Chapter 5, we described the STEP program, which changes school environments to prevent these effects (Felner & Adan, 1988).

Daily Hassles The study of daily hassles and uplifts extends the life-events approach to short-term, smaller-scale events (Kanner, Coyne, Schaefer, & Lazarus, 1981). Examples of daily hassles include family arguments and traffic jams. Although many daily hassles grow from ambient or chronic stress, daily hassles scales do not identify their larger causes. Scores are based on the frequency or intensity of the hassles themselves. Despite the fact that daily hassles scales do not address long-term causal factors, this method produces a more individualized understanding of the immediate antecedents of stress. The approach of Kanner and colleagues also includes measurement of daily uplifts. Uplifts are the small, mood-lifting, commonplace things that occur day to day, such as the kind gesture of a coworker or a phone call from a friend. Uplifts flow from coping resources.

Psychological research on racism shows how a single distal contextual condition may create multiple specific stressors. Harrell and associates studied racism-related stress among a multiracial sample of U.S. students and African-American community members. They measured a variety of stressors. Specific racism-related life events, such as being harassed by police or being unfairly rejected for a loan, were infrequent but stressful. "Micro-aggressions" (similar to daily hassles) such as being followed in stores, being avoided by others, and subtle expressions of disrespect or fear were experienced almost daily. Also stressful were observations of racism that targeted others, seeing one's group blamed for problems, and chronic inequalities of income and material resources. Symptoms of depression, anxiety, and psychological trauma were correlated with each type of stressor, especially with daily micro-aggressions (Harrell, 1997; 2000; Prelow, Danoff-Burg, Swenson, & Pulgiano, 2004).

Disasters These affect entire communities, regions or nations. They include natural disasters such as hurricanes and floods, technological disasters such as an accident at a nuclear power plant, and mass violence such as terrorism and war (Norris, Friedman, Watson, Byrne, Diaz, & Kaniasty, 2002; Norris, Friedman, & Watson, 2002). Reviewing 160 empirical studies involving 60,000 disaster victims, Norris et al. found that the meaning of a disaster makes a difference: mass violence had more damaging psychological consequences than natural or technological disasters. Moreover, prior social context makes a difference: negative impacts of disasters were usually stronger among children and youth; women; ethnic minorities; in developing rather than developed nations; and among those with more severe exposure to the disaster, more prior problems, and fewer resources. Norris et al. also found that in any disaster problems are intertwined: health, mental health, other personal or family distress, fragmented social networks, property loss, and dislocation. An ecological view is needed: societal, community, family, and personal factors contribute to stressful impacts or promote healthy coping.

The psychological effects of the terrorist attacks of September 11, 2001, on New York City residents offer examples. Surveys of adults soon after the attacks showed heightened levels of probable posttraumatic stress disorder (PTSD) and of probable depression among Manhattan residents, especially those nearer the World Trade Center, those whose friends or family died in the attacks, and those who lost jobs because of the attacks. In national surveys shortly after the attacks, one in six respondents reported persistent worries about terrorism that were not psychological disorders but interfered with daily living. These included being less productive at work, avoiding public places, and using alcohol or medications to relax. The highest levels of distress occurred among women and persons of color. Initially, distress rates were higher in New York, but after two months rates were similar across the nation (Galea, Ahern et al., 2002; Schlenger et al., 2002; Stein et al., 2004). However, studies in New York City showed that symptoms subsided to normal levels within six months, indicating resilient coping among the majority of the adult population (Galea, Vlahov et al., 2003). Those who suffered greater exposure to the attacks were more likely to have continued symptoms (Adams & Boscarino, 2005).

Among children and adolescents, effects were more nuanced. Six months after the attacks, one survey found that 30 percent of New York City public school students still reported symptoms of probable anxiety or depressive disorders. Direct or family member exposure to September 11 stressors was correlated with symptom levels (Hoven et al., 2005). (Direct exposure included events such as fleeing for safety or having problems reuniting with family. Family exposure included death or injury to a family member or a family member having to escape the attack area.) However, the mental health impact of exposure to prior community violence (e.g., shootings in one's neighborhood) was greater than the impact of September 11 stressors (Aber, 2005; Aber, Gershoff, Ware, & Kotler, 2004). Thus the psychological consequences of mass violence such as the September 11 attacks, though undeniably serious, must be understood in the context of other traumatic violence and wider community life (Aber, 2005).

Psychological impact of disasters is not limited to mental disorders. The September 11 attacks often created personal distress that interfered with daily life yet fell short of psychological disorder. Moreover, in the Aber et al. (2004) study of children, exposure to either September 11 events or community violence was associated with increased social mistrust and suspicions about others. This outcome is not measured in mental health surveys, but is important for quality of community life.

Vicious Spirals Vicious spirals are cascading patterns of multiple stressors, set in motion when the loss of one resource triggers other losses (Hobfoll, 1998). For example, consider the situation of a low-income single mother whose car breaks down and who cannot afford to have it repaired. Without transportation, she is unable to get to work, which results in the loss of her job. She can no longer afford child care, which makes finding a new job even more difficult. These setbacks also undermine her self-esteem and belief in her ability to cope. Vicious spirals are particularly common for those with fewer material, social, or personal resources. In the case of our single mother, any one resource such as an understanding employer, a community short-term loan fund, a relative who can provide childcare or a friend with car repair skills, might stop the spiral long enough for her to get back on her feet.

Elaine: Proximal Stressors When Elaine's husband was told that his condition was terminal, he began to drink heavily and spend impulsively. He applied for multiple credit cards and ran the balances to the maximum. A major flood damaged their home, and her husband compounded its impact by frivolously spending the funds from the government disaster grant, leaving their home unrepaired. Their son's substance abuse escalated as stress within the family rose, sparking increased discord and the threat of family violence. Although Elaine had little power within the family, societal expectations dictated that she act as caregiver of her husband, son, and elderly mother. She saw a bleak and hopeless future ahead. When her husband died, his disability payments would end. With no marketable skills or job prospects, she could not pay her bills and would probably lose her home. This vicious spiral of life events, natural disaster, transitions, and daily hassles was overwhelming.

Stress Reactions

The personal experience of stress includes physiological, emotional, and cognitive components (Panel D in Figure 8.1). These are interdependent and often cyclical. When a dangerous threat is imminent, brain structures and neural pathways react instantaneously, allowing little time for rational consideration. In a less dangerous circumstance, there is more time for reflection and planning. Detailed description

TABLE 8.2 Illustrative Resources for Coping

Material resources
Social-emotional competencies
Social settings
Cultural resources
Social support
Mutual help groups
Spiritual resources

of these processes exceeds the scope of this chapter (see Folkman & Moskowitz, 2004; Goleman, 1995; Somerfield & McCrea, 2000).

Cognitive Appraisal, Emotions, and Context Appraisal is the ongoing process of constructing the meaning of a stressful situation or event (Lazarus & Folkman, 1984). The most relevant aspects of appraisal include the extent to which the situation is seen as challenging or threatening, expected or unexpected, and largely controllable or not (Folkman & Moskowitz, 2004; Moos, 2002). The person may change an appraisal of stressor or resources over time.

Appraisals are culturally and socially constructed. One's views of divorce, death, or violence, for instance, are influenced by culture and context. Emotional experience and expression also are influenced by culture (Markus & Kitayama, 1991), gender roles, and other contextual factors.

Individual differences in appraisals are most pronounced in circumstances where resources are adequate and threats are modest (Hobfoll, 1998). For instance, in families with ample savings, job loss can be appraised as a temporary setback or as a great personal failure. Individual appraisals vary less when threats are greater and resources weaker. In our case example, Elaine's situation would have to be appraised as extremely serious for anyone.

Elaine: Stress Reactions At the time that she called a crisis line, Elaine was depressed and considering suicide. She felt helpless in the face of stressors largely beyond her control. She also felt distraught, hopeless, and fearful about the future. These emotions were connected to her social context, including family dynamics, housing, economic forces, and cultural gender expectations.

Resources Activated for Coping

To deal with stressors, individuals mobilize resources for coping (Panel E in Figure 8.1). Resources actually are involved at many points in our ecological framework: contextual and personal protective factors are resources; stressors are defined by their threats to resources; interventions often provide resources. A person may not activate all available resources for coping, and coping may strengthen or weaken resources for the future. See Table 8.2 for an illustrative list of resources.

Material Resources Many stressors are related to insufficient material resources, whose psychological impact is greater than many realize. Money, employment, housing, food, clothing, transportation, and health insurance are examples of resources that may be needed. A quiet place to study is a material resource for students. Satisfactory housing is a resource that can circumvent vicious spirals induced by widowhood or divorce.

Social-Emotional Competencies Personal competencies for coping include self-regulation skills: managing emotions, motivations, cognitions, and other intrapersonal processes (Goleman, 1995). Social competencies are needed in order to connect with others and make use of the resources they offer. Empathy, the most basic social skill, involves accurate understanding of the emotions of others. In a United States sample of highly stressed, low-income urban children, empathy was related to resilience and adjustment (Hoyt-Meyers et al., 1995). Making personal connections, building relationships, and managing conflicts are crucial among both adults and children. Assertiveness has been associated with a number of positive outcomes for children, including the ability to resist drug use (Rotheram-Borus, 1988). Social and emotional competencies are a major focus of prevention-promotion programs in community psychology and related fields (Elias & Cohen, 1999; Weissberg & Kumpfer, 2003). We will discuss these in detail in Chapters 9–11.

Social, Cultural, and Spiritual Resources Social resources often reflect the idea stated in the African proverb, "It takes a village to raise a child." Social settings such as youth groups, mutual help organizations, and religious congregations are resources. Cultural traditions, rituals, beliefs, and narratives provide systems of meaning for interpreting stressors, examples of skillful coping, and guides to coping choices. Religious writings, widely read stories, and folk sayings are examples of these. The rituals of bereavement in any culture provide resources to the bereaved. Later in this chapter we discuss social support, mutual help, and social aspects of spiritual resources.

Coping Processes

Panel F of Figure 8.1 represents responses or strategies (e.g., actions, cognitions, self-regulatory practices) that a person uses to reduce stress (Moos, 2002; Moos & Holahan, 2003). Coping is a dynamic process that fluctuates over time according to the demands of the situation, the available resources, and the ongoing appraisal and emotions.

The literature on coping responses is extensive. Researchers have classified coping strategies and styles along a number of descriptive dimensions, such as approach-avoidance, cognitive-behavioral, and prosocial-antisocial (Folkman & Moskowitz, 2004; Hobfoll, 1998; Holahan & Moos, 1994; Lazarus & Folkman, 1984; Moos & Holahan, 2003; Moos, 1984, 2002; Shapiro, Schwartz, & Astin, 1996). Here we will briefly discuss a few key concepts.

Reappraisal Reappraising or "reframing" a problem involves altering one's perception of the situation or its meaning (Lazarus & Folkman, 1984; Watzlawick et al., 1974). (Recall reframing the nine-dot problem that opened Chapter 1.) It may include changing one's view of the stressor's intensity, identifying unrecognized resources, or finding opportunities for growth or meaning in the situation. For example, you might reappraise a stressful circumstance as an opportunity to learn new skills, or reframe an appraised threat as a challenge. Reinterpreting loss of a job as an opportunity for changing careers, or seeking further education, is another example. Cultural values influence what reappraisals are perceived as realistic or constructive. One important role of social support is suggesting reappraisals.

Categories of Coping Empirically based studies have usually found three general categories of coping responses (Folkman & Moskowitz, 2004). **Problem-focused** coping involves addressing a problem situation directly, especially by making a plan to change the situation and following that plan. Changing how one studies for tests, or making a plan to improve one's diet, or learning interviewing skills to search for a new job would be examples. **Emotion-focused** coping addresses the emotions that accompany the problem rather than the stressor itself (Lazarus & Folkman, 1984). For instance, emotion-focused approaches would include exercising or meditating to reduce anxiety, or seeking emotional support from friends or family. **Meaning-focused** coping involves finding meaning in the stressor by reappraising it, especially if this leads to growth or learning of important lessons. It may be based on deeper values, whether secular or spiritual, as when suffering is interpreted as leading to growth (see the accounts in Box 8.1). Whether problem focused, emotion focused, or meaning focused, coping may be primarily individual or may involve help from others.

These categories may overlap, as when a person seeks emotional support from a friend. Each category contains diverse subtypes; for instance, emotion-focused coping includes active emotional regulation and passive avoidance. A person may use both problem-focused and emotion-focused strategies in response to a single stressor (for instance, exercising to reduce anxiety before an exam, then reviewing notes to study). Caregivers for a person with a chronic illness often look for meaning-focused ways to reappraise the situation that promote positive emotions (Folkman & Moskowitz, 2004). Judicious action (Hobfoll, 1998) involves combining several coping strategies, including seeking advice from others.

Coping Is Contextual Action-oriented, individualistic coping strategies are prized in many corners of U.S. society, particularly for men (Hobfoll, 1998; Holahan, Moos, & Bonin, 1997). However, these actions might be considered selfish in East Asia, for example (Shapiro et al., 1996). Whatever your cultural context, think of situations in your life when it was wise to act assertively and other situations when it was wiser to manage your emotions and take no overt action.

From an ecological perspective, coping is contextual. Wise coping choices are based on the context and the person, not on generalities. There is no coping style or strategy that is always superior. Societal and cultural factors, gender and other forms of diversity, ecological level (e.g., community, neighborhood, family), and the stressor itself must all be taken into account.

Virtuous Spirals Earlier we noted how stressors may sometimes trigger each other in a vicious downward spiral. However, adaptive coping may initiate a very different cascade: a virtuous spiral in which resources are increased, successes build on each other, and the stressor is transformed into a catalyst for growth (Hobfoll, 1998). For example, the increased confidence derived from successfully coping with a job layoff may spur an individual to pursue a long-dreamed-of educational degree, which then leads to further accomplishments.

Elaine: Coping When Elaine called the crisis line asking for assistance in committing suicide, she saw few coping options. Her suicidal plan was a maladaptive emotion-focused, avoidant coping strategy. Yet that call initiated a virtuous cycle. With intervention and the activation of increased resources, her coping repertoire expanded. Antidepressant medication and psychotherapy reduced her depression and encouraged the use of more active, problem-focused strategies. Increased resources, such as help with debt management and disaster assistance, increased her coping effectiveness. She learned to drive. When Elaine and her husband began attending a local church, their social support network expanded. Spirituality became an important resource for Elaine.

Later, when her son relapsed in his substance abuse, Elaine employed problem-focused coping strategies. While he was on a binge, his behavior became violent and destructive. Elaine called law enforcement and professional staff and was able to get her son committed to a treatment program. She also called on her expanded support network; these friends encouraged and validated her bold actions. Although her son was initially resentful, he eventually expressed gratitude to his mother.

As the stress of her difficulties subsided, Elaine began to display a lightheartedness and optimistic outlook that had served her well for most of her rather difficult life. This reflected not only a dispositional optimism but also the presence of coping resources and improved emotional and physiological functioning. When her husband "Jimmy" (pseudonym) died some months later, her grief was tempered by positive emotions and humor. She warmly greeted a counselor who visited her shortly after the funeral. While walking in her small vegetable garden, Elaine pointed to the scarecrow and said with a smile, "I put some of Jimmy's old clothes on him. Now I just say, 'There's Jimmy out there, looking out for us.' "

Coping Outcomes

Psychologists have studied coping outcomes mainly with measures of psychological or physical disorders or of distress or dysfunction (Folkman & Moskowitz, 2004). However, this perspective is limited in two ways. It focuses on negative more than positive outcomes, and it often focuses on individuals in isolation rather than also studying how individual functioning is related to outcomes at broader ecological levels (families, organizations, communities, societies). In our ecological framework, Panel G concerns positive outcomes and their relationship to broader ecological levels, and Panel H concerns distress, dysfunction, and disorders.

Wellness This is not simply the absence of symptoms of disorder or of distress; it is the experience of positive outcomes in health and subjective well-being (Cowen, 1994). Life satisfaction, job satisfaction, positive affect, self-esteem, and academic achievement represent wellness outcomes that go beyond mere absence of symptoms (Cicchetti, Rappaport, Sandler, & Weissberg, 2000; Cowen, 1994).

Resilience We refer to resilience as maintaining or returning to a prior level of health during stressful circumstances. Many people experience distress caused by a stressor but recover their prior level of functioning without clinical intervention. Some are able to maintain stable levels of healthy functioning in the face of stressors, with little or no emotional distress or physical symptoms at all. Resilience arises from the interplay of environmental and individual factors (Luthar, Cicchetti, & Becker, 2000).

Thriving For some individuals, an encounter with adversity initiates a process of growth that takes them beyond their prior level of functioning. This positive outcome is referred to as thriving (Ickovics & Park, 1998). It may be thought of as "resilience plus": in the face of stressors, not only holding one's ground but growing through experience. For instance, Abraido-Lanza, Guier, and Colon (1998) studied thriving among Latinas with chronic illness living in impoverished neighborhoods. Thriving in response to stressors often involves meaning-focused coping. Both stories in Box 8.1 illustrate thriving.

Social Embeddedness Many positive outcomes involve closer ties to family, friends, community, or other social groupings. These ties provide meaningful relationships and psychological sense of community meaningful in themselves as well as allies for pursuing goals and coping resources for facing future stressors. Negative outcomes such as family discord and community fragmentation also can occur. Involvement in supportive relationships with professionals, church members, and others was critical to Elaine's recovery, for instance.

Empowerment Wiley and Rappaport (2000) defined empowerment as gaining access to valued resources. This is not the only definition of this term, which we will cover extensively in Chapter 12, but for now it is important to recognize that empowerment involves actually gaining power in some way, not simply feeling more powerful (Riger, 1993). Increased access to resources may be an important outcome of coping. For instance, empowerment occurs when a person with a serious mental illness is able to understand and advocate for his or her rights, gaining more control in case management, treatment planning, family relationships, housing, or employment. Also, mutual help groups bring together persons with experiences in coping with a specific problem, thus sharing their resources and promoting positive outcomes.

Distress, Dysfunction, Clinical Disorders Panel H includes outcomes that are symptoms of mental disorders or illnesses, and outcomes that are problematic but not clinical disorders. The latter may involve internal distress such as anxiety or sadness or dysfunctional behaviors in family or work relationships such as neglect, hostility, or violence. Many psychological outcomes experienced by college students, families, and workers involve distress or dysfunction that is important, and painful, but not a mental disorder.

Elaine and Her Community: Outcomes Resilience among disaster survivors in Elaine's community was common, despite the severity of the flood.

> We now have our lives back to normal, but the flood is not something I would want to experience again. It took several months for us to get our house fixed—to even have a stove to cook on. It was very stressful. But we appreciated all the help we received. It made getting over the flood a lot easier. (Herndon, 1996)

For others, outcomes were less positive. Some expressed continuing anxiety and vigilance 18–24 months afterward.

> Water invades your home and brings you heartache, misery, labor, fatigue, and a very anxious mind each time it rains! (Herndon, 1996, p. 1)

Recent conversations have revealed that Elaine experienced personal growth from her adversity. She reported that she now looks for opportunities to encourage others by sharing her story with them, to show them that options exist even in the direst of circumstances.

Coping Is Dynamic and Contextual Look back at Figure 8.1 for a moment: especially notice its feedback cycles and arrows. Outcomes are not end states but simply one more step in the cyclical processes of coping. They are best understood as snapshots in ongoing processes of living. Those processes are dynamic, changing over time, and contextual, differing in the diverse contexts in which we live.

Hurricane Katrina: A Disaster in Context

Hurricane Katrina and its aftermath illustrate the scope of stressors and coping at multiple ecological levels, especially communities and macrosystems. In August 2005, Hurricane Katrina ravaged portions of Louisiana, Mississippi, and nearby states, creating unrivaled destruction, flooding New Orleans, claiming over one thousand lives, and displacing hundreds of thousands of residents (U.S. Federal Emergency Management Agency, 2006). Governments were unprepared, although a hurricane-related flood in New Orleans had been widely predicted (Bourne, 2004; Fischetti, 2001; Lehrer, 2005; Schleifstein & McQuaid, 2002).

The most affected neighborhoods were often the poorest, and their residents were predominantly African American.

A vicious cycle of interacting events and resource scarcity led to a woefully inadequate response. Recent leadership changes and reductions in funding hampered the response of the Federal Emergency Management Agency (FEMA). Flawed disaster planning and a series of unfortunate decisions on the state and local levels also were involved (DeBose, 2005).

Despite a mandatory evacuation order, about 150,000 residents lacked the resources to leave New Orleans. Many were stranded in attics and on rooftops for days awaiting rescue. The Superdome, opened as a "refuge of last resort," contained only bare-bones provisions. Evacuees waited days without food or water before help arrived.

Dumas Carter, a veteran New Orleans police officer, rode out the storm with five other officers in a hotel near the Convention Center. While the media carried reports of looting and lawlessness, Carter told another side of the story: "Ninety-seven percent of these people were behind us. They wanted us to be the police and they loved that we were still there." He describes how the stranded evacuees sang together at night to keep their spirits up. He relates how "Good Samaritans" retrieved supplies dropped from helicopters blocks away and brought them back to the Convention Center. "And the people got together as a group and disseminated it amongst themselves, without any riots, any fights, anything," he said, "And then these people put together a box of food and water and brought it to us. We didn't take it. We told them, don't worry about us, give it to the kids and the old people" (Priesmeyer, 2005). Under primitive and stressful conditions, people found personal resources such as optimism and altruism and social resources such as mutual aid and sense of community.

Relief efforts gradually gained momentum (U.S. Department of Homeland Security, n.d.). However, the extent of devastation and the dispersal of evacuees presented unique recovery challenges. Transient anxiety, confusion, anger, and sorrow are normal reactions to such a stressor, but loss of community and support networks pose particular risks. Without these key resources, grief is more likely to become depression and anxiety more likely to become chronic (Garloch, 2005; Kohn & Olson, 2005). For those with access, the Internet may play a key role by providing information, linking to services, and facilitating a sense of community among dispersed evacuees (American Psychological Association, 2005; American Red Cross, 2005; Centers for Disease Control and Prevention, n.d.; Center for Mental Health Services n.d.; U.S. Department of Homeland Security, n.d.; Disaster.org, n.d.; National Mental Health Association, n.d.; Recording Katrina, n.d.).

The U.S. Center for Mental Health Services (n.d.) estimates that a third of those affected will develop a stress-related clinical disorder such as depression or post traumatic stress disorder. Over 300,000 people may need longer-term help (Garloch, 2005; Jayson, 2005b). Many who were most exposed to the disaster were African American, but most mental health professionals are European American. Cultural understanding, racial and economic disparities, distrust in government, coordination of services, and funding have been challenges for mental health care following the disaster (Boodman, 2005; Jayson, 2005a,b).

It is important to note that although roughly a third of Katrina's victims may experience clinical-level distress, most will be resilient. Some survivors may even thrive by identifying new strengths, helping others, or organizing for social change. In addition, the economic disparities so publicly revealed by this tragedy may wake Americans up to the realities of poverty and build political will for social change to address those realities.

Interventions to Promote Coping

Conceptualizing stress and coping from an ecological perspective opens up possibilities for better targeted and more holistic interventions (Sandler et al., 2000). It also illustrates how community psychologists, clinical psychologists, and others who implement social and mind/body interventions might work in concert.

Planning interventions requires considering several dimensions (Wandersman, 1990; Wandersman, Coyne, Herndon, McKnight, & Morsbach, 2002). *Timing* concerns the point of intervention in the ecological framework: is the goal to influence distal factors, proximal stressors, stress reactions, resource activation, and/or coping strategies? *Ecological level(s)* concerns the intervention focus (individuals to macrosystems). *Content* goals of the intervention might include increasing awareness (a goal of many psychotherapies and of consciousness raising in liberation movements), behavior change, skill-building, social support, spiritual facilitation (as in twelve-step groups), advocacy for individuals or families, changing social policy, or other goals. The *value system* inherent in the intervention is critical to its nature and effectiveness. For instance, psychotherapy can be successfully enacted by interveners with a value system of expert helping. However, a community health intervention might be more effective with an approach emphasizing citizen participation and empowerment. Many stressors cannot be addressed by individual coping alone (Somerfield & McCrea, 2000). For instance, job stress often is rooted in organizational and macrosystem conditions that require collective action.

The rounded boxes and dashed arrows in Figure 8.1 illustrate interventions and their targeted domains. From left to right, interventions vary from more global to more individual in scope. The figure includes both community and clinical approaches. In our discussion to follow, we leave clinical treatments to other sources, and focus on interventions most relevant to community psychology.

Social and Policy Advocacy Improvements in the well-being of large numbers of persons involves advocacy for community or social change, or for changes in specific policies of macrosystems, localities, and organizations (e.g., laws, organizational practices, social programs, funding decisions). Targets of advocacy may be government officials, private sector or community leaders, or media and the public. Advocacy may involve working to raise public awareness of an issue, such as gaining media attention for the needs of disaster victims. It may involve social action, such as protesting cuts in mental health or youth development programs, or a Take Back the Night rally to call attention to violence against women.

Advocacy can be supported by community research. Community and developmental psychologists recently joined to promote a strengths-building perspective in U.S. government policies regarding children, youth, and families (Maton et al., 2004). This shift of perspective from focusing on individual and family deficits to recognizing and building strengths would affect policies, practices, and budget decisions in mental health, child welfare, education, and other systems. We discuss approaches to community and social change in detail in Chapter 13.

Organizational Consultation Many stressors arise at work. Some human services and schools are less effective because of organizational problems. Community and organizational psychologists consult with these settings, seeking to: change organizational policies; alter organizational roles, decision making, or communication; or deal with issues such as work-family relationships, human diversity, and intergroup conflict. These interventions may lessen stress, increase social support, promote employee job satisfaction, or help make services more effective for clients (e.g., Bond, 1999; Boyd & Angelique, 2002, in press; Shinn & Perkins, 2000; Trickett, Barone, & Watts, 2000).

Alternative Settings At times, the limitations of an agency, clinic, or other setting may be so great that citizens or professionals form an alternative setting to serve clients in a different way. For instance, when many community agencies failed to recognize the needs of battered women and rape victims, concerned women formed women's shelters and rape crisis centers. At first these settings often had very little funding or outside support, but they have grown into an established part of many communities. Self-help organizations provide another example. The Community Lodge (discussed in Chapters 2 and 5) and Oxford House (discussed in Chapter 1) are examples of alternative, supportive housing. Alternative settings provide citizens a choice of services and values systems (Cherniss & Deegan, 2000; Reinharz, 1984). As we noted in Chapter 1, a women's center might have been a valuable resource for Elaine.

Community Coalitions This approach involves bringing together representatives from a local community to address issues such as preventing drug abuse or promoting health or youth development. An effective coalition brings together citizens from many walks of life to discuss community issues and work toward shared goals. It also builds collaboration among multiple agencies, whose separate funding streams and agendas often create a fragmented community service system. For example, community coalitions have increased rates of immunization of young children, effected community changes in drug abuse and domestic violence, and helped decrease levels of local gang violence (Allen, 2005; Butterfoss, Goodman, & Wandersman, 2001; Folayemi, 2001; Snell-Johns, Imm, Wandersman, & Claypoole, 2003; Wolff, 2001a). We discuss this approach in detail in Chapter 13.

Prevention and Promotion Programs These seek to reduce the incidence of personal problems in living, mental disorders, and illness, or to promote health, personal development or academic achievement (see box in top center of Figure 8.1). Examples include school-based programs to promote social-emotional competence, family-based programs to strengthen parenting or promote resilience, and community-wide efforts to promote health or prevent drug abuse (Weissberg & Kumpfer, 2003). Many prevention/promotion programs have grown out of community coalitions or organizational development in schools. They may strengthen coping skills or other protective factors also addressed in clinical treatment, but their focus is on intervention before problems appear. They may address contextual factors such as family functioning, or build personal and social resources for coping. We discuss these approaches in detail in Chapters 9–11.

Moving to the bottom center of Figure 8.1, we next discuss community approaches more closely related to clinical treatments.

Crisis Intervention After the September 11 terrorist attacks, over 1 million New Yorkers received public education or individual counseling through Project Liberty, a public disaster mental health program (Felton, 2004). The most promising crisis intervention approaches immediately after traumatic events focus on providing emotional support, practical assistance, information about coping, and encouraging later use of one's own sources of support and treatment if needed (McNally, Bryant, & Ehlers, 2003). These are consistent with a community-ecological perspective. For mental health professionals, skills for responding to disasters include: helping persons and families deal with multiple problems; working with community resources such as schools, workplaces, and religious congregations; and using mass media to provide information (Felton, 2004). Moreover, programs must be tailored to the specific culture, needs, and resources of a community (Aber, 2005).

An example of crisis intervention with a community-ecological focus is the crisis counseling program that served Elaine and her neighbors. This program emphasizes a wellness perspective, provides social support and practical assistance, and intervenes with multiple problems at multiple ecological levels. Paraprofessionals and community members are used for outreach (Center for Mental Health Services, 2000).

Collaboration with Community Resources Community resources are outside treatment systems. These include mutual help groups, consumer advocates, women's services, spiritual and religious settings, indigenous healers and elders, and holistic health practitioners (Chinman, Kloos, O'Connell, & Davidson, 2002; Pargament & Maton, 2000; Rappaport, 2000). An example is the Alaska Native sobriety initiatives that we discussed in Chapter 7 (Hazel & Mohatt, 2001). Respect for the values underlying these approaches is essential, as is recognition of the practical, experiential knowledge of problems that many community resources provide (and that professionals may not have). Some community resources and alternative settings welcome collaboration with professionals; others do not. Yet they expand the support available to persons in need.

Case Management Complementing professional treatment are innovations in casework and client advocacy. These include Assertive Community Treatment (Bond et al., 1990) and Housing First programs for homeless persons with mental illness (Tsemberis Moran, Shinn, Asmussen, & Shern, 2003). The latter have demonstrated that helping homeless persons find suitable independent housing, then helping them develop a treatment plan, is more effective than transitional housing. Innovations in case management focus on both practical needs, such as housing, and psychological issues such as decision-making and social support.

This list of interventions is not exhaustive. Our purpose is to suggest the richness of intervention options and entry points to address stress and coping.

Elaine and Her Community The disaster crisis counseling program employed multiple interventions. Through communications media, mailings, presentations, and booths at community festivals, the program provided information on resources available to flood victims, common stress reactions of disaster victims, coping strategies, and how others might provide support. In schools and child care centers attended by flood victims, program staff taught teachers how to recognize stress and provide support. They also created a coloring book for children about flooding and recovery from disasters, with input from flood victims to assure its accuracy and relevance. Staff also conducted community meetings with flooded residents in which victims shared their stories and provided training in managing stress.

Staff also built linkages with local service clubs, churches and spiritual settings, and health care providers. These resources donated goods, provided emotional support, jointly participated in community health fairs, and worked with specific disaster victims. Much individual work with flood victims involved case management: acquiring temporary housing, food and clothing; arranging funding for house repairs; and linking victims with disabilities or special needs with appropriate services. Active listening and linking with available services were often the principal interventions.

Some flood victims needed clinical intervention. Individuals and families struggling with many symptoms were identified and referred by crisis counselors or community resources, or sought treatment themselves. Like Elaine, most were flood victims also coping with chronic stressors or in the midst of vicious spirals.

Immediately after the flood, the Red Cross, Salvation Army, National Guard, church groups, and others provided many services. When these groups withdrew, flood victims turned to federal emergency and business agencies for temporary housing, grants and loans for rebuilding and relocation. Maneuvering the regulations of these government agencies was stressful.

> Having to deal with government agencies, and being a widow at the time, was one of the worst times in my life. They didn't want to help me and caused me much stress. I didn't need any more. The recent death of a husband and a daughter with cancer at the same time, and losing all the contents of my home for the second time, was almost too much. I tried to make the best of it, but my health has been going downhill since. (Herndon, 1996, p. 1)

The disaster crisis counseling program helped survivors navigate these obstacles.

One year after the flood, crisis counselors and community members organized "Remember the Flood Day," with food and music for flood survivors. Residents created a display board depicting the disaster and the recovery process. On one side they posted photographs, drawings, and other items expressing the physical, social, and emotional effects of flood; on the other side were items that depicted where survivors were in their recovery a year later. Gathering around the board, residents learned about each other's experiences and connected with each other. It was a time of fellowship for those who shared in this difficult experience.

In the next three sections we describe in detail three important community resources for coping: social support, mutual help organizations, and spirituality and religious settings. These illustrate areas of community psychology research with implications for personal coping and professional services

SOCIAL SUPPORT

Social support is a key resource for strengthening coping and well-being. Interest in social support soared in the 1980s after research showed that social support was associated with lower levels of personal distress and of illness, even in the presence of stressful challenges. Research in a variety of disciplines has found social support of various types was correlated with lesser anxiety, depression, generalized psychic distress, and physical illness among children, adolescents and adults. It also was correlated with stronger cardiovascular and immune functioning, academic performance, parenting skills, and job and life satisfaction. However, later research has indicated that its effects are complicated by many interacting factors, and some negative effects of supportive relationships have become clearer (Barrera, 2000; Barrera & Li, 1996; Cohen, 2004; Cohen, Underwood, & Gottlieb, 2000; Hobfoll & Vaux, 1993; Putnam, 2000, chap. 20; Uchino, Cacioppo, & Kiecolt-Glaser, 1996).

Social support is not a simple, unitary concept. It represents a collection of social, emotional, cognitive, and behavioral processes occurring in personal relationships and social networks.

Generalized and Specific Support

Generalized support occurs in interpersonal relationships sustained over time, providing the individual with a secure base for living and coping. It is not tailored to one specific stressor and does not necessarily involve behavioral helping in a specific situation. It is most clearly measured in terms of **perceived support,** in which research participants are asked about the general quality or availability of support in their lives (Barrera, 1986, 2000). Generalized support thus involves both individual perceptions and environmental support, the presence of meaningful others in one's life (Barrera, 2000; Cohen, 2004). It especially refers to caring and attachment in close personal relationships, such as a strong marriage, parent-child relationship, or friendship. It is there in some form all the time.

Specific support or **enacted support** is behavioral help provided to people coping with a particular stressor. It may be emotional encouragement, information or advice, or tangible assistance such as loaning money. Because it concerns distress already present in the recipient's life, specific support is discernible only when a person needs it, and is tailored to a specific stressor (Barrera, 2000).

Generalized and specific support can intertwine. Stressors such as job loss require both. A close relationship often provides both. Other relationships may involve less caring and more instrumental support, but that too is helpful. For instance, if you are having trouble in a demanding psychology course, caring helps, but so does a tutor.

The meaning of specific support also depends in part on culture and context. Liang and Bogat (1994) found that specific, openly provided support was considered less helpful by mainland Chinese students than by U.S. students. Receiving support in a noticeable way may be embarrassing, especially in a collectivistic culture, where it might reflect poorly on one's family or other ingroup. Even in Western cultures, receiving support from others may lead to feeling patronized or helpless.

The Relationship Context of Support

Social support does not occur in a vacuum, but within relationships with others. It is shaped by the dynamics in those relationships. A number of studies have linked having close, confiding, reciprocal relationships to higher levels of social support and to less loneliness and greater life satisfaction (Hobfoll & Vaux, 1993). Supportive relationships are central to both stories in Box 8.1 and to Elaine's recovery as we have described in this chapter. Yet it is also true that relationships can create stressors as well as provide support. Researchers have studied many support relationships; we will focus on a few examples.

Families and Contexts Family members, particularly parents and spouses, are important sources of support, generalized and specific. Compared with other sources, they often involve greater commitment and personal knowledge of the individual. However, they also involve greater obligation for reciprocity and greater potential for conflict, and they may not be useful for every stressor.

Pistrang and Barker (1998) studied the help provided to women with breast cancer by husbands and by fellow women patients, analyzing audiotaped 10-minute conversations. The women rated both conversations positively, but trained observers of the tapes rated the fellow patients more supportive, empathic, self-disclosing of own feelings, and less critical than husbands. Marital satisfaction did not explain these differences, although other factors may have played a role: gender differences in helping styles, the firsthand experiential knowledge of the fellow patients, and husbands' fatigue with ongoing demands of caregiving.

Settings also influence sources of support. A study of first-year students in a suburban, mainly European-American university found differences in support for African-American and European-American students. For European Americans, peer support was the most important factor in commitment to college during the first year. Peer support for them was easily available on campus. In contrast, for African Americans, for whom fewer peers were available there, family support was a stronger predictor of commitment to college. Among high-achieving African-American male students, family support was especially important (Maton et al., 1996; Maton, Hrabowski, & Greif, 1998).

Natural Helpers, Mentors Natural helpers and mentors are sources of informal support in a community. Some become natural helpers because their jobs lead to conversations with personal-emotional meaning, such as beauticians and bartenders (Cowen, McKim, & Weissberg, 1981). Mentors are older or more experienced persons (other than one's parents) who support and guide younger, less experienced persons (Rhodes, Bogat, Roffman, Edelman, & Galasso, 2002). Mentors may occur naturally in one's social network or may be provided through a program such as Big Brothers/Big Sisters. A review of the effects of mentoring programs for youth found only modest positive effects for mentoring but also identified characteristics of highly effective mentoring relationships that can be built into future mentoring programs (Dubois, Holloway, Valentine, & Cooper, 2002). This review also found that mentoring programs were most helpful with youth in disadvantaged and risky environments. We discuss mentoring programs more fully in Chapter 14 (see also Rhodes & Bogat, 2002).

Relationships as Stressors Of course, relationships create stressors as well as support. Recent studies of HIV-positive persons revealed that depressive symptoms were associated with relationship conflicts with others (Fleishman et al., 2003; Siegel, Raveis, & Karus, 1997). A study of adolescent mothers found that depression was lower when more support was received, but greater when those same relationships involved criticism, conflict, and disappointment (Rhodes & Woods, 1995). A study of Israeli women during the Israel-Lebanon war revealed "pressure cooker" effects (Hobfoll & London, 1986). These occurred because the women all experienced a simultaneous stressor, many individuals sought support, and the shared resources of the group were strained. In other contexts, if support is required over an extended time, for an illness or other chronic problem, conflict often occurs as supporters tire (Coyne, Ellard, & Smith, 1990). Providing support to others takes energy and time. Studying support in the context of relationships helps clarify its positive and negative effects.

Social Support Networks

Social support occurs within networks of relationships. Researchers analyze social networks in terms of many variables related to social support. We will focus on three: multidimensionality, density, and reciprocity.

Multidimensionality Multidimensional relationships are those in which the two persons involved do a number of things together and share a number of role relationships. Multidimensional relationships exist when a coworker is also a friend we see socially or when we share multiple interests and activities with neighbors. Unidimensional relationships are confined to one role: One sees a coworker only at work; neighbors are not friends. As a student, you have a multidimensional relationship with a classmate who is also a neighbor or who is involved in the same organization. With a person you know only in class, you share a unidimensional relationship.

Because a multidimensional relationship means we see the other person more often, forming and deepening friendships is easier. Multidimensional ties are more resilient. For instance, loss of a job effectively means the end of unidimensional relationships with coworkers, whereas multidimensional relationships would survive. However, unidimensional relationships also are valuable for linking with a broader number of people (recall the strength of weak ties, and bridging social capital, in Chapter 6.)

Hirsch (1980) studied multidimensionality in the social networks of two groups: recently widowed young women and adult women students returning to college. In both groups, self-esteem, satisfaction with socializing, and tangible support were associated with having at least some multidimensional relationships.

Density Your social network also contains relationships between the persons in your network other than you. Network density refers to the extent of these relationships. A high-density network exists when many ties exist between network members; for instance, when most network members are friends of each other. Residents of small towns and some urban neighborhoods often live in high-density networks. A low-density network exists when few of the members are closely connected to each other. A person with many friends in different settings who do not know each other has a low-density network. A high-density network and a low-density network could have the same number of persons, but those persons in the high-density network are more interconnected.

High-density networks usually offer greater consensus on norms and advice (Hirsch et al., 1990) and often quicker help in a crisis, because the network members are more interconnected. However, low-density networks often hold a greater diversity of persons with a greater variety of skills and life experiences. Thus, they can provide a diversity of resources needed during life transitions such as divorce, bereavement, or entering college (Hirsch, 1980; Hobfoll & Vaux, 1993; Wilcox, 1981). In such transitions, too much density within one's network may inhibit the development of new roles and personal identities, or adaptation to changed circumstances.

Hirsch (1980) analyzed network density in his study of recently widowed young women and adult women college students. In those samples, low-density social networks were more adaptive than high-density ones. As these women moved into new roles as a single person or college student, they needed a variety of friendships and support resources. In a study of women experiencing divorce, Wilcox (1981) reported similar findings.

Reciprocity Social networks also vary in the extent of reciprocity of support, the extent to which the individual both receives support from others and provides it to others. Reciprocity may be the most important aspect of friendship across the life span (Hartup & Stevens, 1997).

In studies of self-help groups and of a religious congregation, Maton (1987, 1988) found that reciprocity of support was associated with greater psychological well-being. When individuals both provided and received support, well-being was higher. Among those who mostly provided or mostly received support and those who did little of either, well-being was lower. Maton's findings refer to overall reciprocity in the person's social network, not to reciprocity within each dyadic relationship. An individual may primarily provide support to one other person while primarily receiving support from another and still have an overall balance of providing and receiving (Maton, 1987, p. 201).

Maton's correlational findings cannot indicate the direction of cause and effect. A balance of providing and receiving may increase well-being, or it may be that happier individuals create such a balance in their lives or that each factor strengthens the other. However, these findings indicate the general importance of reciprocity. Other studies also show its importance. Stack (1974) analyzed the exchange of assistance among low-income African-American families in a housing project, including providing money, child care, and clothes as well as sharing meals and other costs. These gifts were provided in an atmosphere of reciprocity with the expectation of receiving help from others when it was needed.

MUTUAL HELP GROUPS

Mutual help, self-help, and mutual support groups are "voluntary associations of persons who share some status that results in difficulties with which the group tries to deal" (Humphreys & Rappaport, 1994, p. 218). Examples include an Alcoholics Anonymous (AA) group, a support group for persons who have a disability or illness (or for their family members), and a group for bereaved persons. Over 800 mutual help organizations (each with a network of local groups) exist worldwide (Chinman et al., 2002).

In a representative sample of U.S. citizens, 7 percent of adults attended a mutual help group within the past year and 18 percent have done so within their lifetimes (Kessler, Mickelson, & Zhao, 1997). The proportion of the adult population in mutual help groups appears equal to that engaged in psychotherapy (Borkman, 1990). In just over 50 years, the first widely recognized mutual help organization, Alcoholics Anonymous (AA), has grown from two founders to a worldwide organization with thousands of local groups. A majority of those seeking help for alcoholism in the United States attend AA meetings (Chinman et al.,

2002). Online forms of mutual aid are expanding participation (Madara, 1997). A study of mutual help groups for 20 illnesses, meeting in four U.S. cities and online, found that the highest involvement for face-to-face groups was among persons with alcoholism and AIDS, whereas the highest involvement in online groups was among those with multiple sclerosis and chronic fatigue syndrome. Breast cancer was third in involvement in both forums (Davison, Pennebaker, & Dickerson, 2000).

Mutual help groups vary along a spectrum. **Self-help** groups are facilitated by a person in recovery from the focal problem, and do not have professional involvement (e.g., twelve-step groups like AA). Some **mutual support** groups are peer led, with some professional involvement, and others involve training and supervision by professionals while also using some elements of mutual support (e.g., peer counseling groups in high schools and Reach to Recovery, a group for women with breast cancer) (Borkman, 1990; Schubert & Borkman, 1991). However, terminology in the self-help movement and elsewhere varies. Moreover, self-help advocates have predicted that collaboration between professionals and self-help groups will increase (Riessman & Banks, 2001). For simplicity, and to focus on the communal aspect of these settings, we use the term **mutual help,** although readers should keep in mind the diversity of groups. In addition, mutual help groups are usually chapters of wider (often worldwide) organizations, not isolated microsystems (Borkman, 1991).

Distinctive Features of Mutual Help Groups

Mutual help groups have five distinctive features (Borkman, 1991; Rappaport, 1995, 2000; Riessman, 1990):

- a focal concern: a problem, life crisis, or issue affecting all members
- peer relationships rather than, or in addition to, a professional-client relationship
- reciprocity of helping: each member both receives and provides help
- experiential knowledge for coping
- a community narrative that embodies the experiences of its members

Mutual help is based on peer relationships. It involves an exchange of helping based on interpersonal norms of reciprocity rather than a professional service provided for a fee. Each member both provides aid and receives it. Thus the helping relationship is symmetrical, unlike the asymmetrical professional-client relationship. It also involves the **helper therapy principle** (Riessman, 1990): providing aid to others promotes one's own well-being. For instance, GROW, a group for persons with mental illnesses, emphasizes "If you need help, help others" (Maton & Salem, 1995, p. 641). In addition, needing and receiving aid for one's problems is less stigmatizing if everyone in the group shares similar concerns and if one expects to provide aid also.

Another distinctive element of mutual help is the type of knowledge that is most respected and used for helping. **Experiential knowledge** is based on the personal experiences of group members who have coped with the focal concern, often for years. This practical, insider knowledge is shared in mutual help group meetings. Professional expertise is valuable in many contexts, but professionals usually don't have direct, daily, personal experience in coping with the focal problem.

Mutual help groups offer **community narratives,** expressing in story form a description and explanation of the focal problem, and an explicit guide to recovery or to coping (we discussed these narratives in Chapter 6). The group's belief system, rituals, and mutual storytelling provide ways to make meaning of life experiences, to transform one's identity, and to promote coping. As members become committed to the group, they interpret their own life stories and identities in terms similar to the community narrative. This is especially a concern of spiritually based twelve-step groups (Humphreys, 2000; Rappaport, 1993, 1995).

Professional mental health treatment and mutual help are complementary forms of helping (Chinman et al., 2002). Professional treatment offers, for instance, scientific and clinical knowledge of disabilities and treatments, and it is especially useful in assessing and treating complicated problems. Mutual help offers the benefits of peer relationships, helping others, and experiential-practical knowledge, at very low or no cost. Members of Schizophrenics Anonymous groups in Michigan clearly distinguished between expertise of group members and leaders, and expertise of mental health professionals, yet valued both (Salem, Reischl, Gallacher, & Randall, 2000). In a survey of mental health and rehabilitation professionals in Connecticut, those with more professional experience, and those with personal or family experience with mental disabilities, viewed mutual help groups more positively than other professionals and were more likely to refer clients to them (Chinman et al., 2002).

Mutual help groups are not helpful for everyone. Knowledge, personal contact, and discretion are helpful when professionals refer clients to specific mutual help groups. However, those caveats are also true for referrals to professionals. A recent consensus statement by leading researchers called for strengthening ties between drug abuse treatment professionals and self-help groups (Humphreys et al., 2004). Professionals or students can attend mutual help group meetings to initiate mutual understanding and collaboration (Chinman et al., 2002).

Online Mutual Help

Online mutual help groups provide a resource to those with privacy concerns or who cannot attend face-to-face groups (Madara, 1997). Two studies of online mutual help groups, one for persons with depression (Salem, Bogat, & Reid, 1997) and another for problem drinkers (Klaw, Huebsch, & Humphreys, 2000), found that online group interactions generally resembled interactions in face-to-face groups. Interestingly, both studies found gender involvement was different online. Unlike face-to-face groups, men more often used the online depression group, and women the online problem drinking group. An online professionally moderated support group effectively engaged Asian-American male college students in discussing ethnic identity issues, while face-to-face groups with similar aims had failed (Chang, Yeh, & Krumboltz, 2001). These findings indicate that persons reluctant to participate in face-to-face groups are more willing to join online groups, and can receive similar benefits there.

Online groups also are more accessible for individuals who are less able to leave home. Dunham et al. (1998) developed a local computer mutual-help network for single, low-income mothers of young children. Each mother received a computer donated by local organizations and access to the network. A core group of mothers used the service intensively and experienced declines in parenting stress. Online groups also are helpful for persons with stressful illnesses. As we noted earlier, persons with multiple sclerosis and chronic fatigue syndrome are especially likely to use online mutual help (Davison et al., 2000). In randomized experiments, online social support programs for HIV-positive persons, women with breast cancer, and adults with Type 2 diabetes were effective in providing support (Barrera, Glasgow, McKay, Boles, & Feil, 2002; Gustafson et al., 1999; Gustafson et al., 2001). In the diabetes study, the online support setting had a forum directed by persons with diabetes, where participants discussed day-to-day coping; a forum where professionals introduced topics and led discussion; and real-time chat rooms.

What Really Happens in a Mutual Help Group?

GROW is a mutual help organization primarily for persons coping with serious mental illness (relatives and others are welcome at meetings). It began in Australia when members of an AA meeting, who also experienced serious mental illness, began their own meeting. GROW has become an international organization active in Australia, New Zealand, Ireland, Great Britain, Canada, and the United States (Luke, Rappaport, & Seidman, 1991; Maton & Salem, 1995; Roberts et al., 1991, 1999; Zimmerman, Reischl et al., 1991).

GROW groups meet weekly. Meetings "open and close with group recitation of prayers and pledges" (Roberts et al., 1991, p. 724). Two periods of group discussion of individual participants' problems and progress follow, with a "period of objective discussion and learning of GROW literature" between. GROW meetings studied by Roberts et al. lasted up to two hours, with a mean attendance of eight persons. Behavioral observation of these meetings documented high rates of helping communications: encouragement, advice, or describing a similar experience. Almost one-third of comments in the discussion periods were helping acts or agreement with another speaker. Another one-third of comments shared nonthreatening information intended to be helpful. Most of the rest involved asking questions or self-disclosure. Negative comments and distracting small talk were rare. These practices illustrate reciprocity and sharing of experiential knowledge.

An important GROW objective is the fostering of a "caring and sharing community" among members (Maton & Salem, 1995, p. 648). GROW literature and practice emphasize interdependence and sense of community among members, with sayings such as "If you need help, help others" and "No matter how bad my condition, I am loved by God and a connecting link between persons" (Maton & Salem, 1995, p. 641). Practices such as contacts between pairs of members outside meetings, encouraging friendship among members, and provision of rides and other tangible assistance build a peer-based support system among members (Maton & Salem, 1995).

Within this community atmosphere, GROW encourages members to assume responsibility for their own coping and personal development. Its approach emphasizes member strengths and growth, with sayings such as "I can compel my muscles and limbs to act rightly in spite of my feelings" and "Mostly, when things go wrong they are meant to go wrong, so we can outgrow what we have to outgrow" (Maton & Salem, 1995, p. 641).

Mutual Help Outcomes

Empirical evaluations of GROW programs have documented its efficacy in helping members make changes in their lives. Weekly attenders of GROW meetings have experienced more positive changes in psychological, interpersonal, and community adjustment than infrequent attenders. Compared with matched controls, GROW members spent less than half as many days in psychiatric hospitalization over a 32-month period (Rappaport, 1993; Maton & Salem, 1995). In general, persons with psychiatric disabilities who participate in mutual help groups (not just GROW) have lower symptom levels and hospitalization rates, shorter hospital stays, and enhanced positive functioning and social networks (Chinman et al., 2002).

Studies of participants in Alcoholics Anonymous (AA) and similar twelve-step groups generated similar findings (Kelly, 2003). Humphreys, Finney, and Moos (1994) followed 439 men and women with an alcohol abuse problem in the San Francisco area. Those more involved with AA over a three-year period were more likely to develop active coping strategies, including less use of alcohol. AA participants also develop greater friendship resources, especially support from others committed to abstinence (Chinman et al., 2002; Humphreys & Noke, 1997).

Mutual help groups are not for everyone. Dropout rates are significant (as is also true in professional treatment), and mutual help alone may not be enough for some especially complicated problems (Humphreys, 1997). Moreover, some mutual help groups welcome diverse members and address social injustices underlying some personal problems, whereas others don't (Rapping, 1997).

However, thinking of mutual help as a treatment method overlooks much of its value (Humphreys & Rappaport, 1994). One joins a mutual help group for an extended period, perhaps for life. Membership incurs responsibility not only for working on one's own concerns, but also for helping others. Rappaport (1993) argued that a more revealing view of such groups is that they are normative communities, providing a sense of belonging, identification with the group, and mutual commitment: a psychological sense of community.

One study of a mutual help organization for parents illustrates sense of community in its groups, and outcomes involving empowerment. In Britain, Contact a Family offers mutual help groups for parents of children with physical, mental, or learning disabilities. Solomon, Pistrang, and Barker (2001) studied a sample of these parents (almost all mothers). With the Group Environment Scale, based on Moos's (1986) social climate concepts, participants described their groups as high in cohesion, expressiveness, task orientation, and self-discovery. In focus group discussions, parents described the uncertainties of learning that their child had a disability, and how the groups helped them accept their child's disability and understand the child's strengths. Group members also offered advice on how to advocate assertively with educational professionals for services for the child and helped with that advocacy. Parents also described a sense of belonging, emotional safety, being understood in the group, and increased sense of self-efficacy. These findings represent changes at several ecological levels: in relations with the wider community (schools), sense of community within the group, interpersonal changes in the family, and personal growth.

SPIRITUALITY AND COPING

In times of suffering or loss, but also in times of joy and of deeply felt commitment, many people turn to spiritual practices and communities. They do this not only for support, but also to understand their lives or to experience the transcendent. A spiritual perspective can help make sense of the "incomprehensible, unfathomable, uncontrollable" (Pargament, 1997, p. 8). This is especially meaningful at the limits of an individual's ability to cope, when Western cultural and psychological assumptions about controlling outcomes in one's life are most likely to fall short.

Spirituality and religion offer distinctive personal and social resources for coping. Personal resources include a spiritual relationship with God or other transcendent experience, a set of beliefs that provides meaning in life and may promote coping, and specific coping methods such as prayer and meditation. Social resources include membership and support within a religious congregation or other spiritual setting (including spiritually based mutual help groups), and shared spiritual practices and rituals (Fiala, Bjorck, & Gorsuch, 2002; Folkman & Moskowitz, 2004; Maton & Wells, 1995; Pargament, 1997; Pargament & Maton, 2000).

However, the personal and social impact of religion and spirituality can also be negative. In a survey of U.S. battered women, one-half of respondents reported negative experiences with religion (Horton, 1988, cited in Pargament, 1997). Spirituality and religion can create or worsen stressors, such as when the person interprets a stressor in a spiritual way that prevents helpful coping, or when personal conflicts with a congregation are not resolved (Pargament, 1997). Among a sample of resilient African-American single mothers, some found involvement in a religious community offered "protection and blessing"

(Brodsky, 2000, pp. 213–214), whereas others found spiritual solace and strength outside religious congregations, or avoided them.

Neither religious beliefs and institutions, nor personal and cultural forms of spirituality, exist solely as resources for coping. Both have much larger purposes. Their usefulness for coping must be understood within those larger aims. Spirituality involves a sense of transcendence, of going beyond oneself and daily life (Sarason, 1993). Spiritual persons often view their relationship with God or a spiritual realm as distinct from other relationships. Spirituality cannot be reduced simply to coping resources (Mattis & Jagers, 2001). Our focus here on coping concerns only part of the meaning of spirituality.

Empirical Research on Spirituality and Coping

Empirically, how do spiritual and religious factors affect coping outcomes? Pargament (1997) reviewed empirical studies of spirituality, religion, and coping. Because these studies are correlational, direct conclusions about the causal impact of spiritual-religious coping on coping outcomes cannot be drawn. However, researchers can study the strength of spiritual variables as predictors of coping outcomes, particularly in longitudinal designs. Participants in these studies were mostly North American adults, including persons with chronic and terminal illnesses, bereaved widows and children, victims of automobile accidents and floods, Whites and African Americans, heterosexuals and gay men, and senior citizens. Most who indicated religious involvement were Christian. Researchers measured a variety of coping outcomes, including psychological distress and well-being, and health.

Spiritual-religious coping practices include prayer, a sense of a personal relationship with God or other transcendent experience, framing stressors in spiritual terms, engaging in spiritual practices and rituals, and seeking support from congregation members. Both religious and nonreligious persons may use them in particular circumstances. Pargament's (1997, chap. 10) review revealed five general findings about spiritual-religious coping.

- It was particularly important with stressful, largely uncontrollable situations.
- It often was empirically related to positive coping outcomes even after nonspiritual coping methods were statistically controlled.
- Coping methods most related to positive outcomes included (a) perceiving a spiritual relationship with a trustworthy and loving God, (b) activities such as prayer, (c) religious reappraisal promoting the sense that growth can come from stressful events, and (d) receiving support from fellow members of a religious congregation. These findings have also been supported in more recent studies (Folkman & Moskowitz, 2004).
- Not all studies found significant associations between spiritual-religious coping and outcomes, and some found negative associations. Negative effects included self-blame and lack of support from one's religious congregation.

- Women, those with low incomes, the elderly, African Americans, and the widowed find religion and spirituality more useful for coping than do other groups. What these groups seem to have in common is less access to secular sources of power and resources.

Pargament's (1997) review indicates religious and spiritual coping methods are important for understanding coping. Their impact may be positive or negative. Their most distinctive contributions may occur when other resources are lacking or when stressors are uncontrollable. Yet this research is in its early stages, with much to be learned (Pargament & Maton, 2000; Folkman & Moskowitz, 2004). Especially needed are studies of religion and spirituality in differing social and cultural contexts. For instance, studies have appeared in community psychology on African Americans, Korean Americans, engaged Buddhism, and Native Alaskan spirituality (Bjorck, Lee, & Cohen, 1997; Brodsky, 2000; Dockett, 1999; Hazel & Mohatt, 2001; Mattis & Jagers, 2001).

CONCLUSION

In this chapter we sought to illustrate processes and resources relevant to coping, highlighting community resources and interventions. However, we do not assume that these concepts fully reflect the complex reality of coping, or the diversity of resources and interventions. We encourage you to consider what else needs to be included, and to diagram your own ecological framework of coping.

CHAPTER SUMMARY

1. This chapter presents an ecological framework for understanding the coping process. That framework emphasizes the importance of social, cultural, and situational contexts and resources in coping. The framework includes *risk processes (factors)* and *protective processes (factors).*
2. *Distal factors* are predisposing processes indirectly related to stress and coping. They may involve risk factors or protective factors. Some are *contextual,* others are *personal.*
3. *Proximal stressors* represent a threatened or actual loss or scarcity of resources, and trigger stress. They include *major life events, life transitions, daily hassles,* and *disasters*. Multiple stressors may cascade in *vicious spirals.*
4. *Stress reactions* include cognitive appraisals, emotions, and physiological processes.
5. Persons activate resources for coping with stress. These include *material resources, social-emotional competencies,* and *social, cultural and spiritual resources.*

6. Coping processes include *reappraisal,* and three types of coping: *problem focused, emotion focused,* and *meaning focused.* Coping is contextual: the best approach depends on the situation and persons involved. Effective coping can create *virtuous spirals.*
7. Coping outcomes refer to the psychological or health effects of coping. These include positive outcomes such as *wellness, resilience, thriving, social embeddedness,* and *empowerment* and less pleasant outcomes such as *distress, dysfunction,* and *clinical disorders.*
8. Interventions to promote coping can occur at multiple ecological levels. Community interventions include *social and policy advocacy, organizational consultation, alternative settings, community coalitions, prevention and promotion programs, crisis intervention, collaboration with community resources,* and *case management.*
9. *Social support* includes two types: *generalized* or *perceived support,* and *specific* or *enacted support.* Support occurs in relationships, including families and *natural helpers or mentors.* Relationships can be sources of stressors as well as support. Important qualities of *social support networks* include *multidimensionality, density,* and *reciprocity.*
10. *Mutual help groups* are another important community resource. They vary along a spectrum from *self-help groups* to *mutual support groups* with much professional involvement. They have five key qualities: *focal concern, peer relationships, reciprocity of helping* (involving the *helper therapy principle), experiential knowledge,* and *community narratives.* Online mutual help groups are a growing resource. Mutual help groups are not a cure-all, but they offer positive outcomes for many.
11. *Spirituality and religion* are a third important community resource, providing personal, social, and material resources for many persons. Positive outcomes of spiritual coping include usefulness with largely uncontrollable stressors, especially among groups with less access to secular resources. However, spiritual and religious coping and settings also can have negative effects, and research with more diverse spiritual traditions and populations is needed.

BRIEF EXERCISES

1. Think back to your first year of college. Answer the following questions about it. Discuss them with a friend or classmate.

   What social-emotional competencies were required for you to succeed? Examples might include planning your time, reviewing for tests, organizing papers ahead of time, making conversation with strangers, resolving roommate conflicts, and asking for help of various types.

   What forms of social support were most important for you? Who provided them? What help did you provide to others? What relationships created stressors as well as support?

How did you grow during that year? What personal strengths, skills, and important relationships did you develop? What obstacles did you overcome, and how did others help?

2. Diagram your own ecological framework of processes involved in coping. You can begin with your own ideas or by looking at Figure 8.1. Consider distal and proximal factors, risk and protective processes, resources, coping processes, and outcomes. Consider interventions at various points of your framework. Discuss your diagram with others.
3. Read a psychology journal article on stress, coping, social support, or a related topic. (You can access the *American Journal of Community Psychology* through the InfoTrac College Edition search service.) Consider these questions: Did the article consider multiple ecological levels of analysis? Did it examine contextual factors, community resources, social support, mutual help, social-emotional competencies, and positive outcomes such as resilience, thriving, and empowerment? Did it test or consider interventions? If so, describe them.

RECOMMENDED READINGS

Barrera, M. (2000). Social support research in community psychology. In J. Rappaport & E. Seidman (Eds.), *Handbook of Community Psychology* (pp. 215–246). New York: Kluwer Academic/Plenum.

Dohrenwend, B. (1978). Social stress and community psychology. *American Journal of Community Psychology, 6,* 1–14. Reprinted in T. Revenson et al. (Eds.) (2002), *A quarter century of community psychology* (pp. 103–117). New York: Kluwer Academic/Plenum.

Folkman, S., & Moskowitz, J. (2004). Coping: Promises and pitfalls. *Annual Review of Psychology, 55,* 745–774.

Moos, R. (2002). The mystery of human context and coping: An unraveling of clues. *American Journal of Community Psychology, 30,* 67–88.

RECOMMENDED WEBSITES*

Mutual Help Clearinghouses

American Self Help Clearinghouse, Self Help Group Sourcebook Online
http://mentalhelp.net/selfhelp

Lists local, face-to-face self-help groups and organizations. Readings on self-help, and how to start a group.

*Thanks to Ed Madara of the American Self-Help Group Clearinghouse for help with this list.

Fraternidad de Grupos de Autoayuda y Ayuda Mutua (Self-Help and Mutual Aid Group Fraternity)
http://www.ayuda-mutua.com

Clearinghouse of diverse self-help group materials in Spanish founded by a Mexican psychologist.

National Mental Health Consumers' Self Help Clearinghouse
http://mhselfhelp.org

Consumer-run site, with information on the mental health consumer movement and related organizations.

Psychology Self-Help Resources on the Internet (in PsychWeb site)
http://psychwww.com/resource/selfhelp.htm

Lists and links to online resources for mental health information and self-help clearinghouses.

Self-Help Nottingham
www.selfhelp.org.uk/

Links to self-help group research and listserv for group researchers.

Mental Health

American Psychological Association, Psychology Topics and Help Center
http://www.apa.org/topics
http://www.apahelpcenter.org/

Information on topics related to coping and psychological interventions. Help Center is consumer-oriented.

Mental Help Network
http://mentalhelp.net

Information on mental disorders, treatment, and related issues. Links to self-help resources.

National Alliance for the Mentally Ill
http://www.nami.org

Information on this national advocacy organization with local chapters for persons with mental illness and families.

National Mental Health Association
http://www.nmha.org

Information on this national advocacy organization with local chapters: prevention and treatment of mental disorders.

Psychcentral
http://psychcentral.com

Information on mental disorders and treatments. Chat rooms, support forums, links to online resources.

U.S. Centers for Disease Control and Prevention
http://www.cdc.gov

Information on health and illness: prevention, treatment, health issues in the news; links to other health sites.

U.S. National Mental Health Information Center
http://mentalhealth.org

Provides general and consumer-oriented information on mental health and Federal programs.

INFOTRAC COLLEGE EDITION KEYWORDS

coping, mutual help, religion, resilience(y), self-help, spirituality, stress(or), (social) support, thriving, wellness

INTERCHAPTER EXERCISE

Mapping Your Social Support Network

One way to visualize the personal meaning of social support is by mapping your emotional support network. In this exercise you will list your sources of emotional support, map them in terms of settings and interrelationships, analyze some characteristics of this network, and integrate your learning with social support concepts. We adapted this from a social network exercise developed by David Todd (1979).

NETWORK LIST

First, write a list of the people to whom you would go to seek help with a personal or emotional problem of your own. List only those who you would seek out for this kind of help, not your entire network of friends. (Thus, this map illustrates only your emotional support network, not your entire friendship network.) Include persons you would contact face to face, or by telephone, email, or other means. Write this list down the left margin of your paper, each name on a separate line.

Second, on the line for each person write the relationship(s) you share with that person. You choose the term(s) for these; examples include sister, friend, roommate, fellow worker, neighbor. This is an indicator of the sources of your support and of unidimensional and multidimensional relationships.

Third, on the same line list the setting (just one) where you most frequently encounter that person. Examples include work, residence hall, apartment or home, classes, student union, a campus organization or team, or spiritual setting.

Fourth, put a check mark on the line of each of the persons who you believe would probably seek you out for help with their personal-emotional problems.

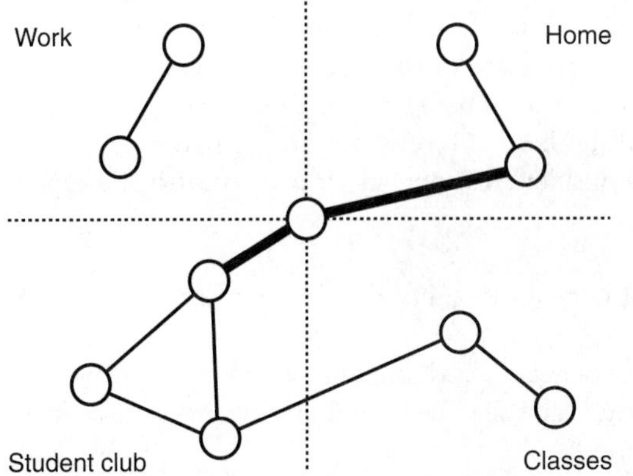

FIGURE 8.2 Social Support Network Map

NOTE: Heavy lines represent multidimensional relationships. Unidimensional relationships between the focal person and others are not drawn. Dotted lines separate segments.

NETWORK MAP

You need a clean sheet of paper for this part. First, in the center of the page, put a small circle or dot, which represents you. Second, use dotted lines to divide the space into segments radiating out from the center like pieces of a pie. Each segment represents a setting in which you encounter at least one person in your emotional support network (from the third step on the previous page). Make a segment bigger if it includes many persons, smaller if it does not.

Third, put small circles or dots in the segments to represent the people on your network list. Label them with initials. You may put your closest confidants closer to you on the map, and others farther away. However, spread all of them out, and use the entire page. That makes the next steps easier. (Remember, everyone on this list is close to you in some way.)

Fourth, draw a heavy line between your circle and the circles of those persons with whom you share a multidimensional relationship. The heavier the line, the more dimensions of relationship you share with that person.

Fifth, draw a light line between any two persons on the map, other than yourself, who you believe to be friends or confidants of each other. (Don't worry about whether these are multidimensional or not.) Lines may cross setting boundaries (dotted lines drawn between segments). This is your indicator of network density.

Figure 8.2 illustrates a network map.

Analyzing Your Network List and Map

Your list and map represent your perceived network for emotional support (see Chapter 8).

Network Size This is simply the number of persons on your list. Network size is not an important predictor of coping outcomes unless it is very low (Sarason, Sarason & Pierce, 1990). A person with few or no confidants is emotionally isolated and lacks a key resource. In addition, conflict or loss in a relationship have a proportionally larger effect when there are only a few supportive ties. On the other hand, there is an upper limit to how many close, emotionally supportive relationships a person can realistically have. More is not always better.

Is there anything you would consider changing about your emotional support network's size?

Sources and Quality of Support Your network list represents a set of relationships.

Which relationships are sources of generalized, ongoing support (see chapter 8)? Are there relationships in which you might seek help for a specific problem or stressor, but not more generalized support?

How many family members are on your list? What is your perception of the quality of their support for you? What sort of support do you perceive to be available from your family? With what stressors are family members able to help you?

How about the number and quality of supportive relationships with friends? What sorts of support are available from them, to cope with what stressors?

Do you have a mentor, an older person who is not a relative and who provides emotional and/or other forms of support? A mentor may provide advice and support in one setting, such as work, or be a source of more generalized support.

This is also a way to consider the diversity of resources in your network. Does your network contain persons of both genders, and of varying ages? Of differing life experiences and backgrounds? Does it contain anyone who has experienced stressors such as bereavement, unemployment, divorce, or serious illness/injury, and who could provide support if one of these stressors happened to you?

Is there anything you would consider changing about your sources of emotional support?

Reciprocity In constructing your network list, you checked persons who you expected would seek emotional support from you for their problems. That is a rough measure of reciprocity within each relationship.

Which relationships in your network are reciprocal? How are they different from those that aren't? Is there an overall balance of providing and receiving emotional support in your life, when all your relationships are considered? What are the psychological benefits for you of providing support to others?

Is there anything you would consider doing to strengthen reciprocity in your emotional support network?

Multidimensionality Heavy lines between you and others in your network map represent multidimensional relationships. Multidimensional relationships often offer high-quality support (e.g., Hirsch, 1980). Do you have any of these? Do they offer more quality of support, or more rewarding contact, than unidimensional ones?

Is there anything you would consider doing to increase multidimensionality in your network?

Network Segments These are separated by dotted lines on your map. Many students have segmented networks, with supportive relationships in each segment, but few connections across segments. Hirsch (1980) found that for young widows and adult women college students, having supportive relationships in different settings or segments of their lives was more adaptive than one densely connected network.

Is there anything you would consider doing to build supportive relationships in each setting in which you spend a lot of time?

Network Density Density refers to the extent of ties among network members other than yourself. A high-density network has many such connections, a low-density network does not. A low-density network has been shown helpful for persons experiencing life transitions that involve forming new relationships, such as divorce, widowhood, and adults re-entering college (Hirsch, 1980; Wilcox, 1981). A high-density network may respond more quickly in a crisis, since its members are more interconnected.

Is there anything you would consider doing to change the density in your network?

Summary The effects of social network variables on your coping is contextual, and some of the ideas and findings we have mentioned may not fit your personal experience. In addition, your emotional support network represents just one form of social support. Your lists and maps for other forms of support (e.g., your friendship network, or for academic guidance, or support at work) would probably look different. Try mapping and analyzing those as well.

9

Prevention and Promotion: Key Concepts

HIRB/Index Stock

OPENING EXERCISE: A PREVENTION PARABLE

A story is told about a man at the side of a river, reaching in and hauling to shore person after person, all of whom were struggling, often drowning, as they were pulled downstream by the strong current. A woman came by, saw what he was doing, and pitched in to help. But despite their hard and constant work, for every body they pulled out, ten more went past them. The condition of those who remained in the river became more and more desperate.

As they worked, the woman asked the man, "How are these people getting into the river?" The man did not know. "Why don't you go upstream and see what the problem is?" she asked. "I am too busy," the man replied. "There is much to do here. Besides, if I stop, even more people will be lost." She thought about what he said and agreed and went back to work. But after more and more days, with the flow of people growing and their own strength diminishing, she decided to go upstream and find out what was going on. "It's true that some extra people may be lost while I am gone, but if I can stop, or even cut down the flow, we all will be better off." And so she went.

Upstream, she saw that one part of a path was leading people to a dropoff directly into the river. As she moved toward it, she realized that this was

> where she would stay; her work would no longer be to fish drowning people out of the river, but rather to keep as many as possible from falling in at all. She would work to redirect people from the path and would also try to change the path. Soon others followed her example, positioning themselves just downstream from the entry point so they could get people out of the river before the current got full hold of them, making them harder to save. Finally, some decided that people needed to live so that they were not drawn to the river at all. They needed to live in a way that kept them away from taking the harmful path in the first place (after all, it did not seem as if everyone was equally likely to take it). Even those people who were reached early, however, had to be prepared so that if they did take the harmful path, they would have the support and strength necessary to resist its pull. The woman and her colleagues began to work toward those goals.

Ask yourself, "What does it mean to prevent something?" No doubt, you have had some experience as the recipient of a prevention program. Perhaps your health classes in high school, middle school, or even elementary school involved programs to prevent drug and alcohol abuse, smoking, teenage pregnancy, violence, and HIV/AIDS. Your college or university probably has programs to prevent bias, sexual harassment, drunk driving, and academic failure. What do you know about these programs? How did they go about trying to help you prevent one problem or another? Were they effective? What accounts for their strengths or shortcomings? For example, were they based in any sound theory of prevention or promotion, specifying when and how programs should take place? In this chapter, we give you some tools to start answering questions like these systematically as well as share ways in which community psychology concepts are leading to new thinking about prevention.

Before we go further, we want to emphasize that a focus on prevention and a focus on treatment can be complementary. Our parable, a version of a story often told by prevention advocates, is intended to highlight the need for a diversity of approaches to mental disorders and other psychological problems in living. Treatment of those already experiencing a mental disorder is a humane goal and often means taking into account biological and individual factors as well as social ones. Prevention, in contrast, focuses on factors that can be changed before disorder develops, whether environmental or personal. Although budget constraints often mean that prevention and treatment advocates may compete for scarce resources, their activities and choices of emphasis are complementary and worthy of mutual respect.

INTRODUCTION: PREVENTION AS A FIELD OF STUDY

What do you think needs preventing now? What two or three areas would you prioritize? Why? You will find that in different eras, different problems seem to be emphasized. In the 1960s, there was a focus on poverty and the way its

BOX 9.1 From "What's Happening?" (Camden County Youth Center, New Jersey, October 1992)

"Dreams Going Up in Smoke"

I used to watch my dad do drugs.
Smokin his pipe. Rock of cocaine on the screen.
Light up with a match or lighter.
I wished he wouldn't.
But what could I do? Thirteen year old.
Talk to him. Hug him. He said he couldn't stop.
They wouldn't tell me how he died.

SOURCE: —T.T., age 15

"If I Gonna Die . . ."

If I gonna die . . . I want people to have good things to say about me—not die from some gunshots or some drug war. I wanta be something—job, church, family—not be the one my aunts hear about shot dead—read about in the papers.
I've got jumped. I've got shot. Next time around I might be dead.

SOURCE: —T., age 17

consequences created disadvantage for children in schools and for all of its victims in terms of health and well-being; in the 1970s, the end of the war in Southeast Asia and the intensification of the Cold War between capitalism and communism highlighted many issues of social and economic justice. In the 1980s, there was a "war" on alcohol, tobacco, and other drugs. Many feel that this war was most successful in the area of smoking prevention. In the early and middle 1990s, the emphasis shifted to the prevention of violence. At the time of this writing, many social issues were being debated, such as abortion; so-called entitlement programs, such as welfare, Social Security, and Medicare; immigration; and racial and ethnic tolerance. These shifts were, in turn, reflected in legislative changes. Among the most noteworthy is the switch of the Drug Free Schools and Communities Act, which funded local, school, and community-initiated substance abuse programs, to the Drug Free, Safe Schools and Communities Act, which added violence to the portfolio but actually reduced the total pool of available funding. Drugs, guns, other forms of violence, and dysfunctional families are continuing sources of harmful influence and are foci for prevention efforts. (See Box 9.1 for an example of what too many youth continue to experience.)

Since September 11, 2001, the focus of prevention has shifted to include terrorism in all of its forms, including suicide bombing, assaults on individual school buildings, transportation systems, or public facilities; attacking water or food supplies with biological agents; and explosion of nuclear devices in public spaces. These concerns, amplified by the occurrence of natural disasters such as Hurricane Katrina in 2005 and the earthquake and tsunami that devastated so many Asian nations at the conclusion of 2004, have created a level of vulnerability, stress, and tension in much of the general public that is unprecedented in recent decades. Yet in many localities these global concerns do not impinge on the enduring difficulties of everyday life as the focus of prevention efforts.

In the previous chapters we presented concepts that community psychologists use to understand individuals and communities and the phenomena that challenge and sustain them. In this chapter and the two that follow we convey how community psychology values, concepts, and tools can be used in the context of preventing problem behaviors, preventing mental health difficulties, and promoting sound mental health and social competence. Because the literature on prevention is growing faster than our ability to keep up with it, our goal is to illustrate rather than be comprehensive. In Chapter 9 we outline key concepts; in Chapter 10 we present a variety of application issues and examples and we use a family case study to highlight how clinical and preventive perspectives come together in practice. In Chapter 11 we review in detail how to "walk the talk" and implement prevention/promotion innovations in a variety of contexts.

What Is Prevention?

Prevention is a common-sense concept that derives from Latin words meaning "to anticipate" or "before something to come." The language of prevention is found in all aspects of public endeavor. Parents try to prevent children from hurting themselves; police try to prevent crimes; the legal system is designed to prevent violation of certain rights; road signs are created and posted to prevent people from getting lost.

In the field of community psychology and community research and action, ideas about prevention have been evolving. Because the field of community psychology is linked to societal events and forces, this evolution will continue. This dynamic makes the field important and exciting, but also hard to capture in a textbook.

As you learned in Chapter 2, the concept and practice of prevention links public health and psychology. Psychiatrists Erich Lindemann and Gerald Caplan were particularly important in forging that link. An analysis of available "person-power" in the mental health field by George Albee (1959) supported the growing interest in prevention. Albee showed that there were not and could not be a sufficient number of clinicians trained to provide all of the needed mental health services for the population. Consider the implications of this extraordinary finding. Therapeutic resources are scarce and will realistically remain scarce. As in the parable that opened this chapter, need will always outstrip the supply of services. Prevention of psychological problems (reduction of need) becomes a justifiable use of scarce resources.

Another issue raised by Albee's (1959) findings concerns how scarce treatment resources are distributed. A series of epidemiological studies (Hollingshead & Redlich, 1958; Myers & Bean, 1972) showed a strong relationship among socio-economic status, ethnicity, and services received. The poor and minority groups were more likely to receive severe diagnoses, to receive medication rather than psychotherapy, and to be seen in groups rather than individually. The preferred clients were those most like the therapists—male, Caucasian, verbal, and successful. Both preventive concepts and innovative services were central to the Community Mental Health Centers Act in 1963, advocated by President John Kennedy. In terms of the parable at the outset of this chapter, there were a growing number of reasons to move upstream and keep people from falling into the river.

Although community psychology has embraced the concept of prevention, another aspect of the concept merits consideration. Take another look at the examples mentioned earlier. Parents try to help children learn how to care for themselves safely; educators encourage learning in different forms; employers train and supervise employees to work effectively; road signs are posted to help people get to where they want to go. These examples focus on developing desired competencies, skills, and abilities. Overall health and quality of life become the goal more than simply preventing psychiatric disorders or types of problem behaviors. Cowen (1991, 2000a) championed the term *wellness* as a more fitting goal of preventive efforts. Although wellness refers to life satisfaction or gratification in living, it is a transactional concept linked to the social ecology within which people live. Again, in Cowen's (1991) colorful words: "The pot-of-gold behind the pursuit of a wellness rainbow might be a genuine betterment of the human condition" (p. 408). Cowen's views have become central to how community psychologists think about prevention of disorder and promotion of competence and wellness.

Box 9.2 features selected quotes from a series of essays on the future of primary prevention. See which ones strike you at this point in your reading. Then, revisit them after you have read Chapters 9, 10, and/or 11 and see how your opinion has changed, if at all.

A FOCUS ON COMPETENCE: BOWER'S MODEL

A focus on the promotion of social competence, wellness, and health and the prevention of problem behavior is common to many professional disciplines. It also is a shared concern among policy makers, elected officials, educators, sports and recreation leaders, and parents. Bower (1972) proposed a useful way of conceptualizing how society is organized to accomplish these goals. He described three types of settings through which all societies prepare their young citizens for adult life, using the catchy acronyms KISS, AID, and ICE.

Key Integrated Social Systems (KISS)

Key integrative social systems (KISS) are formal and informal settings within which individuals interact from conception through childhood. The first of these is the health care system, which includes prenatal care, the management of the birthing process, and postnatal care. The second KISS system is the family, which begins to shape a child's values and outlook on life and provides opportunities to build important cognitive, affective, motor, interpersonal, and academic skills.

School is the third system, and its impact is felt at an increasingly early time as more and more children enter child care and preschools before kindergarten. Head Start, for example, is designed primarily for preschool children from impoverished families and provides not only preacademic skills, but also medical and dental services, housing, parenting support, job training and placement, linkage with social services, and transportation. It is paradoxical that as children move into the public school system, their access to these services tends to become far less organized and systematic. Nevertheless, the school years from kindergarten through twelfth grade exercise substantial influence on a diverse array of skills, of which academic abilities are only a part.

BOX 9.2 Thoughts about Primary Prevention

In its Fall 2000 issue, the *Journal of Primary Prevention* published a set of essays predicting the future of primary prevention. Several quotes capture the range of thoughts expressed:

"Prevention of mental disorders is small potatoes and usually is at the bottom of the social agenda. The Peace Corps was never asked for psychologists or psychiatrists. More immediate needs—for food, clear water, immunization—were more urgent. . . . The best mental health promotion will come with a revolution against social injustice." (George Albee, p. 9)

"With good reason, we have become increasingly concerned that we demonstrate with detail and precision the tremendous potential of prevention initiatives. . . . My concerns about the future of prevention grow, however, from my sense that the calls for precision and detail are frequently misinterpreted. Too often they seem to be equated with honing in on control and detail at the expense of maintaining the big picture. As investigators struggle to narrow in on subtle, albeit potentially important distinctions between and relationships among variables, manipulations can become so restrictive that ecological validity is lost. We risk garnering a tremendous amount of detail about contexts that are so narrowly and rigidly defined that they are highly unlikely to exist or even resemble the real world. . . . The context for human development is a highly dynamic set of interacting systems ranging from micro- to macro-levels. We can't afford to limit our work in primary prevention to any one or small group of these mutually embedded systems." (Lynne Bond, pp. 12–13)

"As one moves from micro- to macro-systems, wellness enhancement issues become more complex and diffuse, access lines to change more difficult, and knowledge about how best to promote change more diverse. Accordingly, it is easier to worship wellness as an ideal, than to achieve it. Amplifying knowledge of how, specifically, micro-, meso-, exo-, and macro-systems operate to affect wellness can solidify the generative knowledge bases needed to bring off diverse wellness enhancing steps at multiple levels. In summary: a) prevention activities, broadly defined, must play a larger role in mental health's overall framework; b) distinctions between risk-disorder prevention and wellness enhancement approaches must be sharpened and more support brought to the latter; c) individual and family strands of a wellness enhancement approach that relate to sound early child formation need further fleshing out; d) steps toward a system-grounded, life-span approach to wellness development and maintenance are needed. The concept of psychological wellness offers a heuristic framework for conceptualization, research, and program development in mental health. The pot of gold at the end of that rainbow is its potential for strengthening the adaptation and enhancing the life satisfaction of many people in modern society." (Emory Cowen, pp. 17–18)

"The world's three richest billionaires (all American, as it happens) have combined wealth greater than 600 million of the poorest people on earth. The combined income of the 200 richest exceeds the combined income of the poorest 40 per cent of the world's population. These 200 more than doubled their net worth—to

An informal KISS system with pervasive influence is peers. Aristotle was among the first to state that humans are *polis* animals, meaning that we are inherently social and that we organize ourselves around relationships. From toddlerhood on, peers serve as models and mirrors, sources of new behaviors, advice, feedback, questions, and support or discouragement. Developmental psychologists have studied how, at different time periods in one's life, peer influences vary in strength and nature. Preadolescence is a time when peer influences begin to compete with those of parents and teachers, increasing in strength into the adolescent years. Shared experiences with peers can strongly influence career, higher education, lifestyle, and religious choices.

Indeed, religion is the final KISS system discussed by Bower (1972). At the time of his writing, religious institutions were in a decline. The late 1960s and early 1970s in the United States were times of disillusionment and confusion

$1 trillion—between 1994 and 1998. Eighty countries have less revenue than they had 10 years ago. In 1960, the richest fifth of the world's population had 30 times the income of the poorest fifth. In 1997, they had 74 times as much. Do these numbers indicate some kind of problem? If so, can anything be done about it? We know that large disparities are associated with reduced life expectancy, more crime, ill health, and so on, but that may be the least of the problems these inequities foretell." (Justin Joffe, p. 33)

"Most people agree that prevention against physical, psychical and social problems of individuals is superior to waiting passively until problems have become manifest and need cure. Most people agree that societies have an obligation to take appropriate measures in some of these areas. Most people agree that educating, convincing and helping people is superior to forcing their compliance with massive coercive interventions. Most people agree that these measures should respect the private sphere of individuals and not violate basic human rights. Most people agree that the preventive strategies chosen should be as effective and efficient as possible, particularly if public money is involved. . . . At the same time many experts are very much aware that what is expected from them and what can be done are miles apart. The reasons for this gap are easily identified but difficult to deal with. In many areas we still do not have a sufficient empirical and/or theoretical basis on which to build preventive strategies. . . . We commonly find ourselves confronted with phenomena that are hard to assess reliably, with a long latency period between intervention and outcome, with low problem incidence in the total population, with a large number of uncontrollable simultaneous influences, and with important context factors that change rapidly over time and vary greatly from region to region. . . . In order to be able to move forward into a more professional and evidence-based direction, we have to be much more precise about terminology and concepts and we have to confront ourselves explicitly with central methodological limitations and principles.

If we put our fingers on the inherent uncertainties encountered in daily prevention and evaluation, emphasize weak spots, reject tasks that are not feasible because of economic, technical and/or ontological restraints, are precise in terminology and do not avoid methodological problems, we risk disappointing potential customers in the short run, but in the long run contribute to the improvement of prevention and evaluation, and help to create a sound foundation for a good and lasting reputation. . . . Some of us, frustrated by the complexity of our task and tempted by the need to contract projects for economic reasons, resort to opportunism or to cynical resignation, but I am very much convinced that we may be quite optimistic about what we can accomplish and about the present developments. Primary prevention and evaluation of primary prevention are challenging tasks, but if we understand our professions, despite all of these limitations, there are many promising approaches, sensible options and solutions available to prevent ourselves from depression and cynicism." (Alfred Uhl, pp. 43–45)

for many, and the role of religion and the operation of religious institutions were questioned or ignored. Yet through the late 1980s, 1990s, and into the earliest twentieth century, there has been a resurgence in the role of religion and religious organizations as sources of influence and support. This trend can be seen dramatically in the Middle East and in Eastern Europe, particularly in the countries of the former Soviet Union. Poland and Russia have seen previously outlawed religious observance flourish, with religious leaders taking strong stands on social issues and the provision of human rights.

The term *secondary KISS contexts* can be used to refer to other key aspects of socialization not mentioned as part of Bower's (1972) initial theory and include the following circumstances.

- Workplaces affect individuals through scheduling, roles and work strain, relationships and interaction, opportunities for growth or frustration.

- Leisure/recreational systems can be formal or informal: country clubs or midnight basketball games, senior citizen centers or a card game with friends, concerts or reading in a coffeehouse.
- Community organizations include parents' groups affiliated with schools; civic groups such as Kiwanis, Scouting, B'nai B'rith, and Mothers Against Drunk Driving; local business associations; and advocates for local beautification/ preservation. These may influence individual development of their members or exist to help others develop (e.g., parenting groups).
- Media/Internet/cyberspace communication is eclipsing more traditional forms of communication and interaction, and "bits" of information flow more quickly. This information influences individual development in many direct and indirect ways but also reduces the control centralizing authorities (e.g., parents, governments) have over socialization messages.

Obviously, the influence of KISS either promotes or thwarts competence. If the KISS settings work as they were designed to, by providing the intended health care, schooling, parenting, friendships, and spiritual supports, individuals passing through them would develop considerable strengths. In such circumstances, KISS would be exercising a substantial preventive effect. But the reality is that KISS settings do not function flawlessly. Inequitable distribution of resources leads some schools, families, and hospitals to work less than optimally. Further, the degree of integration of these social systems with one another varies quite dramatically from country to country, state to state, and municipality to municipality. KISS systems thus may interfere with each other rather than complement each other. For many children, passage through KISS can be quite perilous.

Ailing-in-Difficulty (AID) Institutions

When difficulty is encountered in the KISS settings, society provides AID: ailing-in-difficulty institutions. Those who are not able to function as well as desired in one context of KISS can go to such places for short-term assistance. Following this help, the person is expected to be able to function well. If one thinks of KISS as the main turnpike of socialization, AID can be thought of as rest stops or service areas. Examples of AID include guidance counseling and special services in the schools, outpatient mental health facilities, local police, a short-term detention or crisis center, hospital emergency rooms, and worksite personnel counseling.

Illness Correctional Endeavors (ICE)

The final part of Bower's (1972) model is ICE: illness correctional endeavors. ICE is provided by psychiatric hospitals, prisons, and long-term health care facilities. These may appear to be places where those in need of high degrees of assistance can go so they can return to AID or KISS, but the reality is that it often can be easier to enter ICE institutions than to emerge from them back into KISS systems. Bower viewed these institutions more as agents of social control than as venues for rehabilitation.

Present societal forces (such as greater public scrutiny of care facilities and the rise of cost-oriented managed care and short-term services) make ICE settings less effective as repositories for those felt to be social outcasts and misfits than was the case when Bower (1972) was writing. However, in certain countries, especially those run by dictatorships and other de facto totalitarian regimes, ICE institutions continue to be used overtly as holding tanks for those who do not "fit smoothly" into KISS systems. Bower's point, however, still holds: In ways subtle and not so subtle, people who are deemed "different," "defective," "inferior," "evil," or "bad" are kept away from the social mainstream that constitutes the KISS and even AID systems.

Taken as a whole, Bower's model can be expressed as follows: With a good, loving KISS early in life, people will need less AID and fewer will have to be treated with ICE. From this simple conceptualization, many implications follow about the process of socialization in a nation, community, agency or social organization, or family. If socialization occurs properly throughout life, the large apparatus of repair and diversion can be reduced. Problems of all kinds can be prevented or reduced in severity.

Linkage to Social Ecology and Developmental Psychology

It's helpful to think of KISS in terms of the social-ecological levels of analysis you learned in Chapter 1. Parents and other caregivers, as well as educators, medical personnel, and others whose responsibilities include navigating children through the KISS settings, are themselves embedded within microsystems, organizations, localities, and macrosystems that influence how well they function in their task of socializing children. The macrosystem consists of beliefs about children and child-rearing and such social policies as flexible work scheduling and paternity leave that are of general influence on parents and parenting, but the nature of that influence depends most on the microsystems, organizations, and communities within which parents interact most directly (Belsky, 1984). Among the relevant organizations or communities are religious congregations, tenant associations, neighborhood or town libraries, colleges, chamber of commerce chapters, farmer's cooperatives, neighborhood crimewatch organizations, or political clubs. Some examples of microsystems include families, a small civic group, an informal network of friends, a bowling team, a sewing or quilting group, or a small family-run business.

The social-ecological point of view provides a way of putting Bower's (1972) concepts into motion and applying them dynamically. Central to our thinking is that prevention cannot be thought of as an inoculation. Successful efforts require an ecological and developmental approach, addressing not only people but also the contexts in which they live and interact. For example, macroeconomic trends create financial pressures on corporations, which cut costs by downsizing, laying off workers, and increasing overtime for those who remain. This, in turn, reduces the time and energy of parents for their families and for volunteer organizations related to school, civic, recreational, and religious life. When the KISS systems are deprived of resources and do not work optimally, more individuals require the services of AID stations and ICE institutions.

The practical value of Bower's focus on KISS systems is linked to advances in knowledge that improve socialization efforts. In the social-ecological model, the individual is viewed as developing and adapting at the center of numerous surrounding interactive environments (e.g., Belsky, 1980; Bronfenbrenner, 1979; Holahan & Spearly, 1980). Our biological attributes, knowledge, and attitudes in all domains, personal identity, personal history, socioemotional skills, and physical characteristics all are involved at all times. Seeing this, Masterpasqua (1981) commented on what he saw as the essential synergy between developmental and community psychology. He put forth the notion of **developmental rights** as a key integrative concept, something restated often since then as community psychologists and those interested in the intersection of law and children's rights have been addressing these issues more prominently (Melton, 1991; Wilcox, 1993).

Developmental rights means that children born into a society have the right to conditions that will allow them to grow in a healthy manner, if not also to thrive. These conditions serve as a powerful force for prevention of problem behavior and promotion of competence. Some of these follow from Bower's (1972) model, such as adequate health care in the prenatal period and sound parenting skills. However, research is necessary to constantly fill in the details, help find critical periods of growth and influence, and guide the specific timing and content of interventions and services. Research also is necessary to refine our understanding of variations caused by cultural and racial factors, gender, socioeconomic and education status, and developmental level.

Hence, it was with great wisdom that early community psychologists advised that participant conceptualization should and must precede the onset of interventions and occur throughout them. This strategy acknowledges the richness, complexity, and history of social systems, the individuals within them, and their response to change. And participant conceptualization, as the name implies, is rooted in key concepts for understanding prevention and promotion.

CONCEPTS FOR UNDERSTANDING PREVENTION AND PROMOTION

In this section we describe the historical progression of concepts from prevention of disorder, to promotion of competence, to ideas of strengths and thriving. In so doing, we define and illustrate key concepts in the contexts in which they are used.

Caplan: Primary, Secondary, and Tertiary Prevention

There is a rich history to the concept of prevention, rooted in the field of public health and the mental hygiene movement of the early twentieth century (Heller et al., 1984; Spaulding & Balch, 1983). However, Gerald Caplan is recognized as the individual whose use of the term *prevention* led to its becoming a part of the mental health lexicon. Caplan (1964) made a distinction between the following three types of prevention.

Primary Prevention This is intervention given to entire populations when they are not in a condition of known need or distress. The goal is to lower the rate of new cases (from a public health perspective, to reduce incidence) of disorders. Primary prevention intervenes to reduce potentially harmful circumstances before they have a chance to create difficulty. Examples are such things as vaccinations, fluoridating water, and providing skill-building programs in decision making and problem solving to children in preschool. Similarly, primary prevention also can be thought of as being applied to all persons in a given setting, regardless of potential need (e.g., all fifth graders in preparation for transition to middle school or all first-year college students).

Secondary Prevention This is intervention given to populations showing early signs of a disorder or difficulty. Another term for this is early intervention. This concept is a precursor of current notions of being "at risk," which are discussed shortly. Examples of secondary prevention are programs targeted to children who are shy or withdrawn, those who are beginning to have academic difficulty, or adults who are getting into conflicts with coworkers on the job.

Secondary prevention presupposes some method of determining which individuals are at risk or demonstrating early signs of disorder. Identifying such individuals creates a potential for stigmatization, both because they do not currently have a disorder and because they might never develop one. Improving methods of risk identification represents an important area of work in community psychology.

Tertiary Prevention This is intervention given to populations who have a disorder with the intention of limiting the disability caused by the disorder, reducing its intensity and duration, and thereby preventing future reoccurrence or additional complications.

If it strikes you that it is difficult to differentiate tertiary prevention from treatment, you are not alone. But Caplan had a purpose that often is forgotten by his critics today. A child psychiatrist by training, Caplan was trying to introduce a preventive way of thinking to the treatment-oriented medical, psychiatric, mental health, and social service fields. By emphasizing the similarities of prevention and treatment, he was able to link these concerns. Ultimately, he was successful in that the idea of prevention took hold, becoming a central tenet of fields such as community psychology, school psychology, and, increasingly, clinical and health psychology.

However, Caplan's (1964) framework appealed to those seeking resources for treatment. Some early prevention grants were given to programs designed for such things as the tertiary prevention of schizophrenia: a worthy goal, but not exactly what Caplan had in mind. Yet as many have noted, prevention is a difficult concept to grasp. One is trying to keep away what is not (yet) there. Would it ever arrive if the prevention effort were not in place? Others have stated that if prevention is to be worthwhile, then one must specify what one is preventing. An emphasis on defining specific conditions such as suicide, depression, and conduct disorder as goals of prevention reflects this point of view.

Klein and Goldston (1977) were among a number of community psychologists who attempted to clarify the issues raised by Caplan's (1964) definitions and others' interpretations. Although agreeing with the definition of primary prevention, they felt it important to relabel secondary prevention as treatment given because of early identification and tertiary prevention as rehabilitation services. These definitions help to provide a clearer distinction between prevention and treatment for specific or severe problems. Debate still ensues over whether interventions given to shy children, for example, are best thought of as prevention or treatment. But other models now have risen to prominence, and thus it pays little to dwell on past inconsistencies when current inconsistencies are available for examination.

The IOM Report: Universal, Selective, and Indicated Measures

A report by the U.S. Institute of Medicine (IOM; Mrazek & Haggerty, 1994) is likely to greatly influence thinking about prevention well into the twenty-first century. Its main conceptual contribution is the idea of universal, selective, or indicated measures or methods for prevention.

Universal Preventive Measures These interventions are good for everyone in a given population group, and they typically are administered to populations that are not in distress. This is similar to primary prevention.

Selective Preventive Measures These are desirable for people at above-average risk for developing mental disorders. That risk may be based on their environment (e.g., low income or family conflict) or personal factors (e.g., low self-esteem, difficulties in school). These risk characteristics are associated with the development of particular disorders but are not symptoms of the disorder itself.

Indicated Preventive Measures These are applied to individual people who are at high risk for developing disorder in the future, especially if they show early symptoms of the disorder. However, they do not meet criteria for full-fledged diagnosis of mental disorder.

Interestingly, the IOM Report places mental health promotion (including concepts related to competence and wellness) into a separate area, distinct from prevention. The editors viewed self-esteem and mastery as the main focus of mental health promotion, with competence, self-efficacy, and individual empowerment all terms commonly used in describing such efforts. The IOM Report defined its focus in terms of whether or not an approach prevents a specific disorder, not in terms of competence enhancement.

Weissberg and Greenberg (1997) raised some thoughtful questions about the IOM framework. For instance, should a violence prevention program be considered a universal intervention in a school with few incidents of violence, yet selective in a school where violence is more common? Because depression is diagnosed more often among girls than boys, should a program for prevention of depression be considered universal if given to a troop of Boy Scouts but selective if given to a Girl Scout troop? For disorders such as conduct disorder, what is the boundary between predictors of a disorder (for selective prevention) and early symptoms (for indicated prevention)? Consider a program delivered to a class in which there is a diversity of students: (a) a student with conduct disorder, and another with attention-deficit hyperactivity disorder; (b) several disaffected, underachieving, unmotivated students; and (c) others with no behavioral or emotional difficulty, some even with great strengths. Is the same program considered universal for the latter group, selective for the disaffected students, and indicated for the children with diagnosed disorders? Beneath these definitional questions is a fundamental concern for the direction in which preventive efforts should be headed, both in terms of research and action.

Point/Counterpoint: Prevention of Disorder and Promotion of Wellness and Competence

As the historical overview implies, there is a continuing debate about where the emphasis of time and resources is best placed, on prevention or promotion. In addition, within these areas there are varying options for emphasis (e.g., based on age, socioeconomics, gender, ethnicity). This must be considered against the backdrop of points raised by Uhl and others in Box 9.2. Articulate spokespersons of different points of view arise periodically, and you are urged to engage in this debate on the basis of the current state of knowledge. In general, the debate can be framed between proponents of prevention of disorder and those believing that promotion of wellness and social competence should be emphasized.

Advocates of the prevention view argue that we are learning a great deal about how to prevent specific disorders such as depression, suicide, conduct disorders, and schizophrenia. Research should be directed toward isolating and reducing the operation of risk factors most closely targeted with specific disorders. This view is most likely to be associated with selective and indicated interventions, based on the IOM Report.

Advocates for promotion note that many people are not in a state of sound psychological well-being despite not having specific disorders. We know a great deal about how to promote sound health and social competence, drawing in part from interventions in public health in such areas as prevention of cardiovascular disease, from school settings in areas such as social and emotional skill building, and from workplace efforts to increase organizational effectiveness. Research should be directed toward identifying and understanding the factors that promote health, wellness, and competence in daily living. These will differ in different living environments, cross-culturally and internationally.

Issues of prevention and mental health have never been isolated from political and ideological considerations. As you learned in Chapter 2, in U.S. society the social zeitgeist during conservative times favors individual, illness-oriented conceptions of mental health and other social problems. Prevention in those times tends to be understood in terms of preventing specific disorders. In more progressive times, an environmental focus supports a definition of prevention closer to promotion of overall health and wellness and competence.

The United States is now in a conservative period that moderated in intensity in the 1990s but has accelerated in the shadow of the tragic attacks on September 11, 2001. Research in recent years has focused on biological factors in mental health, and the mental health field is seeking to prove itself to be rigorous (at least as rigorous as medicine is perceived to be) and cost conscious. Insurance companies and federal granting agencies prefer to pay for clear prevention outcomes rather than supporting efforts to improve health. However, organizations such as the World Federation of Mental Health and the World Health Organization tend not to share the view prevalent in the United States. Theirs is a more holistic view of health in which mental health and physical well-being—which extends to basic issues of shelter, food, and freedom from war, societal anarchy, and enslavement—are essential parts of the overall picture. Many community psychologists embrace this broader view of health.

The goals of preventing specific disorders and promoting wellness and competence are not mutually exclusive, and the techniques to pursue them may be the same in particular circumstances. There are strong parallels with physical health, where health-promoting activities such as a sound diet are valuable and may also serve to prevent such problems as cardiovascular disease—but also may not have specific preventive effects on other specific conditions or illnesses. Community psychologists try to keep a perspective on prevention that is best understood as an umbrella providing a common cover for both points of view or as a bridge linking them. Sometimes, community psychology knowledge is used to provide preventive interventions to specific populations to prevent specific disorders, at other times to general populations in KISS settings to promote overall wellness. The outcomes of these interventions are measured in terms of lowered incidence of a specific disorder and/or in terms of increased competence for coping, as appropriate.

We turn next to community psychologists' conceptual frameworks to see how they energize the work of prevention and competence promotion and provide the stimulus for the kinds of creative approaches needed to address diverse settings and circumstances.

Connecting Stress and Coping Concepts with Prevention and Promotion

In Chapter 8 we presented a stress and coping framework. Five key concepts there, *risk, protection, resilience, strengths*, and *thriving*, are especially useful for prevention and promotion at this time. Ultimately, the best conceptualizations of prevention and promotion are those that have the most heuristic value and lead to the most social benefit, in accordance with the values of community psychology. In this chapter we draw from our own experience of what we have found to be heuristic. This includes social ecology, sense of community, and the skill-building orientation that accompanies a stress and coping framework. In addition, we look at the areas where future work in the field is best directed as a guide for those looking toward careers relating to prevention and promotion. The frameworks and examples we present in Chapters 9, 10, and 11 are not complete, but rather serve as webs to which many concepts, examples, and issues can be usefully connected. When our webs can no longer easily connect with current issues, theories, and research findings, we will have to make changes in our conceptualizations. Indeed, we have made some since the previous edition of this book.

As of this writing, momentum toward the concepts of strengths and thriving continues to build, given impetus by theorizing and research in positive psychology (Seligman & Csikszentmihalyi, 2000b) and growing recognition that resources do not exist to equitably deal with social problems primarily on a post-hoc, crisis basis. However, it is important to not view strengths and thriving (or risk, protection, and resilience) as static and unchanging. These concepts are best viewed as dynamic processes that are interrelated and ongoing.

Consider how a community psychology perspective on prevention and promotion is connected to strengths and thriving. A focus on strengths asks the question: What are a person's assets and how can these be used to improve quality of life, especially in times of difficulty? The Search Institute (2004) developed *Frameworks of Developmental Assets* (grouped by age) for children and adolescents. **Developmental assets** are psychosocial protective factors among youth, families, schools, and communities that have been found in research to promote healthy child and youth development. Strengthening these can be the goal of promotion programs. For instance, their youth developmental assets list includes 40 specific assets at ecological levels that vary from individual to locality. This detailed list summarizes a large body of research in practical terms for use by community members. Some examples of assets are: family support; caring adults and neighbors; a caring school climate; parent involvement in schooling; clear expectations for behavior in family, school, and neighborhood; a community that values youth and ensures their safety; access to youth, creative, and/or religious programs; youth commitment to learning and to prosocial values; social competencies such as decision making, interpersonal skills, knowledge of other cultures, and conflict resolution; and having a sense of purpose in life. Community organizations, schools, and other groups have used these assets lists in a variety of ways. The lists are available at: www.search-institute.org/assets/.

Paradoxically, ideas of strengths and thriving draw support from neurobiology, where the concept of compensatory functioning has long been understood as the brain's way of circumventing deficits in its seemingly constant attempt to maximize our functional and adaptive capacities (Sylwester, 1995). Indeed, much of rehabilitation psychology is about finding ways to restore functioning when the primary mechanisms for that functioning are damaged. Clinical and health psychology are recognizing the powerful role of humor and optimism in fighting and preventing disease (Goleman, 1995). Those involved in youth work recognize that at-risk adolescents can be "reclaimed" as their strengths are identified, enhanced, given recognition and value, and then linked to areas of difficulty (Brendtro, Brokenleg, & Van Bockern, 1990; Elias & Cohen, 1999). Community psychology research from a strengths-based perspective is likely to become more prominent in the near future.

We anticipate that the focus on strengths likely will be joined by research driven by the concept of thriving. This stems directly from applying an ecologically based concept of resilience to populations at high risk. It is exemplified by studies such as that of Abraido-Lanza, Guier, and Colon (1998), who examined the process of thriving among Latinas with chronic illness living in impoverished neighborhoods. An individual is deemed as thriving to the extent to which she appears to experience positive growth despite her adverse life circumstances and, additionally, finds strength, insight, or meaning in life as a result of what she goes through. Although the authors acknowledge many methodological complexities in their research, the main finding seems clear: thriving is related to positive affect and self-esteem and represents something beyond coping, or even resilience.

The work of two other investigators sheds some light on ecological factors that might account for individual differences in thriving. O'Leary (1998) reviewed the literature on developing strength in the face of adversity. She identified three stages of response to severe stressors: survival, recovery, and thriving. Thriving is defined as a transformation of one's personal priorities, sense of self, and life roles. Interestingly, this phenomenon was observed by Erich Lindemann and served as the impetus for his work in crisis intervention.

O'Leary (1998) also identified microsystem and organizational level resources that foster thriving. Social relationships appear to be especially powerful for women, to the extent to which having and perceiving strong support is linked with improved immune system functioning. Certain conditions within organizations such as workplaces and schools provide opportunities for thriving to take place. These include caring, openness of communication, encouragement of individual contributions and growth, and organizational risk taking. Under such conditions, individuals appear to be free to contemplate new roles, to make changes in their jobs and roles and still feel accepted within an organization, and to feel involved in organizational decision making.

Thriving also appears to be fostered by nations that respond to challenges in certain ways. O'Leary (1998) reviewed the emergence of the African National Congress and democracy in South Africa, concluding that collectivist traditions and a strong set of positive, supportive, reaffirming rituals in the face of setbacks led to results that have gone beyond recovery to transform a nation. Another example can be found in Armenia (Karakashian, 1998). Over a period of four millennia, Armenia has endured calamities that have led neighboring countries and civilizations to crumble. What accounts for this endurance? Karakashian (1998) identified four main factors that she pointedly labels not as prevention (which implies absence of illness) and not as resilience (which implies a return to former health, a "bouncing back" to prior equilibrium) but thriving (which implies continued strengthening and growth beyond that equilibrium). These factors include (a) development of identity-affirming family traditions and community life; (b) an identity as *dogal,* associated with survival of adversities such as forced deportations and migrations; (c) strong family education in Armenian history, culture, and values; and (d) parenting approaches that appear to equip Armenian children with as much feeling of support and being loved as children from other countries as well as skills of alternative thinking, overcoming obstacles, and communicating their feelings. The latter are among the skills identified as essential aspects of emotional intelligence (Goleman, 1995). By focusing on cultural traditions and practices, Karakashian (1998) identified processes that go beyond individual resilience.

For community psychologists interested in prevention and promotion, strengths and thriving are concepts that hold great promise. They enable us to move beyond an individual perspective and see how prevention, social competence, wellness, and related outcomes result from a convergence of influences at multiple ecological levels. Next, we use the vehicle of the prevention equations to provide a feasible way of conceptualizing and enhancing ecological influences that are associated with the generic term *prevention* but also are linked to a broader set of wellness-related goals.

THE PREVENTION EQUATIONS: INTEGRATIVE GUIDES FOR RESEARCH AND ACTION

> If children are to experience healthy relationships and occupy meaningful and productive roles in society as adults, they must be competent at communicating and working cooperatively with others. They need to be able to express their own opinions and beliefs, to understand and appreciate the perspective of others who differ from them in background, needs, or experiences, and to become skilled at reasoned disagreement, negotiation, and compromise as methods of solving problems when their own needs or interests conflict with those of others. Indeed, in the face of decreasing resources and increasing global interdependence, it can be argued that such qualities are essential to our survival. The question, then, is not whether we must enhance children's social competencies, but rather how to accomplish this goal. (Battistich, Elias, & Branden-Muller, 1992, p. 231)

The complexity of ecological, developmental, and transactional models and their application to notions of risk, protection, resilience, strengths, and thriving can seem daunting. Some simplification strategies are necessary to help make directions for research and action more clear. Prevention equations serve this role.

Two Prevention Equations

The literature concerning social competence promotion over the past decade can be summarized in terms of the prevention equations of Albee (1982) and Elias (1987; see Table 9.1). Albee's (1982) formula is framed at the individual, person-centered, level; its focus is on reducing the likelihood of disorder (or improving the likelihood of wellness) in a single person. Individual risk is heightened to the extent that the individual experiences stress and/or physical vulnerabilities, and is lowered to the extent that the individual possesses coping skills, perceives him or herself as well supported, and has positive self-esteem. For each term in the equation, there is a corresponding approach to intervention that one might take. These are numbered 1–5 in Table 9.1.

TABLE 9.1 Individual and Environmental Level Prevention Equations

Individual Level (Albee, 1982)

$$\text{Incidence of behavioral and emotional disorder in individuals} = \frac{\text{stress}(1) + \text{physical vulnerability}(2)}{\text{coping skills}(3) + \text{social support}(4) + \text{self esteem}(5)}$$

Interventions derived from individual equation:

1. Reduce/better manage perceived stress
2. Reduce the negative impact of a physically/biologically based vulnerability
3. Increase coping skills, problem-solving/decision-making, social skills
4. Increase perceived social support
5. Increase self-esteem/self-efficacy

Environmental Level (Elias, 1987)

$$\text{Likelihood of behavioral and emotional disorder in settings} = \frac{\text{stressors}(6) + \text{risk factors in the environment}(7)}{\text{positive socialization practices}(8) + \text{social support resources}(9) + \text{opportunities for positive relatedness and connectedness}(10)}$$

Interventions derived from environmental equation:

6. Reduce/eliminate stressors in key socialization settings, other aspects of environment
7. Reduce operation/presence of physical risk factors in the environment that result in increased physical/biological vulnerability
8. Improve socialization practices, ways in which key socialization settings carry out their tasks
9. Increase accessible social support resources
10. Increase opportunities for positive relatedness to others and connectedness to positive social institutions, positive social groups, agencies, and other formal and informal settings

Elias (1987) extended these ideas to the level of environments to complement Albee's (1982) equation. In social learning theory, predicting individual risk actually would involve a set of equations for the multiple settings one inhabits. Further, these equations would have to be modified to reflect developmental changes in the individual. Additionally, community psychology calls for ways of examining the risk (and protective) processes for populations and communities, not just for individuals.

The environmental level formula in Table 9.1 indicates that risk is increased as a function of stressors and risk factors in the environment, and decreased to the extent to which protective processes are enhanced: positive socialization practices in key socialization environments, access to social support and socioeconomic resources, and opportunities for positive relatedness and connectedness of the kind that allow for prosocial bonding and the development of a sense of being valued. Note that these terms are attempts to denote properties of settings, not attributes of individuals. The derivative interventions shown in Table 9.1, numbers 6–10, are correspondingly focused on ecological levels that surround individuals.

It might occur to you that the numerators of each equation summarize the literature on risk processes and the denominators do the same for protective processes. Good! It occurred to us, as well! In what follows, we use introductory examples to show how the equations can be used to guide both research and action as well as to illustrate the complementary nature of terms used at the person and environmental levels. Reflecting the perspective of positive psychology, Meyers and Meyers (2003) have introduced an interesting elaboration of the prevention equations to emphasize wellness and positive functioning. Combining individual and environmental levels and integrating recent research in positive psychology (Huebner & Gilman, 2003), they expand the equations to include such elements as:

- Subjective Well-Being: self-concept, life satisfaction, hope
- Competence: emotional and social competence, social cognition, flow, moral sense
- Supports: organizational climate and structure; acceptance; social, educational, functional, and health resources

The implication is that promotion of competence is an end in itself worthy of pursuit by community psychologists without any reference to the prevention of any disorder. Further, it introduces hope, moral sensibilities, supportive organizational conditions, and health resources as essential elements for optimal functioning.

Defining the Terms in the Prevention Equations

Stress (in the individual-level equation) has been linked clearly to individual distress and various types of psychopathology. Although it is recognized that the absence of stress can be as debilitating as an excess of stress (Goleman, 1995), it is generally noted that stress past an optimal level of arousal inhibits optimal performance of specific tasks or life roles. Techniques that teach individuals how to better manage their stress, such as meditation (Kabat-Zinn, 1993) or relaxation training (Cartledge & Milburn, 1989), reduce the likelihood of disturbance, although of course many factors impinge on this.

In a similar way, stressors (in the environmental-level equation), aspects of environments or contexts that engender stress in their inhabitants, are associated with dysfunction. School transitions, especially to kindergarten, to middle school or high school, as a transfer student, and out of high school, are accompanied by increased rates of referrals for mental health and related services as well as decreased academic performance that can set off a trajectory of negative accomplishment and school failure (Carnegie Corporation of New York, 1994; Chung & Elias, 1996; Reyes et al., 1994). Although each student is not automatically affected by these conditions, overall rates of dysfunction increase at times of transition. Programs directed at reducing the factors that engender stress during those transitions, such as the STEP program discussed in Chapter 5, often change structural features of the setting in which transition occurs. As with STEP, that often results in lower rates of problems for students (Elias et al., 1986; Felner & Adan, 1988).

Biologically based vulnerabilities in individuals have many causes but one common effect: they make it more difficult for a person to participate in mainstream KISS contexts. This says far less about the capabilities of such individuals than it does about the willingness and flexibility of social settings to accommodate to their special needs. Person-centered interventions reduce the impact of such vulnerabilities by providing tools that can allow better mainstream access as well as strengthening an individual in areas where help is needed. One positive effect of Head Start for many children is that it gets them earlier access to services for visual, hearing, dental, and health impairments. If children attend school with these vulnerabilities undetected, they encounter academic and social difficulties, loss of motivation, frustration, or self-doubt.

Risk factors in the environment refer to such conditions as lead in paint and water, malnutrition, and poor prenatal care, all of which create physical and psychological vulnerabilities that, in turn, hamper coping and development. Examples include exposure to hazardous wastes that lead to increased incidence of cancer in children. Epidemiological research that uncovers such situations is important in community psychology, as are interventions to correct such factors or ameliorate their effects. For instance, Levine (1982) studied community responses to discovery of the effects of a toxic waste dump at the Love Canal in New York State. When child advocacy groups such as the Association for Children of New Jersey, the National Association of Child Advocacy Organizations, and the Children's Defense Fund advocate against state or federal legislation regarding lead or housing policies that allow children to live in dangerous environments, they are operating within the spirit of intervention term number 7 in the environmental level prevention equation.

Coping skills in individuals are perhaps the most widely studied aspect of prevention. All manner of programs to build individuals' social, emotional, and cognitive skills fall under this term. These represent interfaces with clinical, school, and other branches of applied psychology and allied fields. Many of these focus on teaching skills such as problem solving, communication, self-regulation, and social approach behaviors. Social skills training occurs in schools, mental health programs, and workplaces and with individuals being strengthened for the future as well as those who are experiencing problems and disabilities.

Positive socialization practices denotes the way in which KISS systems fulfill their socializing functions. Much of this involves how caregivers are prepared for their roles and equipped to help individuals learn and use coping and social skills. As Bower (1972) observed, are those in a position to give a good KISS able and willing to do so? Are parents prepared for what they are called upon to do by society? Are teachers? We know, for example, that nearly 50 percent of beginning teachers leave the profession within five years because they are not equipped to handle the behavior of their students and to turn their classes into constructive learning environments. This does not reflect poor capacity on the part of new teachers as a group (although, as in any field, some people are not destined to be teachers and will not find out until they attempt it). The cause is just as much failure of the socializing agents that are supposed to prepare and support them for teaching and oversee the conditions under which they work.

More and more emphasis is being given to the workplace as an ecological context with great relevance for mental health and overall wellness. Think about various jobs you have held. How did your employer prepare you and other new employees for effective role performance? What kinds of ongoing socialization existed? To the extent relevant, how was your family prepared for the nature of working life? As an example, two of your authors (JHD and MJE) vividly recall carrying beepers in earlier clinical jobs, and neither of us was told about the impact of the beeper on our lives and the lives of our spouses. On the other hand, the likelihood of psychological difficulties in such workplaces as factories decreases when supervisors as a group are skilled in training and developing those who work under them. Communities are healthier when, for instance, their teachers know how to deal with children's hearts as well as their minds, and the school administrators know to do the same with their teachers.

In Chapter 8 we discussed the concept of social support as a coping resource, primarily at the individual and microsystem (social network) level. Albee's (1982) individual-level equation recognized this resource. Yet social support resources are accessible and easily used in some settings, but missing or inaccessible in others. Their strength and availability is an important setting characteristic.

Self-esteem and self-efficacy are concepts with long-standing links to positive mental health outcomes. Rotter (1982) and Bandura (1982) showed that individuals with negative expectancies for their ability to impact on their environments and a poor recognition and appreciation of their strengths are more likely to develop a variety of psychological disorders. Similarly, settings vary in the extent to which they provide opportunities for relatedness and connectedness and positive contributions by the people within them (Barker, 1968; Cottrell, 1976; Sarason, 1974; Wicker, 1979). Those settings that do provide such opportunities are likely to have more individuals who feel a positive sense of efficacy; in turn, rates of disorder will be lower in them than in comparable types of settings that do not provide such opportunities.

Recall from Chapter 5 that behavior settings that are optimally populated (Barker & Gump, 1964; Schoggen, 1989) are less likely than underpopulated settings to promote individuals' development and sense of connectedness. Individuals in environments with overpopulated behavior settings are likely to be less loyal, be more disgruntled, feel left out, and leave sooner. You no doubt can think of some settings in which you have had similar feelings. Organizations with many underpopulated behavior settings, however, generate greater perceptions of involvement, connectedness, and individual satisfaction. Many things need doing in an underpopulated setting, and those who do them often recognize they are providing something worthwhile for the setting. Hopefully, you have had this kind of experience as well.

Integrating Person and Environment

Perry and Jessor (1985) have been leaders in linking health and mental health outcomes to risk and protective processes at the person and environmental levels. They identified four domains of health and competence: *physical,* referring to physiological functioning; *psychological,* referring to subjective sense of well-being; *social,* referring to effectiveness in fulfilling social roles; and *personal,* referring to realization of individual potential. Within each domain, knowledge, attitudes, and behaviors comprise health-compromising (risk) or health-enhancing (protective) processes.

In Perry and Jessor's model, three facets of intervention must converge to maximize likelihood of success: environmental contexts, personality, and behavioral (coping) skills. Personality serves an important integrative role, mediating between individual behavioral skills and environmental contexts that influence how the person applies those skills. Subsequently, Jessor (1993) advanced the construct of healthy lifestyles as an elaboration of the role played by personality in his earlier models. Lifestyles embody the meaning and direction that an individual attaches to events, relationships, and one's future. As the way in which one interacts with all aspects of his or her environment, lifestyles imply the embeddedness of problem behaviors in various life contexts. Once these behaviors begin, forestalling their advancement is not simply a matter of addressing a discrete set of skills. Interventions must recognize that a shaped lifestyle is not easily abandoned, and problem behaviors are often reinforced in peer networks. Future work in community psychology is likely to build on integrative models such as Perry and Jessor's.

APPLYING THE CONCEPTS IN THE REAL WORLD: SOME CAVEATS

Our use of equations is not intended to suggest precision regarding prevention and promotion concepts and interventions. As participant conceptualizers, community psychologists are very aware of the complexity of individuals and settings. The prevention equations are merely guides to exploration in a messy, challenging, exciting world.

Moreover, prevention/promotion interventions that work in their original settings may fail miserably in other contexts. Even highly effective interventions will not automatically generalize to new circumstances. As the sage Hillel commented many centuries ago, one can never stand in the shoes of another because time does not stand still. No two situations are identical. Yet we know there are continuities within the diversity of ecological contexts. Respect for uniqueness is balanced with aspects of shared humanity, diversity with commonality, present circumstances with transcendent realities.

How better to think of these high concepts than in terms of a pizza? When we take a bite of a pizza with "everything," it has a certain taste that is hard to attribute to any particular ingredient. What really makes the pizza great? The sauce? The cheese? The spices? The crust? The way it was cooked? The water used to make the dough? Whether we tossed the dough wearing gloves or not? The kinds of toppings used, how much, and where they were placed? Many factors come together to influence an overall outcome. Yet there is still something most can agree is pizza; although it cannot be defined precisely, we can still agree on what great pizza tastes like.

Community psychologists are not content with eating great pizza. We want to know what made it great, who might not have thought it was so great and why not, and how we can make sure that more great pizza reaches more people more consistently. Take as an example Seidman's (1991) Adolescent Pathways Project. His interest is in understanding ways in which five sets of outcomes occur: psychological symptoms, antisocial behaviors, academic achievement, extracurricular achievement, and sound health. For a community psychologist, drawing patterns often occurs from examining a series of cases. Seidman (1991) reviewed studies of 32 elementary and middle/junior high schools in low-income urban areas. Among the findings was the importance of ethnic diversity in understanding pathways. For example, low involvement/participation is significantly related to a negative developmental outcome, antisocial behavior, when one examines the data for the entire sample. Yet when one looks at subgroups, one finds the relationship is not significant for Black and White females, but is so for Latina females.

This is one of many caveats to applying the prevention equations without considering how ethnicity and other mediators refine what predicts developmental outcomes and, therefore, what kinds of preventive efforts are likely to be most effective for what kinds of contexts. Clearly, no single pizza recipe will work across all nations and their ecologies and inhabitants.

From the basic recipes of prevention and competence promotion theory, different ingredients must be added to address the diversity of situations. Often, and appropriately, those additions will reflect the chef, the chef's mentors, the circumstances, the ingredients available, and the nature of the order. The great chefs know the basic recipes, but their greatness comes in knowing how to modify and improvise without compromising the essence of what is being prepared.

In the next two chapters we look at some great recipes and ingredients in the form of effective prevention and promotion programs as well as the challenges of improvisation that arise in particular settings. In Chapter 10 we visit exemplary and promising approaches to promoting competence and preventing problem behaviors applied across different ecological levels, both in the United States and internationally. We begin to answer the question, "How does prevention work?" and examine the application of prevention in everyday life through a family case study. In Chapter 11 we take a more detailed look at implementation and identify key components and processes that are characteristic of viable prevention and promotion efforts.

CHAPTER SUMMARY

1. Prevention is an evolving field of study in community psychology and related disciplines. We began with a parable that illustrates in common sense terms the logic of taking a preventive approach to dealing with mental health problems.
2. Bower's (1972) model illustrates how individual development through the socialization process is related to prevention. These include key integrated social systems (*KISS*), ailing-in-difficulty (*AID*) settings, and illness correctional endeavors (*ICE*) institutions. KISS settings are the focus of preventive efforts. These include prenatal care, schools, parents, peers, religious organizations, and the Internet. The related concept of *developmental rights* emphasizes that persons have rights to conditions that will allow them to cope and thrive.

3. The social-ecological approach stresses the importance of environment, a person's individual attributes, and how these elements interrelate and also impact on the effectiveness of preventive efforts. Prevention occurs not through inoculation but as people pass through social institutions that are strengthening and supportive.
4. Caplan's (1964) concepts of *primary, secondary,* and *tertiary prevention* were an early and highly influential conceptualization of prevention. In 1994, the IOM Report defined prevention in terms of *universal, selective,* and *indicated* approaches. Prevention has become a term that denotes two complementary foci: *prevention* of disorder and problem behavior and *promotion* of wellness and social competence.
5. Concepts for understanding and strengthening prevention and promotion efforts include *risk, protection, strengths, resilience, thriving,* and *developmental assets*. These dynamic processes are important guides for interventions.
6. Albee (1982) and Elias (1987) created two prevention equations useful for integrating the concepts presented. From these equations, one may derive 10 specific types of intervention at either the individual or environmental levels. These are listed in Table 9.1.
7. Community psychology recognizes real-world complexity and tries to avoid overgeneralizing from one context to another. Nevertheless, there are continuities across contexts in prevention and promotion. Understanding prevention and promotion, with all their facets, is like understanding all that goes into making a great pizza.

BRIEF EXERCISES

1. For your community, identify the KISS, AID, and ICE settings. Explain why you placed each setting in each category. A phone book, services directory, or even a walk around the community can help identify settings, as does doing this with a partner. Try to find settings in the health, mental health, educational, justice, and other human service systems. Some of these, especially ICE settings, may serve your community yet be located elsewhere.
2. Look up the Search Institute's Developmental Assets for youth (http://www.search-institute.org/assets). Note that not all assets need be present in an individual's life, but that all are resources for a community. For external assets, consider how these could be strengthened in your hometown or the neighborhood where you live now. For internal assets, consider how these could be better cultivated in children and youth there. Discuss your impressions with neighbors or classmates.
3. One aspect of KISS that has mushroomed since Bower (1972) is media/cyberspace/Internet. This raises critical questions for the future, including the following. Consider these individually and discuss them with classmates or others.

- How can our system of education, both for children and adults, be transformed to take into account the changes in information availability?
- How we can do this in a way that is equitable with regard to communities and individuals of various income levels and conditions of physical or learning abilities?
- How can KISS systems respond to the penetration of information in various forms into our homes, cars, and brains? Is the media/cyberspace/Internet system reducing our involvement in our families, social networks, and communities, or increasing it (or both)?
- Are there differences between a sense of community based on direct personal contact and that derived from cyberspace encounters? Will video technology, such as face-to-face e-mail chats across huge distances, change such perceptions?
- How do families deal with this influx of information into the home? To what should children be exposed? At what ages? For that matter, to what should adults be exposed?

4. Generate some examples of prevention/promotion interventions, and discuss them with a classmate.
   - Choose a problem in living that is at least partly psychological in nature. The problem may be defined by symptoms or behaviors (e.g., depression, anxiety, health problem, poor school performance, criminal arrests) or by a stressful situation (e.g., bereavement, divorce, loss of job, poverty). Also choose an age group in which you are interested that experiences this problem; and a community with which you are familiar, where this problem occurs.
   - For this problem, age group, and community, list the risk and protective processes that you can identify. Write a sentence to define each process; tell why each protective process is protective. Use Table 9.1, the prevention equations, to help identify risk processes (numerators in the equations) and protective processes (denominators).
   - For this problem, age group, and community, identify examples of primary prevention activities and secondary prevention or early treatment activities. List activities that exist and some that you can suggest. Write a sentence or two to describe each existing or suggested intervention. Include what setting that intervention would be based in (e.g., school, neighborhood, workplace). Tell why it represents primary or secondary prevention.

RECOMMENDED READINGS

Albee, G. (1982). Preventing psychopathology and promoting human potential. *American Psychologist, 37,* 1043–1050.

Elias, M. (1987). Establishing enduring prevention programs: Advancing the legacy of Swampscott. *American Journal of Community Psychology, 15,* 539–553.

Maton, K., Schellenbach, C., Leadbeater, B., & Solarz, A. (Eds.). (2004). *Investing in children, youth, families, and communities: Strengths-based research and policy.* Washington, DC: American Psychological Association.

Mrazek, P., & Haggerty, R. (1994). *Reducing risks for mental disorders: Frontiers for preventive intervention research.* Washington, DC: National Academy Press. ["The IOM Report."]

RECOMMENDED WEBSITES

Collaborative for Academic, Social, and Emotional Learning
http://www.casel.org

National Mental Health Association
http://www.nmha.org/children/prevent/index1.cfm

Prevention First
http://www.prevention.org

Search Institute
http://www.search-institute.org

U.S. Center for Substance Abuse Prevention
http://www.samhsa.gov/csap/index.htm

U.S. Center for Mental Health Services
http://www.samhsa.gov/cmhs/cmhs.htm

Information on Social Issues Related to Prevention:

United Nations Children's Fund
http://www.unicef.org

U.S. Federal Interagency Forum on Child and Family Statistics
http://childstats.gov

Annie E. Casey Foundation: Kidscount (influential yearly report on U.S. social indicators regarding children)
http://www.aecf.org/kidscount

National Center for Children in Poverty
http://www.nccp.org

Children's Defense Fund
http://www.childrensdefense.org

(See also Recommended Websites for Chapter 10.)

INFOTRAC® COLLEGE EDITION KEYWORDS

competence(ies), health, intervention, prevention(ive)(ing), primary prevention, promotion(ing), protection(ive), risk, secondary prevention

INTERCHAPTER EXERCISE

Touring the Prevention/ Promotion Literature

The literature in prevention and promotion is expanding far more rapidly than any textbook will ever capture. Relevant literature comes from many fields, including the mass media and the Internet. Particularly for the latter outlets, it becomes important to know how to recognize high-quality work that is useful for prevention/promotion purposes.

The purpose of this exercise is to provide you with ways to do your own investigations of the literature so you can keep up to date and determine what is worth studying in more detail. We invite you to look at a wide array of outlets for examples that reflect prevention and promotion. In addition to research journals, articles in major newspapers and newsmagazines regularly address the social issues that are the central concern of community psychology, although you will rarely see community psychology mentioned. One reason for reading them is our responsibilities as citizens to inform ourselves about those issues. Prevention and promotion are linked to areas that come up for public consideration in the media and in our legislative bodies. The prevention/promotion literature also can inform many college and university policies that impact considerably on students.

The analytic method we recommend is summarized here. It reflects our view that reviews of the literature, as well as your own reviewing of the literature, are best done in a particular context and for particular purposes. We find it is more valuable to read purposefully than generically.

The framework also draws from Bower's (1972) KISS-AID-ICE distinction, social ecological concepts, and the literatures on risk and protective processes and implementation. It provides readers with a way of capturing essential information about articles in a way that we and our students have found useful.

You may find that you will want to add additional questions that are relevant to your particular interests. You might want to keep track of certain problem areas, make a separate file for work done in different parts of the United States and the world, or have a special focus on mass media and Internet sources or doings in your current community or home town. You may find that initial sources you examine will not have the information you need to answer a number of the questions we suggest and that you need to read further. Part of the participant-conceptualizer role of community psychologists is to shed light on knowledge needed for responsible citizenship.

Guidelines for Reviewing Prevention/Promotion Articles/Materials

1. Record full reference information to be sure you know the source and context of this work.
2. What is the purpose of the work? Does it discuss a community or social issue that could be addressed by prevention/promotion initiatives? Or does it report on a specific prevention/promotion intervention?
3. If a prevention/promotion intervention is described, what protective processes is the program trying to strengthen? What risk processes is the program trying to weaken?
4. What population is being focused on? How were particular participants chosen? Some criteria may include age, gender, race or ethnicity, socioeconomic status or class, urban/suburban/rural location or geographic area, nation, or historical/political/cultural context.
5. What Key Integrative Social System(s) is involved? Health care (includes prenatal/birth/postnatal care), parents/families, peers, schools, religious settings, workplaces, leisure/recreational, community organizations, media/Internet/cyberspace, other?
6. What ecological level or levels of analysis does the article address? Individual, microsystems, organizations, localities, and/or macrosystems? What specific persons or groups does it address at that level? Is it targeted at the right level(s)?
7. If a prevention/promotion intervention is described, does it respond to a planned or predictable life situation (such as an education-related transition) or to an unpredictable life event (a reaction to a stressful or crisis event, such as divorce, bereavement, unemployment)?
8. Does the article focus on a wider community or social issue, such as poverty, social injustice, prejudice, or drugs? How might "small wins" thinking be applicable in prevention/promotion efforts on that issue?
9. If a prevention/promotion intervention was conducted, who planned it? How much were various constituencies and stakeholders involved? At what points? Were the persons most affected by decisions made in this program involved in making those decisions? Was there sufficient sensitivity to cultural and contextual factors?
10. How was the intervention implemented? Where? By whom? Under what conditions? When was it carried out? How often? Over what period of time?

Did the program developers check to see if the program was actually implemented as planned?

11. What is the evidence for the effectiveness of the intervention? What are the sources of that evidence?
12. Which of the objectives were clearly met? Not met? Met partially? Did it have an impact on the wider community? How?
13. Was the intervention implemented in multiple settings or contexts? Was it effective in all settings?
14. Are you convinced that the authors' interpretations or claims of effectiveness are true? Why or why not?
15. What are the most important things you think can be learned from what you read? What important questions does it raise?

10

Prevention and Promotion: Current and Future Applications

HIRB/Index Stock

PREVENTION AND PROMOTION ARE ALL AROUND YOU

In *Always Wear Clean Underwear,* Gellman (1997) gives children humor-laced insights into why advice kids get from parents is filled with potential to promote our well-being and to prevent difficulties. We learn, for example, that "share your toys" is a way of saying that people should be more important to you than things. "Always say please and thank you" is important, Gellman believes, because people who steal cars start out by stealing candy bars and people who cheat in business start out by cheating in school. By saying "please," we learn that we are not entitled to anything and everything we want when we want it. Thank-yous teach us that we should be grateful for good things that happen and we should tell people who do good things for us that we appreciate them, because then they will care for us more and do even more for us. What about the title, you are wondering? No, it's not about germs, and it's not about avoiding embarrassment if you get into an accident. The message is that what people don't see about you should still be as good as what they do see about you.

No doubt you are questioning what this has to do with community psychology. Our point is this: Every day, parents and many others conduct prevention/promotion programs without the assistance of community psychologists. Prevention and promotion efforts are ubiquitous. Try this exercise: Think of examples in your own life of efforts (formal programs or informal actions) to promote social competence and prevent problem behaviors. Based on what you learned in Chapters 8 and 9, ask yourself the following: What risk processes were weakened, or protective processes strengthened, by these efforts? Did these efforts promote strengths and thriving? Which efforts had a lasting effect? Why?

In addition, ask yourself this: Does it matter if a formal prevention/promotion program is the work of community psychologists? Snowden (1987) wrote about the "peculiar success" of community psychology: Its approaches are widely adopted, but as a field it is not well known. Since its founding, the field has been interdisciplinary and collaborative, so much so that its members and their work in prevention and promotion appear in many places, including law, education, government, public health, social work, the corporate world, and several fields of psychology (especially developmental, organizational, school, educational, and clinical). Further, members of other disciplines often collaborate on research and interventions that appear as part of collections of work in community psychology. In this chapter we help you recognize some of the work community psychologists are doing in prevention and promotion alongside the work of practitioners in other disciplines and in various countries. We review prevention/promotion programs at multiple ecological levels, emerging areas for the field, and issues in evaluating the effectiveness of prevention/promotion efforts.

AN ECOLOGICAL TOUR OF PREVENTION/PROMOTION

First, we review efforts at prevention and promotion on three ecological levels: microsystems, organizations/settings, and neighborhoods/communities. In the past, many reviews, including ours, have focused on programs across different developmental periods. We have chosen interventions that have been found effective in longitudinal empirical research and that provide an illustration of prevention/promotion practices with an emphasis on the contexts in which they have been carried out.

However, you should understand that most prevention/promotion efforts actually encompass multiple ecological levels, not just one. An effort to change national social policy, for instance, may also concern individuals, families, workplaces, and localities. A program that focuses on classroom curriculum and learning may also lead to changes in the social climate of the school, on the playground, and in the family and neighborhood. Our categorization here is meant to highlight some important differences among the goals of interventions, but not to restrict your thinking about their processes and outcomes.

Taken together, these interventions cover the range of terms and associated kinds of interventions presented in the Prevention Equations in Chapter 9 (see Table 10.1 and Table 9.1). For reasons of space, we omitted a number of exemplary, effective programs and promising innovations. Prevention/promotion is a growing field with many pathways to the future. We encourage you to sample

TABLE 10.1 Interventions Derived from Prevention Equations*

Interventions derived from the individual equation:

1. Reduce/better manage perceived stress.
2. Reduce the negative impact of a physically/biologically based vulnerability.
3. Increase coping skills, problem solving/decision making, social skills.
4. Increase perceived social support.
5. Increase self-esteem/self-efficacy.

Interventions derived from the environmental equation:

6. Reduce/eliminate stressors in key socialization settings, other aspects of environment.
7. Reduce operation/presence of physical risk factors in the environment that result in increased physical/biological vulnerability.
8. Improve socialization practices, ways in which key socialization settings carry out their tasks.
9. Increase accessible social support resources.
10. Increase opportunities for positive relatedness to others and connectedness to positive social institutions, positive social groups, agencies, and other formal and informal settings.

*See also Table 9.1.

the literature, including online resources to learn about additional prevention/promotion initiatives; we provide a partial listing of prevention/promotion websites at the end of the chapter.

MICROSYSTEM-LEVEL PREVENTION/ PROMOTION: HOME, SCHOOL, AND WORKPLACE

Microsystem-level interventions focus on changing patterns of interactions among members of small groups in settings. Because families, schools, and workplaces exert strong, continuous influences on most individuals, we chose to emphasize them.

Family-Based Programs

Prenatal/Early Infancy Project An important target population for preventive efforts is first-time mothers whose children are at risk for birth and early childhood difficulties because the mothers are low income, teenaged, and/or unmarried. The Prenatal/Early Infancy Project, developed by David Olds (1988, 1997) and associates, was designed to provide home-based social support and training in parenting and coping skills to mothers of at-risk infants, leading to reductions in abuse and neglect and improved child health outcomes. The program involved home visits by a trained nurse and health care screenings. Home visits began in the 30th week of pregnancy and continued through the second year of a child's life. The psychological aspects of home-visit discussions were based on developmental

TABLE 10.2 Principles of Effective Family-Based Programs

Effective family-based prevention/promotion programs:

1. Focus on the whole family, not just parents or children.
2. Improve family communication and parenting through changes in cognition, emotion, and behavior.
3. Are appropriate to the age and developmental level of children and the cultural traditions of the family.
4. For families with greater needs, begin early in children's lives, with intensive collaboration between program and family.
5. Employ staff who are genuine, warm, empathetic, confident, and skilled, directive teachers.
6. Involve interactive skills training and practice, not just didactic information.
7. Develop a collaborative process in which families are empowered to identify their own solutions to challenges.
8. Address relationships between family and school or community.

SOURCE: Adapted from Kumpfer & Alvarado, 2003.

concepts of family and community relationships (Bronfenbrenner, 1979), self-efficacy (Bandura, 1982), and mother-child attachment (Bowlby, 1969). The program was first implemented in Elmira, New York, primarily with European-American mothers; later in Memphis, primarily with African-American mothers; and in Denver with a multiracial sample. It has since been adopted in some form in many locales.

A randomized field experiment with the Elmira sample compared mothers and children who received home visits with a group who received only health screenings at a clinic. The comparison group had significantly higher rates of child maltreatment, use of emergency medical services, safety hazards at home, and smoking during pregnancy (a health risk for infants). On average, the comparison group provided a less stimulating environment for intellectual and emotional development. Clearly the home visits made a difference in the lives of young mothers.

Olds's (1997) program is not as effective if funding cutbacks in human services do not allow necessary staff to be employed. When client caseloads were increased for the nurses, the impact of the program was reduced (Schorr, 1988). Yet when long-term effects of the original program were studied, services to low-income families who received the home visits cost over $3,000 less per family than those in the comparison group by the child's fourth birthday. Preventive services thus were significantly less costly than health care and other costs after problems developed (Olds, 1997).

Effective Family-Based Programs Strong evidence exists for the effectiveness of preventively oriented home-based services for parents. Table 10.2 summarizes principles of effective family-based prevention/promotion, adapted from an empirical review by Karol Kumpfer and Rose Alvarado (2003). The most effective ones were often **multicomponent** programs, which worked on multiple goals through involving resources within the family, but also outside it, such as peers, school, and community resources.

Elias and Schwab (2004) proposed that school-based programs focus more explicitly on strengthening parenting. Although many educators and researchers call for greater involvement of parents in schools, other considerations in the home often detract from children's behavior and performance in school: reduced parental time with children at home, differential ability of parents to be genuine participants in school-related concerns, and children not arriving at school ready to learn because of the variety of stressors encountered from the time they awaken to the time they get to the schoolhouse door. Addressing these issues effectively requires more effective parenting as well as more family-based policies at work and in the community and society. Working to promote parenting and to address family-school relationships would build collaboration between family-based and school-based prevention advocates (Christenson & Havsy, 2004). Research has shown that multicomponent family skills training programs such as the Strengthening Families Program effectively address these issues in cost-effective ways (Kumpfer & Alder, 2003; www.strengtheningfamilies.org). Later in this chapter we describe Project Family and the Children of Divorce Program, which link families and schools to promote family competence.

Microsystem Programs in Schools

Schools are a critical KISS, and have been the focus of the greatest amount of research and program development related to prevention and promotion. Research into brain development has made it clear that early childhood is especially important for academic skill development, especially acquisition of reading and language competence. Of particular concern are the executive functions of the left and right frontal lobes that are vital for attention, concentration, frustration tolerance, and social-problem solving skills as well as the right-hemisphere centers for processing nonlinguistic information (Kusche & Greenberg, 2006). When children do not have experiences that provide them with proper stimulation in these areas, especially early in life, they are at risk for falling behind both academically and socially. Thus programs for **social-emotional literacy** (SEL), which build skills in these and related areas, are crucial for healthy development.

Considerable research has been done on prevention/promotion programs in schools. Most of these programs are directed at the classroom level, although many have components that extend to various other aspects of the school environment. Perhaps the best summary of these programs, their characteristics, and the evidence supporting them can be found in *Safe and Sound: An Educational Leader's Guide to Evidence-Based Social and Emotional Learning Programs* (Collaborative for Academic, Social, and Emotional Learning, 2003, downloadable at http://www.casel.org). Reviewing it, one cannot help but be impressed with the quality of research and the strong evidence in favor of many of these programs. Virtually all of the most successful programs are focused on building student skills in key areas. Their components and procedures have been carefully studied and identified. We have space only to highlight several examples, many of which have been designated as Exemplary or Promising Programs by the U.S. Department of Education.

Perry Preschool Project This model program, using the High/Scope curriculum, has become a widely adopted and very important social and educational innovation. Its premise is that comprehensive early childhood education, especially for children at risk for poor public school performance because of growing up in disadvantaged economic circumstances, could avert early school failure, subsequent school dropout, adult poverty, and an array of associated problems. There are many elements to its curriculum; all must be implemented to obtain positive effects. These methods integrate Piagetian and early childhood development theory with findings from developmental neuroscience research. Children become active learners through child-centered, developmentally appropriate activities (Weikart & Schweinhart, 1997).

The Head Start program has often used a High/Scope curriculum in combination with services for parents, a multicomponent model being used in a growing number of school districts in disadvantaged areas. Although there have been some controversies over methodology and specific findings, the consensus is that when Perry High/Scope curricula and Head Start are implemented according to their performance standards, they are powerful interventions. Follow-up studies of Perry Preschool children 20 years later showed positive impact compared with control children on such indices as arrests, educational attainment, income, and duration of marriages (Berreuta-Clement, Schweinhart, Barnett, Epstein, & Weikart, 1984; Weikart & Schweinhart, 1997). Cost-benefit analyses comparing treatment and comparison groups suggest that the program saves $7.16 in future costs (of social, health, and educational services) for each $1 invested (Weikart & Schweinhart, 1997). Nevertheless, these methods are not always implemented rigorously or with full funding, and findings show that without such rigor benefits are diluted.

Concern has surfaced recently about U.S. national policy on early childhood development. Just as research accumulates on critical growth periods, developmental risks associated with poverty, and the benefits of early intervention (Brooks & Buckner, 1996; Carnegie Corporation of New York, 1994; Rickel & Becker, 1997), early childhood policy threatens to revert to local control. This is likely to result in varying eligibility standards and compromises in the comprehensiveness of the model used for Head Start (Ripple & Zigler, 2003). Community psychologists can play an important role in preserving the integrity of Head Start and advocating for universally accessible family and school-based preventive services in the early childhood years.

Interpersonal Cognitive Problem Solving Myrna Shure (1997; Shure & Spivack, 1988) developed a preschool curriculum to increase children's interpersonal cognitive problem solving (ICPS, now known as "I Can Problem Solve") skills. These are critical thinking skills; the focus at the preschool level is on children's feelings vocabulary (words such as *sad, glad, mad, proud, bored*) and prerequisite cognitive concepts, such as "or," "else," "before and after," and "not."

One key premise of ICPS is that children can learn to identify their own problems (e.g., how to share toys, play together, seek help), to imagine possible solutions to these problems, and to consider how each solution may lead to different consequences. A second key premise is that caregivers (e.g., preschool teachers) deliver not only concepts of problem solving, but also give children opportunities to practice the skills being taught, applying their learning throughout the school day.

The centerpiece of ICPS is teaching caregivers to "dialogue" with children. In essence, "dialoguing" involves asking open-ended questions first, to promote children's own thinking and problem solving, reverting to more of a "telling" mode only as needed. Here are two sets of examples of how teachers in a kindergarten classroom context might handle a situation:

Example 1: Who will help Golnar with the blocks?

1. "Golnar, how can you find someone else to work with you in the blocks area to help you build that fort?"
2. "Could you ask Pedro or Liang or Rivka to work with you, or else join Pat's group after lunch and ask them to help you finish?"
3. "Go ask Sara. If she says no, call me and I will tell her to work with you, or else I will tell George to do it."

Example 2: How will Samara and her friends find something to do at recess?

1. "Girls, what are all the things you can think of to do when you get outside?"
2. "Are you going to want to play on the swings, use the jump ropes, or play tag?"
3. "When you get outside, I want Samara to go to the climbing area, Julia to go to the bikes and cars, and Craig to go to the blacktop. We will switch in 15 minutes so everybody has a chance to do at least two different things."

In each set of these examples, there are three levels of caregiver intervention. The first option is an open-ended question, which is likely to result in an interchange between adult and child that requires children to think about their preferences, to envision possibilities, and to make a choice. The second option keeps the ultimate choice in the hands of the child and stimulates possibilities, but the caregiver provides more ideas and structuring than in the first way. The final approach is to tell the child what to do, with or without explanation. ICPS dialoguing is represented by the first two methods in these examples.

If you have sat through many lectures (a fancy form of telling), you can probably guess that telling leads to less skill development than dialoguing. Learning is promoted by actively working with materials and situations, and with creating our own meanings. That is what ICPS, and an entire genre of similar problem solving and decision-making approaches, aspires to do for children of preschool through high school age (Elias & Clabby, 1992; Elias, Zins et al., 1997). The ICPS approach can be used in many preschool settings, and especially in Head Start, although funding constraints now limit widespread staff training and follow-up.

Social Decision Making/Social Problem Solving Elias, Gara, Schuyler, Branden-Muller, and Sayette (1991) examined the impact of an elementary school version of ICPS, the Social Decision Making/Social Problem Solving Program (SDM/SPS; Elias & Bruene-Butler, 2005a), on problem behaviors. SDM/SPS differs from the ICPS program in two major ways. SDM/SPS emphasizes readiness skills designed to build student self-control and group participation and to foster classroom norms to support these skills. SDM/SPS also contains an application phase in which the skills of the program are systematically infused into all aspects of the school routine, including the discipline system, academic areas such as language arts and social studies, and service learning. Elias et al. (1991) found that students followed up six years after receiving a two-year intervention in elementary school showed significantly less likelihood than controls to use alcohol and tobacco. Replications of program effectiveness have been found in settings quite different from the original research site (Bruene-Butler, Hampson, Elias, Clabby, & Schuyler, 1997).

Second Step: A Violence Prevention Curriculum Second Step was developed to teach social and emotional skills to children from preschool to grade 9. Empathy, problem solving for impulse control, and emotion management are the focal skills taught, with extensive amounts of application to interpersonal situations related to bullying and conflict resolution. Second Step has strong empirical and practical support. In perhaps the most rigorous study, longitudinal observation of student behavior on the playground, in the cafeteria, and in class showed that Second Step led to moderate decreases in aggression and increases in prosocial behavior in school. In contrast, students at control schools (those *not* using the curriculum) became more physically and verbally aggressive over the school year (Grossman et al., 1997). One additional feature of Second Step is its strong implementation support system, through the Committee for Children and its international partner organizations. It is now actively used in an estimated 20,000 schools across the U.S. and Canada and in thousands more schools in Europe and Asia (Duffell, Beland, & Frey, 2006).

Life Skills Training (LST) This program provides junior high school–aged children with knowledge, motivation, and skills to resist influences to use tobacco, alcohol, and other drugs (Botvin & Tortu, 1988). The LST curriculum focuses on awareness of negative consequences of substance use, accurate norms regarding peer use, decision-making skills, building self-esteem, coping with social anxiety, and social-communication skills (including building positive relationships and resistance to peer pressure). The curriculum structure includes 15 lessons in grade 7 and "booster" sessions in grades 8 and 9. Teachers are extensively trained and provided with a detailed manual; another version of LST uses eleventh and twelfth graders as peer leaders. Assessments of the research findings on LST program effectiveness have concluded that the program reduces smoking and is promising in its impact on future alcohol and drug use (Botvin & Tortu, 1988; Botvin, Baker, Dusenbury, Botvin & Diaz, 1995; Epstein, Griffin, & Botvin, 2000). Elements of LST have been adopted in many drug abuse prevention programs in schools.

Successful programs directed specifically toward preventing adolescent drug use combine an informational component, training in social influence and skills (often resistance to peer pressure and media advertising), and interventions to alter student norms about the prevalence and acceptability of peer drug use. Reduced alcohol use immediately following programs such as Adolescent Prevention Trial (Hansen & Graham, 1991) and ALERT Drug Prevention (Ellickson & Bell, 1990) have been documented, but enduring effects have been rare, suggesting context effects on ultimate program outcomes.

Lions-Quest Skills for Action Service Learning Module This program of Lions-Quest International has three components: (a) a classroom-based curriculum to develop social-emotional and decision-making skills and to address problem behaviors such as substance use, (b) a highly structured service learning component, and (c) a skills bank containing a series of enrichment activities. Thus, Skills for Action (SFA) involves prevention of problem behaviors and promotion of social-emotional competence and of good citizenship.

An evaluation study involving students in grades 9–12 in 29 high schools in urban, suburban, and rural settings found preliminary support for the effectiveness of the program. In two alternative high schools, where the program was a selective intervention (see the IOM model in Chapter 9), students in SFA were suspended less often and had higher grades than controls. No impact was found on substance abuse. In the other 27 high schools, the strongest overall effect was on prevention of dropping out; ninth graders made the most gains, including lower drug and cigarette use (Laird, Bradley, & Black, 1998). Overall, students reported a high degree of satisfaction with the program.

SFA evaluators also found that if students experienced fewer than 15 hours of service learning, no program effects were obtained. Actual implementation of other program components also varied. These factors make it difficult to form firm conclusions about program impact. However, with 3,500 students performing 29,000 hours of service touching the lives of 12,000 people in the pilot studies alone, SFA clearly is important in many schools and communities. Like Second Step, SFA has an extensive international distribution and implementation support system (Keister, 2006).

Additional School-Based Programs Related evidence-based programs at the elementary level include Open Circle, Responsive Classroom, and PATHS. Later in this chapter, we also discuss the Primary Mental Health Project, the Children of Divorce Program, and the Child Development Project/Caring School Communities program. Effective programs for middle school and/or high school include Resolving Conflict Creatively Program, Social Competence Promotion Program (Weissberg, Barton & Shriver, 1997), Social Decision Making/Social Problem Solving (Elias & Bruene Butler, 2005b), Teenage Health Teaching Modules, Tribes TLC, and Facing History and Ourselves. Updated detailed information and website linkages for these and other programs can be found in CASEL's *Safe and Sound* document, mentioned earlier. At the conclusion of this chapter, we give website addresses for many of these programs.

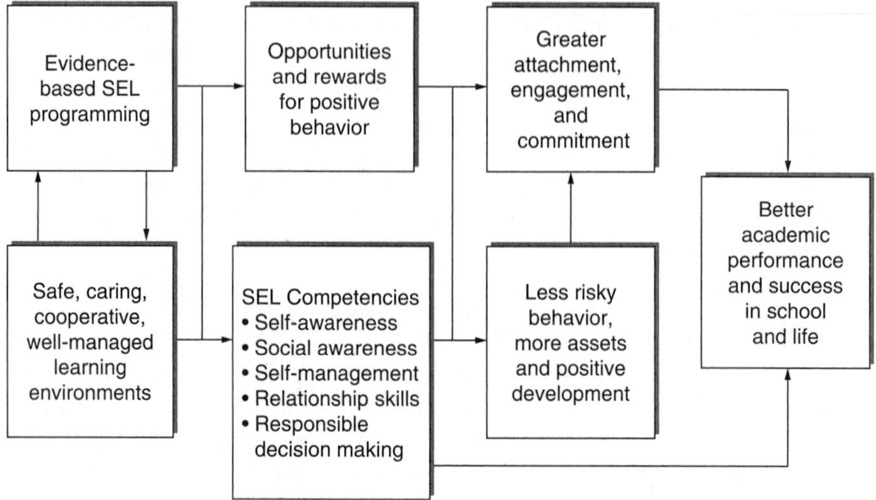

FIGURE 10.1 School-Related Factors Predicting Academic and Life Success

An Integrative Model of School Program Effects Zins, Bloodworth, Weissberg, and Walberg (2004) provided a general model, based on empirical research, of how school-based prevention/promotion programs can create positive long-term effects (see Figure 10.1). Programs for social-emotional literacy (SEL), when embedded within safe, caring, organized, cooperative learning environments, provide opportunity structures for positive school participation and benefit, as well as teaching specific SEL competencies (such as those listed in the figure). These, in turn, promote greater emotional bonding and behavioral engagement in school, build positive behaviors and psychosocial assets, and reduce risky behaviors.

Microsystem Programs in Workplaces

Workplaces are also a critical KISS for adolescents and adults. Workplace prevention/promotion programs have not been as common in community psychology as in schools and families, but several offer important approaches.

JOBS Project Adult workers who lose their jobs are clearly at risk for a variety of psychological problems. The JOBS Project intervenes at the point at which these workers begin looking for new jobs and thus is a selective intervention in the IOM framework. Laid-off workers are offered the opportunity to attend 20 hours of group training focused on problem solving, overcoming setbacks, job search skills, and exchange of social support. Evaluation studies using experimental designs showed the program reduced incidence of serious depression and led to obtaining better jobs. Cost-benefit analysis revealed that the cost of the program, approximately $300 per person, was made up in less than a year in the form of tax revenues contributed by workers once they were back in the work force (Caplan, Vinokur, & Price, 1997; Price, Van Ryn, & Vinokur, 1992; Van Ryn & Vinokur, 1992).

Worksite Coping Skills Intervention Kline and Snow (1994) developed an intervention directed at mothers employed in secretarial positions. Their preliminary research uncovered risk for work and family stressors in this population, and their intervention focused on stress management, problem and emotion-focused coping skills, and cognitive restructuring techniques. It was carried out in four different corporate work sites. Compared with a matched comparison group, participants reported lower role stress, less tobacco and alcohol use, and higher perceived support from others at work. At a six-month follow-up, psychological symptoms were also lower in the treatment group.

Employee Competencies Spencer (2001) reported on a meta-analysis of employee selection programs based on emotional intelligence competencies. Assessment of five clusters of competencies, covering Achievement, Affiliation, Power, Management, and Personal Effectiveness, was used as the basis for attempting to select superior performers and/or avoid marginal performers. Median productivity increased by 19 percent, median turnover decreased 63 percent, and the median economic value added was $1.6 million. Average costs for an emotional intelligence competency selection program were far lower than the costs of hiring employees who later were rated unsatisfactory. Pepsi, Inc. found that emotional intelligence-based assessment led to an 87 percent reduction in turnover and saved $4 million. A large computer firm was able to cut attrition in its staff training from 30 percent to 3 percent based on emotional intelligence assessment procedures, saving $3.15 million. Spencer also reported similar gains from training current employees in emotional intelligence competencies. In addition, training programs for current employees based on emotional intelligence were nearly twice as effective as other training methods.

BEYOND MICROSYSTEMS: PREVENTION/ PROMOTION IN ORGANIZATIONS, COMMUNITIES, AND MACROSYSTEMS

Prevention/promotion also can involve changing the informal environment or formal policies of an organization (e.g., school, workplace), locality, or society. Many settings and larger units create stressors for individuals, and reducing these or increasing protective processes has preventive effects. Next, we review programs that reduce risks and enhance protective processes in whole settings.

Altering Settings

Programs Addressing School Climates Some approaches include skill-building curricula but place greater emphasis on creating a school climate that will promote positive mental health and wellness. The Social Development Model is a universal preventive intervention focused on elementary schools (Hawkins, Catalano,

Morrison et al., 1992; Hawkins & Lam, 1987). It addresses the need to teach skills to children but also to change the norms of home and classroom settings and to create opportunities to practice new skills. Teachers were trained in classroom management, cooperative learning, and the use of the ICPS curriculum described earlier. Parents were trained to create norms in the home for child self-control and for performing academic work. When researchers followed children from first into fifth grade, children in the intervention group were less likely than controls to initiate alcohol use, more psychologically attached to school, their families were stronger in communication and involvement, and school rewards and norms were more positive than among controls (Hawkins, Catalano, and Associates, 1992).

The Character Education Partnership promotes school-based programs to help children live their lives according to core ethical values, which they define in terms similar to social-emotional competence but more general in scope: for instance, caring, honesty, fairness, responsibility, and respect for self and others. School policies, teaching and social climate help create an atmosphere in which individual behavior, thinking and emotions are encouraged in accordance with these principles. Updated information on schools whose overall climate promotes character development can be found at their website (http://www.character.org).

A well-known and effective whole-school approach is the School Development Program (Comer, 1988), which involves multiple interventions, with students, faculty and staff, to promote a cooperative, caring school climate. We examine this program later in this chapter.

Changing School Configurations As we discussed in Chapter 5, Felner and Adan (1988) developed the STEP program, which changed the high school environment to promote peer student support and faculty-student contact. Ninth graders, entering high school, remained with the same classmates for most of their classes and had a smaller number of teachers, who thus knew each student better. Homeroom teachers also were taught to handle more of the students' guidance needs. At year's end, students had better grades, less absenteeism, and a more positive view of school than those in a comparison group. These gains also reduce the risk of conduct disorder (Mrazek & Haggerty, 1994).

Recent research suggests that creating smaller high schools, or schools within schools, with more regular interactions among a limited cohort of students and more stable contacts with a small group of adults, will have similar effects to those obtained by Felner and Adan and will also lead to improved academic performance and decreased school disaffection and dropout, especially in urban areas; however, implementation has been more difficult to accomplish than initially anticipated (Noguera, 2004).

Transforming Religious Education An increasing amount of research is being devoted to religious education, a development that seems long overdue. Of particular interest to community psychologists is the emerging consensus that religious education has not been well served by a predominantly person-centered focus. For example, the well-known African phrase, "It takes a village to raise a child," has been invoked for Jewish education with an appropriate cultural modification, "It takes a Kehilla (entire community) to raise a mensch (moral, unselfish, caring human being)" and then supplemented with some ecological-developmental considerations: "and it requires everyone to do so with integrity and collaboration over a period of many years." This perspective helped shift ways that religious education can be conceptualized and carried out at the local level and beyond (Kress & Elias, 2000). Parallel insights have been made in religious education of other denominations, reinforcing the view that socializing children with a particular religious understanding results from a sustained, coordinated effort across multiple ecological levels, with developmental sensitivity to how different formal and informal instructional experiences interact with emerging levels of spirituality (Kliewer, Wade, & Worthington, 2003).

Creating Emotionally Intelligent Workplaces The paradigm of emotional intelligence has received sustained application in the world of work (Cherniss, 2002; Cherniss & Goleman, 2001; Goleman, 1998). In recent years, companies have recognized that the well-being of their employees can have many economic benefits. American Express, Kimberly-Clark, and Ford Motor Company are among the organizations that have devoted substantial resources to changing their microsystems and organizations to emphasize the emotional competence of work groups and key managers. An example that reflects a community psychology perspective comes from Ford. In their attempt to redesign the Lincoln Continental, executives gave the design team extensive contact with owners and potential owners. The improvements in empathy and perspective taking improved their ability to create a successful design. But beyond that, the employees felt strongly empowered and supported by their larger organization (Goleman, 1998). Some organizations, such as Disney, work extensively to ensure that theme parks and stores create a minimum of stress and a maximum of support for consumers.

Communitywide and Macrosystem Interventions

Prevention/promotion efforts can be pursued at the level of neighborhoods, localities, and macrosystems. These initiatives may involve new programs, as do most of the examples we have just discussed, or changes in the policies and/or practices of localities or larger units, including nations.

Building Community Collaboration Canada has long been committed to pursuing the benefits of prevention/promotion for its children. In the 1980s, the province of Ontario created Better Beginnings, Better Futures as a primary prevention project. Government representatives work actively with local boards comprised of residents and local service providers to create projects to prevent behavioral, emotional, learning, and health problems among children, particularly in economically disadvantaged populations. Research findings indicated that the participation of community residents in developing prevention/programs had many beneficial effects, such as creating a sense of empowerment, fostering new individual and community competencies, and forging informal social support (Nelson, Pancer, Hawward, & Peters, 2005). However, it is difficult for a community to keep resources and energies focused on prevention in children for long periods of time (Sylvestre, Pancer, Brophy, & Cameron, 1994; Nelson et al. 2005).

More recently, municipalities within the York region of Ontario, Canada have been participating in a process termed *Character Matters,* designed to create what they call *Communities of Character.* Beginning with a series of town meetings hosted by local schools, community residents came together to identify and affirm a set of ten common attributes that people pledged to use in their personal, familial, workplace, education, and public contexts. These attributes are: Respect, Responsibility, Honesty, Empathy, Fairness, Initiative, Courage, Integrity, Perseverance, and Optimism. Different communities organized to decide on particular attributes to emphasize, and particular ways to do so. Each year, all municipalities come together to celebrate their accomplishment and share ways in which they have put their ideas into action (York Region District School Board, n.d.; website: http://www.yrdsb.edu.on.ca/).

Many U.S. localities have formed Communities That Care coalitions to promote positive youth development and prevent a variety of youth problems. These coalitions work within a framework based on the Social Development Model (discussed earlier), which promotes both the use of empirically tested programs and local choice of objectives and programs. Each coalition assesses community needs and resources, sets goals, and plans and implements programs to address those goals. Examples of programs include use of school-based, competence-promotion programs (discussed earlier); coordination among schools, youth service agencies, police, juvenile courts, and other community resources; developing volunteer opportunities to connect youth with positive adult and college student role models; and community events to promote awareness of youth and family issues and resources. An evaluation of the Communities That Care approach in twenty-one Pennsylvania localities found that community readiness for the coalition and the capacity of coalition members to work as a team were key factors in coalition effectiveness (Feinberg, Greenberg, & Osgood, 2004).

In Chapters 13 and 14, we consider community and social change and how to evaluate community programs. Some of our coverage of these topics will provide further examples of how citizens in communities can collaborate in promoting health, youth development, and similar positive goals and also in preventing personal and community problems.

Interventions Using Mass Media Leonard Jason (1998a) and associates carried out health promotion interventions at the levels of localities and macrosystems. Among the most effective was collaborating with the Chicago Lung Association and the Chicago Board of Education to work toward smoking prevention among African-American youth. A school-based anti-smoking curriculum developed by the American Lung Association was combined with a three-pronged media intervention: (a) a smoking prevention curriculum run each week on the children's page of *The Chicago Defender,* a local newspaper with a strong African-American readership; (b) eight public service spots on WGCI, a radio station with a listening audience of 1 million, mostly African American, along with a call-in talk show for parents; and (c) an anti-smoking billboard contest, which also posted the five best entries. Findings indicated lower cigarette use among adolescents and lower rates of cigarette, alcohol, and marijuana use in families. Jason's work suggests that media-based interventions must reach directly into microsystems in order to be effective and that careful targeting, including attention to cultural and ethnic issues, is important (Jason & Hanaway, 1997).

Influencing State Education Policies In the United States, individual states are an important ecological level for strengthening prevention/promotion in schools. Efforts are growing to show alignment of social-emotional learning with state education standards (Kress, Norris, Schoenholz, Elias, & Seigle, 2004) and to help states pass legislation mandating character education and related programs (Brown & Elias, 2002). The most concerted efforts are by the Education Committee for the States through its National Center for Learning and Citizenship (NCLC), which has been instrumental in creating the National Voluntary Civic Education Standards to guide state policies. NCLC has defined key civic competencies: Civic Knowledge, Cognitive Thinking Skills, Participatory Civic Skills, and Civic Dispositions (Torney-Purta & Vermeer, 2004). Community psychologists can contribute knowledge and skills on issues such as how to prepare students for sound character and the responsibilities of citizenship. Although public discourse often focuses only on voting as the hallmark of democracy, other voices need to articulate the competencies and sets of actions for genuinely participatory democracy (Gerzon, 1997; Tyack, 1997).

International Examples

Some of the most interesting work in systems-level prevention is not found in peer-reviewed professional journals. Among our favorite sources is *The Community Psychologist,* a quarterly publication of the Society for Community Research and Action, which provided the following prevention initiatives.

Preventing Community Upheaval and Violence in Colombia Guatiguara, Colombia, is a community of 6,000, with 2,500 children, beset by poverty, slum conditions, no social services, and the presence of warring gangs, guerrillas, and paramilitary groups. The Universidad Pontifica Bolivariana and the Pastoral Social Archdiocese of Bucaramanga City led a program designed to prevent community violence and reduce the negative effects of a continuous cycle of poverty. They drew on key community psychology principles: celebrating diversity; sense of community as involving common needs for transcendence; being seen as competent and being deserving of having basic physical, psychological, and spiritual needs met; and a strengths-based perspective. The intervention process began with a series of individual interviews, group discussions, and ethnographic observations. These led to the creation of *Pequenas Comunidades* (Small Communities), each of which consisted of 10 groups of adults (100 people), 20 groups of children (400), and one group of teens (20), guided by facilitators and leaders who themselves were provided with weekly training meetings and ongoing support from the university and archdiocese.

The *Pequenas Comunidades* developed their own projects, including building a chapel, providing more food, and communitywide holiday celebrations attracting over 2,000 participants. Groups within the *Comunidades* met weekly to talk about their rights and develop a positive sense of empowerment via their own folklore, history, and culture; plan programs; and celebrate accomplishments. Martinez, Toloza, Montanez, and Ochoa (2003) reported violence reduction and increased community participation, which they attribute to the effects of organizing the community and fostering individuals' taking collective action.

Substance Abuse Prevention Policy in Mexico Mexico provides an example of a national effort to confront problems of drug abuse through prevention (Garza, 2001). Drawing parallels between Mexico and other developing countries beset by poverty and unemployment, an analysis of public policy on this issue concluded:

> Implementation is much more efficient when carried out in the streets (consumers) rather than on the borders (distributors, producers). This is because in the end, consumers perpetuate the drug chain. They are the ones that encourage drug dealers to risk more. In the end, it is consumers who pay for aggregated values and they are the only ones that can destroy the incentive for the existing supply. (Roemer, 2001, p. 277)

The array of necessary policy changes, however, is daunting (see Box 10.1). Realistic planning at multiple ecological levels and political support will be essential for ultimate success. Mexico and many other countries have found it difficult to develop a comprehensive and effective drug prevention policy.

Preventing Victimization and Bigotry in Turkey Serdar Degirmencioglu (2003), a community psychologist at Istanbul Bilgi University, created a series of preventive interventions for Turkish youth. His first focus was street children, who would come to fleeting public attention after a horrific incident. Degirmencioglu recognized that existing services for these children represented only first-order change. He enlisted representatives from community agencies, community leaders, citizens, and others to form a committee and organize a conference on this issue. An opening panel reviewed children's rights and relevant legal issues; outside keynote speakers brought greater credibility and multiple points of view. Conference work groups developed guidelines for improved practices, and structures were put in place to begin to carry them out.

Another project was inspired by a study Degirmencioglu completed after an earthquake devastated population centers in the Marmara region in 1999. Almost a year later, Degirmencioglu found that the actions of foreigners who provided aid had a positive impact on the relevant attitudes of both the Turkish survivors and the general public. Misconceptions about Greeks and Israelis were especially affected. Degirmencioglu used this experience to provide an intervention at a youth festival that began as an effort of a pan-European student association to

BOX 10.1 Elements of Drug Abuse Prevention Policy in Mexico

Business, education, government, and family must work toward a culture of prevention based on shared values.

Greater resources to train specialists who deal with chronic addicts and low-income users.

Efficient treatment and prevention programs for casual or curious users to prevent abuse.

Anti-doping tests must be extended to companies and universities.

Permanent support of scientific research in neuroscience, immuno-prevention, and replacement therapies, including strong international cooperation to bring existing knowledge and practice to Mexico.

Reinforce educational, cultural, sports, and recreational activities within schools and families that foster creation of fundamental values and keep children away from the risk of drug use.

Campaigns to inform the public about services offered by the National Commission on Addictions must be reinforced, involving radio, television, and print media and sending the message that "just saying no" is not enough, only talking about consequences is no guarantee, and it is essential to explain the problem and its basic causes.

Resources of art, especially theater, must be used to teach young people the truth about drugs.

Major cinema has an affect on people's awareness even though plots are more focused on smuggling than addiction; but official organizations, schools, workplaces, and families must adopt a critical position that will serve as an antidote to productions that seek to achieve sensational effects.

Prevent cigarette and alcohol advertising from being broadcast during children's peak viewing times.

At individual and family levels, policies must be directed toward the following:

Ensure children are given love and trust during their upbringing that will teach them to establish limits on their freedom.

Efforts must be made to strengthen children's willpower from an early age, listen to them, find out about their needs at every stage, and establish direct communications with them.

Parents must be trained to prevent the crises caused by drug use in the family by establishing a dialogue with children that will foster discussion of the issue.

The permissiveness that keeps children from being sanctioned by school and society until they reach a point of no return must be avoided.

Children must be taught about the short-term effects of drugs by emphasizing negative aspects such as unpleasant smell of tobacco and alcohol on clothes, bad breath, stained teeth, etc. This will be more effective for children than warning them about health risks.

Parents must establish a dialogue in which they reward children for their progress while showing them that they are loved unconditionally, regardless of their academic performance.

Parent education programs must be organized and taught regularly at schools because most parents would otherwise be unlikely to implement these practices on their own.

SOURCE: Adapted from Roemer & Garza (2001).

bring Greek and Turkish youth together in a KayaFest, a celebration of the music, dance, and artistry from both cultures.

The history of Greek-Turkish relationships is especially revealing of the arbitrary ways in which negative and hostile attitudes have been fostered by historical actions of governments and then adopted by subsequent generations, often without any realization of the political origins of the initial actions. In many areas, a Population Exchange decree forced Greeks and Turks to uproot themselves from a cooperative and comingled existence and move to separate, segregated villages or neighborhoods. Degirmencioglu conducted a workshop at the KayaFest to show youth the history of their separation and how, through a lack of contact, each group came to see the other as enemies despite the fact that many had relatives from territory in the other's country.

(One author's perspective: My grandparents were Greek and Turkish. However, they would often say that which "side" of the family was Greek or Turkish would depend on which month or year one asked the question, as the territory in which they lived frequently changed hands. My "Turkish" grandmother spoke fluent Greek, and the entire family could never understand late twentieth-century Greek-Turkish conflicts; to them, because they experienced no forced separations, Greeks and Turks were part of a common family. —Maurice Elias)

At KayaFest, Degirmencioglu's youth activities showed the benefits that could result from positive intergroup contact. The final part of the workshop involved a common meal at a local home, including a visit with a 90-year-old Turkish woman who lived in the Festival area before the Population Exchange. She told stories of how everyone lived and worked together and told the youth that they were "all children of the land" (Degirmencioglu, 2003, p. 29). Degirmencioglu concluded, "Now, eighty years later, young people with big hearts and a big dream helped others better understand the big agony of this land. And they also helped them grasp why modern ethnic categories and the overused ethnic adjectives 'Greek' and 'Turkish' can never capture the complex and rich cultures that still exist in this region" (p. 29).

The Importance of Context

The ecological perspective of community psychology makes it clear that forces in macrosystems, localities, and settings strongly influence the nature of prevention/promotion efforts. In many countries, political administrations vary in their belief about the degree of governmental responsibility to fund, mandate, and/or organize interventions that related broadly to mental health. Perhaps the most powerful example in the United States now is the No Child Left Behind Act of 2001, designed to close the achievement gap between disadvantaged and minority students and their more well-to-do, largely White peers. Local schools and state departments of education are judged based on student performance on standardized tests of academic ability, which are focused on math and reading-related skills. Funding and local autonomy, as well as public praise or blame, are contingent on test score increases.

Sadker and Zittleman (2004) point out numerous biases in the tests, their scoring, and the measurement and interpretation of change and significant gain. Davison, Seo, Davenport, Butterbaugh, and Davison (2004) analyzed data from 47,361 students taking standardized tests created in Minnesota for third- and fifth-grade students. Groups of students who were "behind" in third grade in math never caught up with a matched group of students ahead of them when their fifth-grade scores were examined. Low-income students made less progress than did matched peers who were more affluent. Davison and associates (2004) raise this question: "How will low-income and minority students, when necessary, make up lost time by learning *faster* than other students?" (p. 758). Under No Child Left Behind incentives, the answer for schools and districts is to spend more and more time on math and reading and to ask parents to serve as virtual academic tutors. To provide more resources for these efforts, funds have been diverted from programs to prevent smoking, drug, and alcohol use and to promote safe, nonviolent schools. Community psychologists, among others, need to examine existing education policy in light of community research and prevention/promotion concepts.

Interestingly, a number of nations are becoming interested in prevention/promotion initiatives (Elias, 2003). How well do prevention/promotion initiatives developed in North America transfer to other countries and cultures? Sundberg, Hadiyono, Latkin, and Padilla (1995) studied this question. They chose programs with empirical support in the United States and designation as prevention models by the American Psychological Association in *14 Ounces of Prevention* (Price, Cowen, Lorion, & Ramos-McKay, 1988). These included the Prenatal/Early Infancy Project (Olds, 1988), Perry Preschool program (PPP; Schweinhart & Weikart, 1988), Interpersonal Cognitive Problem Solving (ICPS; Shure, 1997), and Life Skills Training (LST; Botvin & Tortu, 1988).

Sundberg and associates asked experts in 12 countries in Asia and Latin America to examine each program, considering the need for such a program in their own nations and the feasibility of applying the program there. With regard to need, only the LST program was ranked highly in Latin American countries. Asian experts showed little consensus on estimations of need but were least interested in the PPP, ICPS, and LST programs. Only the LST program was seen as feasible in most countries.

In India, the Prenatal/Early Infancy project would likely only be applied to married women because of the unacceptability of unwed mothers in that society. Training children to be independent problem solvers was not valued in many countries where respect for elders is paramount. (Recall the concept of individualism-collectivism from Chapter 7 and consider how North American problem-solving training might have to be adapted for use in less individualistic cultures.) Cigarette smoking was not seen as a large problem in many countries outside the United States, and there was little concern about its role as a gateway to more serious substance use. Peer-resistance or refusal skills, part of LST and many other drug-use prevention programs, might conflict with the value of *machismo* in Latin America. Finally, the implicit future orientation of prevention concepts conflicts with the focus on the present in many cultures: the Thai concept of *mai pen rai,* translatable as "don't worry," is an example. Beyond these cultural differences, resource issues such as poverty and population limited the feasibility of these programs.

However, Sundberg et al. (1995) also found that the elements of the prevention equations (Chapter 9) were highly valued across different countries. Specific preventive efforts directed toward the goals in those equations can be tailored to be culturally appropriate, based on a detailed familiarity with the contexts and histories of the local areas and populations involved.

Even within a nation, what is effective in one area or culture may not work in another. For instance, Bierman and associates (1997) found that a conduct disorder prevention program that had been developed in urban areas had to be adapted to rural Pennsylvania localities. Geographic dispersion, limited human services and recreation, predominance of politically conservative climates, stable and insular interpersonal networks among youth and adults, homogeneous populations, and establishing trust were major challenges. Gager and Elias (1997) found that school-based programs in high-risk versus low-risk neighborhoods differed in effectiveness. Having a program coordinator, ongoing training, and explicit linkage of programs to the goals and mission of schools made programs more effective in the most difficult circumstances. As we noted in Chapter 1, Potts (2003) found that an African-centered curriculum for African-American boys in an urban school was more appropriate than a generic ICPS approach.

PREVENTION/PROMOTION: A FAMILY EXAMPLE

How can prevention/promotion efforts address the challenges and strengths of a particular family?

Inez Watson lived with her three children: Jamal (3 years old), Maritza (6 years old) and Carlos (12 years old). (All names are pseudonyms.) Jamal attended preschool, Maritza the first grade, and Carlos was in middle school. Inez's second husband Robert, Jamal's father, had died recently while serving in the U.S. Army in Afghanistan. Inez and her first husband, Rafael, had divorced a few years earlier. Rafael was the father of Maritza and Carlos. Inez, Robert, and Jamal were African American; Rafael was Latino, and Carlos and Maritza thus had both Latino and African-American ancestry. (For simplicity, we have used Inez Watson's surname for all three children.)

The Watson family experienced a number of difficulties. Most obvious was the loss of Robert. Maritza, already shy, was becoming even more withdrawn. Carlos began hanging around with older students in his middle school and was suspended for smoking at school. He also was truant to an increasing degree. Shortly before Robert's death, Inez had been laid off from her job. Her prior income had been adequate, as were the family benefits from the military. Now the benefits remained, but funds were dwindling.

Naturally, the Watsons also had strengths. Inez was a committed mother, determined to give her children a firm foundation in life. She was sensitive to their needs and committed to their safety and well-being. The children loved and respected her, even when they tested her limits. Each child had gifts: Carlos loved to dance and had vocal talent. Maritza enjoyed stories and art. Jamal had a wonderful smile and an uncanny ability to make others laugh. The family attended church in their neighborhood, where the children had friends. Inez sometimes sang in the choir and assisted other members of the congregation.

Inez: The JOBS Project An array of prevention programs were mobilized to assist the Watson family. First, Inez enrolled in the JOBS project (Price et al., 1992), which consisted of eight 3-hour group sessions over a two-week period, led by two trainers. The program provided job search skills as well as rehearsal and practice for job interviews, a problem-solving group discussion process, anticipation of obstacles and strategies for coping with setbacks, social support from trainers and group members, and an extra confidence-boosting endorsement from the trainers. This intervention has shown positive effects on reemployment rates, quality of reemployment, and pay rate, in randomized control studies. Research into the mechanisms underlying these effects—an important but neglected aspect of prevention science—suggested that job search intention and self-efficacy were critical factors. By supporting and strengthening participants' theory of planned action, trainers could energize coping with the anxiety of job loss and the negative effects of setbacks (Caplan et al., 1997; Van Ryn & Vinokur, 1992). For Inez, trainers and fellow group members formed a supportive unit that continued to meet socially after the training ended. She was successful in finding employment after a few months, though at a lower wage than her earlier job.

Family Bereavement Program The entire family participated in the Family Bereavement Program (Sandler et al., 1992). This involved two phases. First, the Watsons joined other bereaved families in a three-session grief workshop. Here, they discussed their grief-related experiences and parents learned how to better communicate with their children around uncomfortable topics and feelings related to death. The second phase was a structured twelve-session program connecting each family with an advisor who focused on four factors:

- emotional support and task assistance
- increasing parent-child warmth, focusing on positive communication, and recognition of strengths
- planning regular positive events such as family meals, story time, and bedtime talks
- specific problem and emotion-focused coping strategies to deal with stressful family events

Randomized control trials of the intervention showed positive impact on parent-child warmth and social support and preventive impact on potential depression and older children's conduct disorder problems (Sandler et al., 1992). Sandler and associates (1992) also explored mediators of the effect of their intervention; the Watsons, for instance, may have benefited from an increased emphasis on promoting parent-child warmth.

School-Based Promotion The Watsons also benefited from school-based prevention efforts. The school district used CASEL's (2003) "Safe and Sound" guide to design a comprehensive curriculum approach to build all students' social-emotional competencies and prevent dysfunction, based on these programs:

- *I Can Problem Solve* curriculum, for preschool, kindergarten, and first grade
- *Responsive Classroom* and *Open Circle* methods to foster positive classroom relationships and build such skills as self-control and empathy in the elementary grades

- *Second Step* and *Social Decision Making/Social Problem Solving* curricula in the middle school to provide skills for nonviolent conflict resolution and promote the integration of problem solving in academics and group guidance to help students with the variety of difficult social pressures and decisions faced during these years
- *Facing History and Ourselves* and the *Lions-Quest Skills for Action Service Learning* program, focusing on applying social-emotional skills and ethical principles to understanding traumatic events in history and the present and how to engage in social action to make the classrooms, school, community, and the world in general a better place

Having these curricula in place in a coordinated plan provides a solid bedrock of skills for all students from which other programs can build as students encounter difficulty.

Jamal Jamal's preschool worked with the Primary Mental Health Project (PMHP), one of the oldest and best researched programs, with over 2,000 sites across the United States and territories (Johnson & Demanchick, 2004). PHMP is overseen by a school mental health professional, such as a school psychologist, social worker, or counselor. The first step is a systematic screening of children in the focal age range, assessing acting out, mood, and learning difficulties. The idea is to identify children who are at risk for future problems based on normative scores but who are not yet severe enough to warrant diagnosis. Hence, this is a secondary prevention, or selective, program. These children are then paired with trained paraprofessionals who provide empathy, acceptance, active listening, and gentle academic tutoring to needy students on a weekly basis. Jamal had elevated scores in Acting Out and Mood problems. He was seen individually twice per week and then met in a small group for a little over a month. If he were older, he would most likely have had 12–15 individual weekly meetings.

In a recent evaluation of PMHP in a multiethnic county in Minnesota, children were found to make significant improvements in behavior control, assertiveness, peer sociability, and task orientation. The warm and caring relationships between children and their PMHP associates emerged once again as an essential element in program success. This study also highlighted the impact of PMHP on shy children like Jamal. Participation in PMHP has a preventive effect on both mental health problems and learning difficulties, so vital as young children enter a critical period for acquisition of language and reading skills.

Maritza In Maritza's elementary school, the school psychologist and guidance counselor co-led groups as part of the Children of Divorce Program (Pedro-Carroll, 1997). Maritza joined four 5- and 6-year-old peers, two boys and two girls, and met in a group for twelve 45-minute sessions once per week in her school. The twelve sessions focused systematically on:

- establishing the group as a safe, supportive place to explore feelings, paving the way for talking about feelings related to divorce

- exploring changes that do and do not occur as a result of divorce, especially children's misconceptions, including viewing themselves as a cause of divorce
- teaching social problem-solving and communication skills to enhance competence and capacity to cope, with particular emphasis on dealing with obstacles they are likely to encounter
- bolstering positive perception of themselves and their families, exemplified by children's creating and keeping an "All About Me Book"

Inez and other parents were kept closely informed via direct contacts, problem-solving assistance, and newsletters focusing on impact of divorce, common reactions and how to deal with them, minimizing parental conflict about childrearing issues, and practical parenting skills.

Pedro-Carroll and Alpert-Gillis (1997) found, in an experimentally controlled study, that children improved in frustration tolerance, in asking for help in getting along with classmates, and in appropriate assertiveness. They appeared less anxious, withdrawn, and disruptive than a matched nonprogram control group of children experiencing divorce.

Carlos Carlos was confronted with perhaps the most serious set of difficulties because of his age and the nature of the problems he displayed. Where and how would you want to intervene with Carlos? How would you decide what to do, in what order, for what duration? What Carlos and other youth often need is a planned, holistic prevention/promotion services system, not just isolated programs.

The potential for Carlos to become involved with intensive, health-threatening addictive behaviors looms large. As a public health issue, prevention of smoking and other tobacco use requires a coordinated strategy, including media campaigns, community interventions that affect the norms and social context of smoking, tobacco excise tax increases, and tobacco use cessation programs for teens (Lantz et al., 2000). From an ecological perspective, the presence of smokers in the adolescent microsystem is the most powerful influence on teen smoking (Wang, Fitzhugh, Eddy, Fu, & Turner, 1997), and it is not a simple task for macro-level, neighborhood, and organizational level interventions to penetrate through to all of the relevant microsystems.

School professionals used a dual approach to help Carlos. First, he was treated as a new smoker and received a prevention program designed to help Latino and African-American inner-city youth develop refusal skills around smoking while also building social decision-making and life skills to enhance overall competence (Epstein, Griffin, & Botvin, 2000). The importance of programs including both of these components was highlighted by a study that showed refusal assertiveness as the most influential factor on smoking rates over a two-year time period in urban sixth and seventh graders, and decision-making skills and a sense of personal efficacy as significant predictors of refusal skills. This reflects the more general conclusion of CASEL (Elias, Zins et al., 1997) that, across problem prevention areas a combination of generic decision-making, problem-solving and social-emotional competence promotion skills and skills specific to a problem area (e.g., bullying, alcohol use, poor health habits) is necessary for significant and lasting preventive effects.

Carlos also was enrolled in the Tobacco Awareness Program (TAP), a type of school-based tobacco cessation program for adolescents. The premise of such programs, which is applicable to other substance use problems, is that behavior change requires movement through five stages: precontemplation (not thinking about changing the behavior), contemplation (starting to evaluate positive and negative consequences of the behavior), preparation (deciding to change and making a plan of action), action (active behavior change), and maintenance (sustaining the change) (Prochaska & DiClemente, 1983).

In a study of implementation of TAP in six high schools over a two-year period (Coleman-Wallace, Less, Montgomery, Blix, & Wang, 1999), the program's key elements were voluntary membership, group format, addressing triggers to use of tobacco and coping strategies, elaborating short- and long-term consequences of smoking, identifying and problem solving around obstacles to quitting and to sustaining changes made, weight management, and individualization of specific approaches to quitting. TAP was developed for use by minority youngsters and has culturally sensitive materials—helpful for Carlos.

At the conclusion of the program evaluation, 16 percent of voluntary TAP students quit smoking (vs. only 9% of those assigned to TAP), significantly better than controls, who rarely quit. TAP also appeared to move a significant number of students to action and maintenance stages. Gains in self-efficacy, along with the influence of close friends, accounted for 53 percent of the variance in tobacco use. For adolescents like Carlos, an organized, school-based program for smoking cessation is a far better option than punishment alone. However, smoking is still subject to microsystem influences beyond students' or professionals' easy control.

Community Support The Watsons benefited from informal support provided by their church. The congregation took seriously its role in promoting child and youth development. It provided religious education designed to involve children actively in promoting values consistent with its tradition, emotional and spiritual development, and social connectedness. This included not just religious education classes, but also involving children and youth with adults in the life of the congregation and in activities that reflect youth talents and interests, such as music and art. The congregation was also a strong, consistent source of emotional support.

Summary This family case example is hypothetical, yet real-life families similar to the Watsons are numerous. Of course, specific dynamics would be different if the family included children of different ages; tilted toward younger or older; were rural, more or less diverse in ethnic background; strong adherents to other religions; wealthy or middle class; recent immigrants; residents of another country; or differed along other dimensions of human diversity. Still, it is exciting to see the advances in knowledge and practice in prevention that can be arrayed in the service of human problems. In this case, there is a blurring of conceptual distinctions among the various levels of prevention and indeed between what we might consider "community" and "clinical" intervention. Many types of interventions have a "preventive" effect; in real life, many families need multiple interventions to stave off potential dysfunction and increase their strengths.

HOW DO WE DETERMINE THE EFFECTIVENESS OF PREVENTION/PROMOTION EFFORTS?

At this point in the development of prevention efforts, anyone implementing a program must move beyond the basic question, "Does it work?" to sophisticated questions such as, "How well does it work, for whom, under what conditions, and what are the mechanisms that account for its effects?" Clear answers are a precursor to making sound decisions about prevention programming, policy, and funding. However, deriving such answers is difficult. In this section we present three approaches to seeking answers to these questions across a broad range of action research studies. The first, *meta-analysis,* represents a quantitative approach. The second, the *best practices approach,* is more qualitative. Third is a *lessons-learned approach*. We illustrate some of the complexities of understanding programs operating with varying target populations and ecological levels by examining three large-scale comprehensive evaluations.

Meta-Analyses of Research on Program Outcomes

Meta-analysis compares statistical findings of all quantitative studies done on a given topic that meet certain methodological criteria (e.g., comparison of home visitor programs and control groups in randomized field experiments, all of which used similar dependent variables). For an experimental study of a prevention program, meta-analysis computes a statistical estimate of effect size: the strength of the effect of that intervention (independent variable) on the chosen outcomes (dependent variables). The average effect size is computed for a set of similar programs tested in multiple studies. Although not without controversy (e.g., Trickett, 1997; Weissberg & Bell, 1997), meta-analysis is one useful tool for broad analyses of the effectiveness of prevention programs.

Durlak and Wells (1997) used meta-analysis to examine 177 primary prevention programs directed at children and adolescents. This is a very broad focus, but it provides a useful overview. The authors included both person and environment (e.g., school) level interventions as well as both universal and selective prevention programs for children at risk (Mrazek & Haggerty, 1994). Their conclusions, which have many qualifiers that are best read in the original study, are that from 59 percent to 82 percent of participants in a primary prevention program surpassed the average performance of those in control groups. This indicates clear superiority of prevention groups to controls. Consistently positive effects resulted from programs that helped people cope with significant life transitions, such as first-time motherhood, children of divorce, school entry or transition, and children dealing with stressful medical and dental procedures (Durlak & Wells, 1997).

Durlak and Wells (1998) conducted a second meta-analysis on 130 secondary or indicated prevention programs for children who were experiencing early signs of difficulty such as persistent shyness, learning difficulties, and antisocial behavior. The average participant in these programs was better off than 70 percent of the control group members. These programs were especially effective for children whose externalizing behaviors put them at risk of conduct disorders and delinquency, for which later treatment is difficult.

More recent reviews have been carried out by Catalano et al. (2002), Greenberg, Domitrovich, and Bumbarger (2001), Roth et al. (1998), Tobler et al. (2000), Wilson, Gottfredson, and Najaka (2001), and Weissberg and Durlak (2006) with newer ones emerging constantly. These reviews confirm the Durlak and Wells findings and add some nuances. Successful preventive interventions are developmentally sensitive. Acquisition of social-emotional competencies seems to reduce expected incidence of academic, social, and behavioral problems, including substance use, conduct problems, school absence and dropout. Two caveats also emerge from this literature: (a) implementation intensity ("dosage") and program quality strongly affect outcomes; and (b) outcomes are stronger when programs mobilize environmental supports from peer groups, schools, parents, and communities. Overall, these meta-analytic studies provide consistent support for the beneficial impact of skills-oriented preventive interventions (Elias, 2004).

Best Practices in Promoting Social-Emotional Learning

The second approach to evaluating prevention/promotion programs is termed the best practices approach. This is not a precise designation. In this section we focus on studying a specific type of program that has been empirically shown to be effective across multiple settings and on gleaning from further studies of those settings the procedures that effective programs of that type have in common. Doing this effectively requires site visits and qualitative research much more detailed and descriptive than is usually found in journal articles.

The Collaborative for Academic, Social, and Emotional Learning (CASEL) identifies best practices in school-based prevention of problem behaviors and promotion of social-emotional competence. CASEL also facilitates effective implementation, ongoing evaluation, and refinement of comprehensive programs in social and emotional learning. Nine action-researchers with many years of experience in the field created a document reflecting their consensus on how best to conduct these programs in schools, *Promoting Social and Emotional Learning: Guidelines for Educators* (Elias, Zins et al., 1997). More recent resources include a special issue of *American Psychologist* (Weissberg & Kumpfer, 2003), CASEL's (2003) *Safe and Sound* document, CASEL's summary and analysis of research on the relationship of social-emotional learning to academic performance (Zins, Weissberg, Wang, & Walberg, 2004), and websites listed at the end of this chapter. Examples of best practices for effective prevention/promotion programs with children and youth are summarized in Table 10.3. (See also Table 10.2, which presented best practices ideas for family-based programs.)

TABLE 10.3 Principles of Effective Prevention/Promotion Programs for Children and Youth

Effective prevention/promotion programs:

1. Address risk and protective processes identified in research.
2. Involve families, peers, schools, and communities to address multiple, interrelated goals.
3. Are appropriate to the age and developmental level of children and sensitive to cultural traditions.
4. Strengthen social-emotional skills and ethical values and foster their applications to everyday life.
5. Use teaching-learning approaches that involve participants actively at multiple points in their development.
6. Focus on second-order change in settings and communities, including changes in formal policies and specific practices and developing resources for postive child and youth development.
7. Involve skills training and support for staff to foster high-quality implementation of programs.
8. Monitor local needs and program quality to promote continuous improvement.

SOURCE: Adapted from Weissberg, Kumpfer, & Seligman, 2003; Zins, Weissberg, Wang, & Walberg, 2004.

Lessons Learned from Large-Scale Prevention/ Promotion Evaluations

The third approach uses comprehensive, large-scale evaluation efforts as a more holistic lens from which to understand the effectiveness of prevention/promotion approaches than can be provided by meta-analyses or best practices compilations alone. The three examples that follow illustrate this approach.

Child Development Project This program, now named Caring School Community, seeks to produce a caring community in the elementary classroom and school by creating environments that foster self-determination, social competence, social connectedness, and moral guidance (Solomon, Watson, Battistich, Schaps, & Delucchi, 1996). Its classroom component consists of developmental discipline (in which students participate in developing and maintaining norms and rules and making decisions about violations and changes), cooperative learning and related collaborative small group pedagogy, and literature-based reading instruction. Schoolwide components increase inclusiveness, reduce competition, and promote a sense of shared purpose and the school as a democratic community. A family component in many settings has parent-teacher teams plan activities designed to increase families' bonds to schools.

A comprehensive evaluation of the program in six districts (three on the West Coast and one each in the Northeast, Southeast, and Midwest) involved two implementing schools in each district, which were then matched to comparison schools based on school size, ethnicity, limited English speakers, and achievement test scores (Solomon, Battistich, Watson, Schaps, & Lewis, 2000). Data were collected over a three-year period and included observations and teacher-completed measures of implementation; student surveys of school environment and academic, personal, and social attitudes and motivation; and cognitive/academic performance. When outcomes in all program schools were tested against those in comparison schools, no significant findings emerged on student social-emotional outcomes, classroom behavior, or achievement. However, five of the twelve program schools showed a pattern of higher-quality implementation of the program. When effects in these five high-implementation schools were compared with their matched comparison schools, a number of small to moderate differences were found, mainly in student attitudes and motivation, sense of community, school engagement, democratic values, conflict resolution, and frequency of self-chosen reading. No such pattern was found in classroom academic behavior or student achievement. Further analyses indicated that quality of program implementation and school sense of community significantly influenced social (but not academic) outcomes. The lessons learned from this evaluation include the following.

- Evaluating outcomes without attending to implementation can yield inaccurate conclusions.
- Even with strong support and resources, implementation of complex, schoolwide programs is difficult.
- The quality of program implementation required to yield consistent, enduring outcomes is not well established, especially for academic indices.
- Case study methods can best identify particular constellations of influences leading to differential implementation within a school or district.

Ultimately, it was the qualitative "stories" of individual schools that the researchers turned to as a way of making sense of the highly complex findings.

School Development Program Developed by James Comer and often known as the "Comer process," the School Development Program (SDP)) is a school-based management approach that transforms the relationships among educators, students, and parents (Comer, 1988; Comer, Haynes, Joyner, & Ben-Avie, 1996; Joyner, Comer, & Ben-Avie, 2004). It combines school decision making with strong community input and a commitment to provide all children with the opportunities to proceed competently along six pathways of healthy development (physical, psychological, linguistic, cognitive, social, and ethical). The program was originally developed in New Haven, Connecticut, a diverse, urban school district with many students from disadvantaged families.

SDP creates and links three teams for each school. A School Planning and Management Team (SPMT) includes school administrators, teachers and other staff, and, at times, students. The SPMT is a governing structure and develops, supports, and monitors a comprehensive school improvement plan. The Social Support Team (also termed a school-based Mental Health Team) includes school psychologists, counselors, social workers, nurses, and special education teachers. It addresses children's special needs and is a vehicle for prevention of problem behaviors via dissemination of information to teachers and parents and organizing skill development and related programmatic interventions. The Parent Team works to increase home-school bonding and support for education by facilitating parents becoming involved in school governance, fundraising, publicity, volunteering, and sharing of parenting skills.

These structures are necessary but not sufficient; the teams, and ultimately the entire school, must operate along four "process" principles that will eventuate in a more humane and effective school:

- working cooperatively
- using a problem-solving (vs. blame-giving) orientation
- reaching decisions by consensus (vs. voting)
- giving primacy to children's needs and keeping them on healthy developmental pathways

Taken as a whole, this model generates powerful radiating effects, which Comer has described as a sense of empowerment that flows into the classrooms and touches the students while also flowing out in the community and touching residents and service providers who interface with the school (Comer, 2004).

Evaluating a process-oriented program such as SDP is a challenge. Cook, Farah-Naaz, Phillips, Stettersten, Shagle, and Degirmencioglu (1999) undertook an independent evaluation of SDP (i.e., not carried out by SDP-associated researchers). Over a four-year period they conducted a field experiment in 23 middle schools in Prince George's County, Maryland, a racially and socioeconomically diverse school district, involving multiple assessments of over 12,000 students, 2,000 staff, and 1,000 parents. Findings suggested that SDP schools carried out more program components than matched controls, but only to a small degree. Key differences were:

- having a program facilitator and more experienced teachers
- more parent and community involvement
- more agreement on a shared vision for the school by staff, students, and parents
- better implementation of School Planning and Management and Parent Teams

No reliable differences were found in shared governance, democratic decision making, or quality of school improvement plans. Improved school climate appeared to affect student well-being but not academic achievement.

As with the Child Development Project evaluation, these findings were disappointing yet revealing. Both evaluations suggest that school climate interventions do make a difference, primarily on social-emotional outcomes, if implemented with high quality.

If there is a clear message from this study, it is that programs must pay very careful attention to their key elements and ensure that they are being implemented strongly, carefully, and consistently. The mere presence of key elements is not sufficient to produce change, particularly in high-risk youth. Consistent, high-quality implementation is necessary. A complicating factor is that intervention components being evaluated in the experimental schools sometimes also appear in the control schools without any input from the program developers. This apparently happened in the SDP study.

The Cook et al. evaluation does not represent a final statement on SDP. The Comer team has used action research to make important adjustments:

> We learned from our academic component experience, reinforced by many subsequent experiences, that it is very important to obtain district-level understanding and support in all aspects of the school improvement or reform process. Otherwise, there can be a notion that the project is the treatment and will lead to the cure without district-level adjustments. Projects can provide a framework, and even content, but improvement can take place only when school people use supportive tools and information effectively at the building and district levels. Also, because of the turnover and change in school systems, support must be broad based and not dependent on one or even a few leaders. The unavailability of support for staff growth can frustrate initiatives and dampen the hope created by good relationships and a more orderly environment. Despite the eventual attention given to the academic program, significant test score gains did not take place until the eighth year of our project. At this point, the staff and parents were functioning very well and the social program had reached its highest level of effectiveness. Student behavior problems were at a minimum. Today, with more knowledge and skills, under average conditions, the model can help poorly functioning schools bring about improved social conditions in a year or two, and improved academic conditions in three to five years. Many schools have achieved both in one year. (Comer, 2004, pp. 126–27)

Project Family This program integrated family, school, and community approaches to substance abuse prevention (Spoth, Redmond, & Shin, 1998; Spoth, Guyll, & Day, 2000). Project Family implemented two family competency promotion programs, Preparing for the Drug Free Years and the Iowa Strengthening Families Program, in rural Iowa communities. Both programs are designed to increase family protective processes and reduce risk processes through family training in group sessions. In an experimental evaluation of Project Family, families linked with 22 experimental schools received the programs; families in another 11 schools served as controls. Results indicated that the program led to changes in specific parenting behaviors, parents' general approach to behavior management, and, in turn, emotional quality of parent-child relationships (Spoth, Redmond, & Shin, 1998).

In practice, such community partnerships involve many components, such as local and state health and social service agencies as well as families and schools. Establishing an organizing structure to operate the partnership and coordinate participation is essential (Adelman & Taylor, 2003). As interventions get more complex, encompassing, and potentially powerful, the quality with which they

are implemented and coordinated becomes more important. In addition, evaluation research becomes more important yet more difficult. In Chapter 14 we discuss evaluation approaches.

EMERGING AREAS FOR PREVENTION/PROMOTION

The areas of prevention/promotion we have discussed will continue to grow. In addition, several areas are emerging as new foci for preventive efforts. These include bullying, violence, victimization, and suicide among children in schools; youth crime and delinquency; the direct and indirect effects of terrorism; and HIV/AIDS. We could have included other issues such as domestic violence and child maltreatment but limited ourselves because of space considerations. Still, the kinds of analyses we have provided for emerging issues have strong parallels for areas we have not covered explicitly.

School-Based Prevention of Bullying and Suicide

Go into a high school assembly and ask students to raise their hands to answer "yes" to any one of these three questions:

> In the past month, have you or has anyone you know in the school actually attempted to harm yourself?
>
> Have you thought about committing suicide or harming yourself in a significant way?
>
> Have you spoken to a classmate who said he or she had similar thoughts?

You are likely to see half of the hands in the room raised.

Go into any elementary, middle, or high school assembly and ask students to raise their hands to answer "yes" to any one of these three questions:

> Have you ever bullied someone in your school, either with your words or actions?
>
> Have you ever been bullied, threatened, or intimidated by someone else in your school?
>
> Have you ever seen or heard someone else in the school being bullied with words or actions, and did not do anything about it?

You are likely to see anywhere from half to three-quarters of the hands up.

These examples are supported by data that indicate that suicide and bullying-related behaviors are problems worldwide (Elias & Zins, 2003; Malley, Kush, & Bogo, 1996; World Health Organization, 2000). Yet, one can certainly find schools where these problems are far less frequent. Suicide and bullying can be conceptualized in ecological terms using the individual- and environmental-level prevention

equations in Chapter 9. Key preventive influences on both of these problems are positive sources of relatedness and connectedness in both school and home life; supportive friends, family members, and other caring adults; and coping skills to deal with frustrations, setbacks, stress, and conflict as well as accurate perception of emotional cues in oneself and others. Suicide and bullying prevention both require multilevel, ecological approaches to intervention (Henry, Stephenson, Hanson, & Hargett, 1993; Kalafat & Elias, 1995; Miller & Du Paul, 1996).

Protective Factors against Violence in School Environments Community psychologists are among those asking how it happens that certain schools are organized so that their levels of violence and vandalism are lower than those of other schools. The following conditions have been identified as conducive to low rates of school violence (Felner & Adan, 1988; Hawkins & Lam, 1987; Pepler & Slaby, 1994; Wager, 1993).

- School courses are perceived as highly relevant to students' lives.
- School rules and structures allow students some control over what happens to them at school.
- School discipline policies are viewed as firm, fair, clear, and consistently enforced.
- A rational reward structure in the school recognizes students for their achievement.
- Strong and effective school governance exists, with strong principal leadership.
- Ongoing, positive contacts occur between students and adults.
- The curriculum includes education in social and emotional competencies.

These characteristics are the foci of a growing number of school-based prevention/promotion programs. School safety can be improved as children learn skills for prosocial participation in school life. However, all students must be given the opportunity for such participation without being marginalized or threatened (Cottrell, 1976; Coudroglou, 1996; Elias, Zins et al., 1997).

Empirical Research on Program Outcomes Despite strong guidelines from theory and research, empirical results for suicide prevention approaches have been inconsistent. For example, it appears that suicide prevention curricula using a stress-based model that attempts to normalize suicidal behavior are either not effective or even harmful (Kalafat, 2003; Miller & DuPaul, 1996). Kalafat (2003) notes the difficulty in providing conclusive empirical evidence about interventions to prevent completed suicides or attempts. Best practices for suicide prevention include in-service training for school staff, identifying suicidal and other at-risk students, handling peer reports sensitively and effectively, and taking appropriate action and making referrals as necessary (Miller & Du Paul, 1996). These appear to apply equally well to preventing other problem behaviors.

With regard to bullying, there is a proliferation of programs in schools and in our understanding of bullying phenomena and their prevention (Zins, Elias, & Maher, in press). However, developing effective interventions is far from simple. Even such well-conceived and carefully implemented programs as the Toronto Anti-Bullying Intervention (Pepler, Craig, Ziegler, & Charach, 1994) showed only limited effects on victimization rates and virtually none on encouraging bystanders to intervene in bullying. Uncertainty remains about the intensity and duration of exposure to key program elements. Recent research (Goldbaum, Craig, Pepler, & Connolly, 2003; Neft & Elias, in press) shows that traditional bully-victim distinctions are too simple. Victims can be categorized into desisters (started with high levels of victimization, decreased over time), late onset (increasing victimization over time), and stable victims. The same distinctions can be made with bullies and bystanders as well as with youth who are both victims and bullies. Related distinctions are being made with regard to sexual harassment and cyber (Internet) bullying and victimization of children with disabilities, which seem to be increasing (Elias & Zins, 2003; Willard, 2005).

Schoolwide Approaches The largest preventive effects for bullying or suicide come from comprehensive schoolwide efforts that create a climate of non-acceptance, a positive social norm of disclosure, a track record of effective action in response to threats and incidents, and curriculum-based training in social-emotional competencies (Elias & Zins, 2003; Silverman & Felner, 1995). Firm, clear, schoolwide policies, referral procedures, and staff training must exist to deal effectively with student reports of problems. But the jury is still out on establishing a set of procedures that is effective in multiple settings, transportable across different contexts, and sustainable over a long period of time and changes in school personnel. Here we review three approaches that have shown success in some contexts.

Olweus: Bullying Prevention Olweus's (Olweus, Limber, & Mihalic, 1999) model has been highly successful in Norway. It focuses on establishing comprehensive school rules for acceptable interaction in all aspects of the environment, including the playground. Intervention components include an educational booklet on bullying used with all students, a parent education booklet, a video depicting the lives of victims of bullying, and a strong school discipline code that labels even nasty verbal comments as bullying and calls for swift consequences, such as removal from the playground or classroom. Repeated offenses quickly bring parents into the school. Evaluation data have indicated significant improvements in satisfaction with school life, feelings of comfort and safety, and less bullying of others. In essence, Olweus's approach creates a school with different patterns of social interaction and a different environmental feel. (This is also a goal of the CDP and SDP programs discussed earlier.) Schools using this approach must have effective ways to promote nonviolent conflict resolution, assertive communication, and ways to respond as a bystander or victim, whether during or after an incident. Research on applying the Olweus model to the United States has had some success but has been challenging to carry out and sustain (Limber, 2004). There is a clear sense that cultural differences between the U.S. and Norway must be addressed in both program structure and implementation processes.

Project ACHIEVE In the United States, comprehensive schoolwide approaches are emerging that incorporate many of the elements necessary for bully/victimization/violence prevention within a broader agenda. Project ACHIEVE (Knoff, in press) illustrates one strategy:

- a schoolwide social skills curriculum focused on friendship development and preventing violence
- individual, grade-level, and schoolwide accountability systems of incentives and consequences related to bullying
- consistent staff and administrative policy and action
- "special situations analysis" of contexts where bullying occurs
- parent and community outreach to communicate the norm that bullying, teasing, taunting, harassing, and aggression are unacceptable and preventable

As with other social-emotional skill-building curricula, ACHIEVE uses a common language of problem solving across grade levels that can be applied to bullying and other problem behaviors (Elias, 2004). Some of its steps include learning to "stop and think," asking "Are you going to make a good choice or bad choice?" and "What are your choices or steps?"

The special situation analysis examines such areas as cafeterias, hallways, buses, and other common school areas and also the specific subgroups of students (and staff) that seem to be most involved with the problem behaviors. This context-sensitive approach is consistent with community psychology principles. Based on extensive reviews of its evaluation data, Project ACHIEVE has been designated as an Exemplary Model Program by the U.S. Substance Abuse and Mental Health Services Administration, a SELect model by the Collaborative for Academic, Social, and Emotional Learning, and an exemplary program by the White House Conference on School Safety (Knoff, in press).

School Mental Health Initiatives Additional comprehensive interventions that address bullying and suicide in the context of other problem behaviors and desired competencies include school mental health initiatives (Hunter et al., 2005), Positive Behavior Intervention Support (Sugai & Horner, 1999), and New Directions for Student Support (Adelman & Taylor, 2006). These initiatives began with relatively narrow goals: addressing mental health problems, misbehavior, and learning difficulties in schools. Yet each has expanded to address the larger climate of education and the academic achievement and social-emotional well-being of all students. All of these initiatives are in early stages and data on their effectiveness across contexts are accumulating slowly. Of the three approaches, New Directions for Student Support is the most detailed and encompassing. Adelman and Taylor (2006) outline three interconnected systems that must be established in coordinated ways to provide integrative and comprehensive mental health services for all students: *Systems to Promote Healthy Development and Prevent Problem Behaviors, Systems of Early Intervention,* and *Systems of Care.* These comprehensive approaches recognize that prevention of bullying and suicide and improvement of school mental health are, in a sense, by-products of longitudinal, multilevel ecological changes in school structure and operation.

Summary Attempting to incorporate all relevant research on comprehensive schoolwide efforts relates to an old tale about the builder and the donkey. A builder was making a house in the next village and wanted to have everything with him so he would only have to make one trip. So he loaded up his donkey but kept thinking of other things he would need. He did not notice the poor donkey's legs beginning to buckle as more got loaded on. When the builder declared, "Let's go!" the donkey replied, "Go yourself. I can't move." That is one ending to the story. Another ending is that the builder, outraged, said, "If you don't start moving right now, I will beat you." The donkey replied by drawing up on its wobbly legs, shaking and shaking until most of the material fell to the ground, and then running toward the village. "You will have to build with what I can carry. Since you could not choose, I did."

Like the builder, schools must choose carefully what to do about suicide and bullying. Chapter 11 addresses the complex issues of implementing interventions and the difficult choices that must be made to reconcile the desired and the feasible. From the perspective of community psychology, future efforts to prevent bullying and suicide seem best directed toward fostering children's positive connections and ensuring that meaningful parts of the school day or week reflects their strengths or interests. As a corollary, destructive behavior toward self or others is likely forestalled by ongoing supportive and caring relationships, such as regular contacts with "buddies," older peer mentors, and/or adults in advisory and other formal and informal counseling contexts. Future research should examine the impact of these processes and how they might be given priority even as more comprehensive schoolwide systems are gradually put into place.

Preventing Youth Delinquency

Delinquency is a legal construct, not a psychological one, because it focuses on behavior by youth that is in violation of law. However, preventing delinquency is a public health concern that is connected with growing public awareness about the operation of gangs in urban and inner-city areas (Roberts, 2004). Community psychology principles provide some insights because delinquency can be conceptualized as one aspect of youth disaffection, which in turn relates to sense of community, empowerment, stress and coping, and other concepts we have discussed. Current research suggests that even though the most powerful predictors of delinquency are parenting factors, additional risk factors are often involved: perinatal risk, cognitive abilities, school achievement, emotion regulation, attachment, family socioeconomic status, marital discord, and levels of community crime and violence.

In a review of delinquency prevention programs, Welsh and Farrington (2003a) identified home visiting programs like the Prenatal/Early Infancy Project (cited earlier), comprehensive child care and preschool programs, and school-based programs as sound strategies. The Houston Parent-Child Development Center (Johnson, 1988) stands as an example of a well-studied child care program. Mothers are taught about child development and provided with parenting, relationship, and cognitive facilitation skills through home visits and group classes. The program also operated a high-quality early child development center. In an eight-year follow-up study, program children were involved in fewer fights and were less impulsive than controls. The Perry Preschool program, described earlier, is marked by high-quality instruction that gives equal emphasis to children's cognitive and social-emotional growth. Welsh and Farrington (2003a) report on a series of studies of the Perry program and similar ones, including a 22-year follow-up, that show such benefits as fewer arrests and chronic offenses in adulthood. Finally, the Seattle Social Development Program (Hawkins, Catalano, Kosterman, Abbott, & Hill, 1999) was tested in eight schools over a six-year period of time. The program's emphasis on parent training, social skills development, and creating climates to foster school bonding led to less violence and less alcohol use when compared to controls. Welsh and Farrington (2003b) note that for adolescents, after-school recreation programs are the most empirically supported strategy for delinquency prevention; mentoring and community-based programs have mixed outcomes.

Roberts (2004) and Yoshikawa (1994) suggest that future efforts to prevent delinquency must address multiple issues, focus on early family supports, community networking, and education as implied earlier, and be consistent with these best practices:

- home-based programs implemented during the first five years of life
- high-quality educational day care and/or preschool
- regular, home-based emotional and informational support relating to child development, parenting, and parents' own educational and social goals
- program length of at least two years

They also note that since chronic delinquents commit a relatively high proportion of serious juvenile crimes, interventions that address this group may be especially important.

Preventing Negative Impacts of Terrorism

Citizens of virtually every nation now live under a threat of terrorism. This state of affairs has had undeniable impact on the lives of individuals, families, and communities. In the coming years, community psychologists will need to examine how the interplay of principles of social justice, individual wellness, collaboration, and sense of community can inform efforts to reduce the negative psychological impacts of terrorism.

Terrorism affects its direct victims, witnesses who feel that they may be future targets, and the surrounding environment. Danieli, Engdahl, and Schlenger (2004) describe how acts of terror and massive trauma infuse themselves into the flow of personal, community, and societal life, coloring relationships and conceptions of life's possibilities. Moghaddam and Marsella (2004) explore the many nuances of terror's impacts, emphasizing how they are related to the extent of direct or indirect personal exposure to the events and the degree to which persons are living in a state of intense fear. Recall from Chapter 8 that research on the effects of the September 11, 2001, terrorist attacks showed widespread effects, with more distress associated with more direct exposure to the attacks. However, follow-up studies also showed resilience among the majority of New York City children and adults, with overall symptom rates returning to prior levels after about six months (Galea, Vlahov et al. 2003; see Chapter 8 for other sources). Explaining such resilience would offer promising angles for preventing or reducing psychological impacts of future terrorism.

Focusing on how schools can respond to terrorism, Alpert and Smith (2003) distinguished between selective or secondary prevention that follows a terrorist attack and universal or primary prevention efforts that prepare schools for possible future terrorist incidents. Secondary prevention following an attack involves working at community and organizational levels to reduce the escalation of chaos and minimize short- and long-term negative outcomes for those affected by the crisis. As we mentioned in Chapter 8, community psychology approaches can help schools and communities publicize accurate information on posttraumatic reactions, developmentally appropriate responses, and available resources. Community psychology concepts also can help in planning crisis services and ensure that research has shown them to be effective and culturally appropriate. For instance, organizational interventions such as critical incident stress debriefing have been shown to be often ineffective, sometimes worsening an already stressful experience. Community-oriented psychologists working in schools and workplaces can organize ongoing mutual support, ensure that the most distressed receive coping assistance, and set up systems to monitor later-emerging effects (Aber, 2005; Felton, 2004; Gist, 2002; McNally, Bryant, & Ehlers, 2003; van Emmerick et al., 2002).

Primary prevention poses larger challenges. Toward what should such efforts be directed? Community psychologists are not in any unique position to prevent actual terrorist events. Should a psychological sense of threat be prevented? What is the balance between prudent preparation and life-altering alarmism? How does this balance change developmentally? Core principles of security and freedom are involved, and divergent reasoning (recall this concept from Chapter 2) is needed to strike balances and to imagine creative solutions. These issues play out, for instance, in decisions about profiling as a means of surveillance, screening in airports and subways, security in workplaces and public spaces, laws about government surveillance of email, and how terror alerts are publicized via the mass media. Developing crisis plans and/or crisis teams also involves these issues. As Alpert and Smith (2003) note, such plans and teams serve to reduce anxiety. But what level of rehearsal and practice is necessary for the effectiveness of these plans to be guaranteed? Indeed, as security drills mount in schools, students seem to become either anxious or habituated; neither response is likely to be adaptive when a crisis occurs. There is no single answer, but rather a need for divergent reasoning and action research on policies, decisions, and their consequences.

Looking beyond schools to communities and societies, can community and other psychologists contribute to public understanding of political and social conflicts involving terrorism and responses to it? How can community psychology concepts of ecological connections among macrosystem forces, communities, and individual lives promote constructive conflict resolution at levels from international to personal? How can ecological-level thinking lead to deeper public understanding of terrorism, and meaning-focused individual coping with its threats? How can community psychology core values of wellness, sense of community, and social justice inform debate? Moghaddam (2005) and Moghaddam and Marsella (2004) gathered some psychological perspectives on related questions. How terrorism is understood involves conflicting social and political values, and deeper understanding requires divergent reasoning and action research. Community psychologists are not the only ones who could contribute to such understanding, but their emphasis on connecting multiple ecological levels and on divergent reasoning can be useful.

HIV/AIDS Prevention

HIV/AIDS continues to be an epidemic that affects all racial/ethnic groups in all parts of the world (Centers for Disease Control and Prevention, 2003). As powerful medical interventions have changed the course of the disease, prevention efforts seem to have become routinized and driven by less urgency. Wolitski (2003) reports an upsurge of "safe sex fatigue" and "AIDS burnout." This leads prevention messages to be ignored, thereby increasing health risks and perpetuating the epidemic. Disturbingly, these trends have been accompanied by a shift toward greater incidence of the disease in people of color and in non-Anglo nations (Centers for Disease Control and Prevention, 2003).

Marsh, Johnson, and Carey (2003) suggest that prevention efforts toward youth may be best directed toward reduction of sexual risk behaviors. Effective interventions tend to include a focus on communication and negotiation skills with potential sexual partners and involve role-play practice; they also need to include information about condom use (Coates, 2004). Structurally, HIV/AIDS programs seem best to include as part of a larger emphasis on sexual health.

For community psychologists, HIV/AIDS prevention contains many challenges and opportunities. Action research can play a meaningful role in identifying subgroups that are gaining or losing ground with regard to HIV/AIDS, so that prevention efforts can be modified accordingly. Ecological theory and our understanding of diversity and context can lead to research on the impact of families, intimate relationships, peer microsystems and cultural norms on positive sexual health in adolescents and adults (Kotchick, Dorsey, Miller, & Forehand, 1999; Power, 1998). As Wolitski (2003) noted,

> HIV prevention messages, like other forms of persuasive communication, have a shelf life and are destined to become monotonous and stale if they are not frequently changed and updated to reflect new scientific information or changes in community perceptions and norms. . . . Qualitative and quantitative research are needed to promote a deeper understanding of how the social, community, and environmental context affect individual risk and to learn from the experiences of those who have successfully maintained safer sex practices. (Wolitski, 2003, p. 15)

Microsystem-level programs, macrosystem social policy, and intermediate ecological levels are all important arenas for HIV prevention (Coates, 2004).

Implementation and Sustainability of Programs

As you have seen, answering the question, "Does prevention work?" is much like answering the questions, "Does surgery work?" or "Does education work?" The answer is "yes," but it must be qualified by knowing how well interventions are implemented. More refined questions are appropriate: "Is this program being implemented as designed, in accordance with theory and research?" and "How does it work with specific populations and contexts?"

Thus, a final emerging area for research and action concerns actual implementation of prevention/promotion initiatives in local contexts. As we have noted throughout this chapter, ideas and approaches may work very well in one organization, locality, culture, or other context yet not be applicable in another. Interventions identified as effective by empirical research in multiple settings, even when backed by meta-analytic findings or best practices and supported by lessons learned in certain situations, must be adapted to the "local and particular" dynamics and resources of each setting. Community psychologists and other prevention advocates are continuously learning about the importance of carefully considering implementation plans in context. An equal concern now is how to sustain effective prevention/promotion initiatives even after they have been brought to the point of adequate implementation. We take up these matters in detail in Chapter 11.

CHAPTER SUMMARY

1. The literature on prevention and promotion is constantly growing. The most reliable conclusions can be gleaned from programs that have been in operation for a number of years and whose effectiveness has been studied empirically. These often focus on factors identified in the prevention equations, listed in Table 10.1.

2. We described a selection of programs focused on *microsystems* in home, school, and workplace settings. Family programs usually focus on parenting skills such as the *Prenatal/Early Infancy Project.* Later in the chapter, we described the *Family Bereavement Program* (pp. 335), and programs that link family-based and school-based efforts, the *Children of Divorce Program* (pp. 336) and *Project Family* (pp. 344). Qualities of effective family-based programs are listed in Table 10.2.
3. School-based programs often focus on teaching *social-emotional competence* or *social-emotional literacy (SEL)*. Examples include the *Perry Preschool Project, Interpersonal Cognitive Problem-Solving (I Can Problem-Solve), Social Decision-Making/Social Problem-Solving, Second Step,* and *Lions-Quest Skills for Action.* School-based programs described later in the chapter include the *Primary Mental Health Project, Children of Divorce Program,* and the *Tobacco Awareness Program* (pp. 338). Workplace programs include the *JOBS Project* and efforts to build coping skills and social-emotional competencies among workers.
4. Other prevention/promotion approaches focus on *altering settings* to promote quality of life. School-based initiatives seek to alter the social climate of schools, including *Character Education,* the *Social Development Project,* the *STEP* intervention, the *School Development Program,* and the *Child Development Project/Caring School Community* program (the latter two are discussed on pp. 341). Other approaches address religious education and creating "emotionally intelligent" workplaces.
5. Broader approaches to prevention/promotion focus on *communities and macrosystems.* Examples include the *Character Matters* initiatives in Canada and *Communities That Care* initiatives in the U.S. We also described Jason's culturally tailored mass media interventions to prevent smoking. Advocacy to influence state and national policies can also serve prevention/promotion goals. We also described how the *Pequenas Comunidades* initiatives empower low-income communities and prevent violence in Colombia, efforts to address substance abuse policy in Mexico, and conferences to prevent victimization and to promote intercultural understanding *(KayaFest)* in Turkey.
6. Context, the ecology of a particular culture, population, community, or setting, is crucial for the effectiveness of prevention/promotion efforts. The *No Child Left Behind Act* in the U.S. has strongly affected the context of prevention/promotion efforts in schools. We also discussed the cross-cultural research of Sundberg et al., which showed that programs developed in North American often translate in limited ways, if at all, in other societies. Even within a society, programs need to be adapted to different cultures or communities.
7. We presented an illustrative family case study, the Watsons, to illustrate how various levels and types of prevention programs come together to serve a

family with multiple needs. This case study included discussion of how programs covered earlier in the chapter could be applied to this family as well as description of several additional programs.

8. How do we determine the effectiveness of prevention/promotion programs? We discussed *meta-analysis,* a quantitative way of summarizing the effects of a prevention/promotion intervention across multiple studies. We discussed examples of meta-analyses for primary and secondary prevention.
9. A qualitative approach to evaluation is the *best practices* approach, which focuses on identifying the elements of effective programs and uses those as criteria for evaluating other programs. We illustrated it through the work of the Collaborative for Academic, Social, and Emotional Learning (CASEL), highlighting their guidelines for school-based programs (see Table 10.3).
10. A third approach is that large-scale program evaluations reveal many *lessons learned* from practical experience as well as complexities related to the effectiveness of prevention/promotion. Local context, working at multiple ecological levels, and the quality of program implementation are key issues.
11. Five emerging areas for prevention/promotion research and action include: school-based efforts to prevent bullying and suicide; preventing delinquency; preventing psychological impacts of terrorism; HIV/AIDS prevention; and implementation and sustainability of prevention/promotion programs.

BRIEF EXERCISES

1. Consider these questions, and then discuss with a classmate:

   Which prevention/promotion programs described in this chapter are most interesting to you? Why?

   In what settings, communities, or cultures might these programs work best? Why?

   In what settings, communities, or cultures might these programs not be effective? Why?

2. Imagine yourself as a member of your local public school board. Which program(s) described in this chapter would you recommend be incorporated into the school curriculum and/or services (spending tax money to do so)? Why?
3. Imagine yourself as a local government official in your community. Which program(s) described in this chapter would you recommend be developed in your community (spending tax money to do so)? Why?

4. Outline a prevention or promotion program. Discuss your ideas with a classmate.
    - Choose a target population (e.g., by age, or those who share the same recent stressor, are in the same setting, or some other similarity).
    - Choose a setting or settings in which to implement your program: an organization, community, or macrosystem. You may focus on changing the setting or on changing microsystems or persons within that setting. You will probably have more useful ideas if you focus on a setting that you know well. You may focus on macrosystems that influence many settings, such as changing state, national, or international policies.
    - Choose at least one goal: a problem to prevent and/or competence to promote.
    - Suggest desired outcomes or objectives that you would use as observable indicators of whether your program attained its goal(s).
    - Describe the specific methods your program would use to accomplish your goal and how these are related to the problem being prevented or competence being promoted.
    - Describe the connection between your program and the concepts of prevention/promotion in Chapters 9–10.

RECOMMENDED READINGS

Albee, G., & Gullotta, T. (Eds.) (1997). *Primary prevention works.* Thousand Oaks, CA: Sage.

Gullotta, T., & Bloom, M. (Eds.) (2003). *Encyclopedia of primary prevention and mental health promotion.* New York: Springer.

Weissberg, R., & Kumpfer, K. (Eds.) (2003). Prevention that works for children and youth [Special issue]. *American Psychologist 58*(6/7).

RECOMMENDED WEBSITES

Partial Listing of Specific Prevention/Promotion Programs

Character Matters Program: York Region District School Board, Ontario, Canada
http://www.yrdsb.edu.on.ca/

Developmental Studies Center: Caring School Community Program (formerly Child Development Project)
http://www.devstu.org

Hope Foundation
http://www.communitiesofhope.org

I Can Problem Solve (ICPS); Social Decision Making/Social Problem Solving
http://www.researchpress.com

Open Circle/Reach Out to Schools Social Competency Program
http://www.open-circle.org

Peace Works
http://www.peaceeducation.com

Promoting Alternative Thinking Strategies (PATHS)
http://www.channing-bete.com

Resolving Conflict Creatively Program (RCCP)
http://www.esrnational.org

Responsive Classroom
http://www.responsiveclassroom.org

Second Step
http://www.cfchildren.org

Skills for Adolescence, Skills for Action, Violence Prevention
http://www.quest.edu

Social Decision Making/Social Problem Solving Program
http://www.umdnj.edu/spsweb
http://www.eqparenting.com

Strengthening Families Program
http://www.strengtheningfamilies.org

Tribes TLC: A New Way of Learning and Being Together
http://www.tribes.com

Information and Best Practices for School-Based Prevention/Promotion

Collaborative for Academic, Social, and Emotional Learning
http://www.casel.org

Character Education Partnership
http://www.Character.org

National Association of School Psychologists
http://www.NASPonline.org

National Mental Health Association
http://nmha.org/children/prevent/index.cfm

National Center for Learning and Citizenship
http://www.ecs.org/nclc

U. S. Dept. of Education, Office of Safe and Drug-Free Schools
http://www.ed.gov/offices/OSDFS/exemplary01/2_intro2.html
Center for Substance Abuse Prevention

U.S. Substance Abuse & Mental Health Services Administration
http://modelprograms.samhsa.gov/template_cf.cfm?page=model_list

U.S. Centers for Disease Control and Prevention
http://www.cdc.gov/hiv/projects/rep/compend.htm

National Institute on Drug Abuse, U.S. National Institutes of Health
http://www.nida.nih.gov/prevention/prevopen.html

Center for the Study and Prevention of Violence, Blueprints Project
http://www.colorado.edu/cspv/blueprints/index.html

National Institutes of Health, consensus findings on youth violence
http://consensus.nih.gov/ta/023/023youthviolencepostconfintro.htm

Center for Social and Emotional Education
http://www.csee.net

School Mental Health Project
http://smhp.psych.ucla.edu

Educators for Social Responsibility
http://www.esrnational.org

Partial International Listing of Prevention/Promotion Resources

United Nations Educational, Social and Cultural Organization
http://www.ibe.unesco.org/International/Publications/Educational/Practices/prachome.htm
(Downloadable, reproducible booklets on social-emotional learning and related topics in multiple languages.)

The World Federation for Mental Health
http://www.wfmh.com/

Center for Social and Emotional Learning (CESEL) of Denmark
http://www.cesel.dk/

Consortium for Research on Emotional Intelligence in Organizations
http://www.eiconsortium.org

German Network for Mental Health
http://www.gnmh.de/

Psychological and Counseling Service/Life Skills Program (SHEFI), Education Ministry, Israel
http://www.education.gov.il/shefi

EQ Japan
http://www.eqj.co.jp/

Youth Education Service (YES) of the New Zealand Police
http://www.nobully.org.nz/

Nasjonalforeningen for Folkehelsen, Norway
http://www.nasjonalforeningen.no/BarnogFamilie/artikler/folkeskikk.htm

Partnerships Against Violence Network
http://www.pavnet.org

Promoting Social Competence Project, Scotland
http://www.dundee.ac.uk/psychology/prosoc.htm

Department of Education Sciences, Rand Afrikaans University, South Africa
http://general.rau.ac.za/cur/edcur/eduscie/krige.htm

6 Seconds (Information on promoting emotional intelligence in schools, organizations, and families.)
http://www.6seconds.org

Social Emotionell Träning, Sweden
http://www.set.st/

Emotional Intelligence of Turkey (Türkiyenin Duygusal Zekasi)
http://www.duygusalzeka.com/

Resources for Service Learning and Citizenship Education

National Center for Learning and Citizenship
http://www.ecs.org/nclc

Center for Information and Research on Civic Learning and Engagement
http://www.civicyouth.org

International Education and Resource Network
http://www.iEARN.org

(See also Recommended Websites for Chapter 9.)

INFOTRAC® COLLEGE EDITION KEYWORDS

community-based, competence(ies), family-based, intervention, prevention(ive)(ing), primary prevention, problem solving, promotion(ing), school-based, social-emotional competence, social-emotional learning

11

Prevention and Promotion: Implementing Programs

HIRB/Index Stock

OPENING EXERCISE: LESSONS LEARNED FROM SUCCESS

It is common to watch TV footage of the latest famine or epidemic somewhere that seems far away and conclude that such problems are too big, that attempting to prevent them is a waste of money, that nothing can be done. Yet many professionals in public health and other fields disagree. The lessons of history support their view.

Levine (2004), in a story published in the *Newark Star-Ledger* for World AIDS Day, assembled a list of some of the prevention successes in the history of public health.

- A global immunization effort, led by the World Health Organization, ended in 1977 with the elimination of smallpox. That outcome probably could have been achieved a decade earlier with money and effort at the right time; in the meantime, many died unnecessarily.
- Focused immunization efforts reduced cases of measles among children in seven southern African nations from 60,000 in 1996 to 117 in 2000.

- In Sri Lanka, a government commitment to "safe motherhood" services has reduced maternal mortality to less than 5% of its former incidence level.
- Across 11 countries in West Africa, a public health program run almost exclusively by African professionals has prevented hundreds of thousands of cases of blindness.
- A national campaign in Egypt that promoted a simple treatment for dehydration (mixing clean water with sugar and salt) helped reduce the number of infant deaths from diarrhea by 82 per cent.
- In Thailand, a government campaign that required sex workers to use condoms led to an 80 per cent reduction in HIV cases, preventing nearly 200,000 new cases.
- In 1985, governments in Latin American and the Caribbean began a major effort to vaccinate every child against polio. This followed earlier, similar large-scale campaigns in developed countries. Today, polio is no longer a threat in the Western Hemisphere.
- In 1990, Poland had the highest rate of tobacco consumption in the world. A combination of health education and stringent tobacco legislation there has prevented 10,000 deaths a year, reduced lung cancer rates by as much as 30%, and boosted the average life expectancy of Polish men by four years.
- The costs of preventing these and other conditions are far less than the costs of treating them, or of dealing with the social disruption and losses they can cause.
- Key elements in such successes have been consensus on the best approaches, sustained funding at adequate levels, political and social leadership, technological innovation, effective delivery of treatments and education, good local management of prevention programs, and ongoing monitoring of program effectiveness. These elements can lead to successes even in countries with very little money. In many successes, international agencies, national governments, private corporations and local professionals and citizens collaborated. (Levine, 2004, pp. 1, 8)

What are your personal reactions to these points? What lessons can we draw from them?

Knowledge from prevention research does little good if it is not implemented. Even if it is implemented, it must be carried out with high quality. Even that is not enough. To have an impact, prevention efforts must be widespread. And they must last. Levine shows that we often know enough to accomplish a great deal, even under highly unfavorable conditions. She provides examples of how such substantial problems as smallpox, polio, maternal mortality, and tobacco use were overcome to extraordinary degrees by focusing on what it took to apply existing knowledge in order to bring it into practice.

In fact, community and preventive psychologists have learned a great deal about the art and science of implementing preventive efforts. Bringing good ideas and sound procedures of the kind you read about in Chapters 9 and 10 into high-quality, enduring practice is possible. The challenge can be likened to the difference between reviewing for a test in the library and actually taking the test, or the difference between pitching in the bullpen and facing live batters in a stadium with a huge crowd roaring on every pitch. Performance in the practice situation does not always match what can be demonstrated under real-world conditions. See what other examples you can think of in which you have noticed a difference in performance under real-world versus more protected conditions. How could those differences be bridged or overcome? Now you can better see why this chapter is an important part of community psychology's understanding of prevention and promotion.

Community psychology has been at the forefront of looking at what happens when a community brings a social action program into a new setting—whether the goals are promoting competence, preventing problems, treating existing difficulties, or a combination of these. This topic integrates personality theory, learning theory, clinical, social, health, environmental, and school psychology, community mental health, public health, and, of course, community psychology. Implementation represents a crucial frontier between action and research.

WHAT REALLY HAPPENS WHEN PREVENTION/ PROMOTION IS CARRIED OUT IN COMMUNITIES?

"What is seen often is not real;
what is real often is not seen."

How does this saying apply to prevention and promotion initiatives? Articles in research journals devoted to these topics describe well-funded demonstration projects involving committed and well-trained staff, occurring in settings that value innovation, supported with a variety of resources, and studied in detail by program evaluation researchers. The unseen is what happens in community contexts: classrooms, Head Start centers, after-school youth groups, workplaces, senior citizen programs, community-based drug abuse prevention coalitions, and other settings where there is rarely an experimental design in place and no one is available to chronicle what actually happens towards reaching prevention/ promotion goals. (See Primavera, 2004, for an example of the importance of local processes and relationships in a community program.)

What else does the saying imply? What does it say to those who want to bring programs into their home settings? From a community psychology perspective, there must be an ecological match, or fit, between the context in which a program has been demonstrated and the context of its future application. Programs developed and studied under conditions of heavy funding, motivation, and resources rarely find their future environments to be similarly endowed. As a result, many failures to replicate "successful" efforts are reported in the literature.

Yet some local settings contain programs that could be quite valuable in other places. However, documentation of how these programs operate may be lacking, inadequate, or not widely distributed. In the previous chapters we reviewed various types of prevention/promotion programs with sound empirical evidence for their effectiveness. In this chapter we describe ways to close the gap between rhetoric and reality, moving from images held out in journal articles, demonstration projects, and well-funded program initiatives toward what will endure in the day-to-day grind of settings with limited resources, such as those in your neighborhood. We seek answers to this question: What can community psychology do to make sure that what we know about prevention/promotion is actually used in communities?

In this chapter we discuss how prevention and promotion initiatives really are complex *operator-dependent innovations.* That is a fancy way of saying that implementing them consistently and with high quality is difficult because they are greatly influenced by numerous critical decisions made by the people who carry them out. First, we ask whether available prevention/promotion interventions are widely implemented effectively and find the answer is often "no." Second, we describe some reasons why this is so, involving ecological contexts and characteristics of prevention initiatives. Third, we present issues to be considered when planning and implementing prevention programs, especially their relationship to setting constraints and resources. Fourth, we propose an analogy to a conductor and orchestra and present a conductor's guide to implementation. We then illustrate that analogy with a description of a two-decades-long process of implementation of one prevention/promotion program. We conclude with thoughts about the current and future importance of attending to implementation issues.

HAVE WELL-IMPLEMENTED PREVENTION/ PROMOTION INNOVATIONS BEEN SUSTAINED OVER TIME?

We illustrate challenges for implementing prevention and promotion approaches with a recent study of the operation of such approaches in schools. As you learned in Chapter 10, the evidence is clear that school-based prevention/promotion innovations can provide children with skills, supportive environments, and positive life opportunities that lessen their risk for a variety of health-compromising actions. Much has been learned about how to implement them effectively, as we have discussed. The next big question for community psychology to address is: Once programs are well implemented, to what extent are they sustained and what factors seem to influence sustainability?

The CASEL Model Site Sustainability Study

In 1997, the Collaborative for Academic, Social, and Emotional Learning (www.CASEL.org) published *Promoting Social and Emotional Learning: Guidelines for Educators* (Elias, Zins et al., 1997). Part of this book contained the results of site visits around the United States designed to identify model sites of schools carrying out high-quality, empirically supported prevention-oriented social-emotional learning (SEL) programs.

TABLE 11.1 Characteristics of Well-Implemented, Sustained Prevention Programs

1. **Active administrative support.** This provides long-term continuity in leadership and the ongoing, high-quality involvement of staff, parents, and community.
2. **Ongoing training and professional development.** This includes staff training, involvement of committed, skillful teachers as role models, and peer support among teams of teachers.
3. **Integration of the program into the school.** This includes institutionalizing the program into school policy, everyday practices, and budget, making the program a routine part of the school.

Five years later, CASEL asked: How many sites were still functioning as model sites? To what extent do they embody features that current research suggests are characteristic of long-lasting programs implemented with fidelity? The theoretical framework used to examine the sustainability of these model sites focused on three elements: the motivation and readiness of the school for the program, the resources available for program implementation, and validation of the program's benefits by key decision makers. Twenty-one interviews were conducted, representing 14 programs in the United States. The interviews covered current program components and the history of changes since inception of the SEL program, satisfaction with the program and changes over time, and factors that sustained (or impeded) the program over time.

The results are summarized in Table 11.1. Six programs were clearly Sustained, and four had retreated significantly in status or quality (Detached or Discontinued). Four other programs were in a status designated as Developing, implying that active steps were being taken to restore them to their prior status. Clearly, not every program was sustainable. Three main areas differentiated Sustained and Developing programs, which sustained their high level of implementation, from those that declined (Elias & Kamarinos, 2003):

First, active administrative support for the program was critical for organizational commitment: for adoption and sustaining of the program by teachers and other staff, for obtaining money and other resources, and for explaining the program to parents and community members. When administrative turnover occurred, programs proceeded with minimal disruption, usually because program developers engaged new administrators and offered program consultation to school staff. Sustainability can take a long-term emotional toll on even its most committed members if the program is in a constant state of reinvention or uncertainty.

Second, sustained implementation required ongoing professional development about the program among teams of committed staff (teachers and others). This required some staff to become program advocates and role models. Sustainability is more likely when professional development is continual and implementers have a constantly deepening understanding of the theoretical principles and pedagogy upon which the program is based. When teams of implementers with a deep commitment to the program work together, they can often maintain program momentum even during times of turnover. Most important, deep understanding of program principles allows implementers to adapt programs in response to changing circumstances yet maintain key program elements.

Third, sustained programs were integrated with other courses and into the mainstream of the school day and routine. This included use of the program in reading, health, and social studies as well as in school assemblies, school discipline and resolution of conflicts among students, and expectations for playground and lunchroom behavior. Integration takes place over a period of years and includes the program's becoming a regular part of the school budget; external funding is often available only for a few years or can change over time.

These findings converge with other studies. McLaughlin and Mitra (2001) analyzed the staying power of school reforms over a five-year period and found that deep learning of theory and planned, proactive training of staff and administrators were important factors. Initial support for an innovation by administration and staff was less important than predicted when the innovation had a clear, feasible path of implementation and its benefits were soon apparent. Lessons about sustaining innovations in schools are similar to those in other workplaces. Administrative energy and direction are essential for sustainability, but overcoming turnover requires an educated, committed workforce. Administrative commitment, deep involvement of the workforce in ongoing change (especially at a face-to-face microsystem level), and innovations that address integral parts of the organization's mission all foster sustainability (Elias & Kamarinos, 2003).

An Action Research Perspective on Program Development

Lewin's concept of action research is a guiding framework for implementing prevention/promotion programs in school and community settings (see Chapters 2, 3, 4, and 14). Action research involves testing theories and methods by putting them into practice, evaluating their impact, and using the results to refine future theory, method, and practice. Action research is seen as involving ongoing cycles of problem analysis, innovation (intervention) design, field trials, and innovation diffusion (dissemination), leading to ever more precise variations and targeting of programs to recipient populations and settings (Price & Smith, 1985). The entire model is cyclical because ongoing monitoring of problem areas yields information about whether or not the program is having a significant impact. This information leads to further cycles of developing, evaluating, and refining prevention innovations. Important models for this process include Fairweather's Experimental Social Innovation and Dissemination (ESID) approach (Fairweather, 1967; Hazel & Onanga, 2003) and the prevention science approach embodied in the IOM Report (Mrazek & Haggerty, 1994).

Rossi (1978) addressed the issue of how a program evolves from its beginnings to having real public health impact. He believed the central question is how the program operates when carried out by agents other than the developers. The process of going from original development of an innovation to its widespread implementation is sometimes referred to as **scaling up** (Schorr, 1997). That process represents the core of this chapter. Combining this work with a community psychology perspective, four stages of program development and implementation can be identified.

- **Experimental development:** A program demonstrates its effectiveness under small-scale, optimal, highly controlled conditions compared to a control group.
- **Technological application:** A program demonstrates effectiveness under real-world conditions, similar to the conditions for which it is eventually intended but still under the guidance of its developers.
- **Diffusion of innovation:** A program is adopted by other organizations or communities and demonstrates effectiveness under real-world conditions when not under the direct scrutiny and guidance of its developers.
- **Widespread implementation:** The diffusion stage brings the program to a few communities only. Implementation becomes widespread when a program continues to show its effectiveness in a wide variety of settings and is transferred from its developers to new implementers, who in turn conduct further program diffusion. The program has widespread impact only when this final stage occurs.

The challenge of widespread implementation can be illustrated in the following example. A developer of innovative science education programs at the American Association for the Advancement of Science noted that he gets calls, requests, letters, and the like from all over the country from people who are excited about the work of his innovative project and want his help to implement it in their communities. He tells them he can't. Why? Because "there are more of you than there are of us" (Rutherford in Olson, 1994, p. 43).

The School Intervention Implementation Study

The School Intervention Implementation Study (SIIS) was an empirical study of what happens when programs developed under carefully controlled conditions are placed into the schools under naturalistic conditions, which means they typically have fewer resources than they did when they were being developed and closely studied. Surveys were sent to the approximately 550 operating school districts in New Jersey, which has a variety of district organizational arrangements and styles that cover the range of what can be found nationally (Elias, Gager, & Hancock, 1993). The overall response rate was 65 percent, highly satisfactory for a study of this kind and scope.

Although the SIIS survey revealed many programs in operation across New Jersey, there was little consistency in their implementation. The vast majority of districts were doing "something" related to the prevention of substance abuse and the promotion of social competence. However, what was taking place was not systematic. In spite of mandates and encouragement for programming from kindergarten to twelfth grade, only 10 percent of the districts had a program running throughout the elementary years, 6 percent had a program throughout middle school, and 12 percent throughout high school. One-third of the districts had at least four grade levels that received no prevention programming. Children receive little continuity in prevention programming within or across communities, and there appears to be an inexplicable neglect of programs for children classified as needing special education services. Further, the programs that were used were not necessarily those supported by a track record of empirical evidence of effectiveness or even a documented history of effective use and positive impact in other, similar districts. One surprise: Even in districts where well-supported programs were implemented under favorable conditions, instances of implementation success were matched by instances of failure. Finally, even the most promising programs showed an uneven record of being adopted (Gager & Elias, 1997).

Goleman (1998) found similar trends in many workplaces. In his study of hotels, police departments, manufacturing plants, teaching hospitals, and other work settings, programs to strengthen employees' social and emotional well-being were often successful in one setting but not in another. Best practices for implementing programs often were not recognized or followed. Therefore, understanding implementation of innovations and ways to bring best practices into common practice is becoming central to a prevention/promotion perspective.

Even those who have created successful demonstration models of school reform and community development, such as Sizer (Coalition of Essential Schools); Slavin (Success for All); Pinnell (Reading Recovery); Levin (Accelerated Schools Project); Dryfoos (Full Service Schools); Comer (School Development Program); Wandersman, Chavis, and Florin (Block Booster and Center for Substance Abuse Prevention Coalition-Building Programs); and Wolff (Community Partners), have found their work spread only to a limited number of settings. They have not solved the problem of how to bring their work to the public more broadly. Similar stories have been told by those working in mental health (Schorr, 1988).

From a community psychology perspective, then, one good way to implement and disseminate prevention/promotion activities is to focus on working with existing settings to help them become more innovative. When this happens, settings become dedicated to the continuous improvement of their own impact on their own members. That leads to adopting innovative practices in ways that are effective in that setting. This is especially true with the KISS settings you learned about in Chapter 9. Creating such organizational cultures, particularly in the schools, is among the most powerful ways to build and maintain competence in children and adolescents and serve the goal of prevention (Elias & Clabby, 1992).

WHY ARE PREVENTION/PROMOTION INNOVATIONS NOT WIDELY ADOPTED?

In *The Path of Most Resistance: Reflections on Lessons Learned from New Futures*, staff of the Annie E. Casey Foundation (1995) described the failure of the New Futures program, which cost in excess of $100 million over five years, to help

10 mid-sized cities develop and implement plans to prevent problem behaviors in at-risk youth. The cities receiving the grant awards ensured that their plans reflected the best-known work in the literature to date. All plans received extensive review and comment. The level of funding was far more than typically is available for implementing prevention/promotion initiatives. Here is an excerpt from their report:

> At the heart of New Futures was the belief that at-risk youth are beset by multiple challenges and served ineffectively by multiple systems of service delivery. Real changes in aggregate youth outcomes would require fundamental and deep changes in existing institutions and systems. Such an approach would not only serve vulnerable children and families more effectively, but it was also the only way to proceed, given the scarce public resources available for significant additions to existing youth-serving systems.
>
> By challenging communities to design comprehensive systems reforms rather than to add programs, New Futures had embarked on the path of most resistance. . . . Vested interests in current practice, fiscal constraints, and political risks created a constant force capable of minimizing system change. Some parts of the reform agenda threatened the stability of the current system, and others seemed to discount the importance of the good aspects of the system that already existed. . . . True integration at the service-delivery level, we learned, requires unprecedented commitments by school boards, child welfare agencies, and other youth-serving institutions to subordinate their traditional authority over critical functions—including budgeting, staffing, and resource allocation—in favor of collective decision making. (Annie E. Casey Foundation, 1995, pp. 1–2)

What lessons must we learn from this? What accounts for what happened? Is there any hope in continuing such efforts? Perhaps you arrived at these thoughts: Money alone will not bring about effective competence promotion and problem prevention efforts, and incorporating best practices into one's plans does not ensure success. Yet despite the failure of New Futures, many other, often smaller and less-well-funded, prevention efforts succeed.

The CASEL, SIIS, and Goleman (1998) studies cited earlier indicate inconsistencies in the content, structure, and effectiveness of prevention/promotion programs. Why? One reason is context, the ecological characteristics of each setting. The qualities of settings that we described in Chapter 5, the nature of a community in Chapter 6, the dimensions of diversity in Chapter 7, and other factors yet to be understood greatly influence the nature and impact of prevention/promotion initiatives.

Let's think of settings in terms of Kelly's (1970) ecological concepts (recall these from Chapter 5). Every setting has a unique set of interdependent relationships among its members. In one workplace, for instance, the supervisors may be more approachable and informal with employees, which may generate employee participation in a workplace exercise program or group meetings designed to foster teamwork. In a different setting, the same programs may fall flat because relationships between supervisors and line staff are more formal and distant.

TABLE 11.2 Seven Characteristics of Prevention/Promotion Innovations in Host Settings

Operator dependent
Context dependent
Fragile, difficult to specify
Core versus adaptive components
Organizationally unbounded
Challenging
Longitudinal

Further, tangible and intangible resources cycle through every setting. A high school may have an English teacher whose interpersonal skills and trustworthiness lead many students to seek her advice. She may be the ideal choice for leading a suicide or drug abuse prevention program, whereas in another setting it may be the soccer coach or even someone from outside the school. These persons will put their stamp on the program, making it different from a program elsewhere that looks the same on paper. Other resources include money, level of support from parents or administrators, and even whether the room where the program occurs is appropriate.

Prevention/promotion innovations inevitably are influenced by the ways in which individuals naturally adapt to their settings. The culture and customs of an urban school mainly attended by students of Caribbean ancestry, for instance, will differ from those in a European-American suburb. The interpersonal skills needed for adaptation will also be different, and any prevention/promotion innovation must recognize and address these circumstances.

Finally, Kelly's (1970) principle of succession means that a setting has a history, representing both continuity and change over time. An effective prevention/promotion innovation must address that history, respecting the culture of the setting while offering new directions for its development. Taken as a whole, Kelly's concepts suggest many issues for prevention/promotion practitioners to consider when transferring an effective, innovative program to a new setting.

Seven Characteristics of Prevention/Promotion Innovations in Host Settings

Table 11.2 lists seven characteristics of prevention/promotion program innovations that affect ecological relationships in a host setting. These characteristics can be obstacles to dissemination or transfer of an effective program from one setting to another. When planners of an innovation address these issues, their efforts are much more likely to be effective.

Operator Dependent Rossi (1978) coined this term to refer to the fact that innovation and social change rely on human beings as the means of change. Clinical trials of a new medication use the same substance, in standardized dosage and treatment procedure, in every setting tested. The nature of a prevention/promotion program, in contrast, depends on the persons involved in it. For instance, consider a school curriculum intended to lessen student drug use. Teacher/staff attitudes and commitment to the program, and their enthusiasm or lack of it, play an important role. Student peer leaders or outside speakers may enhance the program impact, depending on how they are selected, trained, and used. Program leaders may use curriculum activities carefully, or they may devise their own approach. Support from administration and from parents is also crucial for success. Similar factors affect how corporate or community programs are conducted.

In any psychologically relevant prevention/promotion initiative, the decisions made by program staff and participants are perhaps the single greatest influence on its impact. Those decisions are strongly affected by the relationship between the developer of an innovation and the staff who will implement it (Stolz, 1984).

One aspect of operator dependence is that to be taken seriously, an innovation must mesh with the developmental stage and self-conceptions of the staff who implement it. Skilled staff members in any setting take pride in their craft and view their work with a sense of ownership. To gain their approval, an innovation must fit their values and identity: for instance, a police officer's sense of what police work involves. At the same time, an innovation must also offer something new that increases the staff's effectiveness as they define it. Staff members of different ages, ranks in the organization, or levels of seniority may support or resist an innovation, depending on how they understand their work and roles.

Context Dependent Staff members or operators are not the only humans involved in a prevention/promotion innovation. The participants or recipients of the initiative also influence its impact, as does the social ecology of the setting. In the example of a school-based drug use prevention program mentioned earlier, student culture and expectations affect the classroom climate and may even undermine any impact of the program. For instance, research indicates that such a program is more likely to be effective with younger adolescents, before drug experimentation or mistrust of adults becomes more common (Linney, 1990). Thus, developmental stage and self-conception are as important for program participants as for program operators.

Each school, workplace, or community has a mix of ages, genders, races and ethnicities, income levels, and other forms of diversity and personal identity that an innovation must address. These factors affect the social norms of the setting and the skills and resources of its members, and therefore the goals of a prevention/promotion innovation. Furthermore, an innovation may draw a different response in a setting with a strong sense of community among its members compared to one without it.

Finally, the program circuits of the setting (Barker, 1968; recall this from Chapter 5) constrain any prevention/promotion innovation. Middle and high schools restrict most activities to strictly timed periods, for instance. Neighborhood programs must provide child care and other practical support to meet the needs of their participants.

Fragile, Difficult to Specify As with any means of teaching or social influence, the key elements of a prevention/promotion program may be difficult to specify (Tornatzky & Fleischer, 1986). At first, it is easy to assume that the new curriculum in a school-based initiative or the new policy in a corporation or community is the critical element. But a moment's reflection undoes that assumption: psychological innovations are operator dependent, not standardized. Yet what aspect of that operator dependence is the key? Is it participant expectations, staff skill or commitment, extent of staff training or supervision, how much time or money is committed by the organization to the program, whether the top leadership makes clear its support, or other factors? Is a committed, energetic staff the key, regardless of what curriculum they use? Is it the use of small-group exercises and discussion rather than lecture? In one setting one of these factors may be the key, whereas another variable is crucial elsewhere. There are often multiple keys to success. This uncertainty makes the program fragile in the sense that it will assume different forms in different settings, with different effects. It may never be implemented the same way across settings.

In a sense, transferring an effective innovation to a new host setting is impossible (London & MacDuffie, 1985). Operators in the new setting inevitably will make changes in the program to fit their needs, values, and local culture. Indeed, some of these changes are necessary to respect the history and culture of that setting. In the long run, this can be a strength, because a setting committed to innovation can develop prevention/promotion initiatives that fit its context. However, an innovation that is difficult to specify may leave its operators unsure of their roles and responsibilities at first. That uncertainty may be welcomed by bold personalities and by those who are confident of support from their superiors; it may be resisted by others who prefer more structure or who feel unsupported.

Core versus Adaptive Components Despite the challenges we have just mentioned, developers of prevention/promotion innovations need to specify the key components of their programs, especially when they transfer their initiatives to new host settings. Two types of components have been identified. Core components are crucial to the identity and effectiveness of the program and need to be transferred with fidelity and care. Adaptive components may be altered to fit the social ecology or practical constraints of the new host setting (Price & Lorion, 1989).

For one school-based innovation, the core aspect may the written curriculum and skills to be taught. For another, its characteristic method of small-group exercises and discussion is the key; its written curriculum can be adapted to the host setting context. For some innovations, building social support among program participants is the core feature regardless of how that is done. For other innovations, particularly educational ones, learning skills is the core feature, whereas methods of promoting that learning may be adapted to the setting.

Developers and advocates need to pay considerable attention to how core features are being used by the operators in a new host setting. They also need to help those operators develop their own ways of implementing the adaptive features, to fit the circumstances of the setting. Of course, the more difficult it is to specify the core components (see the preceding section), the more difficult this task becomes.

Organizationally Unbounded For many prevention/promotion initiatives, effectiveness means changes in many areas of the host setting or organization (Tornatzky & Fleischer, 1986). Prevention/promotion programs are not isolated; they are connected to many persons and setting activities. (Recall Kelly's principle of interdependence.) For instance, Comer's (1988) approach to improving school climate involves strengthening relationships among teachers, all other staff, students, and parents. Comer (1992) noted that in a middle school using this approach, a new student, whose foot was stepped on by another student, immediately squared off to fight, a behavior expected in his former school. "Hey, man, we don't do that here," he was told by several other students, who succeeded in defusing the tension. That is an organizationally unbounded innovation. It began with strengthening adult-adult and adult-student relationships yet spread to student-student relationships. Those outcomes may be affected as much by a custodian, secretary, or parent volunteer as by teachers or administrators. They may include changes in behavior out of class, not just in it.

An effective, organizationally unbounded innovation is a fine thing to have, but it is difficult to introduce. To members of the host setting, it may seem to lack focus or to require abrupt changes from everyone all at once. Those who believe that a problem is limited to one area of the organization will resist involvement. For instance, a school may implement a number of innovations to prevent violence in school. Those who believe that violence prevention is solely a disciplinary matter will resist changes in curriculum to teach students skills in conflict resolution or training of student peer mediators for informal resolution of conflicts. They may say things like, "That's the vice-principal's job, not mine," or, "Dealing with misbehavior is an adult's job."

Challenging Any innovation is a challenge to a setting. By its nature, it suggests that change is needed. At the same time, that challenge may be understood by staff or program participants as an opportunity for growth or as an answer to a problem. These perceptions may depend on whether the organization is responding to a crisis and whether the innovation is believed to require change that is difficult or feasible, abrupt or gradual. Even the language that innovators use may contribute to those perceptions.

If you have studied developmental psychology, you have no doubt encountered Piaget's distinction between assimilation and accommodation (Flavell, 1963, p. 47). Like individuals in Piaget's theory, organizations also tend to assimilate their experiences to fit their existing ways of thinking if possible. Only if necessary do they accommodate those ways of thinking to incorporate new ideas or practices. Interventions that fail to respect and use the existing culture of a setting—its history, rituals, symbols, and practices—will be rejected or assimilated only partially or in distorted form. A program that is adopted because of pressure from above or outside an organization also is likely to be abandoned as soon as that pressure abates. Innovations that respect organizational culture and that are based on collaboration with stakeholders can lead to accommodation in organizational thinking and practices, and thus to lasting changes.

Weick (1984) mustered evidence from social and cognitive psychology for the conclusion that when extensive changes are required of humans in organizations, their sense of being threatened rises, as does their resistance to change. When the proposed change seems smaller, the perceived threat is smaller, risks seem tolerable, allies are easier to attract, and opponents are less mobilized. **Small wins** is Weick's term for limited yet tangible innovations or changes that can establish a record of success and sense of momentum. In such a context, advocates of prevention/promotion must consider their language. If they portray their innovation as a logical outgrowth of the setting's history to date and as a sensible response to current challenges, resistance is lessened.

When an organization or community believes itself to be in crisis or facing problems that require sweeping change, more challenging innovations may be accepted. Indeed, under those conditions, small wins may be seen as inadequate. However, most innovations take place in a climate less charged by a sense of crisis.

Longitudinal This idea is similar to Kelly's principle of succession. An innovation takes place in a setting with a history and culture. To be effective, it must change that setting in some way (Tornatzky & Fleischer, 1986). To be lasting, it must become part of that history and culture, not dependent on an influential leader or a few staff members, all of whom will eventually leave the setting. It must be **institutionalized**, made a part of the setting's routine functioning. Consider a youth group, a support group for senior citizens, or an organization at your college or university. How would it be different if a new, untrained leader runs it every year versus having a longer-term leader who, when she does leave, trains her successor well?

Moreover, any effective prevention/promotion innovation must be repeated or elaborated periodically for effect. One-shot presentations or activities seldom have lasting impact. Teaching a child to read is a multiyear effort, from identifying letters to reading novels (Shriver, 1992). Should it be any surprise that learning social-emotional skills or developing attitudes that limit risky behavior cannot be done quickly?

Summary Prevention/promotion innovations, by their nature, face obstacles to being adopted within organizations and communities. They are dependent on operators, usually staff who must implement the innovation. They also are dependent on the social context and even physical environment in which the innovation takes place. Their key elements may be difficult to specify or explain and fragile or difficult to transfer to new settings. They challenge organizational thinking and tradition and may generate resistance. They must be sustained over time to be effective.

These qualities represent obstacles for prevention advocates, yet they also suggest the presence of resources. The operators and participants on whom a program is dependent represent potential resources for enriching that innovation, if they are approached as partners and their life experiences and culture respected. Resistance to a proposed change may be rooted in loyalty and commitment to the setting or community, a resource that can also be channeled beneficially.

Advocates of prevention/promotion need to understand these challenges, respect their sources, and work with members of a setting or community to overcome them.

IMPLEMENTING PREVENTION/PROMOTION INITIATIVES WIDELY AND EFFECTIVELY

For an article discussing the challenges of doing effective preventive work in community settings, Kelly (1979b) took his title from a hit song of the 1940s, "Tain't what you do, it's the way you do it." In working to improve community life, means, or how we do things, matter as much as ends, or goals. How implementers of a prevention/promotion effort form relationships with collaborators and citizens is critical to ultimate success and integrity. Our preceding discussion of prevention/promotion as complex, operator-dependent initiatives suggests some reasons why this is so. Human beings (teachers, nurses, parents, program staff) implement programs. The work of community psychologists and others who want to initiate prevention efforts involves forming relationships with these persons. Implementers must communicate clearly the core program elements that must be faithfully replicated while also collaborating with those in the host setting to modify adaptive features so that they will "fit" the local and particular qualities of that setting. Moreover, both the intended and unintended effects of the program must be studied because these are not necessarily going to conform to patterns shown in the original setting in which the program was developed. To paraphrase Kelly (1979b), it's both "what you do" and "the way you do it" that matter.

Ten Considerations for Praxis and Implementation

Prospective implementers of a prevention/promotion initiative must consider many factors. These are summarized in Table 11.3 and are drawn from a number of reviews of community psychology practices (e.g., Chavis, 1993; Elias, 1994; Price, Cowen, Lorion, & Ramos-McKay, 1988; Vincent & Trickett, 1983; Wolff, 1987, 1994).

There is no precise way to express the relationship among the considerations in Table 11.3. Each might be considered a necessary but not sufficient condition for what we describe as **praxis**: program implementation that integrates action, research, and reflection while developing the program and sustaining it over time, and while taking into account the program objectives and the actual ongoing outcomes of the program. Thus praxis refers to implementation that is at least somewhat different in every setting, taking into account the considerations in Table 11.3 and linked with community psychology's commitment to participant conceptualization.

Among the considerations in Table 11.3, **context** refers to the developmental levels and concerns of program staff (e.g., both their age-related concerns and

TABLE 11.3 Considerations in the Praxis of Prevention/Promotion Innovations

Praxis:

Implementation of program, with integration of action, research, and reflection on program objectives and actual ongoing program outcomes.

Considerations:

Context: Developmental, historical, and situational context of the program

Grounding: Understanding of the problem and the literature

Theory: Clarity about theoretical perspectives

Learning: Principles for creating effective, supportive learning environments

Instructional Strategies: Appropriate strategies, tailored to particular groups of learners

Formats: Appealing, engaging delivery systems and formats

Materials: Evidence-based, user-friendly materials

Hospitable Organizational Context: Readiness for the program

Resources: Available, accessible resources to support program implementation

Constraints: Constraints, limitations, and obstacles to program implementation

their seniority in the setting), historical issues in that setting (e.g., prior experiences with similar innovations), and situational factors salient there. Cultural traditions and norms may influence historical or situational forces. **Grounding** in the problem and literature and clarity about **theory** both reflect the need for implementers to understand not only the problem and research literature, but also the conceptual underpinnings of the program. Whose previous work is a useful guide? What theories or concepts are being drawn upon? What are the implicit values? How closely do these match those of the prospective or current host setting? How similar are previous implementation contexts to the one being considered now?

Have you ever attended a class or workshop on an interesting, timely topic, yet found that it was primarily a lecture, with unclear objectives, poor handouts, delivered without evident caring, and with inadequate time for questions? That experience illustrates the importance of the next four considerations: using principles for creating effective, supportive **learning environments**; appropriate **instructional strategies**; appealing and engaging **delivery formats**; and evidence-based, user-friendly **materials**. These terms relate specifically to the mechanics of creating change.

Change often involves some kind of education or reeducation. Much has been learned about techniques for accomplishing this kind of education, although remarkably little of it finds its way into the psychological intervention literature, in part because of traditional research design and publication-related constraints. For a prevention/promotion intervention to be effective, it must use effective learning principles. These include attending to the amount of information presented and the pace of presentation; strategies that are geared to the audiences, whether adults or children, professionals or novices, or members of particular cultural groups; consonant behavioral tactics, which typically involve active learning and examples and a style that communicates caring; and supportive materials that enhance the learning and give people something to take home with them.

Hospitable organizational context refers to the readiness of the host setting for the program. Price and Lorion (1989) and Van de Ven (1986) emphasized that members of an organization must be ready to accept an innovation, preventive or otherwise. There must be a perception that there is environmental pressure, or at least support, for the innovation along with an awareness and acceptance of a problem by the host organization and a set of attitudes, beliefs, and practices held by staff that is compatible with the prevention/promotion effort being proposed. The innovation must be able to find a place within the structures and services already in the host organization, and the staff must be able to imagine how they can relate to it.

In any action-research situation, one must consider the balance of **resources** and **constraints**. Certain types of resources—funds, facilities, and expertise—must be accessible, and potential implementers will require reassurance that all these supports are in place. Constraints—which include shortages of resources but also such factors as a negative history with prior innovations, poor morale, distrust among different levels within the host setting, unstable hiring or retention practices, and other types of organizational instability—all work against effective implementation. If resources are not in place and/or constraints are considerable, more groundwork needs to be laid before the innovation is introduced, a process Sarason (1982) has aptly termed what happens "before the beginning." Even a cursory look at Table 11.3 makes clear the challenge of innovations occurring in contexts of poverty, violence, distrust, and apathy and the need for much groundwork to be laid before embarking upon them with a hope of lasting success.

In summary, change agents interested in prevention must be prepared to immerse themselves into local settings and contexts; to be patient; and to build and extend their ranks through participation, collaboration, and explication (O'Donnell, Tharp, & Wilson, 1993). It is a tenet of the field that the energy and direction for solutions for social problems come from the local level (Cowen, 1977; Price & Cherniss, 1977). As we learned earlier, another tenet is that small wins are powerful and can build momentum for sustained change (Weick, 1984). There is much that can be accomplished in the area of prevention and promotion if innovators are prepared to implement efforts with creativity, tenacity, and integrity.

Applying the Ten Considerations: An Exercise

Imagine that you are in charge of adapting a prevention/promotion program for a middle school to reduce the risk of violence among students in school. Use the implementation considerations in Table 11.3 as a guide to planning your approach.

First, you will gather information about the developmental, historical, and situational **Context** of the school and community. What violent acts are of concern here? What sorts of violence or related problems occur regularly, such as fights, bullying, hazing, or sexual harassment? Are these linked to factors such as cliques among students, gang activity, or drug use? Do adults in the school condone violence as a means of resolving conflicts? What are community attitudes about violence? Who else in the community is conducting similar efforts? What have they learned, and how might they be resources? How has the school addressed this issue before, and what were the results?

Second, you look closely at the research and practice literature about the problem and how it has been addressed (**Grounding**). You identify a program that has been shown to be effective in a demonstration project at a school located near the university where this program was developed. However, the school is different from yours in many ways, including the socioeconomic and racial profile of students, the makeup of the teaching staff, and the extent of monitoring of program implementation by the developers of the innovation. You then look at the way in which the program is structured. You note positively the presence of a skills-oriented approach with many interactive exercises, multimedia, and modules to address different cultural subgroups (**Theory, Learning Environment, Instructional Strategies, Delivery Formats, Materials**). A trip to an educational materials library shows you that the materials are moderately user friendly. As you turn your attention to the middle school in which you will work, you note there is a new principal but an experienced staff and an involved, supportive parents' group. Both teachers and parents believe that something should be done to address the issue of violence, although they have a diversity of ideas about how to do that. Overall, **Resources** appear to outweigh **Constraints**, as long as the experienced staff members support an innovation (**Hospitable Organizational Context**). Your question now is: How can I bring the core elements of the program into my school, retaining its effectiveness while adapting it to the local and particular qualities of my setting?

Box 11.1 illustrates how some of these issues, especially the importance of assembling and organizing resources and paying attention to context, apply when a prevention/promotion is being implemented in multiple countries.

Historical Stages in the Process of Adapting Innovations to Settings

Historically, concepts of how best to transfer effective educational programs and adapt them to new host settings have evolved through four stages (RMC Research Corporation, 1995), which we summarize below.

- **Cookbook:** In the 1970s it was believed that programs had to be thoroughly documented, ideally in "kits" that could be followed precisely, step by step.
- **Replication:** Later, model programs were replicated by having staff trained in the methods used by program developers and then bringing these methods back to their own settings to be carried out as similarly as possible but with some room for individual adaptation.
- **Adaptation:** By the late 1980s, models were understood to require adaptation to the unique context of the host site, ideally by having the developer serve as a consultant in making the necessary changes.

BOX 11.1 Bringing JOBS to Multiple Countries and Contexts

The JOBS program (described in Chapter 10) has been implemented across different cultures. Its chief developer, Richard Price (2002), identified many potential cultural misunderstandings during the collaborative process. Dimensions along which misunderstandings can occur include time orientation, orientation to authority, negotiation style, gender roles, assumptions about the nature of people, sense of the self, task orientation, and communication style. (Recall that we discussed some of these in Chapter 7 in our section on individualism-collectivism.) Price suggests that successful collaborations in multiple countries or localities require "local cultural partners" who serve as guides to the local context. The collaboration thus consists of technical expertise on the part of program developers and consultants and context expertise on the part of local experts. Here is how he describes the work in Finland, China, and California (pp. 3-4):

> Let us first consider Finland. With the breakup of the Soviet Union Finland lost its principal trading partner and unemployment skyrocketed to nearly 20%. Finland still has a strong tradition as a welfare state political economy. Government officials believe that it is important to strengthen the safety net of government services to cushion the blows of unemployment. Furthermore in Finland where the state assumes considerable responsibility for the welfare of its citizens, the government infrastructure already exists for disseminating social services and practices.
>
> A very different picture emerges in the People's Republic of China as the context for implementation of the JOBS program. China is engaged in economic reform and a dramatic shift from socialism to a market economy. The "Iron Rice Bowl" of benefits and services associated with one's job is being broken in favor of market capitalism. This means the security of jobs in state owned enterprises is disappearing and workers "leap into the sea" of an uncertain employment and economic future. At the same time government officials in China are very concerned about social unrest associated with large-scale unemployment and are therefore positively disposed to implement programs to help workers make the transition to a new job when they are laid off from their jobs in state owned enterprises.
>
> In California the picture is different in still other ways. California is subject to a "boom and bust" economy. Like much of the rest of the United States, the social service system in California is in a period of devolution. There is a strong move to get rid of state services and public services are being dismantled in health, labor, education and other arenas. What social services exist in California do so because private nonprofit and for-profit organizations contract with the state to deliver the services, and each agency operates in a competitive entrepreneurial environment. In addition, private foundations attempt to mend some holes in the safety net with private philanthropy in support of service programs for vulnerable populations.

Price also emphasized the importance of local "implementation champions" who served as essential guides for program success (p. 4):

> Each champion did so by understanding the particular problem- framing needed to make an argument that the JOBS program would be crucial to implement in their own particular cultural and political setting. The champion also recognized key challenges or dilemmas to be solved before the JOBS program could be accepted and implemented. To respond to the challenge or dilemma, they had to create an organizational arrangement that worked in their own political and cultural context responding to the challenge. Finally, in making the deal they used their own cultural map in a distinctive way that took advantage of the leverage available in their own cultural and political settings.

The JOBS program champion in Finland, a scientist in the Finnish Institute of Occupational Health, recognized that implementation would not take place until a pilot program demonstrated that JOBS was consistent with Finnish culture and arranged for a study to take place. In China, the champion was a psychologist at the National Academy of Sciences and an influential actor in the People's Consultative Party in China. She recognized that a top-down model was essential and so she used her social network and personal political capital to obtain a "red letter" that directed local agencies in seven cities to cooperate in the JOBS project. California's champion was a social entrepreneur who served as a consultant to a California foundation. He capitalized on the convergence of the JOBS approach and local concerns about the risks of long-term unemployment, which was also part of the mission of the foundation.

BOX 11.1 (Continued)

Summarizing the case studies of implementation, Price (p. 5) identified three key elements that distinguish the work of cross-cultural and cross-context innovation champions:

- **Social capital and network access.** "In the case of China it was connections to the right official, in Finland it was connections to the right government agencies and in California it was connections to the right network of agencies and philanthropic foundations."
- **Knowledge about problem framing.** "They know that the crisis in China's unemployment problem is a source of social unrest, that in Finland unemployment is a government responsibility and requires government action; and that in California unemployment is seen not by the government but by a philanthropic foundation as relevant to the health problems of Californians."
- **Procedural knowledge.** "Procedural knowledge is deeply political and culturally specific in nature. Procedural knowledge tells culturally situated innovation champions how to get things done in unique cultural and political settings. In China a red letter opens doors and commands resources. In Finland intergovernmental agreements and empirical evidence unlock resources. In California building a coalition of agencies and foundations serves multiple interests and makes coalitions possible."

SOURCE: Price (2002).

- **Invention/Innovation:** Recently, models have been seen as sources of ideas and inspiration rather than procedures to replicate or adapt. There is emphasis on creating one's own program, tailored to the unique circumstances at a given time, yet using ideas gleaned from best practices literature. The exercise just presented embodies an invention/innovation approach.

Interestingly, these stages parallel some aspects of individual development illuminated by Jean Piaget and Erik Erikson. Like Piaget's stages of cognitive development (sensorimotor, preoperational, concrete, and formal operations), they progress from concrete experience and thinking to use of abstract principles applied to specific problems (e.g., invention/innovation).

In addition, many adult learners who play major roles in implementing prevention/promotion programs (e.g., teachers, parents, health professionals, community leaders) will be in Erikson's stage of *generativity* in middle adulthood (Erikson, 1950, 1982). At this stage, people have accumulated a certain amount of wisdom. They have "been there, done that." Yet they are open to change if it promises to lead to some positive impact on the next generation, especially something that transcends themselves (Sarason, 1993). They often will value creating more than following. Thus, development and ownership of an innovation are key elements. There is a special sense of fulfillment in being generative as opposed to replicating precisely that which others generated. This directly supports RMC's findings, as well as those of the CASEL Mode Site Study and SIIS discussed earlier, and helps explain why so many schools create their own programs out of existing ones rather than adopting programs developed by others. SIIS and other data indicate that the tendency to invent is greater than the tendency to adapt or adopt.

Thus, successfully disseminating a model program involves implementing and institutionalizing it in a new site while capturing the excellence of practice by linking practice to theory. As noted in the CASEL Model Site Sustainability

Study, what is transferred to others includes not only procedures but also an understanding of the principles that undergird a specific program or practice. From this perspective, it is not only necessary to "talk the talk and walk the walk;" it is necessary to "talk the walk," to explicate practice activities in an articulate and heuristic, generative, instructive, and inspiring manner (Elias, 1994; Fullan, 1994). The ten considerations in Table 11.3 provide guidance for a journey of development for prevention/promotion innovation in a new host setting. The destination and general route are indicated, but specific pathways, timing, obstacles and detours, and resting points are to be chosen by members of the setting. Community psychology, with its rich use of ecological and historical concepts, has much to offer to the study and practice of improving the way in which preventive and health-promoting innovations are organized to influence local settings and beyond.

To return to our example of implementing a program to prevent school violence, you might decide to study the context of the school deeply and to gather the ideas, support, and willing involvement of teachers, administrators and school board, parents, and students before implementing a program. You also might want to allow staff and others involved to exercise creative judgment and control over adaptive features of the program rather than expecting them to implement someone else's program in a concrete way. Yet you would also want to identify the core principles of that program, implementing them in ways faithful to its basic premises that are necessary for it to be effective. How can you balance these expectations? A musical analogy may help.

A CONDUCTOR'S GUIDE TO ENDURING IMPLEMENTATION

Our favorite analogy for implementing prevention/promotion innovations is that of a musical conductor, especially one who also arranges the orchestration of the music. As a conductor begins to practice the piece with a given orchestra's musicians in a given concert hall, the phrasing, tempo, and dynamics of sound may require adaptation from the music as written. In addition, there are times when the music itself has a few gaps in detail. Moreover, performing a piece is more than reading and literally reproducing the written score; performers and conductors must find ways to express the spirit of a composition. Conductors have certain principles that they follow to provide some guidance even as they must make unique and creative decisions. Similarly, there are principles that can guide those who embark on the complex, operator-dependent task of implementing a prevention/promotion initiative (Elias, Zins et al., 1997; Kelly et al., 1988; see Table 11.4).

1. **Carry out environmental reconnaissance** (Trickett, 1984). Do not promise or deliver a totally finished product. Instead, build the basis for action research by discussing the need for modifying any program adapted from elsewhere through careful study of its effects in this setting. The guiding

TABLE 11.4 Conductor's Guide to Orchestrating Prevention/Promotion Innovations

1. Carry out environmental reconnaissance.
2. Ensure strong agreement on program goals among all stakeholders.
3. Ensure connection of program goals to the core mission of the host setting.
4. Consider a coalition with related local settings.
5. Develop strong, clear leadership.
6. Describe the innovation in simple terms, especially in the beginning.
7. When the program begins, ensure implementation of its core principles and elements.
8. Measure program implementation and attainment of program objectives throughout the operation of the program.
9. Search for unintended effects of the program.
10. Plan for institutionalization of the program in the host setting.
11. Establish external linkages with similar programs in other settings.

principle is to start a pilot project using the most basic model that has been used in a similar setting and subsequently modify it. This can be done through the process of monitoring program implementation procedures, evaluating outcomes, providing feedback to the setting, and making appropriate modifications in the program (a process we discuss further in Chapter 14; see also Elias & Clabby, 1992).

2. **Ensure strong agreement on program goals among all stakeholders.** Teachers, administrators, parents, students, and other important groups are stakeholders in a school setting. In a locality, stakeholders include elected or other government officials, representatives of community and private organizations, and interested citizens. Stakeholders need to be included in wide-ranging discussion of the problem to be addressed by a prevention/promotion initiative. For instance, they need to discuss the nature of violence in your school district and community. They also need to set the goals of an intervention or program. Once goals are agreed upon, participants will have a guide for decisions about choice of model programs, implementation details, measuring program effects, and responding to critics.
3. **Ensure connection of program goals to the core mission of the host setting.** A host setting (e.g., school, worksite) is unlikely to adopt a prevention/promotion initiative unless its members can grasp a clear relationship between its purpose and the mission of their setting. For instance, in a school, prevention/promotion relates to students' needs in the areas of behavior and health, but it also relates to their academic education. A prevention/promotion program such as Interpersonal Cognitive Problem Solving (Shure, 1997) that teaches skills for everyday decision making and problem solving also should have implications for reasoning skills needed in academic subject areas (Elias, Zins et al., 1997).

4. **Consider a coalition with related local settings**. Many prevention/promotion initiatives concern a community problem not limited to a single school or setting. If your aims relate to a community-level problem, involve related community settings in the process of goal formation and program development. For a school-based violence prevention program, this might include police, domestic violence agencies, mental health or family guidance agencies, substance abuse treatment facilities, youth centers or recreation programs, local businesses, and religious congregations. Sometimes the stakeholders are more numerous than first appears obvious.
5. **Develop strong, clear leadership.** Hard choices will have to be made and mid-course corrections will be frequent. The effectiveness of a prevention/promotion initiative may require sharing of resources among multiple, often competing groups. Strong leadership helps to build collaboration, especially by listening carefully, working slowly for small wins, and keeping participants focused on shared goals.
6. **Describe the innovation in simple terms, especially in the beginning**. Price and Lorion (1989) emphasized the value of focusing on a few simple objectives and characteristics of the innovative program, even if its implementation ultimately will be more complex and have many components. Articulate to others, "We are here to . . ." and "The way we do this is through 1 . . , 2 . . . , 3. . . ." This allows for mobilization of internal resources and easier project management. Though the reality is more complex, focusing allows communication and key elements to be prioritized planfully (Van de Ven, 1986).
7. **When the program begins, ensure implementation of its core principles and elements.** Identify the core elements of the program innovation and replicate these as faithfully as possible in your setting. This typically requires intensive staff training and ongoing coaching and supervision. Also valuable is consultation by the original program developers or others who have implemented the program in settings similar to yours.
8. **Measure program implementation and attainment of program objectives throughout the operation of the program.** This measurement may range from practical to scientifically precise (see Chapter 14). However, some form of assessment is essential. Foremost, it is a statement of values, of ongoing commitment to goal achievement and accountability to those who are carrying out and receiving the initiative. Secondarily, continuous assessment of process and outcome allows adaptations of a program to be made as its context changes. Finally, measurement provides evidence of program performance that funders and stakeholders require. Many settings find it valuable to use the Levels of Use assessment (see Box 11.2). This involves determining the degree to which a program is being implemented in a knowledgeable and appropriately flexible way by staff. It also requires that those developing and implementing innovations be very clear about the learning curve of its human operators as well as how innovations should be carried out under a range of circumstances.

BOX 11.2 Levels of Use of an Innovation

Level of Use	Qualities of Implementers at This Level
Nonuse	Have little or no knowledge, no involvement and no actions to help them become involved.
Orientation	Are acquiring information about the innovation and its value orientation and what it will require to carry it out.
Preparation	Are preparing to use a new idea or process.
Mechanical	Focus on short-term, day-to-day use, mastering the specific tasks and techniques they must carry out.
Routine	Have established use of the innovation. Regular patterns of implementation predominate and few changes are made in ongoing use.
Refinement	Fine-tune efforts based on feedback from consumers/clients and from their own experience.
Integration	Begin to step back and look at the big picture of the paradigm of the innovation they are doing. They focus on how to combine their own efforts with those of colleagues.
Renewal	Reevaluate practice in light of factors such as changes in population, student needs, staffing patterns, freshness/relevance of materials.

SOURCE: Based on Hord, Rutherford, Huling-Austin, & Hall (1987).

9. **Search for unintended effects of the program.** Any innovation in a host setting will have unintended effects, both positive and negative. Being alert to these possibilities during the assessment process can lead to revision or refinement of the program. In early prevention programs, for example, outside experts would come in and carry out interventions in schools. Teachers were thrilled; they would leave the class and use the time for extra preparation or grading papers. However, when the experts left, there was little of the program left behind and little chance for teachers to reinforce the principles of the program throughout the rest of the school day. Documentation of such unintended effects has led to rethinking about the role of setting members in the implementation of prevention/promotion innovations toward the necessity of their having direct and ongoing involvement.
10. **Plan for institutionalization of the program in the host setting.** Assume that the program will need to outlast the staff members who initiate it. Plan for how to institutionalize it, incorporating it into the host setting's routine functioning so that it survives after its founders have moved on. In addition, develop a process of program renewal so that it can be adapted to changing needs and circumstances in the host setting, including turnover of personnel. Failure to consider this aspect of the implementation process is probably the main reason why good programs do not persist.
11. **Establish external linkages with similar programs in other settings.** Networking is the lifeblood of enduring innovations. Relationships with other implementers—via meetings, distance learning technology, the Internet, shared newsletters, conference calls—provide ideas and technical assistance,

opportunities to share triumphs and frustrations, and social support from individuals who are going through the same things. In addition, networking provides a base for actions on broader issues, such as advocacy or funding.

In case you are wondering if you have to do all of these things in order to be successful, the answer is a definitive "yes and no." The first time you look at a piece of music, you wonder if it can ever be mastered. With practice and attention to feedback and learning, and often through working with others, you learn to play compositions that seemed imposing at first.

Prevention/promotion work is similar. It uses a process of action research so that there is continual feedback and adjusting to the specifics of the context. This feedback often involves both qualitative and quantitative research. The accumulation of feedback through the action-research process leads to modifications that continuously strengthen both core and adaptive features of the program. Prevention/promotion work occurs in teams to an even greater extent than music. Creative leadership, flexible adaptation to context, and appreciation of the interdependencies among stakeholders and the resources each brings to the shared work all converge to create ongoing innovation and high-quality programs.

IMPLEMENTING A PREVENTION/PROMOTION INNOVATION: A CASE EXAMPLE

In this section we describe a case example of implementing a school-based prevention/promotion program in multiple school settings. Its path of implementation took many twists and turns, influenced by action research, a commitment to continuous program improvement, and the practicalities of school and community life. Our example is the Social Decision Making and Social Problem Solving (SDM/SPS) Project (Elias, 1994; Elias & Clabby, 1992), a school-based prevention initiative.

The SDM/SPS Project has used the Conductor's Guide described earlier for over two decades. It has spread from a demonstration project in two experimental and three control classrooms to hundreds of classrooms in schools in two dozen states and several countries. The core of the project involves building the social and emotional skills of students, with a focus on self-control, group participation and social awareness and a decision making strategy to use when faced with difficult choices under stress or when planning. Its ultimate goals include promoting successful social and academic performance and preventing problem behaviors (Elias & Clabby, 1992; Elias & Tobias, 1996).

The task of orchestrating the development and spread of this innovation, with which the primary chapter author (Maurice Elias) was involved from the onset, will appear much more organized in its description than in its reality. Think of orchestrating in a context where all the players are standing on a boat in stormy seas wearing roller blades. The wind is blowing, pages of the musical score are regularly getting washed overboard, even a few members of the orchestra are slipping into the water every now and then, and at times several people believe they are the conductors. If you read the following with this scene in mind, you will be closer to the reality than what the printed page typically allows. Keep in mind, however, that after 20 years the boat is still afloat, many more people have joined the orchestra, and we have learned a lot not only about orchestration but also about sailing in heavy seas.

We drew initial guidance from the principles in the implementation considerations presented earlier, although we were only dimly aware of all of these terms when we started. From the inception of the project, we tried to make the initial implementation conditions match those likely in the school environments where the program would eventually be implemented. Thus little of the available funding went into creating ideal training conditions, providing special resources and materials to implementing teachers, paying for any training or implementation work, having experts work directly in classrooms, or finding locations with strong receptivity to prior innovations. Instead, we sought to work in conditions as close to the real world as possible. Furthermore, we were acutely aware of developmental factors and of the need to modify what we were doing for diverse populations, particularly children with special education classifications.

Evolution of the Elementary School Level Program

The history of much of this effort, as well as the way in which planned and unplanned variations in conditions were addressed, is detailed in Elias and Clabby (1992). Key points in the voyage, however, can be described here. At the elementary school level, we created a scripted curriculum with extensive accompanying materials, all developed through nine years of continuous improvement in an action-research cycle. Other action-research cycles were created to support modifications of the approach for special education and middle and high school populations. In particular, the creation of an acronym for the eight steps of social decision making—FIG TESPN—led to dramatic improvements in delivering the program to special education students (Elias & Tobias, 1996). Another important finding was the need to integrate the learning of problem-solving skills with the application of those skills to academic and interpersonal situations as soon as possible after learning them in class.

We also discovered the value of sharing learning across implementation sites in a systematic way. The Problem Solving Connection Newsletter was created as a resource exchange network for those using social problem solving or related interventions; in the days before e-mail, it became a place to ask questions and to share innovations, to incorporate diversity and change into the implementation context. It is where such creative adaptations as the "Keep Calm Rap" were developed and redeveloped, as well as "Be Your Best," which one class began to sing to the tune of Disney's "Be Our Guest," from *Beauty and the Beast*. Most recently, branches of the project have been focusing on distance learning coalitions and Internet exchanges as vehicles for implementation sharing and support.

Adaptation to Middle School

Although there is far less uniformity among elementary schools than unsuspecting outsiders might think, there is even greater diversity among middle schools. This means that intervention technologies are not easily transferred from elementary to middle school. It also means that successful interventions in one middle school context must be transferred to others with much care. In attempting to provide follow-up for the elementary school level social decision making and problem-solving program into middle school, we found that numerous adaptations had to be made. This was discovered as an outcome of action research and by being clear about the core features and goals of the program. Even after creating successful demonstration projects, however, those involved were not filled with a sense that the work was completed. There was the matter of providing a well-annotated musical score for others to use. This gave rise to the book, *Social Decision Making and Life Skills Development* (Elias, 1993, revised and updated as Elias & Bruene, 2005b).

We were wary of providing a set "score"; therefore, we chose to provide key principles and specific examples as inspiration rather than fully scripted materials. Those who had brought social problem solving successfully into their local settings (in our orchestral analogy, local conductors, the first players of different orchestral sections, and some individual musicians) explained clearly their own use of problem-solving principles in the classroom. This helped readers imagine using program materials; though they began in ways similar to the examples provided, soon thereafter their applications were integrated with their own skills and context.

To introduce each innovation to prospective implementers, we first presented a sales pitch that made the program sound attractive and viable to those who might implement it. Then came a discussion of program materials and how they could be used. Next, we discussed evidence of its effectiveness, accompanied by listings of follow-up and support resources. Finally, we presented sample activities to allow readers to try out specific modules and get a feel not only for the particular details, but also for the flow of the activities with the individuals and groups involved (Elias & Bruene, 2005b). Some examples of modules follow.

1. A video program that shows children how to watch television and then use social decision making and problem solving to create their own programs, series, documentaries, and public service advertisements.
2. A format that allows students to create school and community service projects.
3. A procedure for creating parent newsletters and other school-home communications; the details include such things as what to tell the printer in reproducing photographs.
4. FIG TESPN, an approach to social decision making and problem solving that takes into account the special learning needs of many children. The acronym includes the following:
   Feelings are my cue to problem solve.
   I have a problem.

Goals guide my actions.
Think of many possible things to do.
Envision the outcomes of each solution.
Select your best solution, based on your goal.
Plan, practice, anticipate pitfalls, and pursue it.
Next time, what will you do the same or differently?

5. Troubleshooting sections, where the practitioners in the field talk about the tough issues and how they have dealt with them. Examples include issues of getting started, not having enough time, and working with children who seem to place a positive value on aggressive behavior.

Setting Up an Infrastructure to Support Widespread Implementation

To support the process of widespread implementation with fidelity and effectiveness in diverse contexts, great attention was paid to implementation infrastructure. Using the analogy of music, one can imagine the difficulty in playing a piece of orchestral music one has not heard in its entirety. For this to happen, it is helpful to have ongoing concerts that others can attend; to be able to train master conductors and musicians who will have had experience with the musical work and then can go back and teach it to others; to have the capacity to send out conductors and musicians to local settings to assist them in learning to play; to help them make modifications in light of their own orchestral strengths and weaknesses; and to avoid making modifications that will change the nature of the composition.

A Social Problem Solving Unit was created within the University of Medicine and Dentistry of New Jersey and its affiliated mental health center. The unit's mission is to foster effective implementation of SDM/SPS programs in school districts nationally and internationally, with an action research orientation. Many of the principles of effective implementation in multiple settings that we discussed in this chapter grew out of the experiences of this unit. The SDM/SPS program and implementation unit gained formal recognition from the National Mental Health Association, the National Diffusion Network of the U.S. Department of Education, and the National Education Goals Panel, critical steps in building credibility and opening up contacts with networks of potential and actual implementers from which further refinements in practice and sources of implementation support could be derived.

Evaluation data about implementation of the SDM/SPS Project are available from three major studies. Commins and Elias (1991) undertook an examination of the first four sites to implement the SDM/SPS program. The methodology involved identifying 10 key conditions most likely to facilitate long-term program implementation and comparing the sites on relevant indicators. The two districts showing all 10 conditions were found to have made substantial progress toward institutionalizing the program. A district showing 9 of 10 conditions had made substantial progress. The remaining site met only 4 of 10 conditions and showed almost no progress. This study was the first to show that the program could be disseminated effectively. Anecdotally, it is worth noting that 11 years after the Commins and Elias (1991) study, SDM/SPS had a clear, visible presence in both districts that earlier had met all conditions, had been integrated into the elementary guidance program in the district that met 9 of 10 conditions, and continued to be implemented only on a sporadic basis in the remaining district.

Heller and Firestone (1995) conducted a study of the sources of leadership in schools that had implemented long-term social and emotional learning programs. As part of this study, nine elementary schools that had implemented SDM/SPS for at least three years were identified. An interview procedure was set up to determine the degree of institutionalization of the program. They found that five of nine schools had institutionalized the program to a significant degree. Four were deemed fully institutionalized, meaning that all teachers were using the program with high fidelity. One was designated as mixed because it had a core group of teachers that were high-fidelity users of the program along with other less rigorous users, and four had a partial status, meaning that they maintained affiliation with the SDM/SPS programs and teachers were using the program, although in generally limited, low-fidelity ways.

Detailed analysis of mediating factors indicated that full institutionalization was related primarily to consistent filling of leadership roles by multiple individuals, usually from varied job titles, and to having school-based SDM/SPS coordinating committees. The teachers played the most critical role in institutionalizing SDM/SPS programs. In every school, long-term, high-fidelity institutionalization was more likely when there was an active group of teachers who implemented the program and knew its impact. Essential among the activities of such groups were providing a sustained vision of the program, offering encouragement, and setting up in-house procedures to monitor its progress and improve its effectiveness (Heller & Firestone, 1995).

As the SDM/SPS program expanded through involvement with the National Diffusion Network, trainers were bringing the program to sites inside and outside its New Jersey base. Beyond a focus on implementation, we felt it was important to examine the extent to which teachers and student recipients of the program were developing their skills to the same degrees that they did in the initial validation sample. In the initial samples, of course, the program was smaller, there were fewer implementation sites, and program management was closer and more intensive. For the more recent study, three new sites in New Jersey plus sites in Arkansas and Oregon were studied.

Results are summarized in Bruene-Butler, Hampson, Elias, Clabby, and Schuyler (1997). Briefly, extent of teacher acquisition of skills in dialoguing and facilitative questioning met or exceeded those of the original sample in all of the new sites. Comparing the Oregon and the original New Jersey site, use of inhibitory questioning strategies declined from pretest to posttest; use of facilitative (discussion-oriented) questioning increased greatly. With regard to acquisition of interpersonal sensitivity, problem analysis, and planning skills, students in all of the recent dissemination sites showed significant gains during the program, and the effect sizes in all cases were equal to or as much as twice as large as those in the original validation sample. The Bruene-Butler et al. (1997) data suggest that the implementation of the SDM/SPS program in sites assessed in 1994 and 1995 can occur in ways that allow its impact on teachers and students to be as strong as it was in the initial implementation site, where it was begun in 1980.

Extension to Disadvantaged Urban Settings

The next challenge has been the application of the SDM/SPS approach to an urban, economically disadvantaged school setting. These districts are currently under unprecedented pressure to meet mandates to raise standardized test scores. These efforts have crowded out programs directed at social-emotional and character development. Yet educators also recognize that education is an interpersonal process, occurring in relational contexts and mediated by social-emotional skills. This demands coordination of any SEL or related program with the constraints, and strengths, of urban schools. Few validated social competence or character programs have been systematically applied in urban districts, especially over a period of seven years. Further, there are challenges involved in coordinating programs to allow continuity, synergy, and going to scale with fidelity across multiple schools.

The setting for our work has been Plainfield, New Jersey, an urban setting with a demographic profile that began as 95 percent African American and 5 percent Latino students, shifting to 70–30 percent over seven years. It was deemed a special needs district by the state of New Jersey. Our partnership with Plainfield began in 1998, when the Rutgers Social-Emotional Learning Lab Team approached the superintendent and other administrative staff to discuss a way to address continuing academic and behavior difficulties among students. We spoke in terms of using Price's action-research model as a guide to our collaboration. Agreement was reached on implementing a coordinated, districtwide social-emotional learning initiative, reflecting an analysis of the problem of poor academic performance and high levels of problem behavior and the solutions available to impact on modifiable risk factors. The Plainfield Board of Education adopted a policy concerning Social-Emotional Learning (SEL) for all of its public schools, and accompanied this policy with a vision statement expressing their commitment to the social and emotional development of their children, youth, families, and staff. This policy stated the value position that students' low academic performance is unlikely to transform without also improving their SEL skills.

A full discussion of this aspect of the project is beyond the scope of this chapter, but several important points can be illustrated. First, the existence of a sound curriculum, such as SDM/SPS, is necessary but not sufficient. The curriculum must be modified to be culturally appropriate. Further, for urban schools, it must be linked to mesh with the various mandates, especially those concerning literacy. Second, there must be a distinctive, developmentally sequenced, nonrepetitive curriculum that is capable of being implemented across all grade levels with fidelity despite high levels of student and teacher turnover. Third, a strong implementation support system must be put in place. Finally, there must be a feasible and ongoing procedure for monitoring, evaluation, feedback, and program modification. This last element is very important; for instance, the rapid rise in the proportion of Latino/a students created a need for ongoing monitoring and changes in the cultural grounding of the program.

Mandates The overall umbrella concept of SEL is integrated and monitored within several of the district goals and curriculum standards of the Plainfield Public Schools. It is critical that prevention/promotion programs in schools are related to state and local mandates governing that school. In Plainfield, these mandates included the Abbott/Whole School Reform (WSR) requirements, the New Jersey Core Curriculum Content Standards (NJCCCS), and the New Standards Performance Standards (NSPS). As noted on the website of the Plainfield School District, each of these influences provides a particular set of directions and constraints for the school system. WSR is a set of stipulations required of the 30 districts in New Jersey that have been designated as "high risk" under *Abbott v. Burke* litigation. Each school in these districts must select, adopt, and sustain an approved whole school reform model and then devote the full resources necessary for its proper implementation. Literacy and mathematics, the areas in which standardized testing takes place every year, are emphasized. Any SEL curriculum must be aligned with the district's literacy goals, pedagogy, and implementation plans. Formal and informal lessons have been aligned with specific literacy standards that are a pivotal part of the WSR in Plainfield. A key vehicle for the articulation of literacy and SEL has been the Laws of Life program (see www.lawsoflife.org for more information), which engages students in grades 2 and above in a developmentally appropriate process that results in their writing or using other modalities to express the laws and values that guide their lives (Elias, Bryan, Patrikakou, & Weissberg, 2002). Laws of Life provides a character- and values-linked continuous thread that allows for unified school-wide program-related activities across all grade levels. NJCCCS refers to the set of curriculum standards for all subject areas in schools, adopted by the state of New Jersey. NSPS refers to performance standards in academic areas to which Plainfield is also held accountable. The Board of Education passed a districtwide SEL policy, stating the importance of SEL as part of the core mission of academic education. The five skill areas of SEL (see Chapter 10, Figure 10.1) are aligned with academic standards explicitly named and monitored in two of the six district goals (Goal 1: Student Achievement and Goal 5: Staff) and implicitly in four goals of the Plainfield Accountability System for school administrator performance.

Curriculum In the first year, we collaborated to design and pilot test a variation of the SDM/SPS curriculum, "Talking with TJ," in three of the elementary school's second and third grade classrooms (Dilworth, Mokrue, & Elias, 2002). "Talking with TJ" is a video-based curriculum that provides students with the opportunity to learn and practice prosocial skills. The premise revolves around the fictional T.J., a Black teenage girl who appears in all of the videos as a radio station disc jockey running a radio talk show. Kids call in for advice about solving typical problems faced by children their age pertaining to acceptance issues, difficulty expressing feelings, and difficulty compromising. Subsequent action-research cycles have led to curriculum development. An overall emphasis in grades 2–3 was Teamwork and in grades 4–5 was Conflict Resolution, with character-linked thematic emphases also created for each grade level. A series of topical modules to build readiness skills was created for grades K–1 as well as a supplemental small group intervention for young students with early reading difficulties. After five years, another problem-solving-oriented curriculum, Overcoming Obstacles, was brought in for grades 6–12 and is now being subjected to the action-research cycle. Naturally, as mandates change, curricula and related programming must also be adapted.

Implementation Support Support must be provided at multiple ecological levels. At the administrative level, the superintendent assigned the areas of SEL and Character Education to a special projects coordinator, who was designated the SEL administrative liaison. In this capacity, she worked closely with both the building and district-level administrators as well as SEL staff at the building level. Site coordinators were established in each school building to help with all aspects of implementation. An examination of the role functions of the site coordinators at the elementary school level provides good overall insight concerning the structure of intervention supports:

- monitor implementation of curricula
- foster a positive greeting process each school day, overall and in individual classrooms
- coordinate ways in which curriculum principles can be carried out within the Literacy Block of the Whole School Reform model
- ensure skill-building posters remain on the walls at all times
- encourage practice of skill-building principles in the classroom when children are in group/pair/team situations
- facilitate writing of Laws of Life essays
- collaborate with school staff to create buildingwide applications of SEL, including integration into school discipline procedures
- encourage outreach to parents

A Social Development Coordinating Committee determined overall direction, training, and resource allocation. Note that the term *Social Development* was chosen so that the work of the committee could encompass SEL, character education, and emerging bully/violence prevention mandates. The committee was chaired by the administrative liaison and included at least one member from each elementary school serving as the SEL site coordinator, support staff from secondary schools, some teachers and SEL district administrators, and representation from the Rutgers SEL Lab Team. Initially, team members provided onsite assistance to teachers implementing the curriculum as well as to site coordinators working with buildingwide SEL initiatives; this support, which at its height included using as many as 50 trained undergraduates, faded gradually.

Monitoring and Evaluation A collaborative process between the Social Development coordinating committee and the Rutgers team was used to set goals and develop instruments and reporting systems for feedback (Bryan, Schoenholz, & Elias, in press; Romasz, Kantor, & Elias, 2003). An ongoing problem is the dual nature of data analysis for professional publication purposes and the amount, format, level, and timing of data needed for district-based decisions related to program implementation support and resource allocation. After Year Six of the collaboration, all data systems were turned over to the school district for their subsequent use.

Case Example: Concluding Perspectives

What is the essence of this case example? It chronicles the use of a social decision making approach informed by community psychology principles and implementation considerations, including the prevention and implementation considerations, the four stages of development of innovations, and the Conductor's Guide to Orchestrating Prevention/Promotion Innovations (Table 11.4). The SDM/SPS process by necessity has been context sensitive and operator dependent while trying to remain faithful to basic program principles. The emphasis has been on implementing core features while adapting its methods to diverse host settings, including the challenges of the urban schools. In the spirit of continuous improvement, SDM/SPS developers and adopters conduct ongoing action research to maximize its effectiveness and serve a broad range of populations and settings. Additionally, the uncertainties and adventuresome nature of this kind of work are embraced and become vehicles for deepening the collaborations involved in all community endeavors. The action research process and its related considerations are, in fact, at the core of what community psychology has to contribute as a discipline. There are no shortcuts; every accomplishment, every small win (Weick, 1984) and baby step (Cowen, 1977) is celebrated as a positive action, an instructive example, and part of moving problem prevention and competence and health promotion from rhetoric to reality.

FINAL THOUGHTS, FUTURE THOUGHTS

Conditions like violence, abuse of alcohol and other drugs, AIDS, academic failure, school disaffection and dropout, homelessness, prejudice, and child abuse and neglect require bold, definitive, effective, widespread, sustained efforts. What is at stake is the future health of our youth and what they will become when they are in a position to take over the responsibilities of citizenship in a democracy.

Community psychologists worry when the spread of prevention/promotion innovations is approached naively, unrealistically, or misleadingly. All too often, the result is failure and fatalism about resolving future community problems. There are no shortcuts, inoculations, or preventive approaches that can succeed in the absence of careful oversight, continuous monitoring, and feedback. Policy advocacy also is required if implementation of prevention is to reach the point of having a widespread impact on public health.

The SDM/SPS Project is an example of how health promotion and risk reduction programs can be brought into schools and implemented with integrity, skills acquisition, and generativity in multiple contexts. Space did not allow us to describe initiatives in other community settings, but review the programs in Chapter 10 to understand and imagine the impact of widespread implementation on families, neighborhoods, workplaces, and other settings.

Ultimately, if we do not implement prevention/promotion innovations with care, we are likely to see public interest diminish. Documentation of process and outcomes in ways that policy makers, the public, professionals in caregiving fields, and scientists can all use with confidence is a high priority. Understanding how operator-dependent innovations can be implemented widely in everyday contexts poses intellectual and practical challenges that must be met if we are to have health-enhancing communities. For these reasons, the considerations about program planning and evaluation in Chapter 14 become especially important for the future of the prevention/promotion field.

CHAPTER SUMMARY

1. Successful prevention/promotion programs cited in research journals are not necessarily successfully replicated in multiple settings or sustained over time. Effective, sustained programs in schools have active administrative support, ongoing staff training and support, and integration of the program into the life of the school (see Table 11.1).
2. Action research is a cyclical approach to developing prevention/promotion programs and transferring them to multiple settings. The process of spreading an effective program to many settings consists of four stages: *experimental development, technological application, diffusion of innovation,* and *widespread implementation*. This process is sometimes termed *scaling up.*
3. Many effective prevention/promotion innovations, in schools, workplaces, and other settings are not widely implemented. We used Kelly's ecological concepts of interdependence, resource cycling, adaptation, and succession to explain why encouraging innovation within the context of the local setting is so important.
4. Seven characteristics describe prevention/promotion innovations and the settings where they usually take place (see Table 11.2). Innovations are *operator dependent, context dependent, organizationally unbounded,* and *fragile and difficult to specify.* Effective innovations thus require *identifying core and adaptive components, challenging* the setting while also respecting its key qualities, and *longitudinal* attention to program quality. *Small wins* are often more feasible and accepted in settings. To be effective and sustained, the program or innovation

must be *institutionalized,* made a routine part of the setting's functioning. Because of these factors, prevention advocates must have or acquire specific skills in order to put in place successful, enduring innovations.

5. There are numerous challenges in implementing prevention programs effectively. To meet such challenges, Table 11.3 lists ten considerations in planning and implementing prevention/promotion innovations. Implementing these through action, research, and reflection is termed *praxis.* It concerns both "what you do" and "how you do it."
6. Approaches to exemplary education programs have evolved from *cookbook, replication,* and *adaptation* approaches to an emphasis on *invention/innovation.* Implementing an invention/innovation approach requires taking the developmental levels of implementers into account, such as a desire for generativity in one's work.
7. On the basis of an invention/innovation approach, we presented a Conductor's Guide to Implementing Effective Prevention/Promotion Innovations in Multiple Settings. These guidelines are listed in Table 11.4.
8. The *Social Decision Making and Social Problem Solving Project* is an example of a long-term prevention/promotion effort that has encountered many of the challenges of implementation and has attempted to address them using the principles outlined in this chapter.
9. There is no magic formula for successful widespread implementation of a model program; however, a process of continuous monitoring, feedback, and modification, respecting local ecology and needs of implementers, encouraging diverse inputs, and building a sense of community, allows innovations to have the best chance to adapt to their environments.

BRIEF EXERCISES

1. Recall a prevention/promotion educational program you have experienced. This may, for instance, involve drug abuse prevention, parenting skills classes, conflict resolution training, a program teaching social or communication skills, or other intervention. Using the concepts in this chapter, analyze the quality of its implementation.

   First, use some of the seven characteristics in Table 11.2 to describe this program.

   - Was it operator dependent and context dependent? How?
   - Were its effects organizationally unbounded? How?
   - What were its core and adaptive features, as you perceive them?
   - Do you believe the program was implemented effectively? What factors influenced whether it was effective or not?
   - Was the program evaluated and improved longitudinally?

Second, if possible describe the educational effectiveness of the program using terms from Table 11.3.

- Did it use appropriate instructional strategies? For instance, did it use group discussion, exercises to apply learning, and other ways to strengthen learning?
- Were its materials (e.g., written, visual, computerized) user friendly and helpful?
- Was the organization or setting genuinely committed to the program (hospitable context)?
- What were the constraints, limitations, or obstacles to program implementation? How could these be overcome?
- What persons provided resources of talent, commitment, or other qualities that strengthened the program?
- What aspects of the program would you change or improve? Why?

2. This chapter focused on educational settings. List some other KISS and AID systems, or other systems in society, that are operator-dependent, context-dependent systems whose effects are organizationally unbounded and difficult to specify.

   In what respects might health care, retail sales and services, finance, computer technology, religion, politics, and diplomacy represent such systems? Justify your opinion with recent news stories or with your own experiences.
3. Imagine that you have just been hired as the director of the counseling center at your college or university. While continuing to offer its existing services, you want to take a stronger prevention/promotion approach to serving the campus community. Describe specific innovations and programs that you would develop to pursue this goal.

RECOMMENDED READINGS

Blankstein, A. (2004). *Failure is not an option: Six principles that guide student achievement in high-performing schools.* Thousand Oaks, CA: Corwin Press.

Collaborative for Academic, Social, and Emotional Learning [CASEL]. (2003). *Safe and sound: An educational leader's guide to evidence-based social and emotional learning programs.* Retrieved from http://www.casel.org.

Joyner, E., Comer, J. P., & Ben-Avie, M. (2004). *Comer schools in action: The 3-volume field guide.* Thousand Oaks, CA: Corwin Press.

Novick, B., Kress, J. S., & Elias, M. J. (2002). *Building learning communities with character: How to integrate academic, social, and emotional learning.* Alexandria, VA: Association for Supervision and Curriculum Development.

Osher, D., Dwyer, K., & Jackson, S. (2004). *Safe, suppportive, and successful schools step by step.* Longmont, CO: Sopris West.

RECOMMENDED WEBSITES

Community Tool Box
http://ctb.ku.edu

Resources for planning, implementing, and evaluating community initiatives, including prevention/promotion.

New Century School House
http://www.landmark-project.com/ncsh

A project that asks educators to visit a 1960s-style school building gutted of all relics of industrial age learning and suggest ideas and plans for what space, materials, and learning should look like to build children's competencies for the future.

Center for Effective Collaboration and Practice
http://cecp.air.org

Information and resources on established, effective programs for children and youth.

The Eleven Principles of Character Education Sourcebooks and Institutes
http://www.character.org/files/home/htm

Comprehensive guide to implementation of high-quality character education programs

INFOTRAC® COLLEGE EDITION KEYWORDS

action research, dissemination, experimental social innovation and dissemination, implementing(ation), intervention, prevention(ive)(ing), primary prevention, promotion(ing)

12

Citizen Participation and Empowerment

Lexington-Richland Alcohol and Drug Abuse Commission

If I am not for myself, who will be for me? And if I am only for myself, what am I? (Rabbi Hillel, quoted in Loeb, 1999, p. 1)

INTRODUCTION

I had a contractor build a shower in my basement and a year later, the shower collapsed. I called up the contractor. . . . Three months later, he still had not shown up, so I called the Better Business Bureau. The first questions they asked me were "What block association do you belong to? What community board are you in?" I did not even know at the time that a community board existed. So I called the community board, who filed complaints against the contractor and ultimately restitution was made. Until this point in my life, I literally did not know about citizen participation.

... the East 48th Street Block Association #135 [Brooklyn, New York] was formed to improve the quality of life on our block. Almost immediately changes were visible such as property improvement, communication, and a cleaner block as a whole. Since then we have formed a block watcher group; we have continuous patrols on the block; we have installed outdoor lights in front of almost every home.... Believe it or not, it is a deterrent to crime. We have a youth softball team.... During the summer, we have bus rides to parks for youths and families.... We have a block party about every year.... Even though volunteer service is a lot of hard work, it enhances the quality of life and is quite rewarding. (Louis Burgess, 1990, pp. 159–161; reprinted by permission of Kluwer Academic/Plenum Publishers)

"Some of the adults thought it might never happen. You could tell by the way they looked they were just waiting for it to fail." (Cameron Dary, quoted in Putnam & Feldstein, 2003, p. 143)

About thirty sixth-graders at the Waupun Middle School in Waupun, Wisconsin, met after class to choose projects they could take on to help their school and community. They divided into small groups to discuss possible service activities. Then the groups presented their ideas to the meeting and the students voted on the list of possibilities. They agreed to take on the top three: raising money for a field trip fund for students whose families could not afford to pay the fees; getting new playground equipment for the school; and convincing authorities to install warning lights at a railroad crossing on Edgewood Street, a few blocks away. Only a small sign marked the crossing; brush and mounds of soil obscured the view down the tracks.

Cameron Dary, the sixth grader who led the railroad crossing project, and his fellow students presented their idea to a meeting of the Waupun City Council. Told to collect evidence to support their ideas, they conducted a survey of residents near the crossing. Of 14 residents surveyed, 10 believed the crossing was unsafe, 12 had seen people not stopping, and 13 wanted a better warning device. Continued efforts by the youth for over a year led eventually to action. The railroad installed a series of warning signs and removed the debris to clear sight lines at the crossing. (quoted and paraphrased from Putnam & Feldstein, 2003, pp. 142–144)

"So I went to a town meeting of a couple hundred people, and... I voiced my opinions as best I could, red-faced, hesitant, and embarrassed." That's how Alison Smith began to speak out about community issues. She soon joined the League of Women Voters and became active in environmental issues in her Connecticut town and later in Maine. "I was hesitant at first. I don't have a college degree. I'm more of a behind-the-scenes person. But I've always felt like someone who cares, even if I didn't always know what to do about it."

TABLE 12.1 Myths and Insights About Private Life and Public Life

Myth: Public life is for celebrities, politicians, and activists, people who like to be in the limelight or who want to make waves.

Insight: Every day, at school, where we work, where we worship, within civic or social groups, our behavior shapes the public world and is shaped by it. We are all in public life.

Myth: It's too depressing to get involved in public life, too easy to burn out.

Insight: Public life serves deep human needs: for instance, to work with others or to make a difference. It is as essential as private life.

Myth: Public life is always nasty, cutthroat, all about conflict.

Insight: Public life involves encountering differences, but conflict doesn't have to be nasty. Understood and managed well, conflict can lead to growth for individuals and groups.

Myth: Public life is about pursuing one's own selfish interests.

Insight: Selfishness and enlightened self-interest aren't the same thing. Understanding how our true interests overlap with those of others comes only through involvement in public life.

Myth: Public life interferes with private life.

Insight: Public life often enhances private life, making it more meaningful and enjoyable.

SOURCE: Adapted from Lappe and DuBois (1994, pp. 21, 24, 29, 33, 39).

> When the Maine League of Women Voters asked her to collect signatures for the Clean Elections statewide referendum, she did it. "I just sat at a table with a sign saying 'Do you want to take big money out of politics?' Almost everyone who came over responded and signed." Support for the initiative grew statewide, with Alison as one of over a thousand volunteers. "I felt nervous when the League asked me to do new things like speak at press conferences. . . . But I also found that as an ordinary person, I had more credibility than the political professionals." The Clean Elections Act passed with 56% of the vote, and became a national model for campaign finance reform. "It gave me a sense that I really can do something just by showing up to further a cause. . . . I'm in it, as I said, to challenge the cynicism and despair, both my own and that of our society." (quoted and paraphrased from Loeb, 1999, pp. 63–66)

These stories embody the three themes of this chapter: citizen participation in community decisions, citizen empowerment, and how they are related to sense of community. Stories like the foregoing are surprisingly common. Similar changes occur not only in large-scale social movements, but also in local neighborhoods, schools, spiritual settings, and workplaces.

Citizen participation and empowerment may not seem psychological at first glance, but they involve many psychological dynamics, including cognitions, emotions, values, skills for working with others, personal development, exercising power. Some community settings promote learning these skills, for psychologically meaningful reasons. Understanding citizen participation and empowerment does require debunking myths about private life and community life (See Table 12.1).

In this chapter we first define citizen participation and empowerment, and consider various concepts of power. We discuss how persons become active participants in community decisions and how participation, empowerment, and sense of community are intertwined. Finally, we describe qualities of community settings that empower their members. In Chapter 13, we will continue the discussion by focusing on processes of community and social change. Keep in mind, however, that this division is the result of space limits. In the real world, empowering citizens intertwines with changing communities and macrosystems. In Chapter 14 we consider how program evaluation methods can be used to empower citizens and communities through developing and improving community programs.

WHAT ARE CITIZEN PARTICIPATION AND EMPOWERMENT?

Citizen Participation

A useful definition of citizen participation is:

> a process in which individuals take part in decision-making in the institutions, programs, and environments that affect them. (Wandersman, 1984, p. 339)

Let's unpack this definition. "Institutions, programs and environments" includes workplaces, hospitals or mental health centers, neighborhoods, schools, religious congregations, and society at large. They also include grassroots organizations formed for the purpose of influencing larger environments, including such groups as a block association, political action group, or labor union. Citizen participation involves decision making. It does not necessarily mean holding the power to control all decisions, but it involves making one's voice heard and influencing decisions in democratic ways.

Citizen participation is *not* simply volunteering or community service. Assisting with a school field trip, for instance, is not citizen participation. Participation involves influence in making collective decisions in groups, communities, or society. It occurs in a diversity of forms: for instance, serving on a community coalition, writing a letter to the editor, debating the budget at a school board meeting, meeting with government officials to press for an action, testifying at a public hearing, and voting in elections. Acts of citizen participation are more effective when they are done collectively with others. The Waupun, Wisconsin, youth group and Alison Smith's growing role in community and state affairs illustrate ways of influencing decisions through collective actions.

Participation: Means or End? Citizen participation may be a means, a path to a goal, or an end, a goal in itself. As a means, participation is often encouraged either to improve the quality of a plan or because citizens' commitment to a decision is often greater if they participated in making it (Bartunek & Keys, 1979;

Wandersman & Florin, 2000). As an end, citizen participation is often seen as an essential quality of a democracy, regardless of whether it generates practical benefits such as better decisions or greater commitment.

This means-end distinction is not merely academic. Citizen participation is not always a means to better decisions, particularly if conflicts are not resolved or valid expertise is ignored. Also, participation and efficiency may be contradictory ends. For instance, Riger's (1993) research on feminist movement organizations (e.g., shelters for battered women, rape crisis centers) showed that maximizing participation by staff in decision making can require long meetings and interfere with efficient use of organizational resources (money, staff time, expertise). Similarly, New England town meetings, an institution of local democracy, can involve long discussions and much conflict before reaching decisions. Starnes (2004, p. 4) described neighborhood planning meetings as "raucous democracy."

Klein, Ralls, Smith-Major, and Douglas (2000, pp. 278–279) discussed varying goals for worker participation initiatives in workplaces. Some seek greater equality of power among workers, managers, and owners. Others want to promote worker personal development. Still others seek greater productivity, but little or no change in power relationships. These differing ends shape the means or methods of worker participation.

Nonetheless, citizen participation has many advantages. Reviews of field research in organizations show that participation by members usually (but not always) increases the quality of decisions and overall organizational effectiveness. This is true especially if disagreement is seen as a source of information rather than a threat. Studies of voluntary organizations indicate that participation promotes effective leadership and attaining goals (Bartunek & Keys, 1979; Fawcett et al., 1995; Maton & Salem, 1995; Wandersman & Florin, 2000).

Empowerment

Empowerment is a value-laden term with many meanings. It has been appropriated as a buzzword with varying meanings by both progressive and conservative forces in U.S. politics (Perkins, 1995). Corporations speak of empowering their employees, sometimes with no intent to actually share power. Physical exercise, meditation, and psychotherapy have been described as empowering; those are better understood in terms of personal growth, not empowerment as community psychologists use the term. Riger (1993) criticized varying, inconsistent usages of the term even within community psychology. A word that means everything also means nothing distinctive; sometimes it seems that empowerment has suffered that fate.

However, let's look more closely. In community psychology, Rappaport (1987) originally defined empowerment as "a process, a mechanism by which people, organizations, and communities gain mastery over their affairs" (p. 122). Following an influential critique by Riger (1993), Rappaport and others adopted a more specific, community-oriented definition proposed by the Cornell Empowerment Group:

> an intentional, ongoing process centered in the local community, involving mutual respect, critical reflection, caring, and group participation, through which people lacking an equal share of resources gain greater access to and control over those resources. (cited in Perkins & Zimmerman, 1995, p. 570, and in Wiley & Rappaport, 2000, p. 62)

Empowerment in this definition is accomplished with others, not alone. It involves gaining and exercising greater power (access to resources). It involves individual, community, and social change through collective acts of citizen participation. The Waupun youth group's actions to get the railroad crossing improved and the electoral reforms in which Alison Smith participated fit this definition of empowerment. If the block associations described by Louis Burgess provide citizens with greater access to important resources and influence in community decisions, they also are empowering.

Both empowerment and citizen participation involve exercising power in collective decision making. The principal distinction between them is that participation is a behavior, whereas empowerment is a broader process. At the individual level, it includes cognition (critical reflection in the Cornell definition) and emotion (caring), not just the behavior of participation. Rappaport has intentionally sought to keep the definition of empowerment open, arguing that a simple definition is likely to limit understanding of its multiple forms. Our coverage relies on the theoretical work of Rappaport (1981, 1987, 1995) and Zimmerman (1995, 2000), and the critique of empowerment concepts by Riger (1993).

Qualities of Empowerment Empowerment is a multilevel concept: individuals, organizations, communities, and societies can become empowered (Zimmerman, 2000). A person who becomes more skeptical of traditional authority, more willing to oppose injustice, and more involved in citizen participation is becoming empowered. A work organization may empower small teams to assume responsibility for day-to-day decisions. Through networking with other groups, a community organization may influence the wider locality. Through advocacy at higher levels of government, a locality may gain a greater control over its affairs. Empowerment also can concern dismantling or resisting oppressive systems of injustice at macrosystem or other levels.

Empowerment at one level does not necessarily lead to empowerment at other levels. Feeling empowered does not always lead to actual influence in collective decisions. Empowering individuals does not necessarily empower their organizations or communities. Empowering organizations with competing agendas may unleash competition for resources that weakens the larger community (Riger, 1993). A powerful organization in which leadership is tightly controlled does not empower its members. Empowerment must be understood at multiple levels (Zimmerman, 2000).

Empowerment refers to bottom-up rather than top-down approaches (recall this distinction from Chapter 2). Bottom-up approaches originate at the grassroots level and reflect attempts by ordinary people to assert control over their everyday lives. Top-down approaches, even when well intentioned and containing useful ideas, reflect the perspectives of the powerful and usually preserve the existing power structure (Gruber & Trickett, 1987). The empowerment perspective seeks to understand how bottom-up change works by listening to the views of those most affected by community decisions (Fawcett et al., 1995).

Empowerment is contextual: it differs across organizations, localities, communities, and cultures because of the differing histories, experiences, and environments of each (Zimmerman, 2000). For instance, in a civic group, a person may develop skills for influencing decisions through discussion, teamwork, and compromise. Yet that individual may find these skills ineffective for wielding power in a workplace that rewards directive, task-oriented decision making. The person thus is empowered in the first context but not in the second. Even the nature of what empowerment means may be different in these two settings.

Empowerment is a dynamic process that develops over time. It can deteriorate as well as grow, but it is not reversed by small setbacks (Zimmerman, 2000). It is often best understood by longitudinal research. Louis Burgess and Alison Smith developed from uninvolved citizens into community leaders. The Waupun, Wisconsin, youth group worked for a year to accomplish their goal, but they learned much from their efforts.

Empowerment occurs through participation in a group or organization. It often involves grassroots groups that are limited in size, possess a positive sense of community, involve members in decision making, and emphasize shared leadership and mutual influence (Maton & Salem, 1995). Empowerment also may involve linkages among organizations (Zimmerman, 2000). In the stories that opened this chapter, empowerment occurred through collective action.

Balancing Empowerment with Other Values Empowerment may promote, or conflict with, social justice, equality, respect for diversity, or sense of community. In Western societies, empowerment has often been understood in individualistic terms and used to promote personal self-advancement or individual entrepreneurship without regard for one's community or wider society. Empowerment also may be understood to mean strengthening the position and resources of one's ingroup at the expense of other groups (Riger, 1993). Examples such as an anti-immigration group or a White supremacy group come to mind.

Such issues underscore the need to specify the relationships and potential conflicts between empowerment and values such as sense of community and social justice. Consider these remarks by Stephanie Riger:

> Does empowerment . . . simultaneously bring about a greater sense of community and strengthen the ties that hold our society together, or does it promote certain individuals or groups at the expense of others, increasing

> competitiveness and lack of cohesion? . . . [W]e should consider connection as important as empowerment. (Riger, 1993, p. 290)

Recall Rabbi Hillel's remark that opened our chapter: individual self-determination and community well-being must be balanced. These issues can be clarified by asking questions such as *Who is to be empowered? For what purposes? What communities and other contexts are involved?* (Berkowitz, 1990; Riger, 1993). We try to recognize such issues in discussing examples of empowerment throughout Chapters 12 and 13.

MULTIPLE FORMS OF POWER

Understanding empowerment and citizen participation requires considering concepts of different forms of power. Our intent is to illuminate often-overlooked sources of power that may help to empower citizens and communities. Before reading this section, consider these questions:

In settings and relationships in your own life, how do you exercise power? How do others exercise it? Is the use of power different in different settings or relationships? How?

To what extent do your professors have power over you? Do you experience any differences in power in various classes? How? What forms of power can you exercise as a student? What are the limitations of these?

Now think more broadly about your communities and society. What forms of power exist there? How can citizens like you exert power there?

Power Over, To, and From

One useful formulation recognizes three forms of power (see Hollander & Offerman, 1990, p. 179; Riger, 1993; Rudkin, 2003; van Uchelen, 2000). **Power over** is the capacity to compel or dominate others. It may be used in ways that seem gentle but carry a clear implication that if others do not comply, stronger means will follow. Power over is often rooted in social structures. For instance, one form of power in organizations is "the ability to issue and enforce a command concerning the use of resources" (Levine, Perkins, & Perkins, 2005, p. 382). This ability is created by the organization's structure, regardless of the individuals involved. Also, in systems of oppression that we described in Chapter 7, the dominant group has power over, as when social customs and belief systems empower men more than women. Power over resembles classical sociological (especially Marxian) concepts of power (e.g., Giddens, Duneier, & Appelbaum, 2003). Use of power over involves a hierarchical, unequal relationship and can lead to injustice. Yet it also can be used collectively to promote justice, as when laws compel an end to racial discrimination.

Power to concerns the ability of individuals or groups to pursue their own goals and to develop one's capacities. Unlike power over, this can involve self-determination for each person. It may also involve sharing of power and influencing others by persuasion rather than coercion. However, it is not necessarily cooperative (Hollander & Offerman, 1990, p. 179; Riger, 1993). **Power from** is an ability to resist the power or unwanted demands of others. It can be used to resist a dominant boss or friend or to resist wider forms of social oppression. Some feminist critiques of patriarchy (which involves power over) focus on how women often use power to and power from, to resist domination (Hooks, 1984; Miller, 1976; van Uchelen, 2000).

In a workplace, for instance, a manager may exercise power over by giving orders, by seeking to persuade employees to do what the manager wants, or by delegating decisions to workers (allowing them some power to). Individually or collectively, employees can exercise power to and power from. They can use various persuasive and negotiating strategies. They may circumvent the manager's orders when he or she is not looking, or go "over the boss's head" to higher management. At the extreme, they can withdraw their labor (individually quit the job or collectively strike). This is not to say that the power of employers and employees is equal. Obstacles to employees' use of power (e.g., difficulties in organizing collective action) are greater than the obstacles employers face. However, since employers and employees both hold some forms of power, it is usually in the long-term interest of both to work together.

The power over/to/from framework is applicable to many situations. However, it has no explicit type of power gained through working with others, or *power with* (see Hollander & Offerman, 1990; Riger, 1993).

Integrative Power

Boulding (1989, p. 25) defined **integrative power** as the capacity to build groups, to bind people together and inspire loyalty. This is sometimes termed "people power"; it also resembles sense of community (see Chapter 6). Mohandas Gandhi and others often have asserted that there exist forms of power stronger and more widespread than violence, powers without which human relationships (families, friendships, communities) cannot exist. People enact these forms of integrative power every day. In a sense, the social sources of integrative power are infinite, unlike finite sources such as money (Katz, 1984).

Some of the most remarkable forms of integrative power have been based on moral or spiritual principles. Gandhi proposed the concept of *satyagraha,* literally translated as "clinging to truth" or more broadly as the power of truth (D. Dalton, 1993, p. 249). *Satyagraha* was the basis of Gandhi's nonviolent resistance to British colonialism, of the nonviolent demonstrations of the U.S. civil rights movement, and of more recent nonviolent resistance movements in Poland, South Africa, Chile, and elsewhere (Ackerman & DuVall, 2000; Boulding, 2000; Nagler, 2001). It is based on principled, active, openly expressed resistance to oppression coupled with an appeal to a widely held sense of social justice.

Integrative power also exists in other forms. Labor unions have long used strikes as a form of people power. Boycotts are an exercise of integrative economic power: colonial Americans boycotted tea to protest British policy, and later Americans boycotted cotton and sugar (made with slave labor) to protest slavery. In addition, many government officials will testify to the power of an organized citizen's group demanding specific changes; e.g., the Clean Elections advocacy mentioned by Alison Smith at the beginning of this chapter (we will discuss more examples in Chapter 13). Block associations, mentioned by Louis Burgess at the beginning of this chapter, rely on integrative power, as do support networks and self-help groups. In localities and macrosystems, however, successful use of integrative power often requires access to the media in order to broaden the pool of people who can bring pressure on key decision makers.

Like other forms of power, integrative power can be used for good or ill. It can involve prejudice against an outgroup or be used to enforce conformity within a community.

Reward, Coercive, Legitimate, Expert, and Referent Power

Social psychologists French and Raven (1959; Raven, 1999) identified five forms of power, which they defined as an ability to influence others. **Reward** power involves control of valued rewards; others will shape their actions to obtain these. **Coercive** power is capacity to punish. Both may enforce a target person's behavioral compliance, but both also invite covert or overt resistance. They resemble power over.

French and Raven (1959) originally defined **legitimate power** as "position power," based on a superior position or role in an organization or relationship (similar to power over). Thus an employer has legitimate power to give orders to employees, or a teacher to give grades to students. Position power might also be used in hierarchies of oppression, as when men are considered superior to women. However, if position power is widely considered unjust, its legitimacy may be undermined.

Raven (1999) added concepts of legitimacy based on widely endorsed social norms, not dependent on hierarchical position. For instance, the norm of reciprocity brings expectations that a favor will be returned, and the norm of social responsibility implies that everyone has an obligation to help the less fortunate. These norms can be ignored, but they are widely considered rightful. In some circumstances, they can be used by the less powerful against the more powerful.

Expert power also can be used to offset position power. It is based on the knowledge, skill or experience of a person or group. Mental health professionals are considered experts, but mutual help groups also offer expertise on psychological difficulties and disorders. Writing about workplaces, Klein, Ralls, Smith-Major, and Douglas (2000, p. 277) emphasized the strengths of expert power. In rapidly changing economies, they asserted, the organization's flexibility and productivity is more related to knowledge and ability to learn than to preserving positions and control in a hierarchy. Thus, empowerment efforts in workplaces could usefully focus on gaining and exercising expertise: e.g., skills in gathering new information, problem solving, understanding diverse cultures, and team decision making. The participatory research methods that we discussed in Chapters 3 and 4 also can be a basis of expert power for communities. The Waupun youth group, described at the beginning of this chapter, conducted a survey that was instrumental in exerting pressure on city government and the railroad.

Referent power is based on an interpersonal connection or a social identity the people share. It is potentially involved in any human relationship. It is a key resource for recovery in mutual help groups, for example (Salem, Reischl, Gallacher, & Randall, 2000). Broom and Klein (1999) described three forms of influence involving referent power. One form is based on liking, respect, or a personal relationship. Another form involves appeals to group solidarity or to overarching group values. A third form is networking: seeking help from someone in your social network. Referent power usually refers to interpersonal, microsystem relationships; integrative power usually refers to organizations, communities, or macrosystems.

Three Instruments of Social Power

Gaventa (1980), a social activist, used concepts of political science to describe three instruments of social power (see also Speer & Hughey, 1995). A story provides examples.

> A corporation filed for a permit to use sludge containing human waste on their farm site, which produced grass sod in a rural area along the Walkill River in upstate New York. Under a temporary permit granted by the state without any local input, sludge dumping began. Local citizens discovered the stench without warning, and reacted with understandable anger. The state's Department of Environmental Conservation (DEC) held extensive public hearings on the company's application for a permanent permit before an administrative law judge. These hearings involved hours of testimony by technical experts and local citizens. In theory, all had full input into the DEC decision.
>
> In practice, however, this formal process was distinctly one sided. The local citizens were assigned seats in rows behind attorneys involved in the case. They did not have the legal training or technical background of the corporation's hired experts and knew neither the legal procedure nor the terminology used routinely during the hearings. They made a number of procedural errors until they hired their own attorney. When many of the local farmers became frustrated with their lack of real input, they used their tractors to block access to the sod farm. They were only temporarily successful.
>
> Perhaps most telling, citizens' knowledge of local conditions was discounted. Years of accumulated practical experience had shaped their intuitive understanding of things such as the effects of rainwater runoff on streams and the Walkill River. Yet expert testimony, by consultants who did not live or

work in the community, primarily influenced the judge's decision. When that testimony revealed that the corporation's plans met all state regulations, the permit was granted.

Within five years, virtually every negative outcome predicted by the local citizens had occurred. Wastes had flowed into the Walkill River, groundwater was contaminated with toxic cadmium, and illegal hazardous wastes had been stored at the site. DEC sued the operators of the site for repeated violations and finally had to classify the property as a hazardous waste site for later cleanup. Though they were unsuccessful in this case, local citizens founded Orange Environment, an organization active in community organizing, legal action and policy advocacy on environmental issues. (adapted from Rich et al., 1995, pp. 660–662)

Gaventa's first instrument of power is **controlling resources that can be used to bargain, reward, and punish.** This resembles coercive and reward power, and often power over. In the Walkill River example, the company had the money to hire experts and attorneys, to use or circumvent the law, and to overwhelm local opposition. Yet in other contexts, an organized citizenry can effectively threaten punishments such as negative publicity or boycotts, or offer attractive compromises.

The second instrument of social power is **controlling channels for participation in community decisions.** Speaking at public hearings, signing petitions, and voting are traditional forms of participation. However, Gaventa (1980) also refers to subtler mechanisms, such as controlling meeting agendas to exclude citizen comments and debate, or requiring citizens to hire attorneys to advocate for them. In the Walkill River case, this instrument of power was used to limit citizen testimony. In theory, the DEC public hearings offered citizens the chance to participate in and influence a decision that would affect their health and livelihoods. In practice, legal procedures effectively prevented any meaningful citizen participation. Yet in other contexts, an organized opposition can open other channels of participation, such as public demonstrations or use of the media. Walkill citizens founded Orange Environment in part to provide legal advocacy when needed to participate in decision making.

The third instrument of power, often overlooked, is **shaping the definition of a public issue or conflict.** This is the power of "spin," shaping the terms of public debate on an issue (Gaventa, 1980). For instance, in the Walkill River case, key decision makers favored general scientific expertise over the local, practical knowledge of residents. Communications media shape how social issues are defined, but the third instrument of power is not theirs alone. Behind the media are social institutions and interest groups with the money and perceived credibility to make their voices heard and to create the ideas of the media and the public. The dominant beliefs of a community or society also shape how social issues are interpreted (Rappaport, 2000). An example is Tatum's (1997) metaphor of "breathing smog" for widely accepted social stereotypes (mentioned in Chapter 7). Yet in some situations, citizens who adroitly use the media or word-of-mouth channels

TABLE 12.2 Key Concepts of Power

Power over, to, from
Integrative power
Reward, coercive, legitimate, expert, referent power
Three instruments of social power
Control of resources for bargaining
Control of channels for participation
Shaping definitions of public issues

also shape public opinion. Orange Environment used this instrument of power through public advocacy regarding local environmental issues.

We list key concepts of power in Table 12.2.

Summary Thoughts on Power

What is power, in terms useful to community psychologists?

Exercising power (having an impact on decisions) requires having control of some resources, and ultimately at least some capacity to compel those who resist, so that they go along or compromise. Many resources can empower communities, and personal willingness to get involved and work with others can help mobilize them (recall the examples that began this chapter or the story of Debi Starnes in Chapter 1).

Power is not a purely internal state, such as simply feeling powerful, inspired, or confident. Holding power involves capacity to exert actual influence on decisions (Riger, 1993).

Power is best understood as a dimension, not an all-or-none dichotomy. Seldom is a person or group all powerful or entirely powerless. Those who hold greater power will resist change, yet others may be able to use alternative sources of power. Even small acts may reflect some degree of power. Persons and groups with little or no capacity to compel may find ways to resist the powerful. We do not discount the differences in power in oppressive systems, but seek to call attention to sources of power that citizens can use.

Power is best understood in relationships (Gaventa, 1980; Serrano-Garcia, 1994). It changes as relationships change in families, settings, communities, and societies, and it shifts in unpredictable ways. Power also is contextual: you may hold power in some circumstances, as in influencing decisions in a student group, but not elsewhere, as in a job where you have little voice in decisions. Community psychology as a field still has much to learn about power and about how to balance empowerment with values of community and social justice (Riger, 1993).

HOW DO CITIZEN PARTICIPATION, EMPOWERMENT, AND SENSE OF COMMUNITY INTERTWINE?

How do citizens become participatory, empowered leaders in their communities? Beginning with a developmental perspective, we describe qualities of empowered persons and links between sense of community and participation.

A Developmental Perspective

At a community organizing meeting at her church, Virginia Ramirez raised her hand. "I have this problem. This neighbor lady of mine died because it was too cold and they wouldn't fix her house. I want someone to do something about it."

"What are *you* going to do about it?" the community organizer asked. Angered, Virginia left the meeting. A few days later, an organizer came to Virginia's home. Virginia let her in only because the organizer was a nun. The organizer asked only why Virginia was so angry. She responded with stories not only about her neighbor but also of poor schools and overt racism. Eventually Virginia agreed to hold a meeting of neighbors in her home.

Virginia had never run a meeting, but discussion turned quickly to neighborhood problems: poor housing, poor sewers, few city services. Together the group researched documents at city hall, and discovered that city funds for repairing houses in their neighborhood had been diverted to build a street in an affluent area. When they went to a city council meeting to complain, Virginia froze. "I didn't remember my speech. I barely remembered my name. Then I . . . realized that I was just telling the story of our community. So I told it and we got our money back. It was hard. . . . But I began to understand the importance of holding people accountable. . . ."

The community organizers encouraged Virginia to continue learning in order to make her involvement in social causes more effective. They helped her reflect on each step of participation and learn new skills. Virginia earned her G.E.D. and eventually finished college. Her husband objected strenuously at first. When he yelled at her for studying instead of cleaning house and fixing supper, she trembled but told him, "I'm preparing for my future. If you don't like it, that's too bad, because I'm going to do it. I'm sorry, but this is a priority." Slowly and reluctantly, he accepted and even began to take pride in her accomplishments.

Virginia became a community organizer, supervising volunteers in health education outreach and training members of her church and community, especially women, to speak out. She negotiated with politicians and business leaders to promote community development and better jobs and testified before the U.S. Senate about an innovative job training

> program she helped develop. Through it all, her faith has sustained her personally and directed her efforts. (quoted and paraphrased from Loeb, 1999, pp. 15–20, 55)

One way to understand citizen participation and empowerment is to study how it develops over time among individuals-in-communities like Virginia Ramirez. For instance, Keiffer (1984) studied the development of a sample of 15 adult community activists. They included a working-class mother who had become the prime force in constructing a community health clinic, a migrant laborer who had become an organizer and boycott coordinator, a former junkie and gang leader who had become a leader in an urban homesteading program, and a retired laborer leading efforts against brown lung disease (Kieffer, 1984, pp. 13–14). From another perspective, Watts, Williams, and Jagers (2003) studied sociopolitical development among 24 African American youth and young adult activists. Kieffer looked for similarities among activists in diverse cultural and social contexts; Watts and associates focused on development of persons within African-American culture. Both approaches used qualitative methods that allowed thick description of participants' experiences. Although the processes and outcomes of development were different, some similarities emerged.

In both studies, individuals initially accepted the social and political status quo but increasingly recognized social injustice. They began to see how community and personal events involved power, which benefited only members of dominant groups. For participants in the Watts et al., this involved experiences of racism. For Kieffer's participants, it involved varied, specific provocations: a dam that would flood a mountain community; a betrayal of trust by an employer; being assaulted in one's own yard. For Virginia Ramirez, the process began when she recognized the social injustice behind her neighbor's death. Events like these can lead citizens, however reluctantly, to begin speaking out and confronting those they hold responsible. In both studies, participants passed through intermediate stages of development, leading to a transformed sense of self and to empowered participation in social action. Several themes ran through these participants' and researchers' words. Many also fit Virginia Ramirez's experiences.

- Conflict and growth were intertwined. This included conflicts between competing family and community commitments and conflicts between citizens and powerful elites.
- Practical experience and critical reflection about it were intertwined, leading to insights and learning for the future.
- Kieffer's participants emphasized the importance of being embedded in their communities, obtaining social support from local organizations, and having a personal mentor who provided advice and support. The young activists studied by Watts et al. mentioned similar themes as well as social settings such as training workshops for African-American youth.
- Activists developed an awareness of power relationships in their communities and everyday lives along with a sense that these relationships could be transformed if citizens worked together.

- An inspiring, shared vision of liberation helped frame specific goals for their work and helped sustain activists' personal commitment.
- Sustainable growth from uninvolved citizen to activist-leader took time. In Kieffer's sample, the process averaged four years, but there was much variability.

These developmental insights are useful but are only one standpoint for understanding how participation, empowerment, and community intertwine. Another perspective is to study the qualities of empowered persons.

Personal Qualities for Citizen Participation and Empowerment

> Empowerment appears not to be a spectator sport. (McMillan. Florin, Stevenson, Kerman, & Mitchell, 1995, p. 721)

In research that we reviewed, six personal qualities seem common among empowered persons engaged in citizen participation (see also reviews by Berkowitz, 2000, and Zimmerman, 2000). Empowerment is contextual. It develops in a specific setting, community, and culture and is strongly influenced by those contexts. Thus, the following list of qualities is suggestive; we do not expect it to be characteristic of empowered persons in all circumstances.

Critical Awareness This is an understanding of how power and sociopolitical forces affect personal and community life (Friere, 1970/1993; Zimmerman, 2000). Serrano-Garcia (1984) listed two cognitive elements: "critical judgment about situations [and] the search for underlying causes of problems and their consequences" (p. 178). One form of critical awareness is understanding hierarchies of oppression, dominant and subordinated groups, and social myths that sustain such hierarchies of power (Moane, 2003; Watts et al., 2003). The feminist motto "The personal is political" is an expression of critical awareness.

Critical awareness emerges from three sources: life experiences with injustices, reflection on those experiences and lessons learned, and dialogue with others. It begins with questioning the legitimacy of existing social conditions and existing authority, and involves learning to see problems as social practices that can be changed, not as the natural order of the world. It proceeds with answering questions such as: Who defines community problems? How are community decisions made? Whose views are respected and whose are excluded? Who holds power and how do they use it? How can they be challenged?

The stories of Virginia Ramirez, Alison Smith, and the Waupun youth especially illustrate critical awareness. Virginia Ramirez's group documented that money had been diverted from services for their neighborhood, which deepened their critical awareness of how a city decision had affected their lives and of where to focus their action.

Participatory Skills To be effective in citizen participation, the person also needs behavioral skills. Empirical research and other accounts suggest a variety of these (Balcazar, Seekins, Fawcett, & Hopkins, 1990; Berkowitz, 1987, 1996, 2000; Foster-Fishman, Berkowitz, Lounsbury, Jacobson, & Allen, 2001; Kieffer, 1984; Lappe & DuBois, 1994; Watts et al., 2003):

- articulating community problems using critical awareness
- imagining and articulating visions of a better community
- assertively and constructively advocating one's views
- actively listening to others, including opponents
- identifying and cultivating personal and community resources
- relating well to people of diverse cultures and life experiences
- building collaborative relationships and encouraging teamwork
- identifying, managing and resolving conflicts
- planning strategies for community change
- finding, using and providing social support
- avoiding burnout by finding ways to sustain commitment
- sharing leadership and power

However, participatory competence is contextual; some of these skills are more important in one setting than another.

Skills for identifying and mobilizing resources are particularly important (Zimmerman, 2000). Resources include tangible factors such as time, money, skills, knowledge, and influential allies. They also include less tangible qualities such as legitimacy or status in the community, the talents and ideas of community members, their personal commitment to community change, and social support. Social resources include shared values and the shared rituals and stories that illustrate those values (Rappaport, 1995). Many of the psychological and social resources involved in empowerment (e.g., social support, commitment, knowledge) are multiplied through working together (Katz, 1984; Rappaport, 1987). These skills can be learned, as the stories of Alison Smith and Virginia Ramirez especially illustrate.

Sense of Collective Efficacy This is the belief that citizens acting collectively can be effective in improving community life (Bandura, 1986, pp. 449–453; Perkins & Long, 2002, p. 295). Critical awareness and behavioral skills alone will seldom lead to action unless persons also believe that collective action will lead to constructive changes (Saegert & Winkel, 1996; Zimmerman, 2000).

Others defined this simply as collective efficacy. Our term *sense of* collective efficacy explicitly denotes an individual cognition. Belief in collective efficacy usually arises along with personal experience in citizen participation. Sense of collective efficacy is contextual: a person may believe that citizens can collectively influence community decisions in one situation but not in another (Bandura, 1986; Duncan, Duncan, Okut, Strycker, & Hix-Small, 2003; Perkins & Long, 2002).

In quantitative studies of U.S. urban neighborhoods, citizens with stronger beliefs related to critical awareness and collective efficacy, participated more in community organizations, and experienced a stronger sense of community (Perkins, Brown, & Taylor, 1996; Perkins & Long, 2002; Speer, 2000). Neighborhoods with higher levels of collective efficacy had lower crime rates (Snowden, 2005).

Sense of Personal Participatory Efficacy This is the individual's belief that he or she personally has the capacity to engage effectively in citizen participation and influence community decisions. At its strongest, this includes confidence that one can be an effective leader in citizen action. This is not simply feeling empowered; it must also be connected to behavioral participation. It is a contextual belief; one can feel more effective in some situations than in others. It thus is a specific form of self-efficacy (Bandura, 1986). Virginia Ramirez and Alison Smith grew both in sense of collective efficacy and in sense of personal participatory efficacy.

Research has often concerned similar concepts of sociopolitical control, perceived control, and political efficacy (Zimmerman, 2000). (Again, we added *sense of* to make explicit the cognitive focus.) Such beliefs have been linked to citizen participation among residents of a neighborhood near a hazardous waste site, residents of urban neighborhoods, and in other circumstances (Speer, 2000; Zimmerman, 2000). However, context makes a difference: in one study, involvement in a community service experience led college students to increased feelings of political commitment, but a *decreased* sense of political efficacy (Angelique, Reischl, & Davidson, 2002). Perhaps these students discovered community and social forces that were not as changeable as they had originally expected.

Qualitative studies of community activists have found that long-term citizen participation was sustained by optimism: enjoyment of challenges, can-do spirit, excitement about the work (Berkowitz, 1987; Colby & Damon, 1992). In these studies, experienced citizen activists also attributed setbacks to temporary or situational causes, not personal failures, and sought to learn from them. They celebrated successes and accepted adversity with humor. These optimistic ways of thinking seem related to personal efficacy beliefs about participation.

Participatory Values and Commitment Beliefs about efficacy are not enough to motivate citizen action. Participation is often initiated and sustained by commitment to deeply held values.

Qualitative studies and other accounts have often found that spiritual or moral commitment sustained citizen participation and empowerment (Berkowitz, 1987; Colby & Damon, 1992; Loeb, 1999; Moane, 2003; Nagler, 2001; Schorr, 1997). For some, this involved spiritual faith and practices; for others, it centered on a secular commitment to moral principles such as social justice. Spiritual support for community involvement included a sense of "being called" to their work and certainty of its spiritual necessity. Beliefs that enabled taking risks included a certainty that "God will provide," and a "willing suspension of fear and doubt" as they began new challenges. A capacity for forgiveness in the rough and tumble of community decision making was also important (Colby & Damon, 1992, pp. 78–80, 189–194, and 296). Virginia Ramirez and others in her church illustrate a spiritual basis for participatory commitment.

TABLE 12.3 Personal Qualities for Citizen Participation

Critical awareness
Participatory skills
Sense of collective efficacy
Sense of personal participatory efficacy
Participatory values and commitment
Relational connections

Moane's (2003) account of empowerment in the Irish women's liberation movement included building personal strengths in creativity and spirituality and a larger, positive vision of liberation. Berkowitz (1987, p. 323) found what he called "traditional virtue" among many local activists: caring for others, integrity, persistence, and commitment. Colby and Damon (1992, p. 78) found similar commitments to justice, harmony, honesty, and charity. Schorr's (1997) review of effective community organizations found that many promote a shared group climate based on spiritual or secular ideals that provide shared meaning and purpose related to community change.

Relational Connections Empowerment and citizen participation do not occur in a social vacuum. They involve a wide variety of relationships with others, including both bonding and bridging ties (Putnam, 2000; recall these from Chapter 6). They also include social support and mentoring for participation, neighboring, and participating in community organizations (Kieffer, 1984; Moane, 2003; Putnam & Feldstein, 2003; Speer & Hughey, 1995). Relational connections were essential for Virginia Ramirez, Alison Smith, the Waupun youth, and Louis Burgess in their development as citizen leaders.

Table 12.3 lists the six qualities we have highlighted. Our list is merely suggestive; there is no single profile of empowered persons or citizen activists (Berkowitz, 2000; Zimmerman, 2000).

Sense of Community and Citizen Participation in Neighborhood Organizations

Neighborhood organizations illustrate how grassroots citizen participation and empowerment intertwine with sense of community. For instance, as the story of Louis Burgess illustrates, volunteer block associations offer many opportunities for participation in neighborhood decisions. (A "block" in this sense includes the two facing sides of a street, one block long.) Block associations address a variety of neighborhood issues such as zoning, housing, neighborhood appearance, crime, traffic, and recreation. They form mediating structures between individual residents and city governments. In studies in New York City, resident perceptions of problems on the block decreased over time on blocks with an association, and increased on those without one (Wandersman & Florin, 2000, pp. 263–264).

Community psychologists have studied citizen participation in block associations and larger neighborhood organizations in several U.S. cities: Nashville, New York City, Baltimore, and Salt Lake City. Citizen participation is usually measured as a variable ranging from attending meetings through increasing involvement in association tasks to association leadership. Samples in all four cities were multiracial, multiethnic, and of lower to middle income (Chavis & Wandersman, 1990; Florin, Chavis, Wandersman, & Rich, 1992; Florin & Wandersman, 1984; Perkins, Brown, & Taylor, 1996; Perkins, Florin, Rich, & Wandersman, 1990; Perkins & Long, 2002; Unger & Wandersman, 1983, 1985; Wandersman & Florin, 2000).

In general, these studies demonstrated the interrelationships of five key factors:

- sense of community for the neighborhood
- informal neighboring, such as talking with neighbors or watching someone's house while they are away
- initial dissatisfaction with neighborhood problems
- sense of collective efficacy, regarding working through the neighborhood organization
- extent of citizen participation in neighborhood organizations

These findings suggest a pathway of citizen participation similar to the findings of the developmental studies (Kieffer, 1984; Watts et al., 2003) that we described earlier: embeddedness in a community, recognition of challenges there, a sense that these challenges can be addressed collectively, and a spiraling pattern of participation in a grassroots organization and strengthening sense of efficacy. Though the process is often initiated by neighborhood problems, high levels of crime can inhibit participation (Saegert & Winkel, 2004). Longitudinal analyses of the New York City data indicated that participation led to increased feelings of efficacy (Chavis & Wandersman, 1990). More recent studies have also connected sense of community, social capital, and participation in grassroots organizations (Hughey, Speer, & Peterson, 1999; Peterson & Reid, 2003; Saegert & Winkel, 2004). Of course, not every person, organization, or locality follows the same pattern, but these factors are often involved.

These studies demonstrate that sense of community, neighboring, and citizen participation are resources for communities, even those with fewer material resources. These resources involve not simply individuals, but individuals-in-communities.

HOW CAN COMMUNITY ORGANIZATIONS EMPOWER THEIR MEMBERS?

When I returned to Atlanta [after long involvement in the civil rights movement, and serving as ambassador to the United Nations], I wanted nothing to do with politics. Some of the women in Ebenezer Baptist Church

> wanted me to run for mayor. I was very reluctant, but one of them told me, "We need for you to do this. And we *made* you." I told her, "That's funny, I thought Martin [Luther King, Jr.] made me." "Oh, no" she replied. "We made him, too." (Andrew Young, speech to the Society for Community Research and Action, June 2001)

As this story indicates, Ebenezer Baptist Church in Atlanta was a key setting in the civil rights movement (and as its members hoped, Andrew Young did become mayor of Atlanta). To fully understand citizen participation and empowerment, we must learn how community organizations empower citizens and foster citizen participation. We begin this section with a distinction between empowering and empowered organizations, describe two examples of empowering community organizations, identify nine qualities of such organizations, and conclude by discussing dilemmas in creating and maintaining empowering organizations. In Chapter 13 we will turn to empowered community organizations that influence their communities and societies.

Empowering versus Empowered Community Organizations

Communities and community organizations can be described as empowering or empowered (Zimmerman, 2000; Peterson & Zimmerman, 2004). **Empowering organizations** foster member participation and sharing of power in group decisions and actions. **Empowered organizations** exercise power in the wider community or society, influencing decisions and helping to create community and macrosystem change.

Becoming an empowered organization often requires creating empowering opportunities for members and citizens (McMillan, Florin, Stevenson, Kerman, & Mitchell, 1995). But being empowering and empowered do not always go together. Organizations that exclude rank and file members from any real decision-making power may nonetheless be powerful forces in communities and societies. For instance, Putnam (2000) noted the rise of U.S. national advocacy organizations, which rely on mail and online fundraising, use mass media and lobbying to exercise power, and lack active local chapters.

In addition, some organizations that empower their members choose not to seek wider influence. A mutual help group or spiritual setting, for instance, may empower its members to participate in decision making within the group. Yet many of these settings are not concerned with influencing communities or society. The individualistic focus of psychology, even community psychology, has meant that until recently study of empowerment focused on individual processes of empowerment. Thus when settings or organizations were considered, researchers attended to factors that were empowering for individuals, not how citizen organizations gained and exercised power in community or society (Peterson & Zimmerman, 2004; Riger, 1993). That focus is now broadening to study how empowered community organizations wield wider influence. This is consistent with Rappaport's (1987) original emphasis on empowerment at multiple levels (Zimmerman, 2000).

Next we turn to two stories of empowering community organizations.

Block Booster: Capacity Building in Neighborhood Organizations

The Block Booster Project applied community psychology methods to strengthening block associations in New York City, including the one involving Louis Burgess. The associations were in Brooklyn and Queens, where housing density is less than Manhattan and more typical of other U.S. cities. Neighborhoods were working-class and middle-class areas, and were predominantly European American, predominantly African American, or racially diverse (Florin, Chavis, Wandersman, & Rich, 1992; Prestby, Wandersman, Florin, Rich, & Chavis, 1990; Wandersman & Florin, 2000).

Block associations flourish through citizen participation, or lapse without it. In Block Booster studies, one-quarter to nearly one-half of block associations became inactive over time. Block associations that thrived differed from those that failed in a number of ways. They made more intensive efforts to recruit members, had more ways for individuals to become involved, provided more incentives and fewer barriers for participating, made decisions with more member participation, and carried out more activities.

The Block Booster Project applied these findings by providing organizational development assistance to block associations in order to strengthen their capacity to involve citizens and implement community activities. First, Block Booster staff conducted surveys of each block's residents regarding attitudes about the block association, participation in block activities, and skills that might be useful for the neighborhood. Members of the block association were surveyed about group cohesiveness, leader support, group order and organization, and related concepts from social climate scales (Moos, 1994; recall these from Chapter 5). From these data, Block Booster Profiles were drawn up to describe each block and block association.

Block Booster staff then conducted training for block association leaders. Two leaders from each association participated in a workshop on strengthening block associations as well as in ongoing consultation with Block Booster staff. Training emphasized using member resources, decentralizing decisions, developing leaders, and linking with other organizations and external resources. Staff also explained specific strengths and areas for improvement for each block association as revealed in the profiles. For instance, if member surveys indicated that an association did not focus on tangible goals and tasks, leaders could learn ways to hold more organized meetings and set group goals. If residents indicated that lack of child care limited their meeting attendance, association leaders were encouraged to provide it. Block association leaders also developed action plans for their groups, put these into action, and evaluated their impacts.

An experimental evaluation of the Block Booster training found that 10 months after the workshops, associations that received the Block Booster training and consultation were significantly more active than a control group that received only limited assistance (Florin et al., 1992; Wandersman & Florin, 2000).

Midwest ARC: Conflict and Coempowerment in a Community Organization

> To live is to have conflict. If you don't have conflict, you aren't doing anything. (A community organization leader interviewed by Lappe & DuBois, 1994, p. 247)

Conflict is a fact of life in community work. It may involve polite disagreement or passionate confrontation. Community organizers and researchers agree that a community organization is more effective in the long run if it appreciates and manages conflict, rather than resisting it (Bartunek & Keys, 1979; Chavis, 2001; Kaye & Wolff, 1997; Lappe & DuBois, 1994; Wiesenfeld, 1996). Conflict is a source of new ideas that challenge assumptions. It provides an opportunity for greater inclusion of all members. It often accompanies diversity of backgrounds, life experiences, and viewpoints, and thus can be a positive sign of a truly diverse group. Creatively and wisely resolved, it often leads to better decisions, greater group confidence, increased skills for members, and a stronger organization (Lappe & DuBois, 1994). The following case example by Bond and Keys (1993; Bond, 1999) illustrates how constructive conflict management in a community organization made it more empowering and empowered.

Midwest ARC (a pseudonym) was founded in a U.S. city by families of persons with developmental disabilities. It provided community services for persons with these disabilities, including a day program, vocational services, residences, and an early intervention program. The organization was founded in part because professional services had been patronizing and ineffective, and families initially controlled the organization.

Over time, Midwest ARC broadened its scope and began to bring into its governing board community members (often professionals) who had access to community leaders and resources (including funding for Midwest ARC's expanded programs). However, the organization retained a parents' association, which found ways to overturn or circumvent many governing board decisions. Two subgroups emerged within Midwest ARC: a parents' group and a professionals' group. Parent members tended to be from the working class, valued practical knowledge, and usually had long experience with Midwest ARC. Because their views had often been ignored by professionals, some parents had cultivated confrontational communication styles in order to be heard. Professionals were highly educated and tended to be verbal, confident of their expertise, and impatient with practical details. They had little experience with developmental disabilities or the day-to-day work of Midwest ARC.

A number of conflicts emerged, leading to increasing turnover in staff and in board membership and disrupting the work of the organization. Decisions were often made by a few individuals, sharpening mistrust between subgroups. These conflicts were not simply interpersonal; they involved the differing worlds of the parent and professional subgroups and the wider social context in which professionals had many privileges not shared by the parents.

However, several Midwest ARC members saw that the organization needed both subgroups. Some of these members had interpersonal ties that bridged the conflicting subgroups. One was a community member who often worked in the Midwest ARC crafts store run mostly by family members. Another was a founding parent member who reached out to community and professional board members. A new executive director cultivated strong ties with both subgroups. Their boundary spanning helped each subgroup learn about and begin to respect what the other subgroup had to contribute.

The boundary spanners joined with others to develop an organizational atmosphere of recognizing and using all the resources offered by Midwest ARC members. They also called attention to goals shared by all involved in Midwest ARC, especially a commitment to provide expanded services for persons with developmental disabilities. Both subgroups increasingly recognized that to attain these goals, each needed the other's help.

Organizational bylaws were formalized to ensure that decisions would be made more openly and fairly. Consistent with Midwest ARC's history, the governing board was to have both parent and community representatives, with parents in a majority. This provision enabled parent advocates to accept the board's role. Also, the power of the parents' association was limited. This strengthened community members' confidence that their efforts were useful. More decisions were made by the board, not by a few officers or insiders. The board also made its membership more diverse. It brought in professionals who were also parents of persons with developmental disabilities and community members from working-class communities.

Midwest ARC went on to attain a number of organizational goals, including a successful capital fundraising campaign and increased funding for expanded services. Its process of organizational change has been termed **coempowerment.** It embodied collaboration, community, and empowerment.

Qualities of Empowering Community Organizations

What qualities of community organizations empower their members? We have assembled nine key qualities of empowering community organizations. These were identified in case studies of community settings, personal accounts of community psychologists, and reviews of research on effective neighborhood organizations, community coalitions, and organizational empowerment (Bond & Keys, 1993; Foster-Fishman, Berkowitz, Lounsbury, Jacobson, & Allen, 2001; Peterson & Zimmerman, 2004; Speer & Hughey, 1995; Wandersman & Florin, 2000; Wolff, 2001a). Some factors first identified as important in community settings focused on personal development (Maton & Salem, 1995) and have also proven to be important in settings concerned with citizen participation in community decisions. Our list is suggestive; others might choose a different list from the many important factors.

Group-Based, Strengths-Based Belief System Empowering community organizations promote principles or beliefs that define member and organizational goals, provide meaning and inspiration for action, develop strengths, and promote optimism in the face of setbacks. Shared community events, rituals, and narratives embody core values and strengthen sense of community as well as personal commitment to the group. For example, the belief system of Midwest ARC emphasized the strengths of persons with developmental disabilities and their families. However, identification with a belief system and in-group can create stereotyped images of those outside the group, generate conflict, and foster manipulation by emotional appeals (Pratkanis & Turner, 1996). Fostering external linkages outside the group and awareness of values transcending the group can reduce these risks.

Social Support Empowering organizations promote exchange of social support among members. A case study of effective faith-based community advocacy organizations found that one-to-one meetings among members helped build mutual support and identified issues for action (Speer, Hughey, Gensheimer, & Adams-Leavitt, 1995). Social support and interpersonal ties among members also build organizational solidarity and power for influencing the wider community (Putnam & Feldstein, 2003; Speer & Hughey, 1995).

Shared, Inspiring Leadership Empowering settings have committed leaders who articulate a vision for the organization, exemplify interpersonal and organizational skills, share power, and mentor new leaders (Maton & Salem, 1995). Mentoring was one of the key factors in development of community activists in Kieffer's (1984) study. At Midwest ARC, the ability of new leaders to articulate overall organizational goals and to build interdependence among families and professionals was important in coempowerment. Sharing leadership and developing new leaders were also important in Block Booster.

Participatory Niches, Opportunity Role Structures Empowering organizations create roles and tasks that offer opportunities for members to become involved and assume responsibility: participatory niches (Speer & Hughey, 1995), or opportunity role structures (Maton & Salem, 1995). GROW, the mutual help organization described in Chapter 8, creates new chapters with few members and multiple roles as a way of fostering member participation in the group (Zimmerman et al., 1991). In Block Booster, effective block associations had more offices and committees in which individuals could actively work together (Wandersman & Florin, 2000). These tactics create underpopulated settings that promote member participation (Barker, 1968; Schoggen, 1989; recall this concept from Chapter 5). Participatory niches promote recruitment and training of individuals for roles needed by the setting, increase members' leadership skills, and strengthen their interpersonal ties within the group.

Members bring diverse skills to a community organization: e.g., assertion, emotional sensitivity, financial management, writing, planning events, securing volunteers, or remodeling dilapidated office space. Knowledge of cultures, languages, or community history may be useful. Social networks and connections, prestige or legitimacy as community leaders, and other social resources are important.

An empowering organization has leaders and members who identify and engage such resources (Foster-Fishman et al., 2001; Peterson & Zimmerman, 2004).

Task Focus Citizens prefer to become involved in community organizations that get things done, with clear goals and productive meetings (Wandersman & Florin, 2000). In addition, such organizational structure increases the capacity of the organization to make an impact in its community (Allen, 2005; Fawcett et al., 1995; Foster-Fishman et al., 2001; Wandersman, Goodman, & Butterfoss, 1997). This includes having organization goals and specific objectives for action, meeting agendas, time limits, and leaders who can summarize lengthy discussions and clarify choices to be made. The Block Booster training focused on strengthening this capacity. At Midwest ARC, specifying responsibilities of the governing board and parents' association helped to reduce conflicts.

Inclusive Decision Making This is the essence of citizen participation: widespread, genuine power and voice for citizens in making organizational decisions and plans. Midwest ARC moved from having insiders and officers make key decisions to having a more representative board and committees. Block Booster research demonstrated that more inclusive decision making strengthened both citizen participation and organizational viability. Community coalitions function best when decisions are inclusive (Foster-Fishman et al., 2001).

Allen (2005) studied 43 local domestic violence coordinating councils in one U.S. state. These councils included members from criminal justice, health, education, social services, and other community groups. The best predictor of council effectiveness (as perceived by its members) was an inclusive climate of shared decision making in which members from many community agencies and groups actively participated.

Participatory Rewards Community groups rely on volunteers. If those volunteers don't find their involvement rewarding, or if its personal costs are too high, they will leave. If they find involvement rewarding, they will often become more involved. Empowering community settings provide rewards for citizen participation that outweigh its costs (Prestby, Wandersman, Florin, Rich, & Chavis, 1990; see also Kaye, 2001; Kaye & Wolff, 1997).

Participation is often initiated by concerns such as "How does this problem or decision directly affect me or my family?" Louis Burgess's original motive for involvement in a block association was to gain restitution for a poorly built shower. However, his motivation developed into a broader concern with the quality of life in his neighborhood, and became rewarding in ways he had not anticipated.

Lappe and DuBois (1994, p. 30) informally asked U.S. citizens what rewards they obtained from community involvement. Some illustrative answers included:

- taking pride in accomplishment
- feeling my actions are in tune with my values

- discovering how much I have to contribute
- working with those who share my concerns and hopes
- learning new skills, such as how to negotiate
- knowing my efforts will help create a better world for those I love
- enjoying better communities, schools, jobs, housing, medical care

Barriers to participation include competing demands on time and energy; finding child care; feeling out of place; and unpleasant meetings (e.g., rambling discussions, unproductive conflict). In the Block Booster Project, associations that fostered rewards and lowered barriers to participation had greater levels of member participation and were more likely to remain viable over time (Prestby et al., 1990).

Promoting Diversity Empowering community organizations value member diversity, which can broaden the skills, knowledge, resources, legitimacy, and social connections available to the setting. For community coalitions and other organizations that seek to represent multiple parts of a community, seeking diversity is essential.

However, promoting diversity does not end with a diverse membership list. Often more difficult is the work of building an atmosphere of genuine inclusion of all viewpoints. As with Midwest ARC, when powerful community leaders or professionals (who are used to speaking out and being heeded) dominate discussion, the group must find ways to enable less powerful members to speak out, support each other, and influence decisions.

Promoting diverse participation includes having several members from a disenfranchised group, not just one token member. It also includes taking time to discuss issues of diversity and making organizational language inclusive (e.g. recognizing the presence of women or youth). Finally, diversity is not fully realized until the leadership, not simply the membership, is diverse (Foster-Fishman et al., 2001; Goodkind & Foster-Fishman, 2002).

Fostering Intergroup Collaboration Promoting diversity can generate challenges for a setting. Community members share a macrobelonging or overall sense of community but also have microbelongings, their identifications with other groups within or outside the community (Wiesenfeld, 1996). This also is true of organizations. Diversity multiplies microbelongings, which are often valuable and must be respected, but a viable setting also needs macrobelonging or commitment to the organization.

Midwest ARC demonstrated the power of **boundary spanning.** In organizational psychology (Katz & Kahn, 1978), this refers to relationships that connect groups within an organization, helping each understand the other and building capacity for collaboration. In Midwest ARC, boundary spanners had connections in both subgroups and were respected by both (Bond & Keys, 1993). Boundary spanning is similar to the concept of **bridging** ties (Putnam, 2000; recall this from Chapter 6).

TABLE 12.4 Qualities of Empowering Community Settings

Solidarity
Group-based, strengths-based belief system
Social support
Shared, inspiring leadership
Member participation
Participatory niches, opportunity role structures
Task focus
Inclusive decision making
Participatory rewards
Diversity and collaboration
Promoting diversity
Fostering intergroup collaboration

Organizations also need to develop practices and member skills in identifying, discussing, managing, and **resolving conflicts** (Chavis, 2001; Foster-Fishman et al., 2001). An important skill is recognizing when systems of oppression are involved, not simply interpersonal styles (as in the socioeconomic tensions at Midwest ARC). Conflict often is a useful resource: for learning about problems and for creative ideas for action. It is often helpful to reframe conflicts as shared problems, not simply blame others, and search for shared values or goals based on the organization's belief system.

As a study aid, we suggest organizing these nine factors into three groups: those primarily concerned with group solidarity, with member participation, and with diversity and collaboration (see Table 12.4). Of course, these three functions overlap to some extent, and we encourage you to organize them in a way that makes sense to you.

Dilemmas in Creating Empowering Organizations

Creating a setting that empowers its members is not as easy as it may sound. Dilemmas arise in seeking to empower members. All of them raise two key questions: Who is to be empowered? How?

The Challenges of Success Riger's (1984, 1993) studies of feminist movement organizations, such as women's shelters and rape crisis centers, illustrate how the goal of efficient services for clients (in this case, empowering women) may conflict with the goal of empowering staff members. Many feminist organizations began as small collectives in which decision making was shared widely among volunteers. As demand for services grew, the time-consuming process of bottom-up participation in decision making became very inefficient. Moreover, many feminist organizations began to seek funding and employ staff. As they did so, the need for financial accountability to funders also led to more top-down decision making.

These changes created settings that were less participatory for members/employees. Yet they empowered the organization to provide more services. The less that staff members were involved in participatory decision making, the more women in need could be empowered. Riger (1993) labeled these tradeoffs the "challenges of success."

Stubborn Social Regularities Gruber and Trickett (1987) studied the creation of the High School in the Community, an alternative high school. The school's governing council was comprised of equal proportions of faculty, parents, and students, designed to foster participation by all three subgroups. In practice, however, the council quickly developed conflicts over issues such as faculty hiring and admissions policy. Within three years, the faculty undermined the power of the council by assuming responsibility for important decisions and bringing fewer issues to the council for discussion. Eventually, the council became less important.

One of the main reasons for this outcome was that faculty possessed more organizational knowledge and resources. They had more expertise in educational decisions and more information about day-to-day problems facing the school, and they could more easily perform school-related tasks. When other schools and funding agencies communicated with the school, it was with faculty. Teachers also had the last word in most disputes. They granted grades and credits and could delay or alter implementation of council policies they disliked. As at Midwest ARC, another factor was social class: middle-class teachers did not work well with working-class parents (Trickett, cited in Bond & Keys, 1993, p. 53). Social regularities of traditional schools thus were replicated in the new school (Gruber & Trickett, 1987). (Recall Seidman's (1988) concept of social regularities, or inequalities in roles and relationships, from Chapter 5.) This created an organizational disparity between ideals and practices.

Nonetheless, the parents and students felt empowered in the High School in the Community, perhaps because the school did create a curriculum that increased their educational choices and resources (Gruber & Trickett, 1987, p. 369). It was the distribution of power, resources, and relationships on the school's council that was difficult to change.

The experience of the High School in the Community council also raises a broader question: Can those in more powerful or privileged positions empower others (Gruber & Trickett, 1987)? The **paradox of empowerment** (Gruber & Trickett, 1987, p. 366) occurs when members of a more powerful group seek to share power with those who are less powerful. The social system (and its social regularities) sustains existing power relations, undermining efforts to empower others (e.g., parents, students) (Freire, 1970/1993; Gruber & Trickett, 1987; Tseng et al., 2002). In fact, Gruber and Trickett (1987, p. 370) questioned whether a more powerful group can ever truly empower others.

Summary of Dilemmas These studies pose dilemmas for the creation of empowering community settings.

First, who is to be empowered? The competing aims of empowering staff versus serving women in need were identified in Riger's (1993) "challenges of success." The High School in the Community experienced a similar conflict: empowering faculty interfered with empowering parents and students (Gruber & Trickett, 1987). It is worth noting that both studies in this section took place in work settings. Volunteer organizations must attract and keep committed members, which may include using more participatory, time-consuming decision making. Yet even volunteer organizations may face either tradeoffs between participation and effectively attaining goals, or stubborn social regularities and inequalities that are difficult to overcome.

Second, how can empowerment be genuinely enacted in practice? Verbal commitment to the principle of empowerment does not guarantee behavioral or organizational commitment to empowering practices and behaviour.

Third, we need more studies of how citizen participation and empowerment work among diverse populations and communities. How can diverse cultural traditions be useful in empowerment? When might they be an obstacle rather than a resource? Recall our discussion in Chapter 7 of issues of empowering women in patriarchal cultures (e.g., Brodsky, 2003; Ortiz-Torres, Serrano-Garcia & Torres-Burgos, 2000). A recent special issue of the *American Journal of Community Psychology* provided studies of liberation in diverse contexts (Watts & Serrano-Garcia, 2003).

Understanding and promoting citizen participation and empowerment is challenging. These processes are not simple. Yet as the stories throughout this chapter illustrate, they are deeply rewarding. In the next chapter we take up how empowered organizations can foster social and community change.

CHAPTER SUMMARY

1. Citizen participation, empowerment, and sense of community are intertwining processes through which citizens take part in community life. They are also processes that can strengthen each other.
2. *Citizen participation* occurs when individuals take part in decision making in a community: group, organization, locality, or macrosystem. It is not the same as community service but involves exerting influence in collective decisions. It may be a means, a method of making decisions, or an end, a value about how to make decisions.
3. *Empowerment* occurs when people lacking an equal share of resources gain greater access to and control over those resources. It is a broader and more value-laden term than *citizen participation*. It refers to behavior, cognition, and

emotion, and development over time, but must involve gaining access to external resources or influencing collective decisions.

4. Empowerment occurs at multiple ecological levels: from individual to macrosystems. It originates from a *bottom-up perspective.* It is a process that develops over time and is different in different contexts. It involves collective efforts in relationships with others. Empowering some individuals or some groups, but not others, can create competition or conflicts. Empowerment must be balanced with values of sense of community and social justice.
5. Power takes multiple forms; some are listed in Table 12.2. Power involves control of resources and influence in collective decision making, including at least some capacity to compel others. It is best understood in relationships between persons or groups and as a dimension rather than an all-or-none dichotomy.
6. Personal qualities associated with citizen participation and empowerment are listed in Table 12.3. These develop over time through citizen participation.
7. Citizen participation in neighborhood organizations is related to sense of community, neighboring, initial dissatisfaction with local problems, and sense of collective efficacy (that citizens together can address these problems effectively).
8. *Empowering* settings promote citizen participation and empowerment by their members. *Empowered* settings exert power and influence in wider community life. Characteristics of empowering community settings are summarized in Table 12.4.
9. Creating empowering settings involves several dilemmas. These include the challenges of success and stubborn social regularities. Questions about these include: Who is to be empowered? How can empowerment be put into action? How is it different in diverse contexts?

BRIEF EXERCISES

1. Interview a community leader or activist. (Your instructor may be able to help you find one locally.) Here are some questions to ask: What is the community work that you do? How did you become involved in it? What community decisions does it involve? Does it involve challenging the community's status quo? Who has influenced you in this work? Did you have mentors or role models for this work? Do you have partners now in this work? Has a sense of community been a part of your work? What are the rewards of your work? What sustains you during difficult times in this work? How have you grown through this work? If possible, apply concepts in Tables 12.2, 12.3, and 12.4 to this person's experiences.

2. Attend a meeting of a neighborhood or community group that is devoted to community or social change. Interview group members if you can as well. Learn as much as you can about the purposes and history of the group, how it makes decisions, how it encourages participation by its members, and what its impact on the wider community has been.
3. Read about community activists. Many books offer engaging profiles of individuals and movements (e.g., Ackerman & DuVall, 2000; Berkowitz, 1987; Boulding, 2000; Colby & Damon, 1992; Collier-Thomas & Franklin, 2001; Loeb, 1999; Nagler, 2001; Putnam & Feldstein, 2003). Biographies of individuals are another source. Feature articles in newspapers and magazines sometimes profile activists. Consider the questions in Exercise 1 while you read.
4. Read a recent article in a community psychology journal concerning empowerment, citizen participation, liberation, or related topics. (You can access the *American Journal of Community Psychology* through the InfoTrac® College Edition search service that comes with this textbook.) Does this article concern any of the concepts in this chapter? How? What did you learn from this article?

RECOMMENDED READINGS

Berkowitz, B. (1987). *Local heroes.* Lexington, MA: D.C. Heath.

Loeb, P. (1999). *Soul of a citizen: Living with conviction in a cynical time.* New York: St. Martin's Griffin.

Putnam, R. & Feldstein, L. (2003). *Better together: Restoring the American community.* New York: Simon & Schuster.

Riger, S. (1993). What's wrong with empowerment. *American Journal of Community Psychology, 21*, 279–291.

Wandersman, A. & Florin, P. (2000). Citizen participation and community organizations. In J. Rappaport & E. Seidman (Eds.), *Handbook of community psychology* (pp. 247–272). New York: Plenum.

RECOMMENDED WEBSITES

Community Tool Box
http://ctb.ku.edu

Excellent site for learning about citizen participation and planning community change, maintained by community psychologists. Includes tools and recommendations for planning, implementing, and evaluating community initiatives, and links to many related sites.

Innovation Center for Youth and Community Development
http://www.atthetable.org

Website on youth development and civic activism. Includes stories of youth impacts on communities, tools and resources for actions by young people, research on youth and community development, online surveys and discussion forums.

INFOTRAC® COLLEGE EDITION KEYWORDS

citizen, citizen participation, collective efficacy, community organization, empowering(ed)(ment), liberation(tory), participation(tory), power, sense of community

13

Community and Social Change

GrantPix/Index Stock

Never doubt that a small group of thoughtful, committed citizens can change the word; indeed, it's the only thing that ever does. (Margaret Mead)

OPENING EXERCISE AND INTRODUCTION

Let's begin with an exercise to illustrate the psychological aspects of community and social change. It is best to do this in writing.

- Choose a specific problem or challenge that your locality or society faces. Examples include poverty, violence in various forms, access to health care, unemployment, homelessness, or an environmental problem. Be specific.

- List the psychological difficulties associated with that problem. Consider whether particular age groups (e.g., infants, children, adolescents, senior citizens) are more vulnerable.
- List likely causes of this problem, at multiple ecological levels of analysis.
- Consider how this *problem* may actually be an *issue* with opposing viewpoints, each with its own understandable reasons. Briefly identify at least two sides of this issue and how they disagree.
- Write briefly how each problem involves your locality and your society as a whole.

How can communities and societies address such issues? That is what this chapter is about. In Chapter 12 we examined the intertwining processes of sense of community, citizen participation, and empowerment. In this chapter we continue the discussion by focusing on this question: How do citizens, acting collectively, acquire and use power to promote changes in their communities and in society?

We devote this chapter primarily to change at the levels of communities and societies. Yet change at those levels is intertwined with changes at individual, microsystem, and organizational levels. It sometimes seems to students of psychology that community and social change is exceedingly difficult, beyond their capabilities. To that concern we have three initial answers. First, individual, community and social change intertwine. All three are involved when members of a citizen coalition work together to promote positive youth development, when a battered woman leaves the batterer to pursue her own life, or when any disenfranchised person asserts his or her legitimate rights. Second, individual, community and social changes occur around us, all the time. In every act of living, we involve ourselves in dynamic processes of change at many ecological levels. Third, in this chapter we present conceptual and practical tools and inspiring stories that are useful in choosing goals and taking action. By chapter's end, we hope that you will see how often Margaret Mead's oft-quoted adage about changing the world comes true—and how you can become involved.

CASE EXAMPLES OF COMMUNITY AND SOCIAL CHANGE

We begin with examples of real-life, effective change initiatives.

PICO: Community Organizing for Social Power

The PICO Network (originally Pacific Institute for Community Organizing) is a national network of local faith-based groups. Their community organizing strategies combine building strong interpersonal and community relationships with assertive group tactics to influence community leaders and institutions. Paul Speer, Joseph Hughey, and associates worked with community organizations and studied the processes and outcomes of PICO methods (Speer & Hughey, 1995; Speer, Hughey, Gensheimer, & Adams-Leavitt, 1995).

PICO organizations are based in religious congregations in low-income communities. PICO always begins with permission of a religious congregation to form a community organization among its members and other citizens. Religious values of social justice and compassion, the community visibility of clergy and religious workers, and the institutional legitimacy of the congregation all are resources for community change.

PICO community organizing proceeds through a **cycle of organizing.** In the initial phase, *assessment,* members of the community organization meet one-to-one with citizens to define community issues and to develop working partnerships that strengthen the group. This stage builds interdependence and mutual support.

In the second phase, *research,* organization members meet as a whole to identify the most pressing community issue for the group, based on their conversations with citizens. Members gather further information on that issue from interviews, searching documents, or other sources. A key goal is to identify contradictions between stated policies and actual practices of government, business, and community services.

The third phase, *mobilization/action,* follows. Organization members meet to decide on an action plan and a person or office to be targeted to discuss community changes. If preparatory meetings with an official do not succeed, a public "accountability meeting" is arranged with that official. The key function of the meeting is to confront the target official: presenting the reality of the community problem and actions that citizens demand to resolve it. Meetings often have brought together city officials with large groups of well-informed citizens making clear, focused demands (due to the extensive groundwork conducted by the organization). They often result in commitments being made by the target official, as in the following accounts.

> Members of one organization discovered in the research phase that a private social services agency was placing its immigrant clients in substandard housing owned by absentee landlords, in effect subsidizing the landlords' lack of property maintenance. This practice endangered not only the immigrants but also their neighbors, since the apartments did not meet health and fire codes. Officials of the social service agency refused to cooperate with members of the community organization in getting the landlords to comply with the codes. However, when confronted at a public meeting with 500 community residents, most of whom indicated their intent to write to the agency's funding sources about the problem, the agency capitulated on the spot. (Adapted from Speer & Hughey, 1995, p. 742)

> Members of 14 organizations in the same city had worked independently on a variety of youth issues, including prevention of drug abuse and violence. They had learned that obtaining the resources needed for positive youth development was beyond the capacity of any one group. Working together, they discovered that because city schools, government, and recreation commission did not collaborate with each other, inner-city youth and

> families were denied access to gyms, pools, computers, and health facilities after school hours. After a year of research and planning, about 1,000 citizens met with the mayor, school superintendent, various board members and representatives of civic groups, and citywide media. Testimony from adults and children documented the need for access to the facilities. The organizations demanded a specific agreement for such collaboration among the city, schools, and recreation commission. Officials signed the agreement at that meeting and later provided the services. (Adapted from Speer & Hughey, 1995, p. 741)

Especially for a public official, it is a potent experience of citizen power to face a unified crowd of hundreds of citizens making clear demands for a policy change. Moreover, the community organization hosts the public meeting and carefully scripts its agenda, exercising the second and third instruments of power discussed in Chapter 12: framing the issues for discussion and channeling participation to maximize the strength of citizen voices.

The final phase, *reflection,* returns to the one-to-one relationships where the cycle began to evaluate outcomes and lessons learned. Meetings of the whole organization then discuss these themes. PICO organizations also monitor the keeping of promises made by the target officials and institutions. The organization begins the cycle again with a new assessment phase.

Speer and Hughey's (1995) studies of PICO organizations in one Midwestern U.S. city showed that they effectively mobilized citizens and produced specific changes in the policy and practices of city government and other organizations. Speer et al. (1995) compared the effectiveness of congregation-based PICO organizations and neighborhood-based organizations that did not spend as much time building relationships among organization members. Over a three-year period, the congregation-based organizations had much higher attendance at community events. Their ideas also were covered in the local media at a much higher rate, which widened their impact.

Several psychological factors contribute to the effectiveness of PICO organizations: strong interpersonal networks, mutual support, an institutional and values base in religious congregations, participatory niches (recall this from Chapter 12) created by rotating offices and identifying emerging leaders, targeting specific issues and institutions for change, and mobilizing large meetings to make specific demands. With these tools, PICO organizations representing low-income communities can influence powerful private and public institutions.

The Harvard Union of Clerical and Technical Workers

> I realized right then we were going to lose to these people. I could sell them a good benefits package; I could sell them competitive wages. But I couldn't sell them a sense of belonging, of being part of something bigger. . . .
>
> An employer will never beat a union that has a singing group. Singing together builds unity and harmony and commitment. (Anne Taylor, attorney for Harvard University, quoted in Putnam & Feldstein, 2003, pp. 175, 177)

> Our group is bizarre in the labor movement. We try to solve conflict in a way that deepens the relationship between labor and management. . . . People aren't looking for a fight when they come to work. They want a good job and good relationships. (Kris Rondeau, union organizer, quoted in Putnam & Feldstein, 2003, p. 178)

Clerical and technical workers are vital to a university: secretaries, laboratory assistants, and medical workers in a university hospital. Yet these workers' pay and benefits are often far below that of the faculty and administration, and their contributions are seldom recognized. At Harvard University, through the 1980s, low pay and high living expenses undermined worker satisfaction and well-being. Yet efforts to unionize employees met resistance among workers (mostly women), who disliked traditional, confrontational labor union approaches. University administration also fought unionization stiffly. Its resources included high-powered attorneys, well-connected alumni, money, and Ivy League prestige. The administration promised to improve pay, benefits, and working conditions, then failed to enact these measures after employees voted against unionizing (Putnam & Feldstein, 2003).

At that point, the Harvard Union of Clerical and Technical Workers (HUCTW) decided to rely on its own distinctive, community-building approach. This method involves building face-to-face relationships among members, first with one-to-one conversations, then in small groups, then in larger meetings (note this parallel with PICO). This is done with maximum personal communication and by creating participatory niches in the union. HUCTW members met in pairs and small groups for lunch, created a singing group and sang at meetings, and fostered supportive ties that went well beyond union work, such as shopping for a colleague whose mother is ill. The metaphor of "finding one's voice" is frequently cited by HUCTW to explain how members who considered themselves extremely shy learned to speak out: first with a friend, then in larger meetings, then at work. HUCTW has many of the qualities of an empowering setting that we described in Chapter 12.

Over time, HUCTW developed strong worker support and was insistent on its aims yet willing to build constructive working relationships with administrators. Administration began to work with HUCTW to create better pay and benefits as well as a creative problem-solving process to resolve employer-employee conflicts. Despite this early success, in the late 1990s the Harvard administration returned to a confrontational approach. HUCTW had little choice but to oppose it openly, including picketing administration offices, in order to resolve disputes.

The person-to-person method of community building takes time. HUCTW continues to listen to employee voices and insist that the university listen also, resolving over a thousand work conflicts a year through its problem-solving process (Putnam & Feldstein, 2003, chap. 8).

Spanning Community Networks

Strengthening cohesion within a grassroots community organization builds their integrative power, but that alone may not be enough to create community changes.

Organizations often need resources from outside the group, such as funding, respect within the wider community, or access to influence key decision-makers. Hughey and Speer (2002, especially pp. 77–82) described how a community coalition used *boundary spanning,* a strategy that we discussed in Chapter 12, in order to gain access to resources in the wider community. Their case example also illustrates some concepts of power from Chapter 12. It forms a story in three acts.

In a small Kentucky city, a community coalition was formed to address issues of substance abuse in a disadvantaged neighborhood. Local community service agencies chose this goal and obtained funding for the coalition. When representatives of those agencies attempted to organize neighborhood residents to join the coalition, the residents resisted. They certainly felt that substance abuse was a problem, but not the most important problem in their neighborhood. They had not been consulted in planning the coalition or choosing its goal. Discussion at meetings was dominated by professionals who did not live in the neighborhood and who related mainly to each other. Residents were concerned about retribution from drug dealers (which they would face directly, but the professionals would not). These differences in power echo the early conflicts at Midwest ARC, described in Chapter 12.

To their credit, the professionals soon recognized these problems and turned the coalition over to the residents. A primary lesson of this first act was that top-down planning by professionals from outside the neighborhood was not effective; citizens had to take matters into their own hands (a bottom-up approach). However, the top-down approach had yielded funding for a coalition coordinator, which was important in the coalition's work.

In the second act of this story, citizens adopted methods similar to PICO community-building strategies. They began by working through existing social ties and institutions in the neighborhood, met with residents in individual home meetings, collected stories about neighborhood concerns, and discussed these in community organization meetings. These steps strengthened the cohesion and organizational capacity of the organization considerably. They now had important ties within the neighborhood, and were developing the ability to speak on its behalf.

Discussions focused on residents' dissatisfaction with local police. While verbally committed to "community policing," the department continued to have officers patrol in cars, rarely speaking with residents, and rotated officers from neighborhood to neighborhood frequently. An interpersonal gulf existed between officers and residents. This undermined efforts to address the illegal drug trade.

Meetings between police representatives and the neighborhood coalition revealed that some police officers agreed with residents. Yet in the top-down hierarchy of the police department and city government, neither group possessed the power to implement genuine community policing practices. Neither had the ability to influence the mayor, who could order such changes. A primary lesson of this second act was that building strong social networks within the neighborhood and organization was necessary to speak out as a community. However, that was not sufficient to create needed changes, even with some sympathetic police.

In the third act, members of the coalition renewed ties with the community service professionals who had left the coalition. However, those professionals' contribution was not their expert power but their professional and personal relationships with key community leaders who could influence the mayor (referent power). Those connections led to a retired philanthropist, who met with citizens and professionals, and then arranged meetings including the mayor, police, and citizens. With the mayor's support, police obtained funding and implemented genuine community policing.

In this third act, change occurred when boundary-spanning relationships were formed among citizens, police, influential community members, and the mayor. A shift to genuine community policing may have been attractive to the mayor because it had communitywide appeal and support both from police and citizens. In summary, both cohesive strength within the group and boundary spanning beyond to key decision makers were crucial for success. Recall bonding and bridging forms of social capital from Chapter 6 (Putnam, 2000). Both were necessary in this case (Hughey & Speer, 2002).

CINCH: A Community Health Coalition

Health is often understood as an individual responsibility. It is easy to think of encouraging exercise, a healthy diet, and avoiding smoking as individual choices. Yet health is also a community issue. Community problems such as youth and family violence, drug abuse, sexism, racism, poverty, and unemployment are linked to health outcomes, reflected in emergency rooms and clinics as wounds and injuries, rape trauma, drug dependence, infectious diseases, lung cancer, prenatal and child health problems, and other outcomes. Health care is unaffordable for many in the United States, especially in urban and rural areas. Addressing this deficit is important for social justice and community well-being. It also is important for another reason: contagious illnesses can spread quickly and widely, and the best defense against them for any individual is that all citizens have affordable, preventive health care. These issues raise questions such as: What happens when a community takes responsibility for improving its collective health? What would a healthy community be like?

Building healthy communities often involves creating a **community coalition,** an organization composed of representatives of multiple community groups who bring together their resources to achieve a common goal that none of them could attain alone (Kaye & Wolff, 1997; Wolff, 2001b).

Child immunizations against infectious disease were the focus of the Consortium for Immunization of Norfolk's Children (CINCH), a community coalition in Norfolk, Virginia. Despite its economic wealth, the United States has recently lagged behind other countries in this basic method of disease prevention. A measles epidemic and a resurgence of whooping cough in the 1990s prompted nationwide public health efforts to increase immunization rates. In Norfolk, only 48 percent of the city's children had been fully immunized by 2 years of age, a situation not unusual for urban areas (Butterfoss, Goodman, & Wandersman, 2001).

In 1993, representatives of several Norfolk community groups founded the CINCH coalition. For six months they gathered personal and material resources. They recruited 55 representatives of community organizations, including health care providers, service organizations, civic groups, and academic and religious institutions. CINCH reflected Norfolk's diversity in age, occupation, race and ethnicity, and religion; it also included members with skills in planning, teaching, media presentations, community outreach, and mobilizing volunteers. Coalition members garnered grant monies, and local organizations provided staff time.

CINCH members worked to develop a clear task focus (recall this quality of empowering settings from Chapter 12). They developed a mission statement with five goals: increasing public awareness of childhood immunization in Norfolk, determining the causes of low immunization rates, forming and implementing plans to increase immunizations, evaluating and revising these strategies, and sharing results with other communities. The coalition hired staff to provide training for coalition volunteers. They established procedures for meetings and making decisions and roles for members, leaders, and staff. These steps helped to overcome a common problem with community coalitions: lack of direction early in the coalition's existence, leading to loss of membership and effectiveness (Butterfoss et al., 2001; Kaye & Wolff, 1997).

CINCH also built cohesion and commitment among members. Members excluded titles from name tags and discussions and worked to recognize each other's skills and contribution to the coalition. They emphasized overarching, shared community goals. Leadership was decentralized by assigning many of CINCH's tasks to work groups dealing with specific issues. Members discovered that some were skilled planners and others were skilled doers (Butterfoss et al., 2001). This cohesion and commitment to shared goals helped to resolve conflicts and strengthened ties among coalition members.

The coalition conducted a needs assessment to learn about the problem of underimmunization in Norfolk. Focus groups with parents, patient interviews at clinics, and surveys of health care providers and households revealed that underimmunization existed at all socioeconomic levels. CINCH work groups then developed strategic plans for education of parents and health care providers, support for families at risk, and improvements in delivery of immunizations. Coalition leaders combined the various specific plans into an overall strategic plan with a budget.

Coalition members and organizations then implemented these plans, evaluating and revising them when needed. Over three years, the coalition effectively implemented 77 percent of its strategies, many of which were adopted as routine practices of health institutions and community agencies. Community impact was measured by the overall immunization rate, which rose from 48 percent to 66 percent by the program's third year. Without experimental controls this cannot be attributed to CINCH alone, but its impact seems clear. CINCH's efforts also led to development of a statewide immunization coalition and a nationwide training institute. The coalition expanded to six nearby cities and broadened its mission to child health issues beyond immunization (e.g., asthma, obesity, child health insurance, injury prevention) and is now known as the Consortium for Infant and Child Health (Butterfoss et al., 2001).

CINCH benefited from its focus on children's health, a population and issue that have few public opponents. In addition, its effectiveness could be measured in simple terms, such as immunization rates, that provided clear goals. However, similar coalition-building methods have worked with more controversial and less easily measured objectives, such as curbing substance abuse, as we shall see next.

The Lexington/Richland Coalition

Based in central South Carolina, including the capital of Columbia, the Lexington/Richland Alcohol and Drug Abuse Coalition grew out of state and local initiatives to reduce the social and personal costs of drug abuse (including alcohol and tobacco). Among its most important accomplishments have been locality-level changes in laws, policies, and community norms regarding drug abuse. These have led to measurable changes in indicators of access to drugs and incidents related to drug abuse. To do this, the coalition assumed three roles: developing policies, facilitating policy development by other community institutions, and mediating community disputes related to drug abuse (Snell-Johns, Imm, Wandersman, & Claypoole, 2003).

The Coalition's Policy Development Committee is one of the most active committees within the coalition, bringing together representatives of the police and criminal justice system, schools and universities, community agencies, and citizen groups. Early actions were helping to develop a no-smoking policy for Richland County schools and a no-drug-use (including alcohol and tobacco) policy for county recreation fields, implemented by the recreation authority. The coalition developed a model program for training coaches of youth sports as role models and educators for youth about the importance of not using drugs. This program grew in popularity, training was mandated for all coaches, and the program and policy were adopted statewide.

The coalition organized a merchant education program to decrease sales of alcohol and tobacco to minors. This initially met with reluctance among merchants, but as positive relationships developed with coalition members, merchants became proud to be associated with the program. In 1995 research in Richland County stores, 77 percent of minors who attempted to purchase tobacco products were offered a sale. The 2003 rate was only 8 percent.

The coalition also worked with the University of South Carolina student affairs staff and police to develop new policies for intervening in underage alcohol use and drug abuse on campus. A social norms campaign aims to influence student attitudes about the frequency of drinking among students and the seriousness of alcohol abuse. Recidivism rates for drug offenses at university events have dropped significantly.

The coalition was asked to mediate a community controversy about St. Patrick's Day celebrations (with much alcohol use and noise) at a street fair near the university. This event was popular with students and merchants and unpopular with neighborhood associations. Feelings ran high. City government acknowledged the problem but was uncertain of what to do. Coalition members insisted that the alcohol issue be addressed, researched how other communities handled similar events, and offered a compromise. A Beer Garden area would be open for drinking in a one-block area, cordoned off and patrolled by police, with ID required for admission. Open containers of alcohol would be banned elsewhere. At the same time, family-oriented events would be held in a local park. This compromise was accepted and has worked satisfactorily for five years.

After their teenage son was killed in an alcohol-related boating accident on nearby Lake Murray, one family asked the coalition to help prohibit boating under the influence of alcohol. The coalition worked with the family, state legislators, and others to promote public awareness of the problem, draft the proposed law and testify in the legislature, and organize grassroots support. In 1999, the bill was signed into law. A public awareness campaign for boating safety also began at Lake Murray. Alcohol-related boating accidents there have dropped 30 percent.

Snell-Johns et al. (2003) concluded that these efforts succeeded for several related reasons. The coalition included broad community representation and worked to develop relationships with other community groups. It was persistent in pursuit of its goals. Its core values regarding drug use and abuse were clearly stated and attracted wide support, yet the coalition was not perceived as having an overtly political or one-sided agenda. The coalition also had paid staff and some outside funding, and was able to act quickly when opportunities occurred. Yet the coalition's successes also rested on the volunteer efforts of a broad representation of citizens.

Preventing Homelessness: Policy Research and Advocacy

According to studies by community psychologists and other social scientists, at least 7 percent of U.S. residents, perhaps as many as 10 percent, experience being homeless at least once in their lifetime. About two-thirds of Americans would support slightly higher taxes to help the homeless and prevent homelessness. Yet the problem persists and may worsen: for the poor, housing costs are climbing but incomes are not (Toro & Warren, 1999; Tsemberis, Moran, Shinn, Asmussen, & Shern, 2003).

Generalizations are difficult about the many people who are homeless. In U.S. cities, homeless persons include adult individuals (often single men), families (often young mothers and children), and adolescents who have run away or been kicked out of their homes (Roll, Toro, & Ortola, 1999). Less than 30 percent of homeless persons (in some studies only 20%) have a serious mental illness. About 30 percent currently are abusing drugs or alcohol (Toro & Warren, 1999). Half or more of homeless persons have neither problem currently. Research has identified a number of individual and situational risk factors for homelessness, yet all of them are more common among persons who do *not* become homeless, reducing the ability of researchers to predict homelessness or target prevention programs (Shinn, Baumohl, & Hopper, 2001; Shinn et al., 1998). Moreover, factors influencing homelessness are dynamic, shifting as economic trends rise and fall and varying by locality.

Even the definition of homelessness is complex (Shinn et al., 2001; Toro & Warren, 1999). Should it refer only to those in emergency shelters and on the streets, or include, for instance, women and children in shelters for battered women and persons who have lost their housing but moved into crowded arrangements for long periods with relatives or friends? Persons in these situations are homeless in the sense of lacking their own stable housing arrangements.

Community psychologists, with allies including homeless persons, have helped clarify the complexity and diversity of homelessness and have studied the effectiveness of programs and policies designed to reduce it. Moreover, they are influencing how policy makers and the public think about homelessness.

In a primarily individualistic culture, it seems natural to think of homelessness as an individual problem, requiring programs to help homeless individuals change: for example, treating mental illness or substance abuse, providing education or job training. Yet recall an analogy from Chapter 1: homelessness resembles the game of musical chairs. The best predictor of the extent of homelessness in a community is the ratio of affordable housing units to the number of persons and families seeking them. Strengthening the capacity of a homeless person or family merely changes which persons will be most likely to find stable housing. It will not increase the supply of affordable housing.

Public policy makers are beginning to think of homelessness in terms of access to housing, not simply individual deficits. This shift in perspective has occurred over a period of years and is not the result of any one researcher, study, advocate, or advocacy strategy (Shinn, personal communication, September 22, 2004). It reflects a growing change in the way that government officials, community service and public health administrators, advocates for the homeless, researchers, and others think and speak about the issue. Such an indistinct yet noticeable change in the "policy culture," indirectly influencing public policy decisions, is often the outcome of policy research and advocacy (Phillips, 2000). Many social, political, and economic players will determine what specific public policies are adopted to deal with homelessness. Yet perspectives seem to be shifting among some of the players. An example is that New York City has adopted a "right to shelter" policy, taking responsibility for providing shelter for its homeless.

This shift in perspective has been supported by community psychology research. Marybeth Shinn and others have conducted studies that demonstrated the importance of access to housing in reducing homelessness. For instance, in longitudinal studies, access to public housing or government subsidies for rental costs is the most important factor in helping homeless persons and families find and keep stable housing (Shinn et al., 2001). Even among homeless persons with serious mental illness, programs that put housing first are more effective and less costly. These programs place homeless persons with mental illness in subsidized housing first, then offer other treatment and support services, rather than requiring them to receive mental health treatment in transitional housing programs before becoming eligible for their own housing (Gulcur, Stefancic, Shinn, Tsemberis, & Fischer, 2003; Tsemberis et al., 2003).

Yet research alone is not enough to influence policy. Shinn also has written a report with recommendations for the Federal Interagency Council on Homelessness, cochaired a New York City government task force that wrote a multiyear plan for how the city will address homelessness, and helped to founded a research advisory panel for the City Department of Homeless Services (Shinn, personal communication, September 22, 2004). Another community psychologist, Paul Toro, has worked with homeless persons and advocates in policy research and advocacy. Toro and associates have surveyed homeless persons themselves to determine needs for services, studied homelessness issues and policies across the United States and internationally, and helped develop local services for homeless persons in Detroit (Acosta & Toro, 2000; Tompsett et al., 2003; Toro & Warren, 1999). As we described in Chapter 1, Debi Starnes (2004) has been a leader in developing city policy and funding for services for the homeless in Atlanta. They and others have brought a community psychology perspective to discussions of public policy on homelessness: recognizing multiple ecological levels, attending to the voices of the diversity of homeless persons, cultivating collaborative relationships with policy makers and citizens, developing innovative research methods, and translating findings into policy.

SEVEN APPROACHES TO COMMUNITY AND SOCIAL CHANGE

We next discuss seven general approaches to community and social change. Each actually represents a family of related strategies for collecting and using forms of power. Although these seven approaches are conceptually separable, most community organizations and social movements combine several in practice.

Consciousness Raising

Consciousness raising involves increasing citizens' critical awareness of social conditions and energizing their involvement in challenging and changing those conditions. Paulo Freire's (1970/1993) *Pedagogy of the Oppressed* and many branches of the feminist movement embody this approach. Consciousness is raised as women and men become aware of personal experiences with sexism in the workplace and in the family. However, consciousness raising is not solely cognitive or emotional. New personal understanding is connected to working with others and to actions for change. Action and reflection feed each other. Actions may include other social change approaches, but consciousness raising distinctively emphasizes personal *and* social transformation.

Consciousness raising is reflected in some persons we described in Chapter 12: Virginia Ramirez, Alison Smith, Kieffer's (1984) community activists, and African-American youth leaders (Watts et al., 2003). Life experiences, personal reflection, and discussion with others led them to critical awareness of social injustice. They questioned the credibility of community and corporate leaders and began to oppose injustice and insist on citizen participation. In all the case examples described earlier in this chapter, consciousness raising occurred, but to differing degrees. In the community-building process of PICO and HUCTW, citizens meet to identify and analyze community problems and their causes. CINCH and the Lexington/Richland coalition achieved changes in public views, which began with the personal commitment of their members.

Geraldine Moane's (2003) study of the Irish women's liberation movement illustrated consciousness raising. Participants in women's groups created new understandings of personal, interpersonal, and political pathways to change. At the personal level, women described liberation as a process of building strengths: finding positive images of oneself; personal role models; becoming more assertive; and exploring one's own creativity, sexuality, and spirituality. Interpersonally, women made supportive connections, learned how other women faced similar challenges, and cultivated sense of community. These led to critical awareness of power in relationships, to a vision for liberating political change, and to action at different levels in one's life, whether insisting on help with housework and child care or joining a public protest.

Of the seven approaches we discuss here, consciousness raising most directly addresses personal values, awareness, and commitment. It often precedes or accompanies use of the other approaches, in cycles of deepening critical awareness, supportive relationships, and liberatory actions.

Consciousness raising can be extended to whole communities. The concept of **community readiness** refers to how much a locality recognizes a problem and takes steps to address or prevent it. Action researchers at the Tri-Ethnic Prevention Research Center in Colorado proposed a nine-stage model of community readiness, especially for substance abuse and health issues (Edwards, Jumper-Thurman, Plested, Oetting, & Swanson, 2000). In their model, readiness involves knowledge of the problem and of methods to address it, existing efforts to address it, strength of community leadership on that issue, presence of other resources for action, and overall community climate of attitudes and commitment on the issue. Their nine stages include:

- no awareness of the problem
- denial that it is a local problem, even if a problem elsewhere
- vague awareness of the problem but without local efforts to address it
- preplanning and local information gathering about the problem
- preparing strategies for community change, led by a local team
- initiating programs or policy changes to address the problem
- establishing changes within local organizations such as schools, with local resources
- evaluating, improving and expanding them over time
- maintaining strong program support, evaluation and excellence

Strategies for moving through the stages include identifying and influencing opinion leaders in the community, gathering and disseminating information in focus groups and the media, focusing on local examples and statistics regarding the problem, fostering local leadership, planning everything within the local cultural context, integrating programs or policies within local organizations, and evaluating to promote ongoing program or policy improvement. Outside consultants can provide assistance, but moving through the stages requires local leadership, resources, and commitment. The community readiness model has been validated in research and used to develop culturally valid health interventions in Native American, Mexican American, and Anglo communities (Engstrom, Jason, Townsend, Pokorny, & Curie, 2002; Jumper-Thurman, Edwards, Plested, & Oetting, 2003; Oetting, Jumper-Thurman, Plested, & Edwards, 2001).

Social Action

Grassroots groups use social action to offset the power of organized money with the power of organized people (integrative power) (Alinsky, 1971). Social action identifies specific obstacles to empowerment of disadvantaged groups, and creates constructive conflict to remove these obstacles through direct, nonviolent action.

Social action has a long history, with roots including the Boston Tea Party, labor movements in many countries, Gandhi's movement to free India, and the U.S. civil rights movement. Social action also was used in Poland to defy and ultimately help to bring down an unjust communist state, in Chile to help end a murderous dictatorship, and in South Africa to help bring a relatively peaceful transformation to democracy when many expected widespread violence (Ackerman & Duvall, 2000). The effectiveness of social action methods in attaining their immediate goals depends on the context, but in the right circumstances they can lead to surprising changes.

Saul Alinsky's classic *Rules for Radicals* (1971) delineated social action principles. To effectively oppose organized, powerful interests, citizens must identify their capacities (the strengths of community group members and their potential to act together), and the capacities of the opposing group or community institution. In addition, they need to identify a situation that dramatizes the need for change and that calls forth citizens' strengths. It is best if that situation is something their opponents have never encountered before and that they cannot dominate.

Social action involves power and conflict. If powerful elites limit citizen participation in a decision, adroit choice of a social action can assert citizen views and frame the issue in their terms. The following example of social action aptly illustrates the uses of people power to create a situation that the opponent had never experienced.

> A large, prominent department store in a U.S. city traditionally hired African Americans only in very menial positions and was more discriminatory in its hiring than its competitors. The store had resisted appeals to halt these practices. Boycotts called by African-American community groups had failed due to the prestige of the store. African-American community groups met and decided to plan a "shop-in."
>
> The plan called for busloads of African-American customers to arrive at the store at its opening on a busy Saturday. In small groups they would shop every department in the store, carefully examining merchandise, asking sales clerks for help, doing nothing illegal yet occupying the store's space. These groups would rotate through the various departments in the store. Regular customers would arrive only to find the store crowded, and if they were hurried or uncomfortable with being in largely Black crowds they might go to another store. Finally, shortly before closing, customers would begin purchasing everything they could, to be delivered on Monday, with payment

due on delivery. They planned to refuse these deliveries, causing even more expense for the store. (adapted from Alinsky, 1971, pp. 146–148)

The community groups deliberately leaked these plans to the store while going ahead with arrangements. The next day, officials of the store called to ask for an urgent meeting with African-American groups to plan new hiring practices before the shop-in. The shop-in never had to be carried out.

The shop-in had several elements that mark effective social action (Alinsky, 1971). The goal was clear and tangible: specific changes in hiring policy and practices. Shopping was something that protesters knew how to do; it would even be enjoyable. Social action generates more participation if it asks citizens to do familiar things. At the same time, the situation was outside the experience of their opponents. Store management had ignored boycotts and public appeals, but they had never faced a shop-in. The tactic would cause disruption, potential bad publicity, and increased expenses for the store, yet it was entirely legal; store security or police would have little recourse to stop it. The threat was credible because the African-American community was organized and willing to act. The threat of competition from other retailers not being targeted increased the pressure on the targeted store. The goal was just and the tactic shrewd; its power was revealed when the store quickly capitulated (Alinsky, 1971).

The "accountability meetings" of the PICO approach are another example of social action. They draw power from an organized community making specific demands on specific targets. However, effective social action requires bringing out numbers of committed, organized citizens to oppose powerful interests. Thus, it often requires prior consciousness raising and also community development, which we discuss next.

Community Development

Community development involves a process of strengthening relationships among community members to define community problems, resources, and strategies for actions. It broadens opportunities for citizen participation and influence in community decision making. Unlike social action, community development does not rely on conflict. "Community" usually means a locality, such as a neighborhood, but it can also mean a community organization. Community development approaches often bring together the resources of multiple groups in a locality, such as neighborhood and civic organizations, religious congregations, businesses, schools, youth groups, libraries, and other community resources (Kaye & Wolff, 1997; Kretzmann & McKnight, 1993; Lappe & DuBois, 1994; Nation, Wandersman, & Perkins, 2002; Putnam & Feldstein, 2003; Saegert, Thompson, & Warren, 2001). Perkins, Crim, Silberman, and Brown (2004) give a useful overview.

Community development focuses on one or more of four domains (Perkins et al., 2004)

- economic development: e.g., of businesses and jobs
- political development: of community organizations to influence decisions in the community and at wider levels

- improving social environment: e.g., health, education, policing, promoting youth development
- improving physical environment: e.g., housing, transportation, city services, parks, public spaces

The Block Booster Project that we described in Chapter 12 exemplifies locality-based community development. Louis Burgess's block association in New York City initiated crime watch patrols, improved street lighting, encouraged property cleanup, discouraged illegal drug sales, sponsored outdoor parties and recreational trips, and met regularly to discuss block activities and problems. These collective acts lowered crime, increased neighboring, and strengthened the sense of community. Effective locality-based community development often leads to such outcomes (Wandersman & Florin, 2000).

The Grameen Bank movement blends economic development with microsystem cooperatives. In rural Bangladesh, the Grameen Bank network operates in 18,000 villages to provide small loans to more than a million landless poor women for their own small businesses. Loans are made to small groups of four to seven women, who are responsible for repayment as a group and must have a business plan approved by the bank. The Grameen idea has spread internationally in urban and rural settings, with women and men as borrowers, helping to create working businesses among the poor with very low default rates (Lappe & DuBois, 1994, pp. 99–100). In a similar effort in rural West Virginia, a coalition of churches and community groups provided the loan that began Wellspring, a crafts cooperative run by women in isolated communities (Kretzmann & McKnight, 1993, p. 308).

Community development can support social action. PICO community organizing begins with citizens meeting one-to-one and in groups to identify community problems and agree upon actions. These steps precede and strengthen public advocacy. The Harvard Union of Clerical and Technical Workers' chief resource in dealing with university administration was its membership loyalty and sense of community. Women's consciousness raising often involves community development (Moane, 2003, p. 98).

In the lower Rio Grande Valley of Texas, Valley Interfaith, a grassroots coalition of church and school groups, blends community development, consciousness raising, and social actions similar to those of PICO. Valley Interfaith works with Mexican Americans and Mexican immigrants. One goal is securing better services for local *colonias,* areas where developers sold lots, promising sewers, water, electricity, and paved roads, yet never provided them. Valley Interfaith also has advocated a living wage (minimum wage that reflects the true cost of living), developed job training and placement programs, and offered citizenship classes (Putnam & Feldstein, 2003). Virginia Ramirez in Chapter 12 was involved in a similar group in San Antonio.

Community Coalitions

One outgrowth of community development is the community coalition approach. Community coalitions bring together a broad representation of citizens within a locality, to address a community problem. Coalitions may involve citizens, community organizations (e.g., community agencies, schools, government, religious congregations, businesses, media, grassroots groups), or both. Coalitions agree on a mission, then write and implement action plans. Those plans may involve action by the coalition itself or by affiliated organizations, and may lead to changes in policies or to development of community programs. CINCH and the Lexington/Richland Coalition represent this approach. Coalitions have become a popular and often effective means for strengthening citizen participation and catalyzing community change (Allen, 2005; Fawcett et al., 1995; Feinberg, Greenberg, & Osgood, 2004; Hawkins, Catalano, & Associates, 1992; McMillan, Florin, Stevenson, Kerman, & Mitchell, 1995; Wolff, 2001a).

The Healthy Communities movement often uses community coalitions. Healthy Communities models grew out of the recognition that environmental forces influence individual health and that prevention is needed in addition to treatment. For instance, asthma requires both medical treatment and managing environmental factors. After a local Asthma Coalition pointed out that breathing engine exhaust can trigger asthmatic symptoms, a Connecticut school district changed its school bus contract to require that bus engines be turned off while waiting for riders at school (Wolff, 2004). In Massachusetts, local Healthy Communities coalitions have begun a mobile health van program, initiated a campaign to lessen sales of tobacco products to teens, hosted planning for economic and housing development, started a shelter for the homeless, developed a health outreach program for a low-income neighborhood, brought a dental clinic to an area without dental care, and developed health programs for children (Hathaway, 2001; Wolff, 1995, 2004).

The Communities That Care movement provides another example. Its mission is communitywide action to prevent drug abuse, foster positive youth development and promote psychosocial competence, including many concepts that we emphasized in Chapters 9–11. The Communities That Care coalition model involves developing a local coalition to match prevention/promotion methods backed by empirical research with local community needs and resources (Feinberg et al., 2004; Hawkins, Catalano & Associates, 1992).

Community coalitions have become popular for several reasons (Wolff, 2001b). During the conservative period since 1980, funding for social services has fallen, increasing pressure on localities to do more with less. Agencies are swamped by clients needing treatment, with little time for prevention or for considering community strengths. Categorical funding of government social services (e.g., separate funding streams for mental health, public health, education, child protective services, criminal justice) complicates coordination among agencies. Community coalitions bring organizations together for coordinated action, create or coordinate preventive programs, and engage the resources of nongovernmental community institutions, such as religious congregations, philanthropic foundations such as United Way, and civic and business groups.

These multiple roles involve choices about the coalition's mission and methods, beginning with the recruitment of coalition members (Foster-Fishman et al., 2001). Community coalitions may take a top-down approach, involving existing community leaders, such as the chief of police, superintendent of schools, and elected officials. Or they may seek to also involve ordinary citizens and members of disadvantaged populations in the community. If a diversity of members is involved, the coalition must work to empower the least powerful to participate and the more powerful to listen. CINCH, for instance, omitted professional titles from its discussions. The coalition also needs to think of conflict as a way to learn and find ways to resolve or manage it. Thus a coalition that truly represents the diversity of a community has the qualities of an empowering setting described in Chapter 12.

For instance, the Pro-Youth Coalition in Santa Barbara, California, was founded to reduce youth and gang violence. It brought together representatives of community agencies, juvenile courts, religious congregations, parents, and former gang members, seeking to involve them in constructive leadership and to learn from their experiences. This approach worked: gang violence dropped by 53 percent in three years, and gang-related homicides dropped to zero (Folayemi, 2001).

A community coalition also makes choices about its mission (Chavis 2001; Himmelman, 2001). Will the coalition focus its resources and efforts on one issue, or will it address a broader set of related issues? For instance, CINCH initially focused on immunization only, then moved to broader issues of child health, while the Lexington/Richland coalition focused on multiple drug-abuse issues. Healthy Communities and Communities That Care focus more widely still, on broad issues that concern health or youth development. Will the coalition confine its focus to its immediate locality, or will it work for changes in a wider sphere? For instance, the Lexington/Richland Coalition originally focused on one region but eventually advocated and won safe boating laws at the state level. CINCH moved from a local to a regional consortium and helped develop statewide and nationwide initiatives.

Will the coalition work within the status quo of political and social conditions or seek to change those conditions? For instance, CINCH largely worked within the existing system of health care to educate providers and citizens. In contrast, the Lexington/Richland Coalition challenged community behavioral norms of alcohol use in recreation fields and boating along with the excesses of the St. Patrick's Day event; this no doubt also challenged some business interests. As another example, in Provincetown, Massachusetts, HIV infection rates were high, and residents had to travel to a Boston hospital for treatment. Those without cars faced a bus ride that usually could not be completed in one day, and once in Boston a trek by city bus and foot to reach the hospital. The Lower Outer Cape Community Coalition convinced various bus companies to coordinate their buses so that reaching Boston was more direct. After riding the bus himself, the director of the company delivering riders in Boston agreed to include a stop at the hospital itself (Wolff, 2004).

A community coalition usually doesn't challenge the powerful as much as a social action organization does. The emphasis on collaboration in coalitions may hinder frank discussion of conflicts (Chavis, 2001; Himmelman, 2001). Yet coalitions that truly represent a diversity of community members can be the meeting ground where conflicting views are openly discussed, collaboration forged, and actions taken.

Community psychologist Tom Wolff, a leader in the community coalition movement, has summarized much of the existing practitioners' wisdom about them in various sources (Kaye & Wolff, 1997; Wolff, 2001a, 2004). The Community Tool Box website (http://ctb.ku.edu), developed by community psychologists, contains valuable, practical guidance and resource materials for community coalitions and similar organizations. Empirical research on the qualities of effective community coalitions is growing (Allen, 2005; Foster-Fishman et al., 2001; Feinberg et al., 2004).

Organizational Consultation

This involves professionals working as consultants with workplaces, for-profit or nonprofit, to make changes in the organization's policies, structure, or practices. To qualify as community or social change, this must alter the organization, not simply individual workers, and be connected to wider changes in community or society. Organizational consulting may change organizational policies; alter roles, decision making, or communication in the organization; or deal with organizational issues such as work–family relationships, understanding human diversity, and intergroup conflict. The Block Booster Project and CINCH involved consultation with community organizations, helping them to become more effective in changing communities. The Midwest ARC case example in Chapter 12 used organizational concepts such as boundary spanning (Bond & Keys, 1993). Bond (1999) discussed her work in consulting with a workplace regarding conflicts about human diversity. An evaluation of planned organizational change in nonprofit organizations involved local and national settings working for changes in schools, fostering resources for families, and promoting citizenship for immigrants (Neigher & Fishman, 2004). (Reviews of organizational concepts and approaches in community psychology include Boyd & Angelique, 2002, in press; Shinn & Perkins, 2000; Trickett, Barone, & Watts, 2000.)

Alternative Settings

What do these settings have in common: women's shelters, rape crisis services, alternative schools, mutual help groups, community gardens, a street health clinic bus that operates at night to distribute HIV prevention information and condoms, self-governing cooperative housing for low-income residents, Oxford Houses, and Community Lodges?

All of these are alternative settings that grew out of dissatisfaction with mainstream services and were intended to provide an alternative to those services (Cherniss & Deegan, 2000; Reinharz, 1984). Women dissatisfied with conventional mental health and social services created their own settings for battered women and rape victims. Those settings not only help clients, but also promote public awareness of sexism. Mutual help groups such as Alcoholics Anonymous arose out of dissatisfaction with treatment services, fostering the idea that people with a shared problem could help each other. Community psychology is, in effect, an alternative setting. Distinctions between mainstream and alternative settings are often a matter of degree rather than a simple dichotomy. For instance, mutual help groups differ in the extent to which they collaborate with professionals.

Alternative settings can promote values such as sense of community, social justice, respect for human diversity, and citizen self-governance in ways that conventional organizations often do not. Their organizational structures are often less bureaucratic or hierarchical. They usually foster a spirit of mutual commitment that formal organizations do not. Alternative settings have a centuries-long history, including many spiritually based settings, women's organizations, and utopian communities. Alternative settings may be politically progressive, conservative, or apolitical.

Alternative settings provide a fertile ground for social change. Instead of working within the system to reform mainstream institutions or using social action and conflict to demand changes in those institutions, this approach goes around the mainstream institutions to create new settings. Alternative settings provide a choice for citizens or consumers of services. They can provide a safe haven and support for individuals experiencing discrimination and injustice. They often develop settings or services that later become widely accepted, such as some mutual help groups and women's services.

However, alternative settings encounter characteristic dilemmas (Cherniss & Deegan, 2000; Reinharz, 1984). They often begin with few resources other than the ideals and commitment of their founders. That can lead to burnout among their workers. Their values focus and lack of resources can lead to resisting evaluation and improvement of services (Wandersman, Keener et al., 2004). Alternative settings founded to empower the disenfranchised also may encounter dilemmas of who exactly is to be empowered (we discussed these in Chapter 12; see Riger, 1993). Finally, the existence of an alternative setting may, paradoxically, reduce the pressure on mainstream services to change because an alternative is available. However, many alternative settings have found ways to overcome these obstacles and have pioneered constructive, lasting changes in communities and societies. Cherniss and Deegan (2000) reviewed processes that contribute to their effectiveness and longevity.

The Experimental Social Innovation and Dissemination (ESID) approach can be used to develop and evaluate an alternative setting, then promote its adaptation in multiple contexts. This addresses some of the dilemmas that alternative settings often face. The Community Lodge, which we discussed in prior chapters, was the prototype of this approach (Fairweather, 1979; Fairweather, Sanders, Cressler, & Maynard, 1969). In ESID, an innovative community program or setting is developed, refined, and rigorously evaluated in research. If its outcomes are documented in that research, it can then be promoted for adoption, with appropriate refinements, in multiple settings (see Chapter 11). Sullivan (2003) discussed this process with an innovative advocacy program in women's shelters (see Chapter 4). Hazel and Onanga (2003) edited a special journal issue on ESID.

Policy Research and Advocacy

This approach involves conducting research and seeking to influence public (usually government) decisions, policies, or laws. It often involves persuading government officials but may influence leaders in the private sector, journalists, or others. It especially involves framing how a social issue is understood. This advocacy does not bargain or bring pressure based on threats but seeks to persuade with information (especially research findings) and reasoned arguments.

Policy research and advocacy may be focused on legislative, executive, or judicial branches of government at local, state or provincial, national, or international levels. Examples of policy advocacy by community psychologists include expert testimony in public interest lawsuits, filing "friend of the court" briefs in court cases, serving on advisory commissions (e.g., the Federal Interagency Council on Homelessness), contacts with lawmakers or government officials, testimony in legislative hearings on proposed bills, interviews or writing for mass media, working with advocacy organizations such as the Children's Defense Fund or the National Mental Health Association, working as a staff member for legislators or in executive or judicial branches of government, and even serving as an elected official, from the local school board to wider office (Mayer & Davidson, 2000; Melton, 1995, 2000; Meyers, 2000; Phillips, 2000; Rickel & Becker, 1997; Shinn et al., 2001; Solarz, 2001; Toro, 1998; Vincent, 1990).

Policy advocacy is often based on policy research, which is conducted to provide empirical information on social issues. An early instance of research-based public advocacy was the use of social science research findings in the 1954 Supreme Court desegregation case, *Brown v. Board of Education*. Psychological research was also used for community mental health reforms and early childhood programs such as Head Start (Phillips, 2000).

Policy research may generate findings showing the nature of a social problem, or the need for a new policy or a change in existing policy. Evaluation research studies the effectiveness of programs or policies, including their intended and unintended consequences. Reviews of research literature offer strong implications for policy because they are based on multiple studies in multiple contexts. The community research we have cited in this book offers many examples of policy-relevant studies and findings. Several qualities of community psychology equip it especially for policy concerns: concern with both research and action, emphasis on multiple ecological levels, and participatory approaches to working with citizens (Melton, 1995; Perkins, 1988, 1995; Phillips 2000; Vincent, 1990).

Advocacy is more than simply sharing research findings impartially. It usually involves allying with those on one side of a controversial issue, which demands clarity of values and wise choice of allies (Price, 1989). Advocacy demands making the best case for the side one has chosen, with available evidence and reasoning. However, distortion of research findings is neither ethical nor wise advocacy. To be influential, an advocate must be credible to policy makers and be able to answer research or arguments advanced by opponents. For example, Head Start and the Women, Infants and Children (WIC) nutrition program have survived in a conservative political era in part because of their base in empirical research and in values regarding positive child-family development. ESID, mentioned in the previous section, can also be used to develop, evaluate, and disseminate social policies. The Lexington-Richland coalition and homelessness policy researchers described at the beginning of this chapter developed and evaluated social policies, such as the safe boating law.

Important differences do exist between policy making and scientific research (Phillips, 2000; Solarz, 2001). Policy debates seldom allow room for the cautious interpretation of findings that careful scientists make or for the time to accumulate findings from multiple studies. Whereas a scientist seeks to strengthen a position with more data, a policy maker seeks to strengthen a position by recruiting allies. Communication in science is often in writing, emphasizing precision and long-term accumulation of knowledge. Among policy makers, communication is often in person, emphasizing practical utility and immediate relevance. A term such as *empowerment,* for example, may have different meanings in opposing political ideologies. Understanding the " policy culture" is essential for dealing with these dilemmas.

Box 13.1 presents an account of policy advocacy testimony by a community psychologist in the U.S. Congress.

Persuasion is not effective unless policy makers listen, and thus access to those in power or to media is necessary to influence public debate. Wise policy advocates also ally themselves with grassroots community groups and often conduct participatory research. Policy makers and the public are often persuaded (for good or ill) by a vivid story of a real person affected by a social problem. Thus policy making can be a bidirectional process, bottom-up and top-down (Phillips, 2000).

Policy making is the art of the possible, constrained by factors such as budgetary pressures and how issues are framed in the eyes of the public. U.S. democracy in particular is decentralized, with many checks and balances on the power of different levels and arms of government. This decentralization means that to gain momentum for change, a social issue must be widely considered a crisis. Yet that atmosphere of crisis inhibits taking a long-term perspective (Heller, 1984).

Policy making also involves management of conflict. Social issues have multiple sides, even multiple definitions (Rappaport, 1981; Sarason, 1978). Policy thus inevitably reflects processes of contention, negotiation, compromise, and swings in power over time. It is constrained by prior decisions, often made in response to crises, and seldom develops in an orderly sequence (Phillips, 2000; Solarz, 2001). Moreover, once a policy (e.g., a law) is written, its practical value depends on how it is implemented: for example, determining specific regulations and how changes in practices will occur (e.g., in schools, police departments).

The impact of social science research on policy making is diffuse (Phillips, 2000). Seldom does it involve a technical recommendation for a specific regulation, program, or element of policy. Instead, policy advocacy often involves educating policy makers, influencing their overall perspective on an issue. As we noted in our earlier case example on homelessness policy, Marybeth Shinn and many others have been advocating for years, with research supporting their contentions, that homelessness must be understood in part as a problem of access to affordable housing. Policy makers at local, state, and national levels are increasingly speaking and acting from this perspective. This shift in perspective is occurring after years of work, and the "influence is more on ways of thinking" about policy issues than on particular research findings or programs (Shinn, personal communication, September 22, 2004).

A similar effort to inform policy makers engaged community and developmental psychologists in promoting a strengths-based perspective on policies for

BOX 13.1 "Dr. Jason Goes to Washington": Advocacy Testimony

Following is an abridged version of an account by community psychologist Leonard Jason of his appearance in a congressional committee hearing during consideration by Congress of a national settlement of tobacco lawsuits. The full version appears in Jason (1998b). His team's research on youth access to tobacco appears in Jason, Berk, Schnopp-Wyatt, and Talbot (1999).

On Tuesday, December 2nd, I was called by a staff member of the House Commerce Committee, Subcommittee on Health and Environment, and asked to testify about behavioral aspects of teenage tobacco use. The Congressional staff person asked me to address prevention strategies, particularly issues involving youth access to tobacco products. He mentioned that I had 3 days to prepare my testimony, and I naively agreed to this request. I would have about 5 minutes to present my perspective on issues involving behavioral aspects of smoking and teenagers, and there would be two other presentations [one by a public health official and one by a consultant for the tobacco industry]. There would then be a question and answer period.

The issues involved ways to restrict youth access to tobacco, smoking reduction targets, excise taxes, public education, advertising, international sales, and funding for science. The challenge was to be concise and focus on those pieces of information that might have the largest influence on the Congresspeople at the hearing. I religiously read dozens of new bills on the tobacco settlement being introduced into Congress and continued to seek consultation from American Psychological Association (APA) staff. During that week, I was also being called by Congressional staffers. I had written twenty pages of double spaced text, and I wasn't sure how to reduce this text to a few pages. I finally did write up a brief outline that summarized some of the issues I would cover in my testimony. By Monday morning, after spending the weekend with different drafts of the testimony, I finally had a document, although I continued to incorporate new ideas into it until I boarded the plane to Washington. Pat from APA and I went to the Rayburn House Office Building on Tuesday morning. We were among the first people to enter the room where the testimony was to occur. There were television cameras from CSPAN and chairs for about 100 people. As people began filtering in, the tension began to rise. Faithfully, I practiced my deep breathing exercises. Each of the speakers gave their testimony, and I was the last person to present my views. I had rehearsed my testimony about 5 times that morning. As the minutes [of my presentation] ticked away, my confidence gained. . . . My voice grew strong and clear.

I stressed that there was a considerable amount of behavioral data to indicate that it is possible to reduce the number of young people who smoke. Starting, continuing, and quitting smoking are fundamentally behavioral processes. I next indicated that it is possible to appreciably reduce the percent of vendors that sell to youth. I then mentioned that scientifically based school prevention programs can effectively reduce the percentage of children who later smoke, and that the most exemplary programs include anti-smoking ads in the mass media and comprehensive school programs. I then talked about how even with the settlement [of lawsuits against the tobacco industry], children will be exposed to imagery-laden tobacco advertisements, and that to deal with this we need a ratio of anti-smoking ads to cigarette ads to be 1:4 or greater. I would have preferred saying that all ads should be banned, but I knew that this would raise First Amendment rights issues. I then mentioned that while the federal government can provide leadership on initiatives to reduce tobacco-related disease and death, it should not manage state or local initiatives, and I added that we need to encourage grass roots efforts. In summing up my testimony, I mentioned that psychological research has led to a better understanding of the effects of tobacco advertisements, youth access laws, school and community prevention programs.

For the next hour and fifteen minutes, each of the Congress people had 5 minutes to ask us questions. They were attentive and rarely engaged in side conversations, and I was rather surprised at this high level of interest. Questions posed to me frequently involved issues of youth access to tobacco. One Congressperson asked me if I thought that smoking should be completely banned. In a set of subsequent questions, he kept using the terms "ban" and "restricting youth access to tobacco" interchangeably, and I had to constantly point out the differences in these two concepts. The time flew by, and the hour and a half of session ended.

So what do I make of this experience? First, it is great fun to be able to testify in Congress, and actually have policymakers interested in your research and points of view. To do this type of work, one needs to be able to relatively quickly develop a position that addresses key points and reduces the cognitive complexity of a particular topic. Good stress management and public speaking skills are necessary but not sufficient. Working collaboratively with other organizations, in this case APA, are key attributes for reaching these types of audiences. Keeping a sense of humor, and being diplomatic, are prudent.

children, families, and communities. This initiative produced a book on key areas of research, created brief summary materials for policy makers, built the capacity of professional groups to influence policy, and established relationships with national policy makers (Maton et al., 2004; Solarz, 2001).

This long-term process of influencing ways of thinking means that the relationships among policy makers, citizens, and researchers are important elements of advocacy. Trust is as essential as expertise. An intermediary is often helpful: trained in social science research yet experienced in policy culture, and engaged in social networks that include policy makers and their staffs (Phillips, 2000). Solarz (2001) and Meyers (2000) described their experiences in such roles.

We have described seven approaches to social and community change. No one approach is always effective; each has strengths and limitations. These approaches to change can be integrated in a myriad of ways.

ISSUES FOR COMMUNITY AND SOCIAL CHANGE

How do top-down and bottom-up approaches differ in community change? Do effective efforts for community change have common elements? What processes promote social change? We now turn to these questions that concern the approaches just described.

Community Betterment and Community Empowerment

Efforts to promote community change, especially locality-based coalitions, involve choices between the goals and methods of community betterment and community empowerment (Himmelman, 2001).

Community betterment involves a primarily top-down approach. It often is initiated by professionals who provide services in a community but who may not be personally affected by community problems. Community members or residents may be invited to join the process, but professionals retain primary influence. Betterment efforts often proceed by identifying needs or deficits in a community, then planning and implementing services to meet those needs. This process requires a community to highlight its problems rather than its assets (Kretzmann & McKnight, 1993). In the Spanning Community Networks case example earlier in this chapter, the initial phase involved community betterment (Hughey & Speer, 2002).

Community empowerment uses a primarily bottom-up approach. Members or residents of a community are involved in initiating the effort, and they retain primary influence and control. Empowerment efforts assess community resources as well as problems and focus on community changes (Kretzmann & McKnight, 1993). Community changes may involve services similar to those in a betterment model or may involve other changes defined by the community. The crucial difference is that in the empowerment approach community members retain control. Decisions are made by those whose lives will be most affected (Himmelman, 2001; Kaye & Wolff, 1997). In the Spanning Community

Networks case example, the second and third phases involved community empowerment (Hughey & Speer, 2002).

Kaye and Wolff (1997) described a community meeting in which members of a community coalition described their visions, ideas, and hopes for "their" community. When asked how many actually lived in this community, less than half raised their hands, which indicated a betterment rather than an empowerment approach. In another example, a community health center joined with a community organization of persons of color to obtain a minority health grant. When the grant was received, no members of the community organization were hired and only a few were given positions on the advisory board for the project. Community members were largely excluded from influence. In contrast, the CINCH coalition took steps to make its efforts empowering: involving citizens representing the diversity of Norfolk's population, eliminating titles on name tags, and emphasizing the value of contribution to coalition work rather than professional status (Butterfoss et al., 2001).

Both betterment and empowerment approaches have advantages and drawbacks. Their effectiveness depends in part on context. A betterment approach may obtain useful external resources. An empowerment approach uses community resources more fully and retains local control. As we will discuss shortly, community organizations can take steps to use some features of both approaches.

Elements of Effective Community Change Initiatives

What qualities promote effective community-level change? Schorr (1997, pp. 360–368) reviewed organizations seeking to improve neighborhood and community quality of life and suggested key elements for effective locality-level change. Peterson and Zimmerman (2004) reviewed research on qualities of empowered community organizations that have played effective roles in community and social change. We have integrated their ideas into a list of eight qualities.

Effective Community Actions Empowered community organizations effectively exert power in community decisions, policies, and practices (Peterson & Zimmerman, 2004). They may directly **implement actions:** for example, directly influencing decisions or providing community programs. PICO public accountability meetings with officials and other social action approaches illustrate one type of action. HUCTW won and uses the right to bargain collectively with the university. The Lexington/Richland Coalition helped write local and state policies and helped resolve the St. Patrick's Day controversy. CINCH implemented many community changes regarding child health.

Community organizations may also **disseminate information** to influence decision makers or the public (Peterson & Zimmerman, 2004). The contentious world of community and social change often requires much initial groundwork to influence viewpoints. PICO efforts in one Midwestern city influenced media coverage and public perceptions of the issues they raised, both for immediate impact on decisions and for long-term change in public opinion (Speer & Hughey, 1995). Policy research and advocacy primarily relies on dissemination of information.

The effectiveness of community actions can be assessed in terms of their influence on actual policy and decisions; on creation of alternative settings, community programs, and similar initiatives; and on deployment of resources in the community and wider society (Peterson & Zimmerman, 2004).

Multiple Areas of Action Community problems seldom involve just education, or families, or crime, or economic development. Advocates for change often focus on a single problem, assuming that improvement there will lead to wider changes. Yet the research evidence reviewed by Schorr (1997) and the practical knowledge of community leaders she interviewed, indicated that change in one area seldom leads to wider community change on its own. Effective change initiatives must address multiple, related issues (see also Caughey, O'Campo, & Brodsky, 1999; Wolff, 2001a).

A community cannot address all things at once. Yet it can develop a comprehensive perspective in which linkages are recognized (Schorr, 1997, p. 361). This can lead to linking community initiatives, such as economic development to provide local jobs for graduates of a job training program, or finding senior citizens to volunteer in child care centers.

In Savannah, Georgia, the Youth Futures Authority (YFA) pursued community development in a low-income neighborhood. After an initial single-focus phase failed, the YFA took a comprehensive perspective. It developed a family resource center providing preventive programs regarding health and nutrition, substance abuse, school readiness, and child development. It fostered scout groups, athletics, neighborhood murals, and conflict resolution classes. Because the center exists in a predominantly African-American neighborhood, many of these services use an Africentric format emphasizing family and community ties, self-discipline, and constructive work. YFA initiatives have also included changes in policing and zoning (Schorr, 1997).

The New Community Corporation (NCC) in Newark, New Jersey, is often considered the most successful community development corporation in the United States. Begun by William Linder, a Catholic priest, the NCC now has spawned 30 organizations that own and manage housing, provide a variety of family services and programs for youth, run a credit union, provide home health care and a nursing home, administer a job-training program, and own a shopping center and other retail ventures in the center of Newark (Schorr, 1997).

Local Control Effective community initiatives have substantial local control of planning and implementing changes. Local citizens know best the resources, culture(s), most pressing issues, and workable methods of change for their community. Moreover, when citizens collectively determine their own goals, their talents are used and their commitment mobilized. Of course, decisions need to be based on participation by a cross-section of a community, not just by powerful leaders pursuing only their own visions of community interest. PICO organizations strengthen local control; CINCH also emphasized local planning.

Alliances among local organizations strengthen access to local resources, public legitimacy, and allies in conflicts (Peterson & Zimmerman, 2004). Community coalitions such as the Lexington/Richland Coalition and CINCH provide such linkages. PICO organizations affiliate with local religious congregations that share a commitment to social justice.

External Linkages and Resources Few communities facing serious problems can make significant headway completely on their own. Thus, although community change is best controlled locally, it often requires resources from outside the community. These resources come in three forms: funding, knowledge, and clout (Schorr, 1997, p. 363). External funding is required if change efforts exhaust local resources. Expertise is needed, not to define problems or dictate goals (these are best done within the community), but to provide technical skills and knowledge of what has worked for other communities. Finally, a community needs to influence key decisions by outsiders that affect the community.

Communities can cultivate these resources through **interpersonal networks** with persons outside the community and **organizational alliances** with other organizations (Peterson & Zimmerman, 2004).

The Spanning Community Networks case example involved using external interpersonal networks (Speer & Hughey, 2002). The local grassroots neighborhood organization advocating for genuine community policing, even with support from some police, could not secure a change in police practices until it gained access to persons who could influence the mayor. Those persons were outside the organization and neighborhood.

Building organizational alliances outside the locality can gain access to funding, allies in conflicts, and exchange of strategies that have worked elsewhere. In Boston, the Dudley Street Neighborhood Initiative (see Chapter 5) formed linkages with city government, universities, and foundations that provided resources for neighborhood transformation. To obtain these, Dudley Street residents had to insist on keeping control of decisions and on outsiders respecting that control (Kretzmann & McKnight, 1993; Medoff & Sklar, 1994; Putnam & Feldstein, 2003). CINCH founded a statewide coalition to promote immunization and worked with many outside resources to pursue its aims. Homelessness policy researchers have pursued state, national and international collaborations (Shinn et al., 2001;Tompsett et al., 2003). African-American women in a rural North Carolina county overcame local government resistance to new community programs by working directly with state authorities to obtain funding, employing both bottom-up and top-down approaches (Lopez & Stack, 2001).

A Plausible Theory of Community Change To be successful, a community change initiative needs to be guided by a theory or plan (Nation et al., 2003; Schorr, 1997, p. 364). Theory can be based on social science research, but also on citizen practical experience. Every citizen has some conception of how community change occurs, and evidence of whether an initiative is working is often available with simple measurement. A plausible theory is based on citizens' careful, shared reasoning about how their community can be improved. Such theorizing is not merely exchange of opinions, nor is it solely based on expert advice. In the PICO approach described earlier in this chapter, citizens conduct fact-finding research on the nature of community problems, conduct actions to pressure for change, and then meet to evaluate their work and to plan further efforts (Speer & Hughey, 1995). That reflection builds a plausible, useful theory of change.

Effective Intensity Initiatives for community change must involve changes that are strong enough to make a detectable difference in everyday life. There is a threshold for effective response to a community problem; initiatives below that threshold will not be effective. Small businesses that create only a few jobs will not significantly affect neighborhood unemployment. Educational innovations by a few dedicated teachers will make a difference in some students' lives but do little to change the overall climate of a school or improve overall education for a community. A crime prevention initiative will not be sustained if it makes little visible difference to citizens on the street.

Intense initiatives involve significant amounts of resources, usually funding and citizen involvement. In the United States, many community programs have never been funded at a sufficient level of intensity. Although these initiatives were effective in demonstration projects in specific communities, they were then applied more widely without sufficient resources to reach the threshold needed to create wider social change. Thus they have made little headway against entrenched social problems. Community change initiatives need to generate sufficient intensity through mobilization of sufficient resources, both monetary and human (Nation et al., 2003; Schorr, 1997).

Strengthening Sense of Community A factor implicit in Schorr's (1997) discussion is the importance of sense of community among community members as a resource for community change. Effective community change initiatives both use and enhance this resource by strengthening individuals' sense of community membership, mutual influence of individuals and the community, members' integration and support of each other, and their shared emotional connections. Do you recognize these ideas? They are the McMillan and Chavis (1986) elements of sense of community from Chapter 6.

Long-Term Perspective A final factor, also implicit in Schorr's (1997) discussion and examples, is the necessity for a long-term perspective. Community change does not occur overnight. The community initiatives described in this chapter are often the products of years of effort. The work of coalitions such as CINCH usually is in its second or third year before measurable community outcomes occur (Fawcett et al., 1995; Butterfoss et al., 2001). PICO organizations build their base of interpersonal relationships and commitment carefully for months (Speer et al., 1995). HUCTW took years to win Harvard's recognition and collaboration (Putnam & Feldstein, 2003). When decisions are made through genuine citizen participation, time is a necessary resource. Yet initiatives that build slowly and steadily, with citizen input, are likely to be sustained even if conditions change, because their participatory base is solid.

There are no exact formulas for community change (Alinsky, 1971). These eight elements are best understood as rules of thumb, with many possible ways to apply them in practice. Each community and community issue involves a unique mix of resources, obstacles, allies and opponents, means and ends, intentions and unanticipated consequences. Community change initiatives are an art, but a collective art, involving personal relationships and shared successes and failures.

Larger obstacles also must be considered. For instance, Caughy et al. (1999) found that maternal health programs, highly effective in many Baltimore neighborhoods, had less impact in areas of poverty and high unemployment. Macrosystem forces that create such economic inequalities also need to be addressed. That is the focus of the next section.

Issues in Promoting Social Change

Tseng et al. (2002) proposed a conceptual framework for promoting social change. We will summarize their discussion of three issues in social change: values, contexts, and dynamic processes of social change. See Tseng et al. (2002) for their full perspective.

Values and Language Tseng et al. emphasize the guiding role of values in social change. Although perfect agreement on values is not necessary for effective action, candid discussion of core values and aims is needed, and reexamination of these over time is often healthy. Values such as social justice, respect for diversity, community collaboration, and strengthening sense of community may guide efforts for community and social change, but as we have discussed in prior chapters, conflicts among these values may arise.

Language is also important, because much of community and social change involves communication: defining issues and positions, framing issues, articulating values and visions for change, resolving or managing conflicts. Tseng et al. especially advocate language that calls attention to multiple ecological levels, not just individual factors. They also call for language that recognizes conflict, for instance referring to social *issues,* with multiple, often opposing positions, rather than social *problems,* for which we usually expect to have *solutions* (Sarason, 1978).

Dynamic, Changing Systems Tseng et al. also emphasize the dynamic processes of social change. Social systems (organizations, localities, macrosystems) are ever changing, not stable. Linear thinking that focuses on simple causes and effects will oversimplify complex, unpredictable processes. Thus Tseng et al. call for thinking in terms of ongoing cycles of change and growth for individuals and communities. For instance, our earlier PICO case example described a cycle of community organizing. Each cycle of community action leads to a process of reflection on lessons learned and to a new cycle of change.

To begin cycles of change, Tseng et al. suggest looking for social regularities in role relationships and power (Seidman, 1988). For instance, the STEP program (see Chapter 5) altered many social regularities of high schools, keeping students together for most classes to build a sense of community and support networks, and strengthening ties between students and homeroom teachers (Felner & Adan, 1988). STEP also exemplified a focus on turning points in individual lives (e.g., entering high school). Social systems also have turning points, as when a school faces a critical incident such as a student suicide or a when a locality's major employer closes.

Tseng et al. also are skeptical of focusing too much on specific outcomes of social change. Once an outcome is attained, we may assume that no further change is needed. In reality, community life involves ongoing changes. However, it also often true that showing how a program or policy leads to tangible, desirable outcomes can attract allies and influence decision making. The crucial point is not assuming that those outcomes are permanent or that future changes are not needed.

Social change processes need to be considered at multiple ecological levels. A social change initiative that changes individual behaviors may not change settings or other social systems. Tseng et al. call for targeting social systems for change, including schools, community institutions, and social policies.

Contextual Processes Tseng et al. identify three aspects of social contexts important for engaging in efforts to promote social change. Efforts for social change must understand **time:** how history influences the present and how change occurs over time. Such efforts also must consider **culture** and take into account shared cultural values and practices (which also are continually changing). Tseng et al. also call attention to **power:** understanding existing power relationships at multiple ecological levels, considering who is to be empowered and how that change is to occur. One point of agreement among Schorr (1997), Peterson and Zimmerman (2004), and Tseng et al. (2002) is that contexts must be considered in designing change initiatives.

CONCLUSION

In Table 13.1, we list the key elements and issues for effective community and social change that we have discussed.

TABLE 13.1 Elements and Issues in Community and Social Change

Elements of Effective Community Change Initiatives
Effective community actions
Multiple areas of action, linkages among programs
Local control
External linkages and resources
A plausible theory of community change
Effective intensity of intervention
Strengthening sense of community
Long-term perspective
Issues in Promoting Social Change
Values, language
Dynamic, changing systems
Contextual processes: time, culture, power

SOURCE: Adapted from Schorr (1997, pp. 360--368); Peterson & Zimmerman (2004); Tseng et al. (2002).

If you are inspired to become involved in community or wider social change, an excellent place to learn about practical action steps is the Community Toolbox website, developed by community psychologists to offer an online, accessible resource for citizens. Its address is http://ctb.ku.edu.

CHAPTER SUMMARY

1. How do citizens, acting collectively, acquire and use power to promote changes in their communities and in society? This question concerns psychology because individual, community, and societal quality of life are intertwined.
2. We described six case examples of community and social change initiatives: community organizing in PICO community organizations; the Harvard Union of Clerical and Technical Workers; spanning community networks to influence a community decision; two community coalitions, CINCH and the Lexington/Richland Coalition; and policy research and advocacy concerning homelessness. The PICO approach involves a *cycle of organizing:* assessment, research, mobilization/action, and reflection.
3. Seven approaches to community and social change include *consciousness raising, social action, community development, community coalitions, organizational consulting, alternative settings,* and *policy research and advocacy* . The concept of *community readiness* refers to a form of community-level consciousness raising. These differ in their purposes and methods, but many community organizations use a combination of several approaches.
4. One overarching issue concerning community change initiatives is whether they involve a top-down *community betterment* approach or a bottom-up *community empowerment* approach. Some community organizations use elements of both.
5. We described eight elements of effective community change initiatives and three issues to consider in promoting social change. These are listed in Table 13.1. *Effective community actions* include *implementing actions* and *disseminating information. External linkages and resources* involve *interpersonal networks* and *organizational alliances.*

BRIEF EXERCISES

1. Review the community or social issue you chose for the opening exercise. Suggest how each of the seven approaches to community and social change (consciousness raising, social action, community development, community coalitions, organizational consulting, alternative settings, policy research and advocacy) could be applied to that issue. How would each affect the lives of community members? Which approaches are most interesting to you or are ones that you could imagine yourself becoming involved in?

2. Learn about a community or social change initiative in your community or society. You can do this, for instance, by reading an in-depth newspaper article, interviewing someone involved, or attending a related event. Identify how any of the seven approaches to community and social change are implemented in this initiative. Does it embody any of the eight elements of effective community change or the three issues for social change listed in Table 13.1? Did the change initiative attain its goals? Why or why not, in your view?
3. Write an action letter that advocates a policy change. Choose an issue you have personal experience or background knowledge of and that you have a viewpoint on. Choose also a person or organization you want to address, the more specific the better. (Examples include a legislator, a city mayor, the president of your university, a newspaper editor, the head of a business.)

   Your letter should include the following elements:

   - Define the specific problem or issue you are addressing.
   - Describe aspects of this issue that have gotten too little attention. This may include causes that have been overlooked. Cite sources of specific information.
   - Advocate a specific, feasible course of action to address these aspects of the issue. Examples include a new policy, new practices or ways to carry out an existing policy, a new or modified community program, or research to analyze the issue further. Recognize that your ideas will have costs (e.g., money, time, collaboration among groups). Advocate your course of action assertively.
   - Remember that the likelihood of close reading by your addressee decreases with each page. Be as succinct as you can but cover all the elements listed. A suggested length is two pages double-spaced.

   It is your choice whether or not to send your finished letter.

RECOMMENDED READINGS

Hughey, J., & Speer P. (1995). Community, sense of community, and networks. In A. Fisher, C. Sonn, & B. Bishop, (Eds.), *Psychological sense of community: Research, applications, and implications* (pp. 69–84). New York: Kluwer Academic/ Plenum.

Perkins, D., Crim, B., Silberman, P., & Brown, B. (2004). Community development as a response to community-level adversity: Ecological theory and research and strengths-based policy. In K. Maton, C. Schellenbach, B. Leadbeater, & A. Solarz (Eds.), *Investing in children, youth, families and communities: Strengths-based research and policy* (pp. 321–340). Washington, DC: American Psychological Association.

Peterson, A., & Zimmerman, M. (2004). Beyond the individual: Toward a nomological network of organizational empowerment. *American Journal of Community Psychology, 34,* 129–146.

Phillips, D. (2000). Social policy and community psychology. In J. Rappaport & E. Seidman (Eds.), *Handbook of community psychology* (pp. 397–419). New York: Kluwer Academic/Plenum.

Tseng, V., Chesir-Teran, D., Becker-Klein, R., Chan, M., Duran, V., Roberts, A., & Bardoliwalla, N. (2002). Promotion of social change: A conceptual framework. *American Journal of Community Psychology, 30,* 401–427.

Wolff, T. (Ed.) (2001). Community coalition building: Contemporary practice and research [Special section]. *American Journal of Community Psychology, 29*(2), 165–330.

Action Guidebooks for Community and Social Change

Kaye, G., & Wolff, T. (Eds.). (1997). *From the ground up: A workbook on coalition building and community development.* Amherst, MA: AHEC/Community Partners.

Kretzmann, J., & McKnight, J. (1993). *Building communities from the inside out: A path toward finding and mobilizing a community's assets.* Chicago: ACTA Publications.

Wollman, N., Lobenstine, M., Foderaro, M., & Stose, S. (1998). *Principles for promoting social change: Effective strategies for influencing attitudes and behaviors* (booklet). Ann Arbor, MI: Society for the Psychological Study of Social Issues. [To order, email: spssi@spssi.org]

 RECOMMENDED WEBSITES

Community Tool Box
http://ctb.ku.edu

Excellent site for learning about citizen participation and planning community change, maintained by community psychologists. Includes tools and recommendations for planning, implementing, and evaluating community initiatives as well as links to many related sites. The best single, practical resource for community and social change initiatives.

PICO National Network
http://www.piconetwork.org

This website includes much information on PICO values, people, work, and local affiliates. On the website, go to Resources for multimedia clips with individual stories of personal and social change.

Psychologists for Social Responsibility
http://www.psysr.org

An organization of psychologists concerned with international and U.S. social issues, including peace and war, ethnopolitical violence, conflict resolution, social justice, and other issues. Includes entries on scholarly works and action initiatives as well as links to other organizations.

INFOTRAC® COLLEGE EDITION KEYWORDS

advocacy, alternative settings, community coalition, community change, community development, community initiative, community organizing(ation), consciousness raising, empowering(ed)(ment), policy research, social action, social change

14

Program Evaluation and Program Development

Lexington-Richland Alcohol and Drug Abuse Commission

ACTING ON EVALUATION IN EVERYDAY LIFE

What Can Eating in Restaurants Teach Us about Evaluation?

You stop by a restaurant where you have never eaten before. There is a menu on the outside window. The dishes sound interesting and the environment looks attractive. You are seated at a table and then you wait and wait. Your server finally appears and gives his name and says he will be right back to take your order. You wait again for 10 minutes and he returns. He then takes your drink order and returns 10 minutes later with your drinks. He does not take your food order until he comes back 10 minutes later. After your food order has been taken, you wait 10 minutes for your appetizer. It is really good. You then wait an additional 20 minutes for your entrée, which comes mildly warm. The fish is tasty but not as hot as you like and the vegetables taste like they came out of a can. You finish your food because you are hungry. After you finish the entree, you don't want to wait longer for dessert and coffee so you tell the waiter that you don't want any. The waiter apologizes for the delays—one of the other servers was sick and he had to cover both shifts, and he gives you a check.

Will you go to this restaurant again? You think over the quality of the service, the quality of the food, and the atmosphere. You are about to decide no, it is not worthwhile. Then you think about what you learned in community psychology about ecological levels of analysis. Maybe there is more here than meets the eye. The problem may be more than an individual waiter who lacks competence.

A restaurant should function as a team: waiters, greeters, chef, management. The restaurant as an organization was not prepared for what might be a common occurrence, an employee absence. Perhaps the restaurant is trying to maximize profits by hiring fewer staff. Perhaps the employee's illness may even be related to stress at work. Perhaps the real problem is a demand for profits at corporate headquarters, not with local management.

Still, you have evaluated your experience and decide that you don't want to invest your time and money in this restaurant again. You tell the waiter that you understand that the situation may not have been his fault, but your feedback to management is that this is not satisfactory and you don't plan to come back. The restaurant manager comes to your table and apologizes. She is pleased to have your feedback and says that she has heard about this problem before and has two new servers starting next week to ease the load. She offers you a coupon for a free dinner.

The manager and the employees are concerned about evaluation. The manager seeks to bring you back to the restaurant when you may be more satisfied. Even the wait staff is concerned with your impressions, since these strongly influence how much you will tip them. Even though profits and losses drive many of these decisions, they must be considered in long-term perspective and must address variables such as customer and staff satisfaction as well as the reputation of the restaurant in the community.

What Can Football Teach Us about Evaluation?

Any major college football coach knows all about evaluation. He knows his won and lost record, the scores of each game and how each player performed in the last game. He knows the players' capacities, such as how fast they can run 40 yards, and he knows what they did in the last game (tackles made, passes caught, penalties committed). The coaching staff reviews game films among themselves and with players. They figure out what plays worked and what plays did not. They show the players how they need to improve next time. Coaches use all of this information, and more, to plan for the next game. They are interested in improvement and in results.

Not only does the coaching staff know these statistics; so do many of the loyal fans. A coach gets plenty of advice, such as from callers on a radio talk show: what was good and what was bad about the last game, who played well and who played poorly, and plenty of suggestions for improvement.

In addition to winning and losing, there are other values involved in collegiate football: sportsmanship, the university's reputation, and at least some allegiance to academic values (e.g., as reflected in athletes' graduation rates). Programs are evaluated according to multiple values, at multiple levels: evaluations of individual players, the coaching staff, and the university itself. A college football program is all about program evaluation. Indeed, sports at many levels, whether to win or just to play, are about evaluation and improvement, for players, coaches, and fans.

What Can Project DARE Teach Us about Evaluation?

DARE (Drug Abuse Resistance Education) is the most popular school-based drug-use prevention delivery network in the United States. Millions of students and citizens have participated in the programs designed for grades K–12. At its outset, this program represented a common-sense prevention approach: involve community resources such as the police in the schools; inform students of the dangers of drug abuse, and teach refusal skills that would enable students to say "no" to peer pressure for drug use. (The curricula that were developed for the DARE Network were based on knowledge about effective programming in the 1980s).

Yet a number of evaluations of school curricula delivered by DARE have provided only limited evidence of its effectiveness when children are most at risk: in middle, junior high, or senior high school. For instance, results from a longitudinal evaluation of the program in 36 schools in Illinois showed only some impact on student's drug use immediately following the intervention and no evidence of impact on drug use one or two years after receiving DARE instruction. In addition, evaluations indicated that DARE programs had only limited positive effects on variables such as self-esteem and no effect on social skills variables such as resistance to peer pressure (Enett et al., 1994, p. 113). Evaluations of other programs indicate that other approaches *are* effective in reducing adolescent drug use over time, especially if they teach a broader array of social and emotional-regulation skills (e.g., Botvin & Tortu, 1988; Greenberg et al., 2003; Hawkins, Catalano, & Associates, 1992). However, many school systems have continued to use the DARE approach, in part because it is familiar, and sometimes also because law enforcement and other funds have been used so that a school system can spend less of its own money. Clearly, evaluations of outcomes were not the only factor in these decisions. This is a familiar story in community programs, not limited to DARE or to the issue of drug abuse.

Yet the DARE story is not over. After many years of evaluations showing disappointing results, DARE has undertaken a major revision of its curriculum and techniques, using knowledge from research on substance abuse prevention and on how children learn. This new program is being used and evaluated in a number of communities; results are not out yet (Z. Sloboda, personal communications, January 7, 2005; February 13, 2005).

This sequence illustrates several themes of this chapter. Program evaluation and program development need to be linked so that empirical information can influence decisions. Without that linkage, decisions about community programs are made with much misinformation and wishful thinking about what the actual effects of the program are. With such a linkage in place, even initially disappointing results can lead to systematic improvements in a program.

We acknowledge that evaluating a community program like DARE is not simply identical to evaluating a college sports program or the success of a restaurant. In the contexts of sports and business, wins or profits and losses are very important, salient outcomes. They are not everything, at least in some contexts: a university may choose to keep a football coach without a winning record, and a high-quality restaurant may appeal to a small clientele. Yet the bottom line cannot be ignored. A restaurant that loses money will be held accountable for those losses in some way. For a community program such as DARE, however, there is often not as much agreement among citizens or decision makers on underlying values or measurable objectives. Thus it can be more challenging to determine whether the program is effective.

Yet evaluation is essential to program improvement and effectiveness, *especially* when values and viewpoints conflict. Evaluation of community programs can be done with sensitivity to the contexts within which programs operate, with attention to values issues, and with a focus on program improvement over time. It can provide information on real-world outcomes and impacts and inform debates on values, goals, and methods.

It Seemed Like a Good Idea, But Is It Really Working?

Each year billions of dollars in tax money, charitable contributions, and grants by philanthropic foundations are spent to do good things in communities. Millions of citizens volunteer time and effort to promote these goals. Even paid staff in community organizations often choose to work for a low salary to promote those goals. Is that time, effort, and money making a difference? Government, nonprofit, and private sectors are being challenged to show results (U.S. General Accounting Office, 1990; United Way of America, 1996). At first, this can be a frightening prospect. These are some common complaints and fears about program evaluation (compiled by the Northwest Regional Educational Laboratory, 1999):

- Evaluation can create anxiety among program staff.
- Staff may be unsure how to conduct evaluation.
- Evaluation can interfere with program activities or compete with services for scarce resources.
- Evaluation results can be misused and misinterpreted, especially by program opponents.

Imagine yourself as a board member of a foundation who has to make funding decisions about community programs. You get many more requests for funding than you could possibly fund. It makes sense to ask grantees, "How can we know if your program, supported by our grant money, actually accomplishes its goals?" Schorr (1997) described several types of answers to this question often given by nonprofit organizations and government agencies.

- *Trust and values.* "Trust us. What we do is so valuable, so complex, so hard to document, so hard to judge, and we are so well intentioned that the public should support us without demanding evidence of effectiveness. Don't let the bean counters who know the cost of everything and the value of nothing obstruct our valiant efforts to get the world's work done" (Schorr, 1997, p. 116).

  A potential problem with this answer: Citizens and funders don't know the process of how the program works, and don't know whether there are any results.

- *Process and outputs.* "Our agency sees 200 eligible clients yearly in the 20 parent education programs we offer with our two licensed staff who are funded by your grant." This is probably the most typical answer, with detailed documentation of programs or services provided and resources expended.

  A potential problem: Simply providing services does not mean that those services are effective. Services may be misdirected, thus not addressing the real problem. They may be well planned but not strong or well funded enough to make a difference. They may have unintended side effects. Hopeful but undocumented expectations underlie many community programs.
- *Results-based accountability.* Using program evaluation, agency staff and evaluators can show that a specific program achieved its intended effects. They can also modify it to become even more effective. This is similar to the idea of continuous improvement discussed in Chapter 11.

  Potential problems: Often, agency staff is not trained to do evaluation. Also, what happens if the evaluation shows that the program does not have its intended results? Will the program be given a chance to improve and the resources it needs to do so?

Yet program evaluation does not have to be frightening. Results-based accountability requires us to understand program evaluation and how programs can be improved to achieve their goals. Done well, it can strengthen a program's quality as well as its ability to resist critics.

THE LOGIC OF PROGRAM EVALUATION

We noted earlier how community decisions about using Project DARE have often not been influenced by empirical evaluations. How can a community program remain so popular even when evidence of positive results is scarce?

For DARE, as for many community programs, evaluation studies were designed to yield a final verdict on the program's effectiveness, not to provide specific information on how to improve it. Such studies often compare an intervention group who received a program with a comparison group who did not. Whether the groups differ significantly or not, such a study cannot tell us why specifically the intervention worked (or did not work), or what specifically to do to improve outcomes. Without such information, program staff and community members have little guidance for their decisions about the future of the program.

There are at least two reasons why programs don't work: *theory failure* and *implementation failure.* Theory failure concerns program theory: the rationale for why a particular intervention is considered appropriate for a particular problem with a specific target population, in a particular cultural and social context. Program theory also helps choose appropriate measurements or methods to study the effects of the program. Implementation failure concerns quality of program implementation. You may have an excellent program that has been demonstrated elsewhere to work with your target population, but the implementation in your location may be weak because of a lack of resources, inexperienced personnel, insufficient training, or other reasons (see Chapter 11).

Since the 1960s, the field of program evaluation has developed concepts and methods based on the methods of the social sciences to study program theory and implementation. This chapter uses many of these basic program evaluation concepts. However, we focus on approaches that make program evaluation user friendly and accessible to a wider audience. (For a more detailed review, see Patton, 1997; Rossi, Lipsey, & Freeman, 2004; Worthen, Sanders, & Fitzpatrick, 1997.)

Professional evaluators are trained to think causally. They recognize that an intervention or prevention activity is based on an underlying program theory or model of the causal factors contributing to the problem to be prevented. This model may be clearly stated by the prevention program's developers, or the program may only be based on implicit assumptions. The desired effects are not likely to occur if:

- The underlying assumptions of the program theory are not appropriate for the program's context.
- The program is implemented well, yet doesn't affect the variables specified by program theory.
- The activity or program is not implemented adequately.

For social scientists, this type of thinking becomes so automatic that it is easy to forget it is not universal. Agency staff often need a "critical friend" to help them identify their underlying assumptions about their program theory, goals, and implementation.

For instance, a common community prevention activity is sponsoring a Red Ribbon Awareness Campaign. A local group wants to significantly reduce alcohol, tobacco, and other drug (ATOD) use by getting citizens to display red ribbons. Why would wearing a red ribbon lead to reductions in ATOD use? For example, the logic may be that a red ribbon stimulates awareness of the hazards of alcohol use, which then either reduces one's own consumption of alcohol or at least stimulates a sober friend to drive. Questioning the connections between the display of red ribbons and the ultimate outcome of reduction of drunk driving requires critical thinking about cause and effect. It is important for school and community practitioners to use causal thinking and, as much as possible, to develop a causal model for a community program. That logic model can then indicate questions for evaluation of program process and outcome, which will help demonstrate program effectiveness.

The principal purpose of a causal logic model is to show, in a simple, understandable way, the logical connections among the conditions that contribute to the need for a program in a community, the activities aimed at addressing these conditions, and the outcomes and impacts expected to result from the activities (Julian, Jones, & Dey, 1995; McEwan & Bigelow, 1997).

The logic model is a graphic representation of how the program works. Figure 14.1 illustrates a four-step logic model that can be applied to program evaluation. Its top row consists of four circles, representing program conditions, activities, outcomes, and impacts. The circles are linked together with

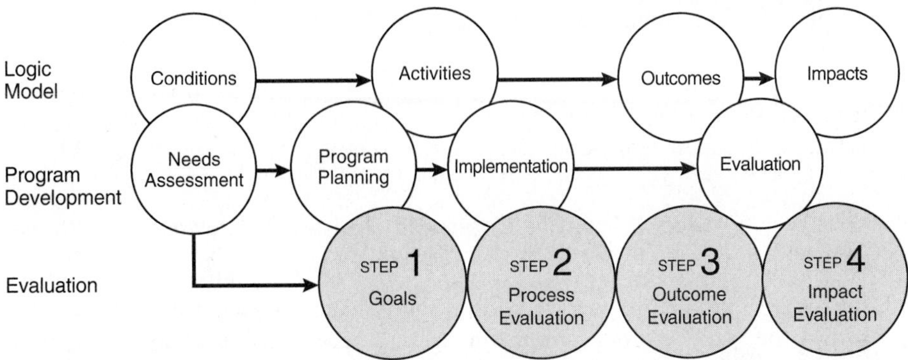

FIGURE 14.1

lines that show the expected logical relationships among them, based on the program theory. These relationships among circles also show the sequence of intended events that occur as a result of program activities.

In the first circle, **conditions** include risk factors or processes, community problems, or organizational difficulties that the program seeks to address. The second circle includes the **activities** that address each condition; one or more activities can aim at solving each of the conditions. The third circle contains the immediate **outcomes** that result from the activity (e.g., changes in knowledge or attitudes of program participants, or changes in local laws or organizational policy). The fourth circle concerns the eventual **impacts** of the program on the community at large. For example, impacts in alcohol, tobacco, and other drugs (ATOD) might include lowering alcohol and other drug abuse in a community, as well as related consequences such as lower crime and better personal health.

In Figure 14.1, the middle row illustrates the steps in program development and their relationships to the logic model. A program developer assesses the need for a program (often with community surveys or interviews), plans a program to address the need, implements the program, and evaluates whether the program has been successful. The bottom row of Figure 14.1 shows how the four-step model of program evaluation relates to the logic model and to program development.

In 1996, the United Way network of community philanthropy organizations began to promote a workbook on outcome measurement, which extends the logic model above and has revolutionized evaluation among many nonprofit community organizations. For instance, the United Way approach also calls attention to resources dedicated to a program (United Way of America, 1996; see also http://national.unitedway.org/outcomes/resources/mpo/model.cfm).

A FOUR-STEP MODEL OF PROGRAM EVALUATION

Linney and Wandersman (1991) sought to design materials that would stimulate analytical thinking about the ways in which prevention programs might affect outcomes, realistic thinking about the effect of any one preventive effort, and careful planning for implementation. Their volume, *Prevention Plus III,* was developed to teach people at the local level the basics about evaluation and how to do elementary evaluations of their own programs. The book boils program evaluation down to four basic steps (goals and desired outcomes, process evaluation, outcome evaluation, and impact evaluation) that relate to the logic model (see Figure 14.1).

Step 1: Identify Goals and Desired Outcomes

Starting with goals sets the project's sights. Goals represent what a project is striving for (e.g., children who have positive social relationships and are well educated so that they will be productive members of society). Goals tend to be ambitious and set a framework for outcomes. Outcomes are more specific and represent what the project is accountable for. Goals can be general; outcomes must be specific and measurable (Schorr, 1997).

If a community program has prevention/promotion aims (see Chapters 9–11 of this book), goals, and outcomes concern problems to be prevented or competencies and health outcomes to be promoted. Alternatively, if a community initiative addresses a wider community issue or problem (see Chapter 13), the changes it seeks to create indicate its goals and outcomes.

In Step 1, program developers describe the program's:

- *Primary goals,* such as increasing parent involvement in the schools, or reducing drug use.
- *Target group(s),* for instance, teachers, children, parents, or general public. Target groups can be described by demographic characteristics (e.g., age, sex, race, socioeconomic status), developmental transitions (e.g., entering middle school, divorce, bereavement), risk processes (e.g., low grades, multiple conduct incidents in school), locality, or other criteria.
- *Desired outcomes,* such as increases in attitudes rejecting smoking or decreases in school absences. Well-formulated outcomes are clearly defined and specific, realistic and attainable, and measurable.

Figure 14.2 illustrates the four-step evaluation method with worksheets adapted from *Prevention Plus III* (Linney & Wandersman, 1991). Step 1 in that figure shows the questions that program planners need to ask themselves to specify program goals, target groups, and desired outcomes.

Step 2: Process Evaluation

In Step 2, the activities designed to reach the desired outcome are described. They answer the question, "What did the program actually do?"

Purposes of Process Evaluation Process evaluation has several purposes. First, monitoring program activities helps organize program efforts. It helps ensure that all parts of the program are conducted as planned. It also helps the program use resources where they are needed (e.g., not spending most of its money on only

Step 1: Identify Goals and Desired Outcomes

A. Make a list of the primary goals of the program.

Ask yourself: "What were we trying to accomplish?"

1.
2.
3.

B. What groups did you want to involve?

Ask yourself: "Whom were we trying to reach?"

For each group, how many persons did you want to involve?

1.
2.
3.

C. What outcomes did you desire?

Ask yourself: "As a result of this program, how would we like participants to change? What would they learn? What attitudes, feelings, or behaviors would be different?"

1.
2.
3.

Step 2: Process Evaluation

A. What activities were implemented?

Ask yourself: "What did we actually do to implement this program?" Form a chronology of events.

Date *Description of Activity*

1.
2.
3.

For each activity given, indicate the following:

Activity length (hrs.) *Percentage of time goal* *Activity attendance* *Percentage of attendance goal*

Total duration of all activities (in hours) =

Total attendance at all activities =

Other services delivered:

B. What can you learn from this experience?

What topics or activities were planned but not delivered? What happened that these were not accomplished?

Activity Problem

FIGURE 14.2 Specific Questions in Four-Step Program Evaluation (*Continued*)

Who was missing that you had hoped to have participate in the program?

What explanations can you give for any discrepancy between the planned and actual participation?

What feedback can be used to improve the program in the future?

Step 3: Outcome Evaluation

Desired Outcome	Measure
1.	1.
2.	2.
3.	3.

Step 4: Impact Evaluation

Desired Impact	Measure
1.	1.
2.	2.
3.	3.

FIGURE 14.2 *(Continued)*
SOURCE: Adapted from Linney & Wandersman (1991, pp. 44–51).

one activity or target group). Furthermore, it provides information to help manage the program and modify activities, leading to midcourse corrections that enhance the project's outcomes.

Second, information in a process evaluation provides accountability that the program is conducting the activities it promised to do. This can be furnished to administration, funding sources, boards of directors, or other stakeholders.

Third, after a later evaluation of outcomes and impacts, the process evaluation can provide information about why the program worked or did not work. By providing information on what was done and who was reached, program planners can identify reasons for achieving outcomes or not achieving them. Process evaluation information also can provide information for future improvements and for sharing practical tips with others planning similar programs.

Fourth, process evaluation can help you decide whether or not you are ready to assess the effects of your program. For example, if a program has been in existence for only a short time and you have implemented only the first activity of a seven-activity program, then it is premature to assess program outcomes.

Fifth, sometimes conditions change and what was planned isn't what actually happens. Process evaluation helps keep track of such changes. Answering process evaluation questions before, during, and after the planned activities documents what actually happened.

Conducting a Process Evaluation A process evaluation centers on two related questions: What were the intended and actual activities of the program? After it was implemented, what did program planners and staff learn from their experiences?

Regarding activities, process evaluation asks: *Who* was supposed to do *what* with *whom* and *when* was it to be done?

Who refers to the staff delivering the services. How many staff? What kinds of qualifications and training do they need?

What refers to what the staff actually does (e.g., hold classes, show movies, model behavior).

Whom refers to the target groups for each activity.

When refers to the time and setting of the activity (e.g., during school assemblies, after school).

The more clearly the questions are answered, the more useful the process evaluation will be. All of the information gathered in the process evaluation can be used to improve (or discard) the activity in the future.

Step 3: Outcome Evaluation

Outcome evaluation assesses the immediate effects of a program. The bottom line of program evaluation concerns these immediate effects and ultimate program impacts. (Note that the field of program evaluation uses the terms *outcomes* and *impacts* as they are described in this chapter. The field of public health reverses these terms and uses *outcomes* to mean long-term indicators and *impacts* to mean short-term indicators.)

Outcome evaluation, as the term is used in program evaluation and community psychology, is concerned with measuring the short-term or immediate effects of a program on its participants or recipients. It attempts to determine the direct effects of the program, such as the degree to which a drug-use prevention program increased knowledge of drugs and the perceived risk of using drugs.

Basically, Step 3 looks at the desired outcomes defined in Step 1 and seeks evidence regarding the extent to which those outcomes were achieved. Evidence of program outcomes for a drug-abuse prevention program could include increased awareness of drug dangers or improved scores on a measure of social skills for resisting pressure to use drugs. Planning how to collect this data or evidence is best begun along with planning program goals and outcomes.

Outcome Measures These should be closely linked to goals, but they are more specific. There are several potential ways to measure outcomes.

Self-report questionnaires are commonly used to measure outcomes. As you probably know from prior methodology courses, they must be chosen with care, and their reliability and validity should be considered. The test-retest reliability (stability) of a measure is a particular concern if it is to be given before and after an intervention. Construct validity, the extent to which a questionnaire measures what it claims to measure, also is an important concern. Does a particular measure of problem-solving skills actually measure those skills? Predictive validity is also a concern. Does a measure of attitudes about drug use predict actual drug use one year later? Program developers and evaluators need to consider these questions in light of their program theory. What measures of what constructs will best reflect the true outcomes of the program? A measure of self-esteem useful for adults may not work well for adolescents or for drug-related outcomes.

Self-report questionnaires are not the only means of collecting outcome data. For some purposes, it is useful to obtain information from other sources about a participant, such as ratings of a child by a parent or ratings of students by teachers. Persons completing questionnaires who are not reporting on themselves are termed *key informants.* Interviews with key informants or participants are excellent sources of qualitative data. *Behavioral observation* ratings may be useful, although they are often challenging to collect and analyze.

Step 4: Impact Evaluation

Impact evaluation is concerned with the ultimate effects desired by a program. In alcohol and other drug prevention programs, the ultimate effects might include reduction in overall drug use (prevalence), reduction in rate of new students starting drug use (incidence), decreases in drunk-driving arrests, and decreases in school disciplinary actions for drug or alcohol offenses.

Outcomes (Step 3) are immediate or short-term results of a program, whereas impacts (Step 4) are ultimate or longer-term effects of the program. Sound program theory and planning of goals and outcomes help delineate what are expected outcomes and impacts.

Archival data, based on records collected for other purposes, help assess impacts. Examples include medical records, juvenile court or police records, or school grades and attendance records.

Summary Illustration of the Four-Step Evaluation Model

Suppose a coalition in your community implemented a prevention program to reduce adolescents' use of alcohol, tobacco and other drugs. The four-step *Prevention Plus III* evaluation model would be applied as follows. Figure 14.3 presents each step using adaptations of *Prevention Plus III* forms (Linney & Wandersman, 1991).

Step 1: Identifying Goals This step involves specifying program goals, objectives, and target groups. The overall program goals are to reduce overall drug use and drug-related arrests, accidents, and illnesses among youth (and eventually, adults). Two specific program objectives are to increase citizen knowledge of drug-related issues and their commitment to action on those issues. Additional objectives are to increase adolescents' skills in resisting pressure from peers and media to use drugs and to decrease local sales of tobacco to minors. Specific target groups include the community, parents of adolescents, students in Grades 7–9, and local stores that sell tobacco products.

Step 2: Process Evaluation The program is to be implemented in several ways. A media campaign and public meetings will be conducted to raise public awareness of drug-related issues. School classes (Grades 7–9), including exercises and

Step 1: Identify Goals and Desired Outcomes

A. Make a list of the primary goals of the program.

Ask yourself: "What were we trying to accomplish?"

1. Decrease adolescent use of alcohol, tobacco, and other drugs
2. Decrease rates of accidents, illness, and other drug-related conditions and drug-related arrests

B. What groups did you want to involve?

Ask yourself: "Whom were we trying to reach?"

For each group, how many persons did you want to involve?

1. Local citizens (all residents of locality)
2. Parents in training course (20 families in first year)
3. Adolescents in school grades 7–9 (500 in first year)
4. Local stores selling tobacco (25 stores)

C. What outcomes did you desire?

Ask yourself: "As a result of this program, how would we like participants to change? What would they learn? What attitudes, feelings, or behaviors would be different?"

1. Increase citizen knowledge of drug-related issues and problem
2. Increase citizen commitment to action on these issues
3. Increase parent skills in communicating with children about drug use
4. Increase teens' skills in resisting pressure to use drugs
5. Decrease local sales of tobacco to minors

Step 2: Process Evaluation Worksheet

A. What activities were implemented?

Ask yourself: "What did we actually do to implement this program?" Form a chronology of events.

	Date	*Description of Activity*
1.		Public awareness campaign: TV, radio, newspapers (ads, letters, columns, brochures, interviews)
2.		Public meetings: schools, religious congregations, etc.
3.		Curriculum and materials in school health classes
4.		Dramatic skits in schools by student team
5.		Parent communication skills training (6 sessions)
6.		Intervention to test and reduce store willingness to sell tobacco to teens, modeled on Biglan et al. (1996)

For each activity given, indicate the following:

Activity length (hrs.)	*Percentage of time goal*	*Activity attendance*	*Percentage of attendance goal*
2. 46 hours	92%	250	50%
3. 100 hours	80%	400	80%
4. 10 hours	100%	400	80%

FIGURE 14.3 Four-Step Program Evaluation Example

Activity length (hrs.)	*Percentage of time goal*	*Activity attendance*	*Percentage of attendance goal*
5. 12 hours	100%	18	90%
6. 25 hours	25%	25 store visits	25%

Total duration of all activities (in hours) = 293 hours

Total attendance at all activities = 1,068 persons

Other services delivered:

1. 100 total actions to increase community awareness, involving media campaigns (Activity #1)
2. Guest lectures in community college classes

B. What can you learn from this experience?

What topics or activities were planned but not delivered? What happened that these were not accomplished?

Activity	*Problem*
Tobacco sales testing not completed	Training, logistics took longer than planned
Who was missing that you had hoped to have participate in the program?	Youth, parents from high-risk family and neighborhood environments Not enough business, civic, and religious leaders
What explanations can you give for any discrepancy between the planned and actual participation?	Competing news events overshadowed some media campaigns Courses, materials for youth need to be more appealing
What feedback can be used to improve the program in the future?	Improve "teen appeal" of course materials Skits were a hit, use that format more Identify potential student and community leaders, involve them Involve youth, parents from high-risk environments in planning

Step 3: Outcome Evaluation

Desired Outcome	*Measure*
1. Increased citizen knowledge of drug abuse issues	Scores on survey of knowledge
2. Increased citizen commitment to action to prevent drug abuse	Number of volunteers for anti-drug activities
3. Increased parent communication skills with teens re: drug use	Self-report survey of parent skills before and after training sessions
4. Increased student resistance	Teacher ratings, student questionnaires on student resistance skills before and after training
5. Decreased sales of tobacco	Number of times clerks were willing to sell when teen assessment teams attempted purchases before and after behavioral intervention

FIGURE 14.3 *(Continued)*

Step 4: Impact Evaluation

Desired Impact	*Measure*
1. Decreased drug-related traffic accidents, arrests	Police records: number of drug-related accidents, arrests; before and after program
2. Decreased school disciplinary actions related to drug use	School records: number of drug-related disciplinary actions before and after program
3. Decreased incidence of drug- related conditions, accidents	Hospital records: number of drug-related emergency room visits; number of admissions for drug-related conditions before and after program

FIGURE 14.3 (*Continued*)

SOURCE: Adapted from Linney & Wandersman (1991).

dramatic skits, and school assemblies will be conducted on drug-related issues, including skills for resisting drug use. A parent training course will focus on communications skills with adolescents. A behavioral intervention for testing stores' willingness to sell tobacco products to minors, and reinforcing their refusals to sell, will be implemented (see Biglan et al., 1996, discussed in Chapter 4). To conduct the process evaluation, the following will be recorded: the number of meetings, classes, assemblies, and training workshops planned and actually held, the staff time spent on each, and attendance at each session. The time and persons involved in training of student testers and implementation of the behavioral intervention for testing stores would also be recorded. After each program component is implemented, the process evaluation also will include a discussion of what program staff and planners learned from the experience.

Step 3: Outcome Evaluation Before and after public meetings, and in surveys of community members conducted before and after the media campaign, a questionnaire would assess changes in citizens' knowledge of drug abuse issues and the number of volunteers for coalition activities. A questionnaire measuring parenting skills for communicating with adolescents would be given before and after the parent training course to measure changes in these areas among course participants. In the schools, questionnaires completed by students and teachers would measure students' gains in skills for resisting drug use (measured before and after the classroom intervention). Student questionnaires could also be used to measure changes in attitudes and behavior regarding drug use. Finally, behavioral tests of store clerks' willingness or refusal to sell tobacco to minors would be conducted and recorded.

Step 4: Impact Evaluation Long-term effects of the program could be measured, for example, by changes in drug-related school disciplinary actions, police arrest and accident records for youth, and hospital records of drug-related treatment.

Although the four-step program evaluation method in *Prevention Plus III* was initially developed for evaluation in the alcohol, tobacco, and other drug abuse domain, it is adaptable to any program area, such as community-based mental health prevention programs (McElhaney, 1995) and delinquency prevention (Morrissey, 1998).

MENTORING: A PROGRAM EVALUATION PERSPECTIVE

In this section, we further illustrate program evaluation concepts by applying them to mentoring programs.

The term *mentoring* comes from Greek mythology where Mentor was a trusted friend of Odysseus and served as a guardian and tutor to Odysseus' son when Odysseus was away (Haskell, 1997). Mentoring relationships generally involve an older, more experienced person (the mentor) and a younger, less experienced person (the mentee). The mentor helps develop the character and competence of the mentee or assists the mentee in reaching goals, while also displaying trust, confidence, and praise, modeling positive behavior and serving as an advocate for the mentee (Haensly & Parsons, 1993; Haskell, 1997; Rhodes, 1994, Rhodes & Bogat, 2002; Slicker & Palmer, 1994). Yet consider the following summary of findings on mentoring programs.

> The evidence from the ten available evaluations consistently indicates that noncontingent, supportive mentoring relationships do not have desired effects on outcomes such as academic achievement, school attendance, dropout, various aspects of child behavior including misconduct, or employment. This lack of demonstrated effects has occurred whether mentors were paid or unpaid, and whether mentors were college undergraduates, community volunteers, members of the business community, or school personnel. However, when mentors used behavior management techniques in one small, short-term study, students' school attendance improved. . . . In another larger, longer-term experimental evaluation by the same researchers, unspecified mentoring relationships significantly increased delinquency for youth with no prior offenses but significantly decreased recidivism for youth with prior offenses. (Office of Juvenile Justice and Delinquency Prevention [OJJDP], 1995, p. 95)

This summary of findings of mentoring programs makes us want to know more about specific programs, since many programs did not have desired effects, but some did. Is it worth the necessary time, energy, and money to ensure that a mentoring program is having positive effects? An examination of mentoring programs in terms of stated goals, process, outcomes, and ultimate impacts is essential if we are to understand why some mentoring programs fail while others flourish.

A case in point is the Big Brothers/Big Sisters (BB/S) mentoring program. At almost the same time as the OJJDP report just cited, Public/Private Ventures (PPV) issued a report concluding that the Big Brothers/Big Sisters mentoring program worked.

> The most notable results are the deterrent effects on the initiation of drug and alcohol use, and the overall positive effects on academic performance that the mentoring experience produced. Improvement in grade-point average among Little Brothers and Little Sisters, while small in percentage terms, is still very encouraging, since non-academic interventions are rarely capable of producing effects in grade performance. (Sipe, 1996, p. 65)

The PPV study of BB/S followed 487 children with mentors in "noncontingent" mentoring relationships over a period of 18 months. Children in mentoring relationships were markedly less likely to use drugs or alcohol, engage in violence, or be truant from school. What can account for the contrast between the studies reviewed by OJJDP and those reported by PPV? There are several possibilities. Studies emphasized by OJJDP included programs that matched groups of children or adolescents to a single mentor. In fact, the negative effects attributed by OJJDP to mentoring were interpreted by the original researchers (Fo & O'Donnell, 1974) as stemming from negative peer influences from contact between students mentored in groups. This spreading of maladaptive behavior occurred between student group members and does not seem applicable to individual student-mentor pairs (characteristic of BB/S and similar programs). Another prominent difference between the PPV study and those reviewed by OJJDP is the length of time the mentoring relationships were studied. Few of the programs reviewed by OJJDP examined mentoring relationships beyond one year, whereas BB/S mentoring was studied over longer periods. Finally, the OJJDP review summarized program evaluations of mentoring programs for both adolescents and children without distinguishing between them.

Both the BB/S mentoring program and the programs reviewed by OJJDP began with similar goals and desired outcomes (prevention of delinquency, promotion of mental health and achievement). They differed, however, in the manner in which processes and activities were logically linked to desired outcomes. Consider the differences between a mentoring relationship at 6 months and again at 18 months. Or consider the same adult mentoring a 17-year-old adolescent versus an 11-year-old. We can see how two simple procedural variables (duration of mentoring relationship and age of child to be matched with a mentor) may have profound influence on the kinds of outcomes we may expect.

In a more recent elaborate empirical review, DuBois, Holloway, Valentine, and Cooper (2002) performed a meta-analysis of 55 evaluations of mentoring programs. They found that mentoring had modest significant outcomes. Several program features were shown to make significant contributions to effects such as: "ongoing training for mentors, structured activities for mentors and youth as well as expectations for frequency of contact, mechanisms for support and involvement of parents, and monitoring of overall program implementation" (p. 187–188).

Other program features that are assumed to be important were not shown to make significant contributions, including screening of mentors, initial training and orientation, and matching of youth and mentors. O'Donnell (2005b) similarly described several practices that may be important for ensuring positive effects of mentoring programs on youth; he also suggests additional considerations (e.g., peer network influences) that are particularly important when targeting high-risk populations for delinquency (e.g., have incarcerated parents) or targeting youth who are in the juvenile justice system. Although both reviews are cautious about the implications of the results, the results do show that a program evaluation must look carefully at process and outcomes. In the following section we describe an evaluation of a mentoring program that used the four-step method from *Prevention Plus III* as a guide.

Mentoring: Applying the Four-Step Evaluation Method

The COPE mentoring program in a rural county in South Carolina paired at-risk middle school students with adult volunteer mentors who met with their mentees during school hours. Teachers and other school staff identified at-risk students based on characteristics such as social withdrawal, aggression, academic failure, or truancy. The evaluators became involved in the project's third year. The COPE program is summarized in Figure 14.4 and described in more detail in Wandersman, Morrissey et al. (1998), and Davino, Wandersman, and Goodman (1995).

The first step in the evaluation was to work with the school staff in the clarification of the mentoring program's goals and desired outcomes (Step 1 of the four-step method). The broad goal of the mentoring program was to improve mentees' quality of life in three domains: relationships, self-esteem, and school-related problems. Next, this goal was developed into a more specific set of measurable outcomes for the program. Desired outcomes included high satisfaction with the program and with the mentoring relationship among mentees and mentors, high scores on a mentee self-esteem measure, increased school grades, increased school attendance, and decreased school behavioral problems.

In order to assess the degree to which the program was successfully achieving its goals and desired outcomes, both process and outcome evaluation components were conducted. Several different stakeholders in the program were surveyed in an attempt to get their feedback about satisfaction with the current program and suggestions for improvement. These stakeholders included mentors, mentees, teachers, and school staff who ran the program. In addition, worksheets were completed to document important program components (e.g., mentor recruitment, support meetings, luncheons) as well as components that were desired by participants but that had not yet been included as part of the program (e.g., mentor orientation sessions, group outings with mentors and mentees).

Process evaluation results also showed that 53 percent of the mentees had contact with their mentor once a week or more; 23 percent met at least once a month but less than once a week, and 24 percent less than once a month. On an open-ended question asking for suggested improvements, almost all mentees wanted to

Step 1: Identify Goals and Desired Outcomes

A. Make a list of the primary goals of the program.

Ask yourself: "What were we trying to accomplish?"

1. Build satisfying and consistent mentoring relationships
2. Improve mentee self-esteem
3. Decrease school problems

B. What groups did you want to involve?

Ask yourself: "Whom were we trying to reach?"

For each group, how many persons did you want to involve?

1. At-risk middle school students: withdrawn, aggressive, academically failing, truant, pregnant, those with social problems
2. As many as possible (100 currently)

C. What outcomes did you desire?

Ask yourself: "As a result of this program, how would we like participants to change? What would they learn? What attitudes, feelings, or behaviors would be different?"

1. Have high satisfaction with program and mentor relationship
2. Increased scores on self-esteem measures
3. Increased grades and school attendance
4. Decreased school behavior problems

FIGURE 14.4 Mentoring Program Goals and Outcomes
SOURCE: Adapted from Linney & Wandersman (1991).

see their mentors more often. Many students were not able to count on the mentor to come often or at the scheduled time.

Results of the COPE mentoring program were mixed. The stakeholder surveys showed consistently positive responses among participants in all groups. For example, the majority of mentees and mentors saw the program as "helpful" or "very helpful" to the students. Both groups also rated the quality of their relationships as "good" or "great," saw their relationship as "improving," and reported the fit between mentor and mentee as "good" or "great." However, comparisons between mentees and a comparison group (children on a waiting list for mentors) on self-esteem, grades, school attendance, and decreased school behavior problems were not statistically significant.

Program participants felt good about the program, but measures of behavioral changes showed no effect of mentoring. Perhaps the program was not long enough or intensive enough to affect outcomes such as grades and self-esteem, or the mentors were not sufficiently trained, or the program needed to be conducted for more hours per week or in a different way. Whatever the reasons, results such as these suggest that program planners need to step back and reexamine their goals and methods more closely. That is the topic of the next section.

LINKING PROGRAM EVALUATION TO PROGRAM DEVELOPMENT

The outcome results of the COPE mentoring program were disappointing. The measured outcomes of many treatment, prevention, and educational programs are often disappointing (e.g., the early results from DARE). The frequent occurrence of disappointing results has spurred a strong movement for accountability in community and social programs. Yet, as with COPE, many participants and observers of a community program may believe that a program has the kernel of a good idea and will be effective if the program is improved. Traditionally, program evaluation has been concerned with whether a program already developed is working, and why. However, this approach does not study how to develop an effective program in the first place.

As you learned in Chapter 11, continuous improvement of programs relies on the use of evaluation data to plan and implement program modifications. Many barriers prevent program planners and staff from using such feedback well. First, programs may use an outside evaluator, a person with no stake in the success or failure of the program (thus presumably more objective). Such an approach can set up an "us versus them" relationship that can limit the quality and usefulness of the evaluation findings. Yet program practitioners often believe that they do not have the time, resources, or expertise to conduct their own evaluation. Second, program evaluation usually provides evaluation feedback at the end of program implementation, without opportunities for midcourse corrections. Program staff thus often view evaluation as an intrusive process that results in a report card of success or failure, but no useful information for program improvement. A third, related barrier is the general perception of evaluation research and findings as too complex, theoretical, or not user-friendly.

Program evaluation can provide information about processes and outcomes. This information is important, but it is much more meaningful if community program staff and citizens understand how and why the program outcomes were or were not produced. If the outcomes were positive, stakeholders can pinpoint some of the processes that led to program success. Conversely, if the outcomes were less than expected, they can identify what needs to be improved.

Empowerment Evaluation

An innovative approach to program evaluation grew out of discussions of new and evolving roles for evaluators, designed to encourage the self-determination of program practitioners (e.g., Dugan, 1996; Fetterman, 1994, 1996, 2001; Fetterman, Kaftarian, & Wandersman, 1996; Fetterman & Wandersman, 2005; Linney & Wandersman, 1991; Stevenson, Mitchell, & Florin, 1996). Empowerment evaluation (EE) breaks down barriers inherent in traditional evaluation methods, promoting an empowerment and citizen participation perspective (Fetterman, 1996). It is an evolving approach in which program planners and developers learn the basics of program evaluation so that they can more systematically plan and implement their programs, and thereby increase the probability of obtaining desired outcomes, as reflected in the following definition:

> *Empowerment Evaluation:* An evaluation approach that aims to increase the probability of achieving program success by: (a) providing program stakeholders with tools for assessing the planning, implementation, and self-evaluation of their program, and (b) mainstreaming evaluation as part of the planning and management of the program/organization. (Wandersman, Snell-Johns, Lentz et al., 2005, p. 28)

Empowerment evaluators collaborate with community members and program practitioners to determine program goals and implementation strategies, serve as facilitators or coaches, provide technical assistance to teach community members and program staff to do self-evaluation, and stress the importance of using information from the evaluation in ongoing program improvement. In sum, empowerment evaluation helps program developers and staff to achieve their program goals by providing *them* with tools for assessing and improving the planning, implementation, and results of their own programs.

EE Principles EE shares some values and methods with other approaches to evaluation, including traditional evaluation and EE's close relatives: collaborative, participatory, and utilization-focused evaluation. However, it is the set of EE principles considered in their entirety that distinguishes EE from other evaluation approaches. The numbering of the principles does not reflect any type of hierarchy or prioritization of one principle over another. Instead, the principles are to be considered as a set of core beliefs that, as a whole, communicate the underlying values of EE and guide our work as empowerment evaluators; these principles are compatible with and overlap with some of the values of community psychology (Chapter 1). The description of the principles is an abbreviated description excerpted from Wandersman, Snell-Johns, Lentz et al. (2005, p. 29–38). The ten principles are listed in Table 14.1.

Principle 1: Improvement EE theory and practice are guided by the fundamental assumption that the vast majority of programs desire to achieve positive results in the lives of those affected by the program (e.g., education, health, social welfare). Empowerment evaluators want programs to succeed. Toward that end, EE values improvement in people, programs, organizations, and communities. Empowerment evaluators use the methods and tools of EE to help programs, organizations, and communities achieve results. This is in contrast to traditional evaluation, which values neutrality and objectivity and wants to examine programs in their natural state in order to determine a program's effect without the influence of the evaluator. Many funders are interested in EE because they are tired of receiving evaluations that show no results and would like evaluation to be helpful to grantees in achieving results (e.g., W. K. Kellogg Foundation, 1999).

Principle 2: Community Ownership Empowerment evaluators believe that the community has the right to make decisions about actions that affect their lives.

TABLE 14.1 Principles of Empowerment Evaluation

Principle 1:	Improvement
Principle 2:	Community ownership
Principle 3:	Inclusion
Principle 4:	Democratic participation
Principle 5:	Social justice
Principle 6:	Community knowledge
Principle 7:	Evidence-based strategies
Principle 8:	Capacity building
Principle 9:	Organizational learning
Principle 10:	Accountability

Empowerment evaluators also believe that evaluation is most likely to lead to program improvement when the community is empowered to exercise its legitimate authority to make decisions that direct the evaluation process. In EE, the stakeholders, with the assistance of the empowerment evaluators, conduct the evaluation and put the evaluation findings to use. Program stakeholders have the responsibility of making critical decisions about the program and the evaluation. This commitment to community ownership is in contrast to typical traditional evaluation approaches, where evaluators and funders hold decision making power regarding the purpose, design, and use of the evaluation.

Principle 3: Inclusion EE is committed to community ownership that is inclusive and that involves direct participation of key stakeholders in decision making whenever possible. Empowerment evaluators believe the evaluation of a program or organization benefits from having stakeholders and staff from a variety of levels involved in planning and decision making. Being inclusive is distinct from how people make their decisions as a group, such as democratic forms of participation (see principle 4).

Principle 4: Democratic Participation The definition of EE assumes that stakeholders have the capacity for intelligent judgment and action when supplied with appropriate information and conditions. This assumption echoes John Dewey's characterization of participatory democracy as a way of personal life controlled, not merely by faith in human nature in general, but by faith in the capacity of human beings for intelligent judgment and action if proper conditions are furnished (Dewey, 1940, p. 224). As with the principles of community ownership and inclusion, democratic participation is a principle that is seen as critical for establishing stakeholder buy-in. Democratic participation also: (1) underscores the importance of deliberation and authentic collaboration as a critical process for maximizing use of the skills and knowledge that exist in the community, and (2) emphasizes that fairness and due process are fundamental parts of the EE process.

Principle 5: Social Justice Empowerment evaluators believe in and have a working commitment to social justice: a fair, equitable allocation of resources, opportunities, obligations, and bargaining power (Dalton, Elias, & Wandersman, 2001; Nelson & Prilleltensky, 2005). This means that empowerment evaluators recognize that there are basic social inequities in society and strive to help ameliorate these conditions by helping people use evaluation to improve their programs so that social conditions and communities are positively impacted in the process. As people become more confident, self-determined, and ready to take control of their lives, they are better able to confront inequities in their lives. The aim of EE is to make a difference with an eye toward the larger social good.

EE is well suited for most programs and populations that are interested in improving their performance. Not all programs identify directly with social justice as part of their mission. However, EE advocates believe that almost any program that is designed to help people and communities at any level (individuals, families, neighborhoods) and domain (e.g., education, health, economic), ultimately contributes to the larger goal of social justice.

Principle 6: Community Knowledge Several participatory and collaborative evaluation approaches view community members as experts on their community. In transformative, participatory evaluation, popular knowledge is as valid and useful as scientific knowledge (Cousins & Whitmore, 1998). In EE, community-based knowledge and wisdom are also valued and promoted. EE embraces local community knowledge and believes that people typically know their own problems and are in a good position to generate their own solutions. For the empowerment evaluator, respect or community knowledge often involves recognizing the tacit (know-how) knowledge of stakeholders and making this knowledge explicit so that it can be shared through communicative action and synthesized to create new knowledge.

Principle 7: Evidence-Based Strategies EE values the role of science and evidence-based strategies and believes that a review of relevant evidence-based or best practice interventions is important to consider early in the process of designing and/or selecting a program to address a community need. Just as EE respects the work of the community and its knowledge base, it also respects the knowledge base of scholars and practitioners who have provided empirical information about what works in particular areas (e.g., prevention, treatment). This value of using existing knowledge is part of the commitment to avoid re-inventing the wheel and to build from existing literatures/practices. However, evidence-based strategies should not be adopted blindly and without regard for the local context (Fetterman, 1998; Green, 2001; Wandersman, 2003).

Principle 8: Capacity Building Patton (1997) defines capacity building as individual changes in thinking and behavior and program or organizational changes in procedures and culture that result from the learning that occurs during the evaluation process (Patton, 1997, p. 90). Empowerment evaluators believe that when stakeholders learn the basic steps and skills involved in conducting program evaluation, they are in a better position to shape and improve their lives and the lives of those who participate in their programs. EE is designed to simultaneously enhance the stakeholders' capacity to conduct evaluation (evaluation capacity) and to improve program planning and implementation (program capacity).

Principle 9: Organizational Learning Improvement is a basic principle of EE (see principle 1). Improvement is enhanced when there is a process that encourages learning (organizational learning) and an organizational structure that encourages learning (a learning organization). There is a vast literature on organizational learning and learning organizations in the organization and management literature (e.g., Ang & Joseph, 1996; Argyris & Schon, 1978; Argyris, 1999; Senge, 1990).

Principle 10: Accountability EE provides an innovative vehicle for helping programs be accountable to themselves and to the public by generating process- and outcome-oriented data within an evaluation framework that heightens an organization's sensitivity to its responsibility to the public and to itself (R. Miller, personal communication, March 12, 2001). Like most approaches to evaluation, EE is committed to accountability and focuses on the final outcomes achieved by a program. At the same time, EE is based on the proposition that the likelihood of achieving results is greatly enhanced when stakeholders collect process evaluation information and hold staff accountable to their activities and plans. Thus, because process evaluation is viewed as a vehicle toward results-based accountability, EE places a high priority on process accountability. In addition, the principle of accountability in combination with other EE principles, especially improvement, community ownership, inclusion, and democratic participation, creates a self-driven approach to program development and improvement.

Case Examples of Empowerment Evaluation

Foundation for the Future Realizing that the youth they served were exposed to multiple risk factors (e.g., poverty, lack of family support), the Boys and Girls Club of Metro Spartanburg, South Carolina, created a community partnership, the Foundation For the Future (FFF). This organization would provide additional services to families of Boys and Girls Club members while simultaneously increasing the capacity of other existing agencies to reach populations their programs typically did not serve. The FFF partnership was founded on the belief that existing organizations and programs in the community could achieve more working together than each could operating independently. Those programs include five arts programs, a Junior Achievement program, a Parents as Teachers program for parents of young children, and a Parent University program for parents of Boys and Girls Club members. A major FFF component was an enhanced after-school program. Although each agency had its own unique set of desired outcomes, the partnership was unified around the overall goal of increasing families' sense of belonging, usefulness, influence, and competence (Keener, Snell-Johns, Livet, & Wandersman, 2005).

The FFF initiative capitalized on evidence-based programs that already existed in the Spartanburg area. The evaluation contract stated that the first objective of the evaluation team was to help establish and maintain an effective self-evaluation system. To fulfill this task, the evaluation team worked closely with FFF member organizations to develop individual evaluation plans and products. However, the major responsibility for the evaluation belonged to FFF (not the evaluators). This is consistent with EE principles of community ownership, inclusion, democratic participation, and capacity building.

A portion of the evaluation findings gives a sense of the FFF approach. One of its objectives was to improve student scores on standardized tests in schools, to be accomplished by after-school programs at the Boys and Girls Clubs. Those programs included a daily homework completion hour and a program for educational and career development. Local Boys and Girls Clubs committed to having over one-third of their weekly programs in these areas, and staff prepared weekly tracking reports on programs. An outcome evaluation compared 334 program participants in multiple FFF programs with a group of 836 similar students from the same schools, on a yearly standardized test in schools. In English, math, social studies, and science, FFF participants outperformed the comparison group. The largest program effects were moving students from the lowest-scoring category into the basic proficiency category, although positive effects were seen at multiple levels.

Evaluating Empowerment Evaluation Campbell and associates (2004) conducted an evaluation of the EE approach, studying all state-funded rape prevention and victim services programs in Michigan. The state wanted to build the evaluation capacity of each agency so that staff could evaluate their own programs. The authors were involved in using an empowerment evaluation approach with all of the organizations that included training, technical assistance and manuals. They then studied what happened and found that 90 percent of the prevention programs and 75 percent of the victim services programs successfully developed and launched program evaluations and 90 percent sustained evaluation processes one year after the formal program funding ended. Campbell et al. also measured increases in evaluation capacity and found significant increases over time. The study provides empirical support for a number of key concepts in empowerment evaluation.

GETTING TO OUTCOMES

Empowerment evaluations sounds good and is attractive to many funders and practitioners. How can you actually do EE? How can you achieve accountability? Using the empowerment evaluation philosophy, Wandersman, Imm, Chinman, and Kaftarian (1999, 2000) developed a 10-step approach to results-based accountability called Getting To Outcomes (GTO). By asking and answering ten key questions, interventions can be guided to results-based accountability and program improvement.

TABLE 14.2 The Ten Accountability Questions and How to Answer Them

Accountability Questions	Strategies for Answering the Questions
1. What are the needs and resources in your organization/school/community/state?	Needs assessment; resource assessment
2. What are the goals, target population, and desired outcomes (objectives) for your school/community/state?	Goal setting
3. How does the intervention incorporate knowledge of science and best practices?	Science and best practices literature
4. How does the intervention fit with other programs already being offered?	Collaboration; cultural competence
5. What capacities do you need to put this intervention into place with quality?	Capacity building
6. How will this intervention be carried out?	Planning
7. How will the quality of implementation be assessed?	Process evaluation
8. How well did the intervention work?	Outcome and impact evaluation
9. How will continuous quality improvement strategies be incorporated?	Total quality management; continuous quality improvement
10. If the intervention (or a component) is successful, how will it be sustained?	Sustainability, institutionalization

The Ten GTO Accountability Questions

GTO is a straightforward approach that demystifies the evaluation process and demonstrates to program practitioners the value of evaluation in implementing quality prevention programs. Whether beginning a new program or continuing an existing one, program practitioners can start thinking about program effectiveness and program improvement by answering the ten GTO accountability questions, which serve as a beginning guide to successful planning, implementation, and evaluation of programs. Each question involves a number of self-assessment steps. The answers to each question lead to the next question. With careful consideration of each question and its answers, an organization should significantly increase the likelihood that it will achieve desired outcomes and demonstrate that it is acting with accountability.

Table 14.2 presents the ten GTO questions and strategies for answering them. In the table, these are presented in chronological order for a project in the planning stage. However, GTO questions can be used at any stage in the life cycle of a program. They often serve as a useful teaching device to demonstrate to program practitioners and funders the relevance and importance of evaluation and program accountability (Wandersman, Imm, Chinman, & Kaftarian, 2000).

In Table 14.2, especially Strategies 2, 6, 7, and 8, we can see that GTO expands upon the four steps of *Prevention Plus III* (discussed earlier in this chapter). What Wandersman et al. realized was that the *Prevention Plus III* approach can help program developers conduct their programs better, but it did not help them ask whether they were doing the right program. Thus, using only Prevention Plus III would be like tuning up your engine and making it run better so that you could drive at 70 mph instead of 30, but you might just be going down the wrong road faster. Questions 1–5 in the GTO questions help the program developers choose the right program, and Questions 6–10 help the program developers plan, implement, and improve the program and keep it going.

Question 1. What are the needs and resources in your organization/school/community/state? How do you know you need a program? Often, programs are selected because they are popular or have been implemented at other local sites rather than because they have been demonstrated to effectively prevent a specified problem in your setting. For example, Kaskutas, Morgan, and Vaeth (1992) described the experience of a guidance counselor who was working on a project as part of an interagency collaboration who discovered after two months of planning a drug group [for] the senior high school kids in the project who were nonworking, that there were no senior high kids in the project who did not have jobs! (p. 179). Therefore, there was no need for the program.

In order to determine which types of programs are needed in a given community, school, or other agency, a planning strategy called a needs assessment is often used (Soriano, 1995; Witlein & Altschuld, 1995). This assessment is designed to gather information about the issues most in need of improvement or intervention in a community or organization (e.g., youth violence, alcohol, drug abuse). A good needs assessment also includes a resource assessment and identification of individual, organizational, and community strengths that can be used to address community needs. Assets may include individual talents, microsystems that can offer social support systems for persons involved in the program, or organizations that can provide funding, a meeting space, or a venue for public discussion of program goals. Resource assessment also provides a counterpoint to needs assessment. The identification of community problems involved in needs assessment is balanced by an assessment of community strengths (Kretzmann & McKnight, 1993). An assets-based approach (Search Institute's Development Assets) to Getting To Outcomes has been developed for positive youth development (Fisher, Imm, Chiman, & Wandersman, 2006).

Question 2. What are the goals, target population, and desired outcomes (objectives) for your school/community/state? After the need for a program has been determined, it is essential to specify the goals of the program, the specific target group(s) of the program, and the desired outcomes. (This is Step 1 of the *Prevention Plus III* four-step evaluation method covered earlier in this chapter.)

Question 3. Which evidence-based interventions can be used to reach your goal? Once program personnel have decided that there is a need to address a specific program, how do they decide which program or intervention to use? For example, administrators of school and community programs are showered with glossy mailings advertising multimedia curriculum products for programs such as violence prevention, sex education, and substance abuse prevention. How does one decide which program to choose? This decision is frequently based on convenience or availability. Does one rely on the program used last year, regardless of success, or use the program that can be borrowed for free from another source, or maybe use the program advertised at the last convention? It is important to keep in mind that although convenience and availability are important, they do not ensure program effectiveness.

A goal of prevention science is to provide two kinds of information. One is empirical findings (usually quantitative) about the effectiveness of programs in attaining identified goals. Another is information, usually qualitative, about best practices, the elements and methods of programs that work best for a particular type of problem within a particular type of population (recall this idea from Chapter 11). These types of knowledge are useful in answering the question of what program to select. To be effective, programs need to be based on a theory of the target problem and be tied to current and relevant research (Buford & Davis, 1995; Goodman & Wandersman, 1994; Green & Lewis, 1986; Leviton, 1994; Nation et al., 2003; Weiss, 1995). Science and best practices knowledge helps not only in program selection, but also in program planning and implementation. Several federal agencies such as the Center for Substance Abuse Prevention and the U.S. Department of Education have websites with information about evidence-based programs (see Recommended Websites for Chapter 10).

Question 4. How does the intervention fit with other programs already being offered? Will this program enhance, interfere with, or be unrelated to other programs that are already offered? Will it be part of a comprehensive and coordinated package or just a new program in a long list of programs?

When a new program is being designed, it is important to ensure that it fits well with the community's needs as well as the available services already in place (Elias, 1995). When a new program is to be implemented in a school or other community setting, a primary consideration should be to make sure that the new intervention will enhance existing efforts. To reduce duplication, practitioners should be familiar with the programs already existing in their school or community. In order to prevent overlap of programs or the implementation of a program that does not fit with overall agency or community goals, a process called program mapping can be used. Question 4 about fit also includes the important concept of cultural competence (see Chapter 7).

Program mapping is an assessment of how well a proposed programs goals and methods will fit with the broader goals or motivating philosophy of the sponsoring organization. Programs can fit into an organization in three basic ways. They can have an add-on effect (one program adds to another), a synergistic effect (one program multiplies the effect of another), or an interference effect (one program diminishes another).

Question 5. What capacities do you need to put this intervention into place with quality? Organizational capacity consists of the resources the organization possesses to direct and sustain the prevention program (Livet & Wandersman, 2005). Some model programs may be too difficult or resource intensive for an organization to deliver. In GTO, organizational capacities to assess include having: (a) adequate numbers of staff, with appropriate credentials and experience to implement the program; (b) clearly defined staff roles and strong staff commitment to the program; (c) strong program leadership, by leaders who understand the program; (d) adequate funding and technical resources for the program, or a plan to get them.

Question 6. How will this intervention be carried out? What are the steps that program personnel will take to carry it out? During this planning stage, program developers must identify how they will implement the program. Outlining how a program will be implemented includes determining specific steps to carry out the program, identifying and training persons to carry out each of these steps, and developing a timeline or schedule for this plan. Program staff should specify what will happen during scheduled program activities and where these activities will take place. All of these components must be clearly defined in order to plan and implement a program effectively.

Question 7. How will the quality of implementation be assessed? Was the program actually implemented as planned? Was the complete program delivered? If not, which components were not delivered? What went right and what went wrong? Evaluating how a program was implemented is called process evaluation (step 2 of the *Prevention Plus III* method discussed earlier).

Question 8. How well did the intervention work? Did the program have the desired effects and proposed outcomes? Were there any unanticipated consequences? Evaluating outcomes and impacts comprised steps 3 and 4 of the *Prevention Plus III* method discussed earlier.

Question 9. How will continuous quality improvement strategies be incorporated? Many programs are repeated. Given that no program is perfect, what can be done to improve the program's effectiveness and efficiency in the future? If the process and outcome of a program are well documented, the opportunity to learn from previous implementation efforts is enormous. Keeping track of program components that worked well ensures that such components will be included in the future. Assessing what program components did not work provides the opportunity for refinement and improvement.

Lessons about what went well with a program and what areas can use improvement come from such informal sources as personal observations and verbal reports from participants and staff, or such formal sources as participant satisfaction measures and evaluations of the program process and outcome. However gathered, information for program improvement is obtained from the answers to Questions 1–8.

Program staff who are open to learning from the results of evaluation can continuously improve their programs. Instead of seeing evaluation as purely a documentation tool, they should view it as a feedback mechanism that can guide future planning and implementation.

Question 10. If the intervention (or a component) is successful, how will the intervention be sustained? After service providers have gone through the time, energy, and money to develop a successful program, what will they do to see it continued? Unfortunately, this question is often neglected in prevention programming. Even when programs have successful outcomes, they often are not continued because of lack of funding, staff turnover, or loss of momentum. Lerner's (1995) review of prevention programs for youth development concluded that there are numerous effective programs to prevent risks and problem behaviors, but unfortunately these programs were rarely sustained over time (recall similar findings from Chapter 11).

Goodman and Steckler (1987) defined institutionalization as developing community and organizational supports for health promotion and prevention programs so that they remain viable in the long term. They have identified factors related to successful institutionalization, such as identifying resources and making program components accessible and user friendly to host organization staff. In Chapter 11, we covered similar issues of program implementation in host settings.

GTO never ends. Even for an effectively implemented, thoroughly institutionalized program, its staff starts over again with question 1.

An Example of GTO in Action: The WINNERS Program

In a medium-sized rural community in South Carolina, the middle school leadership was growing concerned because of developing trends toward increased problems among youth, including increased numbers of referrals to the office, increased incidents of trouble with the law, climbing rates of alcohol and tobacco use, and poor academic performance. Within this atmosphere of concern, a sixth-grade student attending the middle school was caught showing marijuana to his friends. This specific incident generated widespread attention, alarm, and scrutiny by community members who reacted by calling for action to address the growing problems among the middle school students. Community leaders met at a PTA/town meeting that was organized by a small coalition of school administrators, parents, local businesses, and teachers in response to the many calls to the school and city agencies. The coalition contacted a professor at a local university, who agreed to have his graduate students assist with the program development, implementation, and evaluation (called the GTO team). The students and the professor used the GTO system as the basis of their consultation (see Chinman, Imm, & Wandersman, 2004; Everhart & Wandersman, 2000).

Step 1: Needs/Resources The coalition quickly realized that the school incident that occurred was a symptom of larger problems in their school. As a result, the principal called on the teachers, guidance counselors, and community leaders to form a coalition to examine the larger problems in the targeted area. This initial formation worked out well and a coalition of school and community-based leaders were established.

The coalition decided to conduct a complete needs/resources assessment with the targeted population of their students and families. This would help determine the real and underlying problems associated with the incident in the school. The GTO team was useful in helping them establish what methods and assessment questions needed to be asked. In order to gather as much information as possible, several methods of data collection were implemented. Several parent forums were held in the school to have parents respond to particular questions such as: What are the significant stressors for you and your family? What particular stressors do you see in the life of your child? What solutions do you see as being the most helpful? Because not all parents could attend the forum, it was decided that a follow-up survey mailed to parents would be useful in gathering the same information. Archival data was also collected from various sources of records.

The archival data revealed that school grades had declined and school disciplinary referrals had increased in the sixth and seventh grades. In addition, archival sources indicated that 50 percent of school-aged children were living at or below the poverty level, and 70 percent received subsidized lunches. Also, 40 percent of students came from single-parent families or had four or more siblings.

Parent forum findings indicated that parents cared deeply about their children and were feeling overwhelmed by various challenges. The welfare to work initiative had placed many of the parents in jobs, yet resulted in less structure and supervision for the children while parents were at work. Parents also noted that their kids had little contact with adults, especially male role models.

On written surveys, parents reported subjective feelings of being overwhelmed, many financial problems, concerns about their children's inappropriate behavior (e.g., stealing, lying, fighting), suspicions about alcohol and other drug use, and increasing rates of youth smoking.

There were few programs available in the community to address these needs and issues. However, assessments also identified community assets and resources. Schools in the district were willing to open their doors for after-school activities, and the YMCA had a van in which they could transport individuals. Public-private partnerships were possible; for instance, a local manufacturer reported that they had no money to donate but could contribute time from their employees.

Step 2: Goals, Target Population and Desired Outcomes The coalition identified goals, target populations, and desired outcome they would like to see achieved. These are listed in Figure 14.5.

Step 3: Best Practices The coalition reviewed potential science-based programs to meet the needs of the targeted population. However, no programs were easily identified as suitable for the needs of the population, its demographics, and larger goals of the project. As a result, it was determined that the coalition must develop its own program to meet its needs.

An initial review of the literature showed that there was a program designed to build on the character of fifth graders. This program, called *Character Counts,* was highlighted in the literature and showed positive results. Further analyses indicated that it was a curriculum-based program emphasizing specific character traits (e.g.,

Goals:

1. To increase the age of initiation of smoking and drinking from age 11 to age 14.
2. To improve the school performance in the targeted youth.
3. To improve the character and discipline of youth in school.

Target Population:

50 students in the fifth grade at the elementary school, chosen as being at high risk

Desired Outcomes: (based on the GTO format)

Objective 1:

What will change: Grade point average

By how much: 10% increase

By when will the change occur: After 1 year

How will it be measured: Report cards

Objective 2:

What will change: Disciplinary referrals

By how much: 10% decrease

By when will the change occur: After 1 year

How will it be measured: Office records

Objective 3:

What will change: Character, principally defined as specific problem behaviors

By how much: 20% increase

By when will the change occur: After 1 year

How will it be measured: Surveys, including a scale of problem behaviors

FIGURE 14.5 WINNERS Program Goals and Desired Outcomes

honesty, integrity, trust) each week. The coalition contacted the program developer, who shared the basic structure of the curriculum with them. The coalition began to develop its own (i.e., local) curriculum for character building but was challenged in planning how other parts of the goals could be accomplished.

The principal reminded them that the local manufacturer wanted to be involved and had suggested situations (e.g., lunch breaks) where employees could devote their time to the community. As a result of the synergy between the needs of the youth and what the business was ready to deliver, a mentoring program was started within the school. The majority of the program was conducted at the school and was designed to foster critical skills within students. For example, mentors were asked to devote weekly time to:

- reinforce lessons taught in the character-building classroom segment
- build skills in the areas of communication, responsibility, and honesty

- determining what social support students needed in order to decrease their risk for drug (including alcohol and tobacco) use in the future
- determine what special skills (e.g., sports, academics) students had that could be useful in their future

These results suggested that the already established *Character Counts* curriculum could be useful for the students. In order to address issues of social supports and relationship building, it was determined that a mentoring program would be a critical piece of the program. As a result, the coalition began developing structures to include a school-based character-building program in conjunction with a mentoring program.

Step 4: Program Fit Prior to beginning the program, the coalition partners examined what programs were already available in the community serving this particular target population. Other than a Sunday school class held by one of the churches and some recreational activities at the local YMCA, there were no ongoing programs that served this target population. Given the rural nature of this school district, it was clear that transportation was an issue and most likely that many of the students did not attend outside programs (about 25% attended the church class).

After it was determined that this program was not a duplication of efforts for the targeted group, the coalition began to examine how the potential program fit with the values of the lead agency (e.g., school) and the larger community. The coalition easily determined that the fit was a good one in that the community wanted a solution to the problem, the public-private partnership was viewed as advantageous, and the program contained no controversial issues.

Step 5: Capacities The coalition members found that they had the necessary funding (fiscal capacity), commitment from the community (structural/linkage capacity), and access to individuals with appropriate credentials and experience (human capacity) to implement the program. The GTO team was able to enhance the coalition's technical capacities in evaluation. The assessment did show a clear need for training staff and citizens.

Step 6: Planning After school officials and community stakeholders approved the selected program, it became necessary to develop the details of the plan. A part-time project director was hired with the funds from the local alcohol commission to help organize and run the program. The project director and the coalition together used the GTO tools to develop a plan for program implementation with a flexible timeline. First, the team determined specific program components that would link to the identified objectives. For example, having mentors assist certain students with their homework and provide tutoring was linked to the objective of increasing students' commitment to school. After linking the program's major components to the objectives, it became necessary to select specific tasks that would be implemented within each component. For example, it was necessary to determine what role the teachers and mentors would play in implementing the curriculum and providing extra academic assistance to the children. The team also needed to develop a plan for recruiting, selecting, and training mentors.

Step 7: Implementation and Process Evaluation The GTO team and the coalition designed several methods to promote the integrity of program implementation and track its progress. Mentors completed weekly logs documenting meetings with mentees and evaluated the children's progress using the character education curriculum. The log also included questions related to relationship development and allowed mentors to report problems or concerns. In addition, teachers completed a checklist to document the use of curriculum materials and rated its effectiveness and age appropriateness. Open-ended questions were presented to team and committee leaders once a month to determine what elements facilitated or served as barriers to implementation. They used the implementation tool to organize information about how much and how well WINNERS was implemented, comparing the anticipated outputs with the original plan.

Step 8: Outcome Evaluation The GTO team members selected a research design that would best allow them to measure changes on the specific outcomes targeted. The team determined that the most appropriate design would be the Pre-Post with a Comparison Group, since the children receiving services had not been randomly selected, but chosen because of their high-risk status. The comparison group consisted of the same number of children in a nearby school who were similar in terms of socioeconomic status, grade level, and gender. The GTO team helped the coalition choose the Teacher-Child Rating Scale as the primary outcome measure because it had been used before successfully with similar programs. Grades were collected, and other survey items were developed according to unique attributes of the program and desired outcomes. The results of the evaluation indicated improvement in the program group's classroom behavior (i.e., disciplinary referrals) compared with children in the comparison school, who did not have the program. The program group also demonstrated significantly improved character scores compared to the comparison group. Not all desired outcomes were obtained; no changes in grade point average were evident between the two groups. Both groups demonstrated the same level of improvement in grade point averages from pre to post, suggesting that this change did not result from the program, but from some other unmeasured factor.

Step 9: Continuous Quality Improvement The coalition members used tools suggested by the GTO team to organize feedback from process and outcome evaluations in order to make program improvements. This included survey feedback from children, mentors, teachers, and parents. Changes included identifying additional resources, improved communication between mentors and teachers, increased efforts to attend to the children's perceptions of the mentoring relationship, reductions in participant paperwork, a more systematic method of identifying participants for the mentoring program, and the use of more sensitive outcome measures. In addition, it was determined that the tutoring sessions should not take place in the school gym.

Step 10: Sustainability When it became clear that the WINNERS program would demonstrate positive outcomes, the persons running the program at the elementary school obtained continuing funding in the school district budget, including the part-time project director position. In addition, the local manufacturing company that supplied the mentors then decided to include descriptions about the program in its new-hire orientation to ensure a steady flow of new mentors.

CONCLUSION

Chelimsky (1997) described three purposes of evaluation:

- program development (e.g., information collected to strengthen programs or institutions)
- accountability (e.g., measurement of results or efficiency)
- broader knowledge (e.g., increasing understanding about factors underlying public problems)

Traditional evaluation is primarily oriented to the second purpose. The methods explained in this chapter expand the focus to include the first and second objectives, and can inform research concerning the third. However, this does not preclude more traditional evaluation approaches (Fetterman, 2001). The value of any evaluation approach depends upon the purpose of the evaluation (Chelimsky, 1997; Patton, 1997).

As we have seen in this chapter, program evaluation concepts can be incorporated into program planning and program implementation. When this is done, the boundaries between program development and program evaluation are blurred for the sake of improving process and increasing the probability of successful results. GTO is an example of this approach. Although the GTO emphasis so far has been on the accountability of practitioners who receive money for prevention (or treatment or education), Wandersman (2003) noted that the accountability questions also apply to funders and to researchers or evaluators. For example, when funders consider developing a new initiative, the questions of how they know they need a new initiative, how it will use science and best practices, how it fits with other initiatives, and so on should be asked and answered. For evaluators, the same questions would concern whether a new or intensified evaluation process is needed or justified, how well it fits with existing evaluation procedures, and how best practices for program evaluation will be used in planning this evaluation.

As societies, funders, and citizens become more concerned about accountability and results for schools, health care, human services, and related areas, evaluation can lead to fear and resistance or to openness, honesty, empowerment, and improvement. Evaluation and accountability need not be feared—if we work together for results.

CHAPTER SUMMARY

1. Program success depends upon having a good theory of why something works, implementing it with quality, and evaluating it for continuous improvement. Logic models link community *needs or conditions* with *activities, outcomes,* and *impacts*. Program development and program evaluation thus have similar components.
2. A four-step program evaluation model (from *Prevention Plus III*) boils program evaluation down to *identifying goals and desired outcomes, process evaluation, outcome evaluation*, and *impact evaluation*. Figures 14.1, 14.2, 14.3, and 14.4 illustrate this approach. *Archival data* can be used to measure program impact.
3. Accountability involves linking program evaluation to program development. Though the four-step evaluation model helps improve an existing program, it does not address what program is needed or whether a program is the best one for the context. Methods of *Empowerment Evaluation (EE)* and *Getting To Outcomes (GTO)* help interventions reach results-based accountability, which does address these issues. Table 14.1 summarizes the ten EE principles. Table 14.2 summarizes the ten accountability questions of GTO.

BRIEF EXERCISE

1. Consider how you might use the four-step evaluation model in practice. For each example that follows, think about how a program like this might work in a locality or setting that you are familiar with. Be sure to identify:
   - overall goals
   - specific objectives
   - a target population
   - how to gather process evaluation information
   - how to measure or assess program outcomes and impacts

   Examples:
   - A program in middle school to reduce violence, through training students in conflict resolution and related skills
   - A set of coordinated community programs to reduce risk of alcohol, tobacco and other drug use among adolescents
   - A program to promote parenting skills among first-time parents
   - A program to promote academic and personal support and sense of community among adult students in a college
   - Another community program of your choice

RECOMMENDED READINGS

Fettermann, D. & Wandersman, A. (Eds.) (2005). *Empowerment evaluation: Principles in practice.* New York, Guilford.

Fetterman, D., Kaftarian, S., & Wandersman, A. (Eds.) (1996). *Empowerment evaluation: Knowledge and tools for self-assessment and accountability.* Thousand Oaks, CA: Sage.

Linney, J. A., & Wandersman, A. (1996). Empowering community groups with evaluation skills: The Prevention Plus III Model. In D. Fetterman, S. Kaftarian, & A. Wandersman (Eds.), *Empowerment evaluation: Knowledge and tools for self-assessment and accountability* (pp. 259–276). Thousand Oaks, CA: Sage.

Rossi, P. H., Freeman, H. E., & Lipsey, M. (1999). *Evaluation: A systematic approach (7th ed.).* Newbury Park, CA: Sage.

W. K. Kellogg Foundation. (1998). *Kellogg evaluation handbook.* Battle Creek, MI: Author.

Worthen, B. R., Sanders, J. R., & Fitzpatrick, J. L. (1997). *Program evaluation: Alternative approaches and practical guidelines (2nd ed.).* White Plains, NY: Longman.

RECOMMENDED WEBSITES

American Evaluation Association
http://www.eval.org

Evaluation Exchange (online evaluation journal) http://www.gse.harvard.edu/hfrp/eval/issue27/index.html

Getting To Outcomes 2004 workbook (Chinman, Imm & Wandersman, 2004)
http://www.rand.org/publications/TR/TR101/

Step-by-step instructions for the GTO accountability questions. Free for downloading.

INFOTRAC® COLLEGE EDITION KEYWORDS

evaluation (or preceded by *impact, outcome, process, empowerment*, or *program*), *evaluation research*

15

Looking Ahead

HIRB/Index Stock

Where is community psychology going? Where are the communities and societies in your own life going? These are risky yet important questions. In this chapter we consider some emerging directions and challenges for community psychology research and action. We then consider some issues involving time and change in communities and societies, and describe some examples of successful changes. We conclude by inviting you to envision how you would like to see a community and society in your life to develop in the future.

EMERGING TRENDS IN COMMUNITY PSYCHOLOGY

Growing Awareness of the Global Diversity of Human Communities

Over half of the members of community psychology professional organizations now live outside the United States. Regular community psychology conferences occur in Australia/New Zealand, Europe, Japan, and Latin America. Among members of the Society for Community Research and Action (SCRA), the proportion of members who identify themselves as ethnic minorities (23%) is about four times the proportion of such members in the American Psychological Association (Toro, 2005). (Of course, persons of color are "minorities" only in a U.S. perspective; globally, European Americans are a minority.)

Community psychology journals increasingly contain culturally anchored research and interventions. We have highlighted a number of these projects throughout this book. These trends in published work and in membership are only examples of a growing realization in community psychology that its values and perspective lead to including the voices of diverse persons in the field. This recognition is transforming how community psychologists conduct research, collaborate with community members, design interventions, and conceptualize their work. It is a work in progress in which day-to-day practices and published works must continue to develop toward our ideals (Martin, Lounsbury, & Davidson, 2004).

Diversity and community form a creative tension. Both concepts are needed to understand human communities. It is important for community psychologists to foster genuine understanding and respect for the many forms of human diversity and to conduct careful research to deepen that understanding. There is much to learn. At the same time, it is also important to articulate widely shared human ideals and to articulate the particular ideals of our field so that in conversations with diverse persons and communities we can understand both ourselves and others more completely.

Broadening Concern with Social Justice

In community psychology, many trends are coalescing to bring increased energy to advocacy for social justice, liberation, and social transformation. A social justice perspective emphasizes access to resources (material, social, personal) for all citizens to promote individual and family wellness and the quality of community life. Moreover, understanding many forms of human diversity, and many communities, requires understanding issues of social justice, both historical and current. Moreover, it requires an understanding of macrosystems, even global forces.

A few recent examples come from a special section of *The Community Psychologist*. In Chapter 10 we described the work of Degirmencioglu (2003) to promote better Greek-Turkish youth relations and to improve the lives of street children in Turkey. Martinez, Toloza, Montanez, and Ochoa (2003) reported on their community development work with those displaced by political violence in Colombia. Mulvey, Guzman, and Ayala-Alacantar (2003) discussed feminist opposition to the Iraq war and conflicting views in community psychology on how to speak out about it. Conway, Evans, and Prilleltensky (2003) created Psychologists Acting with Conscience Together (Psy-ACT), a network of psychologists advocating for social justice, initially through local efforts such as letters to newspaper editors to raise awareness of poverty issues. Sloan, Anderson, and Fabick (2003) reported on Psychologists for Social Responsibility, which since 1982 has involved psychologists in promoting social justice. Two of their current projects concern public education about group conflicts and developing approaches to helping victims of trauma caused by political violence. Olson (2003) reported a conference discussion of ideas for fostering community action and social change. Israel and Toro (2003) elaborated actions by researchers, service providers, and others to address issues of poverty and homelessness. These included increasing emphasis in psychology courses on the psychological effects of economic inequalities, working with homeless parents to empower them to speak out for their children's interests with schools, and creating ways for businesses and community groups to provide resources for homeless children. At the 2005 SCRA conference, Lykes (2005) discussed her 20 years of involvement in liberatory action research with local communities in Guatemala, South Africa, Northern Ireland, and the United States (see also Lykes, 2003). These are only some illustrations of how community psychologists can enact concerns for social justice. Participatory research, policy research, and empowerment evaluation provide additional examples of how community research can be concerned with social justice (see Chapters 3, 13, and 14).

Community psychologists are not the only psychologists moving in this direction. The 2004 awards addresses to the American Psychological Association on child maltreatment, HIV prevention, international health promotion, and ethnocentrism in psychology all advocated policy initiatives involving social justice (Cichetti, 2004; Coates, 2004; Stout, 2004; Sue, 2004). Another address endorsed empowerment and challenging social myths as elements of clinical treatment with battered women (Paul, 2004).

Concern for social justice can conflict, for instance, with cultural traditions or with community or organizational norms. For instance, in Chapter 7 we described the work of Ortiz-Torres, Serrano-Garcia, and Torres-Burgos (2000) in promoting liberatory values and sexual practices for Latina teens, which involved both commonalities and conflicts with traditional gender roles in their societies, communities and families. We also noted the work of the Revolutionary Association of the Women of Afghanistan, which advocates for women's and human rights and has garnered international support (Brodsky, 2003). In both of these examples, activists recognized values conflicts and identified approaches that promoted both cultural strengths and social justice.

As a core value of the community psychology, social justice must be balanced with respect for diversity and sense of community. Each perspective provides important truths. Understanding values conflicts and finding ways to resolve or transcend them are important challenges for community psychology.

Collaborative, Participatory Research and Action

One of the most distinctive contributions of community psychology to the social sciences is our development of concepts and practical strategies for culturally anchored, truly collaborative action research that promotes genuine citizen participation in making decisions. Throughout this book, especially in Chapters 3, 4 and 14, we have highlighted examples of collaborative, participatory work (see also Jason et al., 2004). Not all participatory-collaborative approaches are the same. Even within community psychology and closely related fields, approaches such as community coalitions, empowerment evaluation, participatory action research, and various approaches to culturally anchored research are based on differing values and worldviews (Trickett & Espino, 2004). This diversity of ideals and practices provides many rich resources and options for promoting community collaboration and participation. It also provides the basis for many future conversations about their differences, strengths, and limitations as applied in real-life community contexts. Because communities are diverse, it also is likely that different conceptions of collaboration and citizen participation will be useful in different communities.

Community Science

Wandersman (2003) proposed this term for an interdisciplinary field that would bridge gaps among empirical research, development of programs and policy, and everyday practice in communities. His focus was primarily on prevention and promotion, but much of Wandersman's definition of community science also fits efforts for broader policy advocacy and social change. A special issue of the *American Journal of Communty Psychology* (Wandersman, Kloos, Linney, & Shinn, 2005) provided specific examples of methods and issues involved in community science.

Wandersman (2003) contrasted community science with the prevention science research and development approach advocated by the Institute of Medicine (IOM; Mrazek & Haggerty, 1994). In the IOM approach, research identifies a disorder or behavior problem and its associated risk and protective factors. Preventive interventions are developed to address the risk and protective factors and are refined through research. The most promising are tested in intervention and effectiveness trials with experimental designs, ultimately including large-scale replications in multiple sites. Finally, experts promote generalization and implementation of the effective programs in many communities, in forms as close as possible to the proven intervention.

There are some critical differences between this approach and the approaches of many community psychologists. Decades of experience in efforts for change in localities and community settings have shown the wisdom of being highly sensitive to community and cultural context (especially its strengths), of collaborative and participatory approaches that involve citizen control and commitment, and of developing or adapting interventions for the local context and local organizational capacity to implement a program (e.g., Miller & Shinn, 2005; Wandersman & Florin, 2003). The effectiveness of a prevention program (or a social policy) developed in a few selected communities will not necessarily generalize everywhere. This perspective is the basis of Chapters 11 and 14 in this book. Wandersman (2003, p. 229) argued that prevention science is useful but not sufficient for meeting these challenges. A new field, community science, is needed.

Community science as defined by Wandersman incorporates many concepts we have discussed in this book. It involves:

- clear core values that help guide goals for change, and processes of working in communities

- understanding historical, cultural, community, and other contexts and incorporating this awareness in research and action
- a participatory approach that enables citizens to be active shapers of community programs and policies and that builds the community's capacity for initiating and sustaining its own processes of innovation and change
- recognizing multiple ecological levels of analysis, and targeting multiple social and community systems for change
- empirical, contextual research involving multiple methods of inquiry, practical as well statistical significance, and longer timelines for longitudinal and community research
- interdisciplinary collaboration to address community issues at multiple levels
- using knowledge for community change, including local self-evaluation for continuous improvement over time (Wandersman, 2003 pp. 236–237)

Biglan and Smolkowski (2002) proposed a role description for community psychologists at the local level involving elements of collaboration, citizen participation, and empirical research. It represents what could become a local base for community science. In their conception, a local community psychologist would facilitate strategic planning and implementing of programs and policies by local citizens for promoting community well-being. This would include four general tasks.

Monitoring local community well-being involves collecting information from surveys, archival information sources, and other local resources, on behavioral and community problems (e.g., health, drug abuse, juvenile crime, personal and family problems). A community psychologist also would need skills in effectively presenting these findings to large, diverse citizen audiences.

Facilitating planning includes helping to organize community coalitions to address local issues and fostering a planning process in which citizens identify specific goals and strategies for community change. As we discussed in Chapter 13, coalitions need to truly represent community diversity. As part of this process, the community psychologist would also provide research findings from the monitoring activities above.

For a problem or goal that citizens have chosen, the community psychologist also would *articulate what works:* identifying community interventions and policies have been empirically demonstrated to be effective elsewhere. This would not assume that any empirically supported intervention would automatically succeed in the local context, but such support does indicate its potential value there.

Through *consultation, training, and evaluation*, community psychologists would assist communities and organizations in implementing and evaluating programs and policies. This will require attention to the process of intervention and to the capacity of the community to sustain it. This resembles the approaches to implementation in Chapter 11 and evaluation in Chapter 14 of this book.

Biglan and Smolkowski's approach describes one local role for community psychologists. However, this is only one of many possible roles for community psychologists, at multiple ecological levels, to promote community and social change.

For instance, advocacy for social justice involves skills and roles that go beyond the Biglan and Smolkowski list (e.g., Nelson & Prilleltensky, 2005; Tseng et al., 2002). However, the diversity of approaches in community psychology share a value for grounding action in empirical research. Thus they all embody the role proposed at the Swampscott conference: the participant conceptualizer.

Community Psychology: A Conversation within a Big Tent

In this book we have presented many examples of roles for community psychologists that involve the core values of the field. Not every community psychologist must play every role, nor can each focus in equal depth on every value. Some may primarily pursue individual/family wellness and sense of community. Others may primarily pursue social justice and citizen participation. Some may focus on building the empirical knowledge base for action, while others involve themselves in community or wider social action itself. All of these efforts will need to respect and understand human diversity and community strengths, and work collaboratively with citizens.

As the variety of concepts and action approaches in this book indicates, community psychology is a "big tent," bringing together psychologists and others with shared values, but also with many ways of acting on those values in communities (Toro, 2005). That variety can be a strength. Its contradictions foster discussions that deepen understanding. Another useful metaphor for community psychology is a conversation in which multiple views are articulated, considered, modified through consideration of other views, and developed over time. Perhaps the field comprises a conversation in a big tent, with diverse participants and views and illustrating Rappaport's Rule: "When everyone agrees with you, worry" (Jozefowicz-Simbeni, Israel, Braciszewski, & Hobden, 2005; Olson, 2003, 2004; Toro, 2005).

TIME AND COMMUNITY AND SOCIAL CHANGE

The history of social and community change illustrates the value of two seemingly contradictory ideas about time: **seizing the day,** and **taking the long view.** Early in the history of community psychology, Kelly (1970b) articulated the importance of both.

Democratic forms of government are designed to balance power among diverse, competing interests, with systems of checks and balances often divided among branches and levels of government. Although this decentralized structure has many strengths, a disadvantage is that it makes it difficult to muster sufficient agreement that a social problem exists, much less on how to respond. To gain wide attention, a social issue (e.g., homelessness, drug abuse, poverty, racism) often must assume crisis proportions. In the heat of such a crisis, citizens and decision makers prefer quick fixes. Support for longer-term, difficult changes becomes difficult to sustain, especially within short political election cycles (Heller, 1984; Marris & Rein, 1973; Riger, 1993; Schorr, 1997).

For community psychologists, *seizing the day* means applying their concepts, perspectives, research, and skills to today's social and community problems. That involves taking advantage of opportunities for learning: community events, processes, and resources (Kelly, 1970b). It also often involves calling attention to the views and experiences of those who are powerless and ignored, through research and advocacy (Price, 1989; Rappaport, 1981). It means speaking out, alongside citizens and communities, with views grounded in empirical research whenever possible.

Taking the long view means understanding historical swings of perspective and power that influence how social and community issues are addressed (Levine & Levine, 1992). It also means learning the histories of communities and populations with whom community psychologists collaborate and recognizing how those histories influence the issues of the day (Tseng et al., 2002). Moreover, it involves sustained commitment and involvement to particular communities, perhaps for years, attending carefully to the process (e.g., personal-emotional relationships and power dynamics) of that work (Elias, 1994; Kelly, 1970b, 1990; Primavera & Brodsky, 2004). It means devising, implementing, evaluating, and refining community interventions that can offer sound, scientific evidence of effectiveness in addressing clearly defined objectives. By doing that, we can provide empirically supported approaches that are not only more tailored to local context, but also more likely to weather the changes of social, political, and economic climate (Heller, 1984 p. 47). Finally, it means articulating core values in ways that sustain persons and communities through setbacks and challenges (Tseng et al., 2002). In these ways, community psychologists can continue to pursue community and social transformation despite changes in the current social context.

Taking the long view also involves recognizing the ongoing, dynamic nature of social and community change (Tseng et al., 2002). It is easy, especially for psychologists, to conclude that nothing can be done about complex social or community problems. This view misses a fundamental reality: social change occurs all around us, every day. Don Klein, a founder of community psychology in the United States, mused in a 1995 interview that when he began his career in the 1950s it was inconceivable that someday smoking would be widely considered a health problem and banned in many public places. Yet that is today's reality (Klein, 1995). In the 1950s and 1960s, African-American college students took practical steps to resist segregation and (soon learning to work with others in their communities) conducted sit-ins, voter registration, and other actions of the civil rights movement, against violent opposition and seemingly insurmountable odds (Lewis, 1998). Their highest aims have yet to be realized, but substantial changes took place. The women's movement is transforming societies around the world. Berkowitz (1987) interviewed 22 community activists who had played leadership roles in sustained community and social changes. Some were famous, and their initiatives well known; many were not, but their contributions were valuable nonetheless, if only at a local level. These and other examples illustrate that social change, though not easy, is pervasive (Ackerman & DuVall, 2000; Loeb, 2004).

Another dimension of time concerns the need for the field of community psychology to listen both to its youth, including students, and its seniors, including those whose involvement stretches back to its emergence as a distinct discipline (Olson, 2004). Youthful community psychologists bring passion and a sense of immediacy to the field. Their concerns are often not based on the traditions (and limitations) of the field. This is a strength: it promotes the questioning of assumptions, enables fresh perspectives and innovative practices to emerge, and helps to focus on the issues of the day. At the same time, seasoned community psychologists, if they are willing to listen and share their views in collaborative ways, can offer the wisdom of personal experience and growth over time. Nuances and lessons to learn can be difficult to understand at first, but awareness of them emerges in the rough and tumble of community action, sometimes through dealing with misunderstandings, opponents, painful experiences, and failure (Sarason, 2003a). In understanding the complexities of community and social life, all community psychologists are students. Both the visions of youth and the wisdom of experience are too valuable to overlook.

Qualities for a Community Psychologist

Soon after the emergence of the field of community psychology, James Kelly (1971) described seven desirable personal qualities for community psychologists. These qualities remain an insightful, useful summary for today's community psychologists (Rudkin, 2003). They address many themes of the field and of this book.

A Clearly Identified Competence The community psychologist must demonstrate skills useful to a community, whether as a participatory researcher, program evaluator, policy analyst, advocate, grant writer, clinical helper, consultant, workshop leader, or other role. This competence must also be taught in some way to community members, sharing it as a resource, not simply imparting it as expert.

Creating an Eco-Identity This involves immersing oneself in a community, identifying with it, caring about it. This emotional engagement with a community supports enduring commitment, deeper understanding, and respecting its members' choices.

Tolerance for Diversity This actually goes well beyond passive tolerance to understanding and embracing diversity. It involves relating to people who may be very different from oneself and understanding how those differences are resources for the community even when they involve conflict. It also involves understanding differences among community members and looking for ways to use those resources.

Coping Effectively with Varied Resources All community members are or have resources, but these may not be visible in community life. It becomes essential to identify hidden skills, knowledge, and other resources and to draw on them while working together. This often involves stepping out of the professional-expert role to collaborate with citizens as true partners, respecting their skills and insights.

A Commitment to Risk Taking This involves being an advocate for a real cause or person, seeking positive community change. This will often involve taking sides with a marginal, unpopular, low-status person or group against more powerful interests. It may involve risking failure, advocating a course of action before knowing if it will succeed. This risk taking is not impulsive, but a careful expression of one's values for the community.

A Metabolic Balance of Patience and Zeal To remain engaged in a community, one needs to feel passionate about the values and goals of one's work, but also be patient with the time required for community change. Knowing when to speak out and when to be silent is an art to be learned, as is finding ways to sustain oneself through successes and failures.

One element for this is supportive relationships with people who promote learning about the community and risk taking in one's work. That may be a network of personal relationships or a community setting or group.

A second element is awareness of the emotions involved in community work. Videos of interviews with early community psychologists in the United States reveal emotions not visible in journal articles or books (Kelly, 2003). These included anger that propelled advocacy, pride and sense of personal connection with a community setting, glee when injustice was confronted, the excitement of finding like-minded allies, the ability to laugh about the ironies of community work, and a mixture of pride and loss when a community was ready to pursue its own future, saying goodbye to the psychologist. Emotions can express values, energize commitment, and strengthen community solidarity. Community psychology can be passionate.

Giving Away the Byline The goals of community psychology are to strengthen community resources, work with community partners, and accomplish positive community change. Seeking or basking in personal recognition interferes with the long-term pursuit of those goals. It is important to celebrate successes, but also to share the credit.

SIGNS FOR HOPE, EXAMPLES OF CHANGE

As successful examples of seizing the day and taking the long view, and to illustrate many of Kelly's skills, we will describe four hopeful yet empirically grounded examples of tangible change in communities. These examples are directly linked to the efforts of citizens and community psychologists. There are certainly many other success stories in community psychology, some of which we have highlighted in prior chapters. All four examples here concern education, just one of the multiple social systems where community psychologists work. Yet they illustrate some of the overarching themes and values of community psychology.

Social-Emotional Literacy / Character Education

Exciting changes are happening in the United States in social-emotional learning/ character education (SEL/CE), which we discussed in Chapters 10 and 11. A number of states, including New Jersey, Illinois, Ohio, Iowa, Rhode Island, New York, and Georgia, have significant state-level policies, mandates, and/or guidelines for educators on carrying out SEL/CE in schools. Many municipalities and individual schools are including SEL/CE as part of their local educational goals and policies. In addition, many states are developing community service learning as an educational experience with similar goals.

Community psychology research and action has played a role in this development. There is a strong empirical base for SEL/CE programs. Much attention has been paid to fidelity of program implementation in local contexts, ensuring that thousands of teachers and literally hundreds of thousands of students have been recipients of high-quality SEL/CE. Further, community psychologists, including Maurice Elias, have been instrumental in establishing the New Jersey Center for Character Education, an action-research and technical assistance center for the schools of New Jersey as they implement SEL/CE. A major concern of the NJCCE is how to help schools coordinate different, well-established programs, such as a K–5 curriculum, a middle school curriculum, and SEL/CE-related modules in high school courses. The school districts involved represent a range of sizes, locations, and socioeconomic profiles of students, and the goal is creating approaches applicable in a diversity of contexts. Innovations in these areas can be reviewed at the websites of the Collaborative for Academic, Social, and Emotional Learning (www.CASEL.org) and the Character Education Partnership (www.character.org).

SEL/CE initiatives capitalize on a concern arising in many U.S. communities with addressing prosocial values and social responsibility as a part of education. Many educators, parents, and citizens see a need to address these issues, not just in families and spiritual settings but also in public schools, in ways that respect the diversity of students.

Empowerment Evaluation in Schools

As noted in Chapter 10, the U.S. No Child Left Behind Act of 2001 was a centerpiece of President George W. Bush's efforts to improve K–12 education. It was "designed to change the culture of America's schools by closing the achievement gap". Schools whose students test below national standards must first provide supplemental services such as tutoring, and if this does not raise scores, "make dramatic changes in the way the school is run" (U.S. Department of Education, n.d.). Those "dramatic changes" can include firing principals and teachers or diverting public school funds into private or charter schools. Clearly the act's intent to improve student performance is noteworthy, but the reliance on standardized tests and punitive remedies has created many problems (Sadker & Zittleman, 2004). Moreover, as implemented under both federal and state standards, schools face penalties but often receive little or no additional funding to address these problems. In a prosperous locality, local funding can be used for this purpose, but in a low-income area, money simply is not present. These were some of the issues for two rural and impoverished school districts in the Arkansas Delta that had been classified as "academic distressed" by the state (Fetterman, 2005).

David Fetterman, a pioneer of the empowerment evaluation approach described in Chapter 14, was asked to apply empowerment evaluation in these districts. Arkansas law defines "academic distress" as having over 40 percent of students scoring at or below the 25th percentile on the Arkansas state assessment of grade-level student achievement (a standardized test mandated by the state). One district had been in academic distress for over six years, beginning under Arkansas requirements that predated the federal No Child Left Behind law. By law, the state has the right to take over schools in "academic distress" status and to replace the entire staff (Fetterman, 2005).

Firing all the principals and teachers was neither appropriate nor realistic. First, as is true in many rural and inner-city areas, the schools were the largest local employer. Second, these remote, impoverished communities found it difficult to recruit credentialed teachers. Fetterman and state and local school officials therefore worked collaboratively to strengthen the existing capacity of the local schools to improve student learning, raise test scores, and exit the "distressed" status.

Fetterman reported, "An initial needs assessment documented that there was potential for improvement. The aim was to build individual, program, and school district capacity in order to construct a firm foundation for future improvements. Everyone was focused on improvement in critical areas (which they identified as a group). Specifically, we focused on improving test scores, discipline, parental involvement, and administrative support and follow-through. School district teachers, administrators, staff members, and community members documented their improvement or progress using the taking-stock (baseline) data and comparing the baseline data with a second data point (a posttest following the intervention of improved teaching and discipline)" (Fetterman, 2005 pp.).

The schools made tangible improvements in each of these areas, including raising student test scores. Arkansas state education officials considered the empowerment evaluation, with its focus on building local capacity and documenting processes and outcomes, to be instrumental in producing these improvements (Fetterman, 2005). For instance, at the beginning of the intervention in fall 2001, 59 percent of students in one school district scored below the 25th percentile on standardized tests. By the end of the empowerment evaluation intervention in spring 2003, only 38.5 percent of students scored below the 25th percentile. This 20 percent improvement was very significant in practical terms and removed the schools from the "distressed" list. Similar results were obtained in another school district (Fetterman, 2005 p. 116). In both districts, efforts are continuing to further improve student learning. Empowerment evaluation addressed a pressing issue for these schools and communities, but also helped develop a process for continuous improvement of learning over the long term.

Meyerhoff Scholars

Even though individual African Americans have attained visible success in U.S. life, the overall proportion of African Americans in some professions remains low. This is especially true in the natural sciences, technology, engineering, and mathematics (STEM) fields. At the University of Maryland at Baltimore County, a predominantly European-American university, the Meyerhoff Scholars program successfully prepares a largely African-American student group for graduate study and careers in STEM fields. It reflects a strengths-based approach: instead of focusing on deficits to be remedied, it identifies strengths to be built upon and enhanced. These include personal talents, family and community resources, and university settings that promote learning and achievement. Community psychologist Ken Maton has been involved in developing and evaluating the Meyerhoff program (Maton & Hrabowski, 2004; Maton, Hrabowski, & Greif, 1998; Maton & Salem, 1995).

Meyerhoff Scholars combines several components that research has shown to be critical to academic success in STEM and other fields: financial aid to allow a focus on studies; high standards for performance in classes; program values that emphasize achievement and support; community building among program members; peer study groups; individualized academic advising and personal support; faculty involvement outside the classroom; mentoring by STEM professionals; summer research internships; family involvement; and community service (Maton & Hrabowski, 2004).

Research on Meyerhoff Scholars has compared the academic careers of its participants to a comparison group of similar students who were offered admission to the program but chose to attend other universities (where they may or may not have had access to resources similar to what Meyerhoff Scholars offers). Nearly 30 percent of Meyerhoff Scholars graduates were enrolled in or graduated from Ph.D. programs in STEM fields, *five times* the rate for the comparison group. Seventy-one percent of Meyerhoff Scholars graduates were enrolled in or graduated from Ph.D., M.D., and master's STEM programs, compared to 56 percent of the comparison group. Surveys and interviews with graduates indicated the importance of these factors in student achievement: sense of community in the Meyerhoff Scholars program, peer study groups, the involvement of program staff in advising and counseling, faculty accessibility, research and mentoring opportunities, and financial aid. Because the comparison group included similarly talented students, these program elements appear to have been critical factors in the graduates' success (Maton & Hrabowski, 2004).

Meyerhoff Scholars African-American students arrived at college with considerable family support. Research on this support showed these particular family strengths: persistent engagement in the child's schooling, child-focused love and support, strict discipline and limit-setting, and connectedness with outside community resources, including extended family, religious congregations, and extracurricular activities at school (Maton & Hrabowski, 2004). Before and during college, these resources complemented the support offered in the program. The strengths perspective and multiple resources of Meyerhoff Scholars can be adapted for a diversity of students of many interests and backgrounds.

The Power of a Place

Catherine Stein and associates have conducted action-research projects that elucidate the strengths and personal lives of persons with serious mental illnesses and build ways to for them to teach psychology students through personal contacts.

In an article entitled "The Power of a Place," Stein, Ward, and Cislo (1992) developed a college course that integrated traditional college students with a group of community students: persons with serious mental illnesses. Their course was not like courses on many campuses in which students are helpers or companions for "patients," an approach that has value but that tends to create an unequal helper–patient role relationship. Instead, Stein et al. developed and led a course in social relationship skills in which traditional and community students were defined as equals. This illustrates the impact of altering social regularities (Seidman, 1988) to enhance student learning and interdependence.

The Stein et al. course had several distinctive elements. The class, a three-credit psychology course, met twice a week: once for didactic teaching and structured exercises, and once for a group meeting patterned as a mutual help group (drawing from the approach of GROW, a mutual help group described in Chapter 8.) Students formed pairs of one traditional student and one community student who met for homework assignments and discussion outside class. The instructors and course materials emphasized that each person in the class had unique life experiences and skills for teaching others as well as something to learn from classmates.

Evaluation findings were heartwarming. Informal observation indicated that the course methods engaged both traditional and community students. Observation and student journals also revealed that substantial interdependence and support developed between the two groups. Journals from both groups described personal gains made during the course. Several members of each student group reported that they began the course with some stereotypes about the other group, but that those were dispelled by the course. In addition, both groups of students reported more positive changes in their personal relationships than did similar members of control groups.

The Stein et al. (1992) course clearly fostered development of interdependent, supportive relationships as equals between the two groups. Moreover, this occurred in a college classroom, "home ground" for the traditional students but not for community students. By blending methods of community psychology, cooperative learning, and mutual help, the class promoted personal development, fostered networks of social support, undermined stereotypes about persons with mental illness, and linked both groups of students with each other and with the wider community.

In a later study that we discussed in Chapter 4, Stein and Wemmerus (2001) interviewed persons with serious mental illness and their family members (see also Stein & Mankowski, 2004). That study led Stein to develop a course in which persons with schizophrenia are paired with clinical psychology graduate students, teaching them about daily coping with the illness. Both of these studies used the opportunity of college courses and the resources of persons with mental illness to enliven learning, build community, and promote a strengths perspective.

As a way of closing the circle of this book, we especially invite you to review two other examples that we presented in Chapter 1:

- the case study of "Elaine" that we presented in Chapters 1 and 8, illustrating individual coping and thriving in relation to community resources
- Debi Starnes's (2003) work on the Atlanta City Council, illustrating community psychology principles in city-wide leadership and advocacy

A FINAL EXERCISE: VISIONING A FUTURE COMMUNITY AND SOCIETY

We conclude this book with an exercise designed to elicit your visions of the future.

Visioning the future is not simply daydreaming. It helps to identify values for individual, community, and social life. It also helps articulate goals and steps toward them. Visioning further helps to understand the interrelationships and conflicts among values and goals. Multiple visions are often needed to deepen our understanding and discern what values and goals deserve our commitment.

Visioning the future helps to articulate voices and ideas that differ from those of experts, leaders, pundits, interest groups, and other voices that dominate public discussion. Discussing visions with others, especially in small groups, can articulate ideals and actions that are not necessarily recognized or taken seriously elsewhere in public life.

Visioning can be motivating. Exploring our feelings about community and social life enriches visions and helps to generate energy for working together and for living out our most deeply held values.

To create your own visions of the future, consider one or more of the following sets of questions. You might enrich your visions by writing down your ideas or by drawing pictures, maps, or diagrams of them. Discuss your visions with others (Community Tool Box, 2005, chap. 8; Dobson & Vancouver Citizen's Committee, 2005).

- What is your vision of the ideal local community or neighborhood in which you would wish to live? What would the most important values shared by its members be? What would its physical layout look like? What community organizations or settings would it have? Compared to existing communities in your life today, would your ideal community promote greater individual or family wellness, sense of community, social justice, respect for human diversity, or citizen participation in community decision making? How?
- Choose an existing locality, organization, or community setting that you care about deeply. How could it be transformed and strengthened? Would this transformation strengthen individual or family wellness, sense of community, social justice, respect for human diversity, or citizen participation in

community decision making? How? What existing community values, strengths, or resources might contribute to the transformation you envision?

- What is your vision of an ideal society in which you would wish to live? What would be the most important values shared by its members? Compared to your existing society today, would your ideal society promote greater individual or family wellness, sense of community, social justice, respect for human diversity, or citizen participation in decision making? How?
- How might your existing society be transformed and strengthened? Would this transformation strengthen individual or family wellness, sense of community, social justice, respect for human diversity, or citizen participation in community decision making? How? What existing societal values, strengths, or resources might contribute to the transformation you envision?

Finally, for any of these sets of questions, consider how to enact your visions:

- What is one step that you could take, today or in the near future, toward making your vision come true? How might that step involve collaborating with others in your community or society? What are the strengths or talents that you could contribute to that work?

Remember these principles of change for individuals and communities:

> *In your own life, be the change you wish to see in the world.* (Mohandas Gandhi)

> *Never doubt that a small group of thoughtful, committed citizens can change the world; indeed, it's the only thing that ever does.* (Margaret Mead)

CHAPTER SUMMARY

1. We identified and described emerging directions in community psychology: growing awareness of human diversity in all its forms; broadening concern with social justice; collaborative, participatory research and action; and the concept and practice of *community science.* We suggested the metaphor of a conversation within a big tent for the diverse concerns of community psychology.
2. We described how *seizing the day* and *taking the long view* are both important time orientations for community psychology, and how listening to the voices of both youth and experience can facilitate the progress of the field.
3. We discussed seven qualities for the community psychologist, first identified by James Kelly in 1971 yet still relevant today. They are: *Demonstrate a clearly identified competence, create an eco-identity, understand and embrace diversity, collaborate effectively with community resources, cultivate a commitment to taking risks, continuously balance patience and zeal, and give away the byline.*
4. We provided four examples of successful community change illustrating these themes: social-emotional literacy and character education programs in

schools, empowerment evaluation to promote student learning in "distressed" schools, the Meyerhoff Scholars program for African-American students in science-related fields, and Stein's college courses that enable students to learn from persons with mental illness.

5. Finally we asked readers to envision their visions for future communities and society and to identify at least one step to take toward putting those visions into action.

BRIEF EXERCISE

1. Consider making this pledge at your graduation:

   "I pledge to explore and take into account the social and environmental consequences of any job I consider and will try to improve these aspects of any organization for which I work."

   This graduation pledge has been adopted by colleges and graduate schools, and signed by students, in many countries. Graduates who sign the pledge must define for themselves how to apply this promise in their own lives, but their actions have included removing racist language in a training manual, working for gender parity in school athletics, convincing an employer to refuse a contract related to chemical weapons, and promoting recycling at work. The pledge works at multiple ecological levels: personal commitment and action, promoting education about values as well as about skills, and action in the workplace and community. (Information provided by psychologist Neil Wollman at Manchester College.) You can find more information on organizing graduation pledge activities for your college or university at the Graduation Pledge Alliance website: http://www.graduationpledge.org

References

Abdul-Adil, J. K., & Jason, L. A. (1991, Fall). Community psychology and Al-Islam: A religious framework for social change. *The Community Psychologist, 24,* 28–30.

Aber, J. L. (2005, June). *Children's exposure to war and violence: Knowledge for action.* Keynote address presented at the Biennial Meeting of the Society for Community Research and Action, Champsign-Urbana, Illinois.

Aber, J. L., Gershoff, E., Ware, A. & Kotler, J. (2004). Estimating the effects of September 11th and other forms of violence on the mental health and social development of New York City's youth: A matter of context. *Applied Developmental Science, 8,* 111–129.

Abraido-Lanza, A., Guier, C., & Colon, R. (1998). Psychological thriving among Latinas with chronic illness. *Journal of Social Issues, 54,* 405–424.

Ackerman, P., & DuVall, J. (2000). *A force more powerful: A century of nonviolent conflict.* New York: Palgrave.

Acosta, O., & Toro, P. A. (2000). Let's ask the homeless people themselves: A needs assessment based on a probability sample of adults. *American Journal of Community Psychology, 28,* 343–366.

Adams, R., & Boscarino, J. (2005). Stress and well-being in the aftermath of the World Trade Center attack: The continuing effects of a communitywide disaster. *Journal of Community Psychology, 33,* 175–190.

Adelman, H. S., & Taylor, L. (2000). Moving prevention from the fringes into the fabric of school improvement. *Journal of Educational and Psychological Consultation, 11,* 7–36.

Adelman, H. S., & Taylor, L. (2003). Creating school and community partnerships for substance abuse prevention programs. *Journal of Primary Prevention, 23* (3), 329–368.

Adelman, H. S., & Taylor, L. (2006). *The implementation guide to student learning supports in the classroom and schoolwide.* Thousand Oaks, CA: Corwin Press.

Adler, A. (1979). On the origin of the striving for superiority and of social interest. In H. Ansbacher & R. Ansbacher, (Eds.), *Superiority and social interest: A collection of later writings* (pp. 29–40). New York: Norton. (Essay originally published 1933.)

Albee, G. W. (1959). *Mental health manpower trends.* New York: Basic Books.

Albee, G. W. (1982). Preventing psychopathology and promoting human potential. *American Psychologist, 37,* 1043–1050.

Albee, G. W. (1995). [Untitled videotape interview]. In J. G. Kelly (Ed.), *The history of community psychology: A video presentation of context and exemplars.* Chicago: Society for Community Research and Action.

Albee, G.W. (2000). The future of primary prevention. *Journal of Primary Prevention, 21* (1), 7–9.

Albee, G. W., Bond, L., & Monsey, T. (1992). *Primary prevention of psychopathology,* Vol. 14: *Improving children's lives: Global perspectives on prevention.* Thousand Oaks, CA: Sage.

Albee, G. W., & Gullotta, T. (Eds.). (1997). *Primary prevention works*. Thousand Oaks, CA: Sage.

Alinsky, S. (1971). *Rules for radicals: A practical primer for realistic radicals*. New York: Random House.

Allen, N. E. (2005). A multi-level analysis of community coordinating councils. *American Journal of Community Psychology, 35,* 49–64.

Allport, G. (1954). *The nature of prejudice*. Cambridge, MA: Addison-Wesley.

Alpert, J., & Smith, H. (2003). Terrorism, terrorism threat, and the school consultant. *Journal of Educational and Psychological Consultation, 14* (3/4), 369–385.

American Anthropological Association (1998). Statement on "race." Retrieved July 28, 2005, from http://www.aaanet.org/stmts/racepp.htm

American Psychiatric Association (1994). *Diagnostic and statistical manual of mental disorders* (4th ed.). [DSM-IV]. Washington, DC: Author.

American Psychological Association (2000). Resolution on poverty and socioeconomic status. Retrieved September 18, 2003 from http://www.apa.org/pi/urban/povres.html

American Psychological Association (2005, September 12). *APA Hurricane Katrina relief activities.* Retrieved October 1, 2005 from http://www.apa.org/releases/apakatrina.html

American Red Cross (2005, October 20). *American Red Cross response to Hurricanes Katrina and Rita.* Retrieved October 25, 2005 from http://www.redcross.org/news/ds/hurricanes/katrina_facts.html

Ang, S., & Joseph, D. (1996, August 9–12). *Organizational learning and learning organizations: Triggering events, processes and structures*. Proceedings of the Academy of Management Meeting, Cincinnati, OH.

Angelique, H., & Culley, M. (2000). Searching for feminism: An analysis of community psychology literature relevant to women's concerns. *American Journal of Community Psychology, 28,* 793–814.

Angelique, H., & Culley, M. (2003). Feminism found: An examination of gender consciousness in community psychology. *Journal of Community Psychology, 31,* 189–209.

Angelique, H., Reischl, T., & Davidson, W. S. (2002). Promoting political empowerment: Evaluation of an intervention with university students. *American Journal of Community Psychology, 30,* 815–835.

Annie E. Casey Foundation. (1995). *The path of most resistance: Reflections on lessons learned from New Futures.* Baltimore, MD: Author.

Argyris, C. (1999). *On organizational learning*. Malden, MA: Blackwell Business.

Argyris, C., & Schon, D. (1978). *Organizational learning.* Reading, MA: Addison-Wesley.

Astin, A., Vogelsang, L., Ikeda, E., & Yee, J. (2000). *How service learning affects students.* Los Angeles: Higher Education Research Institute, UCLA.

Balcazar, F., Seekins, T., Fawcett, S. B., & Hopkins, B. (1990). Empowering people with physical disabilities through advocacy skills training. *American Journal of Community Psychology, 18,* 281–296.

Bandura, A. (1982). Self-efficacy mechanisms in human agency. *American Psychologist, 37,* 122–147.

Bandura, A. (1986). *Social foundations of thought and action: A social cognitive theory.* Englewood Cliffs, NJ: Prentice-Hall.

Barker, R. (1965). Explorations in ecological psychology. *American Psychologist, 20,* 1–14.

Barker, R. (1968). *Ecological psychology.* Stanford, CA: Stanford University Press.

Barker, R. (1978). Behavior settings. In R. Barker & Associates, *Habitats, environments, and human behavior* (pp. 29–35). San Francisco: Jossey-Bass.

Barker, R., & Associates. (1978). *Habitats, environments and human behavior.* San Francisco: Jossey-Bass.

Barker R., & Gump, P. (Eds.). (1964). *Big school, small school.* Stanford, CA: Stanford University Press.

Barker, R., & Schoggen, P. (1973). *Qualities of community life: Methods of measuring environment and behavior applied to an American and an English town.* San Francisco: Jossey-Bass.

Barker, R., & Wright, H. (1955). *Midwest and its children.* New York: Harper & Row.

Barker, R., & Wright, H. (1978). Standing patterns of behavior. In R. Barker & Associates, *Habitats, environments and human behavior* (pp. 24–28). San Francisco: Jossey-Bass. (Original work published 1955.)

Barrera, M. (1986). Distinctions between social support concepts, measures, and models. *American Journal of Community Psychology, 14,* 413–445.

Barrera, M. (2000). Social support research in community psychology. In J. Rappaport & E. Seidman (Eds.), *Handbook of community psychology* (pp. 215–246). New York: Kluwer/Plenum.

Barrera, M., Glasgow, R., McKay, H., Boles, S., & Feil, E. (2002). Do Internet-based support interventions change perceptions of social support?: An experimental trial of approaches for supporting diabetes self-management. *American Journal of Community Psychology, 30,* 637–654.

Barrera, M., & Li, S. A. (1996). The relation of family support to adolescents' psychological distress and behavior problems. In G. R. Pierce, B. R. Sarason, & I. G. Sarason (Eds.), *Handbook of social support and the family* (pp. 313–344). New York: Plenum.

Bartunek, J. M., & Keys, C. B. (1979). Participation in school decision-making. *Urban Education, 14,* 52–75.

Bateman, H. V. (2002). Sense of community in the school: Listening to students' voices. In A. Fisher, C. Sonn, & B. Bishop (Eds.), *Psychological sense of community: Research, applications and implications* (pp. 161–180). New York: Kluwer/Plenum.

Battistich, V., Elias, M. J., & Branden-Muller, L. (1992). Two school-based approaches to promoting children's social competence. In G. W. Albee, L. A. Bond, & T. Monsey (Eds.), *Primary prevention of psychopathology,* Vol. 14: *Improving children's lives: Global perspectives on prevention* (pp. 217–234). Thousand Oaks, CA: Sage.

Baum A., & Fleming, I. (1993). Implications of psychological research on stress and technological accidents. *American Psychologist, 48,* 665–672.

Belenky, M., Clinchy, B., Goldberger, N., & Tarule, J. (1986). *Women's ways of knowing: The development of self, voice and mind.* New York: Basic Books.

Bellah, R., Madsen, R., Sullivan, W., Swidler, A., & Tipton, S. (1985). *Habits of the heart: Individualism and commitment in American life.* New York: Harper & Row.

Belsky, J. (1980). Child maltreatment: An ecological integration. *American Psychologist, 35,* 320–335.

Belsky, J. (1984). The determinants of parenting: A process model. *Child Development, 55,* 83–96.

Benjamin, L., & Crouse, E. (2002). The American Psychological Association's response to *Brown vs. Board of Education:* The case of Kenneth B. Clark. *American Psychologist, 57,* 38–50.

Bennett, C., Anderson, L., Cooper, S., Hassol, L., Klein, D., & Rosenblum, G. (1966). *Community psychology: A report of the Boston Conference on the Education of Psychologists for Community Mental Health.* Boston: Boston University.

Bennett, E. (2003). Emancipatory responses to oppression: The template of land-use planning and the Old Order Amish of Ontario. *American Journal of Community Psychology, 31,* 173–184.

Berger, P., & Neuhaus, R. (1977). *To empower people.* Washington, DC: American Enterprise Institute.

Berkowitz, B. (1987). *Local heroes.* Lexington, MA: Lexington Books.

Berkowitz, B. (1990, Summer). Who is being empowered? *The Community Psychologist, 23,* 10–11.

Berkowitz, B. (1996). Personal and community sustainability. *American Journal of Community Psychology, 24,* 441–460.

Berkowitz, B. (2000). Community and neighborhood organization. In J. Rappaport & E. Seidman (Eds.), *Handbook of community psychology* (pp. 331–358). New York: Kluwer/Plenum.

Bernal, G., & Enchautegui-de-Jesus, N. (1994). Latinos and Latinas in community psychology: A review of the literature. *American. Journal of Community Psychology, 22,* 531–558.

Bernal, G., Trimble, J., Burlew, A. K. & Leong, F. (Eds.). (2003). *Handbook of racial and ethnic minority psychology.* Thousand Oaks, CA: Sage.

Bernard, J. (1973). *The sociology of community.* Glenview, IL: Scott, Foresman.

Berrueta-Clement, J. R., Schweinhart, L. J., Barnett, W. S., Epstein, A. S., & Weikart, D. P. (1984). *Changed lives: The effects of the Perry preschool program on youths through age 19.* (Monographs of the High/Scope Educational Research Foundation, 8). Ypsilanti, MI: High/Scope Press.

Berry, J. (1994). An ecological perspective on cultural and ethnic psychology. In E. Trickett, R. Watts, & D. Birman (Eds.), *Human diversity: Perspectives on people in context* (pp. 115–141). San Francisco: Jossey-Bass.

Berry, J. (2003). Conceptual approaches to acculturation. In K. Chun, P. Organista, & G. Marin (Eds.), *Acculturation: Advances in theory, measurement and applied research* (pp. 17–38). Washington, DC: American Psychological Association.

Berry, J. & Sam, D. (1997). Acculturation and adaptation. In J. W. Berry, M. Segall, & C. Kagitçibasi (Eds.), *Handbook of cross-cultural psychology,* Vol. 3: *Social behavior and applications* (pp. 291–325). Needham Heights, MA: Allyn & Bacon.

Bess, K., Fisher, A., Sonn, C., & Bishop, B. (2002). Psychological conceptions of community: Theory, research and application. In A. Fisher, C. Sonn, & B. Bishop (Eds.), *Psychological sense of community: Research, applications and implications* (pp. 3–22). New York: Kluwer/Plenum.

Betancourt, H., & Lopez, S. R. (1993). The study of culture, ethnicity, and race in American psychology. *American Psychologist, 48,* 629–637.

Bierman, K., & the Conduct Problems Prevention Research Group (1997). Implementing a comprehensive program for the prevention of conduct problems in rural communities: The Fast Track experience. *American Journal of Community Psychology, 25,* 493–514.

Biglan, A., Ary, D., Koehn, V., Levings, D., Smith, S., Wright, Z., James, L., & Henderson, J. (1996). Mobilizing positive reinforcement in communities to reduce youth access to tobacco. *American Journal of Community Psychology, 24,* 625–638.

Biglan, A., & Smolkowski, K. (2002). The role of the community psychologist in the 21st century. *Prevention & Treatment, 5,* Article 2. Retrieved August 1, 2002, from http://journals.apa.org/prevention/volumes

Birman, D. (1994). Acculturation and human diversity in a multicultural society. In E. J. Trickett, R. J. Watts, & D. Birman (Eds.), *Human diversity: Perspectives on people in context* (pp. 261–283). San Francisco: Jossey-Bass.

Birman, D. (1998). Biculturalism and perceived competence of Latino immigrant adolescents. *American Journal of Community Psychology, 26,* 335–354.

Birman, D., Trickett, E. J., & Buchanan, R. (2005). A tale of two cities: Replication of a study on the acculturation and adaptation of immigrant adolescents from the former Soviet Union in a different community context. *American Journal of Community Psychology, 35,* 83–102.

Birman, D., Trickett, E. J., & Vinokurov, A. (2002). Acculturation and adaptation of Soviet Jewish refugee adolescents: Predictors of adjustment across life domains. *American Journal of Community Psychology, 30,* 585–607.

Bishop, B., Coakes, S., & D'Rozario, P. (2002). Sense of community in rural communities: A mixed methodological approach. In A. Fisher, C. Sonn, & B. Bishop (Eds.), *Psychological sense of community: Research, applications and implications* (pp. 271–290). New York: Kluwer/Plenum.

Bjorck, J., Lee, Y., & Cohen, L. (1997). Control beliefs and faith as stress moderation for Korean American versus Caucasian American Protestants. *American Journal of Community Psychology, 25,* 61–72.

Bloom, B. (1977). *Community mental health: A general introduction.* Monterey, CA: Wadsworth.

Bonanno, G. (2004). Loss, trauma, and human resilience: Have we underestimated the human capacity to thrive after extremely aversive events? *American Psychologist, 59,* 20–28.

Bond, G., Witheridge, T., Dincin, J., Wasmer, D., Webb, J., & De Graaf-Kaser, R. (1990). Assertive community treatment for frequent users of psychiatric hospitals in a large city: A controlled study. *American Journal of Community Psychology, 18,* 865–892.

Bond, L.A. (2000). Prevention's adolescent identity struggle. *Journal of Primary Prevention, 21* (1), 11–14.

Bond, L. A., Belenky, M. F. & Weinstock, J. (2000). The Listening Partners Program: An initiative toward feminist community psychology in action. *American Journal of Community Psychology, 28,* 697–730.

Bond, M. A. (1989). Ethical dilemmas in context: Some preliminary questions. *American Journal of Community Psychology, 17,* 355–360.

Bond, M. A. (1990). Defining the research relationship: Maximizing participation in an unequal world. In P. Tolan, C. Keys, F. Chertok, & L. Jason (Eds.), *Researching community psychology* (pp. 183–185). Washington, DC: American Psychological Association.

Bond, M. A. (1999). Gender, race and class in organizational contexts. *American Journal of Community Psychology, 27,* 327–356.

Bond, M. A., Hill, J., Mulvey, A. & Terenzio, M. (Eds.). (2000). Special issue part I: Feminism and community psychology. *American Journal of Community Psychology, 28* (5).

Bond, M. A., Hill, J., Mulvey, A., & Terenzio, M. (Eds.). (2000). Special issue part II: Feminism and community psychology. *American Journal of Community Psychology, 28* (6).

Bond, M. A., & Keys, C. B. (1993). Empowerment, diversity, and collaboration: Promoting synergy on community boards. *American Journal of Community Psychology, 21,* 37–58.

Bond, M. A., & Mulvey, A. (2000). A history of women and feminist perspectives in community psychology. *American Journal of Community Psychology, 28,* 599–630.

Boodman, S. G. (2005, September 13). Uncharted territory: Mental health experts struggle to forecast Katrina's psychological impacts—and best treatments. *The Washington Post,* HE01.

Borkman, T. (1990). Self-help groups at the turning point: Emerging egalitarian alliances with the formal health care systems? *American Journal of Community Psychology, 18,* 321–332.

Borkman, T. (Ed.). (1991). Self-help groups [Special issue]. *American Journal of Community Psychology, 19* (5).

Botvin, G. J., Baker, E., Dusenbury, L., Botvin, E. M. & Diaz, T. (1995). Long-term follow-up results of a randomized drug abuse prevention trial in a white middle-class population. *Journal of the American Medical Association, 273,* 1106–1112.

Botvin, G., & Tortu, S. (1988). Preventing adolescent substance abuse through life skills training. In R. Price, E. Cowen, R. Lorion, & J. Ramos-McKay (Eds.), *Fourteen ounces of prevention* (pp. 98–110). Washington, DC: American Psychological Association.

Boulding, E. (2000). *Cultures of peace: The hidden side of history.* Syracuse, NY: Syracuse University Press.

Boulding, K. (1989). *Three faces of power.* Newbury Park, CA: Sage.

Bourne, J. K. (2004, October). Gone with the water. *National Geographic Magazine* [Electronic version]. Retrieved October 10, 2005 from http://magma.nationalgeographic.com/ngm/0410/feature5/?fs=www3.nationalgeographic.com

Bower, E. (1972). Education as a humanizing process. In S. Golann & C. Eisdorfer (Eds.), *Handbook of community mental health* (pp. 37–50). New York: Appleton-Century-Crofts.

Bowlby, J. (1969). *Attachment and loss,* Vol. 1: *Attachment.* New York: Basic Books.

Boyd, N., & Angelique, H. (2002). Rekindling the discourse: Organization studies in community psychology. *Journal of Community Psychology, 30,* 325–348.

Boyd, N., & Angelique, H. (Eds.) (in press). Exploring the intersection between organization studies and community psychology [Special issue]. *Journal of Community Psychology.*

Bradford, L., Gibb, J., & Benne, K. (1964). *T-group theory and laboratory method: Innovation in re-education.* New York: Wiley.

Bradley, R., & Corwyn, R. (2002). Socioeconomic status and child development. *Annual Review of Psychology, 53,* 371–399.

Brendtro, L., Brokenleg, M., & Van Bockern, S. (1990). *Reclaiming youth at risk: Our hope for the future.* Bloomington, IN: National Educational Service.

Brewer, M. (1997). The social psychology of intergroup relations: Can research inform practice? *Journal of Social Issues, 53,* 197–211.

Bringle, R., & Hatcher, J. (2002). Campus-community partnerships: The terms of engagement. *Journal of Social Issues, 58,* 503–516.

Brodsky, A. E. (1996). Resilient single mothers in risky neighborhoods: Negative psychological sense of community. *Journal of Community Psychology, 24,* 347–364.

Brodsky, A. (2000). The role of spirituality in the resilience of urban, African American, single mothers. *Journal of Community Psychology, 28,* 199–220.

Brodsky, A. (2001). More than epistemology: Relationships in applied research with underserved communities. *Journal of Social Issues, 57,* 323–336.

Brodsky, A. (2003). *With all our strength: The Revolutionary Association of the Women of Afghanistan.* New York: Routledge.

Brodsky, A., Loomis, C., & Marx, C. (2002). Expanding the conceptualization of PSOC. In A. Fisher, C. Sonn, & B. Bishop (Eds.), *Psychological sense of community: Research, applications and implications* (pp. 319–336). New York: Kluwer/Plenum.

Brodsky, A., & Marx, C. (2001). Layers of identity: Multiple psychological senses of community within a community setting. *Journal of Community Psychology, 29,* 161–178.

Brodsky, A., O'Campo, P. J., & Aronson, R. E. (1999). PSOC in community context: Multi-level correlates of a measure of psychological sense of community in low-income, urban neighborhoods. *Journal of Community Psychology, 27,* 659–680.

Brodsky, A., Senuta, K., Weiss, C., Marx, C., Loomis, C., Arteaga, S., Moore, H., Benhorin, R., & Castagnera-Fletcher, A. (2004). When one plus one equals three: The role of relationships and context in community research. *American Journal of Community Psychology, 33,* 229–242.

Bronfenbrenner, U. (1979). *The ecology of human development: Experiments by nature and design.* Cambridge, MA: Harvard University Press.

Brooks, M., & Buckner, J. (1996). Work and welfare: Job histories, barriers to employment, and predictors of work among low-income single mothers. *American Journal of Orthopsychiatry, 66,* 526–537.

Broom, M., & Klein, D. C. (1999). *Power: The infinite game.* Ellicott City, MD: Sea Otter Press.

Brower, A., & Ketterhagen, A. (2004). Is there an inherent mismatch between how Black and White students expect to succeed in college and what their colleges expect from them? *Journal of Social Issues, 60,* 95–116.

Brown, P., & Elias, M. J. (2002). Character education in New Jersey Schools: A status report. *The New Jersey Journal of Supervision and Curriculum Development, 46,* 23–42.

Bruene-Butler, L., Hampson, J., Elias, M. J., Clabby, J., & Schuyler, T. (1997). The Improving Social Awareness-Social Problem Solving Project. In G. Albee & T. Gullotta (Eds.), *Primary prevention works* (pp. 239–267). Thousand Oaks, CA: Sage.

Bryan, K., Schoenholz, D.A., & Elias, M, J. (in press). Applying organizational theories to action research in community settings: A case study in urban schools. *Journal of Community Psychology.*

Brydon-Miller, M., & Tolman, D. (Eds.) (1997). Transforming psychology: Interpretive and participatory methods [Special issue]. *Journal of Social Issues, 53(4).*

Bryk, A. S., & Schneider, B. (2002). *Trust in schools: A core resource for improvement.* New York: Russell Sage Foundation.

Buckner, J. C. (1988). The development of an instrument to measure neighborhood cohesion. *American Journal of Community Psychology, 16,* 771–791.

Buford, B., & Davis, B. (1995). *Shining Stars: Prevention programs that work.* Louisville, KY: Southeast Regional Center for Drug-Free Schools and Communities.

Bullock, H. Wyche, K. & Williams, W. (2001). Media images of the poor. *Journal of Social Issues, 57,* 229–246.

Burgess, L. (1990). A block association president's perspective on citizen participation and research. *American Journal of Community Psychology, 18,* 159–162.

Burlew, A. K. (2003). Research with ethnic minorities: Conceptual, methodological, and analytical issues. In G. Bernal, J. Trimble, A. K. Burlew, & F. Leong (Eds.), *Handbook of racial and ethnic minority psychology* (pp. 179–197). Thousand Oaks, CA: Sage.

Burman, E. (1997). Minding the gap: Positivism, psychology, and the politics of qualitative methods. *Journal of Social Issues, 53,* 785–802.

Buss, A. (1995). *Personality: Temperament, social behavior, and the self.* Boston: Allyn & Bacon.

Butler, J. (1992). Of kindred minds: The ties that bind. In M. Orlandi (Ed.), *Cultural competence for evaluators* (pp. 23–54). Rockville, MD: U. S. Department of Health and Human Services, Office for Substance Abuse Prevention.

Butterfoss, F., Goodman, R., & Wandersman, A. (2001). Citizen participation and health: Toward a psychology of improving health through individual, organizational and community involvement. In A. Baum, T. Revenson, & J. Singer (Eds.), *Handbook of health psychology.* Mahwah, NJ: Erlbaum.

Bybee, D. & Sullivan, C. (2002). The process through which an advocacy intervention resulted in positive change for battered women over time. *American Journal of Community Psychology, 30,* 103–132.

Caldwell, C., Kohn-Wood, L., Schmeelk-Cone, K., Chavous, T., & Zimmerman, M. (2004). Racial discrimination and racial identity as risk or protective factors for violent behaviors in African American young adults. *American Journal of Community Psychology, 33,* 91–106.

Campbell, R. (2002). *Emotionally involved: The impact of researching rape.* New York: Routledge.

Campbell, R., Dorey, H. Naegeli, M., Grubstein, L., Bennett, K., Bonter, F., Smith, P., Grzywacz, J., Baker, P. & Davidson, W. (2004). An empowerment evaluation model for sexual assault programs:

empirical evidence of effectiveness. *American Journal of Community Psychology, 34,* 251–262.

Campbell, R., & Salem, D. (1999). Concept mapping as a feminist research method: Examining the community response to rape. *Psychology of Women Quarterly, 23,* 67–91.

Campbell, R., Sefl, T., Wasco, S., & Ahrens, C. (2004). Doing community research without a community: Creating safe space for rape survivors. *American Journal of Community Psychology, 33,* 253–260.

Campbell, R., & Wasco, S. (2000). Feminist approaches to social science: Epistemological and methodological tenets. *American Journal of Community Psychology, 28,* 773–792.

Canning, S. S. (1999, Winter). Stretching Procrusteus: True confessions on the road to cultural competence in community research and action. *The Community Psychologist, 32,* 30–32.

Caplan, G. (Ed.). (1961). *Prevention of mental disorders in children.* New York: Basic Books.

Caplan, G. (1964). *Principles of preventive psychiatry.* New York: Basic Books.

Caplan, G. (Ed.). (1974). *Support systems and community mental health.* New York: Human Sciences Press.

Caplan, R., Vinokur, A., & Price, R. (1997). From job loss to reemployment: Field experiments in prevention-focused coping. In G. Albee & T. Gullotta (Eds.), *Primary prevention works* (pp. 341–379). Thousand Oaks, CA: Sage.

Carli, L. (1999). Gender, interpersonal power, and social influence. *Journal of Social Issues, 55,* 81–100.

Carli, L. (2003). Gender and social influence. *Journal of Social Issues, 57,* 725–742.

Carnegie Corporation of New York. (1994). *Starting points: Meeting the needs of our youngest children.* New York: Author.

Cartledge, G., & Milburn, J. (Eds.). (1989). *Teaching social skills to children.* New York: Pergamon Press.

Catalano, R.F., Berglund, M. L., Ryan, J. A., Lonczak, H. S., & Hawkins, J. D. (2002). Positive youth development in the United States: Research findings on evaluations of positive youth development programs. *Prevention & Treatment, 5,* Article 15. Retrieved August 1, 2002, from http://journals.apa.org/prevention/volume5/pre0050015a.html

Caughey, M. O., O'Campo, P., & Brodsky, A. (1999). Neighborhoods, families and children: Implications for policy and practice. *Journal of Community Psychology, 27,* 615–633.

Center for Mental Health Services. (2000). *Training manual for mental health and human services workers in major disasters* (2nd ed.). (No. 90-538). Washington, DC: D. J. DeWolf.

Center for Mental Health Services, National Mental Health Information Center. (n.d.). *Emergency mental health and traumatic stress: Crisis counseling training and assistance.* Retrieved October 5, 2005 from http://www.mentalhealth.samhsa.gov/cmhs/EmergencyServices/progguide.asp *Hurricane and other disaster relief information: Disaster relief and mental health resources from CMHS.* Retrieved October 5, 2005 from http://www.mentalhealth.samhsa.gov/cmhs/katrina/

Centers for Disease Control and Prevention. (2003). *HIV/AIDS Surveillance Report, 13* (No. 2), 1–44. Retrieved from: http://www.cdc.gov/hiv/stats/hasrlink/htm.

Centers for Disease Control and Prevention (n.d.). *Disaster mental health resources.* Retrieved October 5, 2005 from http://www.bt.cdc.gov/mentalhealth/

Chang, T., Yeh, C., & Krumboltz, J. (2001). Process and outcome evaluation of an on-line support group for Asian American male college students. *Journal of Counseling Psychology, 48,* 319–329.

Chataway, C. (1997). An examination of the constraints on mutual inquiry in a participatory action research project. *Journal of Social Issues, 53,* 747–766.

Chavis, D. M. (1993). A future for community psychology practice. *American Journal of Community Psychology, 21,* 171–184.

Chavis, D. (2001). The paradoxes and promise of community coalitions. *American Journal of Community Psychology, 29,* 309–320.

Chavis, D. M., Hogge, J., McMillan, D. W., & Wandersman, A. (1986). Sense of community through Brunswik's lens: A first look. *Journal of Community Psychology, 14,* 24–40.

Chavis, D. M., & Pretty, G. M. H. (Eds.). (1999). Sense of community II [Special issue]. *Journal of Community Psychology, 27* (6).

Chavis, D. M., Stucky, P., & Wandersman, A. (1983). Returning basic research to the community:

A relationship between scientist and citizen. *American Psychologist, 38,* 424–434.

Chavis, D. M., & Wandersman, A. (1990). Sense of community in the urban environment: A catalyst for participation and community development. *American Journal of Community Psychology, 18,* 83–116. Reprinted in T. Revenson, A. D'Augelli, S. E. French, D. Hughes, D. Livert, E. Seidman, M. Shinn, & H. Yoshikawa (Eds.), (2002), *A quarter century of community psychology* (pp. 265–292). New York: Kluwer Academic/Plenum.

Chelimsky, E. (1997). The coming transformation in evaluation. In E. Chilemsky & W. Shadish (Eds.), *Evaluation for the 21st century: A handbook.* Thousand Oaks, CA: Sage.

Chen, S.-P. C., Telleen, S., & Chen E. H. (1995). Family and community support of urban pregnant students: Support person, function and parity. *Journal of Community Psychology, 23,* 28–33.

Cherniss, C. (2002). Emotional intelligence and the good community. *American Journal of Community Psychology, 30,* 1–11.

Cherniss, C., & Deegan, G. (2000). The creation of alternative settings. In J. Rappaport & E. Seidman (Eds.), *Handbook of community psychology* (pp. 359–378). New York: Kluwer/Plenum.

Cherniss, C., & Goleman, D. (Eds.) (2001). *The emotionally intelligent workplace.* San Francisco: Jossey-Bass.

Cherry, F., & Borshuk, C. (1998). Social action research and the Commission on Community Interrelations. *Journal of Social Issues, 54,* 119–142.

Chesir-Teran, D. (2003). Conceptualizing and assessing heterosexism in high schools: A setting-level approach. *American Journal of Community Psychology, 31,* 267–280.

Chinman, M., Imm, P., & Wandersman, A. (2004). *Getting to outcomes 2004: Promoting accountability through methods and tools for planning, implementation, and evaluation.* Santa Monica, CA: RAND Corporation. Available at http://www.rand.org/publications/TR/TR101/

Chinman, M., Kloos, B., O'Connell, M. & Davidson, L. (2002). Service providers' views of psychiatric mutual help groups. *Journal of Community Psychology, 30,* 349–366.

Chipuer, H. M., & Pretty, G. M. H. (1999). A review of the Sense of Community Index: Current uses, factor structure, reliability, and further development. *Journal of Community Psychology, 27,* 643–658.

Christenson, S, & Havsy, L. (2004). Family-school-peer relationships: The significance for social, emotional, and academic learning. In J. E. Zins, R. P. Weissberg, M. C. Wang, & H. J. Walberg, H. J. (Eds.), *Building academic success on social and emotional learning: What does the research say?* (pp. 59–75). New York: Teachers College Press.

Chun, K., & Akutsu, P. (2003). Acculturation among ethnic minority families. In K. Chun, P. Organista, & G. Marin (Eds.), *Acculturation: Advances in theory, measurement and applied research* (pp. 95–120). Washington, DC: American Psychological Association.

Chun, K., Organista, P., & Marin, G. (Eds.). (2003). *Acculturation: Advances in theory, measurement and applied research.* Washington, DC: American Psychological Association.

Chung, H., & Elias, M. J. (1996). Patterns of adolescent involvement in problem behaviors: Relationship to self-efficacy, social competence, and life events. *American Journal of Community Psychology, 24,* 771–810.

Cichetti, D. (2004). An odyssey of discovery: Lessons learned through three decades of research on child maltreatment. *American Psychologist, 59,* 731–741.

Cicchetti, D., Rappaport, J., Sandler, I., & Weissberg, R. P. (Eds.). (2000). *The promotion of wellness in children and adolescents.* Washington, DC: Child Welfare League of America.

Clark, K. (1953). Desegregation: An appraisal of the evidence. *Journal of Social Issues, 9* (4), 2–76.

Clark, K., Chein, I., & Cook, S. (1952). The effects of segregation and the consequences of desegregation. [Appendix to the appellants' briefs in *Brown v. Board of Education of Topeka, Kansas; Briggs v. Elliot;* and *Davis v. Prince Edward County, Virginia.* Signed by 29 other social scientists. September 22, 1952.] Reprinted in *American Psychologist, 59,* 495–501 (2004).

Coates, T. (2004). A plan for the next generation of HIV prevention research: Seven key policy investigative challenges. *American Psychologist, 59,* 747–757.

Cohen, L. H., Hettler, T. R., & Park, C. L. (1997). Social support, personality, and life stress adjustment. In G. Pierce, B. Lakey, I. G. Sarason, & B. R. Sarason (Eds.), *Sourcebook of social support and personality* (pp. 215–228). New York: Plenum.

Cohen, S. (2004). Social relationships and health. *American Psychologist, 59,* 676–684.

Cohen S., Underwood, L., & Gottlieb, B. (2000). *Social support measurement and intervention.* New York: Oxford University Press.

Colby, A., & Damon, W. (1992). *Some do care: Contemporary lives of moral commitment.* New York: Free Press.

Coleman-Wallace, D., Lee, J., Montgomery, S., Blix, G., & Wang, D. (1999). Evaluation of developmentally appropriate programs for adolescent tobacco cessation. *Journal of School Health, 69* (3), 314–319.

Collaborative for Academic, Social, and Emotional Learning [CASEL]. (2003). *Safe and sound: An educational leader's guide to evidence-based social and emotional learning programs.* Retrieved October 1, 2002, from http://www.casel.org

Collier-Thomas, B., & Franklin, V. P. (Eds.) (2001). *Sisters in the struggle: African-American women in the civil rights-Black power movement.* New York: NYU Press.

Comas-Diaz, L., Lykes, M. B., & Alarcon, R. (1998). Ethnic conflict and the psychology of liberation in Guatemala, Peru, and Puerto Rico. *American Psychologist, 53,* 778–792.

Comer, J. P. (1988). Educating poor minority children. *Scientific American, 259,* 42–48.

Comer, J. P. (1992). Video segment in *The world of abnormal psychology: An ounce of prevention* (T. Levine, Producer). New York: A. H. Perlmutter. (Available from Annenberg/CPB Collection, 1–800–LEARNER).

Comer, J. P. (2004). *Leave no child behind: Preparing today's youth for tomorrow's world.* New Haven, CT: Yale University Press.

Comer, J. P., Haynes, N., Joyner, E., & Ben-Avie, M. (1996). *Rallying the whole village: The Comer process for reforming education.* New York: Teachers College Press.

Commins, W., & Elias, M. J. (1991). Institutionalization of mental health programs in organizational contexts: The case of elementary schools. *Journal of Community Psychology, 19,* 207–220.

Community Tool Box. (2005). Retrieved July 28, 2005, from http://ctb.ku.edu

Conduct Problems Prevention Research Group. (1999). Initial impact of the Fast Track prevention trial for conduct problems: II. Classroom effects. *Journal of Consulting and Clinical Psychology, 67,* 648–657.

Conger, R., Conger, K., Matthews, L., & Elder, G. (1999). Pathways of economic influence on adolescent adjustment. *American Journal of Community Psychology, 27,* 519–541.

Conway, P., Evans, S., & Prilleltensky, I. (2003, Fall). Psychologists acting with conscience together (Psy-ACT): A global coalition for justice and well-being. *The Community Psychologist, 36,* 30–31.

Cook, T. D., Farah-Naaz, H., Phillips, M., Stettersten, R. A., Shagle, S. C., & Degirmencioglu, S. M. (1999). Comer's school development program in Prince George's County, Maryland: A theory-based evaluation. *American Educational Research Journal, 36,* 543–597.

Cook, T. D., Murphy, R. F., & Hunt, H. D. (2000). Comer's School Development Program in Chicago: A theory-based evaluation. *American Educational Research Journal, 37,* 535–597.

Cortes, D. E., Rogler, L. H., & Malgady, R. G. (1994). Biculturality among Puerto Rican adults in the United States. *American Journal of Community Psychology, 22,* 707–721.

Cosgrove, L. & McHugh, M. (2000). Speaking for ourselves: Feminist methods and community psychology. *American Journal of Community Psychology, 28,* 815–838.

Cottrell, L. S. (1976). The competent community. In B. H. Kaplan, R. N. Wilson, & A. H. Leighton (Eds.), *Further explorations in social psychiatry* (pp. 195–209). New York: Basic Books.

Coudroglou, A. (1996). Violence as a social mutation. *American Journal of Orthopsychiatry, 66,* 323–328.

Coulton, C., Korbin, J., Chan, T. & Su, M. (2001). Mapping residents' perceptions of neighborhood boundaries: A methodological note. *American Journal of Community Psychology, 29,* 371–383.

Cousins, J. B., & Whitmore, E. (1998). Framing participatory evaluation. *New Directions for Evaluation, 80,* 5–23.

Cowen, E. L. (1973). Social and community interventions. *Annual Review of Psychology, 24,* 423–472.

Cowen, E. L. (1977). Baby steps toward primary prevention. *American Journal of Community Psychology, 5,* 1–22.

Cowen, E. L. (1991). In pursuit of wellness. *American Psychologist, 46,* 404–408.

Cowen, E. L. (1994). The enhancement of psychological wellness: Challenges and opportunities. *American Journal of Community Psychology, 22,* 149–180. Reprinted in T. Revenson, A. D'Augelli, S. E. French, D. Hughes, D. Livert, E. Seidman, M. Shinn, & H. Yoshikawa (Eds.), (2002), *A quarter century of community psychology* (pp. 445–475). New York: Kluwer Academic/Plenum.

Cowen, E. L. (2000a). Community psychology and routes to psychological wellness. In J. Rappaport & E. Seidman (Eds.), *Handbook of community psychology* (pp. 79–100). New York: Kluwer/Plenum.

Cowen, E. L. (2000b). Prevention, wellness enhancement, Y2K and thereafter. *Journal of Primary Prevention, 21* (1), 15–19.

Cowen, E. L. (2000c). Psychological wellness: Some hopes for the future. In D. Cicchetti, J. Rappaport, I. N. Sandler, & R. P. Weissberg (Eds.), *The promotion of wellness in children and adolescents* (pp. 477–503). Washington, DC: Child Welfare League of America Press.

Cowen, E. L., Hightower, A. D., Pedro-Carroll, J., Work, W., Wyman, P., & Haffey, W. (1996). *School-based prevention for children at risk: The Primary Mental Health Project.* Washington, DC: American Psychological Association.

Cowen, E. L., & Kilmer, R. (2002). "Positive psychology": Some plusses and some open issues. *Journal of Community Psychology, 30,* 449–460.

Cowen, E. L., McKim, B. J., & Weissberg, R. P. (1981). Bartenders as informal, interpersonal help-agents. *American Journal of Community Psychology, 9,* 715–729.

Cowen, E. L., Pedersen, A., Babigian, H., Izzo, L. D., & Trost, M. A. (1973). Long-term follow-up of early detected vulnerable children. *Journal of Consulting and Clinical Psychology, 41,* 438–446.

Coyne, J., Ellard, J., & Smith, D. (1990). Social support, interdependence, and the dilemmas of helping. In B. R. Sarason, I. G. Sarason, & G. Pierce (Eds.), *Social support: An interactional view* (pp. 129–148). New York: Wiley.

Craigslist Online Community (2005, May). Retrieved July 24, 2005 from http://www.craigslist.org

Crosby, F., Iyer, A., Clayton, S., & Downing, R. (2003). Affirmative action: Psychological data and the policy debates. *American Psychologist, 58,* 93–115.

Dalton, D. (1993). *Mahatma Gandhi: Nonviolent power in action.* New York: Columbia University Press.

Dalton, J. H., Elias, M. J., & Wandersman, A. (2001). *Community psychology: Linking individuals and communities* (1st ed.). Belmont, CA: Wadsworth/Thomson.

Danieli, Y., Engdahl, B., & Schlenger, W. (2004). The psychosocial aftermath of terrorism. In F. Moghaddam & A. J. Marsella, (Eds.), *Understanding terrorism: Psychosocial roots, consequences, and interventions* (pp. 223–246). Washington, DC: American Psychological Association.

D'Augelli, A. (2003). Coming out in community psychology: Personal narrative and disciplinary change. *American Journal of Community Psychology, 31,* 343–354.

Davidson, W. B., & Cotter, P. (1989). Sense of community and political participation. *Journal of Community Psychology, 17,* 119–125.

Davidson, W. B., & Cotter, P. (1993). Psychological sense of community and support for public school taxes. *American Journal of Community Psychology, 21,* 59–66.

Davino, K., Wandersman, A., & Goodman, R. M. (1995). Cherokee County mentoring program evaluation interim report. Unpublished manuscript, University of South Carolina.

Davison, K., Pennebaker, J. & Dickerson, S. (2000). Who talks? The social psychology of illness support groups. *American Psychologist, 55,* 205–217.

Davison, M., Seo, Y., Davenport, Jr., E., Butterbaugh, D., & Davison, J. (2004). When do children fall behind? What can be done? *Phi Delta Kappan, 85* (10), 752–761.

DeBose, B. (2005, September 10). Blacks fault lack of local leadership. *The Washington Times* [Electronic version]. Retrieved October 5, 2005, from http://washingtontimes.com/20050909-113107-31804.htm

Degirmencioglu, S. M. (2003, Fall). Action research makes psychology more useful and more fun. *The Community Psychologist, 36,* 27–29.

Denzin, N., & Lincoln, Y. (Eds.). (1994). *Handbook of qualitative research.* Thousand Oaks, CA: Sage.

Dewey, J. (1940). Creative democracy—the task before us. In S. Ratner (Ed.), *The philosopher of the common man: Essays in honor of John Dewey to celebrate his eightieth birthday* (pp. 220–228). New York: Greenwood Press.

Dilworth, J. E., Mokrue, K., & Elias, M. J. (2002). The efficacy of a video-based teamwork-building series with urban elementary school students: A pilot investigation. *Journal of School Psychology, 40* (4), 329–346.

Disastersearch.org (n.d.). *Disastersearch: Home.* Retrieved October 20, 2005 from http://www/disastersearch.org

Dobson, C. & Vancouver Citizen's Committee. (2005). The citizen's handbook. Retrieved July 28, 2005, from http://www.vcn.bc.ca/citizens-handbook/welcome.html

Dockett, K. H. (1999, June). Engaged Buddhism and community psychology: Partners in social change. In J. Kress (Chair), Bringing together community psychology and religion/spirituality towards an action research agenda for SCRA. Symposium conducted at the Biennial Meeting of the Society for Community Research and Action, New Haven, CT.

Dohrenwend, B. S. (1978). Social stress and community psychology. *American Journal of Community Psychology, 6,* 1–14. Reprinted in T. Revenson, A. D'Augelli, S. E. French, D. Hughes, D. Livert, E. Seidman, M. Shinn, & H. Yoshikawa (Eds.), (2002), *A quarter century of community psychology* (pp. 103–117). New York: Kluwer Academic/Plenum.

Dokecki, P. R., Newbrough, J. R., & O'Gorman, R. T. (2001). Toward a community-oriented action research framework for spirituality: Community psychological and theological perspectives. *Journal of Community Psychology, 29,* 497–518.

Dollard, J. (1937). *Caste and class in a Southern town.* Garden City, NY: Doubleday.

Dooley, D., & Catalano, R. (2003). Underemployment and its social costs: New research directions [Special issue]. *American Journal of Community Psychology, 32* (1).

Drew, N., Bishop, B., & Syme, G. (2002). Justice and local community change: Towards a substantive theory of justice. *Journal of Community Psychology, 30,* 623–634.

DuBois, D. L., Holloway, B. E., Valentine, J. C., & Cooper, H. (2002). Effectiveness of mentoring programs for youth: A meta-analytic review. *American Journal of Community Psychology, 30,* 157–197.

DuBois, W. E. B. (1986). *The souls of black folk.* Republished in N. Huggins (Ed.), *W. E. B. DuBois: Writings* (pp. 357–548). New York: Library of America. (Original work published 1903)

Dudgeon, P., Mallard, J., Oxenham, D., & Fielder, J. (2002). Contemporary Aboriginal perceptions of community. In A. Fisher, C. Sonn, & B. Bishop (Eds.), *Psychological sense of community: Research, applications and implications* (pp. 247–269). New York: Kluwer/Plenum.

Dudley Street Neighborhood Initiative (Boston, MA). (n.d.) DSNI historic timeline. Retrieved September 24, 2004, from http://www.dsni.org/

Duffell, J., Beland, K., & Frey, K. (2006). The Second Step Program: Social and emotional skills for violence prevention. In M. J. Elias & H. Arnold, (Eds.), *The educator's guide to emotional intelligence and academic achievement: Social-emotional learning in the classroom* (pp. 161–174). Thousand Oaks, CA: Corwin Press.

Duffy, K. G. & Wong, F. (2003). *Community psychology* (3rd ed.). Boston, MA: Allyn & Bacon.

Dugan, M. A. (1996). Participatory and empowerment evaluation: Lessons learned in training and technical assistance. In D. Fetterman, S., Kaftarian & A. Wandersman (Eds.), *Empowerment evaluation: Knowledge and tools for self-assessment and accountability* (pp. 277–303). Thousand Oaks, CA: Sage.

Dumka, L., Gonzales, N., Wood, J., & Formoso, D. (1998). Using qualitative methods to develop contextually relevant measures and preventive interventions: An illustration. *American Journal of Community Psychology, 26,* 605–637.

Duncan, T., Duncan, S., Okut, H., Strycker, L., & Hix-Small, H. (2003). A multilevel contextual model of neighborhood collective efficacy. *American Journal of Community Psychology, 32,* 245–252.

Dunham, P. J., Hursham, A., Litwin, E., Gusella, J., Ellsworth, C., & Dodd, P. W. D. (1998). Computer-mediated social support: Single young mothers as a model system. *American Journal of Community Psychology, 26,* 281–306.

Durlak, J. A., & Wells, A. M.. (1997). Primary prevention mental health programs for children and adolescents: A meta-analytic review. *American Journal of Community Psychology, 25,* 115–152.

Durlak, J., & Wells, A. (1998). Evaluation of indicated preventive intervention (secondary prevention) mental health programs for children and adolescents. *American Journal of Community Psychology, 26,* 775–802.

Edgerton, J. W. (2000). [Untitled videotape interview]. In J. G. Kelly (Ed.), *The history of community psychology: A video presentation of context and exemplars.* Chicago: Society for Community Research and Action.

Edgerton, J. W. (2001). The community is it! *American Journal of Community Psychology, 29,* 87–97.

Edwards, R., Jumper-Thurman, P., Plested, B., Oetting, E., & Swanson, L. (2000). Community readiness: research to practice. *Journal of Community Psychology, 28,* 291–307.

Ehrenreich, B. (2001). *Nickel and dimed: On (not) getting by in America.* New York: Henry Holt.

Elias, M. J. (1987). Establishing enduring prevention programs: Advancing the legacy of Swampscott. *American Journal of Community Psychology, 15,* 539–553.

Elias, M. J. (Ed.). (1993). *Social decision making and life skills development: Guidelines for middle school educators.* New Brunswick, NJ: Center for Applied Psychology, Rutgers University.

Elias, M. J. (1994). Capturing excellence in applied settings: A participant conceptualizer and praxis explicator role for community psychologists. *American Journal of Community Psychology, 22,* 293–318.

Elias, M. J. (1995). Primary prevention as health and social competence promotion. *Journal of Primary Prevention, 16,* 5–24.

Elias, M. J. (2002). Education's 9/11 report card. *Education Week, 22* (1), 47.

Elias, M. J. (2003). *Academic and social-emotional learning.* (Educational Practices Booklet #11.) Geneva: International Academy of Education and the International Bureau of Education (UNESCO).

Elias, M. J. (2004). The connection between social-emotional learning and learning disabilities: Implications for intervention. *Learning Disability Quarterly, 27* (1), 53–63.

Elias, M. J., & Bruene-Butler, L. (2005a). *Social Decision Making/Social Problem Solving: A curriculum for academic, social, and emotional learning Grades 4–5.* Champaign, IL: Research Press.

Elias, M. J., & Bruene-Butler, L. (2005b). *Social Decision Making/Social Problem Solving for middle school students: Skills and activities for academic, social, and emotional success.* Champaign, IL: Research Press.

Elias, M. J., Bryan, K., Patrikakou, E., & Weissberg, R. P. (2003). Challenges in creating effective home-school partnerships in adolescence: Promising paths for collaboration. *The School Community Journal, 13* (1), 133–153.

Elias, M. J., & Clabby, J. (1992). *Building social problem-solving skills: Guidelines from a school-based program.* San Francisco: Jossey-Bass.

Elias, M. J., & Cohen, J. (1999). *Lessons for life: How smart schools build social, emotional, and academic intelligence.* Bloomington, IN: National Education Service/ National Center for Innovation and Education (Available online at www.communitiesofhope. org)

Elias, M. J., Gager, P., & Hancock, M. (1993). Prevention and social competence programs in use in New Jersey public schools: Findings from a statewide survey (Working paper no. 3, School Intervention Implementation Study). New Brunswick, NJ: Rutgers University.

Elias, M. J., Gara, M. A., Schuyler, T. F., Branden-Muller, L. R., & Sayette, M. A. (1991). The promotion of social competence: Longitudinal study of a preventive school-based program. *American Journal of Orthopsychiatry, 61,* 409–417.

Elias, M. J., Gara, M. A., Ubriaco, M., Rothbaum, P., Clabby, J., & Schuyler, T. F. (1986). Impact of preventive social-problem-solving intervention on children's coping with middle school stressors. *American Journal of Community Psychology, 14,* 259–275.

Elias, M. J., & Kamarinos, P. (2003, August). *Sustainability of school-based preventive social-emotional programs: A model site study.* Presentation at the meeting of the American Psychological Association, Toronto, Canada, August 8.

Elias, M. J., & Schwab, Y. (2004). What about parental involvement in parenting? The case for home-focused school-parent partnerships. *Education Week, 24* (8), 39, 41.

Elias, M. J., & Tobias, S. E. (1996). *Social problem-solving interventions in the schools.* New York: Guilford.

Elias, M. J., Zins, J., Weissberg, R. P., Frey, K., Greenberg, M., Haynes, N., Kessler, R., Schwab-Stone, M., & Shriver, T. (1997). *Promoting social and emotional learning: Guidelines for educators.* Alexandria, VA: Association for Supervision and Curriculum Development.

Ellickson, P., & Bell, R. M. (1990). Drug prevention in junior high: A multi-site longitudinal test. *Science, 247,* 1299–1305.

Enett, S., Rosenbaum, D., Flewelling, R., Bieler, G., Ringwalt, C., & Bailey, S. (1994). Long-term evaluation of drug abuse resistance education. *Addictive Behaviors, 19,* 113–125.

Engstrom, M., Jason, L. A., Townsend, S., Pokorny, S., & Curie, C. (2002). Community readiness for prevention: Applying stage theory to multi-community interventions. *Journal of Prevention and Intervention in the Community, 24* (1), 29–46.

Epstein, J., Griffin, K., & Botvin, G. (2000). Role of general and specific competence skills in protecting inner-city youth from alcohol use. *Journal of Studies on Alcohol, 61,* 379–386.

Erikson, E. (1950). *Childhood and society.* New York: Norton.

Erikson, E. (1982). *The life cycle completed: A review.* New York: Norton.

Evans, G. W. (2004). The environment of childhood poverty. *American Psychologist, 59,* 77–92.

Everhart, K., & Wandersman, A. (2000). Applying comprehensive quality programming and empowerment evaluation to reduce implementation barriers. *Journal of Educational and Psychological Consultation, 11* (2), 177–191.

Eyler, J. (2002). Reflection: Linking service and learning–Linking students and communities. *Journal of Social Issues, 58,* 517–534.

Fairweather, G. W. (1967). *Methods for experimental social innovation.* New York: Wiley.

Fairweather, G. W. (1979). Experimental development and dissemination of an alternative to psychiatric hospitalization. In R. Munoz, L. Snowden, & J. G. Kelly (Eds.), *Social and psychological research in community settings* (pp. 305–342). San Francisco: Jossey-Bass.

Fairweather, G. W. (1994). [Untitled videotape interview]. In J. G. Kelly (Ed.), *The history of community psychology: A video presentation of context and exemplars.* Chicago, IL: Society for Community Research and Action.

Fairweather, G. W., Sanders, D., Cressler, D., & Maynard, H. (1969). *Community life for the mentally ill: An alternative to institutional care.* Chicago: Aldine.

Fanon, F. (1963). *The wretched of the earth.* New York: Grove Press.

Farrell, S., Aubry, T., & Coulombe, D. (2004). Neighborhoods and neighbors: Do they contribute to personal well-being? *Journal of Community Psychology, 32,* 9–26.

Fawcett, S. B., Paine-Andrews, A., Francisco, V., Schulz, J., Richter, K., Lewis, R., Williams, E., Harris, K., Berkley, J., Fisher, J., & Lopez, C. (1995). Using empowerment theory in collaborative partnerships for community health and development. *American Journal of Community Psychology, 23,* 677–698.

Fawcett, S. B., White, G., Balcazar, F., Suarez-Balcazar, Y., Mathews, R., Paine-Andrews, A., Seekins, T., & Smith, J. (1994). A contextual-behavioral model of empowerment: Case studies involving people with physical disabilities. *American Journal of Community Psychology, 22,* 471–496.

Feinberg, M., Greenberg, M., & Osgood, D. W. (2004). Readiness, functioning and perceived effectiveness in community prevention coalitions: A study of Communities That Care. *American Journal of Community Psychology, 33,* 163–176.

Felner, R., & Adan, A. (1988). The School Transition Environment Project: An ecological intervention and evaluation. In R. Price, E. Cowen, R. Lorion, & J. Ramos-McKay (Eds.), *Fourteen ounces of prevention* (pp. 111–122). Washington, DC: American Psychological Association.

Felner, R. D., Felner, T. Y., & Silverman, M. (2000). Prevention in mental health and social intervention: Conceptual and methodological issues in the evolution of the science and practice of prevention. In J. Rappaport & E. Seidman (Eds.), *Handbook of community psychology* (pp. 9–42). New York: Kluwer/Plenum.

Felsinger, J., & Klein, D. (1957). A training program for clinical psychologists in community mental health theory and practice. In C. Strother (Ed.), *Psychology and mental health* (pp. 146–150). Washington, DC: American Psychological Association.

Felton, B., & Berry, C. (1992). Groups as social network members: Overlooked sources of social support. *American Journal of Community Psychology, 20,* 253–262.

Felton, B., & Shinn, M. (1992). Social integration and social support: Moving "social support" beyond the individual level. *Journal of Community Psychology, 20,* 103–115.

Felton, C. (2004). Lessons learned since September 11th 2001 concerning the mental health impact of terrorism, appropriate response strategies and future preparedness. *Psychiatry, 67,* 147–152.

Ferrari, J., Jason, L., Olson, B., Davis, M., & Alvarez, J. (2002). Sense of community among Oxford House residents recovering from substance abuse: Making a house a home. In A. Fisher, C. Sonn, & B. Bishop (Eds.), *Psychological sense of community: Research, applications, and implications* (pp. 109–122). New York: Kluwer Academic/ Plenum.

Fetterman, D. (1994). Steps of empowerment evaluation: From California to Cape Town. *Evaluation and Program Planning, 17,* 305–313.

Fetterman, D. (1996). Empowerment evaluation: An introduction to theory and practice. In D. Fetterman, S. Kaftarian, & A. Wandersman (Eds.), *Empowerment evaluation: Knowledge and tools for self-assessment and accountability* (pp. 3–46). Thousand Oaks, CA: Sage.

Fetterman, D. (1998). *Ethnography: Step by step* (2nd ed.). Thousand Oaks, CA: Sage.

Fetterman, D. (2001). *Foundations of empowerment evaluation.* Thousand Oaks, CA: Sage.

Fetterman, D. (2002). Empowerment evaluation: Building communities of practice and a culture of learning. *American Journal of Community Psychology, 30,* 89–102.

Fetterman, D. M. (2003). Interim report on districts in Phase III: Empowerment evaluation report to the State Board of Education. Stanford, CA: Stanford University. Available online at http://homepage.mac.com/profdavidf

Fetterman, D. M. (2005). Empowerment evaluation: from the digital divide to academic distress. In D. Fetterman & and A. Wandersman, (Eds.), *Empowerment evaluation principles in practice* (pp. 107–121). New York: Guilford.

Fetterman, D., Kaftarian, S., & Wandersman, A. (Eds.). (1996). *Empowerment evaluation: Knowledge and tools for self-assessment and accountability.* Thousand Oaks, CA: Sage.

Fetterman, D. & Wandersman, A. (Eds.). (2005). *Empowerment Evaluation Principles in Practice.* New York: Guilford Press.

Fiala, W., Bjorck, J. & Gorsuch, R. (2002). The Religious Support Scale: Construction, validation, and cross-validation. *American Journal of Community Psychology, 30,* 761–786.

Fine, M. & Burns, A. (2003). Class notes: Toward a critical psychology of class and schooling. *Journal of Social Issues, 59,* 841–860.

Fischetti, M. (2001, October). Drowning New Orleans. *Scientific American* [Electronic version]. Retrieved October 10, 2005 from http://www.sciam.com/article.cfm?articleID=00060286-CB58-1315-8B5883414B7F0000

Fisher, A. & Sonn, C. (2002). Psychological sense of community in Australia and the challenges of change. *Journal of Communty Psychology, 30,* 597–609.

Fisher, A., Sonn, C., & Bishop, B. (Eds.). (2002). *Psychological sense of community: Research, applications and implications.* New York: Kluwer/Plenum.

Fisher, D., Imm, P., Chinaman, M., & Wandersman, A. (2006). *Getting To Outcomes with Developmental Assets: Ten Steps to Measuring Success in Youth Programs and Communities.* Minneapolis: Search Institute.

Fisher, P. & Ball, T. (2003). Tribal participatory research: Mechanisms of a collaborative model. *American Journal of Community Psychology, 32,* 207–217.

Fitzgerald, F. S. (1995). *The great Gatsby.* New York: Simon & Schuster. (Original work published 1925)

Flad, H. (2003, April 30). *Sense of places, senses of place.* Spring convocation address, Vassar College, Poughkeepsie, NY.

Flavell, J. H. (1963). *The developmental psychology of Jean Piaget.* New York: Van Nostrand.

Fleishman, J., Sherbourne, C., Cleary, P., Wu, A., Crystal, S., & Hays, R. (2003). Patterns of coping among persons with HIV infection: configurations, correlates, and change. *American Journal of Community Psychology, 32,* 187–204.

Florin, P., Chavis, D., Wandersman, A., & Rich, R. (1992). A systems approach to understanding and enhancing grassroots organizations: The Block Booster Project. In R. Levine & H. Fitzgerald (Eds.), *Analysis of dynamic psychological systems: Methods and applications,* Vol. 2 (pp. 215–243). New York: Plenum.

Florin, P., & Wandersman, A. (1984). Cognitive social learning and participation in community development. *American Journal of Community Psychology, 12,* 689–708.

Fo, W. S., & O'Donnell, C. R. (1974). The Buddy System: Relationship and contingency conditions in a community intervention program for youth with nonprofessionals as behavior change agents. *Journal of Consulting and Clinical Psychology, 42,* 163–169.

Folayemi, B. (2001). Case story #1: Building the grassroots coalition. *American Journal of Community Psychology, 29,* 193–197.

Folkman, S. & Moskowitz, J. (2004). Coping: Promises and pitfalls. *Annual Review of Psychology, 55,* 745–774.

Fondacaro, M., & Weinberg, D. (2002). Concepts of social justice in community psychology: Toward a social ecological epistemology. *American Journal of Community Psychology, 30,* 473–492.

Foster-Fishman, P., Berkowitz, S., Lounsbury, D., Jacobson, S., & Allen, N. (2001). Building collaborative capacity in community coalitions: A review and integrative framework. *American Journal of Community Psychology, 29,* 241–262.

Fowers, B., & Richardson, F. (1996). Why is multiculturalism good? *American Psychologist, 51,* 609–621.

Frable, D. (1997). Gender, racial, ethnic, sexual and class identities. *Annual Review of Psychology, 48,* 139–162.

Frankl, V. (1984). *Man's search for meaning: An introduction to logotherapy* (3rd ed.). New York: Simon & Schuster. (Original work published 1959.)

Freire, P. (1993). *Pedagogy of the oppressed (Rev. ed.).* New York: Continuum. (Original work published 1970.)

French, J. R. P., & Raven, B. (1959). The bases of social power. In D. Cartwright, (Ed.), *Studies in social power* (pp. 150–167). Ann Arbor, MI: Institute for Social Research.

Friedman, T. (2000). *The Lexus and the olive tree.* New York: Random House.

Fryer, D., & Fagan, R. (2003). Toward a critical community psychological perspective on unemployment and mental health research. *American Journal of Community Psychology, 32,* 89–96.

Fullan, M. (1994). *Change forces: Probing the depths of educational reform.* Bristol, PA: Falmer Press.

Gager, P. J., & Elias, M. J. (1997). Implementing prevention programs in high-risk environments: Applications of the resiliency paradigm. *American Journal of Orthopsychiatry, 67,* 363–373.

Galea, S., Ahern, J., Resnick, H., Kilpatrick, D., Bucuvalas, M., Gold, J., & Vlahov, D. (2002). Psychological sequelae of the September 11 terrorist attacks in New York City. *New England Journal of Medicine, 346* (13), 982–987.

Galea, S., Vlahov, D., Resnick, H., Ahern, J., Susser, E., Gold, J., Bucuvalas, M., & Kilpatrick, D. (2003). Trends of probable post-traumatic stress disorder in New York City after the September 11th terrorist attacks. *American Journal of Epidemiology, 158,* 514–524.

Gallimore, R., Goldenberg, C., & Weisner, T. (1993). The social construction and subjective reality of activity settings: Implications for community psychology. *American Journal of Community Psychology, 21,* 537–559.

Garbarino, J., & Kostelny, K. (1992). Child maltreatment as a community problem. *Child Abuse and Neglect, 16,* 455–464.

Garcia, I., Giuliani, F. & Weisenfeld, E. (1999). Community and sense of community: The case of an urban barrio in Caracas. *Journal of Community Psychology, 27,* 727–740.

Garloch, K. (2005, September 19). Some Katrina victims face lifetime of anxiety. *Charlotte Observer,* 1E.

Garza, A. (Ed.) (2001). *Drug addiction in Mexico: Indifference or prevention.* Mexico City: ING Seguros.

Gatz, M., & Cotton, B. (1994). Age as a dimension of diversity: The experience of being old. In E. J. Trickett, R. J. Watts, & D. Birman (Eds.), *Human diversity: Perspectives on people in context* (pp. 334–355). San Francisco: Jossey-Bass.

Gaventa, J. (1980). *Power and powerlessness: Quiescence and rebellion in an Appalachian valley.* Urbana, IL: University of Illinois Press.

Gellman, M. (1997). *Always wear clean underwear. New* York: William Morrow.

Gergen, K. (1973). Social psychology as history. *Journal of Personality and Social Psychology, 26,* 309–320.

Gergen, K. (2001). Psychological science in a post-modern context. *American Psychoogist, 56,* 803–813.

Giddens, A., Duneier, M., & Appelbaum, R. (2003). *Introduction to sociology* (4th ed.). New York: Norton.

Gilens, M. (1996). Race and poverty in America: Public misperceptions and the American news media. *Public Opinion Quarterly, 60,* 515–541.

Gilliam, F., & Iyengar, S. (2000). Prime suspects: The influence of local television news on the viewing public. *American Journal of Political Science, 44,* 560–574.

Gillock, K. L., & Reyes, O. (1996). High school transition-related changes in urban minority students' academic performance and perceptions of self and school environment. *Journal of Community Psychology, 24,* 245–262.

Gist, R. (2002). What have they done to my song? Social science, social movements, and the debriefing debates. *Cognitive and Behavioral Practice, 9,* 273–279.

Glidewell, J. (1994). [Untitled videotape interview]. In J. G. Kelly (Ed.), *The history of community psychology: A video presentation of context and exemplars.* Chicago: Society for Community Research and Action.

Glidewell, J., Gildea, M., & Kaufman, M. (1973). The preventive and therapeutic effects of two school mental health programs. *American Journal of Community Psychology, 1,* 295–329.

Glover, M., Dudgeon, P., & Huygens, I. (2005). Colonization and racism. In G. Nelson & I. Prilleltensky (Eds.), *Community psychology: In pursuit of liberation and well-being* (pp. 330–347). New York: Palgrave Macmillan.

Glynn, T. J. (1986). Neighborhood and sense of community. *Journal of Community Psychology, 14,* 341–352.

Goeppinger, J., & Baglioni, A. (1985). Community competence: A positive approach to needs assessment. *American Journal of Community Psychology, 13,* 507–523.

Golann, S. & Eisdorfer, C. (Eds.). (1972). *Handbook of community mental health.* New York: Appleton-Century-Crofts.

Goldbaum, S., Craig, W., Pepler, D., & Connolly, J. (2003). In M. J. Elias & J. E. Zins (Eds.), *Bullying, peer harassment, and victimization in the schools: The next generation of prevention* (pp. 139–156). New York: Haworth.

Goldston, S. (1994). [Untitled videotape interview]. In J. G. Kelly (Ed.), *The history of community psychology: A video presentation of context and exemplars.* Chicago: Society for Community Research and Action.

Goleman, D. (1995). *Emotional intelligence.* New York: Bantam.

Goleman, D. (1998). *Working with emotional intelligence.* New York: Bantam.

Gonsiorek, J. C., & Weinrich, J. D. (1991). The definition and scope of sexual orientation. In J. C. Gonsiorek & J. D. Weinrich (Eds.), *Homosexuality: Research implications for public policy* (pp. 1–12). Newbury Park, CA: Sage.

Gonzales, N. A., Cauce, A. M., Friedman, R. J., & Mason, C. A. (1996). Family, peer, and neighborhood influences on academic achievement among African-American adolescents: One-year prospective effects. *American Journal of Community Psychology, 24,* 365–388. Reprinted in T. Revenson, A. D'Augelli, S. E. French, D. Hughes, D. Livert, E. Seidman, M. Shinn & H. Yoshikawa (Eds.), (2002), *A quarter century of community psychology* (pp. 535–556). New York: Kluwer Academic/Plenum.

Goodkind, J., & Deacon, Z. (2004). Methodological issues in conducting research with refugee women: Principles for recognizing and re-centering the multiply marginalized. *Journal of Community Psychology, 32,* 721–740.

Goodkind, J., & Foster-Fishman, P. (2002). Integrating diversity and fostering interdependence: Ecological lessons learned about refugee participation in multiethnic communities. *Journal of Community Psychology, 30,* 389–410.

Goodman, R. M., & Steckler, A. (1987). A model for the institutionalization of health promotion programs. *Family and Community Health, 11,* 63–78.

Goodman, R. M., & Wandersman, A. (1994). FORECAST: A formative approach to evaluating community coalitions and community-based initiatives. In S. Kaftarian & W. Hansen (Eds.), *Journal of*

Community Psychology Monograph Series, Center for Substance Abuse Prevention Special Issue, 6–25.

Goodstein, L., & Sandler, I. (1978). Using psychology to promote human welfare: A conceptual analysis of the role of community psychology. *American Psychologist, 33,* 882–891.

Gottlieb, B. H. (1997). *Coping with chronic stress.* New York: Plenum Press.

Gould, S. J. (1981). *The mismeasure of man.* New York: Norton.

Granovetter, M. (1973). The strength of weak ties. *American Journal of Sociology, 78,* 1360–1380.

Green, L. (2001). From research to "best practices" in other settings and populations. *American Journal of Health Behavior, 25* (3), 165–178.

Green, L., & Lewis, M. (1986). *Measurement and evaluation in health education and health promotion.* Palo Alto: Mayfield.

Greenberg, M. T., Domitrovich, C., & Bumbarger, B. (2001). The prevention of mental disorders in school-aged children: Current state of the field. *Prevention & Treatment, 4,* Article 1. Retrieved March 1, 2002 from http://journals.apa.org/prevention/volume4/pre0040001a.html

Greenberg, M. T., & Kusché, C. A. (1998). *Blueprints for violence prevention: The PATHS Project* (Vol. 10). (D. S. Elliott, Series Ed.). Boulder, CO: Institute of Behavioral Science, Regents of the University of Colorado.

Greenberg, M., Weissberg, R., O'Brien, M., Zins, J., Fredericks, L. Resnik, H., & Elias, M. (2003). Enhancing school-based prevention and youth development through coordinated social, emotional, and academic learning. *American Psychologist, 58,* 466–474.

Greenfield, P., Keller, H., Fuligni, A., & Maynard, A. (2003). Cultural pathways through universal development. *Annual Review of Psychology, 54,* 461–490.

Gridley, H., & Turner, C. (2005). Gender, power and community psychology. In G. Nelson & I. Prilleltensky (Eds.), *Community psychology: In pursuit of liberation and well-being* (pp. 364–381). New York: Palgrave Macmillan.

Grossman, D. C., Neckerman, H. J., Koepsell, T. D., Liu, P. Y., Asher, K. N., Beland, K., Frey, K. S., & Rivara, F. P. (1997) Effectiveness of a violence prevention curriculum among children in an elementary school: A randomized controlled trial. *Journal of the American Medical Association, 277,* 1605–1611.

Gruber, J., & Trickett, E. J. (1987). Can we empower others? The paradox of empowerment in the governing of an alternative public school. *American Journal of Community Psychology, 15,* 353–371.

Gulcur, L., Stefancic, A., Shinn M., Tsemberis, S., & Fischer, S. (2003). Housing, hospitalization, and cost outcomes for homeless individuals with psychiatric disabilities participating in continuum of care and housing first programmes. *Journal of Community and Applied Social Psychology, 13,* 171–186.

Gurin, P., Nagda, B. & Lopez, G. (2004). The benefits of diversity in education for democratic citizenship. *Journal of Social Issues, 60,* 17–34.

Gustafson, D., Hawkins, R., Boberg, E., Pingree, S., Serline, R., Graziano, F., & Chan, C. (1999). Impact of a patient-centered, computer-based health information/support system. *American Journal of Preventive Medicine, 16,* 1–9.

Gustafson, D., Hawkins, R., Pingree, S., McTavish, F., Arora, N., Mendenhall, J., Cella, D., Serlin, R., Apantaku, F., Stewart, J. & Salner, A. (2001). Effect of computer support on younger women with breast cancer. *Journal of General Internal Medicine, 16,* 435–445.

Hacker, A. (1992). *Two nations: Black and white, separate, hostile, unequal.* New York: Ballantine.

Haensly, P. A., & Parsons, J. L. (1993). Creative, intellectual, and psychosocial development through mentorship: Relationships and stages. *Youth and Society, 25,* 202–221.

Hall, C. C. I. (1997). Cultural malpractice: The growing obsolescence of psychology with the changing U. S. population. *American Psychologist, 52,* 642–651.

Hamby, S. (2000). The importance of community in a feminist analysis of domestic violence among American Indians. *American Journal of Community Psychology, 28,* 649–670.

Hansen, W., & Graham, J. W. (1991). Preventing alcohol, marijuana, and cigarette use among adolescents: Peer resistance training versus establishing conservative norms. *Preventive Medicine, 20,* 414–430.

Harper, G. (2005). A journey towards liberation: Confronting heterosexism and the oppression of lesbian, gay, bisexual and transgendered people. In G. Nelson & I. Prilleltensky (Eds.), *Community psychology: In pursuit of liberation and well-being* (pp. 382–404). New York: Palgrave Macmillan.

Harper, G., Bangi, A., Contreras, R., Pedraza, A., Tolliver, M., & Vess, L. (2004). Diverse phases of collaboration: Working together to improve community-based HIV interventions for adolescents. *American Journal of Community Psychology, 33,* 193–204.

Harper, G., Lardon, C., Rappaport, J., Bangi, A., Contreras, R., & Pedraza, A. (2004). Community narratives: The use of narrative ethnography in participatory community research. In L. A. Jason, C. Keys, Y. Suarez-Balcazar, R. Taylor, & M. Davis (Eds.), *Participatory community research: Theories and methods in action* (pp. 199–217). Washington, DC: American Psychological Association.

Harrell, S. P. (1997, May). Development and initial validation of scales to measure racism-related stress. Poster presentation at the Biennial Conference of the Society for Community Research and Action, Columbia, SC.

Harrell, S. P. (2000). A multidimensional conceptualization of racism-related stress: Implications for the well-being of people of color. *American Journal of Orthopsychiatry, 70,* 1–16.

Harrell, S., Taylor, S., & Burke, E. (Eds.). (1999, Winter). Cultural competence in community research and action [Special section]. *The Community Psychologist, 32,* 22–54.

Hartup, W. W., & Stevens, N. (1997). Friendships and adaptation in the life course. *Psychological Bulletin, 121,* 355–370.

Haskell, I. (1997). The effectiveness of character education and mentoring: An evaluation of the Troopers school-based program. Unpublished manuscript, University of South Carolina.

Hathaway, B. (2001). Case story #2: Growing a Healthy Community: A practical guide. *American Journal of Community Psychology, 29,* 199–204.

Hawkins, J. D., Catalano, R. F., & Associates. (1992). *Communities that care: Action for drug abuse prevention.* San Francisco: Jossey-Bass.

Hawkins, J. D., Catalano, R. F., Kosterman, R., Abbott, R., & Hill, K.G. (1999). Preventing adolescent health-risk behaviors by strengthening protection during childhood. *Archives of Pediatric Adolescent Medicine, 153,* 226–234.

Hawkins, J. D., Catalano, R. F., Morrison, D., O'Donnell, J., Abbott, R., & Day, L. (1992). The Seattle Social Development Project: Effects of the first four years on protective factors and problem behaviors. In J. McCord & R. E. Tremblay (Eds.), *Preventing antisocial behavior: Interventions from birth through adolescence* (pp. 139–161). New York: Guilford.

Hawkins, J. D., & Lam, T. (1987). Teacher practices, social development, and delinquency. In J. D. Burchard & S. N. Burchard (Ed.), *Prevention of delinquent behavior* (pp. 241–274). Newbury Park, CA: Sage.

Hazel, K. L., & Mohatt, G. V. (2001). Cultural and spiritual pathways to sobriety: Informing substance abuse prevention and intervention for Native American communities. *Journal of Community Psychology, 29,* 541–562.

Hazel, K., & Onanga, E. (2003). Experimental social innovation and dissemination [Special issue]. *American Journal of Community Psychology, 32* (4).

Heilman, M. (2001). Description and prescription: How gender stereotypes prevent women's ascent up the organizational ladder. *Journal of Social Issues, 57,* 657–688.

Heller, K. (1984). Historical trends in mental health beliefs and practices. In K. Heller, R. Price, S. Reinharz, S. Riger, & A. Wandersman, *Psychology and community change* (2nd ed.) (pp. 26–48). Homewood, IL: Dorsey.

Heller, K., Jenkins, R., Steffen A. & Swindle, R. (2000). Prospects for a viable community mental health system: Reconciling ideology, professional traditions, and political reality. In J. Rappaport & E. Seidman (Eds.), *Handbook of community psychology* (pp. 445–470). New York: Kluwer/Plenum.

Heller, K., & Monahan, J. (1977). *Psychology and community change.* Homewood, IL: Dorsey.

Heller, K., Price, R. H., Reinharz, S., Riger, S., & Wandersman, A. (1984). *Psychology and community change: Challenges of the future.* Homewood, IL: Dorsey Press/Pacific Grove, CA: Wadsworth.

Heller, M., & Firestone, W. (1995). Who's in charge here? Sources of leadership for change in eight schools. *Elementary School Journal, 96,* 65–86.

Helm, S. (2003, June). Rural health in Molokai: Land, people and empowerment. In C. O'Donnell (Chair), *Interdisciplinary training and rural capacity.* Symposium at the Biennial Meeting of the Society for Community Research and Action, Las Vegas, New Mexico.

Helms, J. E. (1994). The conceptualizations of racial identity and other "racial" constructs. In E. J. Trickett, R. J. Watts, & D. Birman (Eds.), *Human diversity: Perspectives on people in context* (pp. 285–310). San Francisco: Jossey-Bass.

Henry, C., Stephenson, A., Hanson, M., & Hargett, W. (1993). Adolescent suicide and families: An ecological approach. *Adolescence, 28,* 291–308.

Hermans, H., & Kempen, H. (1998). Moving cultures: The perilous problems of cultural dichotomies in a globalizing society. *American Psychologist, 53,* 1111–1120.

Herndon, E. J. (1996). [TSA flood victim follow-up survey]. Unpublished raw data.

Hill, J. (1996). Psychological sense of community: Suggestions for future research. *Journal of Community Psychology, 24,* 431–438.

Hill, J. (2000). A rationale for the integration of spirituality into community psychology. *Journal of Community Psychology, 28,* 139–150.

Hill, P., & Pargament, K. (2003). Advances in the conceptualization and measurement of religion and spirituality: Implications for physical and mental health research. *American Psychologist, 58,* 64–74.

Hillier, J. (2002). Presumptive planning: From urban design to community creation in one move? In A. Fisher, C. Sonn, & B. Bishop, (Eds.), *Psychological sense of community: Research, applications and implications* (pp. 43–68). New York: Kluwer/Plenum.

Himmelman, A. (2001). On coalitions and the transformation of power relations: Collaborative betterment and collaborative empowerment. *American Journal of Community Psychology, 29,* 277–284.

Hirsch, B. J. (1980). Natural support systems and coping with life changes. *American Journal of Community Psychology, 8,* 159–172.

Hirsch, B. J., Engel-Levy, A., DuBois, D. L., & Hardesty, P. (1990). The role of social environments in social support. In B. R. Sarason, I. G. Sarason, & G. Pierce (Eds.), *Social support: An interactional view* (pp. 367–393). New York: Wiley.

Hobfoll, S. E. (1988). *The ecology of stress.* New York: Hemisphere.

Hobfoll, S. E. (1998). *Stress, culture and community: The psychology and philosophy of stress.* New York: Plenum.

Hobfoll, S. E., & London, P. (1986). The relationship of self-concept and social support to emotional distress among women during war. *Journal of Social and Clinical Psychology, 4,* 189–203.

Hobfoll, S. E., & Vaux, A. (1993). Social support: Social resources and social context. In L. Goldberger & S. Breznitz (Eds.), *Handbook of stress: Theoretical and clinical aspects,* (2nd ed.) (pp. 685–705). New York: Free Press.

Hochschild, J. (2003). Social class in public schools. *Journal of Social Issues, 59,* 821–840.

Hofstede, G. (1980). *Culture's consequences: International differences in work-related values.* Newbury Park, CA: Sage.

Holahan, C. J., & Moos, R. H. (1994). Life stressors and mental health: Advances in conceptualizing stress resistance. In W. Avison & I. Gotlib (Eds.), *Stress and mental health: Contemporary issues and prospects for the future* (pp. 213–238). New York: Plenum.

Holahan, C. J., Moos, R. H., & Bonin, L. (1997). Social support, coping, and psychological adjustment: A resources model. In G. Pierce, B. Lakey, I. G. Sarason, & B. R. Sarason (Eds.), *Sourcebook of social support and personality* (pp. 169–186). New York: Plenum.

Holahan, C. J., & Spearly, J. (1980). Coping and ecology: An integrative model for community psychology. *American Journal of Community Psychology, 8,* 671–685.

Hollander, D. & Offerman, L. Power and leadership in organizations: Relationships in transition. *American Psychologist, 45,* 179–189.

Hollingshead, A., & Redlich, F. (1958). *Social class and mental illness: A community study.* New York: Wiley.

Holmes, T. H., & Rahe, R. H. (1967). The social readjustment rating scale. *Journal of Psychosomatic Research, 11,* 213–218.

hooks, b. (1984). *Feminist theory: From margin to center.* Boston, MA: South End Press.

Hord, S. M., Rutherford, W. L., Huling-Austin, L., & Hall, G. E. (1987). *Taking charge of change.*

Alexandria, VA: Association for Supervision and Curriculum Development.

Hoven, C., Duarte, C., Lucas, C., Wu, P., Mandell, D., Goodwin, R., Cohen, M., Balaban, V., Woodruff, B., Bin, F., Musa, G., Mei, L., Cantor, P., Aber, J. L., Cohen, P., & Susser, E. (2005). Psychopathology among New York City public school children 6 months after September 11. *Archives of General Psychiatry, 62,* 545–552.

Hoyt-Meyers, L., Cowen, E. L., Work, W. C., Wyman, P. A., Magnus, K., Fagen, D. B., & Lotyczewski, B. S. (1995). Test correlates of resilient outcomes among highly stressed second- and third-grade urban children. *Journal of Community Psychology, 23,* 326–338.

Huebner, E. S., & Gilman, R. (2003). Toward a focus on positive psychology in school psychology. *School Psychology Quarterly, 18* (2), 99–102.

Hughes, D. (2003). Correlates of African American and Latino parents' messages to children about ethnicity and race: A comparative study of racial socialization. *American Journal of Community Psychology, 31,* 15–33.

Hughes, D., & DuMont, K. (1993). Using focus groups to facilitate culturally anchored research. *American Journal of Community Psychology, 21,* 775–806. Reprinted in T. Revenson, A. D'Augelli, S. E. French, D. Hughes, D. Livert, E. Seidman, M. Shinn, & H. Yoshikawa (Eds.), (2002), *Ecological research to promote social change: methodological advances from community psychology* (pp. 257–289). New York: Kluwer Academic/Plenum.

Hughes, D., & Seidman, E. (2002). In pursuit of a culturally anchored methodology. In T. Revenson, A. D'Augelli, S. E. French, D. Hughes, D. Livert, E. Seidman, M. Shinn, & H. Yoshikawa (Eds.), (2002), *Ecological research to promote social change: methodological advances from community psychology* (pp. 243–255). New York: Kluwer Academic/Plenum.

Hughes, D., Seidman, E., & Williams, N. (1993). Cultural phenomena and the research enterprise: Toward a culturally anchored methodology. *American Journal of Community Psychology, 21,* 687–704.

Hughey, J., & Speer, P. (2002). Community, sense of community, and networks. In A. Fisher, C. Sonn, & B. Bishop, (Eds.), *Psychological sense of community: Research, applications and implications* (pp. 69–84). New York: Kluwer/Plenum.

Hughey, J., Speer, P. W., & Peterson, N. A. (1999). Sense of community in community organizations: Structure and evidence of validity. *Journal of Community Psychology, 27,* 97–113.

Hughey, J., & Whitehead, T. (2003, June). Institutions and community: Where power and ecology meet. In P. Speer (Chair), *Power and empowerment: Institutions, organizations and the grass-roots.* Symposium at the biennial meeting of the Society for Community Research and Action, Las Vegas, New Mexico.

Humphreys, K. (1996). Clinical psychologists as psychotherapists: History, future, and alternatives. *American Psychologist, 51,* 190–197.

Humphreys, K. (1997, Spring). Individual and social benefits of mutual aid self-help groups. *Social Policy, 27,* 12–19.

Humphreys, K. (2000). Community narratives and personal stories in Alcoholics Anonymous. *Journal of Community Psychology, 28,* 495–506.

Humphreys, K., Finney, J. W., & Moos, R. H. (1994). Applying a stress and coping framework to research on mutual help organizations. *Journal of Community Psychology, 22,* 312–327.

Humphreys, K., & Noke, J. M. (1997). The influence of posttreatment mutual help group participation on the friendship networks of substance abuse patients. *American Journal of Community Psychology, 25,* 1–16.

Humphreys, K., & Rappaport, J. (1993). From the community mental health movement to the war on drugs: A study in the definition of social problems. *American Psychologist, 48,* 892–901.

Humphreys, K., & Rappaport, J. (1994). Researching self-help/mutual aid groups and organizations: Many roads, one journey. *Applied and Preventive Psychology, 3,* 217–231.

Humphreys, K., Wing, S., McCarty, D., Chappel, J., Gallant, L., Haberle, B., Horvath, A., Kaskutas, L., Kirk, T., Kivlahan, D., Laudet, A., McCrady, B., McLellan, A. T., Morgenstern, J., Townsend, M., & Weiss, R. (2004). Self-help organizations for alcohol and drug problems: Toward evidence-based practice and policy. *Journal of Substance Abuse Treatment, 26,* 151–158.

Hunsberger, B. (1995). Religion and prejudice: The role of religious fundamentalism, quest and right-wing authoritarianism. *Journal of Social Issues, 51,* 113–130.

Hunter, A., & Riger, S. (1986). The meaning of community in community mental health. *Journal of Community Psychology, 14,* 55–70.

Hunter, L., Elias, M. J., & MacNeil, G. (2004). School violence. In A. Roberts (Ed.), *Juvenile justice sourcebook: Past, present, and future* (pp. 101–128). New York: Oxford University Press.

Hunter, L., Hoagwood, K., Evans, S., Weist, M., Smith, Paternite, C., Horner, R., Osher, D., Jensen, P. and the School Mental Health Alliance. (2005). *Working together to promote academic performance, social and emotional learning, and mental health for all children.* New York: Center for the Advancement of Children's Mental Health at Columbia University.

Hurtado, A. (1997). Understanding multiple group identities: Inserting women into cultural transformations. *Journal of Social Issues, 53,* 299–328.

Ickovics, J., & Park, C. (Eds.). (1998). Thriving: Broadening the paradigm beyond illness to health [Special issue]. *Journal of Social Issues, 54* (2).

Inequality.org. (2004). An inequality briefing book: July 2004. Retrieved July 17, 2004, from http://www.inequality.org/facts.html

Iscoe, I. (1974). Community psychology and the competent community. *American Psychologist, 29,* 607–613.

Iscoe, I., Bloom, B., & Spielberger, C. (Eds.). (1977). *Community psychology in transition: Proceedings of the national conference on training in community psychology.* Washington, DC: Hemisphere.

Isenberg, D. H., Loomis, C., Humphreys, K., & Maton, K. (2004). Self-help research: Issues of power-sharing. In L. A. Jason, C. Keys, Y. Suarez-Balcazar, R. Taylor & M. Davis (Eds.), *Participatory community research: Theories and methods in action* (pp. 123–138). Washington, DC: American Psychological Association.

Israel, N., & Toro, P. (2003, Fall). Promoting local action on poverty. *The Community Psychologist, 36,* 35–37.

Jacobs, J. (1961). *The death and life of great American cities.* New York: Random House.

Jahoda, M. (1958). *Current conceptions of positive mental health.* New York: Basic Books. (Reprinted in 1980. New York: Arno Press.)

Jahoda, M., Lazarsfeld, P., & Zeisel, H. (1971). *Marienthal: The sociography of an unemployed community.* London: Tavistock. (Originally published in German, 1933.)

James, S., Johnson, J., Raghavan, C., Lemos, T., Smith, M., & Woolis, D. (2003). The violent matrix: A study of structural, interpersonal and intrapersonal violence among a sample of poor women. *American Journal of Community Psychology, 31,* 129–142.

Jason, L. A. (1998a). Tobacco, drug, and HIV prevention media interventions. *American Journal of Community Psychology, 26,* 151–188.

Jason, L. A. (1998b, February). Dr. Jason goes to Washington. *The Community Psychologist, 31,* 27–30.

Jason, L. A., Berk, M., Schnopp-Wyatt, D. L., & Talbot, B. (1999). Effects of enforcement of youth access laws on smoking prevalance. *American Journal of Community Psychology, 27,* 143–160.

Jason, L. A., Ferrari, J., Davis, M., & Olson, B. (2006). *Creating communities for addiction recovery: The Oxford House model.* New York: Haworth. [Also published as *Journal of Prevention and Intervention in the Community, 31* (1/2).]

Jason, L. A., & Hanaway, E. K. (1997). *Remote control: A sensible approach to kids, TV, and the new electronic media.* Sarasota, FL: Professional Resources Press.

Jason, L. A., Keys, C., Suarez-Balcazar, Y., Taylor, R., & Davis, M. (Eds.). (2004). *Participatory community research: Theories and methods in action.* Washington, DC: American Psychological Association.

Jayson, S. (2005, September 13). Culture gaps could inhibit counseling of Katrina victims. *USA Today* [Electronic version]. Retrieved October 1, 2005 from http://www.usatoday.com/printedition/life/20050913/d_katrina_race13.art.htm

Jayson, S. (2005, September 14). Emotional toll is brewing. *USA Today* [Electronic version]. Retrieved October 1, 2005 from http://www.usatoday.com/news/health/2005-09-13-katrina-stress_x.htm

Jessor, R. (1993). Successful adolescent development among youth in high-risk settings. *American Psychologist, 48,* 117–126.

Joffe, J. M. (2000). Millenial musings: Another 1000 years of prevention? *Journal of Primary Prevention, 21* (1), 31–34.

Johnson, D., & Demanchick, S. (2004). Primary Mental Health Project: Expanding your reach through prevention. *NASP Communique, 33* (1), 28–30.

Johnson, D. L. (1988). Primary prevention of behavior problems in young children: The Houston Parent-Child Development Center. In R. Price, E. Cowen, R. Lorion & J. Ramos-McKay (Eds.), Fourteen ounces of prevention: A casebook for practitioners (pp. 44–52). Washington, DC: American Psychological Association.

Joint Commission on Mental Health and Mental Illness. (1961). *Action for Mental Health: Final Report.* New York: Basic Books.

Jones, J. M. (1997). *Prejudice and racism* (2nd ed.). New York: McGraw-Hill.

Jones, J. M. (1998). Psychological knowledge and the new American dilemma of race. *Journal of Social Issues, 54,* 641–662.

Jones, J. M. (2003). Constructing race and deconstructing racism: A cultural psychology approach. In G. Bernal, J. Trimble, K. Burlew, & F. Leong (Eds.), *Handbook of racial and ethnic minority psychology* (pp. 275–290). Thousand Oaks, CA: Sage.

Jordan, L., Bogat, A. & Smith, G. (2001). Collaborating for social change: The Black psychologist and the Black community. *American Journal of Community Psychology, 29,* 599–620.

Joyner, E., Comer, J. P. & Ben-Avie, M. (2004). *Comer schools in action: The 3-volume field guide.* Thousand Oaks, CA: Corwin Press.

Jozefowicz-Simbeni, D., Israel, N., Braciszewski, J., & Hobden, K. (2005). The "big tent" of community psychology: Reactions to Paul Toro's 2004 presidential address. *American Journal of Community Psychology, 35,* 17–22.

Julian, J. A., Jones, A., & Dey, D. (1995). Open systems evaluation and the logic model: Program planning and evaluation tools. *Evaluation and Program Planning, 18,* 333–341.

Jumper-Thurman, P., Edwards, R., Plested, B. & Oetting, E. (2003). Honoring the differences: Using community readiness to create culturally valid community interventions. In G. Bernal, J. Trimble, K. Burlew, & F. Leong (Eds.), *Handbook of racial and ethnic minority psychology* (pp. 589–607). Thousand Oaks, CA: Sage.

Kabat-Zinn, J. (1993). Mindfulness meditation: Health benefits of an ancient Buddhist practice. In D. Goleman & J. Gurin (Eds.), *Mind-body medicine* (pp. 259–276.) New York: Consumer Reports Books/St. Martin's Press.

Kagitçibasi, C. (1997). Individualism and collectivism. In J. W. Berry, M. Segall, & C. Kagitçibasi (Eds.), *Handbook of cross-cultural psychology,* Vol. 3: *Social behavior and applications* (pp. 1–50). Needham Heights, MA: Allyn & Bacon.

Kalafat, J. (2003). Suicide, adolescence. In T.P. Gullotta & M. Bloom (Eds.), *Encyclopedia of primary prevention and health promotion* (pp. 1099–1105). New York: Kluwer.

Kalafat, J., & Elias, M. J. (1995). Suicide prevention in an educational context: Broad and narrow foci. *Suicide and Life-Threatening Behavior, 25* (1), 123–133.

Kamenetz, A. (2005, September 5–11). Talking about my generation: There's passion among today's youth—if only people would pay attention. *Washington Post Weekly Edition,* 22.

Kaniasty, K., & Norris, F. H. (1995). In search of altruistic community: Patterns of social support mobilization following Hurricane Hugo. *American Journal of Community Psychology, 23,* 447–478.

Kanner, A., Coyne, J., Schaefer, C., & Lazarus, R. S. (1981). Comparison of two modes of stress measurement: Daily hassles and uplifts versus major life events. *Journal of Behavioral Medicine, 4,* 1–37.

Karakashian, M. (1998). Armenia: A country's history of challenges. *Journal of Social Issues, 54,* 381–392.

Kaskutas, L., Morgan, P., & Vaeth, P. (1992). Structural impediments in the development of community-based drug prevention programs for youth: Preliminary analysis from a qualitative formative evaluation study. *International Quarterly of Community Health Education, 12,* 169–182.

Katz, D., & Kahn, R. L. (1978). *The social psychology of organizations.* New York: Wiley.

Katz, R. (1984). Empowerment and synergy: Expanding the community's healing resources. In J. Rappaport, C. Swift, & R. Hess, (Eds.), *Studies in empowerment: Steps toward understanding and action* (pp. 210–226). New York: Haworth Press.

Kaye, G. (2001). Grassroots involvement. *American Journal of Community Psychology, 29,* 269–276.

Kaye, G., & Wolff, T. (Eds.). (1997). *From the ground up: A workbook on coalition building and community development.* Amherst, MA: AHEC/Community Partners.

Keener, D., Snell-Johns, J., Livet, M., & Wandersman, A. (2005). Lessons that influenced the current conceptualization of empowerment evaluation: Reflections from two evaluation projects. In D. Fetterman & A. Wandersman (Eds.), *Empowerment evaluation principles in practice* (pp. 73–91). New York: Guilford Press.

Keister, S. (2006). Fostering caring, character, and responsibility in schools. In M. J. Elias & H. Arnold, (Eds.), *The educator's guide to emotional intelligence and academic achievement: Social-emotional learning in the classroom* (pp. 175–187). Thousand Oaks, CA: Corwin Press.

Kelly, J. F. (2003). Self-help for substance-use disorders: History, effectiveness, knowledge gaps, and research opportunities. *Clinical Psychology Review, 23,* 639–663.

Kelly, J. G. (1966). Ecological constraints on mental health services. *American Psychologist, 21,* 535–539.

Kelly, J. G. (1970a). Toward an ecological conception of preventive interventions. In D. Adelson & B. Kalis (Eds.), *Community psychology and mental health* (pp. 126–145). Scranton, PA: Chandler.

Kelly, J. G. (1970b). Antidotes for arrogance: Training for community psychology. *American Psychologist, 25,* 524–531.

Kelly, J. G. (1971). Qualities for the community psychologist. *American Psychologist, 26,* 897–903.

Kelly, J. G. (Ed.). (1979a). *Adolescent boys in high school: A psychological study of coping and adaptation.* Hillsdale, NJ: Erlbaum.

Kelly, J. G. (1979b). "Tain't what you do, it's the way you do it." *American Journal of Community Psychology, 7,* 244–258.

Kelly, J. G. (1984). In honor of Erich Lindemann. *American Journal of Community Psychology, 12,* 513–514.

Kelly, J. G. (1986). Context and process: An ecological view of the interdependence of practice and research. *American Journal of Community Psychology, 14,* 581–605.

Kelly, J. G. (1990). Changing contexts and the field of community psychology. *American Journal of Community Psychology, 18,* 769–792.

Kelly, J. G. (1997). [Untitled vidotape interview]. In J. G. Kelly (Ed.), *The history of community psychology: A video presentation of context and exemplars.* Chicago: Society for Community Research and Action.

Kelly, J. G. (2002a). The spirit of community psychology. *American Journal of Community Psychology, 30,* 43–63.

Kelly, J. G. (2002b). The National Institute of Mental Health and the founding of the field of community psychology. In W. Pickren, (Ed.), *Psychology and the National Institute of Mental Health.* Washington, DC: American Psychological Association.

Kelly, J. G. (Producer, Director). (2003). *Exemplars of community psychology* [DVD set]. Society for Community Research and Action. Available through: SCRA Membership Office, 1800 Canyon Park Circle, Building 4, Suite 403, Edmond, OK 73103 USA. Email: scra@telepath.com

Kelly, J. G., Azelton, S., Burzette, R., & Mock, L. (1994). Creating social settings for diversity: An ecological thesis. In E. J. Trickett, R. J. Watts & D. Birman (Eds.), *Human diversity: Perspectives on people in context* (pp. 424– 450). San Francisco: Jossey-Bass.

Kelly, J. G., Azelton, S., Lardon, C., Mock, L., Tandon, S. D., & Thomas, M. (2004). On community leadership: Stories about collaboration in action research. *American Journal of Community Psychology, 33,* 205–216.

Kelly, J. G., Dassoff, N., Levin, I., Schreckengost, J., Stelzner, S., & Altman, B. (1988). *A guide to conducting prevention research in the community: First steps.* New York: Haworth.

Kelly, J. G., Ryan, A. M., Altman, B. E. & Stelzner, S. P. (2000). Understanding and changing social systems: An ecological view. In J. Rappaport & E. Seidman (Eds.), *Handbook of community psychology* (pp. 133–160). New York: Kluwer Academic/Plenum.

Keppel, B. (2002). Kenneth B. Clark in the patterns of American culture. *American Psychologist, 57,* 29–37.

Kessler, R. C., Mickelson, K. D., & Zhao, S. (1997, Spring). Patterns and correlates of self-help groups membership in the United States. *Social Policy, 27,* 27–46.

Keys, C., McMahon, S., Sanchez, B., London, L. & Abdul-Adil, J. (2004). Culturally-anchored research: Quandaries, guidelines, and exemplars for community psychology. In L. A. Jason, C. Keys, Y. Suarez-Balcazar, R. Taylor & M. Davis (Eds.), *Participatory community research: Theories and methods in action* (pp. 177–198). Washington, DC: American Psychological Association.

Kieffer, C. (1984). Citizen empowerment: A developmental perspective. In J. Rappaport, C. Swift, & R. Hess (Eds.), *Studies in empowerment: Steps toward understanding and action* (pp. 9–36). New York: Haworth.

Kim, U., & Berry, J. (Eds.). (1993). *Indigenous psychologies: Research and experience in cultural context.* Newbury Park, CA: Sage.

Kim, U., Triandis, H., Kagitçibasi, C., Choi, S.-C., & Yoon, G. (Eds.) (1994). *Individualism and collectivism: Theory, method, and applications.* Thousand Oaks, CA: Sage.

King, M. L., Jr. (1968). The role of the behavioral scientist in the civil rights movement. *American Psychologist, 23,* 180–186.

Kingry-Westergaard, C., & Kelly, J. G. (1990). A contextualist epistemology for ecological research. In P. Tolan, C. Keys, F. Chertok, & L. Jason (Eds.), *Researching community psychology* (pp. 23–32). Washington, DC: American Psychological Association.

Kingston, S., Mitchell, R., Florin, P. & Stevenson, J. (1999). Sense of community in neighborhoods as a multi-level construct. *Journal of Community Psychology, 27,* 681–694.

Klaw, E., Huebsch, P. & Humphreys, K. (2000). Communication patterns in an on-line mutual help group. *Journal of Community Psychology, 28,* 535–546.

Klein, D. (1984). Zen and the art of Erich Lindemann. *American Journal of Community Psychology, 12,* 515–517.

Klein, D. (1987). The context and times at Swampscott: My/story. *American Journal of Community Psychology, 12,* 515–517.

Klein, D. (1995). [Untitled videotape interview]. In J. G. Kelly (Ed.), *The history of community psychology: A video presentation of context and exemplars.* Chicago: Society for Community Research and Action.

Klein, D. C., & Goldston, S. E. (1977). Primary prevention: An idea whose time has come. Proceedings of the Pilot Conference on Primary Prevention, April 24, 1976 (Department of Health, Education, and Welfare Pub. No. ADM 77–447). Washington, DC: U.S. Government Printing Office.

Klein, D., & Lindemann, E. (1961). Preventive intervention in individual and family crisis situations. In G. Caplan (Ed.), *Prevention of mental disorders in children* (pp. 283–306). New York: Basic Books.

Klein, K., Ralls, R. S., Smith-Major, V. & Douglas, C. (2000). Power and participation in the workplace. In J. Rappaport & E. Seidman (Eds.), *Handbook of community psychology* (pp. 273–300). New York: Kluwer Academic/Plenum.

Kliewer, W., Wade, N., & Worthington, E. (2003). Religion and spirituality, childhood. In T. P. Gullotta & M. Bloom (Eds.), *Encyclopedia of primary prevention and health promotion* (pp. 859–867). New York: Kluwer.

Kline, M., & Snow, D. (1994). Effects of a worksite coping skills intervention on the stress, social support, and health outcomes of working mothers. *Journal of Primary Prevention, 15,* 105–121.

Kloos, B. (2005). Creating new possibilities for promoting liberation, well-being and recovery: Learning from experiences of psychiatric consumers/survivors. In G. Nelson & I. Prilleltensky (Eds.), *Community psychology: In pursuit of liberation and well-being* (pp. 426–447). New York: Palgrave Macmillan.

Kloos, B., & Moore, T. (Eds.) (2000a). Spirituality, religion, and community psychology [Special issue]. *Journal of Community Psychology, 28* (2).

Kloos, B., & Moore, T. (2000b). The prospect and purpose of locating community research and action in religious settings. *Journal of Community Psychology, 28,* 119–138.

Kloos, B., & Moore, T. (Eds.) (2001). Spirituality, religion, and community psychology II: Resources, pathways, and perspectives [Special issue]. *Journal of Community Psychology, 29* (5).

Knoff, H. M. (In press.) Teasing, taunting, bullying, harassment, and aggression: A school-wide approach to prevention, strategic intervention, and crisis management. In J. Zins, M. J. Elias, & C. A. Maher (Eds.), *Handbook of bullying, victimization, and peer harassment research and intervention.* New York: Haworth.

Kohn, D., & Olson, B. (2005, September 28). Unrooted, disconnected. *The Baltimore Sun* [Electronic version]. Retrieved October 20, 2005 from http://www.baltimoresun.com/news/weather/hurricane/bal-te.home28sep28,1,6957426.story?coll=bal-nationworld-utility&ctrack=1&cset=true

Kotchick, B., Dorsey, S., Miller, K. & Forehand, R. (1999). Adolescent sexual risk-taking behavior in single parent ethnic minority families. *Journal of Family Psychology, 13,* 93–102.

Kress, J. S., & Elias, M. J. (2000). Infusing community psychology and religion: Themes from an action-research project in Jewish identity. *Journal of Community Psychology, 28,* 187–198.

Kress, J. S., Norris, J. A., Schoenholz, D., Elias, M. J., & Seigle, P. (2004). Bringing together educational standards and social and emotional learning: Making the case for educators. *American Journal of Education, 111,* 68–89.

Kretzmann, J. P., & McKnight, J. L. (1993). *Building communities from the inside out: A path toward finding and mobilizing a community's assets.* Chicago, IL: ACTA Publications.

Kroeker, C. J. (1995). Individual, organizational and societal empowerment: A study of the processes in a Nicaraguan agricultural cooperative. *American Journal of Community Psychology, 23,* 749–764.

Kroeker, C. J. (1996). The cooperative movement in Nicaragua: Empowerment and accompaniment of severely disadvantaged persons. *Journal of Social Issues, 52,* 123–137.

Kropotkin, P. (1955). *Mutual aid.* Boston: Extending Horizons Books. (Original work published 1914.)

Kumpfer, K., & Alder, S. (2003). Dissemination of research-based family interventions for the prevention of substance abuse. In Z. Sloboda & W. J. Bukowski (Eds.), *Handbook of drug abuse prevention* (pp. 75–119). New York: Kluwer Academic.

Kumpfer, K., & Alvarado, R. (2003). Family-strengthening approaches for the prevention of youth problem behaviors. *American Psychologist, 58,* 457–465.

Kuo, F. E., Sullivan, W. C., Coley, R. L., & Brunson, L. (1998). Fertile ground for community: Inner-city neighborhood common spaces. *American Journal of Community Psychology, 26,* 823–852.

Kusche, C., & Greenberg, M. (2006). Teaching emotional literacy in elementary school classrooms: The PATHS curriculum. In M. J. Elias & H. Arnold, (Eds.), *The educator's guide to emotional intelligence and academic achievement: Social-emotional learning in the classroom.* Thousand Oaks, CA: Corwin Press.

LaFromboise, T., Coleman, H. L. K., & Gerton, J. (1993). Psychological impact of biculturalism: Evidence and theory. *Psychological Bulletin, 114,* 395–412.

Laird, M., Bradley, L., & Black, S. (1998). *The final evaluation of Quest International's Skills for Action.* Newark, OH: Lion's-Quest International.

Lal, S. (2002). Giving children security: Mamie Phipps Clark and the racialization of child psychology. *American Psychologist, 57,* 20–28.

Lambert, S., & Hopkins, K. (1995). Occupational conditions and workers' sense of community: variations by gender and race. *American Journal of Community Psychology, 23,* 151–180.

Langhout, R. D. (2003). Reconceptualizing quantitative and qualitative methods: A case study dealing with place as an exemplar. *American Journal of Community Psychology, 32,* 229–244.

Lantz, P. et al. (2000). Investing in youth tobacco control: A review of smoking prevention and control strategies. *Tobacco Control, 9,* 47–63.

Lappe, F. M., & DuBois, P. M. (1994). *The quickening of America: Rebuilding our nation, remaking our lives.* San Francisco, CA: Jossey-Bass.

Lawler, E. E., III, Mohrman, A. M., Jr., Mohrman, S. A., Leford, G. E., Cummings, T. G., & Associates (1985). *Doing research that is useful for theory and practice.* San Francisco: Jossey-Bass.

Lazarus, R. S., & Folkman, S. (1984). *Stress, appraisal, and coping.* New York: Springer.

Lee, C. (Ed.) (2000). Australian indigenous psychologies [Special issue]. *Australian Psychologist, 35* (2).

Lehrer, J. (2005, September 1). Calling Katrina. *NOVA Science NOW: Dispatches.* Retrieved October 5, 2005 from http://www.pbs.org/wgbh/nova/sciencenow/dispatches/050901.html

Lerner, R. M. (1995). *America's youth in crisis: Challenges and options for programs and policies.* Thousand Oaks, CA: Sage.

Levine, A. (1982). *Love Canal: Science, politics, and people.* Lexington, MA: Heath.

Levine, M. (1981). *The history and politics of community mental health.* New York: Oxford University Press.

Levine, M., & Levine, A. (1970). *A social history of helping services.* New York: Oxford University Press.

Levine, M., & Levine, A. (1992). *Helping children: A social history.* New York: Oxford University Press.

Levine, M., Perkins, D. D., & Perkins, D. V. (2005). *Principles of community psychology: Perspectives and applications* (3rd ed.). New York: Oxford University Press.

Levine, M., & Perkins, D. V. (1987). *Principles of community psychology: Perspectives and applications.* New York: Oxford University Press.

Levine, R. (2004, November 28). How to win the AIDS battle. *Newark Star-Ledger,* Section 10 (Perspective), 1, 8.

Leviton, L. C. (1994). Program theory and evaluation theory in community-based programs. *Evaluation Practice, 15,* 89–92.

Lewin, K. (1935). *A dynamic theory of personality.* New York: McGraw-Hill.

Lewis, J. (1998). *Walking with the wind: A memoir of the movement.* New York: Simon & Schuster.

Liang, B., & Bogat, G. A. (1994). Culture, control, and coping: New perspective on social support. *American Journal of Community Psychology, 22,* 123–147.

Liang, B., Glenn, C., & Goodman, L. (2005, Summer). Feminist ethics in advocacy relationships: A relational vs. rule-bound approach. *The Community Psychologist, 38,* 26–28.

Limber, S. (2004). Implementation of the Olweus Bullying Prevention Program: Lessons learned from the field. In D. Espelage & S. Swearer (Eds.), *Bullying in American schools: A social-ecological perspective on prevention and intervention* (pp. 351–363). Mahwah, NJ: Erlbaum.

Lindemann, E. (1944). Symptomatology and management of acute grief. *American Journal of Psychiatry, 101,* 141–148.

Lindemann, E. (1957). The nature of mental health work as a professional pursuit. In C. Strother (Ed.), *Psychology and mental health* (pp. 136–145). Washington, DC: American Psychological Association.

Linney, J. A. (1986). Court-ordered school desegregation: Shuffling the deck or playing a different game. In E. Seidman & J. Rappaport (Eds.), *Redefining social problems* (pp. 259– 274). New York: Plenum.

Linney, J. A. (1989). Optimizing research strategies in the schools. In L. A. Bond & B. E. Compas (Eds.), *Primary prevention in the schools* (pp. 50–76). Newbury Park, CA: Sage.

Linney, J. A. (1990). Community psychology into the 1990's: Capitalizing opportunity and promoting innovation. *American Journal of Community Psychology, 18,* 1–17.

Linney, J. A. (2000). Assessing ecological constructs and community context. In J. Rappaport & E. Seidman (Eds.), *Handbook of community psychology* (pp. 647–668). New York: Kluwer/Plenum.

Linney, J. A., & Reppucci, N. D. (1982). Research design and methods in community psychology. In P. Kendall & J. Butcher (Eds.), *Handbook of research methods in clinical psychology* (pp. 535–566). New York: Wiley.

Linney, J. A., & Wandersman, A. (1991). *Prevention plus III: Assessing alcohol and other drug prevention programs at the school and community level: A four-step guide to useful program assessment.* Rockville, MD: U.S. Department of Health and Human Services, Office for Substance Abuse Prevention.

Lipset, S. M. (1996). *American exceptionalism: A double-edged sword.* New York: Norton.

Lipsey, M., & Cordray, D. (2002). Evaluation methods for social intervention. *Annual Review of Psychology, 51,* 345–375.

Livet, M., & Wandersman, A. (2005). Organizational functioning: Facilitating effective interventions and increasing the odds of programming success. In D. Fetterman & A. Wandersman (Eds.), *Empowerment evaluation principles in practice* (pp. 123–154). New York: Guilford Press.

Loeb, P. (1999). *Soul of a citizen: Living with conviction in a cynical time.* New York: St. Martin's Press.

London, M., & MacDuffie, J. (1985). *Implementing managerial and technical innovations: Case examples and guidelines for practice.* Basking Ridge, NJ: AT&T Communications.

Long, D., & Perkins, D. D. (2003). Confirmatory factor analysis of the Sense of Community Index and development of a Brief SCI. *Journal of Community Psychology, 31,* 279–296.

Lonner, W. (1994). Culture and human diversity. In E. J. Trickett, R. J. Watts, & D. Birman (Eds.), *Human diversity: Perspectives on people in context* (pp. 230–243). San Francisco: Jossey-Bass.

Loo, C., Fong, K., & Iwamasa, G. (1988). Ethnicity and cultural diversity: An analysis of work published in community psychology journals, 1965–1985. *Journal of Community Psychology, 16,* 332–349.

Loomis, C., Dockett, K., & Brodsky, A. (2004). Change in sense of community: An empirical finding. *Journal of Community Psychology, 32,* 1–8.

Lopez, M. L., & Stack C. B. Social capital and the culture of power: Lessons from the field. In S. Saegert, J. P. Thompson, & M. Warren, (Eds.), *Social capital and poor communities* (pp. 31–59). New York: Russell Sage.

Lott, B. (2001). Low-income parents and the public schools. *Journal of Social Issues, 57,* 247–260.

Lott, B., & Bullock, H. (2001). Who are the poor? *Journal of Social Issues, 57,* 189–206.

Lounsbury, J., Leader, D., Meares, E., & Cook, M. (1980). An analytic review of research in community psychology. *American Journal of Community Psychology, 8,* 415–441.

Lounsbury, J., Loveland, J., & Gibson, L. (2003). An investigation of psychological sense of community in relation to Big Five personality traits. *Journal of Community Psychology, 31,* 531–542.

Luke, D. (2005). Getting the big picture in community science: Methods that capture context. *American Journal of Community Psychology, 35,* 185–200.

Luke, D., Rappaport, J., & Seidman, E. (1991). Setting phenotypes in a mutual help organization: Expanding behavior setting theory. *American Journal of Community Psychology, 19,* 147–168. Reprinted in T. Revenson, A. D'Augelli, S. E. French, D. Hughes, D. Livert, E. Seidman, M. Shinn & H. Yoshikawa (Eds.) (2002), *Ecological research to promote social change: Methodological advances from community psychology* (pp. 217–238). New York: Kluwer Academic/Plenum.

Luthar, S., Cicchetti, D. & Becker, B. (2000). The construct of resilience: a critical evaluation and guidelines for future work. *Child Development, 71,* 543–562.

Lykes, M. B. (2003, Fall). Developing an activist liberatory community psychology: One step at a time. *The Community Psychologist, 36,* 39–42.

Lykes, M. B. (2005). Narratives and representations of survival: The politics and praxis of action research and liberatory community psychology in a post-9/11 world. Keynote address, Biennial Conference of Society for Community Research and Action, Champaign-Urbana, Illinois.

Lykes, M. B., Blanche, M. T., & Hamber, B. (2003). Narrating survival and change in Guatemala and South Africa: The politics of representation and a liberatory community psychology. *American Journal of Community Psychology, 31,* 79–90.

Madara, E. (1997, Spring). The mutual aid self-help online revolution. *Social Policy, 27,* 20–26.

Mahan, B., Garrard, W., Lewis, S., & Newbrough, J. R. (2002). Sense of community in a university setting: Campus as workplace. In A. Fisher, C. Sonn, & B. Bishop (Eds.), *Psychological sense of community: Research, applications and implications* (pp. 123–140). New York: Kluwer/Plenum.

Malley, P., Kush, F., & Bogo, R. (1996). School-based suicide prevention and intervention programs. *The Prevention Researcher, 3* (3), 9–11.

Mankowski, E., & Rappaport, J. (Eds.). (2000a). Qualitative research on the narratives of spiritually-based communities. [Special Section]. *Journal of Community Psychology, 28*(5).

Mankowski, E., & Rappaport, J. (2000b). Narrative concepts and analysis in spiritually-based communities. *Journal of Community Psychology, 28,* 479–494.

Mankowski, E., & Thomas, E. (2000). The relationship between personal and collective identity: A narrative analysis of a campus ministry community. *Journal of Community Psychology, 28,* 517–528.

Marecek, J., Fine, M., & Kidder, L. (1997). Working between worlds: Qualitative methods and social psychology. *Journal of Social Issues, 53,* 631–643.

Marin, G., & Gamba, R. (2003). Acculturation and changes in cultural values. In K. Chun, P. Organista, & G. Marin (Eds.), *Acculturation: Advances in theory, measurement and applied research* (pp. 83–94). Washington, DC: American Psychological Association.

Markus, H. T., & Kitayama, S. (1991). Culture and the self: Implications for cognition, emotion, and motivation. *Psychological Review, 98,* 224–253.

Marris, P., & Rein, M. (1973). *Dilemmas of social reform (2nd. ed.).* Chicago: Aldine.

Marrow, A. J. (1969). *The practical theorist.* New York: Basic Books.

Marsella, A. (1998). Toward a "global-community" psychology. *American Psychologist, 53,* 1282–1291.

Marsh, K., Johnson, B., & Carey, M. (2003). HIV/AIDS, adolescence. In T. P. Gullotta & M. Bloom (Eds.), *Encyclopedia of primary prevention and health promotion* (pp. 541–548). New York: Kluwer.

Martin, P., Lounsbury, D. & Davidson, W. (2004). AJCP as a vehicle for improving community life: An historic-analytic review of the journal's contents. *American Journal of Community Psychology, 34,* 163–174.

Martin-Baro, I. (1990). Religion as an instrument of psychological warfare. *Journal of Social Issues, 46,* 93–107.

Martin-Baro, I. (1994). *Writings for a liberation psychology.* [Eds. A. Aron & S. Corne.] Cambridge, MA: Harvard University Press.

Martinez, F., Toloza, S., Montanez, N., & Ochoa, H. E. (2003, Fall). An alternative model of development with a displaced community. *The Community Psychologist, 36,* 25–27.

Mason, C., Chapman, D., & Scott, K. (1999). The identification of early risk factors for severe emotional disturbances and emotional handicaps: An epidemiological approach. *American Journal of Community Psychology, 27,* 357–381.

Masterpasqua, F. (1981). Toward a synergism of developmental and community psychology. *American Psychologist, 36,* 782–786.

Maton, K. I. (1987). Patterns and psychological correlates of material support within a religious setting: The bidirectional support hypothesis. *American Journal of Community Psychology, 15,* 185–207.

Maton, K. I. (1988). Social support, organizational characteristics, psychological well-being, and group appraisal in three self-help group populations. *American Journal of Community Psychology, 16,* 53–77.

Maton, K. I. (1989). Community settings as buffers of life stress? Highly supportive churches, mutual help groups, and senior centers. *American Journal of Community Psychology, 17,* 203–232. Reprinted in T. Revenson, A. D'Augelli, S. E. French, D. Hughes, D. Livert, E. Seidman, M. Shinn & H. Yoshikawa (Eds.) (2002), *A quarter century of community psychology* (pp. 205–235). New York: Kluwer Academic/Plenum.

Maton, K. I. (1993). A bridge between cultures: Linked ethnographic empirical methodology for culture anchored research. *American Journal of Community Psychology, 21,* 747–774.

Maton, K. I. (2000). Making a difference: The social ecology of social transformation. *American Journal of Community Psychology, 28,* 25–58.

Maton, K. I. (2001). Spirituality, religion, and community psychology: Historical perspective, positive potential, and challenges. *Journal of Community Psychology, 29,* 605–613.

Maton, K. I., & Hrabowski, R.A. (2004). Increasing the number of African American PhDs in the sciences and engineering: A strengths-based approach. *American Psychologist, 59,* 547–556.

Maton, K. I., Hrabowski, R. A., & Greif, G. L. (1998). Preparing the way: A qualitative study of high achieving African American males and the role of the family. *American Journal of Community Psychology, 26,* 639–668.

Maton, K. I., & Salem, D. A. (1995). Organizational characteristics of empowering community settings: A multiple case study approach. *American Journal of Community Psychology, 23,* 631–656.

Maton, K., Schellenbach, C., Leadbeater, B. & Solarz, A. (Eds). (2004). *Investing in children, youth, families and communities: Strengths-based research and policy.* Washington, DC: American Psychological Association.

Maton, K. I., Teti, D. M., Corns, K. M., Vieira-Baker, C. C., Lavine, J. R., Gouze, K. R., & Keating, D. P. (1996). Cultural specificity of support sources, correlates and contexts: Three studies of African-American and Caucasian youth. *American Journal of Community Psychology, 24,* 551–587.

Maton, K. I., & Wells, E. A. (1995). Religion as a community resource for well-being: Prevention, healing, and empowerment pathways. *Journal of Social Issues, 51,* 177–193.

Mayer, J. & Davidson, W. S. (2000). Dissemination of innovation as social change. In J. Rappaport & E. Seidman (Eds.), *Handbook of community psychology* (pp. 421–443). New York: Kluwer Academic/ Plenum.

Mattis, J., & Jagers, R. (2001). A relational framework for the study of religiosity and spirituality in the lives of African Americans. *Journal of Community Psychology, 29,* 519–540.

McClure, L, Cannon, D., Allen, S., Belton, E., Connor, P., D'Ascoli, C., Stone, P., Sullivan, B., & McClure, G. (1980). Community psychology concepts and research base. *American Psychologist, 35,* 1000–1011.

McElhaney, S. (1995). *Getting started: NMHA guide to establishing community-based prevention programs.* Alexandria, VA: National Mental Health Association.

McEwan, K. L., & Bigelow, D. A. (1997). Using a logic model to focus health services on population health goals. *Canadian Journal of Program Evaluation, 12,* 167–174.

McIntosh, P. (1998). White privilege and male privilege: A personal account of coming to see correspondences through work in women's studies. In M. Andersen & P. H. Collins (Eds.), *Race, class and gender: An anthology* (pp. 94–105). Belmont, CA: Wadsworth.

McLaughlin, M., & Mitra, D. (2001). Theory-based change and change-based theory: Going deeper, going broader. *Journal of Educational Change, 2*(4), 301–323.

McLoyd, V. (1998). Socioeconomic disadvantage and child development. *American Psychologist, 53,* 185–204.

McMahon, S., & Watts, R. (2002). Ethnic identity in urban African American youth: Exploring links with self-worth, aggression and other psychosocial variables. *Journal of Community Psychology, 30,* 411–432.

McMillan, B., Florin, P., Stevenson, J., Kerman, B., & Mitchell, R. E. (1995). Empowerment praxis in community coalitions. *American Journal of Community Psychology, 23,* 699–728.

McMillan, D. W. (1996). Sense of community. *Journal of Community Psychology, 24,* 315–326.

McMillan, D. W., & Chavis, D. M. (1986). Sense of community: Definition and theory. *Journal of Community Psychology, 14,* 6–23.

McNally, R., Bryant, R. & Ehlers, A. (2003). Does early psychological intervention promote recovery from posttraumatic stress? *Psychological Science in the Public Interest, 4,* 45–79.

Medoff, P., & Sklar, H. (1994). *Streets of hope: The fall and rise of an urban neighborhood.* Boston, MA: South End Press.

Melton, G. B. (1991). Socialization in the global community: Respect for the dignity of children. *American Psychologist, 46,* 66–71.

Melton, G. B. (1995). Bringing psychology to Capitol Hill: Briefings on child and family policy. *American Psychologist, 50,* 766–770.

Melton, G. B. (2000). Community change, community stasis, and the law. In J. Rappaport & E. Seidman (Eds.), *Handbook of community psychology* (pp. 523–540.). New York: Kluwer Academic/Plenum.

Meyers, J. (2000). A community psychologist in the public policy arena. In J. Rappaport & E. Seidman (Eds.), *Handbook of community psychology* (pp. 761–764). New York: Kluwer/Plenum.

Meyers, J., & Meyers, B. (2003). Bi-directional influences between positive psychology and primary prevention. *School Psychology Quarterly, 18* (2), 222–229.

Miles, M., & Huberman, A. (1994). *Qualitative data analysis* (2d ed.). Thousand Oaks, CA: Sage.

Miller, D., & DuPaul, G. (1996). School-basd prevention of adolescent suicide: Issues, obstacles, and recommendations for practice. *Journal of Emotional and Behavioral Disorders, 4* (4), 221–230.

Miller, J. B. (1976). *Toward a new psychology of women.* Boston: Beacon Press.

Miller, K. (2004). Beyond the frontstage: Trust, access, and the relational context in research with refugee communities. *American Journal of Community Psychology, 33,* 217–228.

Miller, K., & Banyard, V. (Eds.) (1998). Qualitative research in community psychology [Special issue]. *American Journal of Community Psychology, 26*(4).

Miller, R. L., & Shinn, M. (2005). Learning from communities: Overcoming difficulties in dissemination of prevention and promotion efforts. *American Journal of Community Psychology, 35,* 169–184.

Mirowsky, J., & Ross, C. (1989). *Social causes of psychological distress.* New York: Aldine de Gruyter.

Moane, G. (2003). Bridging the personal and the political: Practices for a liberation psychology. *American Journal of Community Psychology, 31,* 91–102.

Mock, M. R. (1999, Winter). Cultural competency: Acts of justice in community mental health. *The Community Psychologist, 32,* 38–41.

Moghaddam, F. (2005). The staircase to terrorism: A psychological explanation. *American Psychologist, 60,* 161–169.

Moghaddam, F., & Marsella, A. J. (Eds.). (2004). *Understanding terrorism: Psychosocial roots, consequences, and interventions.* Washington, DC: American Psychological Association.

Mohatt, G., Hazel, K., Allen, J., Stachelrodt, M., Hensel, C. & Fath, R. (2004). Unheard Alaska: Culturally anchored participatory action research on sobriety with Alaska Natives. *American Journal of Community Psychology, 33,* 263–274.

Mokrue, K., Elias, M. J., & Bry, B. H. (2005). Dosage effect and the efficacy of a video-based teamwork-building series with urban elementary school children. *Journal of Applied School Psychology, 21* (1), 67–97.

Molock, S. D., & Douglas, K. B. (1999, Summer). Suicidality in the Black community: A collaborative response from a womanist theologian and a community psychologist. *The Community Psychologist, 32,* 32–36.

Montero, M. (1996). Parallel lives: Community psychology in Latin America and the United States. *American Journal of Community Psychology,* 24, 589–606.

Montero, M. (Ed.). (2002). Conceptual and epistemological aspects in community social psychology [Special issue]. *American Journal of Community Psychology, 30*(4).

Moore, T., Kloos, B., & Rasmussen, R. (2001). A reunion of ideas: Complementary inquiry and collaborative interventions of spirituality, religion and psychology. *Journal of Community Psychology, 29,* 487–496.

Moos, R. (1973). Conceptualizations of human environments. *American Psychologist, 28,* 652–665.

Moos, R. (1975). *Evaluating correctional and community settings.* New York: Wiley.

Moos, R. (1984). Context and coping: Toward a unifying conceptual framework. *American Journal of Community Psychology, 12,* 5–25.

Moos, R. (1994). *The social climate scales: A user's guide* (2nd. ed.). Palo Alto, CA: Consulting Psychologists Press.

Moos, R. (1996). Understanding environments: The key to improving social processes and program outcomes. *American Journal of Community Psychology, 24,* 193–201.

Moos, R. (2002). The mystery of human context and coping: An unraveling of clues. *American Journal of Community Psychology, 30,* 67–88.

Moos, R. (2003). Social contexts: Transcending their power and their fragility. *American Journal of Community Psychology, 31,* 1–14.

Moos, R. H., & Holahan, C. S., (2003). Dispositional and contextual perspectives on coping: Toward an integrative framework. *Journal of Clinical Psychology, 59,* 1387–1403.

Moos, R., & Moos, B. (1986). *Family Environment Scale manual* (2nd ed.). Palo Alto, CA: Consulting Psychologists Press.

Moos, R., & Trickett, E. J. (1987). *Classroom Environment Scale manual* (2nd ed.). Palo Alto, CA: Consulting Psychologists Press.

Moynihan, D. (1969). *Maximum feasible misunderstanding: Community action in the war on poverty.* New York: Free Press.

Mrazek, P., & Haggerty, R. (1994). *Reducing risks for mental disorders: Frontiers for preventive intervention research.* Washington, DC: National Academy Press.

Muehrer, P. (Ed.). (1997). Prevention research in rural settings [Special issue]. *American Journal of Community Psychology, 25*(4).

Mulvey, A. (1988). Community psychology and feminism: Tensions and commonalities. *Journal of Community Psychology, 16,* 70–83.

Mulvey, A. (2002). Gender, economic context, perceptions of safety,and quality of life: A case study of Lowell, Massachusetts (U.S.A.), 1982–96. *American Journal of Community Psychology, 30,* 655–680.

Mulvey, A., Bond, M. A., Hill, J., & Terenzio, M. (2000). Weaving feminism and community psychology: An introduction to a special issue. *American Journal of Community Psychology, 28,* 585–598.

Mulvey, A., Gridley, H., & Gawith, L. (2001). Convent girls, feminism and community psychology. *Journal of Community Psychology, 29,* 563–584.

Mulvey, A., Guzman, B. & Ayala-Alcantar, C. (2003, Fall). Women from the margins: Challenging U.S. military aggression, policies and SCRA. *The Community Psychologist, 36,* 31–34.

Murray, H. (1938). *Explorations in personality.* New York: Oxford University Press.

Murrell, S. (1973). *Community psychology and social systems.* New York: Behavioral Publications.

Myers, J. K., & Bean, L. L. (1968). *A decade later: A follow-up of "Social class and mental illness"*. New York: Wiley.

Myers, L. J., & Speight, S. (1994). Optimal theory and the psychology of human diversity. In E. J. Trickett, R. J. Watts, & D. Birman (Eds.), *Human diversity: Perspectives on people in context* (pp. 81–100). San Francisco: Jossey-Bass.

Nadler, A. (2002). Inter-group helping relations as power relations: Maintaining or challenging social dominance between groups through helping. *Journal of Social Issues, 58,* 487–501.

Naegele, K. (1955). A mental health project in a Boston suburb. In B. Paul (Ed.), *Health, culture and community* (pp. 295–323). New York: Russell Sage Foundation.

Nagler, M. (2001). *Is there no other way? The search for a nonviolent future.* Berkeley, CA: Berkeley Hills Books.

Nation, M., Crusto, C., Wandersman, A., Kumpfer, K. Seyboldt, D. Morriessey-Kane, E. & Davino, K. (2003). What works in prevention: Principles of effective prevention programs. *American Psychologist, 58,* 449–456.

Nation, M., Wandersman, A., & Perkins, D. D. (2002). Promoting healthy communities through community development. In D. Glenwick & L. Jason, (Eds.), *Innovative strategies for preventing psychological problems* (pp. 324–344). New York: Springer.

National Mental Health Association (n.d.). *Katrina: NMHA responds.* Retrieved October 1, 2005 from http://www.nmha.org/katrina/index.cfm

Neft, D., & Elias, M. J. (in press). The social, emotional, and academic competencies of elementary school bullies: "Thugs" or "Thinkers"? *American Journal of Orthopsychiatry.*

Neigher, W., & Fishman, D. (2004, Spring). Case studies in community practice. *The Community Psychologist, 37,* 30–34.

Nelson, G., Pancer, S. M., Hayward, K., & Peters, R. DeV. (2005). *Partnerships for prevention: The story of the Highfield Community Enrichment Project.* Toronto: University of Toronto Press.

Nelson, G., & Prilleltensky, I. (Eds.). (2005). *Community psychology: In pursuit of liberation and well-being.* New York: Palgrave Macmillan.

Nelson, G., Prilleltensky, I., & MacGillivray, H. (2001). Building value-based partnerships: Toward solidarity with oppressed groups. *American Journal of Community Psychology, 29,* 649–678.

Newbrough, J. R. (1995). Toward community: A third position. *American Journal of Community Psychology, 23,* 9–38.

Newbrough, J. R. (Ed.). (1996). Sense of community [Special issue]. *Journal of Community Psychology, 24*(4).

Newbrough, J. R. (1997). [Untitled videotape interview]. In J. G. Kelly (Ed.), *The history of community psychology: A video presentation of context and exemplars.* Chicago: Society for Community Research and Action.

Newbrough, J. R., & Chavis, D. M. (Eds.). (1986a). Psychological sense of community: I. Theory and concepts [Special issue]. *Journal of Community Psychology, 14*(1).

Newbrough, J. R., & Chavis, D. M. (Eds.). (1986b). Psychological sense of community: II. Research and applications [Special issue]. *Journal of Community Psychology, 14*(4).

Nobles, W. W. (1991). African philosophy: Foundations of Black psychology. In R. L. Jones (Ed.), *Black psychology* (3rd. ed.) (pp. 47–64). Berkeley, CA: Cobb & Henry.

Noguera, P. (2004). Transforming high schools. *Educational Leadership, 61* (8), 26–32.

Norris, F., Friedman, M., & Watson, P. (2002). 60,000 disaster victims speak: Part II. Summary and implications of the disaster mental health research. *Psychiatry: Interpersonal and Biological Processes, 65,* 240–260.

Norris, F., Friedman, M., Watson, P., Byrne, C., Diaz, E. & Kaniasty, K. (2002). 60,000 disaster victims speak: Part I. An empirical review of the empirical literature, 1981–2001. *Psychiatry: Interpersonal and Biological Processes, 65,* 207–239.

Northwest Regional Educational Laboratory (National Mentoring Center). (1999). *Making the case: Measuring the impact of your mentoring program* (pp. 41). Available online at: http://www.nwrel.org/mentoring/pdf/makingcase.pdf

Novaco, R., & Monahan, J. (1980). Research in community psychology: An analysis of work published in the first six years of the American Journal of Community Psychology. *American Journal of Community Psychology, 8,* 131–145.

Novick, B., Kress, J. S., & Elias, M. J. (2002). *Building learning communities with character: How to integrate academic, social, and emotional learning.* Alexandria, VA: Association for Supervision and Curriculum Development.

Obst, P. & White, K. (2004). Revisiting the Sense of Community Index: A confirmatory factor analysis. *Journal of Community Psychology, 32,* 691–706.

Obst, P., Zinkiewicz, L., & Smith, S. (2002). Sense of community in science fiction fandom, Part 2: Comparing neighborhood and interest group sense of community. *Journal of Community Psychology, 30,* 105–118.

O'Donnell, C. R. (2005a, June). Beyond diversity: Toward a cultural community psychology. Presidential address at the Biennial Meeting of the Society for Community Research and Action, Urbana-Champaign, Illinois.

O'Donnell, C. R. (2005b). Juvenile delinquency: Peers, mentors, and activity settings. In C. R. O'Donnell

& L. A. Yamauchi (Eds.), *Culture and context in human behavior change: Theory, research, and applications* (pp. 85–100). New York: Peter Lang.

O'Donnell, C. R., Tharp, R. G., & Wilson, K. (1993). Activity settings as the unit of analysis: A theoretical basis for community intervention and development. *American Journal of Community Psychology, 21,* 501–520.

O'Donnell, C. R., & Yamauchi, L. (Eds.) (2005). *Culture and context in human behavior change: Theory, research, and applications.* New York: Peter Lang.

Oetting, E., Jumper-Thurman, P., Plested, B., & Edwards, R. (2001). Communty readiness and health services. *Substance Use and Misuse, 36,* 825–843.

Office of Juvenile Justice and Delinquency Prevention. (1995). *Guide for implementing the comprehensive strategy for serious, violent, and chronic juvenile offenders.* Washington, DC: U. S. Department of Justice.

Olds, D. (1988). The Prenatal/Early Infancy Project. In R. Price, E. Cowen, R. Lorion, & J. Ramos-McKay (Eds.), *Fourteen ounces of prevention* (pp. 9–23). Washington, DC: American Psychological Association.

Olds, D. (1997). The Prenatal/Early Infancy Project: Fifteen years later. In G. Albee & T. Gullotta (Eds.), *Primary prevention works* (pp. 41–67). Thousand Oaks, CA: Sage.

O'Leary, V. (1998). Strength in the face of adversity: Individual and social thriving. *Journal of Social Issues, 54,* 425–446.

Olson, B. (2003, Fall). Ten primary notions for the SCRA community action interest group. *The Community Psychologist, 36,* 34–35.

Olson, B. (2004, Fall). Thoughts on attending SCRA at the APA convention this year. *The Community Psychologist, 37,* 48–49.

Olson, L. (1994, November 2). Learning their lessons: Scaling up; bringing good schools to every community. *Education Week, 14*(9), 43–46.

Olsson, J., Powell, B., & Stuehling, J. (1998). *Cultural bridges training manual* (Available from Cultural Bridges, 341 Ontelaunee Trail, Hamburg, PA 19526).

Olweus, D., Limber, S., & Mihalic, S. (1999). *The Bullying Prevention Program: Blueprints for violence prevention* (Vol. 10). Boulder, CO: Center for the Study and Prevention of Violence.

O'Neill, P. (1989). Responsible to whom? Responsible for what? Some ethical issues in community intervention. *American Journal of Community Psychology, 17,* 323–342.

Ortiz-Torres, B., Serrano-Garcia, I. & Torres-Burgos, N. (2000). Subverting culture: Promoting HIV/AIDS prevention among Puerto Rican and Dominican women. *American Journal of Community Psychology, 28,* 859–882.

Osher, D., Dwyer, K., & Jackson, S. (2002). *Safe, supportive, and successful schools, step by step.* Rockville, MD: U.S. Department of Health and Human Services, Substance Abuse and Mental Health Services Administration, Center for Mental Health Services.

Ostrove, J., & Cole, E. (2003). Privileging class: Toward a critical psychology of social class in the context of education. *Journal of Social Issues, 59,* 677–692.

Oxley, D., & Barrera, M. (1984). Undermanning theory and the workplace: Implications of setting size for job satisfaction and social support. *Environment and Behavior, 16,* 211–234.

Pager, D. (2003). The mark of a criminal record. *American Journal of Sociology, 108,* 937–975.

Paradis, E. (2000). Feminist and community psychology ethics in research with homeless women. *American Journal of Community Psychology, 28,* 839–858.

Pargament, K. I. (1997). *The psychology of religion and coping: Theory, research and practice.* New York: Guilford.

Pargament, K. I., Maton, K. I., & Hess, R. (Eds.). (1992). *Religion and prevention in mental health: Research, vision, and action.* New York: Haworth.

Park, R. (1952). *Human communities: The city and human ecology.* New York: Free Press.

Patton, M. Q. (1997). *Utilization-focused evaluation* (3rd ed.). Thousand Oaks, CA: Sage.

Paul, B. (Ed.) (1955). *Health, culture and community.* New York: Russell Sage Foundation.

Paul, M. (2004). Clinical implications in healing from domestic violence: A case study. *American Psychologist, 59,* 809–816.

Payne, C. (1995). *I've got the light of freedom: The organizing tradition and the Mississippi freedom struggle.* Berkeley, CA: University of California Press.

Pedro-Carroll, J. (1997). The Children of Divorce Intervention Program: Fostering resilient outcomes for school-aged children. In G. W. Albee & T. Gullotta (Eds.), *Primary prevention works* (pp. 213–238). Thousand Oaks, CA: Sage.

Pedro-Carroll, J., & Alpert-Gillis, L. (1997). Preventive interventions for children of divorce: A developmental model for 5 and 6 year old children. *Journal of Primary Prevention, 18* (1), 5–23.

Pepler, D., Craig, W., Ziegler, S. & Charach, A. (1994). An evaluation of an anti-bulllying intervention in Toronto schools. *Canadian Journal of Community Mental Health, 13* (2), 95–110.

Pepler, D., & Slaby, R. (1994). Theoretical and developmental perspectives on youth and violence. In L. Eron, J. Gentry, & P. Schlegel (Eds.), *Reason to hope: A psychosocial perspective on violence and youth* (pp. 27–58). Washington, DC: American Psychological Association.

Perkins, D. D. (1988). The use of social science in public interest litigation: A role for community psychologists. *American Journal of Community Psychology, 16,* 465–486.

Perkins, D. D. (1995). Speaking truth to power: Empowerment ideology as social intervention and policy. *American Journal of Community Psychology, 23,* 765–794.

Perkins, D. D., Brown, B. B., & Taylor, R. B. (1996). The ecology of empowerment: Predicting participation in community organizations. *Journal of Social Issues, 52,* 85–110.

Perkins, D. D., Crim, B., Silberman, P. & Brown, B. (2004). Community development as a response to community-level adversity: Ecological theory and strengths-based policy. In K. Maton, C. Schellenbach, B. Leadbeater & A. Solarz (Eds.), *Investing in children, youth, families and communities: Strengths-based research and policy* (pp. 321–340). Washington, DC: American Psychological Association.

Perkins, D. D., Florin, P., Rich, R., Wandersman, A., & Chavis, D. (1990). Participation and the social and physical environment of residential blocks: Crime and community context. *American Journal of Community Psychology, 18,* 83–116.

Perkins, D. D. & Long, D. A. (2002). Neighborhod sense of community and social capital: A multi-level analysis. In A. Fisher, C. Sonn, & B. Bishop (Eds.), *Psychological sense of community: Research, applications and implications* (pp. 291–318). New York: Kluwer/Plenum.

Perkins, D. D., & Taylor, R. (1996). Ecological assessments of community disorder: Their relationship to fear of crime and theoretical implications. *American Journal of Community Psychology, 24,* 63–108. Reprinted in T. Revenson, A. D'Augelli, S. E. French, D. Hughes, D. Livert, E. Seidman, M. Shinn, & H. Yoshikawa (Eds.), (2002), *Ecological research to promote social change: Methodological advances from community psychology* (pp. 127–170). New York: Kluwer Academic/Plenum.

Perkins, D. D., & Zimmerman, M. (1995). Empowerment theory, research and application. *American Journal of Community Psychology, 23,* 569–580.

Perkins, D. V., Burns, T., Perry, J., & Nielsen, K. (1988). Behavior setting theory and community psychology: An analysis and critique. *Journal of Community Psychology, 16,* 355–372.

Perry, C., & Jessor, R. (1985). The concept of health promotion and the prevention of adolescent drug abuse. *Health Education Quarterly, 12,* 169–184.

Peterson, N. A., & Reid, R. (2003). Paths to psychological empowerment in an urban community: Sense of community and citizen participation in substance abuse prevention activities. *Journal of Community Psychology, 31,* 25–38.

Peterson, N. A. & Zimmerman, M. (2004). Beyond the individual: Toward a nomological network of organizational empowerment. *American Journal of Community Psychology, 34,* 129–146.

Phillips, D. (2000). Social policy and community psychology. In J. Rappaport & E. Seidman (Eds.), *Handbook of community psychology* (pp. 397–420). New York: Kluwer/Plenum.

Phinney, J. (1990). Ethnic identity in adolescents and adults: Review of research. *Psychological Bulletin, 108,* 499–514.

Phinney, J. (2003). Ethnic identity and acculturation. In K. Chun, P. Organista, & G. Marin (Eds.), *Acculturation: Advances in theory, measurement and applied research* (pp. 63–94). Washington, DC: American Psychological Association.

Phinney, J., Horenczyk, G., Liebkind, K. & Vedder, P. (2001). Ethnic identity, immigration, and well-being: An ineractional perspective. *Journal of Social Issues, 57,* 493–510.

Pickren, W., Tomes H. (2002). The legacy of Kenneth B. Clark to the APA: The Board of Social and

Ethical Responsibility. *American Psychologist, 57,* 51–59.

Pistrang, N., & Barker, C. (1998). Partners and fellow patients: Two sources of emotional support for women with breast cancer. *American Journal of Community Psychology, 26,* 439–456.

Plas, J. M., & Lewis, S. E. (1996). Environmental factors and sense of community in a planned town. *American Journal of Community Psychology, 24,* 109–144.

Pokorny, S., Baptiste, D., Tolan P., Hirsch, B., Talbot, B., Ji, P., Paikoff, R., & Madison-Boyd, S. (2004). Prevention science: participatory approaches and community case studies. In L. A. Jason, C. Keys, Y. Suarez-Balcazar, R. Taylor, & M. Davis (Eds.), *Participatory community research: Theories and methods in action* (pp. 87–104). Washington, DC: American Psychological Association.

Potts, R. (Ed.). (1999, Summer). The spirit of community psychology: Spirituality, religion, and community action [Special section]. *The Community Psychologist, 32.*

Potts, R. (2003). Emancipatory education versus school based prevention in African American communities. *American Journal of Community Psychology, 31,* 173–185.

Power, R. (1998). The role of qualitative research in HIV/AIDS. *AIDS 12*(7), 687–695.

Pratkanis, A. R., & Turner, M. E. (1996). Persuasion and democracy: Strategies for increasing deliberative participation and enacting social change. *Journal of Social Issues, 52,* 187–206.

Prelow, H. M., Danoff-Burg, S., Swenson, R. & Pulgiano, D. (2004). The impact of ecological risk and perceived discrimination on psychological adjustment of African American and European American youths. *Journal of Community Psychology, 32,* 375–389.

Prestby, J., Wandersman, A., Florin, P., Rich, R., & Chavis, D. (1990). Benefits, costs, incentive management and participation in vountary organizations: A means to understanding and promoting empowerment. *American Journal of Community Psychology, 18,* 117–150.

Pretty, G. M. H. (2002). Young people's development of the community-minded self: Considering community identity, community attachment, and sense of community. In A. Fisher, C. Sonn, & B. Bishop (Eds.), *Psychological sense of community: Research, applications and implications* (pp. 183–203). New York: Kluwer/Plenum.

Pretty, G. M. H., Andrewes, L., & Collett, C. (1994). Exploring adolescents' sense of community and its relationship to loneliness. *Journal of Community Psychology, 22,* 346–358.

Pretty, G. M. H., Conroy, C., Dugay, J., Fowler, K., & Williams, D. (1996). Sense of community and its relevance to adolescents of all ages. *Journal of Community Psychology, 24,* 365–380.

Prezza, M., Amici, M., Roberti, T., & Tedeschi, G. (2001). Sense of community referred to the whole town: Its relations with neighboring, loneliness, life satisfaction, and area of residence. *Journal of Community Psychology, 29,* 29–52.

Price, R. (1989). Bearing witness. *American Journal of Community Psychology, 17,* 151–167.

Price, R. (2002). Cultural collaboration for prevention and promotion: Implementing the JOBS program in China, California, and Finland. In C. Hosman (Ed.), *Proceedings of the second world conference on the promotion of mental health and prevention of mental and behavioural disorders.* London: World Federation of Mental Health.

Price, R., & Cherniss, C. (1977). Training for a new profession: Research as social action. *Professional Psychology, 8,* 222–231.

Price, R., Cowen, E., Lorion, R., & Ramos-McKay, J. (Eds.). (1988). *Fourteen ounces of prevention: A casebook for practitioners.* Washington, DC: American Psychological Association.

Price, R., & Lorion, R. (1989). Prevention programming as organizational reinvention: From research to implementation. In D. Shaffer, I. Phillips, & N. Enzer (Eds.), *Prevention of mental disorders, alcohol and other drug use in children and adolescents* (pp. 97–123). Office of Substance Abuse Prevention, Prevention Monograph No. 2 (Department of Health and Human Services Publication No. ADM 89–1646). Washington, DC: U.S. Government Printing Office.

Price, R., & Smith, S. (1985). *A guide to evaluating prevention programs in mental health.* (Department of Health and Human Services Publication No. ADM 85–144). Washington, DC: U.S. Government Printing Office.

Price, R. H., Van Ryn, M., & Vinokur, A. (1992). Impact of a preventive job search intervention on the likelihood of depression among the unemployed. *Journal of Health and Social Behavior, 33,* 158–167.

Priesmeyer, M. (2005, September 20). New Orleans: Survivor stories. *City Pages, 26*(1294). Retrieved October 25, 2005 from http://citypages.com/databank/26/1294/article13694.asp?page=21

Prilleltensky, I. (1997). Values, assumptions, and practices: Assessing the moral implications of psychological discourse and action. *American Psychologist, 52,* 517–535.

Prilleltensky, I. (2001). Value-based praxis in community psychology: Moving toward social justice and social action. *American Journal of Community Psychology, 29,* 747–778.

Prilleltensky, I. (2003). Understanding, resisting, and overcoming oppression: Toward psychopolitical validity. *American Journal of Community Psychology, 31,* 195–202.

Prilleltensky, I. & Gonick, L. (1994). The discourse of oppression in the social sciences: Past, present, and future. In E. J. Trickett, R. J. Watts, & D. Birman (Eds.), *Human diversity: Perspectives on people in context* (pp. 145–177). San Francisco: Jossey-Bass.

Prilleltensky, I., & Nelson, G. (2002). *Doing psychology critically: Making a difference in diverse settings.* New York: Palgrave Macmillan.

Primavera, J. (2004). You can't get there from here: Identifying process routes to replication. *American Journal of Community Psychology, 33,* 181–191.

Primavera, J., & Brodsky, A. (2004). Process of community research and action [Special issue]. *American Journal of Community Psychology, 33*(3/4).

Prochaska, J. O., & DiClemente, C. (1983). Stages and processes of self-change of smoking. *Journal of Consulting and Clinical Psychology, 51,* 390–395.

Puddifoot, J. (1996). Some initial considerations in the measurement of community identity. *Journal of Community Psychology, 24,* 327–336.

Putnam, R. (2000). *Bowling alone: The collapse and revival of American community.* New York: Simon & Schuster.

Putnam, R. (2002). Conclusion. In R. Putnam, (Ed.), *Democracies in flux: The evolution of social capital in contemporary society* (pp. 393–416). New York: Oxford University Press.

Putnam, R., & Feldstein, L., with Cohen, D. (2003). *Better together: Restoring the American community.* New York: Simon & Schuster.

Rapley, M., & Pretty, G. (1999). Playing Procrustes: The interactional production of a "psychological sense of community." *Journal of Community Psychology, 27,* 695–714.

Rappaport, J. (1977). *Community psychology: Values, research, and action.* New York: Holt, Rinehart and Winston.

Rappaport, J. (1981). In praise of paradox: A social policy of empowerment over prevention. *American Journal of Community Psychology, 9,* 1–25. Reprinted in T. Revenson, A. D'Augelli, S. E. French, D. Hughes, D. Livert, E. Seidman, M. Shinn, & H. Yoshikawa (Eds.), (2002), *A quarter century of community psychology* (pp. 121–145). New York: Kluwer Academic/Plenum.

Rappaport, J. (1987). Terms of empowerment/exemplars of prevention: Toward a theory for community psychology. *American Journal of Community Psychology, 15,* 121–144.

Rappaport, J. (1990). Research methods and the empowerment social agenda. In P. Tolan, C. Keys, F. Chertok, & L. Jason (Eds.), *Researching community psychology* (pp. 51–63). Washington, DC: American Psychological Association.

Rappaport, J. (1993). Narrative studies, personal stories, and identity transformation in the mutual help context. *Journal of Applied Behavioral Science, 29,* 239–256.

Rappaport, J. (1995). Empowerment meets narrative: Listening to stories and creating settings. *American Journal of Community Psychology, 23,* 795–808.

Rappaport, J. (2000). Community narratives: Tales of terror and joy. *American Journal of Community Psychology, 28,* 1–24.

Rappaport, J., & Seidman, E. (Eds.). (2000). *Handbook of community psychology.* New York: Plenum.

Rapping, E. (1997, Spring). There's self-help and then there's self-help: Women and the recovery movement. *Social Policy,* 56–61.

Raven, B. (1999). Kurt Lewin address: Influence, power, religion, and the mechanisms of social control. *Journal of Social Issues, 55,* 161–186.

Raviv, A., Raviv, A., & Reisel, E. (1990). Teachers and students: Two different perspectives? Measuring social climate in the classroom. *American Educational Research Journal, 27,* 141–157.

Reason, P., & Bradbury, H. (Eds.). (2001). *Handbook of action research: Participative inquiry and practice.* London: Sage.

Recording Katrina: A collection of survivors' stories and non-traditional reporting on the recovery effort in the Gulf (n.d.). Retrieved October 25, 2005 from http://recordingkatrina.blogspot.com/

Redding, R. (2001). Sociopolitical diversity in psychology: The case for pluralism. *American Psychologist, 56,* 205–215.

Reid, T. R. (1999). *Confucius lives next door.* New York: Random House.

Reiff, R. (1966, May). The ideological and technological implications of clinical psychology. Invited address, Boston Conference on the Education of Psychologists for Community Mental Health.

Reiff, R. (1977). Ya gotta believe. In I. Iscoe, B. Bloom, & C. Spielberger (Eds.), *Community psychology in transition: Proceedings of the National Conference on Training in Community Psychology* (pp. 45–50). Washington, DC: Hemisphere/Wiley.

Reinharz, S. (1984). Alternative settings and social change. In K. Heller, R. Price, S. Reinharz, S. Riger, & A. Wandersman, *Psychology and community change* (2nd ed.) (pp. 286–336). Homewood, IL: Dorsey.

Reinharz, S. (1994). Toward an ethnography of "voice" and "silence". In E. J. Trickett, R. J. Watts, & D. Birman (Eds.), *Human diversity: Perspectives on people in context* (pp. 178–200). San Francisco: Jossey-Bass.

Repetti, R., & Cosmas, K. (1991). The quality of the social environment at work and job satisfaction. *Journal of Applied Social Psychology, 21,* 840–854.

Resnicow, K., Braithwaite, R., Ahluwalia, J., & Baranowski, T. (1999). Cultural sensitivity in public health: Defined and demystified. *Ethnicity and Disease, 9,* 10–21.

Revenson, T., D'Augelli, A., French, S., Hughes, D., Livert, D., Seidman, E., Shinn, M., & Yoshikawa, H. (Eds.). (2002a). *A quarter century of community psychology: Readings from the American Journal of Community Psychology.* New York: Kluwer/Plenum.

Revenson, T., D'Augelli, A., French, S., Hughes, D., Livert, D., Seidman, E., Shinn, M., & Yoshikawa, H. (Eds.). (2002b). *Ecological research to promote social change: Methodological advances from community psychology.* New York: Kluwer Academic/Plenum.

Revenson, T., & Seidman, E. (2002). Looking backward and moving forward: Reflections on a quarter century of community psychology. In T. Revenson, A. D'Augelli, S. E. French, D. Hughes, D. Livert, E. Seidman, M. Shinn, & H. Yoshikawa (Eds.), (2002), *A quarter century of community psychology* (pp. 3–32). New York: Kluwer Academic/Plenum.

Reyes, O., Gillock, K., & Kobus, K. (1994). A longitudinal study of school adjustment in urban, minority adolescents: Effects of a high school transition program. *American Journal of Community Psychology, 22,* 341–370.

Reynolds, A. J., Temple, J. A., Robertson, D. L., & Mann, E. A. (2001). Long-term effects of an early childhood intervention on educational achievement and juvenile arrest: A 15-year follow-up of low-income children in public schools. *Journal of the American Medical Association, 285*(18), 2339–2346.

Rhodes, J. E. (1994). Older and wiser: Mentoring relationships in childhood and adolescence. *Journal of Primary Prevention, 14,* 187–196.

Rhodes, J. E., & Bogat, G. A. (2002). Special issue: Youth mentoring. *American Journal of Community Psychology, 30*(2).

Rhodes, J. E., Bogat, G. A., Roffman, J., Edelman, P., & Galasso, L. (2002). Youth mentoring in perspective: Introduction to the special issue. *American Journal of Community Psychology, 30,* 149–156.

Rhodes, J. E., & Woods, M. (1995). Comfort and conflict in the relationships of pregnant, minority adolescents: Social support as moderator of social strain. *Journal of Community Psychology, 22,* 74–84.

Rice, J. (2001). Poverty, welfare, and patriarchy: How macro-level changes in social policy can help low-income women. *Journal of Social Issues, 57,* 355–374.

Rich, R. C., Edelstein, M., Hallman, W., & Wandersman, A. (1995). Citizen participation and empowerment: The case of local environmental hazards. *American Journal of Community Psychology, 23,* 657–676.

Rickard, K. (1990). The effect of feminist identity level on gender prejudice toward artists' illustrations. *Journal of Research in Personality, 24,* 145–162.

Rickel, A. U., & Becker, E. (1997). *Keeping children from harm's way: How national policy affects psychological development.* Washington, DC: American Psychological Association.

Ridgeway, C. (2001). Gender, status, and leadership. *Journal of Social Issues, 57,* 637–656.

Riessman, F. (1990). Restructuring help: A human services paradigm for the 1990's. *American Journal of Community Psychology, 18,* 221–230.

Riessman, F. & Banks, E. (2001). A marriage of opposites: Self-help and the health care system. *American Psychologist, 56,* 173–174.

Riger, S. (1984). Vehicles for empowerment: The case of feminist movement organizations. In J. Rappaport, C. Swift, & R. Hess (Eds.), *Studies in empowerment: Steps toward understanding and action* (pp. 99–118). New York: Haworth.

Riger, S. (1989). The politics of community intervention. *American Journal of Community Psychology, 17,* 379–385.

Riger, S. (1990). Ways of knowing and organizational approaches to community research. In P. Tolan, C. Keys, F. Chertok, & L. Jason (Eds.), *Researching community psychology* (pp. 42–50). Washington, DC: American Psychological Association. Reprinted in S. Riger, (2000), *Transforming psychology: Gender in theory and practice* (pp. 72–80). New York: Oxford University Press.

Riger, S. (1992). Epistemological debates, feminist voices: Science, social values and the study of women. *American Psychologist, 47,* 730–740. Reprinted in S. Riger, (2000), *Transforming psychology: Gender in theory and practice* (pp. 7–22). New York: Oxford University Press.

Riger, S. (1993). What's wrong with empowerment? *American Journal of Community Psychology, 21,* 279–292. Reprinted in T. Revenson, A. D'Augelli, S. E. French, D. Hughes, D. Livert, E. Seidman, M. Shinn & H. Yoshikawa (Eds.), (2002), *A quarter century of community psychology* (pp. 395–408). New York: Kluwer Academic/Plenum. Also reprinted in S. Riger (2000), *Transforming psychology: Gender in theory and practice* (pp. 97–196). New York: Oxford University Press.

Riger, S. (2001). Transforming community psychology. *American Journal of Community Psychology, 29,* 69–81.

Ripple, C., & Zigler, E. (2003). Research, policy, and the federal role in prevention initiatives for children. *American Psychologist, 58* (6/7), 482–490.

RMC Research Corporation. (1995). *National Diffusion Network schoolwide promising practices: Report of a pilot effort.* Portsmouth, NH: Author.

Roberts, A. (Ed.). (2004). *Juvenile justice sourcebook: Past, present, and future.* New York: Oxford University Press.

Roberts, L., Smith, L., & Pollock, C. (2002). MOOing till the cows come home: The search for sense of community in virtual environments. In A. Fisher, C. Sonn, & B. Bishop (Eds.), *Psychological sense of community: Research, applications and implications* (pp. 223–246). New York: Kluwer Academic/Plenum.

Roberts, L. J., Luke, D., Rappaport, J., Seidman, E., Toro, P., & Reischl, T. (1991). Charting uncharted terrain: A behavioral observation system for mutual help groups. *American Journal of Community Psychology, 19,* 715–738.

Roberts, L. J., Salem, D., Rappaport, J., Toro, P. A., Luke, D., & Seidman, E. (1999). Giving and receiving help: Interpersonal transactions in mutual-help meetings and psychosocial adjustment of members. *American Journal of Community Psychology, 27,* 841–868.

Robinson, W. L. (1990). Data feedback and communication to the host setting. In P. Tolan, C. Keys, F. Chertok, & L. Jason (Eds.), *Researching community psychology* (pp. 193–195). Washington, DC: American Psychological Association.

Roemer, A. (2001). The law and its limits: Public policies. In A. Garza (Ed.), *Drug addiction in Mexico: Indifference or prevention* (pp. 271–278). Mexico City: ING Seguros.

Rogler, L. (2002). Historical generations and psychology: The case of the Great Depression and World War II. *American Psychologist, 57,* 1013–1023.

Roll, C. N., Toro, P. A., & Ortola, G. L. (1999). Characteristics and experiences of homeless adults: A comparison of single men, single women, and women with children. *Journal of Community Psychology, 27,* 189–198.

Romasz, T. E., Kantor, J. H., & Elias, M. J. (2004). Implementation and evaluation of urban schoolwide social-emotional learning programs. *Evaluation and Program Planning. 27,* 89–103.

Roosa, M., Jones, S., Tein, J.-Y., & Cree, W. (2003). Prevention science and neighborhood influences on low-income children's development: Theoretical and methodological issues. *American Journal of Community Psychology, 31,* 55–72.

Rosario, M., Hunter, J., Maguen, S., Gwadz, M., & Smith, R. (2001). The coming-out process and its adaptational and health-related associations among gay lesbian, and bisexual youths: Stipulation and exploration of a model. *American Journal of Community Psychology, 29,* 133–160.

Rosenhan, D. (1973). On being sane in insane places. *Science, 179,* 250–258.

Ross, L. (1977). The intuitive psychologist and his shortcomings. In L. Berkowitz, (Ed.), *Advances in experimental social psychology,* Vol. 10 (pp. 173–220). New York: Academic Press.

Rossi, P. H. (1978). Issues in the evaluation of human services delivery. *Evaluation Quarterly, 2,* 573–599.

Rossi, P., Lipsey, M. & Freeman, H. (2004). *Evaluation: A systematic approach* (7th ed.). Newbury Park, CA: Sage.

Roth, J., Brooks-Gunn, J., Murray, L., & Foster, W. (1998). Promoting healthy adolescents: Synthesis of youth development program evaluations. *Journal of Research on Adolescents, 8,* 453–459.

Rotheram-Borus, M. J. (1988). Assertiveness training with children. In R. Price, E. Cowen, R. Lorion, & J. Ramos-McKay (Eds.), *Fourteen ounces of prevention* (pp. 83–97). Washington, DC: American Psychological Association.

Rotter, J. B. (1954). *Social learning and clinical psychology.* Englewood Cliffs, NJ: Prentice-Hall.

Rotter, J. B. (1966). Generalized expectancies for internal versus external contol of reinforcement. *Psychological Monographs, 80* (Whole No. 609).

Rotter, J. B. (1982). *The development and application of social learning theory.* New York: Praeger.

Rotter, J. B. (1990). Internal versus external control of reinforcement: A case history of a variable. *American Psychologist, 45,* 489–493.

Royal, M., & Rossi, R. (1996). Individual-level correlates of sense of community: Findings from workplace and school. *Journal of Community Psychology, 24,* 395–416.

Rudkin, J. K. (2003). *Community psychology: Guiding principles and orienting concepts.* Upper Saddle River, NJ: Prentice Hall.

Rudman, L. & Glick, P. (2001). Prescriptive gender stereotypes and backlash toward agentic women. *Journal of Social Issues, 57,* 743–762.

Ryan, W. (1971). *Blaming the victim.* New York: Random House.

Ryan, W. (1981). *Equality.* New York: Pantheon.

Ryan, W. (1994). Many cooks, brave men, apples, and oranges: How people think about equality. *American Journal of Community Psychology, 22,* 25–36.

Sadker, D., & Zittleman, K. (2004). Text anxiety: Are students failing tests–or are tests failing students? *Phi Delta Kappan, 85*(10), 740–744.

Saegert, S. (1989). Unlikely leaders, extreme circumstances: Older Black women building community households. *American Journal of Community Psychology, 17,* 295–316.

Saegert, S., Thompson, J. P., & Warren, M. (2001). *Social capital and poor communities.* New York: Russell Sage.

Saegert, S., & Winkel, G. (1990). Environmental psychology. *Annual Review of Psychology, 41,* 441–477.

Saegert, S., & Winkel, G. (1996). Paths to community empowerment: Organizing at home. *American Journal of Community Psychology, 24,* 517–550.

Saegert, S., & Winkel, G. (2004). Crime, social capital and community participation. *American Journal of Community Psychology, 34,* 219–234.

Salem, D., Bogat, G. A., & Reid, C. (1997). Mutual help goes on-line. *Journal of Community Psychology, 25,* 189–208.

Salem, D., Reischl, T., Gallacher, F. & Randall, K. (2000). The role of referent and expert power in mutual help. *American Journal of Community Psychology, 28,* 303–324.

Salina, D., Hill, J., Solarz, A., Lesondak, L., Razzano, L., & Dixon, D. (2004). Feminist perspectives: Empowerment behind bars. In L. A. Jason, C. Keys, Y. Suarez-Balcazar, R. Taylor, & M. Davis (Eds.), *Participatory community research: Theories and methods in action* (pp. 159–176). Washington, DC: American Psychological Association.

Sandler, I. N., Gensheimer, L. & Braver, S. (2000). Stress: Theory, research and action. In J. Rappaport & E. Seidman (Eds.), *Handbook of community psychology* (pp. 187–214). New York: Kluwer/Plenum.

Sandler, I. N., West, S. G., Baca, L., Pillow, D. R. Gersten, J. C., Rogosch, F., Virdin, L., Beals, J., Reynolds, K. D., Kallgren, C., Tein, J., Kriege, G., Cole, E., & Cislo, D. A. (1992). Linking empirically based theory and evaluation: The family bereavement program. *American Journal of Community Psychology, 20,* 491–522.

Santiago-Rivera, A., Morse, G. S., Hunt, A., & Lickers, H. (1998). Building a community-based research partnership: Lessons from the Mohawk Nation of Akwesasne. *Journal of Community Psychology, 26,* 163–174.

Santisteban, D., & Mitrani, V. (2003). The influence of accultration processes on the family. In K. Chun, P. Organista, & G. Marin (Eds.), *Acculturation: Advances in theory, measurement and applied research* (pp. 121–135). Washington, DC: American Psychological Association.

Sarason, S. B. (1972). *The creation of settings and the future societies.* San Francisco: Jossey-Bass.

Sarason, S. B. (1974). *The psychological sense of community: Prospects for a community psychology.* San Fransisco: Jossey-Bass.

Sarason, S. B. (1976). Community psychology and the anarchist insight. *American Journal of Community Psychology, 4,* 243–261.

Sarason, S. B. (1978). The nature of problem-solving in social action. *American Psychologist, 33,* 370–380.

Sarason, S. B. (1982). *The culture of the school and the problem of change* (2nd ed.). Boston: Allyn & Bacon.

Sarason, S. B. (1988). *The making of an American psychologist: An autobiography.* San Francisco: Jossey-Bass.

Sarason, S. B. (1993). American psychology and the needs for the transcendence and community. *American Journal of Community Psychology, 21,* 185–202.

Sarason, S. B. (1994). The American worldview. In S. B. Sarason, *Psychoanalysis, General Custer, and the verdicts of history, and other essays on psychology in the social scene* (pp. 100–118). San Francisco: Jossey-Bass.

Sarason, S. B. (1995). [Untitled videotape interview]. In J. G. Kelly (Ed.), *The history of community psychology: A video presentation of context and exemplars.* Chicago: Society for Community Research and Action.

Sarason, S. B. (2002). *Educational reform: A self-scrutinizing memoir.* Teachers College Press.

Sarason, S. B. (2003a). The obligations of the moral-scientific stance. *American Journal of Community Psychology, 31,* 209–212.

Sarason, S. B. (2003b). American psychology and the schools: A critique. *American Journal of Community Psychology, 32,* 99–106.

Sasao, T. (1999, Winter). Cultural competence promotion as a general prevention strategy in urban settings: Some lessons learned from working with Asian American adolescents. *The Community Psychologist, 32,* 41–43.

Sasao, T., & Sue, S. (1993). Toward a culturally anchored ecological framework of research in ethnic-cultural communities. *American Journal of Community Psychology, 21,* 705–728.

Scheier, M. F., Carver, C. S., & Bridges, M. W. (2001). Optimism, pessimism, and psychological well-being. In E. C. Chang (Ed.), *Optimism and pessimism: Implications for theory, research, and practice,* (pp. 189–216). Washington, DC: American Psychological Association.

Schleifstein, M., & McQuaid, J. (2002, June 23). The big one. *The Times Picayune: Special Edition* [Electronic version]. Retrieved October 25, 2005, from http://www.nola.com/printer/printer.ssf?/washingaway/thebigone_1.html

Schlenger, W., Caddell, J., Ebert, L., Jordan, B. K., Rourke, K., Wilson, D., Thalji, L., Dennis, J. M., Fairbank, J., & Kulka, R. (2002). Psychological reactions to terrorist attacks: Findings from the National Study of Americans' Reactions to September 11. *Journal of the American Medical Association, 288*(5), 581–588.

Schneider, M., & Harper, G. (2003). Lesbian, gay, bisexual and transgendered communities: Linking theory, research and practice [Special issue]. *American Journal of Community Psychology, 31*(3/4).

Schoggen, P. (1988). Commentary on Perkins, Burns, Perry & Nielsen's "Behavior setting theory and community psychology: An analysis and critique". *Journal of Community Psychology, 16,* 373–386.

Schoggen, P. (1989). *Behavior settings.* Stanford, CA: Stanford University Press.

Schoggen, P., & Schoggen, M. (1988). Student voluntary participation and high school size. *Journal of Educational Research, 81,* 288–293.

Schorr, L. (1988). *Within our reach: Breaking the cycle of disadvantage.* New York: Doubleday.

Schorr, L. (1997). *Common purpose: Strengthening families and neighborhoods to rebuild America. New York:* Anchor Books.

Schubert, M., & Borkman, T. (1991). An organizational typology for self-help groups. *American Journal of Community Psychology, 19,* 769–788.

Schwartz, S. H. (1994). Are there universal aspects in the structure and contents of human values? *Journal of Social Issues, 50*(4), 19–46.

Schweinhart, L., & Weikart, D. (1988). The High/Scope Perry Preschool Program. In R. Price, E. Cowen, R. Lorion, & J. Ramos-McKay (Eds.), *Fourteen ounces of prevention* (pp. 53–65). Washington, DC: American Psychological Association.

Scott, J. & Leonhardt, D. (2005, May 15). Class matters: Shadowy lines that still divide. *New York Times* [Electronic version]. Retrieved June 1, 2005, from: http://www.nytimes.com

Search Institute (2004). *40 developmental assets.* Downloaded October 21, 2005, from http://www.search-institute.org/assets/

Seidman, E. (1988). Back to the future, community psychology: Unfolding a theory of social intervention. *American Journal of Community Psychology, 16,* 3–24. Reprinted in T. Revenson, A. D'Augelli, S. E. French, D. Hughes, D. Livert, E. Seidman, M. Shinn & H. Yoshikawa (Eds.), (2002), *A quarter century of community psychology* (pp. 181–203). New York: Kluwer Academic/Plenum.

Seidman, E. (1990). Pursuing the meaning and utility of social regularities for community psychology. In P. Tolan, C. Keys, F. Chertok, & L. Jason (Eds.), *Researching community psychology* (pp. 91–100). Washington, DC: American Psychological Association.

Seidman, E. (1991). Growing up the hard way: Pathways of urban adolescents. *American Journal of Community Psychology, 19,* 173–206.

Seidman, E. (2003). Fairweather and ESID: Contemporary impact and a legacy for the twenty-first century. *American Journal of Community Psychology, 32,* 371–375.

Seidman, E., Aber, J. L., Allen, L., & French, S. E. (1996). The impact of the transition to high school on the self-system and perceived social context of poor urban youth. *American Journal of Community Psychology, 24,* 489–516.

Seidman, E., Aber, J. L., & French, S. E. (2004). The organization of schooling and adolescent development. In K. Maton, C. Schellenbach, B. Leadbeater & A. Solarz (Eds.), *Investing in children, youth, families, and communities* (pp. 233–250). Washington, DC: American Psychological Association.

Seidman, E., Allen, L., Aber, J. L., Mitchell, C., & Feinman, J. (1994). The impact of school transitions in early adolescence on the self-system and perceived social context of poor urban youth. *Child Development, 65,* 507–522.

Seidman, E., & Rappaport, J. (Eds.). (1986). *Redefining social problems.* New York: Plenum.

Seligman, M., & Csikszentmihalyi, M. (Eds.). (2000a). Positive psychology [Special issue]. *American Psychologist, 55*(1).

Seligman, M., & Csikszentmihalyi, M. (2000b). Positive psychology: An introduction. *American Psychologist, 55* (1), 5–14.

Sellers, R. M., Smith, M., Shelton, J. N., Rowley, S., & Chavous, T. (1998). Multidimensional model of racial identity: A reconceptualization of African American racial identity. *Personality and Social Psychology Review, 2,* 18–39.

Senge, P. (1990). *The fifth discipline: The art and practice of organizational learning.* New York: Doubleday.

Serrano-Garcia, I. (1994). The ethics of the powerful and the power of ethics. *American Journal of Community Psychology, 22,* 1–20.

Shadish, W., Cook, T., & Campbell, D. (2002). *Experimental and quasi-experimental designs for generalized causal inference.* Washington, DC: American Psychological Association.

Shapiro, D. H., Schwartz, C. E., & Astin, J. (1996). Controlling ourselves, controlling our world: Psychology's role in understanding positive and negative consequences of seeking and gaining control. *American Psychologist, 51,* 1213–1230.

Shen, B.-J., & Takeuchi, D. (2001). A structural model of acculturation and mental health status among Chinese Americans. *American Journal of Community Psychology, 29,* 387–418.

Shinn, M. (1990). Mixing and matching: Levels of conceptualization, measurement, and statistical analysis in community research. In P. Tolan, C. Keys, F. Chertok, & L. Jason (Eds.), *Researching community psychology* (pp. 111–126). Washington, DC: American Psychological Association.

Shinn, M. (1992). Homelessness: What is a psychologist to do? *American Journal of Community Psychology, 20,* 1–24. Reprinted in T. Revenson, A. D'Augelli, S. E. French, D. Hughes, D. Livert, E. Seidman, M. Shinn, & H. Yoshikawa (Eds.), (2002), *A quarter century of community psychology* (pp. 343–366). New York: Kluwer Academic/Plenum.

Shinn, M. (Ed.). (1996). Ecological assessment [Special issue]. *American Journal of Community Psychology, 24*(1).

Shinn, M., Baumohl, J. & Hopper, K. (2001). The prevention of homelessness revisited. *Analyses of Social Issues and Public Policy,* 95–127.

Shinn, M., & Perkins, D. N. T. (2000). Contributions from organizational psychology. In J. Rappaport & E. Seidman (Eds.), *Handbook of community psychology* (pp. 615–641). New York: Kluwer Academic/ Plenum.

Shinn, M., & Rapkin, B. (2000). Cross-level research without cross-ups in community psychology. In J. Rappaport & E. Seidman (Eds.), *Handbook of community psychology* (pp. 669–696). New York: Kluwer/Plenum.

Shinn, M., & Toohey, S. (2003). Community contexts of human welfare. *Annual Review of Psychology, 54,* 427–459.

Shinn, M., Weitzman, B., Stojanovic, D., Knickman, J., Jimenez, L., Duchon, L., James, S., & Krantz, D. (1998). Predictors of homelessness from shelter request to housing stability among families in New York City. *American Journal of Public Health, 88,* 1651–1657.

Shriver, T. (1992). Video segment in *The world of abnormal psychology: An ounce of prevention* (T. Levine, Producer). New York: A. H. Perlmutter. (Available from Annenberg/CPB Collection, 1–800–LEARNER).

Shure, M. B. (1997). Interpersonal Cognitive Problem-Solving: Primary prevention of early high-risk behaviors in the preschool and primary years. In G. Albee & T. Gullotta (Eds.), *Primary prevention works* (pp. 167–188). Thousand Oaks, CA: Sage.

Shure, M. B., & Spivack, G. (1988). Interpersonal Cognitive Problem-Solving. In R. Price, E. Cowen, R. Lorion, & J. Ramos-McKay (Eds.), *Fourteen ounces of prevention* (pp. 69–82). Washington, DC: American Psychological Association.

Siegel, K., Raveis, V. H., & Karus, D. (1997). Illness-related support and negative network interactions: Effects on HIV-infected men's depressive symptomatology. *American Journal of Community Psychology, 25,* 395–420.

Silka, L., & Tip, J. (1994). Empowering the silent ranks: The Southeast Asian experience. *American Journal of Community Psychology, 22,* 497–530.

Silverman, M., & Felner, R. (1995). Suicide prevention programs: Issues of design, implementation, feasibility, and developmental appropriateness. *Suicide and Life-Threatening Behavior, 25* (1), 92–104.

Simons, R., Johnson, C., Beaman, J., Conger, R., & Whitbeck, L. (1996). Parents and peer group as mediators of the effect of community structure on adolescent problem behavior. *American Journal of Community Psychology, 24,* 145–172.

Singer, J., King, L., Green, M., & Barr, S. (2002). Personal identity and civic responsibility: "Rising to the occasion" narratives and generativity in community action student interns. *Journal of Social Issues, 58,* 535–556.

Sipe, C. L. (1996). *Mentoring: A synthesis of P/PV's Research: 1988–1995.* Philadelphia, PA: Public/ Private Ventures.

Slicker, E., & Palmer, D. (1994). Mentoring at-risk high school students: Evaluation of a school-based program. *School Counselor, 40,* 327–334.

Sloan, T., Anderson, A., & Fabick, S. (2003, Fall). Psychologists for social responsibility. *The Communty Psychologist, 36(4),* 37–39.

Smedley, A., & Smedley, B. (2005). Race as biology is fiction, racism as social problem is real: Anthropological and historical perspectives on the social construction of race. *American Psychologist, 60,* 16–26.

Snell-Johns, J., Imm, P., Wandersman, A., & Claypoole, J. (2003). Roles assumed by a community coalition when creating environmental and policy-level changes. *Journal of Community Psychology, 31,* 661–670.

Snow, D., Grady, K., & Goyette-Ewing, M. (2000). A perspective on ethical issues in community psychology. In J. Rappaport & E. Seidman (Eds.), *Handbook of community psychology* (pp. 897–918). New York: Plenum.

Snowden, L. R. (1987). The peculiar successes of community psychology: Service delivery to ethnic minorities and the poor. *American Journal of Community Psychology, 15,* 575–586.

Snowden, L. R. (2005), Racial, cultural and ethnic disparities in health and mental health: Toward theory and research at community levels. *American Journal of Community Psychology, 35,* 1–8.

Solarz, A. L. (2001). Investing in children, families and communities: Challenges for an interdivisional public policy collaboration. *American Journal of Community Psychology, 29,* 1–14.

Solomon, D., Battistich, V., Watson, M., Schaps, E., & Lewis, C. (2000). A six-district study of educational change: Direct and mediated effects of the Child Development Project. *Social Psychology of Education, 4,* 3–51.

Solomon, D., Watson, M., Battistich, V., Schaps, E., & Delucchi, K. (1996). Creating classrooms that students experience as communities. *American Journal of Community Psychology, 24,* 719–748.

Solomon, M., Pistrang, N., & Barker, C. (2001). The benefits of mutual support groups for parents of children with disabilities. *American Journal of Community Psychology, 29,* 113–132.

Somerfield, M. R., & McCrea, R. R. (2000). Stress and coping research: Methodological challenges, theoretical advances, and clinical applications. *American Psychologist, 55,* 620–625.

Sonn, C. (2002). Immigrant adaptation: Understanding the process through sense of community. In A. Fisher, C. Sonn & B. Bishop, (Eds.), *Psychological sense of community: Research, applications and implications* (pp. 205–221). New York: Kluwer/Plenum.

Sonn, C., & Fisher, A. (1996). Psychological sense of community in a politically constructed group. *Journal of Community Psychology, 24,* 417–430.

Sonn, C., & Fisher, A. (1998). Sense of community: Community resilient responses to oppression and change. *Journal of Community Psychology, 26,* 457–472.

Sonn, C., & Fisher, A. (2003). Identity and oppression: Differential responses to an in-between status. *American Journal of Community Psychology, 31,* 117–128.

Soriano, F. (1995). *Conducting needs assessments: A multidisciplinary approach.* Thousand Oaks, CA: Sage.

Spaulding, J., & Balch, P. (1983). A brief history of primary prevention in the twentieth century: 1908 to 1980. *American Journal of Community Psychology, 11,* 59–80.

Speer, P. (2000). Intrapersonal and interactional empowerment: Implications for theory. *Journal of Community Psychology, 28,* 51–62.

Speer, P., Dey, S., Griggs, P., Gibson, C., Lubin, B., & Hughey, J. (1992). In search of community: An analysis of community psychology research from 1984–1988. *American Journal of Community Psychology, 20,* 195–210.

Speer, P., & Hughey, J. (1995). Community organizing: An ecological route to empowerment and power. *American Journal of Community Psychology, 23,* 729–748.

Speer, P., Hughey, J., Gensheimer, L., & Adams-Leavitt, W. (1995). Organizing for power: A comparative case study. *Journal of Community Psychology, 23,* 57–73.

Spencer, L. M. (2001). The economic value of emotional intelligence competencies and EIC-basd HR programs. In C. Cherniss & D. Goleman (Eds.), *The emotionally intelligent workplace* (pp. 45–82). San Francisco: Jossey-Bass.

Spoth, R. L, Guyll, M., & Day, S. X. (2002). Universal family focused interventions in alcohol-use disorder prevention: Cost-effectiveness and cost-benefit analyses of two interventions. *Journal of Studies on Alcohol, 63,* 219–228.

Spoth, R., Redmond, C., & Shin, C. (1998). Direct and indirect latent-variable parenting outcomes of two universal family-focused preventive interventions: Extending a public health-oriented research base. *Journal of Consulting and Clinical Psychology, 66* (2), 385–399.

Stack, C. (1974). *All our kin: Strategies for survival in a Black community.* New York: Harper.

Stanley, J. (2003). An applied collaborative training program for graduate students in community psychology: A case study of a community project working with lesbian, gay, bisexual, transgender, and questioning youth. *American Journal of Community Psychology, 31,* 253–266.

Starnes, D. (2004). Community psychologists – Get in the arena!! *American Journal of Community Psychology, 33,* 3–6.

Steele, C. (1997). A threat in the air: How stereotypes shape intellectual identity and performance. *American Psychologist, 52,* 613–629.

Stein, B., Elliott, M., Jaycox, L., Collins, R., Berry, S., Klein, D. & Schuster, M. (2004). A national longitudinal study of the psychological consequences of the September 11, 2001 terrorist attacks: Reactions, impairment, and help-seeking. *Psychiatry, 67,* 105–117.

Stein, C. H., & Mankowski, E. S. (2004). Asking, witnessing, interpreting, knowing: Conducting qualitative research in community psychology. *American Journal of Community Psychology, 33,* 21–36.

Stein, C. H., Ward, M., & Cislo, D. A. (1992). The power of a place: Opening the college classroom to people with serious mental illness. *American Journal of Community Psychology, 20,* 523–548.

Stein, C. H., & Wemmerus, V. (2001). Searching for a normal life: Personal accounts of adults with schizophrenia, their parents and well-siblings. *American Journal of Community Psychology, 29,* 725–746.

Steinman, K., & Zimmerman, M. (2004). Religious activity and risk behavior among African American adolescents: Concurrent and developmental effects. *American Journal of Community Psychology, 33,* 151–161.

Stevenson, J., Mitchell, R. E., & Florin, P. (1996). Evaluation and self-direction in community prevention coalitions. In D. Fetterman, S. Kaftarian, & A. Wandersman (Eds.), *Empowerment evaluation: Knowledge and tools for self-assessment and accountability* (pp. 208–233). Thousand Oaks, CA: Sage.

Stewart, E. (2000). Thinking through others: Qualitative research and community psychology. In J. Rappaport & E. Seidman (Eds.), *Handbook of community psychology* (pp. 725–736). New York: Kluwer/Plenum.

Stiglitz, J. (2003). *Globalization and its discontents.* New York: Norton.

Stolz, S. B. (1984). Preventive models: Implications for a technology of practice. In M. Roberts & L. Peterson (Eds.), *Prevention of problems in childhood* (pp. 391–413). New York: Wiley.

Stone, R. A., & Levine, A. G. (1985). Reactions to collective stress: Correlates of active citizen participation at Love Canal. *Prevention in Human Services, 4,* 153–177.

Stout, C. (2004). Global initiatives. *American Psychologist, 59,* 844–853.

Strother, C. (Ed.) (1957). *Psychology and mental health.* Washington, DC: American Psychological Association.

Strother, C. (1987). Reflections on the Stanford Conference and subsequent events. *American Journal of Community Psychology, 15,* 519–522.

Stuber, S. (2000). The interposition of personal life stories and community narratives in a Roman Catholic religious community. *Journal of Community Psychology, 28,* 507–516.

Stukas, A., & Dunlap, M. (2002). Community involvement: Theoretical approaches and educational initiatives [Special issue]. *Journal of Social Issues, 58*(3).

Suarez-Balcazar, Y. (1998, July). Are we addressing the racial divide? *The Community Psychologist, 31,* 12–13.

Suarez-Balcazar, Y., Davis, M., Ferrari, J., Nyden, P., Olson, B., Alvarez, J., Molloy, P., & Toro, P. (2004). University-communty partnerships: A framework and exemplar. In L. Jason, C. Keys, Y. Suarez-Balcazar, R. Taylor, & M. Davis (Eds.), *Participatory community research: Theories and methods in action* (pp. 105–120). Washington, DC: American Psychological Association.

Sue, D. W. (2004). Whiteness and ethnocentric monoculturalism: Making the "invisible" visible. *American Psychologist, 59,* 761–769.

Sue, S. (1999). Science, ethnicity, and bias. *American Psychologist, 54,* 1070–1077.

Sugai, G., & Horner, R. (1999). Discipline and positive behavioral support: Preferred processes and practices. *Effective School Practices, 17* (4), 10–22.

Sullivan, C. (2003). Using the ESID model to reduce intimate male violence against women. *American Journal of Community Psychology, 32,* 295–304.

Sundberg, N., Hadiyono, J., Latkin, C., & Padilla, J. (1995). Cross-cultural prevention program transfer: Questions regarding developing countries. *Journal of Primary Prevention, 15,* 361–376.

Sundstrom, E., Bell, P., Busby, P., & Asmus, C. (1996). Environmental psychology, 1989–1994. *Annual Review of Psychology, 47,* 485–512.

Swift, C., Bond, M. & Serrano-Garcia, I. (2000). Women's empowerment: A review of community psychology's first twenty-five years. In J. Rappaport & E. Seidman (Eds.), *Handbook of community psychology* (pp. 857–896). New York: Kluwer/Plenum.

Sykes, C. (1992). *A nation of victims: The decay of the American character.* New York: St. Martin's Press.

Sylvestre, J., Pancer, M., Brophy, K., & Cameron, G. (1994). The planning and implementation of government-sponsored community-based primary prevention: A case study. *Canadian Journal of Community Mental Health, 13,* 189–196.

Sylwester, R. (1995). *A celebration of neurons: An educator's guide to the human brain.* Alexandria, VA: ASCD.

Tandon, S. D., Azelton, L. S., Kelly, J. G., & Strickland, D. A. (1998). Constructing a tree for community leaders: Contexts and processes in collaborative inquiry. *American Journal of Community Psychology, 26,* 669–696.

Tatum, B. (1997). *Why are all the Black kids sitting together in the cafeteria?* New York: Basic Books.

Tatum, B. (2004). Family life and school experience: Factors in the racial identity development of Black youth in White communities. *Journal of Social Issues, 60,* 117–136.

Tebes, J. (2000). External validity and scientific psychology [Comment]. *American Psychologist, 55,* 1508–1509.

Thoits, P. A. (1983). Multiple identities and psychological well-being: A reformulation and test of the social hypothesis. *American Sociological Review, 48,* 174–187.

Timko, C. (1996). Physical characteristics of residential psychiatric and substance abuse programs: Organizational determinants and patient outcomes. *American Journal of Community Psychology, 24,* 173–192.

Tobler, N. S., Roona, M. R., Ochshorn, P., Marshall, D. G., Streke, A. V., & Stackpole, K. M. (2000). School-based adolescent drug prevention programs: 1998 meta-analysis. *Journal of Primary Prevention, 20,* 275–337.

Todd, D. M. (1979). Appendix: Social network mapping. In W. R. Curtis, (Ed.), *The future use of social networks in mental health.* Boston: Social Matrix Research.

Tolan, P., Keys, C., Chertok, F., & Jason, L. (Eds.). (1990). *Researching community psychology: Issues of theory and methods.* Washington, DC: American Psychological Association.

Tolman, D. & Brydon-Miller, M. (Eds.). (2001). *From subjects to subjectivities: A handbook of interpretative and participatory methods.* New York: NYU Press.

Tompsett, C., Toro, P., Guzicki, M., Schlienz, N., Blume, M., & Lombard, S. (2003). Homelessness in the US and Germany: A cross-national analysis. *Journal of Community and Applied Social Psychology, 13,* 240–257.

Tonnies, F. (1988). *Community and society* [Translation of *Gemeinschaft und Gesellschaft*]. New Brunswick, NJ: Transaction Publishers. (Original work published 1887.)

Tornatzky, L., & Fleischer, M. (1986, October). *Dissemination and/or implementation: The problem of complex socio-technical systems.* Paper presented at the meeting of the American Evaluation Association, Kansas City, MO.

Torney-Purta, J., & Vermeer, S. (2004). *Developing citizenship competencies from kindergarten through Grade 12: Background paper for policymakers and educators.* Denver, CO: Education Commission of the States.

Toro, P. (1998, February). A community psychologist's role in policy on homelessness in two cities. *The Community Psychologist, 31,* 25–26.

Toro, P. (1999). Homelessness [special issue]. *Journal of Community Psychology, 27*(2).

Toro, P. (2005). Community psychology: Where do we go from here? *American Journal of Community Psychology, 35,* 17–22.

Toro, P., Rappaport, J., & Seidman, E. (1987). Social climate comparison of mutual help and psychotherapy groups. *Journal of Consulting and Clinical Psychology, 55,* 430–431.

Toro, P., Reischl, T., Zimmerman, M., Rappaport, J., Seidman, E., Luke, D., & Roberts, L. (1988). Professionals in mutual help groups: Impact on social climate and members' behavior. *Journal of Consulting and Clinical Psychology, 56,* 631–632.

Toro, P., & Warren M. (1999). Homelessness in the United States: Policy considerations. *Journal of Community Psychology, 27,* 119–136.

Triandis, H. C. (1994). *Culture and social behavior.* New York: McGraw-Hill.

Trickett, E. J. (1984). Toward a distinctive community psychology: An ecological metaphor for the conduct of community research and the nature of training. *American Journal of Community Psychology, 12,* 261–279.

Trickett, E. J. (1996). A future for community psychology: The contexts of diversity and the diversity of contexts. *American Journal of Community Psychology, 24,* 209–234. Reprinted in T. Revenson, A. D'Augelli, S. E. French, D. Hughes, D. Livert, E. Seidman, M. Shinn, & H. Yoshikawa (Eds.), (2002), *A quarter century of community psychology* (pp. 513–534). New York: Kluwer Academic/Plenum.

Trickett, E. J. (1997). Ecology and primary prevention: Reflections on a meta-analysis. *American Journal of Community Psychology, 25,* 197–206.

Trickett, E. J., Barone, C., & Watts, R. (2000). Contextual influences in mental health consultation: Toward an ecological perspective on radiating change. In J. Rappaport & E. Seidman (Eds.), *Handbook of community psychology* (pp. 303–330). New York: Kluwer/Plenum.

Trickett, E. J., & Espino, S. L. R. (2004). Collaboration and social inquiry: Multiple meanings of a construct and its role in creating useful and valid knowledge. *American Journal of Community Psychology, 34,* 1–70.

Trickett, E. J., Kelly, J. G., & Todd, D. M. (1972). The social environment of the school: Guidelines for individual change and organizational redevelopment. In S. Golann & C. Eisdorfer (Eds.), *Handbook of community mental health* (pp. 331–406). New York: Appleton-Century-Crofts.

Trickett, E. J., Trickett, P., Castro, J., & Schaffner, P. (1982). The independent school experience: Aspects of the normative environments of single sex and coed secondary schools. *Journal of Educational Psychology, 74,* 374–381.

Trickett, E. J., Watts, R. J., & Birman, D. (Eds.). (1994). *Human diversity: Perspectives on people in context.* San Francisco: Jossey-Bass.

Trimble, J. (2003). Introduction: Social change and acculturation. In K. Chun, P. Organista, & G. Marin (Eds.), *Acculturation: Advances in theory, measurement and applied research* (pp. xvii–xxi). Washington, DC: American Psychological Association.

Trimble, J., Helms, J., & Root, M. (2003). Social and psychological perspectives on ethnic and racial identity. In G. Bernal, J. Trimble, K. Burlew, & F. Leong (Eds.), *Handbook of racial and ethnic minority psychology* (pp. 239–275). Thousand Oaks, CA: Sage.

Trout, J., Dokecki, P., Newbrough, J. R., & O'Gorman, R. (2003). Action research on leadership for community development in West Africa and North America: A joining of liberation theology and community psychology. *Journal of Community Psychology, 31,* 129–148.

Tsemberis, S., Moran, L., Shinn, M., Asmussen, S., & Shern, D. (2003). Consumer preference programs for individuals who are homeless and have psychiatric disabilities: A drop-in center and a supported housing program. *American Journal of Community Psychology, 32,* 305–318.

Tseng, V., Chesir-Teran, D., Becker-Klein, R., Chan, M., Duran, V., Roberts, A., & Bardoliwalla, N. (2002). Promotion of social change: A conceptual framework. *American Journal of Community Psychology, 30,* 401–427.

Tyler, F. (2001). *Cultures, communities and change.* New York: Kluwer/Plenum.

Tyler, F., Pargament, K., & Gatz, M. (1983). The resource collaborator role: A model for interactions involving psychologists. *American Psychologist, 38,* 388–398.

Uchino, B., Cacioppo, J., & Kiecolt-Glaser, J. (1996). The relationship between social support and physiological processes: A review with emphasis on underlying mechanisms and implications for health. *Psychological Bulletin, 119,* 488–531.

Uhl, A. (2000). The future of primary prevention. *Journal of Primary Prevention, 21* (1), 43–45.

Unger, D., & Wandersman, A. (1983). Neighboring and its role in block organizations: An exploratory report. *American Journal of Community Psychology, 11,* 291–300.

Unger, D., & Wandersman, A. (1985). The importance of neighbors: The social, cognitive and affective components of neighboring. *American Journal of Community Psychology, 13,* 139–170.

Unger, R. (2001). Marie Jahoda [Obituary]. *American Psychologist, 56,* 1040–1041.

United Way of America. (1996). *Measuring program outcomes: A practical approach: Effective practices and measuring impact.* Alexandria, VA: Author. (See also http://national.unitedway.org/outcomes/resources/mpo/model.cfm)

U.S. Census Bureau. (n.d.). Frequently asked questions about income statistics from the Current Population Survey. Retrieved July 14, 2004 from http://www.census.gov/hhes/income/incfaq.html

U.S. Census Bureau. (August 30, 2005). News conference: 2004 income, poverty and health insurance estimates from the Current Population Survey. Retrieved September 19, 2005, from http://www.census.gov/hhes/www/income/income04.html

U.S. Department of Education. (n.d.). No Child Left Behind Act: Accountability. Retrieved July 28, 2005, from http://www.ed.gov/nclb/accountability/index.html

U.S. Department of Homeland Security (n.d.). *Hurricane Katrina: What government is doing.* Retrieved March 25, 2006 from http://www.dhs.gov/interweb/assetlibrary/katrina.htm

U.S. Federal Emergency Management Agency. (2006, Feb. 28). FEMA news: Six months after the storms. Retrieved March 29, 2006, from http://www.fema.gov/news/newsrelease.fema?id23903

U.S. General Accounting Office. (1990). *Drug education: School-based programs seen as useful but impact unknown* [GAO/HRD-91-27]. Washington, DC: Author.

Van de Ven, A. (1986). Central problems in the management of innovation. *Management Science, 32,* 590–608.

Van Egeren, L., Huber, M., & Cantillon, D. (2003, June). *Mapping change: Using geographic information systems for research and action.* Poster presented at the biennial meeting of the Society for Community Research and Action, Las Vegas, New Mexico.

van Emmerick, A., Kamphuis, J. Hulsbosch, A., & Emmelkamp, P. (2002). Single session debriefing following psychotrauma, help or harm: A meta-analysis. *The Lancet, 360,* 766–771.

Van Ryn, M., & Vinokur, A. (1992). How did it work? An examination of the mechanisms through which an intervention for the unemployed promoted job-search behavior. *American Journal of Community Psychology, 20,* 577–592.

van Uchelen, C. (2000). Individualism, collectivism and community psychology. In J. Rappaport & E. Seidman (Eds.), *Handbook of community psychology* (pp. 65–78). New York: Kluwer/Plenum.

Varas-Diaz, N., & Serrano-Garcia, I. (2003). The challenge of a positive self-image in a colonial context: A psychology of liberation for the Puerto Rican experience. *American Journal of Community Psychology, 31,* 103–116.

Ventis, W. L. (1995). The relationships between religion and mental health. *Journal of Social Issues, 51,* 33–48.

Vincent, T. (1990). A view from the Hill: The human element in policy making on Capitol Hill. *American Psychologist, 45,* 61–64.

Vincent, T., & Trickett, E. (1983). Preventive intervention and the human context: Ecological approaches to environmental assessment and change. In R. Felner, L. Jason, J. Moritsugu, & S. Farber (Eds.), *Preventive psychology: Theory, research, and practice* (pp. 67–86). New York: Pergamon.

Vinokur, A. D., & Selzer, M. L. (1975). Desirable vs. undesirable life events: Their relationship to stress and mental distress. *Journal of Personality and Social Psychology, 32,* 329–337.

Vivero, V., & Jenkins, S. (1999). Existential hazards of the multicultural individual: Defining and understanding "cultural homelessness." *Cultural Diversity and Ethnic Minority Psychology, 5,* 6–26.

W. K. Kellogg Foundation. (1998). *Kellogg evaluation handbook.* Battle Creek, MI: Author.

Wager, C. (1993). Toward a shared ethical culture. *Educational Leadership, 50*(4), 19–23.

Waldo, C. R., Hesson-McInnis, M. S., & D'Augelli, A. R. (1998). Antecedents and consequences of victimization of lesbian, gay, and bisexual young people: A structural model comparing rural university and urban samples. *American Journal of Community Psychology, 26,* 307–334.

Wallach, M., & Wallach, L. (1983). *Psychology's sanction for selfishness: The error of egoism in theory and therapy.* San Francisco: Freeman.

Walsh, R. (1987). A social historical note on the formal emergence of community psychology. *American Journal of Community Psychology, 15,* 523–529.

Walsh-Bowers, R. (2000). A personal sojourn to spiritualize community psychology. *Journal of Community Psychology, 28,* 221–236.

Wandersman, A. (1984). Citizen participation. In K. Heller, R. Price, S. Reinharz, S. Riger, & A. Wandersman, *Psychology and community change* (2nd ed.) (pp. 337–379). Homewood, IL: Dorsey.

Wandersman, A. (1990). Prevention is a broad field: Toward a broad conceptual framework of prevention. In P. Mueherer (Ed.), *Conceptual research models for preventing mental disorders.* Rockville, MD: National Institute of Mental Health.

Wandersman, A. (2003). Community science: Bridging the gap between science and practice with community-centered models. *American Journal of Community Psychology, 31,* 227–242.

Wandersman, A., Coyne, S., Herndon, E., McKnight, K. & Morsbach, S. (2002, Summer). Clinical and community psychology: case studies using integrative models. *The Community Psychologist, 35,* 22–25.

Wandersman, A., & Florin, P. (1990). Citizen participation, voluntary organizations and community development: Insights for empowerment and research [Special section]. *American Journal of Community Psychology, 18,* 41–177.

Wandersman, A., & Florin, P. (2000). Citizen participation and community organizations. In J. Rappaport & E. Seidman (Eds.), *Handbook of community psychology* (pp. 247–272). New York: Plenum.

Wandersman, A., & Florin, P. (2003). Community interventions and effective prevention. *American Psychologist, 58,* 441–448.

Wandersman, A., Goodman, R. M., & Butterfoss, F. D. (1997). Understanding coalitions and how they operate: An "open systems" organizational framework. In M. Minkler (Ed.), *Community organizing and community building for health* (pp. 261–277). New Brunswick, NJ: Rutgers University Press.

Wandersman, A., & Hallman W. (1993). Are people acting irrationally? Understanding public concerns about environmental threats. *American Psychologist, 48,* 681–686.

Wandersman, A., Imm, P., Chinman, M. & Kaftarian, S. (1999). *Getting To Outcomes: Methods and tools for planning, evaluation and accountability.* Rockville, MD: Center for Substance Abuse Prevention.

Wandersman, A., Imm, P., Chinman, M. & Kaftarian, S. (2000). Getting To Outcomes: A results-based approach to accountability. *Evaluation and Program Planning, 23,* 389–395.

Wandersman, A., Keener, D., Snell-Johns, J., Miller, R., Flaspohler, P., Livet-Dye, M., Mendez, J., Behrens, T., Bolson, B., & Robinson, L. (2004). Empowerment evaluation: Principles and action. In L. Jason, C. Keys, Y. Suarez-Balcazar, R. Taylor, & M. Davis (Eds.), *Participatory community research: Theories and methods in action* (pp. 139–156). Washington, DC: American Psychological Association.

Wandersman, A., Kloos, B., Linney, J.A., & Shinn, M. (Eds.) (2005). Science and community psychology: Enhancing the vitality of community research and action [Special issue]. *American Journal of Community Psychology, 35*(3/4).

Wandersman, A., Morrissey, E., Davino, K., Seybolt, D., Crusto, C., Nation, M., Goodman, R., & Imm, P. (1998). Comprehensive quality programming and accountability: Eight essential strategies for implementing successful prevention programs. *Journal of Primary Prevention, 19,* 3–30.

Wandersman, A., Morsbach, S. K., McKnight, K., Herndon, E. & Coyne, S. M. (2002, Summer). Clinical and community psychology: Complementarities and combinations. *The Community Psychologist, 35,* 4–7.

Wandersman, A., & Nation, M. (1998). Urban neighborhoods and mental health: Psychological contributions to understanding toxicity, resilience and interventions. *American Psychologist, 53,* 647–656.

Wandersman, A., Snell-Johns, J., Lentz, B., Fetterman, D., Keener, D., Livet, M., Imm, P. & Flaspohler, P. (2005). The principles of empowerment evaluation. In D. Fetterman & A. Wandersman (Eds.), *Empowerment evaluation principles in practice* (pp. 27–41). New York: Guilford Press.

Wang, M., Fitzhugh, J., Eddy, J., Fu, Q., & Turner, L. (1997). Social influences on adolescents' smoking progress: A longitudinal analysis. *American Journal of Health Behavior, 21* (2), 111–117.

Wasco, S., Campbell, R., & Clark, M. (2002). A multiple case study of rape victim advocates' self-care routines: The inflence of organizational context. *American Journal of Community Psychology, 30,* 731–760.

Watts, R. J. (1994). Paradigms of diversity. In E. J. Trickett, R. J. Watts, & D. Birman (Eds.), *Human diversity: Perspectives on people in context* (pp. 49–79). San Francisco: Jossey-Bass.

Watts, R., & Serrano-Garcia, I. (2003). The psychology of liberation: Responses to oppression [Special issue]. *American Journal of Community Psychology, 31*(1/2).

Watts, R., Williams, N. C., & Jagers, R. (2003). Sociopolitical development. *American Journal of Community Psychology, 31,* 185–194.

Watzlawick, P., Weakland, J., & Fisch, R. (1974). *Change: Principles of problem formation and problem resolution.* New York: Norton.

Weick, K. (1984). Small wins: Redefining the scale of social issues. *American Psychologist, 39,* 40–49.

Weikart, D., & Schweinhart, L. (1997). High/Scope Perry Preschool Program. In G. Albee & T. Gullotta (Eds.), *Primary prevention works* (pp. 146–166). Thousand Oaks, CA: Sage.

Weinstein, R. (2002a). *Reaching higher: The power of expectations in schooling.* Cambridge, MA: Harvard University Press.

Weinstein, R. (2002b). Overcoming inequality in schooling: A call to action for community psychology. *American Journal of Community Psychology, 30,* 21–42.

Weinstein, R. (2005, June). *Reaching higher in community psychology.* Seymour Sarason Award address, biennial meeting of the Society for Community Research and Action, Champaign-Urbana, Illinois.

Weinstein, R., Gregory, A. & Strambler, M. (2004). Intractable self-fulfilling prophecies: Fifty years after *Brown v. Board of Education. American Psychologist, 59,* 511–520.

Weinstein, R., Soule, C., Collins, F., Cone, J., Mehlhorn, M., & Simontacchi, K. (1991). Expectations and high school change: Teacher-researcher collaboration to prevent school failure. *American Journal of Community Psychology, 19,* 333–364.

Weiss, C. H. (1995). Nothing as practical as good theory: Exploring theory-based evaluation for comprehensive community initiatives for children and families. In J. P. Connell, A. Kubisch, L. Schorr, & C. H. Weiss (Eds.), *New approaches to evaluating community initiatives: Concepts, methods, and contexts* (pp. 65–92). Washington, DC: Aspen Institute.

Weissberg, R. P., Barton, H. A., & Shriver, T. P. (1997). The Social-Competence Promotion Program for young adolescents. In G. Albee & T. Gullotta (Eds.), *Primary prevention works* (pp. 268–289). Thousand Oaks, CA: Sage.

Weissberg, R. P., & Bell, D. N. (1997). A meta-analytic review of primary prevention programs for children and adolescents: Contributions and caveats. *American Journal of Community Psychology, 25,* 207–214.

Weissberg, R. P., & Durlak, J. (2006). *Meta-analysis of the effect of social-emotional learning and positive youth development programs on academic achievement and problem behaviors.* Available from www.CASEL.org.

Weissberg, R. P., & Greenberg, M. T. (1997). School and community competence-enhancement and prevention programs. In I. Sigel & K. Renniger (Eds.), *Handbook of child psychology,* Vol. 4: *Child psychology in practice* (5th ed.) (pp. 877–954). New York: Wiley.

Weissberg, R. P. & Kumpfer, K. (Eds.). (2003). Prevention that works for children and youth [Special issue]. *American Psychologist, 58* (6/7).

Weissberg, R. P., Kumpfer, K. & Seligman, M. (2003). Prevention that works for children and youth: An introduction. *American Psychologist, 58,* 425–432.

Weisstein, N. (1993). Psychology constructs the female: Or, the fantasy life of the male psychologist (with some attention to the fantasies of his friends, the male biologist and the male anthropologist). *Feminism and Psychology, 3,* 195–210. (Originally published 1971. Boston: New England Free Press.)

Welsh, B., & Farrington, D. (2003a). Childhood deliquency. In T.P. Gullotta & M. Bloom (Eds.), *Encyclopedia of primary prevention and health promotion* (pp. 384–390). New York: Kluwer.

Welsh, B., & Farrington, D. (2003b). Adolescent deliquency. In T.P. Gullotta & M. Bloom (Eds.), *Encyclopedia of primary prevention and health promotion* (pp. 390–395). New York: Kluwer.

Werner, C., Voce, R., Openshaw, K., & Simons, M. (2002). Designing service-learning to empower students and community: Jackson Elementary builds a nature study center. *Journal of Social Issues, 58,* 557–580.

White, G. (2005). Ableism. In G. Nelson & I. Prilleltensky, (Eds.), *Community psychology: In pursuit of liberation and well-being* (pp. 405–425). New York: Palgrave Macmillan.

Wicker, A. (1969). Size of church membership and members' support of church behavior settings. *Journal of Personality and Social Psychology, 13,* 278–288.

Wicker, A. (1973). Undermanning theory and research: Implications for the study of psychological and behavioral effects of excess populations. *Representative Research in Social Psychology, 4,* 185–206.

Wicker, A. (1979). Ecological psychology: Some recent and prospective developments. *American Psychologist, 34,* 755–765.

Wicker, A. (1987). Behavior settings reconsidered: Temporal stages, resources, internal dynamics, and context. In D. Stokols & I. Altman (Eds.), *Handbook of environmental psychology,* Vol. 1 (pp. 613–653). New York: Wiley.

Wicker, A., & Sommer, R. (1993). The resident researcher: An alternative career model centered on community. *American Journal of Community Psychology, 21,* 469–482.

Wiesenfeld, E. (1996). The concept of "we": A community social psychology myth? *Journal of Community Psychology, 24,* 337–346.

Wilcox, B. L. (1981). Social support in adjusting to marital disruption: A network analysis. In B. Gottlieb (Ed.), *Social networks and social support* (pp. 97–116). Beverly Hills, CA: Sage.

Wilcox, B. L. (1993). Deterring risky behavior: Policy perspectives on adolescent risk-taking. In N. Bell & R. Bell (Eds.), *Adolescent risk taking* (pp. 148–164). Newbury Park, CA: Sage.

Wiley, A., & Rappaport, J. (2000). Empowerment, wellness, and the politics of development. In D. Cicchetti, J. Rappaport, I. Sandler, & R. Weissberg (Eds.), *The promotion of wellness in children and adolescents* (pp. 59–99). Washington, DC: CWLA Press.

Willard, N. (2005). *A parents' guide to cyberbullying and cyberthreats.* Eugene, OR: Center for Safe and Responsible Internet Use (http://csriu.org).

Wilson, B. D. M., Hayes, E., Greene, G., Kelly, J. G., & Iscoe, I. (2003). Community psychology. In D. Freedheim (Ed.), *Handbook of psychology,* Vol. 1: *History of psychology* (pp. 431–449). New York: John Wiley.

Wilson, D. B., Gottfredson, D. C., & Najaka, S. S. (2001). School-based prevention of problem behaviors: A meta-analysis. *Journal of Quantitative Criminology, 17,* 247–272.

Wingenfeld, S., & Newbrough, J. R. (2000). Community psychology in international perspective. In J. Rappaport & E. Seidman (Eds.), *Handbook of community psychology* (pp. 779–810). New York: Kluwer/Plenum.

Witlein, B., & Altschuld, J. (1995). *Planning and conducting needs assessments.* Thousand Oaks, CA: Sage.

Wittig, M. A., & Schmitz, J. (1996). Electronic grassroots organizing. *Journal of Social Issues, 52,* 53–70.

Wolff, T. (1987). Community psychology and empowerment: An activist's insights. *American Journal of Community Psychology, 15,* 151–166.

Wolff, T. (1994, Summer). Keynote address given at the fourth biennial conference. *The Community Psychologist, 27,* 20–26.

Wolff, T. (1995, Spring). Healthy Communities Massachusetts: One vision of civic democracy. *Municipal Advocate* (Massachusetts Municipal Association), 22–24. (Available from AHEC/Community Partners, 24 S. Prospect St., Amherst, MA 01002.)

Wolff, T. (Ed.). (2001a). Community coalition building: Contemporary practice and research [Special section]. *American Journal of Community Psychology, 29,* 165–329.

Wolff, T. (2001b). The future of community coalition building. *American Journal of Community Psychology, 29,* 263–268.

Wolff, T. (2004). Collaborative solutions: Six key components. *Collaborative Solutions Newsletter, Fall 2004.* Retrieved from http://www.tomwolff.com

Wolff, T., & Lee, P. (1997, June). *The Healthy Communities movement: An exciting new area for research and action by community psychologists.* Workshop presented at the meeting of the Society for Community Research and Action, Columbia, SC.

Wolitski, R. J. (2003, Fall). What do we do when the crisis does not end? *The Community Psychologist, 36,* 14–15.

Wollman, N., Lobenstine, M., Foderaro, M., & Stose, S. (1998). *Principles for promoting social change: Effective strategies for influencing attitudes and behaviors* (booklet). Ann Arbor, MI: Society for the Psychological Study of Social Issues.

World Health Organization (2000). *Preventing suicide: A resource guide for general physicians.* Geneva: Author, Department of Mental Health.

Worthen, B., Sanders, J., & Fitzpatrick, J. (1997). *Program evaluation: Alternative approaches and practical guidelines* (2nd ed.). White Plains, NY: Longman.

Wuthnow, R. (1994). *Sharing the journey: Support groups and America's new quest for community.* New York: Free Press.

Wuthnow, R. (2002). Bridging the privileged and the marginalized? In R. Putnam, (Ed.), *Democracies in flux* (pp. 59–102). New York: Oxford University Press.

Ying, Y. (1995). Cultural orientation and psychological well-being in Chinese Americans. *American Journal of Community Psychology, 23,* 893–912.

York Region District School Board, Ontario, Canada. (no date). *Character matters.* Retrieved October 23, 2005, from http://www.yrdsb.edu.on.ca/

Yoshikawa, H. (1994). Prevention as cumulative protection: Effects of early family support and education on chronic delinquency and its risks. *Psychological Bulletin, 115,* 28–54.

Yoshikawa, H., Wilson, P., Hseuh, J., Rosman, E., Chin, J., & Kim, J. (2003). What front-line CBO staff can tell us about culturally anchored theories of behavior change in HIV prevention for Asian/Pacific Islanders. *American Journal of Community Psychology, 32,* 143–158.

Young, A. (2001, June). Invited address, Society for Community Research and Action Biennial Conference, Atlanta, Georgia.

Zigler, E. (1994). Reshaping early childhood intervention to be a more effective weapon against poverty. *American Journal of Community Psychology, 22,* 37–48.

Zimmerman, M. A. (1995). Psychological empowerment: Issues and illustrations. *American Journal of Community Psychology, 23,* 581–600.

Zimmerman, M. A. (2000). Empowerment theory: psychological, organizational and community levels of analysis. In J. Rappaport & E. Seidman (Eds.), *Handbook of community psychology* (pp. 43–63). New York: Kluwer/Plenum.

Zimmerman, M. A., Reischl, T. M., Seidman, E., Rappaport, J., Toro, P. A., & Salem, D. A. (1991). Expansion strategies of a mutual help organization. *American Journal of Community Psychology, 19,* 251–278.

Zins, J. E., Bloodworth, M. R., Weissberg, R. P., & Walberg, H. J. (2004) The scientific base linking social and emotional learning to school success. In J. E. Zins, R. P. Weissberg, M. C. Wang, & H. J. Walberg, H. J. (Eds.), *Building academic success on social and emotional learning: What does the research say?* (pp. 3–22). New York: Teachers College Press.

Zins, J., Elias, M. J., & Maher, C.A. (Eds.). (in press). *Handbook of victimization, bullying, and peer harassment in the schools: Research and intervention.* New York: Haworth.

Zins, J. E., Weissberg, R. P., Wang, M. C., & Walberg, H. J. (Eds.). (2004). *Building academic success on social and emotional learning: What does the research say?.* New York: Teachers College Press.

Zirkel, S., & Cantor, N. (2004). 50 years after *Brown v. Board of Education:* The promise and challenge of multicultural education. *Journal of Social Issues, 60,* 1–16.

Zuckerman, M. (1990). Some dubious premises in research and theory on racial differences: Social, scientific and ethical issues. *American Psychologist, 45,* 1297–1303.

Credits

Name Index

C

D

S

Y

Z

Subject Index

A

B

T